MEN AND MASCULINITIES

MEN AND MASCULINITIES

A Social, Cultural, and
Historical Encyclopedia

Volume I: A–J

*Edited by Michael Kimmel
and Amy Aronson*

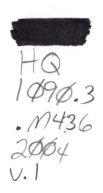

A B C • C L I O

Santa Barbara, California   •   Denver, Colorado   •   Oxford, England

Library of Congress Cataloging-in-Publication Data

Men and masculinities : a social, cultural, and historical encyclopedia
/ edited by Michael Kimmel and Amy Aronson.

   p. cm.

"Also available on the World Wide Web as an e-book."

Includes bibliographical references and index.

   ISBN 1-57607-774-8 (cloth : alk. paper) — ISBN 1-57607-775-6 (e-Book)

   1. Men—United States—Encyclopedias. 2. Masculinity—United
States—Encyclopedias. 3. Sex role—United States—Encyclopedias.
4. Men's studies—United States—Encyclopedias. 5. Men—Encyclopedias.
6. Masculinity—Encyclopedias. I. Kimmel, Michael S. II. Aronson, Amy.

HQ1090.3.M436 2003

       —dc22

                       2003020729

07   06   05   04   10 9 8 7 6 5 4 3 2 1

This book is also available on the World Wide Web as an e-book.
Visit http://www.abc-clio.com for details.

ABC-CLIO, Inc.
130 Cremona Drive, P.O. Box 1911
Santa Barbara, California 93116-1911

This book is printed on acid-free paper.
Manufactured in the United States of America

For Hank Rubin,
"premature antifascist" and dear friend
A "new man" before his time

And for our son, Zachary,
Whose time has come.

CONTENTS

Preface, Michael Kimmel and Amy Aronson, xiii
Introduction, xv

MEN AND MASCULINITIES

A Social, Cultural, and Historical Encyclopedia

PREFACE

All encyclopedias are frauds. The idea that one could collect, in a single volume or set of volumes, the entire corpus of human knowledge, represents the height of Enlightenment optimism. Such was Diderot's stated vision as he sought to accomplish this task in the years before the French Revolution; his "reference work covering all knowledge" captures both the inspiring effort of such an undertaking as well as its hubris.

Even in its more modest claims of "a comprehensive reference work containing articles on a wide range of subjects or on numerous aspects of a particular field, usually arranged alphabetically," as offered by *The American Heritage Dictionary of the English Language,* or "a literary work containing extensive information on all branches of knowledge," which is the second definition in the *Oxford English Dictionary,* any encyclopedia project inevitably falls short. The reach of an encyclopedia will always exceed its grasp. Optimistic in intent, the conclusion of an encyclopedia project is always tinged with sadness.

Optimism first. An encyclopedia announces, summarizes, and presents a sampling of the range and interests of a field of study. The sheer size of an encyclopedia makes clear that there is a "there" there—that a field of study exists and that many scholars are toiling in that field. In the case of the study of men and masculinities, it demonstrates that in three short decades, an entirely new, interdisciplinary field has emerged and is now an accepted part of gender studies. Not that long ago, academic skeptics and antifeminist political pundits suggested that when it came to masculinity, there was "nothing to study." But today, the study of masculinity has begun to be integrated into traditional disciplines as well as to compose a small but significant share of gender studies courses.

An encyclopedia summarizes the field, bringing together all the various strands of research and writing. In the case of the study of men and masculinities, it means fully honoring the interdisciplinary nature of the field. Like gender studies, of which it is a part, the study of men and masculinities draws on all branches of knowledge, all areas of research—from the natural and biological sciences to social and behavioral sciences, and also the humanities. Entries in these volumes range from the biology of male hormones to representations of masculinity in theological texts or in contemporary movies.

As an interdisciplinary field, the study of men and masculinities uses the lens of "gender" through which to view its subject matter and the subject matter that is ordinarily housed within the more traditional academic fields. Most entries fall into one (or more) of these five categories: One type of entry takes already well-known individuals—writers, historical figures, actors—and suggests the ways in which their work both reflects and challenges conventional notions of masculinity. A second set of entries examines pivotal historical or cultural events, social or political movements that are decisive or somehow constitutive in the development of masculinities. A third set of entries takes dynamic psychological or social processes, or cultural or developmental rituals or symbols and explores the meanings of masculinity through them. A fourth set of entries takes well-known—even canonical—works of fiction and drama, and, by reexamining them through a gender lens, reveals new meanings embedded in them. And finally, a fifth set of entries applies this same perspective to new, contemporary representations of gender in more popular cultural works like music and film.

Of course, making "masculinity" visible in the lives and works of well-known figures, or "gendering" processes, events, and experiences, should not mean that we ignore other ways in which identity is organized and that frame and constitute the events and processes we describe here. Any inquiry into gender must be "inter-sectional," by which we mean that we explore the intersections with other arenas—race, class, sexuality, age, religion, ethnicity, and the like. Thus readers will note how many entries discern distinct patterns among men of color, or gay men, or older or younger men—to name just a few of these intersections. At times these different realms collide, at times they reinforce, and at other times they move on parallel tracks. But it is imperative to note the ways in which our understandings of masculinities remain true to the pluralization of the term in the first place.

We've fared less well on being international, at least in the content of the entries. Most entries address the situation in the United States. This U.S. focus was both by design and by default. A fully "encyclopedic" work on masculinities throughout the world was beyond the scope of this project, and beyond the expertise of its editors. And because such projects proceed both by editorial invitation to prospective authors and by various networks of scholars, we also had to choose from among the sources that we had.

On the other hand, while our subject matter is largely United States based, our authors span the globe and draw from the expertise of people working in the English language in all parts of the world. Such diverse authors are able to provide an interesting angle of vision for their decidedly North American subjects.

As we have inevitably failed at collecting *all* information from all branches of inquiry, we sample their offerings. As encyclopedias always emphasize breadth over depth, we have collected samples from the widest range of areas we could conceive to give a small taste of the richness of the arenas in which such work is currently underway. We've drawn especially from the social and behavioral sciences, history, literature, and media studies, and sampled less fully from other fields.

As we suggest above, all encyclopedias are tinged with sadness. At the end of any project, one is aware of all the things that one has omitted, either by choice or accident. This is especially true with an encyclopedia, which bears the additional burden of attempting comprehension of a full field. We are aware of all the entries, all the areas, that could not be encompassed by these two volumes, which suddenly feel so small and so incomplete.

We're buoyed, though, by the other definition of the word *encyclopedia,* in fact the first definition in the *Oxford English Dictionary*— "the circle of learning; a general course of instruction." We offer this work, then, as a general course of instruction, a brief introduction to a field in development. And we leave it to you, the users of these volumes, to complete the circle of learning.

ABA and MSK
New York
April 2003

INTRODUCTION

This is the first encyclopedia on "men and masculinities." As such, it both celebrates the establishment of a new field of study and hopes to participate in the inauguration of a new phase of that field of inquiry.

To be sure, there are libraries filled with volumes about men. And university course catalogs are overflowing with courses about men. But rarely are these volumes or these courses about men *as men*—that is, rarely are they also about gender. Instead they are called "history" or "literature" or "political science." It's probably fair to say that if the course doesn't have the word "women" in the title, it's more than likely about men—except that it's rare for "masculinity" to be discussed at all.

The pioneering efforts by feminist scholars to "make women visible," both in the traditional curriculum and in the newly minted special interdisciplinary field of women's studies, has been a signal success, a sign of dramatic transformation of traditional modes and methods of inquiry into human life. Beginning in the 1960s, scholars redressed what Catharine Stimpson (1988) has called the "omissions, distortions, and trivializations" of women's experiences and began to examine the spheres to which women have historically been consigned, like private life and the family. Women's history sought to rescue from obscurity the lives of significant women who had been ignored or whose work has been minimized by traditional androcentric

scholarship—the now-celebrated painters, composers, writers, and political and military figures who had been consigned to minor footnotes if they were recognized at all. And it also sought to examine the everyday lives of women in the past—the efforts, for example, of laundresses, factory workers, pioneer homesteaders, office workers, sex workers, and housewives to carve out lives of meaning and dignity in a world controlled by men. Through women's studies courses and also in courses about women in traditional disciplines, students have explored the complexity of women's lives, the hidden history of exemplary women, and the daily experiences of women in the routines of their lives.

But women's studies also made *gender* visible as a category of analysis, a set of experiences. Women's studies made it clear that gender—masculinity and femininity—are among the core organizing principles of social life, among the bedrock experiences from which we fashion our identities. Before women's studies, if you wanted to study gender in the 1960s in social science, for example, you would have found but one course designed to address your needs—"Marriage and the Family"—which was sort of the "ladies' auxiliary" of the social sciences. There were no courses on gender. But today, gender has joined race and class in our understanding of the foundations of an individual's identity. Gender, we now know, is one of the axes around which social life is organized and through which we understand our own experiences. And it is from this insight about the centrality of gender in social and individual life that all current work on men and masculinities proceeds.

The central insight of the new field of inquiry, "Studies on Men and Masculinities," is that gender is a central organizing feature of *men's* lives as well as women's; that it composes a foundation of men's identities; that it structures our interactions with other men, women, and children; and that it is part of the framework of the institutions that shape our lives.

Why Not "Men's Studies"?

Why, you might be asking, would we title this work *Men and Masculinities* and not simply the *Encyclopedia of Men's Studies?* This is a complicated issue, as are all issues in the politicized world of gender studies in the academy. "Men's studies" is not the accurate corollary to "women's studies," because women's studies made both women *and* gender visible. Nor is it a "corrective" to the perceived defects of women's studies alleged by antifeminist scholars, who seem to say, "Well, you have *your* women's studies but what about us men?" In short, "men's studies" suggests a defensive reaction to women's studies rather than a building on women's studies' original insights about gender.

Women's studies was itself conceived as a corrective to the androcentric biases of the traditional scholarly canon. And among its greatest successes was the creation of a new discipline; today, entire libraries, course curricula, and books series are devoted to women's lives. We have titled this work *Men and Masculinities: A Social, Cultural, and Historical Encyclopedia* to better distinguish between studies of men—corporeal beings—and masculinities—the ideologies and attitudes that are associated with those corporeal beings. And we use the term *masculinities* to make clear that there is no one singular masculinity, but that masculinity is elaborated

and experienced by different groups of men in different ways.

This encyclopedia brings together many of the world's premier scholars and writers, who provide the reader with a brief guide to each issue and some suggestions for further reading. We cover biological, cross-cultural, psychological, and sociological research, as well as representations from the arts and humanities. Our authors are among the best-known scholars in the field, invited because of both their command of the material and their ability to convey it in a manner that is immediate and accessible.

Gender, Not Sex

Most social and behavioral scientists now use the term *gender* in a different way than we use the word *sex. Sex* refers to the biological apparatus, the male and the female—our chromosomal, chemical, and anatomical organization. *Gender* refers to the meanings that are attached to those differences within a culture. *Sex* is male and female; *gender* is masculinity and femininity—what it means to be a man or a woman. Even the Supreme Court understands this distinction. In a 1994 case, Justice Antonin Scalia wrote:

> The word 'gender' has acquired the new and useful connotation of cultural or attitudinal characteristics (as opposed to physical characteristics) distinctive to the sexes. That is to say, gender is to sex as feminine is to female and masculine is to male. (*J.E.B. v. Alabama,* 114 S. Ct. 1436 [1994])

And while biological sex varies very little, gender varies enormously. What it means to possess the anatomical configuration of male or female means very different things depending on where you are, who you are, and when you are living.

Men as "Gendered Beings"

But what exactly does it mean to examine men "as men"? It means using gender as a way to understand men's lives—both the quotidian experiences of men in various environments, as well as shedding a new and different light on the lives of men whose accomplishments in some field have already distinguished them.

Think of gender as a sort of lens through which we can see the familiar in a different way, colored by a slightly different hue. The goal of this encyclopedia is not to replace all previous ways of understanding the lives of men, but rather to amplify those other ways of understanding, to add another dimension. We do not believe that once we have examined gender or masculinity, we have therefore come to understand everything there is to know about, for example, F. Scott Fitzgerald or the Vietnam War, to take two examples from the book. But we do emphatically believe that without understanding gender and masculinity, you cannot understand the works of F. Scott Fitzgerald, nor fully comprehend the various elements that contributed to America's involvement in Vietnam. The intention of these volumes is to hold men's lives up to that lens.

Take, for example, the famous American composer Charles Ives, debunking "sissy" types of music; he said he used traditional "tough guy" themes and concerns in his drive to build new sounds and structures out of the popular musical idiom. Or take the celebrated architect Louis Sullivan, describing his ambition to create "masculine forms": strong, solid, commanding respect. (He invented the skyscraper.) Or novelist Ernest Hemingway, retaliating against literary enemies by portraying them as impotent or homosexual.

In my university, the course on nineteenth-century British literature includes a deeply "gendered" reading of the Brontes, which discusses their feelings about femininity, marriage, and relations between the sexes. Yet not a word is spoken about Dickens and masculinity, especially regarding his feelings about fatherhood and the family. Dickens is understood as a "social problem" novelist, and his issue was class relations—this despite the fact that so many of Dickens's

most celebrated characters are young boys without fathers who are searching for authentic families. And there's nary a word about F. Scott Fitzgerald's ideas about masculinity and social success in, say, *The Great Gatsby*. And my collaborator and coeditor tells me that in her nineteenth-century American literature class at Princeton, gender was the main topic of conversation when the subject was Edith Wharton, but the word was never spoken when they discussed Henry James, in whose work gendered anxiety erupts variously as chivalric contempt, misogynist rage, and sexual ambivalence. James, we're told, is "about" the form of the novel, narrative technique, the stylistic powers of description, and characterization—certainly *not* about gender.

Or think about the 1840 presidential campaign during which William Henry Harrison's supporters chastised Martin Van Buren as "Little Vanny," a "used up man?" (You might recall that Harrison was actually deceived by his own hypermasculine hype, eschewing a topcoat while taking the oath of office on the coldest day in several years, and dying one month later of pneumonia.) Or consider Andrew Jackson's manly rage at effete bankers and infantilized Indians; or Theodore Roosevelt's thundering about the strenuous life while he prepared invasions of Panama and the Philippines. For all his tough talk, TR suffered an emotional collapse when his son—whom he pushed into the military—died in World War I. And what about President Lyndon Johnson's vainglorious claim during the Tet Offensive of the Vietnam War, when he said that he "didn't just screw Ho Chi Minh. I cut his pecker off!" Or George H. W. Bush, boasting proudly after his vice presidential debate with Geraldine Ferraro in 1984 that he had "kicked a little ass," and then squaring off against television commentator Dan Rather in 1988 to dispel his image as a wimp? Or, perhaps the more recent case of an assistant to Deputy Secretary Paul Wolfowitz who commented in April 2003 that "anyone can go to Baghdad. Real men go to

Tehran!" Indeed, recent political campaigns have revolved, in part, around gender issues, as each candidate attempted to demonstrate that he was not a "wimp" but was a "real man." (Of course, the few successful female politicians face the double task of convincing the electorate that they are not the "weak-willed wimps" that their gender implies in the public mind while at the same time demonstrating that they are "real women.") From the very founding of the country, the political arena has been a primary masculine testing ground. In fact, the pursuit of manhood has been a dominant theme in American history, at least rhetorically or metaphorically.

Above are just a few examples of what we might call gendered speech, language that uses gender terms to make its case. And these are just a few of the thousands of examples one could find in every academic discipline of how men's lives are organized around gender issues and how gender remains one of the organizing principles of social life. Men come to know themselves and their world through the prism of gender.

Yet, too often, we treat men as if they had no gender, as if only their public personae were of interest to us as students and scholars, as if their interior experience of gender was of no significance.

Earlier Efforts to Study Men

Although this is the first effort to bring this lens to bear on an encyclopedic range of topics, researchers have certainly been examining men and masculinities for a long time. Here I want to provide a sort of chronology of those inquiries and suggest some of the ways our project attempts to synthesize them.

Historically, there have been three general models that have governed social scientific research on men and masculinity. Biological models have focused on the ways in which innate biological differences between males and females program different social behaviors. Anthropological models have examined masculinity cross-culturally, stressing the

variations in the behaviors and attributes associated with being a man. And, until recently, sociological models have stressed how socialization of boys and girls includes accommodation to a "sex role" specific to one's biological sex. Although each of these perspectives helps us to understand the meaning of masculinity and femininity, each is also limited in its ability to explain fully how gender operates in any culture.

Relying on differences in reproductive biology, some scholars have argued that the physiological organization of males and females makes inevitable the differences we observe in psychological temperament and social behaviors. One perspective holds that differences in endocrine functioning are the cause of gender difference, that testosterone predisposes males toward aggression, competition, and violence, whereas estrogen predisposes females toward passivity, tenderness, and exaggerated emotionality. Others insist that these observed behavioral differences derive from the differences between the size or number of sperm and eggs. Because a male can produce 100 million sperm with each ejaculation, while a female can produce fewer than 20 eggs capable of maturing into healthy offspring over the course of her life, these authors suggest that men's "investment" in their offspring is significantly less than women's investment. Other authors arrive at the same conclusion by suggesting that the different size of eggs and sperm, and the fact that the egg is the source of the food supply, impel temperamental differences. Reproductive "success" to males means the insemination of as many females as possible; to females, reproductive success means carefully choosing one male to mate with and insisting that he remain present to care for and support their offspring. Still other authors argue that male and female behavior is governed by different halves of the brain. Allegedly, males are ruled by the left hemisphere, which controls rationality and abstract thought, whereas females are governed by the right hemisphere, which controls emotional affect and creativity. (For examples of these works, see Trivers 1972; Goldberg 1975, 1986; and Wilson 1976)

Observed normative temperamental differences between women and men that are assumed to be of biological origin are easily translated into political prescriptions. In this ideological sleight of hand, what is normative (i.e., what is prescribed) is translated into what is normal, and the mechanisms of this transformation are the assumed biological imperative. George Gilder (1986), for example, assembles the putative biological differences between women and men into a call for a return to traditional gender roles. Gilder believes that male sexuality is, by nature, wild and lusty, "insistent" and "incessant," careening out of control and threatening anarchic disorder, unless it can be controlled and constrained. This is the task of women. When women refuse to apply the brakes to male sexuality—by asserting their own or by choosing to pursue a life outside the domestic sphere—they abandon their "natural" function for illusory social gains. Sex education, abortion, and birth control are all condemned as facilitating women's escape from biological necessity. Similarly, he argues against women's employment, because the "unemployed man can contribute little to the community and will often disrupt it, but the woman may even do more good without a job than with one" (Gilder 1986, 86).

The biological argument has been challenged by many scholars on several grounds. The implied causation between two observed sets of differences (biological differences and different behaviors) is misleading because there is no logical reason to assume that one caused the other, or that the line of causation moves only from the biological to the social. The selection of biological evidence is partial, and generalizations from "lower" animal species to human beings are always suspect. One sociologist asks, if these differences are "natural," why should their enforcement be coercive? And why must males and females be forced to observe the rules that they are naturally supposed to play by (see Epstein 1986, 8)? At least one primatologist argues that the evidence adduced to support the current status quo might also lead to precisely the opposite conclusions, that biological differences would impel female promiscuity and male fragility (see Hardy 1981). Biological differences between males and females would appear to set some parameters for differences in social behavior, but would not dictate the temperaments of men and women in any one culture. These psychological and social differences would appear to be the result far more of the ways in which cultures interpret, shape, and modify these biological inheritances. We may be born males or females, but we become men and women in a cultural context.

It fell to anthropologists to detail some of those differences in the meanings of masculinity and femininity. What they documented is that gender means different things to different people—that it varies cross-culturally. Some cultures, like our own, encourage men to be stoic and to prove their masculinity. Men in other cultures seem even more preoccupied with demonstrating sexual prowess than American men. Other cultures prescribe a more relaxed definition of masculinity, based on civic participation, emotional responsiveness, and the collective provision for the community's needs. What it meant to be a man in seventeenth-century France, or what it means among Aboriginal peoples in the Australian outback at the turn of the twenty-first century are so far apart that comparison is difficult, if not impossible. The differences between two cultures is often greater than the differences between the two genders. If the meanings of gender vary from culture to culture, and vary within any one culture over historical time, then understanding gender must employ the tools of the social and behavioral sciences and history.

Some anthropologists have suggested that the universality of gender differences comes from specific cultural adaptations to the environment, whereas others describe the cultural variations of gender roles, seeking to demonstrate the fluidity of gender and the primacy of cultural organization. Lionel Tiger and Robin Fox (1984) argue that the sexual division of labor is universal because of the different nature of bonding for males and females. "Nature," they argue, "intended mother and child to be together" because she is the source of emotional security and food; thus, cultures have prescribed various behaviors for women that emphasize nurturance and emotional connection (Tiger and Fox 1984, 304). The bond between men is forged through the necessity of "competitive cooperation" in hunting; men must cooperate with members of their own tribe in the hunt and yet compete for scarce resources with men in other tribes. Such bonds predispose men toward the organization of the modern corporation or governmental bureaucracy.

Such anthropological arguments omit as much as they include, and many scholars have pointed out problems with the model. Why didn't intelligence become sex linked, as this model (and the biological model) would imply? Such positions also reveal a marked conservatism: the differences between women and men are the differences that nature or cultural evolution intended, and are therefore not to be tampered with.

Perhaps the best-known challenge to this anthropological argument is the work of Margaret Mead. Mead insisted that the variations among cultures in their prescriptions of gender roles required the conclusion that culture was the more decisive cause of these differences. In her classic study, *Sex and Temperament in Three Primitive Societies* (1935), Mead observed such wide variability among gender-role prescriptions—and such marked differences from our own—that any universality implied by biological or anthropological models had to be rejected. And although the empirical accuracy of Mead's work has been challenged in its specific arguments, the general theoretical arguments remain convincing.

Psychological theories have also contributed to the discussion of gender roles, as psychologists have specified the developmental sequences for both males and females. Earlier theorists observed psychological distancing from the mother as the precondition for independence and autonomy, or suggested a sequence that placed the capacity for abstract reason as the developmental stage beyond relational reasoning. Because it is normative for males to exhibit independence and the capacity for abstract reason, it was argued that males are more successful at negotiating these psychological passages and implied that women somehow lagged behind men on the ladder of developmental success.

But these models, too, have been challenged, for example by sociologist Nancy Chodorow (1978), who argued that women's ability to connect contains a more fundamentally human trait than the male's need to distance, and by psychologist Carol Gilligan (1982), who claimed that because earlier research on child development examined only boys' and men's lives, researchers missed alternative possible bases for moral reasoning. This other ethical construct, an "ethic of care" is not simply "women's" ethical framework, but an ethical framework that both women and men may utilize, but that is associated more with femininity.

Regardless of our assessment of these arguments, Chodorow and Gilligan rightly point out that the highly ideological assumptions that make masculinity the normative standard against which the psychological development of both males and females was measured would inevitably make femininity problematic and less fully developed. Moreover, Chodorow explicitly insists that these "essential" differences between women and men are socially constructed and thus subject to change.

Finally, sociologists have attempted to synthesize these perspectives into a systematic explanation of "sex roles." These are the collection of attitudes, attributes, and behaviors that are seen as appropriate for males and appropriate for females. Thus, masculinity is associated with technical mastery, aggression, competitiveness, and cognitive abstraction, whereas femininity is associated with emotional nurturance, connectedness, and passivity. Sex-role theory informed a wide variety of prescriptive literature (self-help books) that instructed parents on what to do to ensure that their children would grow up as healthy boys or girls.

The strongest challenge to all these perspectives, as we have seen, came from feminist scholars, who have specified the ways in which the assumptions about maturity, development, and health all made masculinity the norm against which both genders were measured. In all the social sciences, these feminist scholars have stripped these early studies of their academic facades to reveal the unexamined ideological assumptions contained within them. By the early 1970s, women's studies programs began to articulate a new paradigm for the study of gender, one that assumed nothing about men or women beforehand, and that made no assumptions about which sex was more highly developed. And by the mid-1970s, the first group of texts about men appeared that had been inspired by these pioneering efforts by feminist scholars.

Thinking about Men:
The First Generation

In the mid-1970s, the first group of works on men and masculinity appeared that were directly influenced by these feminist critiques of the traditional explanations for gender differences. Some books underscored the costs to men of traditional gender-role prescriptions, exploring how some aspects of men's lives and experiences are constrained and underdeveloped by the relentless pressure to exhibit other behaviors associated with masculinity. Books such as Marc Feigen-Fasteau's *The Male Machine* (1974) and Warren Farrell's

The Liberated Man (1975) discussed the costs to men's health—both physical and psychological—and to the quality of men's relationships with women, other men, and their children of the traditional male sex role.

Several anthologies explored the meanings of masculinity in the United States by adopting a feminist-inspired prism through which to view men and masculinity. For example, Deborah David and Robert Brannon's *The Forty-Nine Percent Majority* (1976) and Joseph Pleck and Jack Sawyer's *Men and Masculinity* (1974) presented panoramic views of men's lives from within a framework that accepted the feminist critique of traditional gender arrangements. Elizabeth Pleck and Joseph Pleck's *The American Man* (1980) suggested a historical evolution of contemporary themes. These works explored both the "costs" and the privileges of being a man in modern U.S. society.

Perhaps the single most important book to criticize the normative organization of the male sex role was Joseph Pleck's *The Myth of Masculinity* (1981). Pleck carefully deconstructed the constituent elements of the male sex role and reviewed the empirical literature for each component part. After demonstrating that the empirical literature did not support these normative features, Pleck argued that the male sex-role model was incapable of describing men's experiences. In its place, he posited a male "sex role strain" model that specified the contemporary sex role as problematic, historically specific, and also an unattainable ideal.

Building on Pleck's work, a critique of the sex-role model began to emerge. Sex roles had been cast as the static containers of behaviors and attitudes, and biological males and females were required to fit themselves into these containers, regardless of how ill fitting these clusters of behaviors and attitudes felt. Such a model was ahistorical and suggested a false cultural universalism, and was therefore ill equipped to help us understand the ways in which sex roles change, and the ways in which individuals modify those roles through the enactments of gender expectations. Most telling, however, was the way in which the sex-role model ignored the ways in which definitions of masculinity and femininity were based on, and reproduced, relationships of power. Not only do men as a group exert power over women as a group, but the definitions of masculinity and femininity reproduce those power relations. Power dynamics are an essential element in both the definition and the enactments of gender.

This first generation of research on masculinity was extremely valuable, particularly because it challenged the unexamined ideology that made masculinity the gender norm against which both men and women were measured. The old models of sex roles had reproduced the domination of men over women by insisting on the dominance of masculine traits over feminine traits. These new studies argued against both the definitions of either sex and the social institutions in which those differences were embedded.

Shapers of the new model looked at "gender relations" and understood how the definition of either masculinity or femininity was relational, that is, how the definition of one gender depended, in part, on the understanding of the definition of the other.

In the early 1980s, the research on women again surged ahead of the research on men and masculinity. This time, however, the focus was not on the ways in which sex roles reproduce the power relations in society, but rather on the ways in which femininity is experienced differently by women in various social groups. Gradually, the notion of a single femininity—which was based on the white, middle-class Victorian notion of female passivity, langorous beauty, and emotional responsiveness—was replaced by an examination of the ways in which women differ in their gender-role expectations by race, class, age, sexual orientation, ethnicity, region, and nationality.

The research on men and masculinity is now entering a new stage in which the variations among men are seen as central to the understanding of men's lives. The unexamined assumption in earlier studies had been that one version of masculinity—white, middle-aged, middle-class, heterosexual—was the sex role into which all men were struggling to fit in our society. Thus, working-class men, men of color, gay men, and younger and older men were all observed as departing in significant ways from the traditional definitions of masculinity. Therefore, it was easy to see these men as enacting "problematic" or "deviant" versions of masculinity. Such theoretical assertions, however, reproduce precisely the power relationships that keep these men in subordinate positions in our society. Not only does middle-class, middle-aged, heterosexual white masculinity become the standard against which all men are measured, but this definition, itself, is used against those who do not fit as a way to keep them down. The normative definition of masculinity is not the "right" one, but it is the one that is dominant.

The challenge to the hegemonic definition of masculinity came from men whose masculinity was cast as deviant: men of color, gay men, and ethnic men. We understand now that we cannot speak of *masculinity* as a singular term, but must examine *masculinities*: the ways in which different men construct different versions of masculinity. Such a perspective can be seen in several late-twentieth-century works, such as Harry Brod's *The Making of Masculinities* (1987), Michael Kimmel's *Changing Men: New Directions in Research on Men and Masculinity* (1987), and Tim Carrigan, R. W. Connell, and John Lee's "Toward a New Sociology of Masculinity" (1985). Robert W. Connell's *Gender and Power* (1987) and Jeff Hearn's *The Gender of Oppression* (1987) represent the most sophisticated theoretical statements of this perspective. Connell argues that the oppression of women is a chief mechanism that links the various masculinities and that the marginalization of certain masculinities is an important component of the reproduction of male power over women. This critique of the hegemonic definition of masculinity as a perspective on men's lives was one of the organizing principles of my coedited textbook (with Michael Messner), *Men's Lives,* published initially in 1988, and now in its sixth edition. When it first appeared, *Men's Lives* was the first college-level text in this second generation of work on men and masculinities.

Since then the field has mushroomed, and there are now subfields on masculinities in many academic disciplines, as well as a recognition that men and masculinities need to be acknowledged and analyzed within the frameworks established in gender studies.

So, how do we think about men and masculinities in the social and behavioral sciences in the early twenty-first century?

The Social Construction of Masculinities

Men are not born—growing from infants through boyhood to manhood—to follow a predetermined biological imperative encoded in their physical organization. To be a man is to participate in social life as a man, as a gendered being. Men are not born; they are made. And men make themselves, actively constructing their masculinities within a social and historical context.

The meaning of masculinity is neither transhistorical nor culturally universal; it is not carried on the Y chromosome, nor is it somehow a function of testosterone. Rather, the meanings of manhood vary from culture to culture and within any one culture over time. Thus, males become men in the United States in the early twenty-first century in a way that is very different from men in Southeast Asia, or Kenya, or Sri Lanka.

Men's lives also vary within any one culture over time. The experience of masculinity in the contemporary United States is very different from that experience 150 years ago. Who would argue that what it meant to be a "real man" in seventeenth-century France (at least among the upper classes)—high-heeled patent leather shoes, red velvet jackets covering frilly white lace shirts, lots of rouge and white powder makeup, and a taste for the elegant refinement of ornate furniture—bears much resemblance to the meaning of masculinity among a similar class of French men today?

Masculinity also varies within any one society according to the various types of cultural groups that compose it. Subcultures are organized around other poles, which are the primary way in which people organize themselves and by which resources are distributed. And men's experiences differ from one another according to what social scientists have identified as the chief structural mechanisms along which power and resources are distributed. We cannot speak of masculinity in the United States as if it were a single, easily identifiable commodity. To do so is to risk positing one version of masculinity as normative and making all other masculinities problematic.

In the United States of the early twenty-first century, masculinity is constructed differently by class culture, by race and ethnicity, and by age. And each of these axes of masculinity modifies the others. Black masculinity differs from white masculinity, yet each of them is also further modified by class and age. A thirty-year-old, middle-class black man will have some things in common with a thirty-year-old, middle-class white man that he might not share with a sixty-year-old, working-class black man, although he will share with him elements of masculinity that are different from those of the white man of his class and age. The resulting matrix of masculinities is complicated by cross-cutting elements; without understanding this, we risk collapsing all masculinities into one hegemonic version. Imagine, for example, an older, black, gay man in Chicago and a young, white, heterosexual farm boy in Iowa. Wouldn't they have different definitions of masculinity?

If gender varies across cultures, over historical time, among men within any one culture, and over the life course, can we really speak of masculinity as though it was a constant, universal essence, common to all men? If not, gender must be seen as an ever-changing fluid assemblage of meanings and behaviors. In that sense, we must speak of *masculinities,* and thus recognize the different definitions of masculinity and that we construct these definitions. By pluralizing the terms, we acknowledge that masculinity means different things to different groups of people at different times.

At the same time, we can't forget that all masculinities are not created equal. American men must also contend with a particular definition that is held up as the model against which we are expected to measure ourselves. We thus come to know what it means to be a man in our culture by setting our definitions in opposition to a set of "others"—racial minorities, sexual minorities. For men, the classic "other" is, of course, women. It feels imperative to most men that they make it clear—eternally, compulsively, decidedly—that they are unlike women.

For most men, this is the "hegemonic" definition—the one that is held up as the model for all of us. This is what Virginia Woolf called "the quintessence of virility, the perfect type of which all the others are imperfect adumbrations" (142). The hegemonic definition of masculinity is "constructed in relation to various subordinated masculinities as well as in relation to women," writes sociologist R. W. Connell (1987, 183). The sociologist Erving Goffman once described this hegemonic definition of masculinity like this:

> In an important sense there is only one complete unblushing male in America: a young, married, white, urban, northern, heterosexual, Protestant, father, of college education, fully employed, of good complexion, weight, and height, and a recent record in sports. Any male who fails to qualify in any one of these ways is likely to view himself—during moments at least—as unworthy, incomplete, and inferior. (Goffman 1963, 128)

(Of course, women contend with an equally exaggerated ideal of femininity, which Connell calls "emphasized femininity" [1987, 183]. Emphasized femininity is organized around compliance with gender inequality, and is "oriented to accommodating the interests and desires of men" [Connell 1987, 187]. One sees emphasized femininity in "the display of sociability rather than technical competence, fragility in mating scenes, compliance with men's desire for titillation and ego-stroking in office relationships, acceptance of marriage and childcare as a response to labor-market discrimination against women" [Connell 1987, 188]. Emphasized femininity exaggerates gender difference as a strategy of "adaptation to men's power" stressing empathy and nurturance; "real" womanhood is described as "fascinating" and women are advised that they can wrap men around their fingers by knowing and playing by the "rules.")

This Encyclopedia

Men and Masculinities was assembled and edited with this background. These volumes present more than 400 entries of varying lengths. The entries that comprise these volumes can be generally grouped into three large categories:

First, we hold up the lives and accomplishments of many historical figures—political figures, writers, artists, and thinkers—who are well known to readers. Here, we see them through a new lens, a gendered lens that explores their activities and their ideas as they contribute to the larger historical construction of masculinities. Of interest to us here is not that they *were* men themselves, although many were, but rather that what they *did* is somehow exemplary to the construction of masculinities. All subjects are carefully presented to illuminate the ways in which their lives and work expressed and contributed to the construction of masculinities. These are often icons of masculinity, those "role models" or the creators and purveyors of those role models, who are held up as the images of masculinity to which we should aspire. Often, though, these entries also highlight less-well-known figures whose contribution to the construction of masculinities is often overlooked.

Second, we examine the various intersections of masculinity and other experiences and identities. Entries on diverse groups of men—by race, class, religion, ethnicity, sexuality—help give a fuller and richer picture of the meaning of masculinities. Here are the entries that focus specifically on the construction of gay masculinities or African American masculinities that specify the ways in which these "marginalized" masculinities are constructed through racism or homophobia, that is, constructed through an interaction with other, dominant forms of masculinities.

Third, we present a collection of events, processes, movements, and historical moments—all of which are pivotal in the construction of masculinities. These include historical events like wars, or social movements like unions. Organizations that were developed to assist in the construction of masculinity, such as the Boy Scouts or the YMCA, are also featured.

Fourth, we present a set of experiences that constitute men's lives, experiences that are essential for the individual construction of masculinity for men—such as aging—and institutions that shape men's lives, such as marriage, sports, and the workplace. We're especially aware of the different meanings that different groups of men bring to experiences of sexuality, for example, and we present a large number of entries that examine men's bodies and men's sexuality as a central site in the construction of masculinity.

And finally, we present a set of theoretical constructs that have been developed by natural and social scientists as well as humanists to illuminate some essential aspect of men's lives and the construction of masculinities. These include psychological terms that describe men's experiences, as well as the application of more traditional terms to specifi-

cally male populations. Here, readers will find terms such as *gender order, patriarchy, Adonis Complex,* or *Don Juanism.*

We have sought to illuminate the experiences of men and the shaping of masculinities. In the process, we hope these volumes will raise new ideas as well as new pathways to and through more well-trodden ground. Canonized authors like Shakespeare and Cooper and Fitzgerald and Ellison; everyday issues like housework, health, and fatherhood; major historical currents from democracy to colonialism to the Cold War; superstars like Elvis and Tom Hanks and Eminem; American cultural staples like baseball, Bruce Springsteen, and the "self-made man" all gain new dimensions through their treatment here.

We make no claims that the 400 entries that comprise these volumes present a complete and comprehensive compendium of all extant knowledge about men and masculinities. Such a project would be a lifetime's work, worthy, perhaps, of Diderot's magisterial ambition, but impossible to undertake today. As the editors of these volumes, we remain painfully aware of their limitations. For one thing, while we have contributions from around the world and entries on international topics, the overwhelming majority of entries are limited *largely,* but not entirely, to United States–based sources. We have made reference to non-American sources—whether individual characters or movements—but have included mainly those that directly bear on the construction of American masculinities. The work is limited by the vision of its editors, but enlarged by the greater collective wisdom of the advisory editors. Several entries we had hoped to include, and for which we had contracted with authors, failed to materialize.

But in the modern world, an encyclopedia need not be fully comprehensive to be the definitive work in the field. We hope that we have assembled a useful collection of entries that will serve readers for many years to come, providing the best and most complete compendium possible at this moment. We hope that it will prove useful to those who use it, and that it will serve as the basis for future work to make men's lives and masculinities visible.

References:

Brod, Harry, ed. 1987. *The Making of Masculinities.* Boston: Unwin, Hyman.

Carrigan, Tim, R. W. Connell, and John Lee. 1985. "Toward a New Sociology of Masculinity." *Theory and Society* 5, no. 14.

Chodorow, Nancy. 1978. *The Reproduction of Mothering.* Berkeley, CA: University of California Press.

Connell, R. W. 1987. *Gender and Power.* Stanford, CA: Stanford University Press.

David, Deborah, and Robert Brannon, eds. 1976. *The Forty-Nine Percent Majority.* Reading, MA: Addison-Wesley.

Elliott, J. H. 1984. *Richelieu and Olivares.* New York: Cambridge University Press.

Epstein, Cynthia Fuchs. 1986. "Inevitability of Prejudice." *Society* (September/October).

Farrell, Warren. 1975. *The Liberated Man.* New York: Random House.

Feigen-Fasteau, Marc. 1974. *The Male Machine.* New York: McGraw-Hill.

Gilligan, Carol. 1982. *In a Different Voice.* Cambridge, MA: Harvard University Press.

Gilder, George. 1986. *Men and Marriage.* Gretna, LA: Pelican Publishers.

Goffman, Erving. 1963. *Stigma.* Englewood Cliffs, NJ: Prentice-Hall.

Goldberg, Steven. 1975. *The Inevitability of Patriarchy.* New York: William Morrow.

———. 1986. "Reaffirming the Obvious." *Society* (September/October).

Hardy, Sandra Blaffer. 1981. *The Woman That Never Evolved.* Cambridge, MA: Harvard University Press.

Hearn, Jeff. 1987. *The Gender of Oppression.* New York: St. Martin's Press.

Kimmel, Michael S., ed. 1987. *Changing Men: New Directions in Research on Men and Masculinity.* Newbury Park, CA: Sage.

Mead, Margaret. 1935. *Sex and Temperament in Three Primitive Societies.* New York: McGraw-Hill.

Pleck, Elizabeth, and Joseph Pleck, eds. 1980. *The American Man.* Englewood Cliffs, NJ: Prentice-Hall.

Pleck, Joseph. 1981. *The Myth of Masculinity.* Cambridge, MA: M.I.T. Press.

Pleck, Joseph, and Jack Sawyer, eds. 1974. *Men and Masculinity.* Englewood Cliffs, NJ: Prentice-Hall.

Stimpson, Catharine. 1988. *Where the Meanings Are.* New York: Methuen.

Tiger, Lionel, and Robin Fox. 1984. *The Imperial Animal.* New York: Holt, Rinehart and Winston.

Trivers, Robert. 1972. "Parental Investment and Sexual Selection." In *Sexual Selection and the Descent of Man.* Edited by B. Campbell. Chicago: Aldine.

Wilkinson, Rupert. 1986. *American Tough: The Tough Guy Tradition and American Character.* New York: Harper and Row.

Wilson, E. O. 1976. *Sociobiology: The New Synthesis.* Cambridge, MA: Harvard University Press.

Woolf, Virginia. 1938/1966. *Three Guineas.* New York: Harcourt.

Note

This introduction borrows liberally from the Introduction to *Men's Lives,* 6th edition, edited by Michael Kimmel and Michael Messner (Boston: Allyn and Bacon, 2003), and *The Gendered Society,* by Michael Kimmel (New York: Oxford University Press, 2000). It has been modified and revised, but draws on those works' initial formulations.

A

Abolitionists

In a poem dedicated to William Lloyd Garrison, Thomas Wentworth Higginson thanks his fellow abolitionist for what he calls "thy manly life," reflecting a sentiment shared by most nineteenth-century antislavery supporters. Theirs was a manly or masculine endeavor, one that upheld the basic principles of democracy—life, liberty, and the pursuit of happiness—and that did so respectfully, yet sometimes forcefully. At the same time as the abolitionists celebrated traditional masculinity, however, the movement's close association with several of the century's other causes, including the Temperance movement and the Women's Suffrage movement, ensured an alignment with the feminine that often complicated their approach to gender. The speeches and writings of three of the most notable abolitionists—Higginson, Garrison, and Wendell Phillips—reveal precisely this type of complicated approach to gender. By combining elements of traditional masculinity with elements of traditional femininity, these men helped redefine what it meant to be a man in nineteenth-century America.

Despite a shared understanding and sometimes vehement invocation of masculinity, the abolitionists used the term to describe behaviors and ideals that both significantly differed from popular connotations of the word and reinforced them. For example, the typically masculine characteristics of reason, action, and violence find their way into many of Higginson's, Garrison's, and Phillips's speeches. These same men, however, often meld those masculine characteristics with more feminine characteristics, such as passivity and emotion, sometimes even within the same speeches. The ensuing paradox behind messages that call for individuals to embrace aspects of both the masculine and feminine complicates the understanding and use of gender. A man should be passive, yet often must act in violence; he should be courageous, but also sensitive; reasonable, yet also open to emotional appeals.

Garrison exemplifies the abolitionists' complicated definition of masculinity in his "Tribute to Clarkson and Wilberforce," where he systematically lists what he sees as the most positive masculine qualities of the two British activists. They are "venerable men" with "passive hearts" who do not know how to act selfishly. Garrison applauds them for their devotion to the cause, for "enduring shame and reproach," for behaving rationally, and, above all, for not allowing color to blind them. In their actions, they work to stop

This illustration depicts the great antislavery meeting at Exeter Hall in 1841. When the Mexican-American War began in 1846, abolitionists were one of the most outspoken groups in the United States and vehemently denounced the war. They feared that the war was being fought to gain new territory for slavery. (National Archive)

bloodshed and they "break the yoke of oppression." They behave respectfully, sincerely, and passionately toward their cause—attributes of the new, abolitionist masculinity. In contrast, Garrison uses "The Great Apostate," an essay devoted to critiquing Daniel Webster, to demonstrate the lack of manhood and masculinity that fuels the proslavery agenda. Garrison describes Webster as having "thrown away his manhood to gratify a wicked ambition."

Phillips applauds masculine courage also, but he focuses on illuminating another of its important aspects, the courage of black men. In his speech, "Crispus Attucks and the Negroes," Phillips draws a portrait of the Revolutionary War hero that highlights the ig-

nored black soldier's courageous feats, claiming that Attucks is "the emblem of Revolutionary violence in its dawn" and that he should receive the same respect and admiration as Washington. Phillips repeats this theme in other essays, including "Toussaint l'Ouverture," where he outlines courage, contrary to popular belief at the time, as the most notable and defining feature of black men.

On the surface, Higginson's sense of masculinity seems to be the most stereotypical of the three. He often points to the ideals of courage and action in order to fuel the efforts of the cause, and many of his own actions reflect these beliefs, including his participation in the violent storm on Boston's court house when officials in the same city captured and prepared to return Andrew Burns to slavery; his reporting from, and participation in, the Kansas/Missouri conflict over slavery; and his involvement with John Brown's raid as part of the "Secret Six."

Higginson's involvement with abolition, however, also complicated his conception of masculinity. As a supporter of Temperance and Women's Suffrage, Higginson willingly acknowledged his appreciation for femininity. Later, as the colonel of the Union army's first black regiment, Higginson himself even turns toward the feminine. He often refers to himself as a "mother" of his troops, and in letters written to his wife and mother he acknowledges the feminine side of his interactions with the regiment, and of his own personality.

Perhaps the most notable aspect of Higginson's sense of masculinity is his repeated insistence on the importance of the body. For him, masculinity surfaces not only as a state of mind or an emotion, but as a bodily condition, one that enables a person to behave courageously, to rise to action if necessary. Masculinity means, among other things, a keen awareness of the body's abilities and a willingness to cultivate those abilities. On a less personal scale, nonviolence and temperance also helped construct attitudes toward masculinity and the body, but this time as a means of self-control.

All three men exemplified, in their actions, speeches, and writings, a new type of masculinity for the nineteenth century. Rather than relying solely on stereotypical notions regarding gender, these men gleaned what they saw as the best attributes of the masculine—reason, courage, and action—and then combined the attributes with more feminine characteristics, such as appeals to emotion, passivity, and sensitivity. The result often created an image that, in its seemingly oppositional structure, defied popular assumptions regarding what it meant to be a man or a woman, to be masculine or feminine in the nineteenth century.

Kristin N. Sanner

See also American Civil War; Slavery

Further Reading:
Bartlett, Irving H. 1961. *Wendell Phillips: Brahmin Radical.* Boston: Beacon Press.
———. 1979. *Wendell and Ann Phillips: The Community of Reform, 1840–1880.* New York: W. W. Norton.
Cain, William E., ed. 1995. *William Lloyd Garrison and the Fight against Slavery: Selections from* The Liberator. Boston: Bedford.
Garrison, William Lloyd. 1852. *Selections from the Writings and Speeches of William Lloyd Garrison.* New York: Negro Press.
Grimke, Archibald H. 1969. *William Lloyd Garrison: The Abolitionist.* New York: Negro Universities Press.
Harrold, Stanley. 2001. *American Abolitionists.* Harlow, UK: Longman.
Higginson, Thomas Wentworth. 1884. *Wendell Phillips.* Boston: Lee and Shepard.
———. 2000. *The Complete Civil War Journal and Selected Letters of Thomas Wentworth Higginson.* Edited by Christopher Looby. Chicago: University of Chicago Press.
Meyer, Howard N., ed. 2000. *The Magnificent Activist: The Writings of Thomas Wentworth Higginson (1823–1911).* Cambridge, MA: Da Capo Press.
Phillips, Wendell. 1982. *Wendell Phillips on Civil Rights and Freedom.* Edited by Louis Filler. Washington, DC: University Press of America.
Tuttleton, James W. 1978. *Thomas Wentworth Higginson.* Boston: Twayne.

Action Television Series

The male action television series is a genre that was most popular from the late 1970s through the 1980s. The plots tend to be superficial vehicles for the action, which generally entails the "good" male protagonists fighting, either with fists or guns, against their "evil" adversaries. These shows included *CHiPs* (1977–1983), *Dukes of Hazzard* (1979–1985), *Knight Rider* (1982–1986), *The A-Team* (1982–1987), and *Simon & Simon* (1981–1988), among others. Early elements of the genre can be found in shows such as *The Lone Ranger* (1949–1957), *Batman* (1966–1969), and *Mission Impossible* (1966–1973); later shows such as *Walker, Texas Ranger* (1993–2001) suggest that the genre did not disappear entirely. However, there has been a shift toward investigative crime series, in which the protagonist must think instead of fight, exemplified by such shows as *McGyver* (1985–1992), *The Pretender* (1996–2000), and *CSI* (2000–). In the male action TV series, masculinity is presented as exclusively heterosexual through fighting, superfluous romance plots, and supercharged automobiles.

Heterosexual masculinity within these shows is complicated by the close relationship between the multiple male protagonists. By having more than one male protagonist, the shows provide models of male-male interaction, something that our culture does not do often outside of sports. Although most shows use the conventional two—the "buddy narrative"—creating a simple male-male dynamic, a few break this form: *S.W.A.T.* (1975–1976), *Magnum, P.I.* (1980–1988), and *The A-Team* have three or more recurrent male protagonists. *Knight Rider* has a lone male protagonist, although one could easily argue that the protagonist's car, which is endowed with a personality that is gendered male, makes this a "buddy" show.

The male-male pairings within these shows generally fall within the *female* stereotypical pairings of light and dark heroines and/or "butch" and "femme." *Starsky and Hutch* (1975–1979), *CHiPs, Dukes of Hazzard, Simon & Simon, The A-Team, Miami Vice* (1984–1989), and *Walker, Texas Ranger* all have a light-skinned, light-haired protagonist paired with a dark-haired and frequently darker-skinned protagonist. Despite the original audiences being overwhelmingly male, the light-haired male often has a boyish or pretty appearance ("femme"), such as Rick (*Magnum, P.I.*), "Face" (*The A-Team*), A. J. (*Simon & Simon*), and Bo (*The Dukes of Hazzard*). These men are paired with darker-skinned or dark-haired men: T. C. (*Magnum, P.I.*), B. A. (*The A-Team*), Rick (*Simon & Simon*), and Luke (*The Dukes of Hazzard*). Although not all of the latter men are as "butch" as B. A., they do tend to be the tougher men in the pairings.

In the series that include men of color, these men rarely exceed the racially stereotypical component of their masculinity. The most offensive would be the "warrior" Tonto, in *Lone Ranger,* but Ponch (*CHiPs*) is routinely presented as the "Latin Lover," and the African American men in *The A-Team; Magnum, P.I.; Miami Vice;* and *Walker* are primarily present for their strength, and any suggestion of their heterosexuality must be achieved with women of color. Only the shows of the late 1960s and early 1970s, such as *Mission Impossible* and *The Rookies* (1972–1976), present African American men in slightly more complex roles. However, all of these shows present the person of color in the secondary role, making his masculinity less threatening to the predominantly white audience.

Flirtatious and suggestive banter is also part of the homoerotic subtext of many of these shows. Because their heterosexuality is not to be questioned, the men in these shows can makes jokes impugning the masculinity, maleness, and/or heterosexuality of the others, and they can cross-dress. The shows of the 1980s have the greater homoerotic subtext and in retrospect are the most campy.

Heterosexual masculinity is affirmed in these shows through force and violence; most shows use hand-to-hand fighting or big guns. Hand-to-hand fighting proves that the hero is physically stronger than his foe, suggesting that he is not gay (the stereotype of gay men being effeminate underlies this). Or, the shows have the male heroes use excessively large guns (*The A-Team, S.W.A.T.*), the not-so-subtle phallic metaphor.

To defuse the homoerotic potential of male-male interaction, some of these shows employ an overtly sexualized female costar: Daisy (*The Dukes of Hazzard*), Amy and Tania (*The A-Team*), Amy and Bonnie (*Knight Rider*), Bonnie (*CHiPs*). These women have little plot significance, and despite their conventionally attractive appearance, are not physically involved with the male protagonists. These woman are present for the heterosexual male viewer, so that he may participate in the male bonding while having a viable or acceptable release for his heterosexual desire.

Another element that is frequently used to affirm heterosexual masculinity is the male-female kiss. For example, at least half of the episodes of *Knight Rider* end with Michael Knight giving an attractive woman a quick kiss before he leaves. Similarly, a majority of *A-Team* episodes contain at least one scene where "Face" kisses a young woman; the other three men have one or two episodes each where they kiss women, so that all of the team is ultimately confirmed as heterosexual.

A less frequent and less compelling approach is the off-screen girlfriend or wife. The audience can be satisfied with the apparent heterosexuality of the hero, but the plot and male bonding are not interrupted by her presence.

A related device is the foiled wedding. *Magnum, P.I.; Knight Rider;* and *Walker, Texas Ranger* each have an episode where the hero is set to marry, only to have the bride killed or otherwise removed *before* the marriage can be consummated; therefore, heterosexuality is assured, but the hero can still maintain his close male relationships without the continuous plot disruption of a wife.

As if homosexuality were not taboo enough within American culture, the shows generally incorporate a second taboo that would have to be broken for anything sexual to occur: incest (*Simon & Simon, The Dukes of Hazzard*), biracial relationships (*CHiPs; The A-Team; Miami Vice; Walker, Texas Ranger*), or cybernetic relationships (*Knight Rider*).

Finally, given the automobile's long-standing association in the American vernacular with male sexuality, the powerful car (or van) is a prominent element of almost all of the aforementioned shows. For most viewers, the car is the one thing that they could have in common with the men on TV, and thus it is the point of access for the masculinity presented in the shows.

Michael Hardin

See also Buddy Films

Further Reading:

Brown, Jeffrey. 1993. "Bullets, Buddies, and Bad Guys: The 'Action-Cop' Genre." *Journal of Popular Film and Television* 21, no. 2 (Summer): 79–87.

Osgerby, Bill, and Anna Gough-Yates, eds. 2001. *Action TV: Tough Guys, Smooth Operators and Foxy Chicks.* New York: Routledge.

Adolescence

Adolescence has been identified as a critical period of boys' gender socialization during which pressures to accommodate norms of masculinity provide a framework for bodily changes (e.g., cognitive development, sexual maturation), shifts in existing relationships (e.g., with family and friends), experiences of new relationships (e.g., with romantic and/or sexual partners), and introductions to new social roles and responsibilities (e.g., at work). Qualitative and quantitative empirical studies of boys, along with clinical work with boys, indicate that relationships with teachers, family members, and peers are primary contexts in which masculine norms manifest in boys' everyday lives and emphasize that it is often through and within interpersonal relationships that masculine norms are introduced, reinforced, incorporated, and perpetuated in ways that become personally meaningful and directly consequential to adolescent boys. Much of recent discourse on boys' gender socialization focuses on ways in which masculine norms can negatively impact boys' attitudes and behaviors, and thereby be detrimental to boys' psychological and social health. However, studies also show that boys are neither helpless victims of their gender socialization nor passive recipients of culture. Evidence suggests that individual boys are able to play a mediating role, for instance, through their capacity to resist as well as internalize pressures to accommodate masculine norms and through their ability to make meaning of, and give significance to, their experiences of gender socialization. Studies also suggest that having at least one close, confiding relationship, in which boys feel truly known and accepted for who they are, can potentially protect boys from psychological and social risks that may be associated with their gender socialization. That is, as active participants in their gender socialization, boys negotiate their identities, behaviors, and styles of engaging others in light of cultural constructions of masculinity but also in light of their own senses of themselves, their experiences of relationships, and their perceptions of reality.

Over the last two decades of the twentieth century, feminist researchers highlighted ways in which aspects of feminine norms can contribute to the social and psychological oppression of girls and women, and raised questions as to whether aspects of masculine norms may similarly have negative consequences for boys and men, despite the social privileges of being male. Although masculine norms may vary within and between groups (e.g., by race/ethnicity, class, sexuality, age), conventional norms of masculinity, which tend to emphasize physical toughness, emotional stoicism, projected self-sufficiency, and heterosexual dominance over women, have persisted over time and can usually be identified within most cultures. It is boys' socialization toward conventional norms of masculinity that clinicians and researchers suggest can be detrimental to boys' emotional and relational development, linked to risk-related social behaviors, and become a hindrance to boys' overall psychological well-being.

Clinical work with boys has suggested that the content and processes of male socialization may stifle boys' emotional and relational development in the name of proving and sustaining manhood. Kindlon and Thompson (1999) propose that, as emotional stoicism is regarded as a defining feature of masculinity, boys are "emotionally miseducated" through their gender socialization and rendered "emotionally illiterate" in the sense that their ability to articulate their own feelings and their sensitivity to other people's feelings are not valued and, as a result, are not developed.

Pollack (1998) argues that boys' separations from their mothers during early childhood in the name of masculine self-sufficiency, although considered normative in boys' gender socialization, are experienced as traumas that exacerbate their struggles as men to develop close, intimate relationships. Although this work provides an important perspective on how boys may become emotionally and relationally constrained as a result of their gender socialization, a tendency is evoked in this literature to conceptualize boys' socialization as a linear model of cause and effect wherein masculine norms directly impact boys' attitudes and behaviors. As a result, boys are often depicted as passive recipients of culture and helpless victims of their socialization.

Empirical studies of boys have begun to highlight ways in which boys actively participate in their gender socialization, for instance through their ability to resist as well as internalize pressures to accommodate masculine norms and through their ability to interpret or make sense of their experiences, and can thereby influence its effects on their social behaviors and psychological health. Pleck et al. (1994) suggest that the salience of masculine norms to an individual boy can mediate how they impact his attitudes and behaviors and thus account for individual differences in the experiences and consequences of male gender socialization. Pleck and his colleagues found that adolescent boys who placed greater importance on the need for males to adhere to conventional norms of masculinity tended to exhibit more risk-related social behaviors, including being suspended from school, drinking alcohol and using street drugs, tricking or forcing someone to have sex, and engaging in delinquent activities. Likewise, Chu, Porche, and Tolman (2001) found that, despite possible advantages of status and power, adolescent boys' alignment with conventional norms of masculinity was associated with lower self-esteem.

Research also has shown that interpersonal relationships can protect adolescents, boys and girls alike, against psychological and social risks. Resnick and his colleagues from the National Longitudinal Study of Adolescent Health (1977) revealed that, independent of race, ethnicity, family structure, and poverty status, adolescents who feel connected to their parents, families, and school communities are healthier than those who do not, and that having access to at least one close, confiding relationship is the single best protector against psychological and social risks, including emotional distress, suicidal thoughts and attempts, violence perpetration, cigarette use, alcohol use, marijuana use, early sexual involvement, and unintended pregnancy. In Chu's study of boys' relational development, adolescent boys' interview narratives emphasize ways in which their relationships with family members and with friends can be an important source of support as well as pressure and how boys draw strength from these relationships as they work to reconcile their desire to fit in socially (e.g., by accommodating masculine norms) with their desire to be true to themselves (e.g., by expressing their genuine thoughts and feelings), when these desires conflict.

Despite an increasing emphasis on individuation and separation in the name of maturity and manhood, boys' development continues to center on their interpersonal relationships during adolescence. However, boys are observed to experience difficulties in developing close relationships and to have lower levels of intimacy in their relationships, as compared with girls. In contrast to stereotypes that consequently depict adolescent boys as either incapable of, or uninterested in, having close and intimate relationships, evidence indicates that boys' relational capabilities, including their self-awareness and their sensitivity to others, carry forth beyond early childhood (Chu 1998). There is also evidence of adolescent boys' desires to be truly known and accepted, for instance in their friendships.

Rather than being a question of ability or interest, boys' styles of engaging in their relationships, and thereby the quality of boys' re-lationships, seem partly to reflect how boys are actively reading, taking in, and responding to their culture, and particularly constructions of masculinity. In a culture where having and wanting close relationships tend to be associated with being female, and proving masculinity involves devaluing and differentiating oneself from all things feminine, it is not surprising that boys may learn to cover up their capacity and desire for emotional intimacy. In interviews, adolescent boys emphasize the need to protect themselves from ridicule and rejection by being careful about what they reveal to others (Chu 1998). Adolescents also describe how issues of trust can make it difficult to rely on and share their genuine thoughts and feelings with others (Way 1998). Boys indicate that they learn through experience to modify their self-expression and their styles of engaging others in light of their understanding of what is acceptable and desirable, and also what feels safe, in their particular social contexts. That is, boys' gender socialization does not cause boys to lose their relational capabilities and their desire for emotional intimacy in relationships. However, through their experiences of gender socialization, boys do become more savvy about how they express themselves and how they engage in their relationships. Moreover, as they accommodate themselves to conventional norms of masculinity in what may be considered a socially adaptive move, their capacity and desire for relationships become more difficult to detect.

Judy Y. Chu

See also Boyhood; Bravado; Columbine; School Shootngs

Further Reading:

Chu, Judy Y. 1998. Relational Strengths in Adolescent Boys. Paper presented at the American Psychological Association, San Francisco, CA.

Chu, Judy Y., Michelle V. Porche, and Deborah L. Tolman. 2001. Examining Relational Masculinity Ideology and Self-Esteem among Adolescent Boys. Paper presented at the American Psychological Association, San Francisco, CA.

Connell, Robert W. 1996. "Teaching the Boys: New Research on Masculinity, and Gender

Strategies for Schools." *Teachers College Record* 98, no. 2: 206–235.

Kindlon, Daniel, and Michael Thompson. 1999. *Raising Cain: Protecting the Emotional Life of Boys.* New York: Ballantine Publishing Group.

Pleck, Joseph H., Freya L. Sonenstein, and Leighton C. Ku. 1994. "Problem Behaviors and Masculinity Ideology in Adolescent Males." Pp. 165-186 in Robert Ketterlinus and Michael E. Lamb, eds., *Adolescent Problem Behaviors: Issues and Research.* Hillsdale, NJ: Lawrence Erlbaum Associates, Inc.

Pollack, William S. 1998. *Real Boys: Rescuing Our Sons from the Myths of Boyhood.* New York: Random House.

Resnick, Michael D., Peter S. Bearman, Robert W. Blum, Karl E. Bauman, Kathleen M. Harris, Jo Jones, Joyce Tabor, Trish Beuhring, Renee E. Sieving, Marcia Shew, Marjorie Ireland, Linda H. Bearinger, and Richard Udry. 1997. "Protecting Adolescents from Harm: Findings from the National Longitudinal Study on Adolescent Health." *Journal of the American Medical Association* 278, no. 10: 823–832.

Way, Niobe. 1998. *Everyday Courage: The Stories and Lives of Urban Teenagers.* New York: New York University Press.

Way, Niobe, and Judy Y. Chu, eds. Forthcoming. *Adolescent Boys in Context.* New York: New York University Press.

"Adonis Complex"

The Adonis complex refers to the various manifestations of body image problems seen in men today (Pope, Phillips, and Olivardia 2000). Contrary to popular belief, these problems are not only experienced by women. It is this belief that leads many boys and men to suffer silently for fear that they will be perceived as effeminate or weak. Men with these issues struggle with a "feeling and talking taboo" that prevents them from discussing these concerns, even with those closest to them. They often suffer with depression, anxiety, and issues of self-esteem.

The rates of body dissatisfaction in men have risen dramatically over the last several decades. A survey found that close to 50 percent of men are dissatisfied with their appearance compared to only 15 percent of men in 1972 (Cash, Winstead, and Janda 1986). More men are seeking cosmetic surgery to improve their appearance. For example, in 1992 approximately 6,000 men had liposuction to remove unwanted fat, compared to close to 22,000 men in 1997. Approximately 3 to 5 million men in the United States alone struggle with eating disorders, such as bulimia nervosa. These problems are associated with devastating psychological and medical consequences, including depression, social isolation, cardiac problems, and death (Pope, Phillips, Olivardia 2000).

About 1 million men have body dysmorphic disorder (BDD), which causes them to believe that a part of their appearance is ugly and defective in some way, when in reality it looks fine. They may think they are losing their hair, even when sporting a full head of hair. Or they may think that their penis is too small, when it is of average size, or feel their nose is too big, when it looks ordinary. These beliefs lead to various compulsive behaviors in an attempt to disguise or eliminate the perceived defect. Meanwhile, others cannot see what the victim sees. A subcategory of BDD, known as muscle dysmorphia, has emerged in the literature in which men who are very muscular and fit perceive themselves to be too small or weak looking. This preoccupation leads to compulsive exercise and weight lifting (sometimes up to six hours per day), idiosyncratic dietary rituals, compulsive mirror checking and grooming behavior, social avoidance, and occupational and relational impairments (Olivardia 2001).

Once relegated to elite bodybuilding circles, anabolic steroids are being used more and more by young boys and men who are striving for a perfect muscular body. Studies have found that approximately 6 percent of high school boys have admitted using these dangerous illegal substances (Durant et al. 1993, 922). Physical effects include hardening of the arteries, which can lead to stroke and heart attacks at an early age. Psychological effects include psychosis, mania, and aggressive or violent behavior, also known as "roid rage" (Pope, Phillips, and Olivardia 2000).

Various theories have been offered as to why men are now being affected by body-image concerns that have plagued women for centuries. A proliferation of media images over the last twenty years of the twentieth century and into the twenty-first directed at young boys and men dictating the ideal male body may have had some role in this phenomenon (Pope, Phillips, and Olivardia 2000). The popular toy G. I. Joe action figure, Calvin Klein advertisements, muscled athletes and movie stars, and fitness magazines have all been implicated in projecting to young men the type of body for which they should strive. Some have hypothesized that the increased attention to male body image is a result of the increased parity of women (Mishkind et al. 1986; Pope, Phillips, and Olivardia 2000). Men used to define their masculinity through their occupations or income. Because many of these roles are rightfully shared by women today, men may be attempting to demonstrate their masculinity through building their bodies. In addition, men may feel increased pressure to have a good body as a means of competing with other men for the attention of men and women. Muscularity signifies many hyper-masculine traits, such as strength, sexual virility, aggression, and dominance. Outreach, recognition, proper assessment, diagnosis, and further research on treatment of these problems are necessary in order to remedy this significant problem.

Roberto Olivardia

See also Anabolic and Androgenic Steroids; Atlas, Charles; Bodybuilding, Contemporary; Bodybuilding, History of; Men and Eating Disorders; Schwarzenegger, Arnold

Further Reading:

Cash, Tom F., Barbara A. Winstead, and Louis H. Janda. 1986. "The Great American Shape-Up: Body Image Survey Report." *Psychology Today* 20: 30–37.

Durant, Robert H., Vaughn I. Rickert, Carolyn S. Ashworth, Cheryl C. Newman, et al. 1993. "Use of Multiple Drugs among Adolescents Who Use Anabolic Steroids." *New England Journal of Medicine* 328: 922–926.

Mishkind, Marc E., Judith Rodin, Lisa Silberstein, and Ruth H. Striegel-Moore. 1986. "The Embodiment of Masculinity: Cultural, Psychological and Behavioral Dimensions." *American Behavioral Scientist* 29, no. 5: 545–562.

Olivardia, Roberto. 2001. "Mirror, Mirror on the Wall, Who's the Largest of Them All?" *Harvard Review of Psychiatry* 9: 254–259.

Pope, Harrison G., Jr., Katharine A. Phillips, and Roberto Olivardia. 2000. *The Adonis Complex: The Secret Crisis of Male Body Obsession.* New York: The Free Press.

Aging

Aging is a process with enormous psychological, emotional, and—some believe—moral consequences. We can identify the onset of aging when the physiological development of a boy is being completed, at the end of puberty in the late teen years. Adolescent boys typically relish the process of maturation, wanting the privileges and status that accompany being a man.

Maturation takes about twenty years. During the next forty years of mature adulthood, men rarely notice the very slow aging process. Most men continue to grow in discernment and wisdom during this time. When accident or illness brings awareness that recovery to a previous maximum functional ability will not occur, gradually and episodically men become aware of aging and more acutely aware of their mortality. Denial of death is an adaptive mechanism in midlife that enables individuals to focus on planning for the future.

The objective and subjective experiences of men differ enormously (Thompson 1994). Life events and the meanings attributed to them vary by socioeconomic class, education, ethnicity, religion, random occurrence, and personal interpretations.

Tradition has it that sometime in the eighteenth century, Frederick the Great of Prussia asked one of his ministers the average age of death of his citizens. Told that it was sixty-five, he decreed that that age should be the

Runners in the 10K Run of the first U.S. National Senior Olympics (Joseph Sohm; ChromoSohm Inc. / Corbis)

age of retirement—a concept that was not necessary before the Industrial Revolution and the development of modern state bureaucracies that could provide retirement benefits. Had his minister taken into account higher infant mortality and death from infectious disease prior to age 65, the figure would have been closer to forty years. Recognizing that statistics vary by source and country, in the nineteenth century, it appears that men on average lived about two years longer than women, who were vulnerable to the danger of complications in multiple pregnancies and deliveries. In 1900 in the United States, average life expectancy for men was 48.2 and women 51.1; in 1996, 73.0 for men and 79.0 for women (National Institute on Aging). The National Center for Health Statistics reported life expectancy in the year 2000 as 74.1 for men and 79.0 for women. Due to improved health care both sexes live longer than they used to, but women's average life expectancy exceeds that of men by six to eight years. It is

worth noting, however, that the United States ranks only twenty-fourth among nations in life expectancy (World Fact Book 2000), with Japan ranked highest.

Some of this difference may be intrinsic to the biological differences between men and women. Men are more vulnerable to sex-linked disorders. More male than female fetuses are conceived, between 108 and 120 males to 100 females (Tricomi, Seer, and Solish 1960; Parkes 1967) and more spontaneously abort. Still 103 to 105 boys are born for every 100 girls. (World Fact Book 2000). Approximate sex parity, that is equal numbers of men and women, occur approximately at the time of physiological maturity.

Another part of the difference between men and women in life expectancy can be attributed to men's socialization. Boys have far stronger inducement to conform to traditional sex-role expectations than girls. The cultural illusion that men are stronger than women promotes an expression of "masculinity" that honors greater risk taking by men throughout life. More men die early due to accidents and acts of violence than women. The subjective experience of failure to achieve idealized masculine goals results in shame for some men, which is at best psychologically destructive, and surely contributes to men's greater risk for suicide. Traditionally, more men smoke tobacco than women, doubtless as a symbol of masculinity, though smoking rates are declining and equalizing. The health consequences of smoking, greater risk of all types of cancer and coronary and pulmonary diseases, are well documented.

Evidence that difference in life expectancy is not all intrinsic to biological factors but is in part a consequence of behavioral and environmental factors is found in the variation among life expectancy in various countries. Depending on the source of data and method of analysis, specific average figures vary, but trends are clear. According to a World Health Organization (WHO) report rating 191 countries, Japan ranked first with male life expectancy of 74.5 years and the United States ranked twenty-fourth with a male life expectancy of 67.5 years for children born in 1999 (World Health Organization 2000). (Note: Demographic data has multiple parameters. The specific data cited here is illustrative and not intended to be complete. Additional data can be found at www.aoa.dhhs.gov/aoa/stats.)

Increased life expectancy has had a profound impact on society. Not only can a man expect to live longer, but in developed countries the average age of the population is increasing. Historically, a few of the privileged or lucky who survived famine, infectious disease, and war lived to an old age. Now for the first time in history, most men do.

Sixty-five is no longer the standard age for retirement. Gradually the age for receiving Social Security benefits and Medicare is being increased, yet at the same time many men have vested pensions and are retiring at much younger ages. However, the trend to-ward early retirement may be reversing itself due to perceived financial insecurity. Some research suggests that men in general adjust to retirement better than women, but that men who return to some form of work by choice are happier with their lives and marriages than men who retire permanently (Kim and Moen 1999). Men are socialized to be the primary breadwinners, though this no longer holds for the generation approaching retirement age in the early twenty-first century. Nevertheless, adjusting to a domestic-based life can cause both personal and relationship stress.

A man who survives to age sixty-five in good health can expect on average twenty more years of life. These changes in life expectancy have important consequences for social policy. For example, Social Security systems can no longer be based on the assumption that there will be increasing numbers of workers in the preretirement group to provide benefits for the retired. In a healthy economy, there are sufficient resources to provide for all, but considering the trend of an aging population, both political determination and new mechanisms will be required to make retirement systems secure.

Recognizing these changes, universities have established academic programs in gerontology research. Clinical training programs for health care providers now offer specializations in geriatrics. Professional organizations have emerged with journals and annual conferences for early reporting of research and continued education for practitioners. (Note: Two of the most important professional organizations are the Gerontological Society of America and the American Society on Aging.)

In 1974 Congress authorized formation of the National Institute on Aging (NIA) to provide leadership in aging research, education, dissemination of health information, and other programs relevant to aging and older people. Subsequent amendments to this legislation designated the NIA as the primary federal agency for Alzheimer's disease research.

The term *old* is no longer considered sufficient to describe the postretirement group, but new distinctions have appeared in the professional literature. *Young old* is now conventionally used to designate persons between sixty-five and seventy-five, *old* denotes persons between seventy-five and eighty-five, and *old old* describes persons eighty-five and older.

Inevitably the question occurs: Can the increase in human life expectancy that has been experienced in the twentieth century be continued? Most researchers answer in the affirmative, but not at the same rate. Most biological scientists believe that there is an upward cap on human life expectancy somewhat short of 150 years (Moody 1993).

Inevitably the human body, including the brain, slows down, probably as a result of cumulative errors in DNA replication. Vision changes for most people in their fifth decade of life, but in time most people also experience some loss of visual acuity, auditory clarity, and even taste and smell. Although the age of onset varies, this results in a condition called senility, which includes both debility and dementia. Debility and dementia do not proceed at the same rate in all men. For some, death comes from a physiological failure before there is any onset of dementia; for a few, dementia occurs even before the onset of physical weakness.

Dementia is defined as the failure of mental abilities, again with no certain sequence. Typically, recent or short-term memory declines first, and then remote memory. In time comes the failure of abstract thinking, orientation to time and place, and failure of expressive and receptive linguistic ability. In its last stages, dementia can result in the loss of orientation to self, loss of speech, and loss of motor control, with only the brain stem supporting basic vital functions.

Dementia has multiple causative factors, the most significant being the syndrome called Alzheimer's disease. Strokes can also result in death of sufficient brain cells to reduce thinking and motor activity. Other neurological illnesses with unknown causes such as Parkinson's disease and multiple sclerosis can contribute to dementia. Alcohol abuse is a significant factor in memory loss. Failure to fully program the brain through education is also thought to contribute to vulnerability. These causes are additive in their effect, though a few men escape dementia until a very advanced age, when coronary failure becomes the most common cause of death.

The vast majority of men enter one or more domestic relationships during their lives, most frequently in the form of legally sanctioned heterosexual marriages. Due to the higher mortality rate of men, fewer aging men live alone than women. In the year 2000, 73 percent of men sixty-five and older were living with a spouse, 17 percent alone, and 10 percent in other arrangements. Sociologists and psychologists have found that men living alone are at greater risk for reduction in quality of life than women living alone (Velkoff and Lawson 1998). More women become caregivers of domestic partners than men, and in the prime of life more women become caregivers for aging parents and other family elders than do men.

Nevertheless, because of the random unpredictability of life, many men must assume the role of caregiver for chronically ill or demented partners or parents. Some men feel they are more constitutionally suited for these tasks, even when a woman is available (Kraemer and Thompson 2002).

Heterosexual men who survive the death of a domestic partner in later life are advantaged in finding a far larger pool of available women for continued companionship (Moore and Stratton 2002). In the year 2000, the sex ratio for the 65–69 age group was 143 women for every 100 men; for those 85 and older there were 245 women for every 100 men (World Fact Book 2000).

Homosexual men who are coming to an age of retirement in the early 2000s have adequate reliable information and adequate social support systems to facilitate emotional well-being. However those in the "old old" cohort are especially disadvantaged, with few exceptions. They matured during a time of taken-for-granted cultural prejudice resulting in severe negative sanctions, not only against physical intimacy between men but even against expressions of affection. Not only religious leaders, but educational and medical authorities as well, conflated gender roles with sexual orientation, unintentionally promoting widespread anxiety among all men of any behavior that could be considered "feminine."

Many older men living today were shaped by the Great Depression and World War II. Many were economically and emotionally deprived, resulting in anxieties and insecurities. After the war, many men had opportunities for upward social and economic mobility, which sometimes resulted in identifications with structures of domination over women, children, and minorities. These experiences have caused some older men to be defensive about social and cultural developments that have passed them by. However, age alone is not a handicap for growth and adjustment to changing social circumstances. Age is typically accompanied by reduction in both social and internal pressure to conform to sex-role stereotypes. Many older men find sufficient freedom from convention to be themselves for the first time.

Contrary to popular opinion, old men are able to maintain a healthy sexual and sensual life, and medications are becoming available to enhance sexual ability. Physical intimacy is as important as orgasms. Our society, however, retains such negative attitudes about sex that older men are criticized for their expressed interest. The possibilities available are rarely discussed in medical settings for lack of time or perceived importance, and churches and senior centers often fail to help due to ignorance and inhibition. Therefore it is advisable for men to be proactive about such discussions with informed counselors.

Social Security does not provide sufficient income to live above the poverty level, but only a survival minimum. A prudent man will plan for additional retirement income and lay aside some savings to assure more comfort in old age.

Medicare, part of the Social Security insurance system, provides basic outpatient medical care, limited hospitalization, and limited rehabilitation in a skilled nursing facility, but it does not pay for medication at the present time. If long-term care is needed, private payment is required as long as there are personal assets. Medicaid, an emergency welfare program, becomes available for persons who have "spent down" to a minimal reserve fund of several thousand dollars, specified by each state. Medicaid then covers the cost of generic medications, however, Social Security benefits are taken to cover the cost of residential care, except for approximately one dollar per day personal allowance.

Adjustment to life in a nursing home is usually more difficult for men than women. Almost everyone requiring long-term care grieves for the loss of his or her home. The loss of freedom of movement and personal decision making is usually greater for men than for women. Even the best nursing homes are not resort hotels. A private room requires private pay. Individual food preferences and choice of mealtimes and sleep times are structured by the necessities of the setting. Personal control over medications and most toilet articles is usually denied and the guiding principle is safety over comfort or personal preference. Expressions of physical intimacy are strongly discouraged except between legally married couples sharing the same room, and that may not be possible unless both members of the couple qualify for the same level of care.

Enhanced medical technology, a pervasive prolife ideology, and the legal vulnerability of health care providers often results in the use of any life-sustaining technology possible. These may include a ventilator that requires penetration of the trachea and a gastric feeding tube that requires the penetration of the abdomen. In some cases the heart is started after there is no longer sufficient brain function to assure any quality of life. Most men would want these interventions if there were a possibility of recovery. Without that possibility most men would prefer the natural death that would occur without these invasive interventions. Churches could be far more resourceful in assisting old men to cope with the realities of old age but all too often encourage denial of death by promising life after death rather than focusing on the quality of life here and now.

To have some chance that one's personal wishes will be carried out, all men need to prepare a prior directive, or living will, and keep it on file with their physicians. Everyone should designate a family member or trusted friend, as well as a "backup" individual, to exercise a health care power of attorney, which authorizes such friend or relative to make decisions in case of one's temporary or permanent loss of competence. Personal communication to a life partner, friend, relative, or physician regarding one's wishes in such circumstances is not sufficient without documentation of authority. Forms for these documents can be downloaded from the Internet and are available in physicians' offices and county departments of social services.

For the man who has given thought to his future, however, old age can be wonderful. Though there are accidental and genetic factors that are not under personal control, men can optimize their health by not smoking and limiting alcohol use. Weight control and regular, physical activities that maximize range of motion, such as gardening, housecleaning, and sports—especially walking and swimming—are valuable. Most older men want to work part time, if not for the financial reward, then for the change of scene and the opportunities of socialization. Many older men for the first time find opportunity for political activity. For those who do not need or wish to work, old age provides opportunities to enhance their lives by travel and voluntary service.

Aging can also offer opportunity to create better balance in life. Some men will want to remedy past mistakes and mend the fences of broken relationships with children or friends. For others this is an opportunity to make peace with the cosmos and to accept that death is part of life, while living to the fullest until it comes.

James Harrison

See also Male Menopause; "Midlife Crisis"

Further Reading:

Binstock, Robert H., and Linda K. George. 2001. *Handbook of Aging and the Social Sciences.* 5th ed. San Diego, CA: Academic Press.

Brown, Lester B., ed. 1997. *Gay Men and Aging.* New York: Garland.

Eisler, Richard M., and Michael Herson, eds. 2000. *Handbook of Gender, Culture and Health.* Mahwah, NJ: Erlbaum.

Furstenburg, Frank F. 2002. *Adult Transitions in Cross-National Perspective.* Thousand Oaks, CA: Sage Publications.

Kim, Jungeen E., and Phillis Moen. 1999. *APA Monitor Online* 30, no. 9 (October).

Kraemer, Betty J., and Edward H. Thompson. 2002. *Men as Caregivers.* New York: Springer.

Moody, Harry R. 1993. *Aging: Concepts and Controversies.* Thousand Oaks, CA: Pine Forge Press (Sage).

Moore, Alinde J., and Dorothy C. Stratton. 2002. *Resilient Widowers.* New York: Springer.

National Center for Health Statistics. At http://www.cdc.gov/nchs/fastats/lifexpec.html (cited 27 July 2003).

National Institute on Aging. At http://www.originalghr15.com/secrets.html (cited 27 July 2003).

Parkes, A. 1967. "The Sex Ratio in Man." In *The Biology of Sex.* Edited by A. Allison. Baltimore: Penguin Books.

Thompson, Edward H., Jr., ed. 1994. *Older Men's Lives.* Thousand Oaks, CA: Sage.

Tricomi, V., O. Seer, and C. Solish. 1960. "The Ratio of Male to Female Embryos as Determined by the Sex Chromatin." *American Journal of Obstetrics and Gynecology* 79: 504–509.

Velkoff, V., and V. Lawson. 1998. "Gender and Aging." U.S. Department of Commerce. At http://www.census.gov/ipc/prod/ib-9803.pdf (cited 27 July 2003).

World Health Organization (WHO). 2000. "WHO Issues New Healthy Life Expectancy Rankings." At http://www.who.int/inf-pr-2000/en/pr2000-life.html (cited 27 July 2003).

AIDS

AIDS (acquired immune deficiency syndrome) is an infectious disease that suppresses the human body's immune system, greatly increasing the chances for other, opportunistic infections to beset the victim. AIDS is caused by infection with HIV (human immunodeficiency virus). HIV enters the body through the introduction of bodily fluids from an already infected individual. Once in the body, HIV centers in the blood stream, attacking and destroying so-called T4 cells. The depletion of T4 cells weakens the body's immune function, leading to other infections. HIV/AIDS is considered a chronic disease, and one that eventually leads to death. However, it is not AIDS itself that causes death; rather, individuals die of opportunistic infections, which are facilitated by the body's suppressed immune system and weakening state.

The World Health Organization estimated that at the end of 2001 more than 40 million persons worldwide were living with HIV, with more than 20 million having already died. More than one-half (53 percent) of those living with HIV are men, and 54 percent of those who died with AIDS in 2001 were men. Men are expected to continue to bear the brunt of the AIDS epidemic, as 58 percent of new infections in 2001 were in men (WHO 2002).

In the United States, the HIV/AIDS epidemic has taken a serious toll, but not nearly as significant as in other parts of the world. Diagnosed cases of AIDS in North America account for only about 2 percent of all AIDS cases worldwide, according to the World Health Organization. The true brunt of the epidemic has been in Sub-Saharan Africa and South and Southeast Asia, which together account for approximately 85 percent of all cases. As of the start of 2001 the Centers for Disease Control and Prevention reported a total of 748,393 cases of AIDS had been diagnosed in the United States. More than 442,000 Americans had died with AIDS by this time. Deaths among persons with AIDS peaked in the United States in 1995, when more than 50,200 persons died. Since 1995 new treatments and drugs have contributed to the decline in the number of deaths among persons with AIDS; in 2000 only 8,867 deaths among persons with AIDS were reported. Additionally, more than 450,000 individuals were living with HIV infection or diagnosed with AIDS. The total number of persons infected with HIV is unknown, as it is widely believed that as many as one in three persons that are infected do not know of their infection.

HIV infection and AIDS has historically been a primarily male disease in the United States. This is not the case in most other nations, however. In the United States, fully 85 percent of all known cases of AIDS have occurred in men. In the initial stages of the AIDS epidemic in the United States, HIV was concentrated among men, specifically men who have sex with men. Due to this initial concentration, and the ease with which HIV is transmitted during sexual activities, the disease quickly gained a foothold in this segment of the population and has only slowly begun to even out across the sexes. As of the start of 1991, 90 percent of all persons with AIDS in the United States were men. In the early years of the twenty-first century, however, the number and proportion of women with HIV and AIDS is increasing, although the numbers still show a strongly skewed distribution.

The first cases of AIDS in the United States were all men, almost entirely gay men or men who had sex with men. Small, unusual outbreaks of Kaposi's sarcoma, a rare skin cancer, and pneumocystis carinii pneumonia (PCP), were reported on the west and east coasts in 1981, suggesting an immune system failure in the diagnosed men, but the cause of their illnesses was unknown. It was another three years before scientists isolated the cause of the suppression of suddenly sick and dying men's immune systems. The HIV virus as the agency that causes the disease AIDS was identified and named in 1984 by Dr. Joseph Gallo. (Others debate this, crediting the original identification to researchers at the Institute Pasteur in France who pointed to what they called lymphadenopathy-associated virus [LAV] in 1983.) Once a cause was identified, research turned to three new foci: 1) developing a way to test for the infection; 2) developing a treatment, cure, or vaccine for the disease; and 3) developing and implementing prevention programs to thwart new infections. The first test for HIV infection (developed by Dr. Robert Gallo) was approved by the Food and Drug Administration in 1985. Less success has been achieved regarding the other two foci, although significant progress has been made on both. The fact remains, however, that HIV continues to infect perhaps several million additional individuals worldwide every year.

HIV, the virus widely attributed as the cause of AIDS, is concentrated in bodily fluids, especially blood and other fluids containing blood products. As such, transmission of HIV from an infected individual to another requires the transmission recipient to have contact with (and internalize) infected fluids from the transmitting individual. Exchange of blood (through contact following injury or other blood-to-blood contact) is the most efficient means for transmitting HIV. Exchange of bodily fluids via sexual activities and sharing of injection drug paraphernalia are the most common activities for transmitting HIV. Also, HIV-positive women are capable of transmitting the virus to their fetuses prenatally.

According to the United States Centers for Disease Control and Prevention, the most common way men have become infected with HIV is via sex with an infected male sexual partner. More than one-half of all American men with HIV infection report having engaged in sex with another man. When assessing the risk factors for infection among men known to be HIV positive, at the start of 2001 cumulative statistics show 46 percent report sex with a male partner, 13 percent report injection drug use, 6 percent both sex with a man and injection drug use, and 7 percent unprotected heterosexual sexual activity (risk factors are not reported for 27 percent of HIV-positive men).

Largely due to the initial concentration of HIV/AIDS among gay men, Americans quickly came to define AIDS as a "gay disease." The consequences of this meant that homophobia was fueled and gay men were targeted for increased discrimination, including violent attacks. Mainstream American society quickly equated "gay" with "AIDS" and justified their prejudice and discriminatory actions on the foundation of protecting the public health. In the early twenty-first century, the perception of AIDS as a gay disease is dissipating, but does somewhat remain. Although it is widely known today that AIDS is not restricted to gay men (or men who have sex with men), many groups and segments of American society continue to attribute the presence and proliferation of AIDS to gay men.

One positive consequence of the AIDS epidemic—and consequential blaming of gay men for the disease—has been a renewed and invigorated level of social activism. This includes activism directly related to HIV/AIDS issues (e.g., increased access to health care, faster approval for experimental drugs, legal protections against discrimination for infected persons, etc.) and a more visible, more vocal, and stronger gay rights movement. The HIV/AIDS epidemic certainly helped to invigorate these forms of social activism, and the gains that have been made as a result are valuable, but the costs that have accompanied these gains (illness, suffering, and deaths) have been monumental.

In sum, HIV/AIDS in the United States has been a disease that has hit men especially hard. The disease has not only led to the suffering and deaths of many men, but it has also led to many significant social repercussions for men. Men who have sex with men have been the primary group affected by HIV/AIDS in the United States, but in the early twenty-first century this is changing. The fact remains, however, that men are bearing the brunt of AIDS in the United States.

Richard Tewksbury

See also Condom Use; Homosexuality; Reproductive Health; Risk Behaviors, Sexual; Sexually Transmitted Infections

Further Reading:

Shilts, Randy. 1987. *And the Band Played On: Politics, People, and the AIDS Epidemic.* New York: St. Martin's Press.
Smith, Raymond A., ed. 1998. *Encyclopedia of AIDS.* Chicago: Fitzroy Dearborn.
World Health Organization (WHO). 2002. *World Health Report.* Geneva: WHO.

Alcohol

The consumption of alcohol is commonplace in many cultures, serving religious, cultural, social, and nutritional functions. People "drink" for many reasons and in a variety of contexts. Historically and culturally, drinking has been considered to be primarily a male activity that is often associated with men's being together. When men drink, they drink more often, in greater quantities, and with more negative consequences than women. The research literature on alcohol provides a gendered understanding of men's drinking, suggesting that men who use alcohol drink in order to be male, or rather, to be what they perceive to be male within a specific historical or cultural context (Capraro 2001). These gender influences exist alongside other influences on drinking. Thus, although many factors influence drinking, gender in turn exerts an additional influence within these social, cultural, and class differences that results in men drinking more in each group than

women. Yet not all men drink, and many drink without problems.

Research has demonstrated that the causes of drinking and alcoholism are varied and complex, with biology, personality, family background, religion, and culture all contributing to the character of one's relationship with alcohol. Studies of North American and European men have shown that gender expectations and roles exert a significant influence in addition to these other variables, with drinking serving to enhance many activities that are traditionally seen as masculine. Thus, men who identify with more traditional definitions of masculinity drink more. For example, in cultures where risk taking is seen as a male or manly activity, men are more likely to engage in risky behavior while drinking, an often dangerous and fatal combination. Furthermore, men who experience conflicts over being men (i.e., gender-role conflicts) drink with more negative consequences, regardless of how these "masculinities" may be defined in terms of race, class, ethnicity, and historical period.

Men may drink without problems. However, when men feel conflicted about being male, they suffer more negative consequences of their drinking. Men therefore use alcohol to "play out the expectations of the male role and to deal with stresses and perceived role failures about their masculinity" (Brooks 2001, 290). These behaviors are reinforced by the portrayal of men in media and literature and by the behavior of male icons. Like many of the paradoxes of masculinity, men who drink to gain a sense of status and power can pay a serious price for doing so, including loss of status and power as a consequence of the negative effects of their drinking. Interestingly, men who have a greater sense of agency or self-efficacy are protected from drinking problems in comparison with men who are conflicted about their masculinity (McReary, Newcomb, and Sadava 1999).

Drinking can also provide men with the opportunity to express feelings that may not otherwise be considered normative for men.

For example, in American culture celebratory drinking among men is associated with physical contact and bonding that would otherwise feel uncomfortable due to prohibitions about male closeness (i.e., homophobia). As a ritualized, gendered activity, alcohol allows men to feel and express closeness and share experiences that might otherwise create discomfort about intimacy with men.

In addition to the biological and physiological effects of alcohol, psychological expectations regarding the effects of alcohol, along with men's perceptions of other men's drinking, play a significant role in how men drink and how men act when they drink. Most men (and women) think that men (and women) drink more than they really do, a belief that encourages men to drink more than they would otherwise and to act certain ways when they drink. Thus, the stereotypical behaviors associated with men's drinking occur even when men are given nonalcoholic beer that they think is alcoholic, confirming that gendered expectations can directly influence men's drinking behaviors in addition to biology, genetics, and other causes (Critchlow 1986).

Much has been made of the "convergence hypothesis" that women are drinking more like men as strict notions of gender roles relax. Yet even though the frequency of women's drinking has increased slightly in recent years, women still drink in different ways than men, for different reasons, and to a lesser extent (Berkowitz and Perkins 1987; Perkins 1992).

Finally, it is important to note the differences in men's drinking across a range of cultures and identities. For instance, in the United States, Caucasian men drink more often and with greater negative consequences than men of color, with African American men drinking the least often and with the least problems. Among religious groups, Catholics of different ethnicities drink more than Protestants, who in turn drink more than Jews. These ethnic and religious differences exist for women as well.

In summary, drinking is a ritualized behavior that is gendered and scripted for men. Men's drinking can at least in part be explained by the extent to which men try to be male and/or have problems with the inherent conflicts and expectations of the male gender role, and this gender effect is enacted within the different cultures, identities, and contexts that men live.

Alan D. Berkowitz

See also Beer; Chemical Dependence

Further Reading:
Berkowitz, Alan K., and H. Wesley Perkins. 1987. "Recent Research on Gender Differences in Collegiate Alcohol Use: A Review of Recent Research." *Journal of American College Health* 35 (1): 21–28.
Brooks, Gary R. 2001. "Masculinity and Men's Health." *Journal of American College Health* 49: 285–297.
Capraro, Rollo C. 2001. "Why College Men Drink: Alcohol, Adventure and the Paradox of Masculinity." *Journal of American College Health* 48: 307–315.
Critchlow, Barbara. 1986. "The Powers of John Barleycorn: Beliefs about the Effects of Alcohol and Social Behavior." *American Psychologist* 7: 751–764.
McCreary, D. R., M. Newcomb, and S. Sadava. 1999. "The Male Role, Alcohol Use, and Alcohol Problems: A Structural Modeling Examination in Adult Women and Men." *Journal of Counseling Psychology* 46, no. 1: 109–124.
Perkins, H. Wesley. 1992. "Gender Patterns in Consequences of Collegiate Alcohol Abuse: A 10-Year Study of Trends in an Undergraduate Population." *Journal of Studies on Alcohol* 53: 458–462.

Alda, Alan (1936–)

After his star-making turn as Captain Benjamin Franklin "Hawkeye" Pierce in the perennial, award-winning television series *M*A*S*H* (1972–1983) and his appearances in the comedy-dramas *Same Time Next Year* (1978) and *The Four Seasons* (1981, which he also wrote and directed), Alan Alda emerged at the beginning of the 1980s as a representative, if unconventional, icon for a new generation of men. For many television and film viewers, male and female alike, the gangly, sweater-wearing Alda symbolized a charming, certainly milder alternative to the "Raging Bulls" and "Rockys" of the world—a romantic lead whose masculinity was predicated on sensitivity, intelligence, and roguish wit as opposed to testosterone-fueled aggression, machismo, and intimidating physical prowess. Even today, despite reputation-shattering forays into more darkly cynical territory (such as his roles as an arrogant and self-serving filmmaker in Woody Allen's *Crimes and Misdemeanors* [1989], a greedy, Nobel Prize-minded AIDS researcher in Roger Spottiswoode's *And the Band Played On* [1993], and a war-mongering U.S. president in Michael Moore's *Canadian Bacon* [1994]), Alda's name remains synonymous with humanistic awareness and sensitivity to others, due in no small part to his well-documented personal convictions and political consciousness. However, this predictable, knee-jerk depiction of Alda as an emblematic sign of the late-twentieth century's domesticated, demasculinized male presents a rather one-dimensional approach to this actor/director/screenwriter's diverse career, and does little to account for the ways his strategic deconstruction of stereotypical masculinity was propelled and shaped by cultural forces.

With the benefit of historical hindsight, it is possible to excavate Alan Alda's entrenched persona and situate it within a broader continuum—a masculine genealogy rooted in everything from the fleet-footed dandyism and finesse of Fred Astaire to the "everyman" earnestness of James Stewart, from the verbal gymnastics and wise-cracking of Groucho Marx to the trickster intellectualism of Robert Benchley—while gesturing toward subsequent televisual permutations of the well-read, well-bred "New Man" (culminating in the 1990s with Kelsey Grammer's opera-loving, sherry-sipping Frasier Crane in the television series *Frasier*). This historical continuum furthermore links Alda's East Coast brand of moderate liberalism to that of other outspoken media figures sympathetic to women's rights (such as John Lennon, Ed Asner, Gore Vidal, Phil Donahue, and Howard Cosell). Indeed, the intertextual matrix of meaning surrounding Alda's charismatic persona solidified his status as the ideal, nonthreatening "New Man" of the 1970s and early 1980s—a hyperconscious manifestation of American masculinity that hearkened back to male icons of Hollywood's classical studio era (1930s–1950s, during which his father, actor Robert Alda, enjoyed brief success as a matinee idol), while suggesting a contemporary concern for civil liberties that could only have emerged in the post-Vietnam, antiestablishment era. The rise of Alda's star status, and its eventual decline during the Reagan years, thus marks a considerable paradigm shift in the epistemological terrain subtending masculinity studies.

As a longtime advocate of the Equal Rights Amendment (ERA), Alda was able to deploy his New Man image to promote gender equality while refashioning masculinity into a malleable "meta-trope" through which to channel public dissent. A friend of Gloria Steinem and an enemy of all that smacked of male hegemony, Alda rose above the ranks of his profeminist brethren to speak before Senate committees as the chairman of Men for ERA. He successfully lobbied against job discrimination, penned several widely circulated essays (among them the introduction to *A Guide to Non-Sexist Children's Books*), and took great pride in his "emancipated" wife Arlene's successful career as a professional photographer after her twenty years of playing the devoted homemaker. His outspoken attacks on the political status quo performed an implicit critique of patriarchal authoritarianism, deflating, as it were, the "masculine mystique" promulgated by his cinematic and televisual forebears. Though a *New York Times* article proclaimed that the aggressively nonaggressive Alda—after supplanting John Wayne as America's favorite personality in 1981—had "achieved something close to pop cultural sainthood," not everyone leapt onto the sensitivity bandwagon, particularly those who questioned his sincerity or felt that his celebrity was the result of a carefully engineered public relations stunt. Yet Alda persevered and, with the resolve of a self-righteous crusader, stared down the inevitable patriarchal backlash of the 1980s, when rampant "wimp bashing" and diatribes against "quiche-eaters" sparked a nostalgic revival of the conservative ethos and macho posturing of the 1950s.

Besides supporting women's liberation, Alda the humanitarian activist championed workers' rights, abortion rights, and racial equality (notably, in 1964 he costarred alongside African American actress Diana Sands in Broadway's first interracial comedy, *The Owl and the Pussycat*). And yet, for all of the admittedly progressive agendas, contradictions linger. As his biographer, Raymond Strait, points out, "It is difficult to understand how anyone with his clout on *M*A*S*H* was so busy selling feminism that he overlooked the lack of it in his own series" (1983). In order to unpack this key player's import in the cultural rethinking and physical reformulation of the white American male, it will be helpful to at least partially shuck the prevailing wisdom concerning his image. This image continues to be nurtured and manipulated via a well-oiled publicity machine (which, besides guarding his family's privacy under lock and key, occasionally parlays his egalitarian spirit and frequent appearances at fundraisers and marches into headline-grabbing rhetoric).

By sorting through the discursive manifestations of Alda's so-called soft masculinity (in print media, television, and film), scholars can begin to highlight the underlying contradictions of a man who played everyone from a promiscuous, skirt-chasing army surgeon (*M*A*S*H*) to a show-tune-singing patriarch (*Everyone Says I Love You*, 1996), from a misogynistic draft dodger (*Jenny*, 1970) to a convicted California rapist (*Kill Me If You Can*, 1977). Tracking his professional and personal life from his Second City improvisational performances and television work in the late 1960s (for instance, *That Was the Week That Was*

and *What's My Line?*) to his distinguished body of cinematic output (including *The Glass House* [1972], *Free to Be You and Me* [1974], *The Seduction of Joe Tynan* [1979], *Flirting with Disaster* [1996], and *The Object of My Affection* [1998]) throws into relief some of the underlying ruptures and inconsistencies of the modern zeitgeist—a roughly forty-year period that witnessed the birth of feminist as well as masculinist movements. Interestingly, his film debut in 1963 (as Charlie Cotchipee, a tolerant Southerner in *Gone Are the Days*) conveniently coincides with the first printing of Betty Friedan's book *The Feminine Mystique*, a publication that launched the hitherto novel idea that a life for women existed outside of the domestic sphere. Moreover, Alda's midcareer ascendancy ran parallel to the first, middle-class-oriented wave of men's studies scholarship during the late 1970s. Despite his late-career U-turn into less positive territory, one that dovetails with the second, more polycentric wave of academic study on masculinity, few commentators bother to crack the surface of this iconoclastic "do-gooder"—leaving intact the myth of a man who shoots words in lieu of bullets, someone who speaks softly and carries a big conscience. Prospective readings of Alan Alda's masculinity might seek to explore the deeper implications of this contradictivity in hopes that a more nuanced and judicious understanding of his significance to gender studies might come into focus.

David Scott Diffrient

Further Reading:

Brod, Harry, ed. 1987. *The Making of Masculinities: The New Men's Studies*. Boston: Allen and Unwin.

Butler, Judith. 1992. *Gender Trouble: Feminism and the Subversion of Identity*. New York: Routledge.

Filene, Peter. 1998. *Him/Her/Self: Gender Identities in Modern America*. Baltimore, MD: Johns Hopkins University Press, 1998.

Kimmel, Michael S. 1992. *Against the Tide: Pro-Feminist Men in the U.S., 1776–1990*. Boston: Beacon Press.

Penley, Constance, and Sharon Willis, eds. 1992. *Male Trouble*. Minneapolis, MN: University of Minnesota Press.

Strait, Raymond. 1983. *Alan Alda: A Biography*. New York: St. Martin's Press.

Thompson, Cooper. 1991. "We Should Reject Traditional Masculinity." Pp. 17–31 in *To Be a Man: In Search of the Deep Masculine*. Edited by Keith Thompson. Los Angeles: Jeremy P. Tarcher

Alexithymia

Emotional restriction, constriction, and inexpressiveness have long been viewed as central norms for traditional male behavior. Men's studies scholars pointed out the similarity between normative male emotional restriction and a clinical condition known as alexithymia. Alexithymia literally means the inability to put emotions into words. The term is composed of a series of Greek roots: *a* ("without"), *lexus* ("words"), *thymos* ("emotions")—without words for emotions. This condition was originally defined to characterize the severe emotional constriction encountered in (primarily male) psychosomatic, drug-dependent, and posttraumatic stress disorder (PTSD) patients. However traditional male inexpressiveness is less severe than alexithymia.

Emotions consist of three components:

1. The neurophysiological substrate, which includes both autonomic and endocrinological components. For example, in the fight-or-flight response the sympathetic nervous system is activated, and the adrenal glands release epinephrine.
2. The motor/behavioral response, which involves the activation of the skeletal-muscular system in facial expression, tone of voice, and body language, or in direct action, such as a physical attack or an embrace.
3. The cognitive/affective component, which includes the subjective awareness of the emotion and the ability to put it into words.

People who suffer from alexithymia typically have severe deficits in both the second and the third components and also have trouble identifying the first component. On the other hand, normative male emotional restriction typically involves some deficits in the third component (i.e., men can subjectively experience certain classes of emotions, such as anger and lust, but not others, such as vulnerability and dependency) and the requirement to follow rigid display rules to express emotions (the second component). Some men report that their wives know what they are feeling when they themselves do not. This might be accounted for by deficits in the third component of the emotion but not in the second component, from which their wives can read their emotions in their facial expression and tone of voice.

Normative male emotional restriction thus can be viewed as a subclinical form of alexithymia, which is very common among men who subscribe to, or who were raised under, traditional norms of masculinity. This form of alexithymia is termed *normative male alexithymia*. Normative alexithymia is a predictable result of the male gender-role socialization process (*see* Boyhood). Specifically, it is a result of boys being socialized to restrict the expression of their vulnerable and caring/connection emotions and to be emotionally stoic. This socialization process includes both the creation of skill deficits (by not teaching boys emotional skills or allowing them to have experiences that would facilitate their learning these skills) and trauma (including prohibitions against boys' natural emotional expressivity, and punishment, often in the form of making the boy feel deeply ashamed of himself for violating these prohibitions).

This widespread inability among men to identify emotions and put them into words has enormous consequences. It blocks men who suffer from it from utilizing the most effective means known for dealing with life's stresses and traumas—namely, identifying, thinking about, and discussing one's emotional responses to a stressor or trauma with a friend, family member, or therapist. Consequently it predisposes such men to deal with stress in ways that make certain forms of pathology more likely, such as substance abuse, violent behavior, sexual compulsions, stress-related illnesses, and early death. It also makes it less likely that such men can benefit from psychotherapy as traditionally practiced.

Ronald F. Levant

See also Boyhood

Further Reading:

Krystal, Henry. 1982. Alexithymia and the Effectiveness of Psychoanalytic Treatment. *International Journal of Psychoanalytic Psychotherapy* 9: 353–378.

Levant, Ronald F., and Gini Kopecky. 1995. *Masculinity Reconstructed.* New York: Dutton.

Levant, Ronald F., and William S. Pollack, eds. 1995. *A New Psychology of Men.* New York: Basic Books.

Sifneos, Peter E. 1988. "Alexithymia and Its Relationship to Hemispheric Specialization, Affect, and Creativity." *Psychiatric Clinics of North America* 11: 287–292.

Taylor, Graeme J. 1994. "The Alexithymia Construct: Conceptualization, Validation, and Relationship with Basic Dimensions of Personality." *New Trends in Experimental and Clinical Psychiatry* 10: 61–74.

Alger, Horatio, Jr. (1832–1899)

Alger was a prolific author of novels, biographies of public figures, short stories, and poetry, nearly all aimed at boys and young men. Most tell the story of a young male protagonist climbing upward in social status. *Ragged Dick* was one of the bestsellers of 1867, but none of Alger's other books attained such popularity during his lifetime. However, his novels were often reprinted in the twentieth century, and a mistaken notion of the "Horatio Alger tale" as describing a rise "from rags to riches" became a touchstone for successful men who wished to em-

phasize their humble beginnings and masculine virtues.

Alger was born in Chelsea, Massachusetts, trained at Harvard for the ministry, and became pastor of a Unitarian Church on Cape Cod. Early in 1866, a parishioner charged Alger with "a crime of no less magnitude than the abominable and revolting crime of unnatural familiarity with *boys*" (quoted in Scharnhorst and Bales 1985, 67). Alger resigned in disgrace and turned to writing as a career. His pederasty remained unremarked for over a century, but more recently some critics have made the incident a significant aspect of their interpretation of his life and works.

Ragged Dick (1867) set the pattern for Alger's subsequent novels. Its eponymous protagonist begins as a mischievous but honorable bootblack. Through the positive influence of wealthier boys and men, as well as his own honesty, energy, and desire for literacy, by the end of the novel he is working as a clerk, is described as "a young gentleman on the way to fame and fortune," and is ready to aid other young boys in the book's sequels. Though they were undoubtedly sentimental and didactic, Alger's stories had more qualities of realism and material specificity, and they conveyed their morals more subtly, than did most antebellum children's fiction. Surprisingly for those who imagine the Horatio Alger tale as being about a virtuous, hardworking boy pulling himself up by his own bootstraps, typically the boy benefits from a wealthy man's benevolence and a good deal of luck. The hero's appearance and his virtues are inevitably described as "manly," and it is clear that one of Alger's central concerns was to construct a form of genteel masculinity to which humble clerks and other young men could aspire.

In the twentieth century a mythical version of the "Horatio Alger story" emerged, in which a "faith in *laissez-faire,* in the best of all possible worlds, in the inevitability of rags to riches" was evinced (Scharnhorst and Bales 1985, 154). The Horatio Alger myth became a bulwark against criticism of American capitalism and a template for describing the passage from boyhood to manhood, cited by presidents from Eisenhower to Reagan, as well as innumerable businessmen. Herbert Mayes published a wildly inaccurate biography of Alger in 1928; it became the basis for many unreliable encyclopedia entries and books on Alger. Only with Scharnhorst and Bales's 1985 biography did we get a reliable account of Alger's life and works.

Jason Richards

See also "Self-Made Man"
Further Reading:

Cawelti, John. 1965. *Apostles of the Self-Made Man: Changing Concepts of Success in America.* Chicago: University of Chicago Press.

Hendler, Glenn. 1996. "Pandering in the Public Sphere: Masculinity and the Market in Horatio Alger." *American Quarterly* 48, no. 3: 414–438.

Leverenz, David. 1998. "Tomboys, Bad Boys, and Horatio Alger: When Fatherhood Became a Problem." *American Literary History* 10, no. 1: 219–236.

Mayes, Herbert R. 1928. *Alger: A Biography without a Hero.* New York: Macy-Masius.

Moon, Michael. 1987. "'The Gentle Boy from the Dangerous Classes': Pederasty, Domesticity, and Capitalism in Horatio Alger." *Representations* 19: 95–97.

Nackenoff, Carol. 1994. *The Fictional Republic: Horatio Alger and American Political Discourse.* New York: Oxford University Press.

Scharnhorst, Gary, and Jack Bales. 1981. *Horatio Alger, Jr.: An Annotated Bibliography of Comment and Criticism.* Metuchen, NJ: Scarecrow Press.

———. 1985. *The Lost Life of Horatio Alger, Jr.* Bloomington, IN: Indiana University Press.

Alighieri, Dante

See Dante

Allen, Woody
[Allen Stuart Konigsberg] (1935–)

Actor, scriptwriter, and director of more than thirty feature films, Woody Allen is probably the most respected American director outside the United States, and with no doubt the most underrated in his own country in the early 2000s. A man of constructive contradictions, he is fascinated by old movies (Bogart movies, the Marx Brothers, Renoir's *Grand Illusion*), jazz music from the 1940s, French literary classics, Freudian psychoanalysis, and his own New York City.

Woody Allen became a popular filmmaker with comedies that included some mixture of humor and spiritual thoughts (*Take the Money and Run* 1969; *Everything You Always Wanted to Know about Sex but Were Afraid to Ask* 1972). Even though he didn't direct the film *Play It Again, Sam!* (1972, directed by Herbert Ross), Allen wrote the script and starred in this funny tribute to Humphrey Bogart, portrayed here as a model of virility and primitive seduction. In this parody of the cult movie *Casablanca,* Allen's character identifies himself with Bogart's icon image of rude and seductive machismo.

Right from the beginning of the 1970s, Allen more or less created that funny character of the intellectual loser, a kind of adult "Charlie Brown" wearing glasses, who can't succeed with women because of his lack of self-confidence. This character more or less reappears in *Bananas* (1971), when a feeble man rejected by women goes to an obscure country in Latin America where he becomes for a moment a new revolutionary hero. Only then can he reconquer the woman who left him before. One of Allen's funniest films, *Sleeper* (1973), depicts a twentieth-century man who wakes up after a 200-year coma in a totalitarian futuristic society where humans live with robots. His next film, *Love and Death* (1974), a parody of Tolstoy, has a title that could apply to many of his movies, synthesizing his two main preoccupations. This first cycle ends with *Annie Hall* (1976), an award-winning comedy that shows, as in many Woody Allen movies, the professional ascent of a woman combined with the social decline of her lover.

Allen's *Interiors* (1978) marks a rupture in its stylistic opposition to his previous films. It is an austere drama using themes such as the sea, self-destruction, intense women characters with strong personalities, and deep family conflicts, reminiscent of Ingmar Bergman films like *Persona* (1966). Bergman's early film *Smiles of a Summer Night* (1955) also influenced Woody Allen's *A Midsummer Night's Sex Comedy* (1982). As many others did before him, Woody Allen even asked Bergman's Swedish cameraman Sven Nykvist to light three of his own films (*Another Woman* [1988], *Oedipus Wrecks* [1989], and *Crimes and Misdemeanors* [1989]). Even Bergmanian actor Max Von Sydow played once again for Woody Allen his role of a tormented artist in *Hannah and Her Sisters* (1986), as he did so many times for Ingmar Bergman (*The Hour of the Wolf*, 1968). Woody Allen's visual masterpiece *Manhattan* (1979) introduced a cycle of "serious comedies."

Family is the key concept to understanding Woody Allen's vision of human relations. Often reduced to only a few obsessive themes and characters centered on immature sexuality, the marginality of the intellectual living in a superficial society, and fundamental doubts about the existence of God, family ties are present in Woody Allen's films more than in those of any other contemporary American filmmaker. The family, and especially brotherhood, are portrayed in *Take the Money and Run* (1969), the two opposed families in *Annie Hall* (1977), and also in *Zelig* (1983), *Radio Days* (1987), and *Deconstructing Harry* (1997). In *Crimes and Misdemeanors* (1989), a doctor asks his own brother to kill his embarrassing mistress. This, combined with Jewish heritage and major cinematographic inspirations (such as Fellini's classic *8½* in the beginning of Allen's *Stardust Memories* [1980] or *Juliet of the Spirits*'s influence on Allen's *Alice* [1990]), gives a more profound and complex picture of Woody Allen's elaborate universe.

Sometimes we see parents ashamed of their sons. They even wear disguises in case someone might recognize them in *Take the Money and Run* (1969); they are shattered when the despaired-of son (played by Allen) announces he will give up Jewish religion to become Catholic in *Hannah and Her Sisters* (1986). In *Annie Hall* (1977), the adult character played by Allen remembers that his mother brought him to the doctor as he was a boy to cure his anguish about the expanding universe. In *Radio Days* (1987), the son is compared to a young genius seen at the fair and ridiculed by his parents in front of their model "boy." In *Oedipus Wrecks* (a short sketch taken from *New York Stories*, 1989), the old mother is omnipresent and always critical toward her son, who remains powerless. Surprisingly, this same humiliating situation almost reappears in Barbara Kopple's documentary about Woody Allen's tour in Europe as a musician, *Wild Man Blues* (1998), when the actor (and clarinet player) meets his real parents in the company of his new young wife. The final scene when the old mother criticizes her famous son proves that a man, however great he is, always remains a child for his parents. This also illustrates a situation that many previous films had only suggested.

The couple is also a subject of infinite variation in Woody Allen's universe. Unhappy couples are seen in many films, such as *Bananas* (1971), *The Purple Rose of Cairo* (1985), *September* (1987), *Another Woman* (1988), *Alice* (1990), *Husbands and Wives* (1992), *Mighty Aphrodite* (1995), *Sweet and Lowdown* (1999), and *Small Time Crooks* (2000). But dynamic couples exist in *Play It Again, Sam!* (by Herbert Ross, 1972), *Sleeper* (1973), *Manhattan* (1980), *Manhattan Murder Mystery* (1995), or whenever Diane Keaton appears in one of Allen's movies. Superficial couples are portrayed in *Annie Hall* (1977) (those living in California), *Celebrity* (1998), and *Small Time Crooks* (2000). Bad, rude, and brutal husbands are portrayed in many Allen films: *The Purple Rose of Cairo* (1985), *Sweet and Lowdown* (1999), and *Small Time Crooks* (2000). Mature men having a love affair with a younger woman are seen in *Manhattan* (1980), *Husbands and Wives* (1992), and *Sweet and Lowdown* (1999).

Fatherhood can appear as a challenge in Woody Allen's films. In *Interiors* (1978), the retired father abandons his old wife and adult children; that is how they see him, although the father says he always paid and took care of everybody without thinking of himself. In *Crime and Misdemeanors* (1989), the father is honored in a ceremony, although he just got rid of his mistress to save his image and marital union. He is not punished for that; he gets away without any problem, but is left with guilt. The too-busy father in *Alice* (1990) never takes care of his children, but Alice's lover does. In *Husbands and Wives* (1992), the couple can't conceive a child; they even ask their best friend's help to procreate. Procreation is also a problem for the couple in *Mighty Aphrodite* (1995). Fatherhood can simultaneously feature serious problems and laughable situations.

In other Woody Allen films, some images of fatherhood are touching: the rude father who is ashamed to reveal to his son that he is a cab driver in *Radio Days* (1987); the generous uncle who takes care of his niece's education in *Crimes and Misdemeanors* (1989); the nice adoptive father in *Mighty Aphrodite* (1995). But turbulent kids make more critical and questionable the possible union with a divorced French woman in *Stardust Memories* (1982). Adults often say they were beaten by their parents when they were younger in *Zelig* (1983) and *Radio Days* (1987).

Homosexuality is not often portrayed in Woody Allen's films, except in *Sleeper* (1973) when a gay couple use an effeminate robot at home; in *Manhattan* (1980), the character's ex-wife who has become an intransigent lesbian raises their son with her new "mistress." Divorced fathers, separated couples, and new families are frequent in Woody Allen's films. Sisterhood often appears as a motif, such as the strong trio of dominant women in *Interiors* (1978), and also in *Hannah and Her Sisters* (1986). Brother and sister relationships are also present in *Annie Hall* (1977), *Zelig* (1983), and *Crimes and Misdemeanors* (1989).

Woody Allen's resonance with audiences is made possible because of the many problems inherent to the loss of balance and sharing in modern couples and families. Political revolution is seen as pointless in early films such as *Bananas* (1971), *Sleeper* (1973), and *Love and Death* (1974). Unlike in many typical American movies, heroes are vulnerable and deconstructed in Allen's movies (e.g., *Deconstructing Harry*, 1997). In *The Purple Rose of Cairo* (1985), the idolized actor can't deal with reality; in *Alice* (1990), the powerful Chinese doctor is addicted to drugs; in *Sweet and Lowdown* (1999), the champion guitar player is too sensible to tolerate Django Reinhardt's presence and appears to be rude and abusive with vulnerable women. In *Hollywood Ending* (2002), the director becomes blind just before the first shooting day! Even Bogart's image fades at the end of *Play It Again, Sam!* (1972).

Yves Laberge

See also Bergman, Ingmar; Bogart, Humphrey; Fellini, Federico; Jewish Men

Further Reading:

Allen, Woody. 1982. *Four Films of Woody Allen: Annie Hall, Interiors, Manhattan, Stardust Memories.* New York: Random House.

American Civil War

The American Civil War, fought between a pro-Union North and a secessionist, proslavery Confederate South between 1861 and 1865, ended with the defeat of the South and the destruction of chattel slavery. Costing over 600,000 lives, this cataclysmic war tested and subtly transformed American ideals of manhood. Soldier volunteers initially drew upon a concept of manhood that linked patriotism with family honor, morality, and the duty of defending one's home. The stunning loss of life and the dehumanizing environment of total war soon challenged received standards of courage and moral behavior. Soldiers learned to value the shovel as well as the musket, to distrust showy displays of bravery as invitations to death, and to submit to an increasingly rigorous army discipline.

Camp life fostered drinking, swearing, and womanizing, challenging the presumed link between military service and manly virtue. High rates of desertion among white soldiers on both sides suggest that many men came to question the badge of manhood conferred by military service in favor of individual and family survival. By serving with exemplary bravery and loyalty, African American men challenged widely held, racially exclusionary definitions of manliness and established to their own satisfaction their right to political manhood and to freedom and equality for their people. In the post–Civil War period, however, African American manhood came under attack, while combat experience in the Civil War was increasingly sentimentalized. The lessons of racial equality and total war for American ideals of manhood were forgotten until the twentieth century.

Publicly and privately, Americans viewed participation in the war as a test of manhood and as a competition between regional ideals of manhood. Although three-fifths of Civil War enlistees were over twenty-one years of age (old by twentieth-century standards), letters routinely portrayed battle experience as an initiation into manhood (Mitchell 1993, 5). The Northern press predicted that combat would check the creeping effeminacy brought on by Northern commercial success. African Americans sought to fight as a means of establishing their right to the manly independence denied them by slavery and prejudice, a strategy strongly supported by radical abolitionists. The war of words between Northerners and Southerners relied heavily on the vocabulary of manhood. Southerners were vilified as un-American aristocrats; Northerners as money-grubbing cowards. Southern generals were able to capitalize militarily on the Southern soldier's reputation for reckless valor in the opening years of the war. Defeat of the South signaled

a defeat of Southern manhood, symbolized by the song "Jeff in Petticoats," which popularized the image of Confederate president Jefferson Davis trying to escape Richmond disguised as a woman.

As suggested by the fratricidal metaphor informing the portrait of the wartime nation as a "house divided," Northern and Southern soldiers shared many elements of manly identity. Southern and Northern enlistees, including immigrant soldiers, most of whom fought in nonethnic regiments, volunteered to defend the political system of democratic republicanism and the rights of freedom and equality that grounded their self-conception as men. Those patriotic values played havoc with military discipline. Volunteer soldiers on both sides expected their officers, many of whom they had known from childhood or had elected to their offices, to earn their respect through demonstrations of bravery and competence, and to exercise command in a paternal rather than an authoritarian way. As the war dragged on, soldier enthusiasm plummeted, and both sides instituted conscription to supplement flagging enlistment. Authorities abolished elections or supplemented them with performance criteria and tightened military discipline. By 1864 soldiers no longer complained openly about the execution of deserters, the denial of furloughs even in the case of family illness, and the harsh discipline of shirkers.

For the volunteer soldiers who joined up in local and state regiments, fighting conflated the defense of the nation with the defense of home and family. Enlistees knew that their fellow soldiers would report home about battlefield performance. Preserving family honor constituted a primary impetus to bravery. Volunteer soldiers assumed that making war would draw upon manly qualities such as moral righteousness, fair play, loyalty, and fearlessness that would in turn determine who would survive and win. The indiscriminate loss of life to disease and to mass frontal attacks against bored-rifle muskets undermined ideas that individual courage mattered. Loyalty to one's company, rather than the display of particular combat skills or heedless bravery in the presence of whizzing bullets, became the baseline definition of acceptable manly conduct in battle. There is some evidence that Southern officers, preferring to exhibit bravery on the battlefield above all else, had low enthusiasm for surveying potential battlefields, securing necessary supplies, and other such bureaucratic tasks necessary to waging modern war. Both sides came to see skirmishing, defensive tactics, and flanking movements, previously viewed as dishonorable, as consistent with manliness. Similarly, Northern soldiers learned to treat Southern civilians as combatants and both sides sought to sow terror. Still, sniping, night attacks, and mortar shelling were judged by the old standards of combat as personal contest and reviled as unmanly.

The evidence presented by scholars to argue that Civil War combatants were poor soldiers but good fighters is inconclusive. Like their leaders, soldiers came to accept that digging defensive earthworks was necessary to win battles. Nonetheless, ordinary soldiers complained in racial terms about the many menial tasks involved in keeping camp, in occupying a hostile region, and in defensive preparation for battle. White soldiers often felt they were "above" such labor. Assumptions about the servile nature of blacks led most Northern soldiers to welcome them as menial laborers but to oppose their enlistment as soldiers. Free blacks agitated from the beginning of the war to fight, recognizing that it would enhance their claim to equality, a basic component of American manhood. In July 1862 the Union government's Second Confiscation Act and the Militia Act signaled the formal adoption of emancipation and the military employment of fugitive slaves. Northern opposition to black enlistment evaporated with the Conscription Act of 1863. Black men from the North and border states enlisted in droves. Approximately 58

percent of Kentucky's black men of fighting age joined the Union army, as did 28 percent of Maryland's, and 71 percent of the North's (Berlin et al. 1992, 203). Only a handful of men of color and no slaves pleaded to fight for the Confederacy, although slaves were used as support labor. Black Union soldiers were treated with special ferocity by Southern forces. Despite being largely excluded from the officer ranks, discriminated against in pay until Congress abolished such distinctions in 1864, and underutilized as fighting men, African Americans served and died out of proportion to their numbers. By the time the final arduous battles of the war were over, most black soldiers had seen combat; more importantly, their service convinced a reluctant North to recognize their manhood and established a powerful argument for political and civil equality for their people. After Reconstruction, however, Northern and Southern white "brothers" would seek sectional reconciliation to the detriment of hard-won African American rights.

Katherine Chavigny

See also Abolitionists; Slave Narratives; Slavery; War

Further Reading:

Berlin, Ira, Barbara J. Fields, Steven F. Miller, Joseph P. Reidy, and Leslie S. Rowland. 1992. *Slaves No More: Three Essays on Emancipation and the Civil War.* New York: Cambridge University Press.

Burton, William L. 1988. *Melting Pot Soldiers: The Union's Ethnic Regiments.* Ames, IA: Iowa State University Press.

Glatthaar, Joseph T. 1990. *Forged in Battle: The Civil War Alliance of Black Soldiers and White Officers.* New York: The Free Press.

Jimerson, Randall C. 1988. *The Private Civil War: Popular Thought during the Sectional Conflict.* Baton Rouge, LA: Louisiana State University Press.

Linderman, Gerald. 1987. *Embattled Courage: The Experience of Combat in the American Civil War.* New York: The Free Press.

Mitchell, Reid. 1988. *Civil War Soldiers.* New York: Viking.

———. 1993. *The Vacant Chair: The Northern Soldier Leaves Home.* New York: Oxford University Press.

American Men's Studies Association (AMSA)

The American Men's Studies Association (AMSA) is a nonprofit organization of men and women dedicated to teaching, research, and clinical practice in the field of men's studies. Its primary goal is to provide a forum for teachers, researchers, and therapists to exchange information and gain support for their work with men and the study of men's lives and masculinities.

The AMSA's history extends back to the mid-1980s when a small group of mainly academics within the National Organization for Changing Men (now known as the National Organization for Men Against Sexism—NOMAS) created a Men's Studies Task Group (MSTG) devoted to the study of men's lives. During the next several years, the MSTG grew in membership and began hosting a conference on men's studies in conjunction with the annual Men and Masculinity (M&M) conference. By the early 1990s, the MSTG's leadership proposed to incorporate and hold its men's studies conference separate from the M&M conference. This proposal caused a split between the NOMAS and MSTG leadership.

In 1992 Martin Acker, Stephen Boyd, James Doyle, Sam Femiano, Charles Miley, and David Robinson (via phone) met at Stony Point, New York. The primary goal for this meeting was to draft a mission statement outlining a number of issues fundamental to the creation of an organization—the American Men's Studies Association—devoted the analyses of men's lives and experiences as social, historical, and cultural constructions. Besides this overriding goal, plans were set in motion to begin an annual men's studies conference that has occurred every year since (see "AMSA History").

To achieve these goals, the AMSA set for itself a commitment to serve as a multidisciplinary forum of men and women who wished to engage in and promote critical discussion of issues involving men and masculinities, while disseminating knowledge about men's lives to a broad audience through its support of research (see "AMSA Mission Statement").

The major objectives of the American Men's Studies Association are to encourage the refinement of the parameters of men's studies, to generate theory, and to develop methodologies for the study of masculinities from an ethical perspective that eschews oppression in all forms (sexism, racism, homophobia, anti-Semitism, classism, etc.)

Given the pluralistic nature of men's studies, the AMSA recognizes and respects the many voices emerging from among those working with and/or studying men's lives and the many shades of masculinity, all the while being committed to providing a forum of open and inclusive dialogue, which involves a spirit of mutual respect for our common humanity.

During its brief history, the AMSA has hosted a richly diverse annual conference, provided a "spirited" Internet list server, and grown into a vital and dynamic men's studies organization that respects and gives forum to the many voices that are charting the emergent field of men's studies.

James A. Doyle

See also National Organization of Men Against Sexism (NOMAS)
Further Reading:
American Men's Studies Association. "AMSA History." At *http://www.mensstudies.org/history.htm.*
———. "AMSA Mission Statement." At *http://www.mensstudies.org/mis-st.htm.*

Anabolic and Androgenic Steroids

Anabolic and androgenic steroids are drugs designed to ameliorate a variety of medical conditions, including reproductive dysfunction, various protein deficiencies, infections, and burns (Nichols 1996). Anabolic steroids build muscle, while androgenic steroids increase strength. Steroid administration occurs primarily through oral ingestion of the drug and/or intramuscular injection.

Unsafe combinations of steroids may produce medical and psychiatric side effects that can be life threatening and addictive. For instance, steroid abuse has been linked to cardiac problems, liver dysfunction, nonmalignant liver tumors, and the premature closure of growth plates among adolescents (Yesalis 1995). Abuse can further produce paranoid delusions, auditory hallucinations, and depression (Annitto and Layman 1980).

The illegal use and abuse of anabolic and androgenic steroids among male adolescent and adult weight lifters (for the purpose of increasing body size and strength) continues to rise dramatically (Brower 1992). Why do young athletic men continue to use these drugs despite considerable evidence of their destructive nature?

Initially, many athletes experiment with steroids in order to gain lean muscle mass, strength, and aggression. However, initial experimentation often leads to more frequent use. Some biologically minded researchers suggest that steroids are drugs that significantly compromise mood, affect, behavior, thinking, and perception (Brower, Blow, Beresford, and Fuelling 1989). They suggest that male weight lifters abuse steroids for their primary reinforcement effects (e.g., feeling euphoric after use). To this end, Brower et al. (1989) reported that 43 percent of steroid abusers reported feeling "high" for an extended amount of time after use. Biologically minded researchers further note that more steroids are self-administered once tolerance to a previous dose occurs.

Another group of researchers emphasize the role of secondary reinforcement in steroid abuse. Athletes receive social reinforcement by others for obtaining a lean, muscular body. This body type is valued by a society that defines masculinity according to the ideal mesomorph image (i.e., tall and muscular). This avenue of reinforcement is so powerful that it can significantly affect the steroid users' self-image, self-worth, and sense of self (Tucker 1984).

A third group of researchers believes that various components of the traditional male sex role (e.g., competition with other men, fear of humiliation, the lack of intimate emotional expression) significantly contributes to the progression of steroid addiction (Khorrami 2000; Khorrami and Franklin 2002). According to this model, there are two distinct groups of steroid abusers: those men who lift weights recreationally and those who lift weights in order to gain an advantage when competing in atlethic events (e.g., football, ice hockey, weight lifting competitions). Often, the steroid abuse and dependence literature does not separate these two unique groups and implicitly assumes that all steroid abusers have a homogeneous profile.

The steroid user in this first category perceives himself as having a small body, often erroneously. The decision to experiment with steroids is tied to his perception that having a small body causes him to be perceived as unmanly by others. In an attempt to avoid perceived humiliation, the steroid user experiments with these drugs and obtains lean muscle mass in a relatively short period of time; he attempts to become mesomorphic.

The steroid user in this category is hypervigilant, constantly comparing his body size to that of other men. Such a comparison often becomes a competition with other men. When the steroid user believes he is not as big as other men (even considering his newfound muscle gains) there is an increased probability that steroid abuse will begin, ultimately resulting in steroid dependence. "Stacking steroids" illustrates this phenomenon. "Stacking steroids" is the unlawful combination of various types and amounts of steroids in order to combat tolerance to a previously effective dose of the drug. The abuser believes that by taking more steroids in different combinations, he will obtain even more muscle mass, thereby winning the silent competition and avoiding perceived humiliation.

For young athletic men who constitute the second category, steroid use produces increased lean muscle mass, strength, and aggression. It is precisely strength and aggression that are critical commodities for these male athletes who compete in contact sports such as football and ice hockey. When a young athlete believes he lacks strength and/or aggression, he begins to think that he cannot successfully compete in these contact sports. Often, this form of negative thinking results in a high probability of steroid experimentation.

The progression of steroid use to abuse and dependence for men in the second category is more complicated than for men in the first. Most commonly, the steroid user obtains some short-term gains (increased strength and aggression) before tolerance occurs. In this scenario everyone on the team (ranging from other players to coaches) notices the athlete's significant improvement in performance. As a consequence, a new expectation emerges that the athlete will continue to perform at this high level each day, during practices and games. There is additional pressure to maintain his marked improvement in performance if the athlete becomes promoted to "starting status" or is rewarded with more playing time during games. Ultimately, the steroid user cannot maintain his newfound level of strength and aggression when tolerance occurs. Fearing the humiliation of not fulfilling the new expectations, the athlete begins "stacking steroids," initiating the downward spiral of abuse and dependence.

Finally, when steroid users from both aforementioned categories compete with other men, it thwarts the opportunity for them to form close, intimate bonds where emotions, vulnerabilities, and feelings are openly expressed to each other.

Sam Khorrami

Further Reading:
Annito, W. R., and W. A. Layman. 1980. "Anabolic Steroids and Acute Schizophrenic Episode." *Journal of Clinical Psychiatry* 41: 143–144.

Brower, K. 1992. "Addictive Potential of Anabolic Steroids." *Psychiatric Annals* 22: 30–34.
Brower, K., C. F. Blow, T. P. Beresford, and C. Fuelling. 1989. "Anabolic-Androgenic Steroid Dependence." *Journal of Clinical Psychiatry* 50: 31–33.
Khorrami, Sam. 2000. "Risk-Factors and Early-Warning Signs of Steroid Abuse in Male Weightlifters." *Michigan Psychologist* 25, no. 1: 2.
Khorrami, Sam, and J. T. Franklin. 2002. "The Influence of Competition and Lack of Emotional Expression in Perpetuating Steroid Abuse and Dependence among Male Weightlifters." *International Journal of Men's Health* 1, no. 1: 119–133.
Nichols, T. 1996. "Juice Master." *Men's Fitness* 12, no. 2: 38–40.
Tucker, L. A. 1984. "Physical Attractiveness, Somatotype, and the Male Personality: A Dynamic Interactional Perspective." *Journal of Clinical Psychology* 40: 1226–1234.
Yesalis, C. 1995. *An Unvarnished Look at Steroids.* New York: Random House.

Androgyny

Psychological androgyny, according to Nash (1979), is "the integration of both masculinity and femininity within a single individual" (273). Androgynous individuals report high levels of stereotypical masculine and feminine personality traits and, as a result, are more able to cope with and behave appropriately in a wide variety of life situations. Masculine types report high levels of masculine traits (i.e., aggressiveness, competitiveness, ambition, self-reliance, and independence) and low-levels of feminine traits. Feminine types are the opposite, with high levels of feminine traits (i.e., compassion, tenderness, cheerfulness, loyalty, sympathy, and sensitivity) and low levels of masculine traits. An undifferentiated person is one who has low levels of both masculine and feminine traits.

Psychological androgyny correlates with high degrees of emotional independence and self-esteem, a greater likelihood of attributing positive results to one's own effort or ability, and lower reports of psychiatric symptoms among females—making androgynous individuals maximally adaptive to changing situations in their lives (Nash 1979; Viaene 1979; Williams 1979). Nash (1979) also notes that children with a high degree of emotional independence—a characteristic associated with androgyny—are the children most likely to show an increase in IQ scores during adolescence.

Androgynous males are high in masculine traits, but because they are equally high in feminine traits, they are less likely to develop the negative characteristics associated with agency. A balance is created by the integration of a sense of the "other" (communion) into their personality makeup, and as such these males are less likely to be self-centered, self-absorbed, or selfish in general. The androgynous female's sense of the "other" (communion) is balanced by a sense of self (agency), and as such she is less likely to be completely self-sacrificing or easily victimized. Androgynous individuals are more likely to develop such balanced characteristics because they have a high incidence of complimentary characteristics. Guggenbühl (1994) says, "although society may see us as men or women, they should sees us as both" (22). He explains Jung's concept of anima/animus as the quest for the soul—to integrate the feminine part of the soul (for men) in order to achieve "psychic maturity." Psychic maturity is conditional upon integrating a balance of psychological traits that are stereotypically masculine and feminine.

Many cultures perpetuate the myth that masculinity, when compared with femininity, equates with superiority. The ideal male is fully autonomous—financially, physically, and especially emotionally. He must be capable of standing alone, and he must struggle and even fight to protect what is his—property, reputation, and family. He must never reveal his vulnerability, and he must eschew all things feminine, including personality traits that are associated with femininity.

Pollack (1998) explains that the socialization of boys is a traumatic and often damaging process. Boys are expected to separate from their mothers by the time they are five or six years old. Cultural practices and societal constraints demand that the mother push her small son away and harden herself to his initial separation pain in order that he learn early the need to rely on no one but himself. "Only sissy-boys cry for their mommies." First boys must hide their tears and then they must learn to hide their fear, uncertainty, and emotional needs. They must be stoic and strong.

Pollack explains that boys are shamed into complying with the expectations of masculine ideals. The most common shaming taunts involve questioning the boy's commitment to being male. He is called "sissy," "girlie," or "baby." These taunts reinforce the myth that femininity and dependence are somehow related and inferior.

Contrary to the conclusions of Freud and many of his compatriots and followers who believed mental health was contingent upon the successful adoption of the appropriate sex-typed personality characteristics (Williams 1979, 201), modern psychologists and therapists have found this not to be true for females. Masculine sex-typed individuals (both male and female) score high on self-esteem scales, but feminine and undifferentiated individuals report much lower self-esteem scores. Androgynous individuals report the highest self-esteem of all (Boldizar 1991). Rose and Montemayor (1994) discussed traits that are stereotypically assigned to gender. They discovered that both boys and girls that exhibit or describe themselves as having positive masculine traits also claim high self-esteem, whereas having positive feminine traits does not affect self-esteem in either sex.

Rose and Montemayor (1994) applied both the Children's Sex Role Inventory (CSRI)(see Boldizar 1991) and Harter's (1982) Self Perception Profile for Adolescents to their subjects to draw parallels between self-esteem and ownership of gendered traits. They found that the highest perceived self-competency among their subjects was directly related to individuals who claimed a high incidence of masculine traits *and* feminine traits.

Shaver and Papalia (1996) explored sex-role typologies and their relationship with attachment-style typologies. They discovered that individuals who claimed secure attachment styles were more likely to be androgynous. Those scoring low on masculinity scales were more likely to be anxious-ambivalent, and those scoring low on femininity were more often avoidant in their relationships.

In a second study, using Bartholemew's (1991) four attachment-style descriptions (secure, preoccupied, fearful, and dismissing), Shaver and Papalia found that androgyny was related to the secure trait: While feminine subjects were more likely to be preoccupied, masculine subjects were more often dismissing, and undifferentiated subjects were the most fearful.

In their third study, Shaver and Papalia sought the potential relationship between attachment styles and exaggerated masculinity or exaggerated femininity. They found that secure attachment "means being relatively high, but not extreme on either agency or communion" (589).

Lack of security in children is related to the child's evident compliance with gender-normative behavior. Insecure four-year-old boys are "more aggressive, disruptive, assertive, controlling, and attention seeking than secure children and insecure girls showed more dependent behavior" (Turner 1991, 1475). Furthermore, peer relationships among the children in this study, in which at least one insecure child was involved, were less harmonious. Pairings of children with insecure-avoidant or insecure-ambivalent children resulted in the children behaving as victimizers and victims respectively. The presence of at least one secure child in the pair eliminated these patterns of behavior. The secure child is more capable of a healthy reciprocal relationship of give and take. This child believes he or she is worthy of love and kind acts, and that his or her companion is also worthy, and therefore exhibits a willingness to accept kindness and contribute kindness. The avoidant/victimizer is willing only to take and demands love and attention. This masculine orientation may in fact result in the child obtaining that which he or she demands, which accounts for the relatively high self-esteem scores for masculine typologies, even though this type of relationship is not healthy. The ambivalent/victim gives, but seldom receives love and affection. This feminine orientation is by far the least satisfying, and it is very likely that this person will have low self-esteem and low expectations for love and kindness.

Promoting both agency and communion in children allows each to explore more equitable and healthy reciprocal relationships. In effect, encouraging androgyny in children gives them the resources to strengthen their peer relationships and learn the skills necessary for creating and sustaining healthy adult romantic relationships.

Linda Bolton-Holder

Further Reading:

Boldizar, Janet P. 1991. "Assessing Sex Typing and Androgyny in Children: The Children's Sex Role Inventory." *Developmental Psychology* 27, no. 3: 505–515.

Guggenbühl, Allan. 1994. *Men, Power, and Myths: The Quest for Male Identity.* New York: Continuum.

Harter, Susan. 1982. "The Perceived Competence Scale for Children." *Child Development* 53, no. 1: 87–97.

Nash, Sharon C. 1979. "Sex Role as a Mediator of Intellectual Functioning." Pp. 263–302 in *Sex-Related Differences in Cognitive Functioning: Developmental Issues.* Edited by Michele A. Wittig and Anne C. Petersen. New York: Academic Press.

Pollack, William. 1998. *Real Boys: Rescuing Our Sons from the Myths of Boyhood.* New York: Henry Holt.

Rose, Amanda J., and Raymond Montemayor. 1994. "The Relationship between Gender Role Orientation and Perceived Self-Competency in Male and Female Adolescents." *Sex Roles* 31, nos. 9/10: 579–595.

Shaver, Philip R., and Daria Papalia. 1996. "Androgyny and Attachment Security: Two Related Models of Optimal Personality." *Personality and Social Psychology Bulletin* 22: 582–595.

Turner, Patricia J. 1991. "Relations between Attachment, Gender, and Behavior with Peers in Preschool." *Child Development* 62: 1475–1488.

Viaene, Nicole. 1979. "Sex Differences in Explanations of Success and Failure." Pp. 117–139 in *Sex Role Stereotyping: Collected Papers.* Edited by Oohagh Hartnett, Gill Boden, and Mary Fuller. London: Tavistock Publications.

Williams, Jennifer A. 1979. "Psychological Androgyny and Mental Health." Pp. 200–214 in *Sex Role Stereotyping: Collected Papers.* Edited by Oohagh Hartnett, Gill Boden, and Mary Fuller. London: Tavistock Publications.

Andrology

The term *andrology* is derived from the ancient Greek word *andros* ("of a man") and is defined as the branch of Western medicine dealing with the study and treatment of male procreative health. Unlike the men's health movement, which emphasizes the role of social and cultural contexts for men's illnesses, andrology concentrates on biomedical perspectives and has a more specific scope. It looks at the physiology and pathology of male reproductive processes, notably infertility, erection problems, testicular disorders, the effects of so-called sex hormones on health and disease, contraception, and aging. Andrology is predominantly concerned with illnesses and diseases threatening aspects of masculinity that are valued in many cultures and societies, insofar as the male reproductive organs are symbols of manhood. With its growth during the decade of the 1990s and into the 2000s, andrology acquired increasing power to (re)define men's health, sexual behavior, and body norms, and to give biomedical answers to the crisis of masculinity.

As gynecology does for women, andrology defines men as a special group of patients. Whereas gynecology was institutionalized during the eighteenth and nineteenth centuries, andrology has a shorter history, and is still a rather small area of medical theory and practice. Early attempts to establish it as a medical specialty date back to the nineteenth century, but they failed to take hold. For a long time, Western medicine focused almost exclusively on women's bodies when dealing with questions of procreation.

In 1951 the German gynecologist Harald Siebke was the first to use the term *andrology* in a way that became scientifically successful and internationally influential. He looked at male-related problems during the medical examination and treatment of infertile couples, instead of focusing only on the female partner. Andrology's institutionalization as a separate field of professional and academic medicine began to take hold in the late 1960s. In its inception, spermatology, the technology of examining sperm, constituted its basis. Physicians and scientists coming from different professional and disciplinary contexts—mainly urology, endocrinology, and in some cases dermatology—referred to Siebke's neologism and began to label their work on men's health problems, especially on male infertility, "andrology." Soon other specialists joined the branch, among them cell biologists, immunologists, toxicologists, molecular biologists, and geneticists. The first andrological journal, *Andrologie,* has been published since 1969, and the first andrological society Comité Internacional de Andrologia was founded in 1970 (renamed International Society of Andrology in 1981). At the beginning of the twenty-first century, more than 8,000 professionals and scientists are members of andrological societies all over the world. In several countries, the education of students and doctors in the specialty is organized in pre- and postgraduate courses. Andrology has not yet been designated a board specialty in the United States, where it is a subspecialty of urology. In some other countries its institutionalization is more advanced; in Germany, for example, andrology is on its way to becoming a board specialty.

The development of andrology and the spread of its subjects have been especially influenced by the introduction of new technologies and the ongoing exchange with other fields of medicine. In the 1960s, the treatment of infertility and genital disorders and the routinization of vasectomy were basic areas of andrological work. Andrological therapy deals with venereal and sexually transmitted diseases, delayed puberty, ejaculatory disturbances, baldness, and intersexuality. Since the 1990s, andrology has been expanding rapidly and encompasses many aspects of men's health, including sexuality, aging, and the development of new methods of male contraception. One of the biggest impacts on the recent expansion came from the establishment of newer assisted reproductive technologies for the treatment of male infertility (e.g., intracytoplasmatic sperm injection [ICSI]). Focal points of today's andrological research are regulation of testicular processes, molecular biology and genetics of sperm, and cell interaction between sperm and egg.

From a gender studies point of view, andrology's significance is that it is the first time in history that a branch of Western medicine is widening the biomedical scope to include men's bodies. Andrology's approach to men's bodies as male bodies produces new norms of healthy manhood and new ways of defining masculinity. With the rise of andrology, biomedicine discovers men's bodies, establishing a specific field of research and medical practice, "reinventing" these bodies within a binary logic of sex difference, which plays a constitutive role in Western gender orders.

Torsten Wöllmann

See also Reproductive Health
Further Reading:
Huhtaniemi, Ilpo. 1999. "Message from the International Society of Andrology: Current Challenges of Andrology." *Asian Journal of Andrology* 1: 3–5.
Isidori, Aldo. 2001. "Storia dell'andrologia moderna." *Medicina nei Secoli* 13: 255–268.
Niemi, Mikko. 1987. "Andrology as a Specialty. Its Origin." *Journal of Andrology* 8: 201–202.
Nieschlag, Eberhard, and Hermann Behre, eds. 2000. *Andrology: Male Reproductive Health and Dysfunction.* 2d ed. Heidelberg, Germany: Springer.
Siebke, Harold. 1951. "Gynäkologe und Androloge bei der Sterilitätsberatung." *Zentralblatt für Gynäkologie* 5a: 633–637.

Anger

In many cultures, both historically and in the twenty-first century, men have been more authorized to admit and express anger than women. At the same time, men have also faced limits on anger, resulting in some complex tensions. Historians studying emotions have paid increasing attention to the way these tensions have changed over time.

Considerable debate rages over whether men are by nature angry and aggressive, and some careful studies have suggested little difference between men and women in the experience of anger, but just huge differences in the ways cultural conditioning allows the emotion to be acknowledged and expressed. In most societies, men's anger is primarily shaped by social status and culture. Thus, some relatively small cultures, like the Inuit, dramatically play down anger for men as well as women after early infancy. Some religions, in contrast, authorize considerable anger in defense of religious truth or family honor, and men unquestionably lead the way in expressing it. Societies that emphasize the validity of revenge, or other honor-based practices such as dueling, offer particular encouragement to male anger. Even in societies that legitimate anger, social status conditions the expression. Many males in subordinate positions, such as boys, slaves, servants, or laborers, learn the importance of controlling anger in favor of deference and obedience—regardless of what they "really" feel.

Cross-cultural comparisons in contemporary society suggest the continued impact of different cultural rules. Thus, Greek culture places a higher premium on anger than does Chinese culture, where the heritage of Confucian values suggests the importance of limiting aggressiveness for the sake of social harmony. Social differentiation continues to count as well. Thus, some American chief executives delight in expressing anger as a means of controlling subordinates, while insisting that middle managers take lessons in how to control their anger at work.

Male rules for anger change over time. In the nineteenth-century American middle class, a complex set of guidelines developed that simultaneously urged the importance of a capacity for anger and the need for control. Men were urged to restrain all anger in domestic settings, where harmony was supposed to prevail. But anger would remain a useful spur to competitive business activity and to political movements for social reform. Boys were taught to keep their anger in check at home, but to use anger to fight against schoolyard bullies. Boys who lacked an appropriate capacity for anger were labeled with a new term, "sissy," that clearly indicated effeminacy. Sports, including boxing, were seen as ideal to teach boys to use anger constructively, in competition. At the same time, older expressions of anger, like dueling, were now seen as cruel and disruptive in middle-class culture. One historian has noted how complicated these anger rules were for boys seeking to define their masculinity around 1900.

During the twentieth century, rules tended to change yet again in the United States, with more uniform attacks on male anger. Corporate culture, as early as the 1920s, began to urge men to keep anger in check at work, and a variety of training exercises and other programs were designed to drive this lesson home. Women's movements also pressed for new restraints on male anger. In the 1970s the men who urged a greater accommodation to feminism, under the banner of "male liberation," also called for new levels of anger restraint. The term *aggression* began to replace *anger* in child-rearing manuals—another sign that the emotion was under new attack. Of course, not all men lived up to the new norms, and concern about crimes of anger by men (such as "road rage," in the 1990s) continued to suggest both the complexity of men's attitudes toward anger and the effort to keep a lid on it.

Some subcultures, such as the African American culture, had their own dynamic. The Civil Rights movement of the 1950s and 1960s worked hard to persuade African American men that older habits of deference needed to give way to a new willingness to stand up for rights, and a certain amount of anger was legitimated in the process. Change and cultural divisions both made the topic of male anger a lively one by the end of the twentieth century in the United States.

Peter Stearns

Further Reading:

Rotundo, E. Anthony. 1993. *American Manhood.* New York: Basic Books

Stearns, Carol Zisowitz, and Peter N. Stearns. 1986. *Anger: The Struggle for Emotional Control in America's History.* Chicago: University of Chicago Press.

Tavris, Carol. 1989. *Anger: The Misunderstood Emotion.* New York: Touchstone.

Antifeminism

The term *antifeminism* means "opposition to women's equality." Antifeminists oppose women's entry into the public sphere, the reorganization of the private sphere, women's control of their bodies, and women's rights generally. Often this is justified by recourse to religious or cultural norms, and sometimes it is justified in the name of "saving" masculinity from pollution or invasion.

Antifeminism often promotes a frightened or nostalgic retreat to traditional gender arrangements, supported ideologically by religious or pseudoscientific notions of "natural law." Antifeminists typically accept the traditional gender division of labor as natural and inevitable, perhaps also as divinely sanctioned. Women, in this model, are not being "excluded" from the competitive and aggressive public arenas of work, politics, education, or the military, but rather are "exempted" from them because of the fragility of their moral or physical constitutions.

In the nineteenth century, the centerpiece of antifeminism was opposition to women's suffrage. Suffrage would prove too great a burden on women; as one California man proclaimed in 1880:

> I am opposed to woman's sufferage [sic] on account of the burden it will place on her. Her delicate nature has already enough to drag it down. Her slender frame, naturally weakened by the constant strain attendant upon her nature, is too often racked by diseases that are caused by a too severe tax upon her mind. The presence of passion, love, ambition is all to [sic] potent for her enfeebled constitution, and wrecked health and early death are all too common. (cited in Kimmel and Mosmiller 1992, 10).

Opponents of women's entry into institutions of higher learning offered equally dire predictions of the physical consequences of education. In *Sex in Education* (1873), Harvard professor Edward Clarke predicted that if women went to college, their brains would grow bigger and heavier, and their wombs would atrophy. In a masterpiece of faulty social science, his evidence for this preposterous claim was that college-educated women had fewer children than non-college-educated women. (Today, we might see that as the result of increasing opportunities, not decreasing womb size.) Other antifeminists opposed women's entry into the labor force, or their right to join unions, to sit on juries, or to obtain birth control and control of their sexuality.

Some antifeminists opposed women's equality not because of the enfeebling effects public participation might have on the women, but for the corrosive effects it might have on men. Opponents of women's entry into the military, police forces, and fire departments have claimed that women's presence would prove a distraction from the immediate crises the men faced, and that the cohesion necessary to maintain these homosocial institutions required a tenuous process of male bonding. The presence of women would inevitably prevent that bonding, thus rendering the organizations less effective.

Contemporary antifeminists follow these traditions. Some argue that feminists have duped women into abandoning marriage and family life for the unpredictable (but predictably dangerous and taxing) working world. Others claim that feminists have so colonized the government that women have more choices than men and that it is men who are victims of reverse discrimination. The National Organization for Men (NOM), founded by divorce lawyer Sidney Siller, claims that the goal of feminism is to "denigrate men, exempt women from the draft and to encourage the disintegration of the family" (Kimmel 1987). Like most contemporary antifeminists, NOM opposes affirmative action, abortion rights, imprisonment of men for nonpayment of alimony, and giving preference to women in child custody cases.

Opponents of women's entry into the military or military schools maintained that women would corrupt and pollute the pristine homosocial atmosphere of untrammeled masculinity necessary for male bonding. (Other antifeminists want to end women's exclusion from the military because they see it as sexism that forces only men to serve.) Some contemporary antifeminists also support "men's right to choose," which means curtailing women's reproductive freedom. In general, antifeminists believe, along with one antifeminist, Aaron Kipnis, that "the notion that men are somehow more privileged than women" is a "bad joke" (cited in Clatterbaugh 1997, 75).

Among the most visible contemporary antifeminists is Warren Farrell, once heralded as the most "liberated" man in America. To Farrell, men's power is a "myth" and women and men are already equal; in fact, women do men (see Farrell 1993). Farrell proposes reforms to protect men from false accusations of sexual harassment and rape, and recites standard antifeminist claims that women are the perpetrators of domestic violence at least as often as men are; that funding for women's health issues far outstrips funding for men's health issues; and that incest is a problem only because "parental authority becomes undermined because the child senses it has leverage over the parent" (Farrell 1993, 298). (Rarely has anyone suggested that incest is a problem of the *child's* power over the *parent*.)

Many organizations today take up these issues as policy recommendations, lobbying and protesting the contemporary feminist takeover. These antifeminist organizations include Coalition for Free Men; the National Congress for Men; Men's Rights, Inc.; and Men Achieving Liberation and Equality.

Kimmel 1992

See also The Citadel and the Virginia Military Institute (VMI); Men's Rights Movement; Postfeminism; Promise Keepers; "Save the Males!"

Further Reading:
Clatterbaugh, Kenneth. 1997. *Contemporary Perspectives on Masculinity*. 2d ed. Boulder, CO: Westview.
Farrell, Warren. 1993. *The Myth of Male Power*. New York: McGraw-Hill.
Kimmel, Michael. 1987. "Mens Responses to Feminism at the Turn of the Century." *Gender & Society* 1, 2.
Kimmel, Michael, and Thomas Mosmiller. 1992. *Against the Tide*. Boston: Beacon.

Apartheid

Apartheid is an Afrikaans word that literally means "apartness." It entrenched racial segregation—and white supremacy—in almost all areas of life and was the official policy of the Afrikaner Nationalist Government of South Africa from the time it came into power in 1948 until it began negotiations with the banned African National Congress in 1990. In every respect, including the right to vote, all nonwhite South Africans (classified as African, Indian, and Coloured) were discriminated against. Racism impacted the constructions of masculinity of all South African men. Among whites, one might suggest that it bolstered the prejudices that accrued to the colonizing power and extended gendered norms of superiority, privilege, and authority over their own women to all men and women of other race groups. Among black African men, it undermined traditional patriarchies and male-dominated gender systems by corroding traditional cultures and denying men almost every basic human right. That experience is illustrated in several works by black African men. The autobiographies of three black men are exemplary: Ezekiel Mphahlele's *Down Second Avenue* (1959); Bloke Modisane's *Blame Me on History* (1963); and Godfrey Moloi's *My Life: Volume One* (1987). Although content and form differ, all raise issues fundamental to the life stories of black South African men.

The widespread adoption of Christianity undermined, but seldom supplanted, traditional African models of masculinity; this caused uncertainty. Mphahlele (1973, 160), Moloi (1987, 197), and Modisane—albeit with protestations—(1986, 256ff) all paid the customary *lobola* (brideprice) for their wives, despite having been raised as Christians. Mphahlele was forbidden from mixing with "heathens," whereas Moloi was rejected by a Zulu woman because he was not manly enough. Furthermore, Christian models of identity were fraught with contradiction because churches were tainted by racism (as Moloi's father, an Anglican priest, found) and governments—especially the Afrikaner Nationalist Government that instituted apartheid in 1948—proclaimed their Christianity while promoting racism. For Modisane and Mphahlele, this hypocrisy created turmoil.

The 1913 Land Act allocated 87 percent of the country to whites. Black Africans were forced to flock to industrialized centers. But, in the urban ghettoes, the Western nuclear family was the uncommon alternative to collapsing traditional family structures. Mphahlele and Modisane were raised by women in broken families.

Western ideals of masculinity permeated black society, but were unattainable because of job reservation, discriminatory wages, and restrictions on movement, right of abode, and access to education. So, for example, whilst the notion of the male breadwinner (of European origin) was adopted, it was simultaneously frustrated. Mphahlele, Modisane, and Moloi were raised in circumstances of extreme privation. The usual alternative to unemployment was unskilled work. Modisane's father was a lowly messenger. Modisane himself was a reporter, and Mphahlele a teacher, and both earned considerably less than white colleagues.

Men should be strong, but black men had to be servile before whites. Men should command respect; racism denied the means for this. Black adults were perpetually "boys" and "girls." These autobiographers all record experiences of their own and their parents' denigration—a word that conveys the debasements of racism (Segal 1990, 187).

Black men could not be proper fathers, being unable to offer their children security, protection, or hope. There were constant threats of imprisonment or "deportation" to rural "homelands" if necessary permits were missing or if the state decided to supplant a community with whites. For Modisane, the bulldozed rubble of his home township symbolized the compounded failures of successive generations of black men: "I had failed my children as my father and my forefathers and the ancestral gods of my fathers had failed me: they had lost a country, a continent, but I had failed to secure a patch of weeds for my children" (Modisane 1986, 10).

Having bequeathed their children the black skin that imprisoned them in poverty and oppression, black fathers often found that bullying was the only contribution they could make (see Segal 1990, 28–29). Mphahlele's father neglected his family, and was cold and brutal. Modisane's father was distant and authoritarian. He was not loved or respected by his son. Modisane himself failed as a husband and father, and Moloi's claim that he did not know love is borne out by his apparent lack of affection for his wife and children. Fatherhood seems to have provoked crises in Mphahlele and Modisane—understandable, given the fact that fathers would have to admit to their children that they, in turn, would be subjected to vilification and disempowerment. Modisane's father's inability to effect this "castration ceremony of the truth" contributed to a rift between them. But when he became a father himself, Modisane also could not commit this "confessional emasculation" (1986, 76).

Black South Africans often countered social and political impotence with sexual promiscuity. Modisane's manhood craved the sort of validation that his wife, being black, could not provide. His numerous affairs with white lovers, however, being illegal, involved humiliating subterfuge and Modisane's compulsive conquests "left in their wake an emptiness even lonelier than that which had set me on the pursuit" (1986, 210). Both Modisane and Moloi seemed to be afraid of intimacy with women and frightened of fatherhood and the "soft" sentiments it might arouse. For Moloi, love was irrelevant to sex. His wife, chosen by his mother when she felt that he should settle down, is hardly mentioned. Other women (referred to as "dolls," "dames," or "molls") were part of the gangster image. Nevertheless, he presented himself as a protector of women. He tried to kill a man who had beaten up an ex-girlfriend (1987, 126; as it turns out, the wrong man), but was himself not averse to beating a two-timing girlfriend.

For many black men, conflict between shifting and confused masculine ideals and the racist denial of humanity induced self-destruction. Drunkenness usually characterizes masculine behavior of slum dwellers (Connell 1995). Although the state outlawed the sale of liquor to blacks, illegality, combined with poverty, made bootlegging necessary for many urban women, even for Christians, like Modisane's and Mphahlele's mothers. Strong, cheap liquor was thus readily available. Violence was the usual accompaniment: Mphahlele's drunken father brutally assaulted his wife.

Although satisfying the desire for oblivion and allowing men to achieve the masculine ideal of seeming invulnerability and the suppression of feelings, drunkenness, violence, and promiscuity simultaneously remind the downtrodden that they are alive (Modisane 1986, 117). They provide antidotes to the dangerous parallel emotions of joy, compassion, and love. Men and boys must be unemotional. Modisane was warned not to cry at his sister's funeral but battled not to disgrace his masculinity (as he saw it). And when, at the age of fourteen, he saw his father's bloodied corpse, Modisane behaved like a man and did not cry.

Apartheid robbed black children of their childhood: parents could seldom provide adequately—emotionally or materially. Often, children had to contribute to the family's income. Every Monday, Mphahlele rose at four in the morning to collect laundry from white families. Education rarely promised an escape: Overcrowded schools offered "Bantu Education," which "educated" blacks for servility. Furthermore, because of endemic violence in the ghettoes, many boys (like Modisane) were required to be men prematurely if their fathers died. (In many African cultures, in the absence of the father, the young boy becomes the head of the household.)

Boys could not be the sons that they wanted to be: Modisane was helpless when his mother was tormented by police, and Moloi's desire to please his Christian parents was thwarted by the criminal lifestyle that was his only means to status. Wearing American clothes, posing as a township Bogart, listening to American jazz, Moloi adopted an exaggerated masculinity. Anyway, being black meant almost inevitable criminalization. Even law-abiding individuals like Mphahlele were continually in danger of breaking some law. Although breaking the white man's law constituted, for some, an act of antiracist self-assertion, for Modisane (1986) this was not a possibility: "In the name of law and order I accommodated a variety of humiliations. I permitted sidewalk bullies to push me about, spitting insults into my eyes, and other men to castrate me" (124). Fanon (1967) declares that "the black is not a man" (8). Commonly, Africans were denied their names. To whites, Mphahlele (1973) was simply "Jim," "John," or "boy" (137). And Modisane's identity crumbled under the weight of his racial classification. Dropping his given name, William, he accepts anonymity: "I have no face, I have no name, my whole existence slithers behind a mask called Bloke" (1986, 74–75).

In imperialist thought, women and Africans are deemed emotional, illogical, less civilizable, properly submissive. We have seen some of the effects of this—and its racist extreme—on black men. Ultimately, however, Mphahlele and Modisane escaped emasculation by leaving South Africa (see Chapman 1996, 501–502.) Moloi redefined himself in terms of movie discourse. Moreover, the fact that they published their life stories suggests that they—unlike millions of other black men—rose above the morass.

Judith Lütge Coullie

See also Colonialism; Race, Conception of
Further Reading:
Chapman, Michael. 1996. *Southern African Literatures.* London and New York: Longman.
Coullie, Judith Lütge. 1998. "Crazed New World: Reflections on Godfrey Moloi's *My Life: Volume One.*" In *True Relations: Essays on Autobiography and the Postmodern.* Edited by G. Thomas Couser and Joseph Fichtelberg. Westport, CT: Greenwood Press.

————. 2001. "The Race to Be Hero: Race and Gender in Roy Campbell's *Light on a Dark Horse.*" *scrutiny2* 6, no. 2: 3–16.

Fanon, Frantz. 1967. *Black Skin, White Masks.* Translated by Charles Lam Markmann. New York: Grove Weidenfeld.

Modisane, William (Bloke). 1986 [1963]. *Blame Me on History.* Craighall, South Africa: Ad Donker.

Moloi, Godfrey. 1987. *My Life: Volume One.* Johannesburg, South Africa: Ravan Press.

Morrel, Robert, ed. 2000. *Changing Men in Southern Africa.* Pietermaritzburg, South Africa: University of Natal Press.

Mphahlele, Ezekiel. 1973 [1959]. *Down Second Avenue.* London: Faber and Faber.

Segal, Lynne. 1990. *Slow Motion: Changing Masculinities, Changing Men.* London: Virago.

Asian American Men's Studies

In the early stages of men's studies, Asian American men's issues were academic footnotes. Very few scholars mentioned Asian American men's issues until the editors of *Aiiieeee!* formulated a convincing argument in their introduction to their collection of Asian American literature. Their multilayered discourse included analyses of stereotypes of Asian American men, the insistence that Asian Americans contributed to the building of the nation, warnings of the perils of not preserving and creating a uniquely Asian American cultural experience, and an explanation of the need to rejuvenate Asian American manhood. The underlying complaint, however, was the lack of complex and diversified representations of Asian American men in all aspects of American culture.

These editors are largely credited for putting Asian American men's issues into the social discourse among Asian Americans. The argument for reconstructing Asian American manhood was as socially and culturally powerful as it was physically and emotionally visceral. The gender divide was magnified by the financial success of Maxine Hong Kingston's *Woman Warrior* (1976), which won widespread acclaim by American literary critics. Its popularity seemed to support the *Aiiieeee!* editors' point that Asian American writers catered to prevailing stereotypes about Asians living in America and the cultural "qualities" of Asia were being diluted and filtered in order to be accepted by mainstream American society.

Unfortunately, after ten years, the debate within Asian American studies did not expand to a more complex analysis of gender relations within Asian America. However, the production of David H. Hwang's *M. Butterfly* in 1989 stimulated new rounds of debates and Asian American scholars started to rethink Asian American men's issues in much more complex and theoretical ways. More conference papers started to surface, and the discourse on Asian American men started to emerge. In the 1990s, Asian American men's issues grew from conference papers and articles to full scholarly analyses, and the subject of Asian American manhood will continue to grow as a legitimate field for academic studies.

The discourse of Asian American masculinities overlays multiple axes of inquiries. In its simplest form, the lack of Asian male role models in popular culture has precluded serious discussions on the position of Asian men in America's cultural and political landscape. This lack of visibility has led to the creation of highly visible stereotypes such as the evil machinations of Fu Manchu, the effeminate and emasculated Charlie Chan, the high-flying martial arts of Bruce Lee, and the revival of that image by Hong Kong action stars such as Jacky Chan and Jet Li. The prominence of these predominantly Chinese American symbols raises several questions. What is the relationship between Asians who were born and raised in America and those who have immigrated from Asia as children or as adults? What are the linkages and dissimilarities between these groups? What kinds of cultural and social transformations occur when linguistic and cultural divisions are momentarily unified by heroic manifestations of stereotypes? These fictional models of masculinity also lead to another set of inquiries that are directly related to the racial divide within Asian American studies. What are the differences between American men who have racial ties to Asian countries such as Japan, Korea, Taiwan, Singapore, Malaysia, India, Pakistan, Indonesia, the Philippines, Vietnam, Cambodia, and Laos—among many others?

One of the side effects of this lack of diversified representation of Asian men in America is that all Asian men seem to be indistinguishable from mainstream America's perspective. Asian men in America are seldom heterosexualized in the media and the resentment is palpable among some Asian American men, especially those who see Asian women dating Caucasian men. The gender divide widens over the issues of interracial dating and marriage. There are historical contexts, immigration patterns, and racism to consider when tackling this particular topic, but the voice of multiracial children of interracial unions cannot be ignored. The multiracial characteristics of Asian Americans are inextricably linked to Asian American studies and raise perplexing problems of social and cultural identifications. The successes of multiracial individuals, for example, are "claimed" by some Asian Americans as a part of Asian America, and yet these individuals may not have any stake in raising Asian American issues.

Due, in part, to the undersexualized Asian male image, gay Asian American men are often ignored, castigated, and demonized within the Asian American community. For some Asian American men, it is critical to counter negative stereotypes, and reasserting male authority whenever possible serves a clear psychological and political purpose. Positioning oneself against gay men is the easiest way to prove to the larger society that Asian American men are indeed heroic and masculine, just like other hypermasculine Americans.

By placing the voices of gay Asian men in an abject social position, the opportunity of redefining masculinity decreases. Theoretical frameworks on gay and lesbian studies and women's studies are perceived as male bashing, and the regression from a more progressive unpacking of masculinity to a traditional and patriarchal model of masculinity becomes rather appealing.

Nonetheless, as the field of Asian American men's studies continues to expand, more nuanced models of masculinity will emerge. In American sports, an increasing number of Asian athletes are emerging. More Asian Americans are interested in politics. Comparative studies on Asian American men will broaden the scope of inquiry and Asian American men's studies courses will be offered at universities. Asian American artists will continue their struggle to provide insights on the gender divide to a larger audience and Asian American men's issues will become more accessible and less homogeneous.

Jachinson Chan

Atlas, Charles
[Angelo Siciliano] (1892–1972)

For the last sixty years, thousands of comic books and men's magazines have featured what is probably the most successful mail-order advertisement in history, a comic strip called "The Insult That Made a Man out of Mac." Mac, a "ninety-seven-pound weakling" (the term is trademarked) has a bad day at the beach: A bully kicks sand in his face, and then his girlfriend abandons him with a taunting "little boy!" Back home in his room, Mac notices an advertisement for the Charles Atlas program of Dynamic Tension, which promises that isometric exercises instead of the usual weight training will build huge muscles fast. He decides to gamble the price of a stamp to get the free information. Six months later, a built and aggressive Mac returns to the beach, kicks sand in the bully's face, and acquires a new, better girlfriend. "Hey, Skinny!" the well-proportioned but not massive Charles Atlas calls, "Nobody picks on a strong man!"

Charles Atlas (Library of Congress)

Angelo Siciliano (1892–1972), the Italian American immigrant who would enter fitness legend, popular culture, and even English-language dictionaries as Charles Atlas was himself a ninety-seven-pound "runt" in 1905, and like "Mac," he got sand kicked in his face on the beach at Coney Island. Later, in Prospect Park, he was inspired by the statues of Greek gods, who did not belong to gyms, and eschewed weight training in favor of isometrics. The results were amazing. When Bernarr Mcfadden, the quirky publisher of *Physical Culture* magazine, announced a contest to find "The World's Most Perfect Man," Siciliano entered twice and won both times, in 1921 and 1922. Mcfadden stopped holding the contest after that, as obviously Siciliano would always win.

Now fashioning himself "Charles Atlas," Siciliano teamed up with entrepreneur Charles Roman in 1928 to develop his enormously successful mail-order campaign, reaching huge numbers of boys and young men in a remarkably short time. Within months both partners were millionaires. Not even the stock market crash of 1929 slowed the flow of mail-in coupons; in fact, the Atlas empire flourished during the Great Depression, because even men with uncertain personal and financial futures could afford the hard, solid muscles necessary for a minimum of bullying and a maximum of heterosexual accomplishment. Atlas demonstrated his product on nationwide speaking tours, lent his image to dozens of Greek-god-style statues, and was featured on hundreds of magazine covers, both as a fitness expert and as a marketing genius. No one knows how many copies of his program have been sold, but by the early 2000s an estimated 3 million men (and a few women) are learning the principles of Dynamic Tension in seven languages (Bushyeager 1991, 56).

A number of factors contributed to the success of the Charles Atlas program. The price was right: $30 in 1928 and inflated only slightly to $45 in 2003. It required no heavy equipment or inconvenient hours at the gym. It was a simple but rigorous at-home program combining isometrics, diet, and mental hygiene. It drew to a great extent from the physical-culture faddists of the nineteenth and early twentieth centuries: lots of roughage but no white bread, fresh air to avoid tuberculosis, cold baths to limit sexual desire, and a positive mental attitude. And it worked, increasing muscle tone and strength (though not mass) sufficiently for most men to notice a difference within a few weeks. But Atlas's greatest success was in an explicit association of masculinity with bodybuilding.

Early in the twentieth century, bodybuilders and "strong men" received disapprobation: They were oddities, carnival sideshow attractions, or at best narcissistic hobbyists whose hours in the gym ogling each other's bodies surely masked sublimated homoerotic desire. Many social forces conspired to transform the image of the "real" man, the epitome of masculinity, from the slim, sophisticated Clark Gable of the 1930s to the massive, Nautilus-toned Jean-Claude Van Damme of the early 2000s, including an increase in leisure time, an increase in sedentary occupations, and the development of scientific bodybuilding techniques that made sculpted torsos a matter of perseverance rather than genetics.

Charles Atlas capitalized on the tide of invention, stating quite overtly that a muscular frame, far from indicative of narcissism or sublimated homoerotic desire, actually was essential for the successful performance of heterosexual masculinity, defined as the ability to fight bullies and get girls. Later exercise gurus, from Jack La Lanne to Joe Weider to the latest ab-buster pitchmen on late-night infomercials, modernized their programs and sales tactics, but they retained Charles Atlas's dictum that masculinity necessitates bodybuilding, and that every "real" man can and should have a physique resembling Michelangelo's *David*.

Jeffery P. Dennis

See also "Adonis Complex"; Bodybuilding, History of

Further Reading:

Bushyeager, Peter. 1991. "The World of Atlas." *Men's Health* 6, no. 5: 56–61.

Butler, George, and Charles Gaines. 1982. *Charles Atlas: Yours in Perfect Health.* New York: Simon and Schuster.

Dutton, Kenneth R. 1995. *The Perfectible Body: The Western Ideal of Male Physical Development.* New York: Continuum Publishing Company.

Kasson, John F. 2001. *Houdini, Tarzan, and the Perfect Man: The White Male Body and the Challenge of Modernity in America.* New York: Hill and Wang.

Webster, David. 1982. *Bodybuilding: An Illustrated History.* Lawrenceville, NJ: Peterson's.

B

Bachelor

The term *bachelor* has had varied and shifting connotations over the course of American history, and it has had strong, yet differing, relationships to the concept of manhood. Its etymology is uncertain, though it possibly is derived from Old French and Middle English terms relating to farmland. According to the *Oxford English Dictionary,* a bachelor originally was "a young knight, not old enough, or having too few vassals, to display his own banner," also "a junior or inferior member of a trade-guild." Eventually, it came to mean "an unmarried man (of marriageable age)."

Cultures that attach strong values to marriage and family often have viewed bachelors with a jaundiced eye, seeing them as arrogant, selfish, misanthropic, repugnant—even degenerate because they chose not to marry or were rejected as suitable spouses. Some considered bachelors useless and dangerous because they had evaded family responsibilities and seemed to drift aimlessly with nothing to do but cause trouble for communities seeking moral and social stability. One eighteenth-century observer called bachelors "rogue elephants." Both traditional and modern societies often have established marriage as a rite of passage out of childhood into adulthood and have denied to bachelors the status and prerogatives awarded to married men. Lurking at the edges of family life, where they remain members of a kin group but lack their own family of procreation, bachelors have been objects of scorn, yet their apparent independence and freedom from responsibility have at times had an appealing quality.

Any consideration of bachelorhood must distinguish between those who never marry and those who simply have not yet married. Though small variations have occurred, the proportion of males in any society who remain permanently single has been quite small. Such individuals have not married for many reasons, including religion, economics, psychological and/or physical constraints, personal choice, and sexual orientation. Indeed, in some places "bachelor" has been and is a code word for "homosexual."

Every male, regardless of sexual orientation, is a bachelor for at least some portion of his life, and for the most part, the proportion of a society's men who are bachelors depends upon the age at which that society's men normally marry. The average duration of an unmarried existence between puberty and betrothal has differed according to time and place. In premodern societies, the timing of marriage generally was guided by economic circumstances, mainly the ability of a man to own or rent and cultivate his own plot of land. Men often did not marry until their late twenties, having waited until their fathers bequeathed or deeded property to them. In the industrialized world, better access to economic resources reduced the average marriage age, but in the late twentieth and early twenty-first centuries there has been a general trend toward relatively late marriage as patterns of courtship and uses of leisure time have diverted people from early marital commitments. Average marriage age for men, having reached the low twenties in the midtwentieth century, had risen back to the late twenties by century's end. In the United States, for example, men's median age at first marriage stood at 26.1 in 1890, fell to 22.5 by 1960, then rose to 26.7 by 1994. Thus considerable numbers of bachelors populate modern societies in the early twenty-first century, especially in urban areas.

Bachelors also comprise a subculture within male culture. According to historian E. Anthony Rotundo (1993), as traditional inhabitants of the public sphere, consisting of the marketplace and political arena, men have developed their own homosocial associations that have included both married and unmarried members and participants. But within this domain, bachelors also have held roles as "others," individuals whose activities and institutions, as well as their status, differentiated them from married men. Because they seemingly escaped the female-dominated domestic sphere to which married men at least had to pay lip service, bachelors could cultivate a kind of autonomy that served as both an asset and a liability.

Before the modern age, bachelors were social outcasts, often considered pariahs, even criminals, because they functioned outside the basic unit of social organization—the family. In colonial America, for example, the Pennsylvania legislature passed an annual "bachelor's tax" to force unwed males into marrying and supporting a family. Similar levies stigmatized bachelors in Massachusetts and Connecticut, creating a situation in which a man gained more freedom by marrying than by staying single. Bachelors also bore other kinds of discrimination. A Virginia law of 1619 required men to dress according to their marital status. In towns of colonial New England, married men were allocated much larger home lots than were unmarried men.

The accelerated migrations and economic transformations of the nineteenth century not only loosened the social controls over bachelors but also increased their numbers and proportions in certain communities. Mining towns, lumber camps, and seaports, where women were scarce, contained large contingents of unattached, migrant men. In California during the Gold Rush period of the 1850s, for example, an estimated 90 percent of the state's population was male, 70 percent of whom were between the ages of twenty and forty and mostly unmarried. Even in fast-growing cities, such as Chicago and San Francisco, it was common for 40 to 50 percent of males in their twenties and thirties to be single. By 1890, 41.7 percent of all adult American men were unmarried, a proportion not again equaled for the next century. Similar, though slightly lower, proportions of American women also were unmarried, reflecting the relatively high marriage ages of both sexes. In several European regions in this period, especially Scandinavian countries and Ireland, marriage rates were considerably lower than those of the United States, resulting in even higher proportions of bachelors. For the most part, according to historian Howard Chudacoff (1999), by this time the apparent postponement of marriage was related not as much to economic factors and unbalanced sex ratios but rather to the flourishing of a commercial, consumer culture that created institutions and values that diverted people at least temporarily from marital commitments. Though surprisingly large proportions—sometimes close to half—of unmarried men continued to reside in their families of origin, new attitudes of individual freedom and release from traditional constraints of family, church, and community gave people—especially the young—control over what they did with their lives and their time, including when and whether they married.

In various locales, Chudacoff (1999) has noted, aggregations of working-class bachelors formed subcommunities with particular institutions such as boarding houses, saloons, dance halls, pool halls, barber shops, and cheap cafés. Middle- and upper-class bachelors frequented many of these places, as well as literary societies and social clubs. The relationships that men created in these places repudiated social reformers' assumptions that the unmarried state was one of isolation and loneliness. The male-centered sociability of bachelor institutions, with its prevalence of aggressiveness, boisterousness, competitiveness, misogyny, and teasing—often fueled by drinking, smoking, and gambling—contributed to a refashioned masculinity that countered middle-class pressures for male domesticity. Homosexual bachelors also created a thriving subculture with gay relationships located in bars, clubs, boarding houses, and YMCA lodgings. By the 1920s, though marriage rates were climbing and marriage ages were dropping, the various components of bachelor life had achieved some parcel of rootedness within consumer societies, and bachelors' alternative lifestyles had shed at least some of their repugnance. Nevertheless, because most bachelors were (and are) young and in the most crime-prone age range, society tended still to view them with apprehension.

The fall in marriage age halted temporarily during the Great Depression and World War II, but declined again during the marriage boom that followed the war, reducing proportions of unmarried men to historic lows. By the 1970s, however, new attitudes, including greater acceptance of premarital sex, contributed to a sharp rise in the numbers and proportions of unmarried people in the industrialized world. In the United States, a "singles" culture flourished in discotheques, bars, clubs, and apartment complexes that catered to the unmarried. Among males, a new form of masculinity linked to consumer goods arose. According to sociologist Michael Kimmel (1996), the popularity of *Playboy* magazine and its various imitators not only reinforced the male propensity to objectify women but also made bachelorhood respectable—even appealing—by relating high quality cars, stereo equipment, and liquor to the lifestyle of the unmarried man.

At the dawn of the twenty-first century, the roles and subtypes of bachelors span a wide spectrum. Marriage rates in many Western countries as well as in Japan and some other Asian countries remain relatively low, but the category of the unmarried is complicated by large numbers of men and women who cohabit with a partner—of either sex—in a quasi-marital condition. As well, with divorce rates at all-time highs, many societies include large numbers of men who have been previously married but are currently among the bachelor population. These men, along with the never-married and not-yet-married, continue to adapt to social change while at the same time effecting social change with their institutions, associations, and behavior.

Howard P. Chudacoff

See also Family; Husbands; Intimacy

Further Reading:
Cargan, Leonard, and Matthew Melko. 1982. *Singles: Myths and Realities.* Beverly Hills, CA: Sage; Chauncey, George. 1994. *Gay New York: Gender, Urban Culture, and the Making of the Gay Male World, 1890–1940.* New York: Basic Books.
Chudacoff, Howard P. 1999. *The Age of the Bachelor: Creating an American Subculture.* Princeton, NJ: Princeton University Press.
Kimmel, Michael. 1996. *Manhood in America: A Cultural History.* New York: Free Press.
Rotundo, E. Anthony. 1993. *American Manhood: Transformations in Masculinity from the Revolution to the Modern Era.* New York: Basic Books.
Stein, Peter J. 1976. *Single.* Englewood Cliffs, NJ: Prentice-Hall.

Backlash

Backlash is the title and term for the central thesis of the 1991 bestselling book by Susan Faludi that argues that whenever women make gains toward equality, a reactionary period follows in which the women's movement is blamed for all manner of social upheaval and unhappiness, justifying a call for the swift return to traditional feminine roles. According to Faludi, "fear and loathing of feminism is a sort of perpetual viral condition in our culture," but it is "not always in an acute phase; its symptoms subside and resurface periodically" (9). These flare-ups are always triggered by the perception that women are making progress.

The central purveyors of the contemporary antifeminist backlash are a loose coalition of antifeminist women and men, certain conservatives, neocons (neoconservatives), religious groups, and men's rights advocates who are helped—consciously or not—by novelists, journalists, screen writers, and pundits who cooperate in framing or perpetuating the arguments. Faludi calls it "a kind of pop-culture Big Lie": it "stands the truth on its head and proclaims that the very steps that have strengthened women have actually led to their downfall" (8). If women are hopelessly stressed out, desperately unwed, or miserably infertile, the backlash blames feminism's achievements for their pain, not men's and society's resistance to these only partial achievements. Yet, Faludi argues, "these so-called female crises have had their origins not in the actual conditions of women's lives but rather in a closed system that starts and ends in the media, popular culture, and advertising—an endless feedback loop that perpetuates and exaggerates its own false images of women" (6).

Faludi finds over and over that the actual positions and perspectives of women fly in the face of the backlash. She marshals considerable evidence that women consistently rank their own inequality—both at the office and at home—among their most urgent concerns. They complain of a lack of economic, not marital, opportunity. They protest that it is working men, not working women, who don't spend time in the nursery and the kitchen. "It is justice for their gender, not wedding rings and bassinets, that women believe to be in desperately short supply," Faludi writes (7).

With "backlash," Faludi gave a name to a phenomenon with deep historical and cultural roots. Outbreaks of backlash have occurred at the turn of the twentieth century, in the 1920s, during the postwar years, and in the 1980s—always at times when women are perceived to be making gains. Current purveyors of backlash include the men of the Promise Keepers and men's rights movement, who in one way or another criticize the precepts and/or progress of the women's movement and call for a return to traditional gender relations, and antifeminist women such as Wendy Shalit, Danielle Crittendon, Sylvia Hewlett, and Christina Hoff-Somers, who blame women and the women's movement for a range of social ills, including but not limited to women's supposed loss and disappointment over of the widening opportunities in their lives.

Amy Aronson

See also Antifeminism
Further Reading:
Faludi, Susan. 1991. *Backlash: The Undeclared War against American Women.*

Baden-Powell, Robert Stephenson Smyth (1857–1941)

A British army general with extensive experience of colonial warfare (service in India, West and South Africa), Robert Stephenson Smyth Baden-Powell is best known as the founder of the Boy Scout movement. Drawing especially on his experiences in the South African war (1899–1902) and his skills and contacts as a publicist, Baden-Powell published the first version of his popular *Scouting for Boys* in 1908. The movement that he simultaneously founded was the most enduring among a number of contemporary initiatives responding to a perceived crisis in imperial defense: the growth of socialism and the women's and labor movements at home, and the threat of German militarism abroad.

A key aspect of this public panic was the idea of "degeneration." Underpinned by the rising "science" of eugenics, and supported by revelations about the poor physique of army conscripts, there was a widespread belief that urbanization and demographic trends were leading to the sturdy elements of the Anglo-Saxon race being swamped by an increasingly debased underclass. Because this impending national disaster was understood as arising from a crisis of manliness, many resulting interventions—the Boys Brigade, the Church Lads, the Legion of Frontiersmen, and others—took urban male youth as their focus. These movements had in common a set of practices aiming to reinvigorate masculinity through camping and open-air activities, physical and sporting prowess, and loyalty to the group. Critics objected at the time (and have ever since) to the more or less overt militarism, jingoism, and racism of the scouting movement. Viewed as a mode of social control, scouting successfully fused the late nineteenth-century adventure tradition in boys' fiction with some of the most compelling ideological forces of the period. Yet the Boy Scout code and the injunction to "be prepared" were the hallmarks of a movement not directed simply to breeding soldiers, but toward responsible citizenship. B-P (as he was known) who criticized trade unions and strikers—the "despotic power of a few professional agitators"—also attempted to inculcate values opposed to snobbery and class consciousness.

A pedagogical ideal ran through the movement: The self-discipline and attention to others of the model Boy Scout was to be grounded in developed skills in woodcraft and observation. Baden-Powell, who saw espionage and training in tracking and observation as two sides of the same coin, was heavily influenced by his reading of Rudyard Kipling's novel *Kim* (1901), whose story he simplified and retold in *Scouting for Boys.* Implicit in this mythography of the frontier was the construction of an imaginary space in which senior males could symbolically nurture their offspring. It seems indisputable that one object was to do for lower-class boys what the British "public" (private schools in the United States) schools aimed to do for the middle and upper classes: to remove boys from the feminine environment of home and implant values of good form, tribal loyalty, and unquestioning obedience. "Manliness can only be taught by men, and not by those who are half men, half old women" (*Scouting for Boys* 342).

Quotation from Baden-Powell and those close to him can easily demonstrate the prevailing Social Darwinist climate of competition and struggle for mastery. Baden-Powell shared with many contemporary publicists a view given apparent support by the success of the Japanese in their war against Russia (1905–1906) that manly character and self-discipline (rather than economic or technological advancement) provided the foundation for national greatness. Yet as scouting became a mass movement, it became increasingly heterogeneous and thus evaded the attempts of either supporters or critics to turn it into a monolithic movement. The Girl Guides were founded 1912, the year in which Baden-Powell married Olave Soames, who became his coleader. (He had retired from the army in 1910 to devote his attention to the scouts.) Both complementary movements rapidly spread to North America as well as throughout the British Empire and generated a succession of rival and splinter groups, some of them like the Woodcraft Folk (descended in turn from the ominously named Kibbo Kift Kindred) avowedly cooperative and pacifist.

The debate over the significance of Baden-Powell and his movement has veered between hagiography and critique. Though on returning from South Africa as the hero of Mafeking he was able to exploit his status as a public icon, there are aspects of Baden-

Powell that undermine attempts to make him into an uncomplicated emblem of imperial masculinity: his lifelong love of drawing and watercolor, or the pedagogic inventiveness of *Scouting for Boys* with its use of drama and role play. Evidence of his ambiguous sexuality suggests in the context of his time an altogether more troubled and complex figure than a simple critique would imply. Baden-Powell represents a major intervention in the debate about boyhood and male development: an attempt to rebuild the social domain in which manliness and the nurture of men was understood and attempted.

Ben Knights

See also Boy Scouts; Seton, Ernest Thompson
Further Reading:

Baden-Powell, Robert. [1908] 1992. *Scouting for Boys.* London: Stevens Publishing.
Bristow, Joseph. 1991. *Empire Boys.* London: HarperCollins.
Brogan, Hugh. 1987. *Mowgli's Sons: Kipling and Baden-Powell's Scouts.* London: Jonathan Cape.
Jeal, Tim. 1989. *Baden-Powell.* London: Hutchinson.
Macdonald, Robert H. 1993. *Sons of the Empire: The Frontier and the Boy Scout Movement.* Toronto: Toronto University Press.
Rosenthal, Michael. 1986. *The Character Factory: Baden-Powell and the Origins of the Boy Scout Movement.* London: Collins.
Rutherford, Jonathan. 1997. *Forever England: Reflections on Masculinity and Empire.* London: Lawrence and Wishart.
Springhall, John. 1977. *Youth, Empire and Society: British Youth Movements 1883–1940.* London: Croom Helm.
Warren, Allen. 1987. "Popular Manliness." In *Manliness and Morality: Middle-Class Masculinity in Britain and America, 1800–1940.* Edited by J. A. Mangan and James Walvin. Manchester, UK: Manchester University Press.

Bar Mitzvah

In Jewish religious law, called *halakhah*, a boy attains the age of religious responsibility at thirteen. At that time he is called a *bar mitzvah* (plural, *b'nai mitzvah*), a "son of the commandments," from the Aramaic *bar* ("son") and the Hebrew *mitzvah* ("commandment").

At that time, the boy's father is no longer responsible for his son's education or sins, and the boy is allowed to perform certain religious rites—for example, being called to read from the Torah scroll and wearing *tefillin* (phylacteries) at morning services. Jewish men are not required to don *tefillin* until they have become *b'nai mitzvah*. Being allowed to do so at the age of thirteen constitutes a significant rite of passage. The American sociologist William Helmreich (1976), an Orthodox Jew by upbringing, recalls, "More than anything else *tefillin* was the *mitzvah* that made me feel the significance of my newly acquired status. It was the most tangible evidence that I was now a man."

However, contrary to popular belief, the elaborate ceremonies surrounding this milestone are of relatively recent vintage, and in many Jewish communities (particularly among the Sephardic Jews, descendants of the Jews expelled from the Iberian peninsula in the fifteenth century) boys were allowed to read from the scrolls while much younger, and the arrival of the thirteenth year was greeted with relative indifference.

It is important to understand that—popular usage to the contrary—one is not *bar mitzvahed*. That would be like saying you were "sonned" or "daughtered." Or maybe "commandmented." A male becomes a *bar mitzvah* merely by reaching the age of thirteen. No special ceremony is necessary to be a *bar mitzvah;* all one has to do is reach the right age. The designated age is the one at which a Jewish boy is considered by Jewish law to be able and ready to fulfill the *mitzvot,* the central tenets of the Jewish religion—not only ready and able, but obligated to do so. In the eyes of religious law, he is no longer a minor but an adult, both permitted to enjoy the religious privileges and responsible for the religious transgressions he may commit. In essence, he is now a full-fledged recipient of the religious heritage of the Jewish people and member of the community.

The *bar mitzvah* ceremony has only taken on its current importance in the past hundred or so years. Its origins are unclear; it is mentioned in neither the Hebrew Bible nor the Talmud (although the term *bar mitzvah* does occur in the Talmud, referring only to one who observes the commandments). In fact, there is no evidence of the *bar mitzvah* ceremony before 1400. However the Talmud does specify that adolescence for a male child begins at thirteen years and one day. The ceremony as we know it began to evolve in the Rhineland of Germany and France as a response to the Christian rite of confirmation.

In its earliest versions, the *bar mitzvah* ceremony consisted of a boy wearing *tefillin* for the first time and receiving his first *aliyah* (being called to bless the Torah reading), perhaps even reading from the Torah scroll. In Western Europe, a thirteen-year-old would say the blessing for the reading of the Torah, and would chant *Maftir* (the concluding passage of the week's Torah portion) and also the *Haftarah* (the prophetic reading for that week). Gradually other Jewish communities came to regard that set of responsibilities as the standard. After his son had completed the second Torah blessing, the boy's father would recite the *Barukh she-petarni,* a prayer in which he acknowledged his son's new status and asked to be absolved of responsibility for any of the boy's future sins.

Over time, the *bar mitzvah* ceremony became more elaborate, with the boy chanting not only *Maftir* but the entire Torah portion. The event was moved from a weekday morning service to Shabbat, although it can take place on Monday or Thursday, the other days on which Torah is read in synagogue. Some boys would lead the *Kabalat Shabbat* service welcoming the Sabbath the night before. More would deliver a *d'rash* on the week's portion on Saturday morning. The family-sponsored *kiddush* grew in size from a modest offering to the congregation for the Third Sabbath Meal into the occasionally excessive celebration it is today. (Ironically, there are ample examples of rabbis of the medieval period condemning families for turning the event into a veritable orgy of conspicuous

consumption, so the devaluing of this spiritually significant event into a circus of self-congratulation didn't start in the post–World War II suburbs.)

Rabbi Mordecai Kaplan, an Orthodox-trained rabbi who went over to the Conservative movement before finally founding the Reconstructionist stream of American Judaism, considered the exclusion of girls from this rite of passage totally unacceptable. In response he promoted the *bat mitzvah* ceremony; in 1922 his daughter Judith became the first girl to undergo the ceremony. For many years in most Conservative congregations the *bat mitzvah* ceremony took place on Friday night, with the girl reading from the *Haftarah.* Today, the ceremony has evolved to the point that it is indistinguishable from its male counterpart. Even many Modern Orthodox congregations now perform *b'not mitzvah* (the plural of *bat mitzvah*), albeit significantly differently from those one sees in Reform, Reconstructionist, and Conservative synagogues.

George Robinson

See also Circumcision; Jewish Men
Further Reading:
Cooper, John. 1996. *The Child in Jewish History.* Northvale, NJ: Jason Aronson, Inc.
Robinson, George. 2000. *Essential Judaism: A Complete Guide to Beliefs, Customs, and Rituals.* New York: Pocket Books.
Schauss, Hayyim. 1950. *The Lifetime of a Jew, Throughout the Ages of Jewish History.* New York: United Association of Hebrew Congregations Press.

Barnum, Phineas Taylor (1810–1891)

Phineas Taylor "P. T." Barnum considered himself—and was considered by others—to be a "real man," at least as far as the age of "fleece 'em, bunk-um" in which he lived was concerned. This is because he exemplified several of the traits of the real man of this generation: He had the wry wit and cleverness to be able to satirize and exploit for profit the gullibility and "cluelessness" of the

Known as America's greatest showman, P.T. Barnum made popular entertainment, promoted through aggressive publicity, a staple in American life and changed the way Americans viewed leisure time and cultural pursuits. He is best known as the cofounder of the Barnum & Bailey Circus, "The Greatest Show on Earth." (Library of Congress)

"Let's get the show on the road," and will forever be associated with the famous phrase "There's a sucker born every minute," although this satirization of human nature was coined by someone else.

One way Barnum sough to accomplish his goals was through advertising. He had an ability to reinvent himself and the English language to create an image of a man who knew how to rise to celebrity status by selling the gullible public on his "humbugs." For a man to achieve this kind of reputation, he had to have immense confidence in himself and in his shows—a typical "real man" characteristic. That is, he was able to convince people that his exhibits were real, and those who would question these tactics were the ones who needed to be observed in a skeptical way. Also, Barnum always wanted the media to focus on him and his accomplishments. By the same token, he adhered to the Victorian concept that a woman should remain in the home and take care of the children and the man would support his family financially. Barnum toured the world promoting his exhibits and his circus, and his family had to endure his absences.

In showing the public just how successful he believed he was, Barnum wrote in his autobiography, *The Life of P.T. Barnum, Written by Himself, Struggles and Triumphs* (1854) that he had devised the "Rings of Power," which were ten approaches to becoming a successful businessman. Further, Barnum delighted in presenting to audiences his freaks and oddities, claiming that he had the most incredible and fantastic exhibits ever seen by man. For example, he promoted Joice Heth as being the 161-year-old nurse to George Washington (she was really only 86 years old when she died), and claimed to be the one uncovering and discovering the Feejee Mermaid. (This "oddity" was a "mannequin" composed of the head of a monkey connected to the spine of a fish put together by Barnum and his technicians.) Later, he passed off Charles Stratton, actually a child dwarf, as the small-

general public of the time. And even though he was short and stocky, and unprepossessing in appearance, he had a conceited opinion of himself to the point that whatever he did, especially as far as "showmanship spectacle" was concerned, had to make him and the show seem "larger than life." At the age of sixty, Barnum created what he considered to be "the greatest show on Earth": the Barnum and Bailey Circus. Further, such a spectacle reflected Barnum's watchword, that the circus was for "Ladies and Gentlemen and children of all ages!"— something that is carried on even today. Barnum has been credited with signature words and phrases such as "Jumbo" and est "man" in the world, Tom Thumb. Also, Barnum fostered the Cardiff Giant hoax. Originally, a supposed "body" of a "prehistoric" man, made by a Mr. George Hull, who buried, dug up, and then announced the unearthing of a ten-foot stone giant on a farm in Cardiff, New York. When Barnum tried to purchase the "giant" for his collection of oddities, his offer was refused. Nothing daunted, Barnum made a replica of the giant and passed it off as the original. This "Cardiff Giant" sealed Barnum's reputation as a hoaxer; he inspired banker David Hannum to coin the saying "there's a sucker born every minute," when he viewed it. In a final gesture to the media, Barnum added to the "Greatest Show on Earth" by collecting even more oddities and freaks, contributing to the mystique that surrounded him all his later life. The circus proved to be more than a success; indeed, it has shown a universal appeal for all audiences for over a century.

For a man who was considered the prince of the humbug, Barnum honed his skills at serious advertising and reinventing himself whenever he saw a chance to turn a profit. According to Barnum, "there is only one liquid a man could use in excessive quantities without being swallowed up by it, and that was printer's ink" (Werner 1923, 234). Barnum spared no expense to in order to show himself as someone whose work went beyond that of mere humans. He even went so far as to take exhibits such as Tom Thumb to England to meet Queen Victoria. Perhaps Barnum thought he could fool the queen as well. Barnum was especially delighted when reporters wrote negatively about him. The more the public read about him, even in a negative way, the more he felt that he was seen and remembered.

Further, his museum was such a success that one person said, "the people will go to see Barnum despite whether he is good or not" (Barnum 1854, 212). Thus, Barnum kept himself in the public eye. His ability to manipulate audiences with his curiosities and

his continuous belief that people will come to see something advertised as the "greatest," or "smallest," or "oldest" in the world were among Barnum's "masculine" traits that made him—for his time—the world's greatest showman and a great "man."

Karen E. Holleran

Further Reading:
Adams, Bluford. 1997. *E Pluribus Barnum: The Great Showman and the Making of U.S. Popular Culture.* Minneapolis: University of Minnesota Press.
Barnum, P. T. 1999. *Art of Money Getting: Or Golden Rules for Making Money.* Bedford, MA: Applewood Books. Originally published: Philadelphia: Bell, 1880.
———. 1981. *Struggles and Triumphs or, Forty Years' Recollections of P. T. Barnum.* New York: Penguin Books. Second edition published 1869.
———. "What the Fair Should Be." At http://www.boondocksnet.com/expos/wfe_barnum1890.html (cited 2 October 2002).
Benton, Joel. "The P. T. Barnum of the Barnum and Bailey Circus." At http://www.electricscotland.com/history/barnum/chap16.htm (cited 7 August 2003).
Brown, Rick J. 2002. "P. T. Barnum Never Did Say 'There's a Sucker Born Every Minute.'" At http://www.historybuff.com/library/refbarnum.html (cited 26 September 2002).
Hamilton, T. A. "P. T. Barnum: King of the Weird." At http://www.tahamilton.com/11_Museum_of_the_Weird/barnum1.htm (cited 4 September 2002).
Harris, Neil. 1973. *Humbug: The Art of P. T. Barnum.* Chicago: The University of Chicago Press.
Kunhardt, Peter W. 1995. *P. T. Barnum: America's Greatest Showman.* New York: Knopf.
"P. T. Barnum." At http://www.barnum-museum.org/orig/html/barnum.html (cited 7 August 2003).
Saxon, Arthur H. 1989. *P. T. Barnum: The Legend and the Man.* New York: Columbia University Press.
Seaburg, Alan. "P. T. Barnum." At http://uua.org/uuhs/duub/articles/ptbarnum.htm (cited 7 August 2003).
Vitale, Joe. 1998, *There's A Customer Born Every Minute: P. T. Barnum's Secrets to Business Success.* Kansas City, KS: American Management Association.
Wallace, Irving. 1959. *The Fabulous Showman: The Life and Times of P. T. Barnum.* New York: Knopf.
Werner, M. Robert. 1923. *Barnum.* New York: Harcourt, Brace.

Barton, Bruce (1886–1967)

Bruce Barton stands as a seminal figure in defining post–World War I masculinities in the United States. Barton published *The Man Nobody Knows* (1924) as a guide to American men on how to incorporate a masculine spirituality into their lives while maintaining a strong business profile. He became the equivalent of a modern self-help guru, allaying the fears of millions of American men stymied by corporate culture and its perceived feminization. His book was enormously successful, selling over 250,000 copies in its first eighteen months and prompting Barton to write sequels *The Book Nobody Knows* (1924) and *What Can a Man Believe?* (1927). Through these volumes, Bruce Barton revised feminized notions of Protestant Christianity by depicting Jesus Christ as a precursor to the modern businessman, labeling him the essence of white manhood. As such, Barton became one of the most influential figures regarding Jazz Age masculinity, defining it as a combination of persuasive power and virile strength.

Barton's work was not the first attempt to define Christianity in masculine terms. "Muscular Christianity," a Victorian/Progressive ideal of physical strength complementing strong faith, still held sway in the postwar decade. In addition, the progressive Social Gospel movement combined the tradition and prestige of religion with the desire for fraternity as a means of combating the urban alienation expressed by many of its practitioners. The Social Gospel was an ideology of sentiment designed to alleviate anxiety through good feelings and fuzzy brotherhood, though it also contributed to specific material gains such as the rise of the Young Men's Christian Association (YMCA) and the Young Women's Christian Association (YWCA). The "men and religion forward" movement of 1911–1912, echoed by Billy Sunday's popularity, made muscular Christianity a revitalized, and revitalizing, doctrine (Bederman 1989).

But Barton's book is perhaps the most straightforward and popular depiction of the linkages between religion and manhood in the 1920s. Barton cofounded the successful advertising firm of Batten, Barton, Durstine, and Osborn; his central metaphor of Christ as an adman seems indebted to his background. *The Man Nobody Knows* masculinized Jesus within the context of commercial enterprise by presenting him as an effective salesman. Male subjectivity thus becomes a matter of performance rather than an intrinsic set of qualities. Jesus Christ represents the Self-Made Man, rising from the manger of Bethlehem to become the world's most powerful adman for Christian lifestyle, transforming others through virile self-production/promotion. Compelling in his speech and in his imposing physicality, Christ represents the secure manly ideal for 1920s men anxious about their place in postwar corporate culture. In addition, Barton presents Christ's teachings as the means for 1920s men to endure their workplace miseries. The ideals of tolerance, patience, and virtue taught by Jesus become the steps by which men regain control of an emasculating workplace environment, turning the feminizing agents of sedentary office work into a breeding ground for manly vigor.

The central tenets Barton ascribes to Jesus invoke ideals of brotherhood as well. Barton trumpets the fact that men followed Christ as a leader, suggesting the fraternal instincts that Jesus provokes and noting his skill in salesmanship and recruitment. Jesus's advertising skills are nowhere more evident than in his finding of the disciples, where he turns those attributes toward the gathering of a fraternal collective. Descriptions of Christ's muscularity and healthy vigor permeate the text, presenting an idealized physicality to which emasculated men could aspire that paid tribute to physical culture's leaders such as Bernarr Macfadden and Charles Atlas, exemplars of masculinity in and of themselves. Barton rescues Christ from the feminized artists and women to restore him to manliness, reviving religion as a masculinizing brotherhood. As a result, Barton's vision creates a new set of disciples, eagerly subjecting themselves to this masculinized Christian ideal as a means of assuaging anxieties about modernity's feminization of the American male.

David E. Magill

See also Men and Religion Forward Movement; Muscular Christianity; YMCA

Further Reading:

Barton, Bruce. 1925. *The Man Nobody Knows: A Discovery of the Real Jesus.* Indianapolis: Bobbs-Merrill.

Bederman, Gail. 1989. "'The Women Have Had Charge of the Church Work Long Enough': The Men and Religion Forward Movement of 1911–1912 and the Masculinization of Middle-Class Protestantism." *American Quarterly* 41: 432–465.

Davis, Simone Weil. 2000. *Living Up to the Ads: Gender Fictions of the 1920s.* Durham, NC: Duke University Press.

Douglas, Ann. 1995. *Terrible Honesty: Mongrel Manhattan in the 1920s.* New York: Farrar, Straus, and Giroux.

Dumenil, Lynn. 1995. *The Modern Temper: American Culture and Society in the 1920s.* New York: Hill and Wang.

Gerzon, Mark. 1982. *A Choice of Heroes: The Changing Faces of American Manhood.* Boston: Houghton Mifflin.

McWilliams, Wilson Carey. 1973. *The Idea of Fraternity in America.* Berkeley, CA: University of California Press.

Baseball

A descendant of the British ball and bat games of rounders and cricket, baseball was first known in America as townball. With its rules established in the New York area in the 1840s, the game's popularity spread and by the end of the Civil War baseball was the national pastime. Contrary to popular mythology, baseball's roots are thoroughly urban, growing out of a men's culture that featured boardinghouses, saloons, and ward politics. By the end of the nineteenth century, the pastoral myth foisted upon the game by A. G. Spalding, a former player and sporting-goods manufacturer, had taken hold. The positioning of baseball as expressive of American contradictions—ballparks as urban pastures, deliberation countered by spontaneity, work as play and play as work, and the precarious balance between boyhood and manhood—enabled baseball to become an apt metaphor for shifts in culture and masculinity for the next 150 years.

Lacking the legitimacy of a profession, the game drew most of its players from society's margins. Rowdiness prevailed in the early days of the game and persisted once the National League was established in 1876, followed by the American League in 1901. With the owners firmly in power and their players bound to them—in effect for their careers, via the reserve clause—baseball enjoyed a period of general prosperity. The play was aggressive, dirty, physical, violent, and ugly, and fans loved it. Players like Cap Anson, King Kelly, and John McGraw personified tough play on and off the field, passing that baton to Ty Cobb after the turn of the century. Cobb exemplified what would later become known as "little ball," a style of play that stressed speed, aggression, base stealing, place hitting, and scratching out runs one at a time. He was a racist misanthrope widely regarded as the greatest player of the first twenty years of the new century.

The early twentieth century was marked by a crisis in masculinity among white, middle-class men. Urbanization, immigration, an erratic economy, and the appearance of the "new woman"—single and sexually active, professionally ambitious, and upwardly mobile—fueled male insecurity. Baseball was in a similar crisis. The Black Sox scandal of 1919 may be remembered as having hit baseball out of the blue, but the truth is that it was simply the largest and ugliest blight on a game that had been mired in scandal and infighting for several years. During the 1919 World Series, the corruption that gambling brought to baseball reached its pinnacle. Eight players from the Chicago White Sox were involved in the scandal and were suspended from baseball for life, even though they were all acquitted of criminal charges. The harsh ruling by first-year commissioner Judge Kenesaw Mountain Landis restored some faith in the game, but the emergence of

George Herman "Babe" Ruth was far more influential in restoring baseball's place as the nation's pastime.

When he was sold to the New York Yankees from the Boston Red Sox in December 1919, Ruth had already established himself as the Sox's best player and a bankable gate attraction. In his first year with the Yankees he hit fifty-four home runs, while Yankee attendance more than doubled, setting a new league record. Ruth and his home runs signified a shift in the offensive philosophy of the game and a rejuvenation of the game itself. Ruth was lovable, big-hearted, simple, careless, reckless, and charming. Coming on the heels of the Black Sox scandal and in the midst of the rampant urbanization and economic transformation that characterized the 1920s, Ruth rekindled baseball's pastoral connections and embodiment of the American dream. He was living proof that through sports a man can rise from common beginnings to fame and fortune. In the home run, Ruth embodied modernity. He was a machine, dependable and efficient. His home runs were akin to skyscrapers, education, and industrial production as symbols of American greatness. His ability to span two distinct eras, embodying the best of both, is evidence of his efficacy in allaying the era's male fears.

The son of a poor Italian fisherman, Joe DiMaggio became the next male exemplar of an age. He arrived in New York in 1936, the year after Ruth retired, and quickly filled the void. The Yankees enjoyed unprecedented success. During DiMaggio's reign the Yankees won ten pennants and nine World Series. They were solid, dependable, and consistent. DiMaggio was the rock at the center. Where Ruth was all innocence and childish impulse, DiMaggio was poise, self-discipline, and dignity. No record personified DiMaggio more aptly than his fifty-six-game hitting streak in 1941. Still standing in 2003, it records his poised persona and steady playing style as ably as Ruth's sixty home runs represent his explosiveness and ebullience.

DiMaggio was linked with his Italian American heritage from the outset. Much of the early publicity surrounding him called attention to the fact that he was a member of a large Italian family, supporting the traditional American emphasis on a strongly parented, large, close, and affectionate family. That Joe and his brothers, Dom and Vince, all played baseball, breaking from the family's traditional vocation of fishing, was interpreted as part of the process of Americanization. Like Ruth before him, DiMaggio was presented in terms that served to stitch a social fabric that was fraying during his peak years. DiMaggio blossomed in Depression America and his unassuming, self-assured, and humble demeanor fit. Because large-scale immigration was at a lull, Americans were receptive to ethnic heroes, and DiMaggio seemed the ideal. He projected a strong, positive view of Italian Americans that countered their representations as devious criminals in popular culture. His history was one of reassuring proof that the American dream was alive and well. If the streets weren't actually paved in gold, you could, after all, become the quintessential self-made man.

For African American men, the quest for successful masculinity was beset by the additional need for racial equality. The sporting realm relies on the assumption that there exists a level playing field where all are judged by their performance and all perform within an agreed-upon set of rules. More so than any other institution, sports is said to be color-blind. Black baseball players had been denied participation in the major leagues since 1887. Nevertheless baseball thrived in the black community. All-black teams barnstormed their way through the North and South, but were mostly invisible to white America. Under the leadership of Rube Foster, black ballplayers and owners organized and formed the National Negro League in 1920. The league existed in relative prosperity for over thirty-five years, adding an American League, an All-Star game, and a sporadically held World Series. Black ballplayers enjoyed a dignity, notoriety, and prosperity unavailable to them elsewhere in society. As much as anything else, the Negro Leagues were a valiant attempt to display to white America that black America could sustain an economic endeavor as large as a professional sporting league. The Negro leagues were a double-edged exercise that on one hand proved that black athletes, fans, owners, and investors were as capable and zealous as their white counterparts, and on the other provided a symbol and practice of cultural pride and solidarity that assimilation could not furnish.

The 1947 breaking of the color line placed that exercise squarely on Jackie Robinson's shoulders and signaled the beginning of the end for the Negro leagues. Chosen as much for his experience in integrated institutions as his skills on the baseball diamond, Robinson furnished the hardworking, honest, self-sacrificing, and safe model of masculinity demanded by a segregated culture still fearful of miscegenation. As part of his agreement with Branch Rickey, the Dodgers' general manager, Robinson was not to respond to any racial slights on or off the field. Robinson was able to respond by bringing a palpable ferocity to the diamond and returned baseball to the aggressive style of play built on speed and guile that flourished at the turn of the century. He led the league in stolen bases, led the Dodgers to the National League pennant, won the Rookie of the Year Award, and was the main reason Brooklyn drew over a million fans for the first time. His performance erased doubts about black players' abilities and Negro league veterans slowly began popping up in major league lineups, allowing access to the sporting meritocracy. Robinson's celebrity and character enabled him to succeed in economic, social, and political realms in ways that his sporting predecessors could not have imagined.

The frustration with the slow-moving response to assimilation as practiced by the Civil Rights movement and embodied by the nonconfrontational black male gave rise to the late 1960s move to "Black Power," which, in conjunction with a counterculture that coalesced around opposition to the Vietnam War, created a dramatic shift in the construction of popular masculinity. The move to embrace "otherness" and youth was most evident in the long hair and flashy uniforms of the Oakland Athletics. Urged on by their promotions-oriented owner, Charles O. Finley, the A's were a freewheeling bunch that exuded a "cool" requisite for the period. In keeping with the shift, and despite countless death threats and racial epithets, Hank Aaron managed to break Babe Ruth's career home run record. In a structural move that reflected the cultural upheavals of the era, baseball players were finally rid of the reserve clause and able to enjoy, with some limitations, the freedoms of free agency. Players with a minimum of six years' major league experience were allowed to sell their skills to the highest bidder. For the first time since its organization, power in baseball resided with the players. The era was capped by a World Series victory by a Pittsburgh Pirates squad fielding an all-black and Latino starting nine. Further underscoring the shift in and fluidity of male identity during the period, the Pirates unironically appropriated the gay disco anthem "We Are Family" as a rallying cry.

The celebration was short-lived. The 1980s ushered in a new era of conservatism with its thinly veiled indictment of the gains made by minorities in the previous decades. Baseball labor strife characterized the period. The century threatened to end as it had begun with a full-fledged crisis in white, middle-class masculinity stemming from immigration fears, economic woes, and feminism. Baseball's attendance numbers dropped steadily as fans soured on the twice-striking players who were portrayed in the media as spoiled children. After the 1994 players' strike and subsequent canceling of the playoffs and World Series, confidence in baseball was at an all-time low. Cal Ripken's 1995 breaking of Lou Gehrig's consecutive-games-played record stemmed the tide, but it was in the return of the home run as metaphor that baseball and white masculinity was, for the time being, healed. The race to the record for home runs in a single season between Sammy Sosa and Mark McGwire was framed largely as one of competing masculinities. McGwire was the "new man" bridging traditional and evolving notions of masculinity. He was a powerful father who managed to be compassionate and loving. Sosa filled the familiar trope of the "other." Flamboyant and deferential, he was the perfect foil. McGwire's blasts were compared to national monuments and his eventual victory proof of white masculinity's cultural saliency. The relative lack of attention paid to Barry Bonds's breaking of McGwire's record in 2001, particularly during a time when sport was being used to heal the American psyche, is further evidence of baseball's deep connection to inherent American racial and masculine conservative and cultural contradictions.

Although baseball has slipped in popularity and continues to be plagued by labor strife, its metaphoric capabilities have not eroded. Where basketball embraces an urban identity and football relishes its mythic rural roots, baseball articulates both and is second only to soccer in global appeal and youth participation. That being said, competition for a family's entertainment dollar is greater than it has ever been, as is the proliferation of athletic activities available for American youths. The pace of American life has shifted to the point where baseball, once reflective of cultural briskness, is now slow by comparison. Baseball is far from drifting into irrelevancy, but American character is increasingly marked by the immediacy of basketball and football as opposed to the timelessness of baseball.

Julio Rodriguez

See also Basketball; Football; Physical Culture
Further Reading:
Kahn, Roger. 1972. *The Boys of Summer.* New York: Harper and Row.

Messner, Michael, and Donald Sabo, eds. 1990. *Sport, Men, and the Gender Order.* Champaign, IL: Human Kinetic Books.
Moore, Jack B. 1986. *Joe DiMaggio: Baseball's Yankee Clipper.* New York: Praeger.
Sailes, Gary A., ed. 1998. *African Americans and Sport.* New Brunswick, NJ: Transaction Publishers.
Smelser, Marshall. 1975. *The Life that Ruth Built.* New York: Quadrangle.
White, G. Edward. 1996. *Creating the National Pastime: Baseball Transforms Itself, 1903–1953.* Princeton, NJ: Princeton UP, 1996.
Will, George. *Men at Work: The Craft of Baseball.* 1990. New York: Macmillan, 1990.
Zoss, Joel, and John Bowman. 1995. *The History of Major League Baseball.* Greenwich, CT: Brompton.

Basketball

Invented by Dr. James Naismith in December 1891 at the School for Christian Workers in Springfield, Massachusetts, basketball is the result of the specific desire to create an indoor winter game to maintain the interest and physical fitness of young men and women bored with gymnastics and calisthenics. Under the auspices of Muscular Christianity, the belief that sports could build character, help in the acquisition of virtue, and serve as an instrument of moral reform, the game served the needs of the school, later renamed the International Training School of the Young Men's Christian Association (YMCA). Although devoid of its religious connotations, the ethic of Muscular Christianity continues to inform institutionalized sport. By the end of the decade the game had taken on a distinctly urban character that would characterize its nature and its participants throughout the twentieth century and into the twenty-first.

The game proved immediately popular and in the months following its invention, it spread to YMCAs throughout the Northeast. By the following winter, basketball was popular enough to draw significant crowds willing to pay admission. The most successful of the early YMCA teams was the squad from the German YMCA in Buffalo, New York, the Buffalo Germans. They recorded a 30-year record of nearly 800 wins and fewer than 100 losses including an unequaled mark of 111 consecutive wins. Held in conjunction with the 1901 Pan-American Exposition, the Germans also won the first ever World Championship. The YMCA basketball, however, fell victim to its success. Although originally envisioned as a noncontact sport, the game quickly became remarkably physical, and women, who had played since the game's inception, were increasingly relegated to the sidelines. The YMCA directors felt the rough play detracted from the institution's overall mission and systematically eliminated basketball from its gymnasiums. The exile was short-lived.

Amateur basketball found a new home at the collegiate level. Friends and pupils of Naismith's, Amos Alonzo Stagg, Henry F. Kallenberg, and Ray Kaighn spread basketball to colleges in the Midwest and Northeast. By the late 1890s the Intercollegiate League, forerunner to the Ivy League, was playing a regular basketball schedule, and in 1905 the Western Conference, later the Big Ten, began conference play. Regional champions quickly sought national bragging rights and in 1904 a semblance of an annual National Championship Tournament began to be held. During the next decades regional styles of play began to emerge, adding more intrigue to the National Tournament. In the East play was slow and methodical, relying on exact passing, endless give-and-go schemes, and stationary two-handed set shots. In the Midwest and West, play was more open, employing more fast-breaking, free shooting, and running one-handed jump shots. Regardless of the style, college ball was mostly about coaching and a team system. Setting the template for collegiate coaching, Ward Lambert at Purdue, Nat Holman at the City College of New York, and Doc Carlson at Pittsburgh instituted ironclad systems in which the system outshone those playing in it. Basketball was

largely a matter of discipline and repetition. Even though historians point to the 1966 National Collegiate Athletic Association (NCAA) championship game between Texas Western and Kentucky as the turning point from team play—understood as white—to a more individualized style, born from a black urban milieu, the process began earlier with Bill Russell and the San Francisco University Dons, echoing a shift that occurred earlier still with the first professionals.

Having been run out of YMCA gymnasiums, men who were not in the position to pursue a college education turned to renting halls and charging admission to offset the cost—in effect, becoming professionals. Philadelphia was the nexus of the professional game. The urban environment, heavy influx of immigrant athletes, and raucous partisan crowds elevated the rough nature of play and drew the ire of the Amateur Athletic Union and YMCA officials. Undaunted, professional leagues coalesced around teams sponsored by social clubs. Irish, German, and Jewish immigrants fielded teams that dominated the early professional game. The New York Celtics, later the Original Celtics, and the South Philadelphia Hebrew Association (SPHA) in particular used the rugged play and charged atmosphere of games as a site for the creation and maintenance of ethnic and male pride. For immigrant men who were systematically barred from pursuit of the American dream, being able to make a living playing basketball was a means of articulating an ethnic male identity that was elsewhere marginalized and ridiculed.

Professional basketball was a chaotic enterprise for much of its early existence. Although ethnically identified clubs remained, leagues came and went, and players routinely jumped teams in search of better pay. The instability of league play resulted in the most successful teams and players taking up barnstorming as a means to earn a living. For African American men who wanted to play professionally, it was the only option. Although black colleges had been playing basketball since 1910, and there were a number of club teams in major cities, no equivalent to baseball's Negro League existed. Foremost among barnstorming teams were the Harlem Renaissance Big Five. Created in 1922 by Robert L. Douglass, the Rens, as they became known, were the first black owned and operated professional basketball team in the United States. As the premier all-black basketball team, the Rens developed rivalries with the top white teams of the era, the Celtics and the SPHA, producing contests that were only a thinly veiled discourse on racial supremacy.

Emerging five years after the Rens, the Harlem Globetrotters are easily the most famous of the barnstorming teams. A product molded by Chicago entrepreneur Abe Saperstein, the Trotters took the Harlem moniker as a means to identify them with the style of play increasingly associated with urban blackness and made famous by their barnstorming predecessors. As coach and manager, Saperstein, as did many Jewish businessmen of the era, shrewdly circumvented institutionalized anti-Semitism by catering to markets ignored by mainstream institutions—blacks, immigrants, and the white working class. Accusations of racism and paternalism notwithstanding, Saperstein displayed a keen awareness of the racial climate, encouraging buffoonery and clowning on the court and eventually making it the Trotter signature. In an era teeming with racially motivated violence, America could accept black entertainers, but not black athletes routinely defeating whites. The comic antics, harkening back to minstrelsy, and white management allowed the Trotters a level of prosperity and fame not possible for the all-black and nonclowning Rens.

As a means to fill their arenas when other draws were absent, Eastern arena owners created the Basketball Association of America in 1946. The new league had the advantage of large arenas in large cities, but lacked talented players who called the Midwest and the National Basketball League home. After three years of competing for players and fan dollars, the leagues merged, forming the National Basketball Association (NBA). Integrated competition had been the norm at the college level for numerous years, but at the professional level basketball did not become integrated until 1950, when the Boston Celtics, Washington Capitols, and New York Knicks drafted Charles Cooper, Earl Lloyd, and Nat "Sweetwater" Clifton respectively. Even with a steady influx of black players, the NBA remained predominantly white in skin tone and playing style. The game was dominated by defense and set plays. Not until 1967 and the American Basketball Association (ABA) did basketball take on some of the thrilling qualities that quickly became associated with black players. The ABA played a wide-open game and instituted the three-point shot. It also had players who played with an electric quality above the rim that dazzled old-time NBA fans. Television played an integral role in the growing popularity of the league. Like football before it, basketball seemed tailor-made for the medium and cultural age. The constant action of the game fit the pace of modern life more so than baseball and football, and the generation that was coming of age along with basketball was less preoccupied with race—as evidenced by the relatively smooth name change of NBA star Lew Alcindor to Kareem Abdul Jabbar. In spite of the cultural shift, the ABA folded in 1976. It had suffered from poor attendance throughout its nine-year existence and was unable to sustain itself. Its strongest franchises, San Antonio, Denver, Indiana, and New York joined the NBA. The rest of the league simply vanished.

To a great extent, the racial politics of the early 1970s caused the ABA to fold. According to racist logic, professional basketball was drug infested simply because it was too black. The specter of drug abuse within the league was used as evidence of the inherent depravity of the black males who dominated and thus threatened the existence of professional basketball. By the mid-1970s, television revenues had withered and migrating franchises nearly crippled the NBA. The on-court violence that was typical during the decade did not help matters any. Teams had stars and enforcers protecting the stars and brawls were not uncommon. The league remained saddled with financial woes and negative press coverage until the 1980s. The emergence of Larry Bird and Earvin "Magic" Johnson helped cleanse the NBA's drug-tainted, brawling image, but the pair also served as ideal foils for the racial dialogue that characterized the next decades.

During the 1980s Ronald Reagan capitalized on white America's racial fears and argued successfully that racism was no longer a problem, even though the economic divide between black and white was increasing. Reagan-era politics drew on American nostalgia, reinstilling traditional ideas of the nuclear family and contrasting them with images of welfare-cheating, unwed black mothers and absentee black fathers. Bird was the perfect embodiment of the nostalgic American dream. Even though he displayed spontaneity, improvisation, individual expression, and creativity, all staples of a black playing style, Bird was popularly understood as a product of hard work, practice, study, dedication, and team-oriented basketball. The narrative surrounding Johnson was nearly the exact opposite. Johnson was all-black ball, natural ability, and showmanship. It didn't matter that he involved his teammates better than any guard had done prior or that he was studious and skilled enough to play at every position. Johnson returned audiences to an ABA heyday when the likes of Julius Erving, George Gervin, and David Thompson expressed an urban black sensibility on and off the basketball court. However, Johnson's and other black athletes' successes were popularly framed as evidence of America's victory over racism, furthering the racist policies of the Reagan-Bush era.

Although racist rhetoric dominated the airwaves, alternate voices existed, and by the mid-1980s, the Nike corporation had recognized the commercial viability of rebellious blackness. Latching onto the Georgetown Hoyas' success in college basketball in the early part of the decade, Nike capitalized on coach John Thompson's strident support for black youth off the court and his teams' aggressive dominance on it. With an antagonistic racial binary as a backdrop, celebrities, in the form of black athletes, refined endorsement advertising by injecting cultural capital into the equation. Entering the league four years after Bird and Johnson, Michael Jordan managed to personify both sides of the racial dichotomy. By the mid-1990s Jordan was the most recognizable figure in the sporting world. Sensing his broad appeal, Michael and his handlers crafted a palatable version of blackness for Reagan-era America. Off court he espoused family values and the work ethic, sacrifice and responsibility, and, above all, a safe model of black masculinity. On court he was as creative, explosive, imaginative, and innovative as Johnson and countless predecessors. Riding Jordan, the NBA became as consumable worldwide as McDonald's and Coca-Cola.

Basketball continues to expand in Jordan's wake. It is tailor-made for audiences raised with television and video games, which increasingly inform television aesthetics. No other game is as instantly gratifying, incessantly stimulating, or aesthetically pleasing in its controlled violence. Its minimal spatial and equipment requirements make it ideal for emerging populations. At the international level, the once unchallenged reign of the United States is quickly eroding. The NBA has expanded into Canada and showcases superstars from every continent save Antarctica. Even though the central racial tension persists, the game flourishes and remains the most effective canvas on which to render an individualized masculine identity.

Julio Rodriguez

See also Baseball; Football; Physical Culture; YMCA
Further Reading:
Bjarkman, Peter C. 1996. *Hoopla: A Century of College Basketball.* Indianapolis, IN: Masters Press.

Feinstein, John. 2000. *The Last Amateurs: Playing for Glory and Honor in Division I College Basketball.* New York: Little, Brown.

———. 2002. *The Punch: One Night, Two Lives, and the Fight that Changed Basketball Forever.* New York: Little, Brown.

George, Nelson. 1992. *Elevating the Game: Black Men and Basketball.* New York: Harper Collins.

Halberstam, David. 2000. *Playing for Keeps: Michael Jordan and the World that He Made.* New York: Broadway Books.

Battered Husband Syndrome

Battered husband syndrome is the label some researchers and activists give to three phenomena: (1) the notion that violence in couples is mutual combat, (2) the argument that intimate victimization is gender symmetrical, and (3) the fact that a small proportion of victims of violent crimes by intimates are men. In 1978 Steinmetz coined the term *battered husband syndrome* to draw public attention to men's victimization. Literary, anecdotal, and clinical evidence, crime statistics, and common sense cast men as perpetrators and women as victims of battering. Claims that some men are battered and arguments that women and men are equally violent and victimized rest on two facts. First, some men are assaulted or killed by their wives or girlfriends. Second, there is no statistically significant difference in the rates at which women and men report that they use aggression in conflicts with their intimate partners. At best, this evidence evokes compassion and justice for brutalized men. At worst, proponents of the battered husband syndrome claim that men are not any more aggressive in intimate settings than women (this is gender symmetry). Some reporters, politicians, and activists go on to assert that feminists have fraudulently appropriated taxpayer dollars to fund shelters and services for women only.

The empirical evidence undergirding the battered husband syndrome is straightforward and based on three sources. The source of the claim that "Men are victims, too!" is crime statistics such as the U.S. National Crime Victimization Survey (NCVS). The NCVS estimates that 15 percent of victims of intimate violence are men and 26 percent of intimate homicides are men (Rennison 2001; figures are for 1999). Thus, although the vast majority of victims of violent crimes and homicides by intimates are women, some men are also violently assaulted by their wives or girlfriends.

The source of claims about gender symmetry and mutual combat is surveys of married, cohabiting, and dating heterosexual couples. When asked how they respond to relationship conflicts, roughly equal proportions of women and men report using physical aggression. Such studies most commonly use some variant of Straus's Conflict Tactics Scale (CTS; 1979). The CTS asks women and men to report whether and how often they and their partner use aggression to resolve relationship conflicts. An exhaustive meta-analysis of studies of sex differences in CTS-type aggression toward heterosexual partners found that women were slightly more likely than men to use physically aggressive tactics and to use them more frequently (Archer 2000).

The experiences of interviewers asking some clinical and nonsheltered samples of women about couple conflict constitute another source of claims about men's victimization. Some women report that they yell, strike out physically, or brandish weapons against their husbands or boyfriends. This combination of crime statistics, surveys, and interviews forms the empirical basis for the battered husband syndrome. Some commentators use the battered husband syndrome, in turn, to claim that women are as aggressive as men; that men are entitled to sympathy, shelter, and services; and that feminists have maligned men and grossly overstated the extent and meaning of violence against women.

Critiques of the battered husband syndrome take two forms. The first is empirical and methodological. Eighty-five percent of victims of intimate partner violence are women; that is not "gender symmetry" (Rennison 2001). What survey researchers see when they look at aggression between intimates depends on specific questions, respondents, and contexts. For example, when researchers ask about injuries, they find less empirical support for gender symmetry. In Archer's meta-analysis, the exact same studies that showed no significant sex difference in physical aggression also showed that men were more likely than women to injure their intimate partners and the majority (but not all) of those who were injured were women (2000). The national samples on which the battered husband syndrome rests measure "common couple violence" and vastly underrepresent the "patriarchal terrorism" that abusive men use to intimidate and control women (Johnson 1995). Archer's meta-analysis also found that the magnitude of sex differences in reported aggression rates was sensitive to the characteristics of the study sample, including age and marital status. The NCVS shows higher victimization rates for separated women, who are underrepresented in surveys of couples. When researchers rely on self-reports instead of partner reports, women have higher aggression rates than men. Both men and women currently in couples may use aggressive conflict tactics. However, CTS-based surveys seldom ask about violence in past relationships, violence and stalking after separation, self-defense, or broader patterns of control and intimidation. Moreover, there is no evidence that the aggression is "mutual" in cases of woman battering reported in crime statistics, clinical settings such as hospital emergency rooms, and interviews with women who have fled their homes for shelters. Finally, although a focus on specific acts enhances disclosure rates, reliability, and validity, critics argue that battering is not reducible to individual acts of physical aggression. The CTS does not reliably tap into the meaning or context of a threat or a blow, including self-defense and the possibility that battering is completely unrelated to relationship conflicts.

The second critique of the battered husband syndrome is more theoretical. Critics assert that battering "takes two"—not in the sense of mutual combat, but in the sense of an aggressor plus a social system (Goetting 1999). Battering, in this view, is possible and meaningful only in the context of a set of social relations that first deliver a woman into the control of a man and then reinforce his ability to extract deference, sexual access, housekeeping and emotional services, etc., from her through threats, harassment, coercion, and violence. According to this argument, although women can be mean and physically violent, and some men as a consequence are hurt, there are no battered husbands. Men (unlike women) do not live in a social order organized around their own economic, sexual, political, and social subordination. To make these points is not to deny that some men are victimized by women. It is to claim that men's victimization does not constitute a battered husband syndrome.

Lisa D. Brush

See also Batterer Intervention Programs; Battering; Domestic Violence; Marital Violence

Further Reading:

Archer, John. 2000. "Sex Differences in Aggression between Heterosexual Partners: A Meta-Analytic Review." *Psychological Bulletin* 126: 651–680.

Berns, Nancy. 2001. "Degendering the Problem and Gendering the Blame: Political Discourse on Women and Violence." *Gender & Society* 15: 262–281.

Brush, Lisa D. 1990. "Violent Acts and Injurious Outcomes in Married Couples: Methodological Issues in the National Survey of Families and Households." *Gender & Society* 4: 56–67.

Goetting, Ann. 1999. *Getting Out: Life Stories of Women Who Left Abusive Men.* New York: Columbia University Press.

Johnson, Michael P. 1995. "Patriarchal Terrorism and Common Couple Violence: Two Forms of Violence against Women." *Journal of Marriage and the Family* 57: 283–294.

Rennison, Callie Marie. 2001. *Intimate Partner Violence and Age of Victim, 1993–1999.* Bureau of Justice Statistics Special Report NCJ 187635. Washington, DC: U.S. Department of Justice Office of Justice Programs.

Renzetti, Claire, Jeffrey L. Edleson, and Raquel K. Bergen, eds. 2001. *Sourcebook on Violence against Women.* Thousand Oaks, CA: Sage.

Steinmetz, Suzanne. 1978. "The Battered Husband Syndrome." *Victimology* 2: 499–509.

Straus, Murray A. 1979. "Measuring Intrafamily Conflict and Violence: The Conflict Tactics (CT) Scales." *Journal of Marriage and the Family* 41: 75–88.

Tjaden, Patricia, and Nancy Thoennes. 1998. *Prevalence, Incidence, and Consequences of Violence against Women: Findings from the National Violence against Women Survey.* Washington, DC: U.S. Department of Justice,

Batterer Intervention Programs

Batterer intervention is a specialized form of group counseling designed to change the behavior of people who have abused intimate partners. Batterer intervention programs were first established in the United States in the late 1970s, and have since proliferated here and abroad. The pioneering programs included EMERGE in Boston, AMEND in Denver, and RAVEN in St. Louis. In the early years of the twenty-first century, most programs in the United States primarily serve court-referred men who have been convicted of battering an intimate partner. Many programs also serve lesbians and gay men who batter, adolescents who batter dating partners, non-English speakers, and some programs offer groups for women who have battered male partners—although this practice is somewhat controversial. Specialized groups for men of color that address specific cultural issues have also been established in some states in the United States.

Historically, the first batterer intervention programs developed in connection with the battered women's movement and specific battered women's advocacy agencies. Battered women's movement–allied programs often have the goal of promoting individual behavior change and social change simultaneously. These programs typically teach that causes of intimate partner violence include power differences between men and women in society and prescribed gender roles that grant men privilege in heterosexual relationships. Other types of interventions for batterers use cognitive-behavioral or psychodynamic approaches to promote individual transformation. Many battered women's movement–allied practitioners object to the practice of teaching only "anger management" techniques to batterers, as these techniques are believed to endanger victims by suggesting that they provoke or share in the responsibility for abuse.

Reviews of batterer intervention program evaluations have found that the large majority who complete the programs remain nonviolent for follow-up periods ranging from six months to three years (Eisikovitz and Edleson 1989, 395–397; Rosenfeld 1992, 216–217; Tolman and Bennet 1990, 105–108). The largest-scale evaluation to date found that those who completed the programs were two-thirds less likely to reassault their partners than those who dropped out of them, even controlling for demographic and behavioral factors that might otherwise explain this difference (Gondolf 2002, 140). As the author of this study points out, "batterer program success rates are comparable to those in drunk-driving programs, drug and alcohol programs, sex offender programs and check-forging programs" (Gondolf 2002, 48). This evidence should be used to dispel popular myths that batterer intervention programs are generally ineffective—or worse—create better batterers. On the other hand, victims of intimate partner violence should be advised of the high probability of reassault on the part of batterer intervention program attendees. Batterer intervention, while potentially effective for the majority of those who attend it, is not a guaranteed panacea for intimate partner violence perpetration.

Initially, men who believed in the cause of the battered women's movement decided to organize men's consciousness-raising groups in order to discuss men's relationship behavior. During discussions, some men admitted to using physical violence, verbal abuse, or other forms of controlling behavior within their intimate partnerships. Over time, the nature of the consciousness-raising groups shifted from discussion-oriented to confrontational and psycho-educational. Group facilitators began to coordinate their efforts with probation officers, prosecutors, child protection workers, and other social services workers. Beginning in the 1980s, people convicted of assault and battery on intimate partners, or those who violated retraining orders held by intimates, were ordered by courts to attend the programs. During this time, many batterer intervention programs developed curricula, created standard methods for conducting group sessions, and established criteria for training and supervising staff. Beginning in the late 1980s, the Domestic Abuse Intervention Project based in Duluth, Minnesota, created and began to disseminate what is now the most widely used curriculum package for conducting batterer intervention group sessions as part of a coordinated community response to domestic violence (Pence and Paymer 1993). As of 1997, thirty-seven states or regions in the United States had established formal standards for operating community batterer intervention programs (Austin and Dankwort 1999).

Although each batterer intervention program is different, many programs in the United States and other nations adhere to a basic format for group sessions. The widely used Duluth model curriculum is designed for twenty-four consecutive weekly two-hour sessions and provides agendas for each group session. The Duluth model originated the "Power and Control Wheel" diagram of abusive behaviors that is now virtually ubiquitous among battered women's shelters in the United States and provides the basis for batterer intervention group discussions at Duluth-model batterer intervention programs each week.

Many intervention groups are facilitated jointly by males and females in order to model egalitarian cooperation for group participants. Typically, group sessions begin with a "check-in" during which participants describe the incident that resulted in their referral to the program. The facilitators select one educational theme per group session. Typical lessons often include discussions of physical, sexual, verbal, emotional, or economic abuse, coparenting, gender roles, accountability for abuse, resolving conflict, or managing emotions. Programs that use the Duluth-model curriculum normally show short video scenarios or facilitate role playing on the selected theme, and group discussions ensue.

Duluth-model programs spend three weeks devoted to the topic of male privilege and how it may be exploited in intimate partnerships. Other model programs, such as EMERGE, similarly raise issues of gender roles and male privilege. Cultural beliefs that support men's use of violence against intimate partners and in general are explored. In the United States and abroad, the belief of many men that they are "king of the castle" or "should wear the pants in the family" (i.e., be in charge) is challenged and the idea that intimate partnership should be based on a balance of power is promoted (Rothman, Butchart, and Cerda, in press). Discussions of social inequalities that benefit men provide participants with an opportunity to reflect on the experience of maintaining a position of superiority within their partnerships.

Evaluating the capacity of batterer intervention programs to change the behavior of participants is complex. Not only is it difficult to track and measure whether program participants reoffend, but creating experimental conditions is often either unethical or too unnatural to yield meaningful results. Nonetheless, the results of more than thirty batterer intervention program evaluations and five reviews have been published. The largest-scale and most methodologically innovative evaluation found that 49 percent of all court-referred batterers reassaulted their partners within fifteen months of beginning the program and 75 percent were verbally abusive (Gondolf 2002, 115). However, by measuring the frequency of renewed abuse by those who completed the program and those who dropped out, it was possible to observe a positive program effect; the program dropouts were 1.5 times more likely to reassault their partners than those who attended the entire program (Gondolf 2002, 140).

The field of batterer intervention has navigated a series of intense debates regarding nomenclature, theory, and practice. For example, many practitioners and battered women's advocates object to the term "batterer treatment." This objection stems from the fact that "treatment" (such as alcohol or sex offender treatment) implies medical or psychopathological services are being procured. Many battered women's advocates and allied batterer intervention practitioners believe that intimate partner violence is caused in part by social conditions that encourage the subordination of women to men in intimate relationships. Therefore, they rarely endorse "illness/treatment" models of intimate partner violence intervention that focus on individual psychopathology and detract from a broader social change agenda.

Perhaps one of the most pressing challenges in the field of batterer intervention in the United States at this time is the growing number of anger management and conflict resolution programs that serve people who batter. Anger management programs, which are generally available to those who are convicted of assaults on strangers or acquaintances—such as "road rage" or "bar brawl" incidents—fail to distinguish people who batter from other types of violent offenders and are designed to assist participants with controlling impulsive violence. Conflict resolution programs often bring victims and perpetrators together to resolve disagreements mutually and most require that both parties accept partial responsibility for the dispute that has occurred.

Many batterer intervention practitioners feel that attributing intimate partner violence to anger or impulsivity is overly simplistic and endangers victims, as does requiring victims to accept partial responsibility for abuse they have experienced. If intimate partner violence is understood as involving the systematic control of an intimate partner through the use of a variety of coercive behaviors, anger management techniques that focus exclusively on physical or verbal outbursts may be insufficient intervention. Conflict resolution programs that require victims to negotiate with perpetrators may endanger those who are most at risk for further acts of abuse; victims fearing retaliation will either be unable to participate in a genuine negotiation process or may face consequences for advocating for themselves when the process is concluded. Educating judges and probation officers about the potential dangers of anger management and conflict resolution for intimate partner violence offenders remains a major challenge for the field.

There is also continued debate in the field as to how programs can best provide services to females who are convicted of battering male intimates. Although women are increasingly being ordered to batterer intervention by courts, many practitioners believe that a high proportion of those mandated to the programs are in fact victims who have acted in self-defense (Martin 1997). Methods for intervening effectively with women who are referred to batterer intervention programs are being developed by several programs in the United States.

Emily F. Rothman

See also Domestic Violence; Sexual Assault Prevention; "Wife Beaters"

Further Reading:

Austin, Juliet B., and Juergen Dankwort. 1999. "Standards for Batterer Programs: A Review and Analysis." *Journal of Interpersonal Violence* 14, no. 2: 152–168.

Eisikovits, Zvi C., and Jeffrey L. Edleson. 1989. "Intervening with Men Who Batter: A Critical Review of the Literature." *Social Service Review* 37: 383–414.

Gondolf, Edward. 2002. *Batterer Intervention Systems.* Thousand Oaks, CA: Sage.

Martin, Margaret E. 1997. "Double Your Trouble: Dual Arrest in Family Violence." *Journal of Family Violence* 12, no. 2: 139–157.

Pence, Ellen, and Michael Paymer. 1993. *Education Groups for Men Who Batter: The Duluth Model.* New York: Springer.

Rosenfeld, Barry D. 1992. "Court-Ordered Treatment of Spouse Abuse." *Clinical Psychology Review* 12, no. 2: 205–226.

Rothman, Emily F., Alexander Butchart, and Magdalena Cerda. In press. *Intervention with Men Who Batter: A Global Perspective.* Geneva, Switzerland: World Health Organization.

Tolman, Richard M., and Larry W. Bennett. 1990. "A Review of Quantitative Research on Men Who Batter." *Journal of Interpersonal Violence* 5, no. 1: 87–118.

Battering

Marital violence perpetrated by men against women remains a prevalent global problem. In the United States alone, data from a large, representative national survey indicated that one of eight husbands carried out at least one violent act toward his wife, and 1.8 million wives were severely assaulted by their husbands during the year prior to the study (Straus and Gelles 1988). Given its detrimental effects, including injuries and chronic health problems, much effort has been directed at identifying predictors of partner violence. Although these efforts have explored a range of biological, social, and psychological correlates (see Holtzworth-Munroe, Bates, Smutzler, and Sandin 1997), little attention has focused on examining the association between partner violence and masculinity.

One line of research explored whether men who possess traditionally masculine characteristics (e.g., positive attitudes toward violence, conservative sex-role expectations, need for control) are more likely to perpetrate violence against an intimate partner than are men with less traditionally masculine attributes. In relation to attitudes toward violence, there is inconsistent evidence supporting a relationship between men's positive attitudes toward violence and the occurrence of partner violence (Kaufman-Kantor, Jasinski, and Aldarondo 1994; Holtzworth-Munroe, Meehan, Herron, Rehman, and Stuart 2000; see also Sugarman and Frankel 1996). However, Holtzworth-

Munroe et al. (1997) caution against interpreting any positive relationship between attitudes and violence as causal given that many studies used samples of previously violent men who may report more positive attitudes toward violence as a justification or rationalization for the violence.

In relation to sex-role expectations, Hotaling and Sugarman (1986) reviewed studies assessing the relationship between husbands' traditional sex-role expectations and the probability of them inflicting violence on their wives. They found that two of eight studies identified the sex-role expectations of batterers to be more traditional than those of nonbatterers. However, Smith (1990) indicated that Hotaling and Sugarman's review combined studies measuring sex-role "expectations" and "orientations." Sex-role expectations reflect the attitudes, beliefs, and norms of men about men and women, whereas sex-role orientations reflect men's personality traits or adjectives describing masculinity versus femininity.

Despite this distinction, the research findings are mixed when comparing separately the sex-role orientations and expectations of violent and nonviolent men. For instance, Lisak, Hopper, and Song (1996) found no differences in the sex-role orientations of perpetrators compared to nonperpetrators, whereas Ray and Gold (1996) showed that men who scored higher on a measure of hypermasculinity (e.g., seeing violence as manly) were more likely to report using verbal and sexual aggression against an intimate partner.

As for sex-role expectations, Neff, Holman, and Schluter (1995) indicated that among 1,800 households, sex-role traditionalism was not a significant predictor of husband violence, and Neidig, Friedman, and Collins (1986) failed to find differences between abusive and nonabusive military husbands in their attitudes toward women. In contrast, Stith and Farley (1993) found that husband violence was negatively correlated with egalitarian sex-role beliefs, and Sugarman and Frankel's (1996) quantitative review found that assaultive husbands have more traditional gender attitudes than nonassaultive husbands (see also Holtzworth-Munroe et al. 1997).

Compared to men's self-reports, reports from battered women consistently indicate that they view their husbands as having more traditional sex-role expectations. Smith (1990) interviewed wives of abusive and nonabusive husbands and found that patriarchal beliefs reliably predicted whether a woman was abused by her husband. This finding is supported from earlier work that found that battered women perceived their partners as possessing greater traditional sex-role expectations than nonbattered women (Walker 1983). Taken together, these mixed findings suggest that not all partner-violent men possess traditional sex-role expectations and beliefs.

Finally, Hotaling and Sugarman's (1986) review indicated that 33 percent of studies showed that need for power, control, and dominance was related to partner violence. More recently, results from a national survey indicated that men were over 3.5 times more likely to issue threats prior to becoming physically violent with their female partners than were offenders in other relationships or other gender combinations (Felson and Messner 2000). The authors contend that these findings "provide the first quantitative evidence suggesting that males' assaults on female partners are especially likely to involve a control motive" (Felson and Messner 2000, 91). Results from another national survey showed that violent husbands evidenced stronger beliefs that men should have more decision-making power in relationships than did nonviolent husbands (Straus 1990), and Babcock, Waltz, Jacobson, and Gottman (1993) found that wives with greater decision-making power were more likely the victims of partner violence than wives with less decision-making power. These findings suggest that a power imbalance, regardless of which spouse has greater power, may be a critical variable in predicting partner violence (Holtzworth-Munroe et al. 1997).

In summary, research provides support for the relationship between positive attitudes toward violence and the occurrence of partner violence. We may say, tentatively, that men's need for power and power imbalances in intimate relationships may be an important variable placing men at increased risk to engage in partner violence.

As power and control in relationships partly define traditional masculinity, it may be that partner violence is likely to occur in situations that men consider relevant or threatening to their construal of and adherence to the masculine gender role (Eisler, Franchina, Moore, Honeycutt, and Rhatigan 2000). This notion is based on the gender-role conflict/strain paradigm originally formulated by Pleck (1981). This paradigm postulated that gender roles are inconsistent, ever changing, and often violated by men, resulting in negative psychological consequences and overcompensation through the use of dysfunctional behaviors (e.g., violence) to meet gender-role expectations (Brooks and Silverstein, 1995). Thus, when faced with perceived or actual challenges to their masculine gender role, some men may experience significant conflict or stress and engage in traditionally masculine behaviors to maintain their sense of control and power (Eisler 1995).

Two major research programs and their respective empirically validated measures are beginning to produce evidence supporting a relationship between gender-role strain and intimate violence (Eisler and Skidmore 1987; O'Neil, Helms, Gable, David, and Wrightsman 1986). Both O'Neil et al.'s (1986) Gender-Role Conflict Scale (GRCS) and Eisler and Skidmore's (1987) Masculine Gender-Role Stress Scale (MGRS) assess "the extent to which males feel that violating traditional masculinity ideologies is uncomfortable or stressful for them" (Thompson and Pleck 1995, 156).

Early research showed a positive correlation between the GRCS and a measure of hostility toward women, and that men with the highest gender-role conflict reported greater lack of trust and anger at women (Chartier, Graff, and Arnold 1986, as cited in O'Neil, Good, and Holmes 1995). Moreover, Rando, Rogers, and Brittan-Powell (1998) showed that sexually aggressive men evidenced greater scores on the "restrictive affectionate behavior between men" subscale than did nonaggressive men. Similar findings emerge in studies using the MGRS scale. For instance, Eisler et al. (2000) and Franchina, Eisler, and Moore (2001) showed that high MGRS men reported greater anger and endorsed verbally aggressive responses toward their intimate partners more often than did low MGRS men in situations that challenged masculine gender roles. In addition, Copenhaver, Lash, and Eisler (2000) found that high MGRS substance-abusing men reported greater use of abusive behaviors with their intimate partners than did controls.

Although research assessing the relationship between men's gender-role strain and partner violence is in its infancy, the aforementioned studies suggest that men who experience gender-role conflict or stress may be more likely to engage in violent behavior with their intimate partners. However, the relationship between masculine gender-role strain and partner violence remains tentative.

There are several implications. First, the mixed findings regarding masculine attributes and violence supports the notion that there may be numerous culturally constructed masculinities; many likely include a particular constellation of masculine characteristics and attributes, but some may espouse violence while others eschew it. Similarly, it seems important to recognize that the etiology of partner violence is multifactorial, and no singular theory of violence is likely to apply to all violent men (Holtzworth-Munroe and Stuart 1994). Masculinity may play a significant role in the etiology of violence for some violent men, but play a minimal role in the development of violence among other men. Therefore, rather than examining single-factor explanations for masculinity and partner

violence, future research should devise methodologies that address the multidimensional nature of these constructs.

Second, our understanding of the relationship between masculinity and partner violence will be incomplete without examining the processes of socialization as they relate to the development of masculine gender roles and violent behavior. However, this area of study remains largely uncharted, and longitudinal research is needed to understand developmental predictors of violent behavior in order to create programs and strategies to reduce partner violence.

Finally, the efficacy of interventions for men who batter is questionable, and future researchers interested in the health and adjustment problems of men might develop and evaluate psycho-educational programs to promote alternative roles and decision-making strategies that expand men's range of healthy coping behaviors. These programs could examine and challenge men's beliefs and conceptions about gender roles, explore the pressures and influences of socialized masculine gender roles as well as men's feelings about violating gender roles, and provide information-processing skills and social skills to reduce the likelihood of becoming violent toward women.

Todd M. Moore
Richard M. Eisler
Gregory L. Stuart

See also Batterer Intervention Programs; Domestic Violence; Mentors in Violence Prevention (MVP) Model; White Ribbon Campaign

Further Reading:
Babcock, J., J. Waltz, N. S. Jacobson, and J. Gottman. 1993. "Power and Violence: The Relation between Communication Patterns, Power Discrepancies, and Domestic Violence." *Journal of Consulting and Clinical Psychology* 61: 40–50.

Brooks, G. R., and L. S. Silverstein. 1995. "Understanding the Dark Side of Masculinity: An Interactive Systems Model." In *A New Psychology of Men.* Edited by R. F. Levant and W. S. Pollack. New York: Basic Books.

Copenhaver, M. M., S. J. Lash, and R. M. Eisler. 2000. "Masculine Gender Role Stress, Anger, and Male Intimate Abusiveness." *Sex Roles* 42, nos. 5, 6: 405–416.

Eisler, R. M. 1995. "The Relationship between Masculine Gender Role Stress and Men's Health Risk: The Validation of a Construct." Pp. 207–228 in *A New Psychology of Men.* Edited by R. F. Levant and W. S. Pollack. New York: Basic Books.

Eisler, R. M., J. J. Franchina, T. M. Moore, H. Honeycutt, and D. L. Rhatigan. 2000. "Effects of Gender Relevance of Conflict Situation on Attributions." *Journal of Men and Masculinity* 1: 30–36.

Eisler, R. M., and J. R. Skidmore. 1987. "Masculine Gender Role Stress: Scale Development and Component Factors in the Appraisal of Stressful Situations." *Behavior Modification* 11, no. 2: 123–136.

Felson, R. B., and S. F. Messner. 2000. "The Control Motive in Intimate Partner Violence." *Social Psychology Quarterly* 63, no. 1: 86–94.

Franchina, J. J., R. M. Eisler, and T. M. Moore. 2001. "Masculine Gender Role Stress and Intimate Abuse: Effects of Masculine Gender Relevance of Dating Situations and Female Threat on Men's Attributions and Affective Responses." *Psychology of Men and Masculinity* 2, no. 1: 34–41.

Holtzworth-Munroe, A., L. Bates, N. Smutzler, and E. Sandin. 1997. "A Brief Review of the Research on Husband Violence. Part 1: Maritally Violent versus Nonviolent Men." *Aggression and Violent Behavior* 2, no. 1: 65–99.

Holtzworth-Munroe, A., J. C. Meehan, K. Herron, U. Rehman, and G. L. Stuart. 2000. "Testing the Holtzworth-Munroe and Stuart (1994) Batterer Typology." *Journal of Consulting and Clinical Psychology* 68, no. 6: 1000–1019.

Holtzworth-Munroe, A., and G. L. Stuart. 2000. "Typologies of Male Batterers: Three Subtypes and the Differences among Them." *Psychological Bulletin* 116: 476–497.

Hotaling, G. T., and D. B. Sugarman. 1986. "An Analysis of Risk Markers in Husband to Wife Violence: The Current State of Knowledge." *Violence and Victims* 1, no. 2: 101–124.

Kaufman-Kantor, G. K., J. L. Jasinski, and E. Aldarondo. 1994. "Sociocultural Status and Incidence of Marital Violence in Hispanic Families." *Violence and Victims* 9: 207–222.

Lisak, D., J. Hopper, and P. Song. 1996. "Factors in the Cycle of Violence: Gender Rigidity and Emotional Constrictions." *Journal of Traumatic Stress* 9, no.4: 721–741.

Neff, J. A., B. Holman, and T. D. Schluter. 1995. "Spousal Violence among Anglos, Blacks, and Mexican Americans: The Role of Demographic Variables, Psychosocial Predictor, and Alcohol Consumption." *Journal of Family Violence* 10: 1–21.

Neidig, P. H., D. H. Friedman, and B. S. Collins. 1986. "Attitudinal Characteristics of Males Who Have Engaged in Spouse Abuse." *Journal of Family Violence* 2: 223–233.

O'Neil, J. M., G. E. Good, and S. Holmes. 1995. "Fifteen Years of Theory and Research on Men's Gender Role Conflict: New Paradigms for Empirical Research." Pp. 164–208 in *A New Psychology of Men.* Edited by R. F. Levant and W. S. Pollack. New York: Basic Books.

O'Neil, J. M., B. Helms, R. Gable, L. David, and L. Wrightsman. 1986. "Gender Role Conflict Scale: College Men's Fear of Femininity." *Sex Roles* 14, nos. 5/6: 335–350.

Pleck, J. H. 1981. *The Myth of Masculinity.* Cambridge, MA: MIT Press.

Rando, R. A., J. R. Rogers, and C. S. Brittan-Powell. 1998. "Gender Role Conflict and College Men's Sexually Aggressive Attitudes and Behavior." *Journal of Mental Health Counseling* 20, no. 4: 359–369.

Ray, A. L., and S. R. Gold. 1996. "Gender Roles, Aggression, and Alcohol Use in Dating Relationships." *Journal of Sex Research* 33, no. 1: 47–55.

Smith, M. D. 1990. "Patriarchal Ideology and Wife Beating: A Test of a Feminist Hypothesis." *Violence and Victims* 5, no. 4: 257–273.

Stith, S. M. and S. C. Farley. 1993. "A Predictive Model of Male Spousal Violence." *Journal of Family Violence* 8, no. 2: 183–201.

Straus, M. A. 1990. "Social Stress and Marital Violence in a National Sample of American Families." Pp. 141–162 in *Physical Violence in American Families: Risk Factors and Adaptations to Violence in 8,145 Families.* Edited by M. A. Straus and R. J. Gelles. New Brunswick, NJ: Transaction Publishers.

Straus, M. A., and R. G. Gelles. 1998. "Violence in American Families: How Much Is There and Why Does It Occur?" Pp. 181–189 in *Families in Trouble Series,* vol. 3, edited by E. W. Nunnally, C. S. Chilman, and F. M. Cox. Newbury Park, CA: Sage.

Sugarman, D. B., and S. L. Frankel. 1996. "Patriarchal Ideology and Wife Assault: A Meta-Analytic Review." *Journal of Family Violence* 11, no. 1: 13–40.

Thompson, E. H., and J. H. Pleck. 1995. "Masculinity Ideology: A Review of Research Instrumentation on Men and Masculinity." Pp. 129–163 in *A New Psychology of Men.* Edited by R. F. Levant and W. S. Pollack. New York: Basic Books.

Walker, L. E. 1983. *The Battered Woman Syndrome.* New York: Spring Publishers.

Beat Poets

The group of writers collectively known as the Beats, and the literary movement referred to as the Beat Generation, redefined American culture's notion of the male community and

Students, writers, and friends Hal Chase, Jack Kerouac, Allen Ginsberg, and William Burroughs enjoy each other's company in Morningside Heights, near Columbia University Campus, New York City. (Allen Ginsberg / Corbis)

the nature of friendship among artists. Allen Ginsberg, Jack Kerouac, William Burroughs, and Gregory Corso, the core individuals of the group, looked to each other for creative and spiritual guidance, sexual stimulation, and poetic inspiration. Experimental writers exploring the boundaries of the genres in which they wrote, primarily poetry and the novel, they also insistently interrogated the American construction of the male and masculinity, ultimately opening possibilities for alternative visions of the male community during the 1960s and after. In addition, the enduring attraction of the Beat writers is a testimony to their success in establishing the counterculture voice as a powerful instrument in American discourse. Distinctly pitched against the "macho" aesthetic, the collective voice of the Beats reshaped attitudes toward male friendship, community, consciousness, politics, and sexuality.

The Beats were first and foremost interested in writing as it relates to individual consciousness. However, at the time these writers began working—the early and middle years of the 1950s—individual consciousness could hardly be separated from the memory of the Second World War and the dawning of the nuclear age. In addition,

the escalation of the Cold War, manifesting itself in Senator Joseph McCarthy's witch-hunts for communist sympathizers, as well as in American military involvement in Korea and, later, in Vietnam, increasingly aligned American masculinity with social conservatism and military aggression. The Beats sought an alternative to this narrowing concept of what constituted an American male, and their writing, combining a voice of social resistance with an intellectual and spiritual yearning, succeeded in suggesting that men had options other than those of military service, marriage, careers in business, and homes in the suburbs.

The greatest writers of the Beat group were Jack Kerouac (1922–1969) and Allen Ginsberg (1926–1997). Both were poets of considerable talent, though Kerouac remains better known as a novelist, primarily for *On the Road* (1957), the defining prose work of the Beat movement. Ginsberg's career was longer, beginning with his groundbreaking poem "Howl," first read in public in 1955 and published in 1956, and continuing for nearly three more decades, during which he served as a primary spokesperson for first the antiwar movements of the 1960s, and then for the gay liberation movement. Ginsberg first met Kerouac, as well as Burroughs, while in New York City attending Columbia University during the 1940s. He immediately recognized in Kerouac a kindred spirit, a man seeking his place in the world, a searcher eager to confront and discuss major questions about one's existence. Although Kerouac, unlike Ginsberg, was not gay, Ginsberg fell in love with him and began not only to share his living space and his writing with Kerouac, but in turn to encourage Kerouac's writing. Burroughs had introduced Ginsberg to drug experimentation, and drugs became another of the many vehicles the writers used in their efforts to achieve a higher plane of consciousness.

In late 1946 Kerouac and Ginsberg met a man named Neal Cassady (1926–1968) who, although married, quickly became Ginsberg's lover and a major literary inspiration for both Ginsberg and Kerouac. Cassady is the character named Dean Moriarty in *On the Road,* which Kerouac completed in manuscript in 1951, and his energy for life, his spontaneity, intensity, and what Kerouac termed his "madness" in many ways gave a center to the group's fraternal bond. The writers used Cassady's personality as something iconic, an alternate model for masculinity. Cassady seemed to embody the free-spirited westerner, roaming the country in search of intense emotional connectedness, open to conversations that spanned days and sexual union that went beyond the merely physical. Certainly part of the genius of *On the Road* is the way in which it captures the essence of this male community. In a famous passage, the narrator Sal Paradise (Kerouac) describes the first meeting between Moriarty (Cassady) and Carlo Marx (Ginsberg), focusing on the joining of not just their eyes but also their minds, as they wend off down the street together, simultaneously in tune with their surroundings and yet completely focused on one another. Sal sees these two friends as representative of "the mad ones, the ones who are mad to live, mad to talk, mad to be saved, desirous of everything at the same time, the ones who never

yawn or say a commonplace thing, but burn, burn, burn" (Kerouac 1957, 5–6).

A unique level of energy, intensity of friendship, and openness to all forms of experience is a major element of what the Beats sought, and Kerouac is able to capture the quest in his writing style, a "spontaneous prose" that helped inspire what Ginsberg would call the "bop prosody" of "Howl." The group offered a new model for American men disenchanted with the social and political conformity of the 1950s, with, in *On the Road,* a call to the adventure of the open road, and, in "Howl," an invitation to explore "madness," anger, gay sex, meditation, and mantra as an antidote to the military-industrial complex. Ginsgerg's "Howl," which has become the most famous postwar poem in American literature, immediately establishes the sense of a community of resistance fighters in its opening line: "I saw the best minds of my generation destroyed by madness, starving hysterical naked" (Ginsberg 1956, 9). The major thrust of the poem is its powerful description of disenfranchisement and alienation, its rebellion against the "haze of Capitalism" and the "heterosexual dollar" (Ginsberg 1956, 13–14). The poem's evocation of gay sex is frank and direct, and shocked many readers when first published in *Howl and Other Poems* (1956). In fact, the poem and its publisher, Lawrence Ferlinghetti of City Lights Books, were tried on charges of obscenity, but in a landmark ruling by Judge Clayton Horn citing First Amendment rights, were cleared. The significance of "Howl" and the Beat poets for gay literature, and the gay community in general, can not be overstated. According to Barry Miles, in his biography of Ginsberg, the gay community "has clear roots in the kind of open-minded comradeship and male bonding found among the early Beats, particularly between Ginsberg and Kerouac, or Kerouac and Cassady. It was a kind of masculine tenderness out of Walt Whitman, virtually unknown in the late forties and early fifties, which later became a prototype in the gay community" (Miles 1989, 532). In one of his best known shorter poems, "A Supermarket in California," Ginsburg invokes the spirit of Whitman as a psychological guide through mid-twentieth-century America, a place that seems to have lost touch with much of Whitman's vision.

Another key Beat poet is Gregory Corso (1930–2001). Although not a cultural icon like Kerouac and Ginsberg, he began publishing poetry in 1955 and wrote several strong poems that, like the best work of his fellow Beats, question and reconstruct notions of masculinity. One such poem is "Marriage," from his 1960 volume *The Happy Birthday of Death*. The poem expresses a strong desire for love and spiritual union, while resisting what the poet sees as the social construction and confinements of marriage. Blending humor with sociological analysis, the poem begins with the lines "Should I get married? Should I be good?/ Astound the girl next door with my velvet suit and faustus hood?" (Corso 1989, 61) The poem struggles with the notion that marriage brings with it a set of behaviors and attachments that are uniform, rather than exploratory and revelatory in terms of selfhood. Another well-known Corso poem from the same collection is "Bomb," a free associative and at times sarcastic exploration of postnuclear anxiety. Again employing Corso's characteristic humor, the poem implicitly questions male allegiance to a weapon of destruction. In another text titled "Variations on a Generation" included in Ann Charters's *The Portable Beat Reader,* Corso, echoing other seminal texts from the movement, characterized the work of the Beats as inaugurating "a delicate shift of total consciousness in America," aligning it with the democratic belief that "free will is not destructive" (Charters 1992, 185).

Ernest Smith

See also Hippies

Further Reading:

Charters, Ann. 1992. *The Portable Beat Reader.* New York: Penguin.

Corso, Gregory. 1989. *Minefield: New and Selected Poems.* New York: Thunder's Mouth.

Davidson, Michael. 1993. "Beat Poetry and the San Francisco Renaissance." Pp. 581–604 in *The Columbia History of American Poetry.* Edited by Jay Parini. New York: Columbia University Press.

———. 1989. *The San Francisco Renaissance: Poetics and Community at Mid-Century.* Cambridge and New York: Cambridge University Press.

Ginsberg, Allen. 1956. *Howl and Other Poems.* San Francisco: City Lights Books.

Kerouac, Jack. 1957. *On the Road.* New York: Penguin.

Martin, Robert K. 1979. *The Homosexual Tradition in American Poetry.* Austin, TX: University of Texas Press.

Miles, Barry. 1989. *Ginsberg: A Biography.* New York: Simon and Schuster.

Parkinson, Thomas. 1961. *A Casebook on the Beat.* New York: Crowell.

Perloff, Marjorie. 1990. "A Lion in Our Living Room: Reading Allen Ginsberg in the Eighties." Pp. 199–230 in *Poetic License: Essays on Modernist and Postmodernist Lyric.* Evanston, IL: Northwestern University Press.

Beer

Since ancient times, beer, a beverage brewed from malted (roasted) cereal, has been a feature of many civilizations, including those of Mesopotamia, Egypt, and South America. America itself was an "alcoholic republic" from its earliest origins and alcohol remains a staple of many American lifestyles. Although beer was once the favored alcoholic beverage of certain men—white, European ethnic, urban—it is today regarded in the United States as the quintessentially *American* drink. In the year 2000, beer constituted 58 percent of the alcoholic beverage market in the United States. Drawn from the media, the image of a smiling, beer-drinking younger man surrounded by his affirming, beer-drinking buddies, usually watching a sporting event, is one of the most powerful icons of contemporary American masculinity. A late-1990s variation on this theme is brewer Anheuser-Busch's "Wassup?!" highly successful advertising campaign for its top-two beer brand, Bud Lite, featuring men in their twenties who "simply yelled at each and stuck out their tongues" as they ask each other the equivalent of how are you. According to Lachky, the ads "capture the essence of beer and male camaraderie."

Until the mid-nineteenth century, alcohol-consuming American men favored distilled spirits, whiskey in particular, and hard cider. Wine was seen as a pricey import, associated with affluence and the ruling classes. To some extent, wine came to be stigmatized as unpatriotic and antidemocratic. Beer was promoted as a democratic alternative to whiskey and wine: It was "a beverage that could be brewed in America and that the masses could afford" (Rorabaugh 1979, 107). Beer was not yet an economically viable commercial venture, brewed mainly by women in households until the late eighteenth century and "the rise of the male-dominated beer business" (Eames 1990, 2). In the 1840s, German immigrants to America brought with them a special yeast they used to brew *lager*. Lager was a beer of higher quality, lower alcoholic content, and greater appeal than existing domestic beers. The German immigrant brewers and their lager eventually created a commercially sustainable national American brewing industry, centered in the Midwest, including the cities of Milwaukee, Cincinnati, and Saint Louis.

In the years after Prohibition, the German lager beer garden, the Irish saloon, and other European-style drinking establishments gave way to the hegemony of the American bar. The bar was a male domain par excellence, where men drank beer in the company of other men. Pete Hamill recollects his first visit to Gallagher's, a bar in New York City, as a boy with his father, in 1943: "This is where men go, I thought; this is what men do" (Hamill 1994, 17). In fact, virtually anywhere we find men in groups, we find alcohol. The relatively cheap availability of beer assures its presence among men in the military, on college campuses, and in and around men's sports, to name other important male domains. Because of the ascendancy of sports in

American society and the close association between men's sports and masculinity, sport is perhaps the most significant contemporary cultural link between men and alcohol, and therefore, men and beer.

Rocco L. Capraro

See also Alcohol
Further Reading:
Behr, Edward. 1996. *Prohibition: Thirteen Years that Changed America.* New York: Arcade Publishing.
Capraro, Rocco L. 2000. "Why College Men Drink: Alcohol, Adventure, and the Paradox of Masculinity." *Journal of American College Health* 48 (May): 307–315.
Cochrane, Thomas C. 1948. *The Pabst Brewing Company: The History of an American Business.* New York: New York University Press.
Hamill, Pete. 1994. *A Drinking Life.* Boston: Little, Brown.
Messner, Michael A. 1992. *Power at Play: Sports and the Problem of Masculinity.* Boston: Beacon Press.
Oldenburg, Ray. 1991. *The Great Good Place: Cafes, Coffee Shops, Community Centers, Beauty Parlors, General Stores, Bars, Hangouts, and How They Get You through the Day.* New York: Paragon House.
Postman, N., C. Nystrom, L. Strate, and C. Weingartner. n.d. *Myths, Men and Beer: An Analysis of Beer Commericals on Broadcast Television, 1987.* Washington, DC: AAA Foundation for Traffic Safety.
Rorabaugh, W. J. 1981. *The Alcoholic Republic: An American Tradition.* Oxford: Oxford University Press.

Berdache

See Native American Masculinities; Two Spirit People

Bergman, Ingmar (1918–)

This Swedish director is probably the last of the great filmmakers of the twentieth century and no doubt one of the most respected and influential among his peers. Although some of his first movies were comedies (*Smiles of a Summer Night,* 1955; *The Devil's Eye,* 1960), Ingmar Bergman's most famous films offered a deep look into the human mind and soul in a perfect aesthetical conception, with the help of his longtime cameraman, Sven Nykvist. No other director in film history has such a constant visual and thematic unity. Themes with implications for masculinity studies are constants in most Bergman films, especially those made between 1952 and 1983.

A man humiliated by a dominative woman is a figure in many Bergman films. In *The Naked Night* (1953), the clown is publicly humiliated by his wife who goes naked on the beach in front of everybody. Later another artist loses a fight against his wife's lover. In *Dreams* (1955), a model visits an older man to have an illicit affair with him, but his daughter stops them and slaps her in the face while the old man is in a malaise. In *Wild Strawberries* (1957), a celebrated seventy-eight-year-old professor is about to receive high recognition, but when he visits his old mother, she still treats him with distance, as a puerile child. In *The Magician* (1958), the superintendent of police humiliates the magician and his troupe, saying they are not true artists, but then his hypnotized wife insults him and reveals the couple's intimate secrets.

Children are not frequent characters in Bergman's universe, but a young boy (around eight to ten years old), often neglected by his mother, appears in *Monika* (1952), *The Silence* (1963), *Persona* (1966) and *Fanny and Alexander* (1982; 1983 in the U.S.). In *Persona,* the boy's vision of his mother's giant face in a hallucination is the symptom of the absence of parental love. In a dream from *Hour of Wolf* (1968), a young boy bites Johan, the tormented painter, who kills the child. Bergman's last feature film, *Fanny and Alexander,* depicts the world through the eyes of a young boy in the beginning of the twentieth century.

Illicit love affairs are frequent in Bergman's films. The strange *Through a Glass Darkly* (1961) shows sexuality through incest between brother and sister. Eva, in *Shame* (1968), allows herself to be seduced by the colonel, because her husband is weak. In *Cries and Whispers* (1973), a man tries to kill himself because his wife had an affair with

the family's doctor. In a final banquet at the end of *Fanny and Alexander* (1982), the happily married Gustav-Adolf Ekdahl gives a surprising speech (in the presence of his forbearing wife) about the joys of free love: His young mistress has just given birth to his new child!

Suicide is sometimes considered as a solution for masculine characters in Bergman's universe. In *The Serpent's Egg* (1977), after the mad scientist's suicide, Abel (David Carradine) is free but can't face the new era announced by the man who predicted a "New Germany" symbolized by an image of a lonesome crowd (we are in Berlin, 1923); he throws himself out of the car just after being released. Some feminine characters choose self-destruction (or even self-mutilation) in *Persona* (1966) and *Cries and Whispers* (1973).

Maybe Bergman's best attempt to explain the masculine psyche (in this case mixed with latent masculine homosexuality) is a film made in Munich, *From the Life of the Marionettes* (1980), in which a man tries to understand why he killed a prostitute he didn't even know after a quarrel with his wife. The investigation is made by the police, but Bergman prefers to follow the psychiatrist's inquiry and diagnosis; we learn that the murderer had repressed his homosexuality because of his omnipresent and possessive mother.

In most cases, masculinity cannot compensate for existential emptiness, because death and pain represent major obstacles. In *The Seventh Seal* (1957), the fearless knight tries to negotiate directly with death himself, but he just obtains a delay. In *The Virgin Spring* (1960), the fervent father gets vengeance against the three murderers of his beloved daughter, but this ritual doesn't bring her back to life, even though a spring emerges magically at the place where the child was raped. Maybe Bergman's tentative solution to find a meaning in a world without God might be found in the father's final words in *Through a Glass Darkly* (1961), when he says to his child that God is just another word for love, and love can really help to change people.

Bergman's movies are sortileges. His last masterpiece, *Fanny and Alexander*, by counterposing Alexander's late generous father and evil stepfather, shows two opposite images of fatherhood. He then introduces the perfect androgyne, Ismael (a character played by an actress, but supposed to be a man), who gives Alexander the key to eliminate his cruel stepfather. An androgynous character was already present in *The Magician* (1958), where the magician's assistant was not a man but in fact a transvestite woman. The six-hour version of *Fanny and Alexander* is a wonderful synthesis of all Bergman's themes: youth as a paradise lost, marriage as an inferno, illusion in art and life, the possible dangers of religion, and the mysteries of the senses.

Yves Laberge

Further Reading:

Bergman, Ingmar. 1973. *Bergman on Bergman.* Edited by Stig Björkman, Torsten Manns, and Jonas Sima. London: Secker & Warburg.

Bergom-Larsson, Maria. 1978. *Ingmar Bergman and Society.* Translated by Barrie Selman. London: Tantivy Press.

South Brunswick, NJ: A. S. Barnes, with the Swedish Film Institute and the Swedish Institute.

Gervais, Marc. 1999. *Ingmar Bergman: Magician and Prophet.* Montréal, Canada: McGill-Queen's University Press.

Steene, Birgitta. 1987. *Ingmar Bergman: A Guide to References and Resources.* Boston: G. K. Hall.

Birth Control

See Contraception

Bisexuality

Bisexuality can be defined as being attracted sexually to persons of either sex. Bisexual, heterosexual, and homosexual are categories of sexual orientation (sexual desire). One's sexual orientation should not be confused with one's biological gender (male or female); one's gender-role behaviors (masculine, feminine, or androgynous); or one's gender identification (for example, males who identify as males or males who identify as females—transsexuals). Most men who are bisexual do not feel confused about or reject being a man, but they differ from the majority of men in their attraction. They think of themselves as men, but are attracted to both men and women.

People often think of sexual orientation as "either/or" and ignore the large numbers of persons who identify and/or function as bisexual. However, the famous sex survey and interviews of Kinsey, Pomeroy, and Martin (1948) showed that sexual attraction falls on a continuum from "gay" to "straight." Unfortunately, the categories—homosexual, bisexual, heterosexual—tend to assume that the gender of another person is the sole basis for attraction. Sexual attraction is far more complex than that, and gender may not even be the most important issue in a person's "turn on." A man who is generally attracted to other men may not be attracted to a particular man. He may be attracted only to persons whom he perceives as handsome, or only those who seem intelligent, or only those with brown eyes and dark hair. In short, there are many components—both visual and in terms of personality—which play a role in who "turns us on."

In fact, for some bisexuals, gender is not particularly relevant to their attraction. They might state, "I am attracted to warm friendly people who seem to care about others; it doesn't really matter to me if they are male or female." Other bisexuals seem to experience their sexuality in terms of two different desires. These bisexuals report, "I'm not really content except when I have one lover who is male and one who is female" (Matteson 1987).

Because the acknowledgement of one's bisexual orientation is more complex, it typically takes longer for bisexuals to identify as such (Fox 1996). As with gays, bisexuals may try during their early adolescence to conform to heterosexual activities. Because they are in fact turned on by the other sex, bisexuals may succeed in deceiving themselves longer than their gay or lesbian peers; dating the other sex does "work" for them. But gradually they integrate the two experiences and realize that they are aroused by persons of their own sex and by persons of the other sex. Sometimes this recognition comes simply from seeing attractive members of their own sex and sensing their inner response. Other times friendships with persons of their own sex involve touch that leads to experimentation and then the realization. For a period, these "homosexual" feelings may seem frightening, they don't match what society has told them. Yet they may seem more authentic and more important than their heterosexual experiences, and bisexuals may begin to believe that they were deluding themselves about having heterosexual attractions. So they may swing from identifying themselves as "straight" to believing they are totally "gay" or "lesbian." They may function solely as homosexual for a period. But later the feelings and attractions for the other sex reemerge.

Some bisexuals go through a sequence of dating a man, then dating a woman, then a man, etc.; they are sequentially bisexual. Others discover that if they are only having sex with a woman, for example, their dreams and fantasies tend to be about men (or the other way around). It's as if they become "needy" for whatever "type" of sexuality is not being satisfied. Either kind of developmental experience can lead a person to realize, "I am bisexual."

Coming out is an especially difficult process for bisexuals (which is not to say it's easy for gays or lesbians). It is easiest if there is a community of friends who are accepting. In recent decades there has been an increasingly visible gay and lesbian community. It is more difficult to find an accepting bisexual community, though bisexual networks are beginning to emerge. Much of the time bisexuals feel caught between the homophobic "straight" world and the biphobic "gay" world, which accuses bisexuals of refusing to fully acknowledge that they are gay, or of "passing" by "playing" that they are straight (see review in Fox 1996). Neither world is fully accepting.

Bisexuals have to struggle with at least two cultural taboos. First, there is the taboo against same-sex relationships (homophobia). Second, heterosexism sanctions the monogamous marriage as normative (though a very high percentage of married men have sex outside of marriage). Socially progressive heterosexuals may tolerate homosexuality as long as same-sexed couples try to mirror heterosexual marriage as a lifestyle. Few face the possibility of polyamory—the fact that a person can really love more than one other person (Rust 1996b).

Thus, developing a bisexual identity requires noticing the variety of experiences that are genuinely pleasing and negotiating between subcultures rather than letting the subcultures' scripts define you.

Clearly, the categories of our thinking about sexuality are very much a product of our culture. The division of sexual orientations into "heterosexual" and "homosexual" didn't occur until the 1880s (Katz 1995, 17–19), and the concept "bisexual" is even more recent. It should be noted that bisexual behavior has been common in many cultures in the past. Anthropologists have noted that in almost all cultures there are some individuals who exhibit both homosexual and heterosexual behavior. Ford and Beach (1951) and Margaret Mead (1975) went so far as to describe bisexuality as normal except where culturally constrained. Much of what has been claimed as "gay" history is based on biographic data of men and women who in fact behaved as bisexuals. (See Fox 1996 for a review of bisexuality in historical and cross-cultural inquiry).

No evidence of greater psychopathology has been found among either male or female bisexuals than among other groups (see review in Fox 1966, 20–21). A number of studies used intensive interviews with heterosexually married bisexual men. Matteson (1985) followed such men over a seven-year period and showed that such marriages could become stable with the husbands developing positive sexual identities. Research on other bisexual living arrangements is still scarce. The Centers for Disease Control became interested in researching bisexuality in the early 1990s out of concern that bisexuals might be a bridge for transmitting the virus that causes AIDS from the gay to the straight community. As it turned out, the most important path for the spread of HIV from infected males to females was through IV drug users. However, between 11 and 15 percent of women infected with HIV through heterosexual intercourse became infected due to sexual relations with a man who also had sex with men.

The HIV-related studies had the advantage of providing information on bisexual men from various ethnic groups, including African American (Stokes, McKirnan, and Bozett 1993) and Asian American men (Chan 1995; Matteson 1997). An excellent chapter on "Managing Multiple Identities: Diversity among Bisexual Women and Men" by Paula Rust appears in Firestein (1996).

Much remains to be learned about bisexuality, which could shed light on sexuality in general because it fails to neatly fit the categories of society and raises questions about the simplistic views of environmental and biological influences of sexual orientation.

Dave Matteson

Further Reading:

Chan, Connie S. 1995. "Issues of Sexual Identity in an Ethnic Minority: The Case of Chinese American Lesbians, Gay Men, and Bisexual People." Pp. 87–101 in *Lesbian, Gay, and Bisexual Identities over the Lifespan: Psychological Perspectives.* Edited by Anthony R. D'Augeli and C. J. Patterson. New York: Oxford Press.

Firestein, Beth A., ed. 1996. *Bisexuality: The Psychology and Politics of an Invisible Minority.* Thousand Oaks, CA: Sage.

Ford, Clellan S., and Frank A. Beach. 1951. *Patterns of Sexual Behavior.* New York: Harper and Row.

Fox, Ronald C. 1996. "Bisexuality in Perspective: A Review of Theory and Research." Pp. 3–50 in *Bisexuality: The Psychology and Politics of an Invisible Minority.* Edited by Beth A. Firestein. Thousand Oaks, CA: Sage.

Hutchins, Loraine, and Lani Kaahumanu. 1991. *Bi any Other Name.* Boston: Alyson.

Katz, Jonathan N. 1995. *The Invention of Heterosexuality.* New York: Dutton.

Kinsey, Alfred C., Wardell B. Pomeroy, and Clyde E. Martin. 1948. *Sexual Behavior in the Human Male.* Philadelphia: W. B. Saunders.

Matteson, David R. 1985. "Bisexual Men in Marriage: Is a Positive Homosexual Identity and Stable Marriage Possible?" *Journal of Homosexuality* 11, nos. 1 and 2: 149–172.

———. 1987. "The Heterosexually Married Gay and Lesbian Parent." Pp. 139–141 in *Gay and Lesbian Parents.* Edited by Frederick W. Bozett. New York: Praeger.

———. 1997. "Bisexual and Homosexual Behavior and HIV Risk Among Chinese-, Filipino-, and Korean-American Men." *Journal of Sex Research* 34: 93–104.

Mead, Margaret. 1975. "Bisexuality: What's It All About?" *Redbook* (January): 6–7.

Rust, Paula C. 1996a. "Managing Multiple Identities: Diversity among Bisexual Women and Men." In *Bisexuality: The Psychology and Politics of an Invisible Minority.* Edited by Beth A. Firestein. Thousand Oaks, CA: Sage.

———. 1996b. "Monogamy and Polyamory: Relationship Issues for Bisexuals." Pp. 127–148 in *Bisexuality: The Psychology and Politics of an Invisible Minority.* Edited by Beth A. Firestein. Thousand Oaks, CA: Sage.

Stokes, Joseph P., David J. McKirnan, and Rebecca G. Bozett. 1993. "Sexual Behavior, Condom Use, Disclosure of Sexuality, and Stability of Sexual Orientation in Bisexual Men." *Journal of Sex Research* 30, no. 3: 203–211.

Black Masculinities

In the United States, black males are often seen as a social "problem." Terms such as "crisis," "at risk," "marginal," and "endangered" are used with increasing regularity to describe the plight and condition of black males in the United States. The use of such stark and ominous descriptions is due to the fact that a broad array of social and economic indicators suggest that large numbers of individuals who are black and male are in deep trouble. What is not clear is whether such a way of framing the issue, focusing on race and gender, is helpful to understanding the nature of the problems affecting these individuals or in finding solutions to the problems.

The evidence is clear and disturbing. Black males, especially those between the ages of sixteen and twenty-five, experience higher rates of unemployment than any other demographic group within the U.S. population. Black males who are employed on average earn 73 percent of the income earned by white males. Black males are vastly underrepresented in professional and managerial positions, and in some fields (e.g., many high tech and science-related jobs), they are almost entirely absent. Numerous studies indicate that despite the existence of laws prohibiting discrimination in employment, black males are widely regarded as less desirable employees and therefore substantially less likely to be hired in most jobs (Massey and Denton 1993; Hacker 1992; Feagin and Sikes 1994). At the aggregate level, the average black male with a four-year college degree earns less than the average white male possessing only a high school diploma (Hacker 1992).

Health indicators for black males reveal similar hardships. Between 1988 and 2003 black males were the only demographic group within the U.S. population to experience a declining life expectancy. The homicide rate for black males ages fifteen to twenty-five is seven to eight times higher than that for white males (Roper 1991), and since 1980, the suicide rate for black males increased more rapidly than any other group

in the U.S. population. Additionally, black males also lead the nation in the incidence of HIV infection, heart disease, and colon cancer.

In education, black males are typically overrepresented in every category associated with academic failure and underrepresented in areas associated with academic success. They are more likely to drop out of school than any other ethnic group (with the exception of Latinos), more likely to be suspended or expelled from school, and substantially more likely to be placed in special education classes. Conversely, black males are vastly underrepresented in advanced placement and honors courses, gifted and talented programs, and among the ranks of national merit scholars. From 1973 to 1977 black male enrollment in college steadily increased. However, since 1977 there has been a sharp and continuous decline in black male college enrollment (National Research Council 1989). At most colleges and universities throughout the United States, fewer than 40 percent of black males admitted graduate within six years (Carnoy 1994).

For a growing numbers of black males, prison rather than college is a more probable destination during adolescence and young adulthood. In 1995 one of every three black males (for white males the rate is one of ten) between the ages of eighteen and thirty were either incarcerated or under the control of the criminal justice system. In states like California, Florida, Texas, and Alabama, 40 percent of black males find themselves ensnared by the criminal justice system (*San Francisco Examiner,* 18 February 1996). Black males constitute less than 6 percent of the U.S. population but nearly 50 percent of the prison population (Waquant 2000).

Although the evidence of serious problems confronting individuals who are black and male is overwhelming, what is less clear is what race and gender have to do with these problems. Likewise it may be that by emphasizing the significance of race and gender in framing these social problems, the significance of other factors are overlooked or negated.

One indication that a broader analytical lens may be needed is the significant number of black males who are relatively successful, prominent, and highly visible in the United States. For example, several major politicians and a number of highly visible entertainers, athletes, and celebrities are black and male. Does the status and wealth of such individuals suggest that some black males may be immune to this crisis? If so, what might their immunity tell us about the nature of the problem afflicting others?

Additionally, if black males are in a state of crisis, what does this mean for black women? Are black women also in a state of crisis, or have the hardships facing black males resulted in improved social and economic status for black women? Does the crisis afflicting certain black males imply that patriarchy as a cultural system and the norms and values associated with it are in decline among black Americans? Or, could it be that the problems confronting black males are merely manifestations of broader problems confronting poor and marginalized people generally?

As awareness of the acute nature of the problems facing young black males has grown, an array of interventions aimed at preventing hardships and addressing the particular needs of black males have been initiated. These have included various mentoring and job training programs; rites of passage programs aimed at socializing and preparing young males for adulthood, fatherhood, and community responsibility (Watson and Smitherman 1996); and the creation of a small number of all-black, all-male schools (Leake and Leake 1992). The common theme underlying each of these initiatives is an assumption that the needs of black males can best be served through efforts specifi-

cally targeted at them, even if it may require isolating them in order to apply the intervention (Ampim 1993). Often this assumption is combined with the belief that adult black males are the most appropriate persons to provide the services and support needed by black male youth.

Yet, regardless of how benevolent or well intentioned these efforts may seem, history suggests that great risks are involved with advocating and promoting separate treatment for African Americans, whether they be male or female. Slavery and Jim Crow segregation were rationalized and sustained by the notion that blacks should be separated and accorded different treatment from the rest of the population because of their racial inferiority.

In more recent times, awareness has been growing that special education programs and schools specifically designed for dealing with troubled youth often target black males because of racial prejudice, assumptions of innate inferiority, and deeply ingrained fear and hostility (Wilson 1992).

Rather than helping those served, such interventions have frequently been criticized for stigmatizing black youth and depriving them of access to mainstream programs (Taylor-Gibbs 1988). Although programs such as special education were not created for the purpose of addressing the needs of black males, the fact that black males often comprise a disproportionate number of those served has furthered the perception that these young people are deficient and different from the rest of the population. Increasingly, many of these programs have come under attack because there is now considerable evidence that more often than not placement in such a program does not lead to improvement in academic achievement or behavior for those served (Wilson 1992).

Some attempts to address the "crisis" facing young black males have been designed, managed, and directed by individuals who empathize with those served and who share a similar background and experience. Such initiatives are rationalized as being better able to help black male youth because they are "culturally authentic" and "culturally appropriate" (Girabaldi 1992). These initiatives differ from past efforts to separate black youth in that they are not based on the premise that those served are intellectually deficient or culturally deprived. Rather, the new efforts are based on the assumption that black youth from low-income urban areas possess the potential to succeed if provided with proper guidance and support in a culturally affirming environment.

What is missing from efforts to understand and address the problems and issues confronting black males is an awareness of the ways in which social environment, and even more importantly, the political economy, constrain opportunities. By focusing almost exclusively on race and gender, other factors that are relevant to understanding the causes of social problems like crime, drug trafficking, or violence often go ignored. Most important among the omitted factors are the influence of class and geographic location. Many, though not all, of the problems cited as afflicting black males are most prevalent in poverty-stricken urban areas. These are typically communities that lack a sustainable local economy, where community institutions are weak or barely existent, and where environmental degradation and an absence of social services are primary characteristics of the social landscape.

Too often, the problems facing black males are not discussed in the context of their interaction with these types of conditions. Instead, race and gender are employed as explanatory categories, resulting in an explanation of the crisis facing black males that focuses almost exclusively on cultural rather than structural factors. For the scholars and writers who advocate this perspective, these cultural factors can include the matriarchal black family; oppositional attitudes and behavior (Solomon 1992); or the violent and destructive culture of inner-city streets (Anderson 1990). Even when not intended, such explanations tend to reinforce and affirm many of the negative images and stereotypes that have historically been associated with black males.

By focusing exclusively on race and gender, some of the initiatives undertaken to address the needs of black males inadvertently reinforce the negative images of black males that permeate the media and society generally. This can even be an unintended consequence of initiatives like the Million Man March of 1995. Though organized to encourage and empower black men to take action to improve black communities, the event was advertised as a "Day of Atonement." Throughout the day, numerous speakers called on black men to be responsible fathers and role models in their communities and to reject drugs and violence. Few of the organizers of the march questioned the logic behind one million black men appealing for atonement in the nation's capitol at a time when Congress and the federal government were eliminating social programs that serve poor black communities through their Contract on America.

At the root of most of the problems facing poor black communities are desperate economic and social conditions shaped by deindustrialization and the flight of the middle class. Should black men be held responsible for countering the failure of public schools, the lack of access to adequate health care, and the general decline in the quality of life that has been exacerbated by federal and state cutbacks in social services? The possibility that the problems facing young black males and poor black communities could be solved through self-help initiatives or through mentoring programs is at best naive. Given the structural nature of the problems facing poor black people throughout the United States, it is imperative that we devise strategies to compel those with power and resources to view these issues not as black male problems, but as problems of American society that must be addressed.

The point of this analysis is not to discount the hardships experienced by black males. The central point is that by focusing exclusively upon race and gender as an explanation for these hardships, the issues can become distorted, and consequently, the remedies employed to bring relief may be either ineffective, or worse, contribute to further marginalization.

Black males don't exist in isolation. Most belong to families, live within communities, and are members of complex societies. It is therefore impossible to understand and address the issues confronting black males out of context, for it is in relation to others and to the structure of power and privilege in society that the issues confronting black males have meaning and significance.

Pedro A. Noguera

See also Blues; *Invisible Man;* Masculinities; Men of Color; Race, Conception of; Rap

Further Reading:
Ampim, Michael. 1993. *Towards an Understanding of Black Community Development.* Oakland, CA: Advancing the Research.
Anderson, Elijah. 1990. *Street Wise: Race, Class and Change in an Urban Community.* Chicago: University of Chicago Press.
Carnoy, Martin. 1994. *Faded Dreams: The Politics and Economics of Race in America.* New York: Cambridge University Press.
Feagin, Jerome, and Matthew Sikes. 1994. *Living with Racism: The Black Middle-Class Experience.* Boston: Beacon Press.
Fordham, Signithia. 1996. *Blacked Out: Dilemmas of Race, Identity, and Success at Capitol High.* Chicago: University of Chicago Press.
Girabaldi, Antonio. 1992. "Educating and Motivating African American Males to Succeed." *Journal of Negro Education* 61, no. 1 (Winter): 62–87.
Glassgow, David. 1980. *The Black Underclass: Poverty, Unemployment and Entrapment of Ghetto Youth.* New York: Vintage Books.
Hacker, Andrew. 1992. *Two Nations: Black and White, Separate, Hostile, Unequal.* New York: Charles Scribner and Sons.
Kunjufu, Jawanza. 1985. *Countering the Conspiracy to Destroy Black Boys.* Chicago: African American Images.
Leake, Diana, and Bernard Leake. 1992. "Islands of Hope: Milwaukee's African American Immersion Schools." *Journal of Negro Education* 61, no. 1 (Winter): 23–47.
Madhubuti, Haki. 1990. *Black Men, Obsolete, Single Dangerous?* Chicago: Third World Press.
Massey, Douglas, and Nancy Denton. 1993. *American Apartheid.* Cambridge, MA: Harvard University Press.
Memi, Albert. 1965. *The Colonizer and the Colonized.* Boston: Beacon Press.
Solomon, Rovell Patrick. 1992. *Black Resistance in High School.* Albany, NY: SUNY Press.
Tabb, William. 1970. *The Political Economy of the Black Ghetto.* New York: W. W. Norton.
Taylor-Gibbs, Jewell. 1988. *The Black Male as an Endangered Species.* New York: Auburn House.
Watson, Carol, and G. Smitherman. 1996. *Educating African American Males: Detroit's Malcolm X Academy.* Chicago: Third World Press.
Wilson, Amos. 1992. *Understanding Black Adolescent Male Violence.* New York: Afrikan World Infosystems.

Black Panthers

The term *Black Power* achieved popularization in 1966, the year after the Watts riots that resulted in more than thirty deaths and countless injuries. The Black Panther Party (BPP) was founded in Oakland, California, in October 1966, and the two terms have been intimately associated ever since. Founded by Bobby Seale and Huey Newton, the BPP broke with the peaceful, integrationist agenda of the Civil Rights movement and emphasized the necessity of claiming self-determination for black communities in the United States and abroad, as well as those communities' right to resist violent oppression with violence. Working from a black-nationalist, Marxist/socialist orientation and openly cynical about the possibility of justice for African Americans within the U.S. legal system, the BPP soon found itself the object of the FBI's notorious Counter-Intelligence Program (COINTELPRO). Partially as a result of law enforcement's concerted efforts to infiltrate the party and to jail Panthers, by 1971 the BPP was split by dissension, and many commentators consider this the end of the Panthers' time as an influential organization. Still, the party continued until 1982, placing increasing emphasis on its community work and distancing itself from the militant ideology and imagery that had typified its earlier form. Emphasis by scholars and media on male party leaders has had the dual result of highlighting male bias in the BPP and conflating the BPP's value as a movement with its male leaders' individual failings, such as drug dependency and misogyny. It is important to note, however, that the BPP pioneered new ways of grassroots activism in black communities, officially allied itself with homosexuals as an oppressed group, and denounced sexism as a function of class oppression, a position that was consistent with its Marxist/socialist orientation.

Prominent male Panthers gave some justification to the view that the BPP's understanding of black liberation was male centered and that black liberation essentially meant liberating black men. In 1968, Eldridge Cleaver, the party's minister of information, advocated that women claim the power specific to them, which he degradingly termed "pussy power." Moreover, Cleaver's *Soul on Ice* (1968) promoted a notorious exaggeration of black masculinity; in it, he recounts raping both black and white women, claiming the rape of white women as a blow for revolution. As the BPP withered in the 1970s, he marketed pants outfitted with a codpiece. By 1976 the tragic backlash against the BPP's members, both men and women (great numbers of whom had been jailed or killed in shootouts), had become, in Cleaver's case, a male farce. Under Huey Newton's influence, though, party leadership early showed maturity in banning the "pussy power" slogan and in allying itself with the emerging gay rights movement in 1970. Despite these official positions, prominent black women such as Angela Davis, Alice Walker, and Michele Wallace would grow frustrated with men's dominance in the BPP.

Eldridge Cleaver (Library of Congress)

Thus, while there is no doubt that real gender discrimination existed in the BPP's actual practice, the party's official platform showed considerable complexity and prescience in its understanding of male privilege. Indeed, we may in part judge the complexity of the place of masculinity in Panther politics by its involvement with homosexual French author Jean Genet. On one hand, the Panthers' willingness to go to Paris to solicit the intervention of a white figure primarily renowned for explicit depictions of gay sex gives the lie to the ill-informed notion that the Panthers were uniformly homophobic and antiwhite. On the other hand, Genet biographer Edmund White indicates that it was partially the Panthers' hypermasculine, male-dominated aesthetic that attracted Genet to them (Genet 1989, x).

The BPP's "uniform" was both a powerful aesthetic marker serving to identify members on the street and in the media and, ultimately, an easily caricatured style that lent itself to facile media appropriation and dismissal. Consisting of black leather jackets, berets, and form-fitting pants, the uniform projected a neat, masculine, and militant image that was in consonance with its platform and rules of conduct: purity of body, at least when doing party business; strict, military-style discipline; and, of course, the right to resist oppression with violence when necessary. However, Angela Davis has written movingly of how, today, references to the Panthers cite primarily the party's style, especially the Afro hairstyle, while its grassroots activism and substantive messages about systemic racism in the legal system, housing, and access to health care have been obscured. Even in the late sixties and early seventies, though, the media emphasized Panther men with guns rather than the rank-and-file Panthers, many of them women, doing tough community work. During the critical years 1969–1971, while black America was subjected to the Nixon administration's policy of "benign neglect" and Panthers were rapidly jailed, the BPP was already being dismissed—in books such as Tom Wolfe's *Radical Chic* (1970)—as merely a chic fad for wealthy liberals.

Douglas Steward

See also Cleaver, Eldridge; Race, Conceptions of
Further Reading:

Cleaver, Eldridge. 1992 [1968]. *Soul on Ice*. New York: Laurel.

Davis, Angela Y. 1998. *The Angela Y. Davis Reader*. Edited by Joy James. Malden, MA: Blackwell.

Genet, Jean. 1989. *Prisoner of Love*. Translated by Barbara Bray. Introduction by Edmund White. Hanover, NH: Wesleyan University Press.

Jones, Charles E., ed. 1998. *The Black Panther Party Reconsidered*. Baltimore: Black Classic Press.

Newton, Huey. 1973. *Revolutionary Suicide*. New York: Writers and Readers.

Staub, Michael. 2000. "Setting Up the Seventies: Black Panthers, New Journalism, and the Rewriting of the Sixties." Pp. 19–40 in *The Seventies: The Age of Glitter in Popular Culture*. Edited by Shelton Waldrep. New York: Routledge.

Ture, Kwame [Stokely Carmichael], and Charles V. Hamilton. 1992. *Black Power: The Politics of Liberation*. New York: Vintage.

Wallace, Michele. 1999. *Black Macho and the Myth of the Superwoman*. 2d ed. London: Verso.

Wolfe, Tom. 1970. *Radical Chic and Mau-Mauing the Flak Catchers*. New York: Farrar, Straus and Giroux.

Blackface Minstrelsy

The blackface minstrel show—known in nineteenth-century America as "Negro" or "Ethiopian" minstrelsy—was an extremely popular form of commercial theatrical entertainment in which white men brutally caricatured African Americans for fun and profit. Northern stage mimics such as George Washington Dixon and T. D. Rice began in the late 1820s and early 1830s to "black up" (with either greasepaint or burnt cork), parodying black dress, dance, speech, and song, and developing enduring stereotypes such as the happy-go-lucky rustic slave, Jim Crow, and the ludicrous urban dandy, Zip Coon. By the 1840s, minstrel bands or troupes had formed and elaborated the minstrel show's basic three-part form—an opening section featuring songs, dances, broad jokes, and riddles; a middle or "olio" section of novelty set-pieces like burlesque sermons or stump speeches; and a final, extended skit usually set in the South. After the Civil War, African American performers took the stage, and though they performed in blackface, they reworked even as they adopted racist performance conventions. The final decade of the nineteenth century became famous for its "coon shows," in which black performers caricatured black chicken thieves and razor-wielding hustlers. Despite its investment in racist stereotype, minstrelsy was nearly the only outlet for African American stage talent—the coon show provided work for such artists as Will Marion Cook, Paul Laurence Dunbar, Bert Williams, and George Walker, while musicians such as Ma Rainey and W. C. Handy got their start in black minstrelsy.

If early minstrelsy depended on the appropriation by whites of what they believed to be black styles, to put on "blackness" was also to mimic black maleness—for an audience consisting predominantly of white men. To perform or witness blackface acts was to briefly become black, to inhabit the "cool," virility, humility, or abandon that marked white men's fantasies of black men. For all its ridicule, the minstrel show displayed a secret envy of black manhood. The special achievement of minstrel performers was to have intuited and formalized a broad, general white male fascination with black men, which still may be one means through which conventional adult masculinity is assumed or negotiated. The male bonding between white performers and white audience members that characterized minstrelsy could often enough include the imaginary black men that this bonding was meant to ostracize. At the same time, there is evidence that minstrel shows afforded something closer to a homo-erotic charge. Not only did some blackface songs jokingly reference same-sex love— "Oh, Sally is de gal for me/ I would'nt hab no udder/ If Sal dies to-morrow night/ I'll marry Sally's brudder" (1850)—in a context where occasional black female characters were played by cross-dressed, blacked-up white men. The minstrel show itself provided the first public venue for drag performance in its popular "wench" acts. Usually these female impersonations ridiculed black women as unremittingly as other minstrel acts did black men. Later in the nineteenth century, however, certain specialists such as Francis Leon performed so seductively, as one writer remarked of him, as "to make a fool of a man if he wasn't sure." Such female impersonations more frankly acknowledged the same-sex desire evident in many other minstrel acts, texts, and pictorial illustrations.

As a kinetic art, the minstrel show put "black" men's bodies on display through the intimate fantasies of white men. And the permutations of those fantasies were numberless—extending at least to white male envy of black men, desire for them, and cross-racial identification with "potent" black heterosexuality that displaces homoerotic desire for them. The longstanding interest that blackface minstrelsy has held in U.S. culture in any case testifies to the continuing racial and sexual power of black images in white minds.

Eric Lott

See also Race

Further Reading:

Lhamon, W. T. 1997. *Raising Cain: Blackface Performance from Jim Crow to Hip Hop.* Cambridge, MA: Harvard University Press.

Lott, Eric. 1993. *Love and Theft: Blackface Minstrelsy and the American Working Class.* New York: Oxford University Press.

Rogin, Michael. 1996. *Blackface, White Noise: Jewish Immigrants in the Hollywood Melting Pot.* Berkeley, CA: University of California Press.

Blaxploitation

Providing a critical, if contradictory, shift in mainstream cinematic representations of African American men and women, the so-called blaxploitation era of the early 1970s was a landmark moment in American film history. Ossie Davis's 1970 film *Cotton Comes to Harlem* is generally cited as the first example of the new black-action cinema of the early seventies, but it was the overwhelming success of both *Sweet Sweetback's Baadasssss Song* (Melvin van Peebles) and *Shaft* (Gordon Parks) in 1971 that truly sparked the blaxploitation boom. Although blaxploitation films varied dramatically in formal style, politics, genre, and tone, they generally focused on inner-city environments and tales of corruption, violence, sexual excess, and revenge. Black macho protagonists—private investigators, pimps, gangsters, or revolutionaries—typically dominated the narratives, but Pam Grier's *Coffy* (Jack Hill, 1973) and Tamara Dobson's *Cleopatra Jones* (Jack Starrett, 1973) were successful female variations on the formula. Although short-lived (approximately 1970–1976), the era of blaxploitation cinema helped revitalize the Hollywood film industry during one of its weakest economic periods, provided unprecedented opportunities for African American actors, and presented a variety of perspectives on what it meant to be a black man.

Although seventies' cinema and culture was addressing, critiquing, and even assaulting white patriarchal masculinity, blaxploitation films such as *Sweet Sweetback's Baadasssss Song, Shaft,* and *Superfly* (Gordon Parks, Jr., 1972) rewrote this critique as a cinematic fantasy of black male empowerment. Haunted by the accommodations of "ebony saint" Sidney Poitier to white America in 1960s cinema, blaxploitation films—borrowing from the Black Power movement—turned their back on a nonviolent approach to racial progress and instead elevated the confrontational, hypersexualized, figure of the black macho male to unforeseen heights. But the widespread controversy that contributed to the genre's dubious name was in part a result of the fascinating, yet ambiguous, ways that blaxploitation cinema also threatened black male empowerment and troubled notions of black male authenticity.

Blaxploitation cinema frequently involves a reversal of the gendered and racialized hierarchies that have typically marked the history of American cinema and culture. White male impotence, vulnerability, and femininity become hyperbolized in these films alongside a striking hyperphallicization of black men (e.g., *Shaft*). And yet, the gendering of blaxploitation is far from simple. Black women also adopt phallic power, black male bodies are both fetishized and spectacularly assaulted, queer characters (black and white) abound, and narrative excesses encourage camp readings that trouble the promotion of "authentic" black manhood. Consequently, black masculinity in blaxploitation cinema remains fraught, conflicted, decentered, and in flux. Even the black male stars of the period such as Richard Roundtree, Ron O'Neal, Fred Williamson, Jim Brown, Godfrey Cambridge, and Antonio Fargas suggest remarkably diverse visions of masculinity *and* blackness that are crucial to the operations of the genre. Although rarely acknowledged in the commonly reductive or iconic references to the films today, blaxploitation cinema nevertheless offers a revealing, if ambiguous, look at the intersections of race, gender, class, and sexuality in seventies' America.

Joe Wlodarz

See also *Shaft*

Further Reading:

Bogle, Donald. 1994. *Toms, Coons, Mulattoes, Mammies, & Bucks.* 3d ed. New York: Continuum.

Brody, Jennifer Devere. 2000. "The Returns of Cleopatra Jones." Pp. 225–247 in *The Seventies: The Age of Glitter in Popular Culture.* Edited by Shelton Waldrep. New York: Routledge.

George, Nelson. 1994. *Blackface: Reflections on African-Americans in the Movies.* New York: HarperCollins.

Guerrero, Ed. 1993. *Framing Blackness: The African American Image in Film.* Philadelphia: Temple University Press.

James, Darius. 1996. *That's Blaxploitation: Roots of the Baadasssss 'Tude.* New York: St. Martin's Press.

Martinez, Gerald, Diana Martinez, and Andres Chavez, eds. 1998. *What It Is . . . What It Was!: The Black Film Explosion of the '70s in Words and Pictures.* New York: Hyperion.

Medovoi, Leerom. 1998. "Theorizing Historicity, or the Many Meanings of *Blacula*." *Screen* 39, no. 1 (Spring): 1–21.

Blues

Blues is a musical form that evolved from oral traditions, work songs, and spirituals. It was a way for people to combat society's unfair treatment of the African American. In *The Story of Blues,* Paul Oliver explains that "[blues] can't be sung widout *a full heart and a troubled spirit*" (Oliver 1997, 6). Blues was a combination of exploring the depths of depression and despair, while foraging a sign of hope at the end of the song. The idea took root that "anyone male who grew into manhood, had enough material and insight to sing the blues" (Jones 1999, 82). However, the blues was not a designated style of music, at first.

African American male slaves in the United States were forced to work in the fields. In order to endure the hardships this work entailed and keep their spirits intact, a "leader-and-chorus form of singing" (Oliver 1977, 7) was introduced around the 1850s. (The leader being the male in charge and the chorus all the other male field hands.) To escape the isolation and quiet, the field workers conceived "field calls." Thus, field hands were able to "talk" to each other through these calls and were referred to as "shouters." Each person's "call" had a distinct identity; this type of music was referred to as "primitive blues."

One of the main components of the blues was that it was for men, who would perform music with themes. According to Alan Lomax, "the blues tradition was considered to be a male discipline" (Baker 2001, 1). Not only were field hands credited with inventing this male discipline, but prisoners also contributed to the blues tradition with songs of prison, death row, murder, and prostitutes. In line with this male tradition, the "father" of the Delta blues was Charley Patton (1891–1931). Blind William McTell (1901–1959) was considered the "dean of Atlanta's blues." One of the most influential Delta blues men was Son House (Eddie James Jr., 1902–1988), who was born in Riverton, Mississippi, and made his name with the use of the bottle-necked slide guitar.

The main reason blues was a male discipline was because, even though families were free to travel after the Emancipation, the men were the ones who would go where work was available—and this was generally field work. When African American men traveled North, field work was not as plentiful, and men had to change how they sang. They now relied on singing the blues, instead of "shouting" as they had done in the fields. After a while, groups such as the Georgia Minstrels, the Pringle Minstrels, and McCabe and the Young Minstrels began to employ blues singers. These employers provided male blues singers with a steady income. (Women did not have the same problems finding work, in that they could obtain employment as maids, etc.)

One thing that set blues apart from traditional music was the emotional impact of each song. Blues was a deeply felt music and

musicians wanted to expose their angst through lyrics. Early blues was "the most impressive expression of the Negro's individuality within the superstructure of American society" (Jones 1999, 66). Within this society, men would travel throughout the South and elsewhere and entertain through performing the blues. The instruments most often used to accompany the songs were the piano, the guitar, and the harmonica. Because each region of the South was different, singers would exchange their ways of performing with fellow blues men. As a result each singer could tailor his songs to the style most comfortable to his audience. Singers wanted the audiences to react to the lyrics and to feel as if the instruments were playing only to them.

Classical blues was first introduced around World War I and was composed of two or three instruments and no lyrics. Unlike country blues, or Delta blues, which were performed by musicians with no formal musical training, classical blues required musical training. These more polished performances proved to be one route for the African American male to be integrated into American society. This type of blues also demonstrated that the African American male's life had improved substantially. He was now recognized as a musician and not a field "hollerer."

The Great Migration (1919–1926) ocurred when African Americans traveled from the South to the North, specifically New York City and Chicago, and precipitated numerous changes for the African American male. After years of being slaves, oppressed, and treated unfairly, African Americans began to envision some hope during the 1920s, 1930s, and 1940s, and the New Negro Movement emerged as the "Harlem Renaissance" to express their optimism. This Great Migration was referred to by Alain Locke in *The New Negro* (1925) as "something like a spiritual emancipation" (*Encarta*). African Americans began to be treated in a more positive manner as their unique contributions to the American musical genre caught on with a wider public. People would flock to speakeasies to hear blues men. Women's contribution to the blues focused on physical abuse and marital infidelity, and in a more emotional way. One way women found their creative talent could be seen and appreciated was in the minstrel and vaudeville shows. "To be in a minstrel or vaudeville show, it helped blues women to polish their skills" (Jones 1999, 93). One of the most recognized vaudeville singers was Lucille Hegamin (1894–1980), who was also referred to as "The Cameo Girl." Hegamin chose to perform in speakeasies and cabarets. Alberta Hunter (1895–1984) was considered the "Prima Donna of Blues Singers." Ida Cox (1896–1967) was considered the "Uncrowned Queen of the Blues," and the "Empress of the Blues" was Bessie Smith (1894–1937). Like the male singers, the women provided entertainment for mainstream audiences, as well as the intellectuals. Mamie Smith (1883–1946) recorded the first blues song. Memphis Minnie (1897–1963) was considered one of the "most prolific and influential women of the blues." Just as W. C. Handy is considered the "father of the blues," Ma Rainey (1886–1939) is considered the "mother of the blues."

For the male musicians who had moved from the South, obtaining recognition for their talents was a long and arduous battle, sometimes thwarted and stifled; however, through their music, they could express their disillusionments and frustrations, and in the end, their spirits always prevailed with the sounds of hope. Some of the early blues singers, along with Charley Patton, Eddie James, and Blind Willie McTell, who influenced later blues musicians were: Blind Lemon Jefferson (1897–1929), who was one of the first successful recording artists; Robert Johnson (1911–1938), who influenced later musicians through his lyrics; Nehemiah "Skip" James (1902–1969), who was influential with country blues and developed the "Bentonia Style"; and W. C. Handy, who was known as the "father of the blues."

Even after the disappearance of the Harlem Renaissance, the African American blues men's influence on music goes on. Blues was played solely by African American musicians until the 1950s, when white musicians began to adapt their styles to blues singers. Blues is still popular into the twenty-first century with performers such as B. B. King, Buddy Guy, and Eric Clapton. Big Mama Thornton (1926–1984) was the first to record a song made famous by Elvis Presley, "Hound Dog," as well as "Ball n' Chain," made popular by Janis Joplin. Indeed, the blues form is as strong as ever, and the songs are still driven by sadness over personal tragedies and injustices; however, they still manage not only to bring a feeling of hope for the musicians, but also to speak of a better life for the audience.

Karen E. Holleran

See also Jazz; Rap

Further Reading:

Baker, Robert M. 2001. "A Brief History of the Blues." At http://www.island.net/~blues/history.html (cited 17 August 2001).

Davis, Angela Y. 1999. *Blues Legacies and Black Feminism: Gertrude "Ma" Rainey, Bessie Smith, and Billie Holiday.* New York: Random House.

Encarta Schoolhouse. "Harlem Renaissance." At http://encarta.msn.com/schoolhouse/harlem/harlem.asp (cited 1 November 2001).

Harrison, Daphne Duval. 1990. *Black Pearls: Blues Queens of the 1920s.* New Brunswick, NJ: Rutgers University Press.

Herman, Hawkeye. "History of the Blues." At http://www.blues.org/history/essays/hawkeye2.html (cited 9 November 2001).

Hilliard, Kenneth B. 2001. "The Impact of the Music of the Harlem Renaissance on Society." At http://www.yale.edu/ynhti/curriculum/units/1989/1/89.01.05.x.html (cited 25 October 2001).

Huggins, Nathan Irvin. 1971. *Harlem Renaissance.* London: Oxford University Press.

Jones, LeRoi. 1999. *Blues People: Negro Music in White America.* New York: Quill.

Oliver, Paul. 1997. *The Story of the Blues.* Boston: Northeastern University Press.

Urton Art. 2003. "The Harlem Renaissance." At http://eyeconart.net/history/harlem.htm (cited 22 August 2003).

Bly, Robert Elwood (1926–)

Robert Elwood Bly was a renowned poet before he emerged in the 1980s as the key figure in what came to be known as the mythopoetic branch of the men's movement. Bly was born on 23 December 1926, in the small town of Madison, Minnesota. His Norwegian Lutheran parents were farmers, though his mother also worked off the farm in the town courthouse, during the day. After high school, Bly joined the navy for two years (1944–1946), attended St. Olaf College for a year after his discharge, and in 1947 transferred to Harvard. He graduated from Harvard in 1950.

After college, Bly returned briefly to Minnesota, then moved to New York, where he wrote and worked odd jobs for several years. A brief stint (1954–1955) at the University of Iowa Writers' Workshop was followed by a Fulbright scholarship to study in Norway and translate Norwegian poetry into English. When he returned to the United States, Bly founded a poetry journal, *The Fifties* (which later became *The Sixties* and *The Seventies*), that brought the translated works of European and South American poets to the attention of American audiences. In 1968 Bly received the National Book Award in poetry for *The Light around the Body*. Altogether Bly has published over forty books of poems and translations.

The ideas that Bly brought to his work as a men's movement leader were forged through his study and craft as a poet. As a poet, Bly has sought to conjure images that stir the imagination and evoke repressed emotion. His images, however, are not simply evocative sketches of concrete realities; nor are they easily grasped metaphors for emotional experience. Rather, Bly often uses irrational images—of objects, events, and actions that are literal impossibilities—to represent the energies and passions that exist in psychic realms unruled by and troubling to the rational mind. Poetry, for Bly, is a doorway to these realms, and thus a means to self-discovery.

Bly's thinking about the psychological import of poetic imagery borrows heavily from the work of the Swiss psychologist Gustav Jung (1875–1961). Following Jung, Bly sees certain images as archetypal, meaning that they represent psychic energies that are part of the collective unconscious. These images are said to have an emotional resonance that transcends time and place. Individuals can use such images to explore, activate, and harness their psychic energies. But more than this, the universality of archetypal images, according to Jung and Bly, reveals deeper connections that unite humans with each other and with nature.

In the early 1970s, Bly became especially interested in the imagery found in ancient myths and fairy tales. Within a few years, he was explicating these images to workshop audiences. The first major workshop, which Bly called "The Conference on the Great Mother," was held in Colorado in 1974. Under the influence of Jung and of mythology popularizer Joseph Campbell (see *The Hero With a Thousand Faces* [1972]), Bly came to see these stories as offering a theory of psychological growth. A key part of this growth process was, as Bly discerned it, initiation—the ritual by means of which the transition from childhood to adulthood is effected.

Through workshops and weekend seminars, Bly began to teach people how to extract from myths and fairy tales wisdom useful for coping with everyday struggles and for pursuing spiritual growth. For some years, his audiences were composed of both men and women. In 1980 at the Lama Commune in New Mexico, Bly offered his first workshop for men only. This marked a turn toward teaching men how to explore and activate their specifically "masculine energies." One of Bly's favorite vehicles for doing this was the Grimms's fairy tale "Iron John," which Bly interpreted as a story about initiation and the stages of male growth.

Bly's visibility was boosted through an interview published in the May 1982 issue of *New Age Journal*. In the interview Bly expounds his notion of the "soft male," a type of man who is peaceful, socially aware, and accommodating toward women and women's equality, yet unhappy, unassertive, and enervated. Bly then recounts the "Iron John" tale, using it to argue that soft males need to get in touch with the deep, wild masculine energies allegedly present in every male psyche that Western society has taught them to repress. To do this, Bly says, men need an initiation through which they can learn to tap these energies and use them wisely. The routine opportunity for such initiation, Bly further argues, was lost when industrial society separated fathers from their sons.

The *New Age* interview was a watershed piece, summarizing Bly's ideas and attracting thousands of men to his form of "men's work." Bly gained a national audience in January 1990, when PBS television aired a ninety-minute Bill Moyers special, "A Gathering of Men," which prominently featured Bly as the main teacher at a three-day men's workshop in Austin, Texas. Bly's *Iron John: A Book about Men* was published later that year. The PBS program and *Iron John,* which remained a best-seller throughout 1991, brought Bly to the peak of his fame.

Over the next few years, Bly and the "mythopoetic men's movement" were widely written about in the popular media. Television news programs and a few sitcoms examined the movement. An academic literature also sprang up. Although much of the commentary by outsiders was mocking or critical, Bly's workshops and poetry readings were often filled to capacity. His themes of men's needs for mentoring, initiation, and emotional communion appealed not only to the thousands of men, most of whom were white, middle aged, and from the middle class, who came to hear him, but also to millions more who read his work or read about him.

Although Bly and his followers claimed that the mythopoetic movement was not antifeminist, many observers were skeptical. Some feminist critics were disturbed by Bly's attribution of differences in women's and men's behavior to biologically based psychic energies, rather than to culture and social organization. The role of political and economic inequalities in producing those differences was thus obscured, feminists argued. Critics also charged that the archetypal images Bly urged men to embrace, especially images of the king, the warrior, and the wild man, arose from and reinforced male supremacy.

Bly's treatment of men's violence was similarly criticized for being reductionist and ignoring inequality. According to Bly, men's violence arises from shame they feel at not knowing how to be good men and from consequent insecurity about their worth as men. Feminists, on the other hand, point to thwarted expectations of privilege, men's efforts to control women, men's institutionalized power, and the link between masculinity and domination—all factors that disappear in Bly's rendering. And again scholars criticized Bly for claiming expertise about these matters while largely ignoring decades of social science research on gender and masculinity.

Although publicity and participation waned by the mid-1990s, the mythopoetic movement carried on. Bly and his main collaborators, storyteller Michael Meade and Jungian psychologist James Hillman, continued to give workshops. Hundreds of men's groups around the country continued to hold gatherings that involved storytelling, poetry, drumming, dancing, and faux Native American rituals (e.g., sweat lodges), all of which had become staple parts of mythopoetic practice. In the summer of 2002, a seventy-five-year-old Robert Bly held his twenty-eighth annual conference on "The Great Mother and the New Father" in Nobleboro, Maine.

Michael Schwalbe

See also Consciousness Raising; Fraternities; The ManKind Project; Mythopoetic Men's Movement

Further Reading:

Bly, Robert. 1990. *Iron John: A Book about Men.* Reading, MA: Addison-Wesley.

Male Bodybuilders posing, Venice Beach, CA (Robert Landau / Corbis)

————. 2000. "An Interview with Robert Bly." *Paris Review* 154 (Spring): 36–75.

Campbell, Joseph. 1972. *The Hero with a Thousand Faces*. Princeton, NJ: Princeton University Press.

Kimmel, Michael, ed. 1995. *The Politics of Manhood: Profeminist Men Respond to the Mythopoetic Men's Movement (And the Mythopoetic Leaders Answer)*. Philadelphia: Temple University Press.

Schwalbe, Michael. 1996. *Unlocking the Iron Cage: The Men's Movement, Gender Politics, and American Culture*. New York: Oxford University Press.

Sugg, Richard P. 1986. *Robert Bly*. Boston: Twayne.

Bodybuilding, Contemporary

The use of progressive resistance exercise to control and develop one's musculature is the defining feature of contemporary bodybuilding. Progressive resistance exercise is made possible by using barbells and dumbbells, or machine stations, at progressively heavier weights. When done effectively, in conjunction with appropriate nutrition, bodybuilding can enhance a man's appearance and sense of his own masculinity. Most bodybuilders train for personal pleasure, self-esteem, and health. A limited number train for weight lifting, power lifting, or competitive bodybuilding competitions. Almost all bodybuilders who compete do so as amateurs, but a few are sanctioned as professionals, earning money with contest wins. The dream of going "pro" keeps many men in the gym, despite the small number who achieve professional status.

The history of bodybuilding as a performance of masculinity is the history of "name" bodybuilders and of the promoters who helped them achieve fame. Bodybuilding's origins in Europe in the late nineteenth century coincided with the advent of photography, which distributed striking images of muscular men to a worldwide audience. The first famous bodybuilder, Eugen Sandow (born Friedrich Müller in 1867), got his start under the employ of Oscard Attila (born Louis Durlacher in 1844), who had converted his music hall act into a career as a professional strongman. Taking Sandow under his wing, Attila taught his protégé how to transform his gymnast's build into a bodybuilder's physique. (Sandow had what is now termed "good genetics"—a physiology ideal for building muscles.) Attending Attila's training school in Brussels, Sandow used a shot-loading barbell (one with globes at each end that could be filled with shot or sand at various weights), the forerunner of the plate-loading barbell. Sandow later invented and popularized other equipment, such as spring-grip dumbbells.

With Sandow, bodybuilding was born. In 1898, when he started publishing the magazine *Physical Culture* (later *Sandow's Magazine of Physical Culture*), he was one of the most famous men alive. He appeared on countless postcards and cabinet cards, often wearing only an imitation fig leaf. World tours with showman Florenz Ziegfeld, who billed him as "the World's Most Perfectly Developed Man," cemented Sandow's fame. At first giving demonstrations of strength or posing as a "living" Greek statue, he later only had to show up and let a sold-out audience witness his physique. A cottage industry of magazines, contests, exercise devices, and diets helped Sandow commodify his personal brand of masculinity. By his death in 1925, Sandow had pioneered much of what has made bodybuilding a profitable enterprise.

Two major names in bodybuilding promotion in the early twentieth-century were Bernarr Macfadden and Charles Atlas. Macfadden, an American who moved to England to promote his chest expander (a metal or rubber spring strand with side grips), founded the magazine *Physical Development* in 1898 to market his exercise philosophy. His greatest contribution was the physique contest he sponsored in 1903 at New York's Madison Square Garden, the first of its kind. The posing styles in today's bodybuilding competitions developed at Macfadden's annual events. The $1,000 prize winner in Macfadden's 1921 contest for "The Most Perfectly Developed Man in America" was Angelo Siciliano, an Italian immigrant who achieved fame as "Charles Atlas." Mythologizing an experience he'd had as a teenager on a Coney Island beach—when a bully had kicked sand in his face—Atlas sold "Dynamic Tension" mail-order courses to generations of boys who wished to face down their own bullies. The larger-than-life Charles Atlas handling the beach bully has never lost its appeal as a masculine icon.

The location typifying bodybuilding in the 1930s and 1940s was another American beach: Muscle Beach in Santa Monica, California. During the summer, bodybuilders flocked to the spot to perform hand-balancing stunts before admiring crowds. Among the leading figures at Muscle Beach were Jack La Lanne, later a TV fitness expert; Joe Gold, founder of Gold's Gym; Harold Zinkin, inventor of the Universal Gym, the most widely used exercise machine; and John Grimek, Mr. America for 1946. When Muscle Beach closed in the 1950s, America's west coast remained the destination of bodybuilding aspirants—now centered at Venice Beach, California, site of the first Gold's Gym, still the facility of choice for many current pros.

Mr. America competitions sponsored by the American Athletic Union (AAU) have existed since 1939, but the dominant modern bodybuilding organization is the International Federation of Bodybuilders (IFBB), begun in 1946 by Ben Weider, a Canadian promoter. His brother Joe, who won bodybuilding contests in the 1950s, directed an empire of magazines promoting the "Weider philosophy" of training and fitness. In 1965 Joe Weider professionalized competitive bodybuilding by founding the Mr. Olympia contest, which drew top bodybuilders away from rival organizations and contests—including Mr. Universe, sponsored by the National Amateur Body Builders' Association (NABBA). One such bodybuilder was an Austrian immigrant to America named Arnold Schwarzenegger (born in 1947). By the time Schwarzenegger won his seventh Mr. Olympia title in 1980, the IFBB dominated most competitive bodybuilding, and the National Physique Committee (NPC) had severed its ties with the AAU, becoming an independent amateur organization, the only one qualifying contest winners for an IFBB pro card. The influence of other sponsoring organizations was broken, and now only a few other organizations remain.

Since Schwarzenegger left the bodybuilding world for Hollywood stardom, no single competitor has exerted the charisma and influence he did. Bodybuilding now faces a crisis of legitimacy, even as its popularity as a form of training has flowered. Although competitive bodybuilders consider what they do a sport, the mainstream sports world rejects it as such. Only specialized bodybuilding magazines and Internet websites note winners of competitions. Outside of a devoted subculture, competitive bodybuilding often remains misunderstood, and bodybuilders themselves demeaned as stupid or emotionally stunted. Even a sophisticated recent ethnographic study by Alan M. Klein claimed that men are drawn to bodybuilding by feelings of insecurity. Bodybuilding has never shaken its association with strongman sideshows; indeed, being called a "freak" can be a compliment to some bodybuilders. The willingness of bodybuilders to possibly risk their long-term health for muscular size and strength through the use of anabolic steroids—illegal in many nations without a prescription, and criminalized in America—has further eroded its legitimacy. Exploitation of bodybuilders is common, since little money can be made in competition, and paraprofessional work like personal training in gyms is undependable as a source of income.

Still, new generations of boys and men are drawn to bodybuilding for the same reasons Sandow, Atlas, and Schwarzenegger were. Although limited, the fandom of bodybuilding is loyal. Images of bodybuilding have transformed pop culture. Most important,

bodybuilding has changed the lives of many men by offering them a sense of masculine empowerment their career paths and personal relationships do not. Bodybuilding has helped them establish a firmer sense of self and given them a means by which to pursue their personal best.

Michael J. Emery

See also "Adonis Complex"; Macfadden, Bernarr; Schwarzenegger, Arnold

Further Reading:

Budd, Michael Anton. 1997. *The Sculpture Machine: Physical Culture and Body Politics in the Age of Empire.* New York: New York University Press.

Chapman, David L. 1994. *Sandow the Magnificent: Eugen Sandow and the Beginnings of Bodybuilding.* Urbana, IL: University of Illinois Press.

Dutton, Kenneth R. 1995. *The Perfectible Body: The Western Ideal of Male Physical Development.* New York: Continuum.

Fair, John D. 1999. *Muscletown USA: Bob Hoffman and the Manly Culture of York Barbell.* University Park, PA: Pennsylvania State University Press.

Fussell, Samuel Wilson. 1991. *Muscle: Confessions of an Unlikely Bodybuilder.* New York: Poseidon Press.

Gaines, Charles, and George Butler. 1974. *Pumping Iron: The Art and Sport of Bodybuilding.* New York: Simon and Schuster.

Klein, Alan M. 1993. *Little Big Men: Bodybuilding Subculture and Gender Construction.* Albany, NY: State University of New York Press.

Monaghan, Lee F. 2001. *Bodybuilding, Drugs and Risk.* New York: Routledge.

Schwarzenegger, Arnold, with Bill Dobbins. 1998. *The New Encyclopedia of Modern Bodybuilding.* New York: Simon and Schuster.

Zinkin, Harold, with Bonnie Hearn. 1999. *Remembering Muscle Beach: Where Hard Bodies Began.* Santa Monica, CA: Angel City Press.

Bodybuilding, History of

The muscular male body with a V-shaped torso is a distinctly Western cultural ideal, one that is traceable to the ancient Greek valorization of muscularity as evidence of manly agency and willpower (Kuriyama 1999). Yet as a mainstream phenomenon, bodybuilding is a distinctly modern development that reflects a number of changes in Western culture since the late nineteenth century, including the growing importance of physical appearance in social situations, an emerging obsession with youthfulness, and anxieties about a loss of manhood in an age of changing gender structures. Like many body techniques of this period (including the sport and fitness movements), developing the male physique may be seen as an attempt to resist modernity's erosion of tradition by seizing upon the apparently stable foundation of the body. Despite the emergence of many female bodybuilders in recent decades, the muscular, hardened, and striated male physique is often presented as the ideal masculine body.

The West has a long tradition of strongmen who dramatized their physical strength for popular audiences, either as performers in city streets and country fairs or, in modern times, in traveling circus troupes. When coupled with the late-nineteenth-century interest in health and physical culture, however, the dramatization of masculine force became much more acceptable to middle-class tastes. The Prussian-born strongman Eugen Sandow (Friedrich Müller) was the most famous of bodybuilders of the late nineteenth century, and in addition to his well-attended displays of strength and beauty before fashionable audiences, he founded his own magazines and invented his own exercise equipment to encourage other men to develop their bodies. Thanks to fellow travelers like Bernarr Macfadden in America and Edmond Desbonnet in France, by 1900 the promise of physical development attracted many middle-class men who felt that sedentary lifestyles and excessive mental labor left their bodies weak, sickly, and unattractive.

Early bodybuilding was nevertheless a controversial pastime, mainly because it seemed to glorify the sensation and spectacle of manly force for narcissistic rather than practical or social ends. It was also dogged by the belief that portraits of seminude men in eroticized poses attracted homosexual onlookers (Waugh 1996). Interest in bodybuilding nevertheless increased after World War One, perhaps as a means of reconstructing bodies that had been wounded in the conflict. From the 1930s onward popular enthusiasm for bodybuilding was fueled by entrepreneurs who appealed to the gender anxieties of young men. In the back advertisement pages of many magazines, Charles Atlas (Angelo Siciliano) famously promised that his method of bodybuilding would "turn Weaklings into He-Men," while Joe Weider did much to promote this activity, notably with his magazine, *Muscle and Fitness,* which by the 1990s reached a monthly circulation of 6 million copies. The growing respectability of the pastime was capped off in the United States by the formal recognition of bodybuilding as a sport by the Amateur Athletic Union, which created the "Mr. America" competition in 1940. Unlike the early days, when "heroic" displays of muscular force were as important as the spectacle of male beauty, by the 1940s the "erotic/aesthetic" dimension of bodybuilding achieved prominence. In 1947 bodybuilders united in the International Federation of Bodybuilders, an organization that has steadily grown to include 134 member organizations by the 1990s. Finally, in the 1970s and 1980s anxieties about the homoerotic potential of the sport were largely put to rest by Arnold Schwarzenegger, whose aggressively heterosexual self-presentation conferred upon the sport a new respectability among boys and men (Dutton 1995).

Although muscular development continues to be a preoccupation of many men, the quest for physical perfection has also generated criticism. One ethnography of bodybuilding subculture draws attention to the dialectic of control and weakness in the identities of many bodybuilders, thus revealing how cultivating the appearance of muscular bulk and definition often compensates for feelings of physical weakness or a lack of autonomy (Klein 1993). This use of muscularity as a sort of protective psychic shell was famously described by Sam Fussell (1991), who in his popular memoir recalled how his compulsive weight training and steroid use merely masked a range of personal insecurities. More recently compulsive bodybuilding has been described as a form of "body dysmorphic disorder" in which male body obsessions are understood within a wider framework that includes anorexia and bulimia. Pope, Phillips, and Olivardia (2000) have dubbed this body obsession "the Adonis complex," a condition whose personal dimensions clearly reflect Western culture's growing insistence on unrealistically developed male bodies. This is particularly true in the fictional characters and toys marketed to boys. Whereas comic book superheroes have always boasted muscular and well-defined bodies, their physical dimensions have expanded considerably over the years, thus providing a male counterpart to the unrealistic female body ideal marketed to girls through Barbie and other dolls. Given the proliferation of such imagery in popular culture, most boys today grow up measuring themselves against body ideals that are rarely attainable without drugs.

Christopher E. Forth

See also "Adonis Complex"; Bodybuilding, Contemporary; Macfadden, Bernarr; Physical Culture; Schwarzenegger, Arnold

Further Reading:

Dutton, Kenneth R. 1995. *The Perfectible Body: The Western Ideal of Male Physical Development.* New York: Continuum.

Fussell, Sam. 1991. *Muscle: Confessions of an Unlikely Bodybuilder.* London: Sphere Books.

Klein, Alan M. 1993. *Little Big Men: Bodybuilding Subculture and Gender Construction.* Albany, NY: State University of New York Press.

Kuriyama, Shigehisa. 1999. *The Expressiveness of the Body and the Divergence of Greek and Chinese Medicine.* New York: Zone Books.

Pope, Harrison G., Jr., Katharine A. Phillips, and Roberto Olivardia. 2000. *The Adonis Complex: The Secret Crisis of Male Body Obsession.* New York: The Free Press.

Waugh, Thomas. 1996. *Hard to Imagine: Gay Male Eroticism in Photography and Film from Their Beginnings to Stonewall.* New York: Columbia University Press;.

Bogart, Humphrey (1899–1957)

Actor and legendary tough guy, Humphrey Bogart was the son of a wealthy Manhattan surgeon and a magazine illustrator. His privileged circumstances resulted in his being sent to the Phillips Academy in Andover, Massachusetts, to be groomed as a gentleman. He was expected to pursue medical studies at Yale, but he dropped out of Andover and joined the U.S. navy during World War I. After he was discharged from the navy for insubordination, Bogart took up acting. In classical Hollywood, he came to exemplify the lonely, self-reliant, and cynical representation of masculinity. The "Bogey" image was a direct reflection of his unusual attractiveness. He was a medium-sized man with a scarred upper lip, but Bogart's tough-guy persona helped erect, reflect, and reevaluate the construction of American masculinity. Unlike his resurrection as the paragon of virility in the 1960s, Bogart's career represented an unstable masculinity that was always in crisis. He played figures who continually redefined manhood, from wartime individualism, through the postwar reconsideration of male homosociality, to the frequently failed identity of the 1950s male.

Although Bogart achieved popular success with his portrayal of the brooding gangster Duke Mantee in *The Petrified Forest* (1936) and later as the pathetic killer "Mad Dog" Earle in *High Sierra* (1941), the "Bogey" legend was born with the release of John Huston's directorial debut, *The Maltese Falcon* (1941). Bogart was the embodiment of the solitary male with a private moral code, Detective Sam Spade, who is forced into action when his partner is killed. As the reluctant warrior, Spade personifies the isolationism of a nation wary of being dragged into World War II. But if Spade parallels the official American stance of neutrality, Rick Blaine in *Casablanca* (1942) represents the moral obligation to get involved. Here, the notion of masculinity is tied to political engagement (Trice and Holland 2001, 65). As the quiet but subversive bar owner who risks it all for love and patriotism, Bogart came to represent ethical manhood.

The heroic involvement of the tough male, however, began to evince an underlying vulnerability in postwar masculinity. In *To Have and Have Not* (1945), Bogart played a doubting fishing-boat privateer, who finally supports the Free French for the girl he loves (Lauren Bacall), and in *The Big Sleep* (1946), he was private eye Philip Marlowe, who tries to restore stability to a corrupt world through romance. After the war, Bogart's secure persona yielded to the interrogation of normative heterosexuality, which had defined masculinity until this time. Indeed, in *Dead Reckoning* (1947), he explored the complexities of being a "man's man." He played Rip Murdock, a returning vet who discovers "the incompatibility of postwar heterosexual civilian life and wartime buddy love" (Cohan 1997, 88). Rip's obsession for his dead friend Johnny Drake (William Preston) threatens, and ultimately disrupts, the postwar desire for a return to domestic heterosexuality.

Throughout the 1950s, Bogart's characters regarded aggressive and self-assured manhood with ambivalence. In *In a Lonely Place* (1950), Bogart portrayed Dixon Steele, a self-destructive and violent screenwriter under investigation for murder. Dix's reckless bravado draws on Bogart's infamous nightclub brawls. But Dix's angry outbursts are not glorified; the film remains skeptical of the star's own tough-guy image. Unlike the invincible heroes he had embodied in the past, Bogart appeared quite ordinary in *The African Queen* (1951), where he played Charlie Allnut, a riverboating trader who helps a missionary (Katharine Hepburn) escape the Germans during World War I. In *The Desperate Hours* (1955), on the other hand, he became the ultimate antisocial deviant, the fugitive Glenn Griffin, who terrorizes a middle-class suburban family. Bogart's Griffin represents masculinity gone awry, thereby finally shattering his earlier masculine image of complete self-control.

Although Bogart's oeuvre is complex and diverse, he is remembered as the indomitable male. Jean-Luc Godard canonizes the actor's romantic masculinity in *Breathless* (1959). With the trademark cigarette dangling from his lips, Michael Poiccard (Jean-Paul Belmondo) performs the classic gangster-hero by imitating Bogey's gestures. In *Play It Again, Sam* (1972), Woody Allen resurrects the ghost of Humphrey Bogart. As Michael Kimmel points out, Bogart returns as a cultural phantasm to impart "a series of lessons in manhood for Allen-as-nebbish-Everyman to follow" (1996, 289). Of course, Bogey remains inimitable. His image rests on a nostalgic formation of masculinity—ideal because it is unattainable. The Bogey legend endures as the incomparable tough guy, contrasted with Woody Allen's lament: "I'm not like that and I never will be."

Rashna Wadia

Further Reading:
Cohan, Steven. 1997. *Masked Men: Masculinity and the Movies in the Fifties.* Bloomington, IN: Indiana University Press.

Gardiner, Judith Kegan, ed. 2002. *Masculinity Studies and Feminist Theory: New Directions.* New York: Columbia University Press.

Kimmel, Michael. 1996. *Manhood in America.* New York: Free Press.

Krutnik, Frank. 1991. *In a Lonely Street: Film Noir, Genre, Masculinity.* London: Routledge.

Sedgwick, Eve Kosofsky. 1985. *Between Men: English Literature and Male Homosocial Desire.* New York: Columbia University Press.

Sklar, Robert. 1992. *City Boys: Cagney, Bogart, Garfield.* Princeton, NJ: Princeton University.

Sperber, A. M., and Eric Lax. 1997. *Bogart.* New York: William Morrow and Company.

Trice, Ashton D., and Samuel A. Holland. 2001. *Heroes, Antiheroes, and Dolts: Portrayals of Masculinity in American Popular Films, 1921–1999.* Jefferson, NC: McFarland.

Bond, James

Created by ex-Commander of (British) Naval Intelligence Ian Fleming in the 1950s, James Bond is the hero of many spy books and a host of movies made from them, all spectacular financial successes. Combining many elements of sexuality and violence, these works have often been derided as sadistic, adolescent boy fantasies and criticized for overt sexism, with some critics even claiming to identify the propagation of an imperialist British supremacy in them. Bond, however, has been a hit with adult audiences for nearly half a century. Clearly, the character embodies aspects of masculinity pleasing to both men and women, however outdated those aspects are.

Ian Fleming (1908–1964) was a womanizer, fond of gambling, and a connoisseur of food and drink, and so is his creation, Bond. When a married woman became pregnant with his child, Fleming wrote the first of the Bond novels, settling down at last, as John Cork says, "like a grown-up."

Like Peter Pan, Bond rarely gets injured, and women have no hold on him—only Mother. An orphan, the supremely competent spy's only parent is his beloved country and its personal representative, M. (Compare the parody character "Mother" in *The Avengers* television spoof of the Bond series.) "M" was Fleming's nickname for his own mother, and one can easily relate this situation to the Oedipus complex, as John Cox has done. At one point M replaces Bond's "weapon" with a different model, and when the agent tries to exit M's womb-like padded office with his old gun, M orders him to leave it. (We are told Bond hates M at that revealing moment.) In films from the late 1990s, Bond's boss is played by Judi Dench. The Secret Service head retains the name "M," slyly indicative of an almost physical sex change.

Bond is often criticized as a romanticized, idealized depiction of masculinity, who is both deeply conservative and intrinsically homophobic: only bad guys are gay. The flaming stereotypical two villains in *Diamonds Are Forever* (1971), for instance, are played for laughs.

In both books and films, women are willing sexual objects. Bond's relations with women, however, are invariably brief. *Diamonds Are Forever* ends with Bond and lover happily united, but the reader is told in the next novel that the couple split. In *On Her Majesty's Secret Service* (1963), Bond marries a countess. She is gunned down by an asexual villainess within hours.

Although women are viewed as erotic objects, so are men, such as Largo, the villain of *Thunderball* (1961), a novel admired by President Kennedy: "[M]uscles bulged under his exquisitely cut shark-skin jacket. An aid to his athletic prowess were his hands . . . almost twice the normal size" (1961, 75).

In his first appearance, *Casino Royale* (1953), Bond's affair with the spy Vesper turns sour: He discovers she is a double agent working for the Russians. Bond finds her murdered body and reports to London, "The bitch is dead," to end this novel with a Mickey Spillane tough-guy punch. Of this sort of hero, sociologist Robert Connell explains, "In contemporary Western society, masculinity is strongly associated with aggressiveness and the capacity for violence. . . . In much of the writing about men produced by the 'men's movement' of the 1970s it was assumed that [if we] change the macho image, . . . violence would be reduced." But "violence is not just an expression; it is a part of the process that divides different masculinities from each other. There is violence within masculinity; it is constitutive" (1984, 24).

Reinvented by a new actor, Pierce Brosnan, Bond faces enemies of the 1990s such as despots who want to control the world oil supply. Bond seems more sensitive in this post–Cold War world in which he is partnered with sexy, powerful women such as a Chinese agent (Michelle Yeoh).

The question of whether Bond's killings serve the cause of the faded British Empire—there are paeans to England scattered throughout the fifteen books, spoken by the patriotic agent—never truly arises. The role was attempted by George Lazenby and Timothy Dalton, but the public perceived them as not macho enough. It is the violent stereotypes that still fuel public fantasies.

Carl Jay Buchanan

Further Reading:

Black, Jeremy. 2000. *The Politics of James Bond: From Fleming's Novels to the Big Screen.* New York: Praeger.

Connell, Robert W. 1984. "A New Man." *The New Internationalist* 136 (June): 24.

Cork, John. 2003. (The Ian Fleming Foundation). "The Life of Ian Fleming." At http://www.klast.net/bond/flem_bio.html (cited 3 January 2003).

Fleming, Ian. 1961. *Thunderball.* New York: Signet.

Lycett, Andrew. 1996. *Ian Fleming: The Man behind James Bond.* London: Phoenix.

Boxing

As a sport, boxing has a long history, filled with colorful characters, sordid backroom corruption, and constant fan support.

Although stories of fistfighting are found in ancient Greece and the Old Testament, it was in the late nineteenth century that boxing became a legitimate and major sport in the United States. Boxing was seen as the ultimate test of manliness at a time when cultural fears that men had grown soft and effeminate were on the rise. Boxing heralded the triumph of the simple, hard-working man over the desk-bound office worker.

In his fascinating study of bare-knuckle prizefighting in America, historian Elliot Gorn describes the ways that working-class bachelor subcultures resurrected the language of the virtuous worker to describe the skills and the spectacle of the boxing match. Boxing was a "profession," and boxers were "trained" in various "schools" of combat. Newspapers reported that the combatants "went to work" or that one "made good work" of another. Admirers spoke of the ways that particular fighters "plied their trades" or understood the "arts and mysteries" of the pugilistic métier. It was, as Gorn described it, a "manly art."

Boxing was celebrated by President Theodore Roosevelt, himself an amateur boxer, as one of the "manly sports" to revitalize American manhood. Boxing was a good example of the "strenuous life." Perhaps no one symbolized this elemental virility better than John L. Sullivan, perhaps the "greatest American hero of the late nineteenth century." With his manly swagger and well-waxed moustache, this Irish fighter symbolized "the growing desire to smash through the fluff of bourgeois gentility and the tangle of corporate ensnarements to the throbbing heart of life" (Kimmel 1996, 139). At the other end of the spectrum, though, stood Jack Johnson, the first black heavyweight boxing champion. Flamboyant and powerful, Johnson came to symbolize the black "menace" to white society, and his celebrated prowess produced a swell in racist reaction as well as black pride.

In the twentieth century, boxing has also been an avenue of upward mobility for newly arrived ethnic groups in the United States. As new waves of immigrants came to the United States, it was through boxing, especially at the lower-weight classes, that ethnic succession patterns were established. At the turn of the last century, the great lightweight boxers were Italian and Irish; by the 1920s and 1930s, they were largely Jewish. Black lightweight fighters replaced Jewish boxers in the 1940s, and by the 1950s, it was Puerto Ricans who claimed the titles. The post–World War II era has witnessed a succession of Latin and Central American fighters, who now vie with Southeast Asians for flyweight and bantamweight titles.

Boxing has also generated its share of controversy over the years, as evidence of corruption and the involvement of organized crime was coupled with periodic moral outcries against the brutality of the sport and the occasionally lethal boxing match, such as the death of Benny "The Kid" Paret in 1962 and Ray "Boom Boom" Mancini's lethal beating of Duk Koo Kim in 1982.

On 24 March 1962, Paret met Emile Griffith for the third time for the welterweight championship. (They had split the earlier meetings.) At the weigh-in Paret made derisive remarks about Griffith and his manhood. In the twelfth round, Griffith backed Paret into a corner and hit him with a series of hooks and uppercuts. Paret was hanging defenseless on the ropes, and by the time the referee, Ruby Goldstein, intervened, Paret slumped to the canvas. He never regained consciousness, but lapsed into a coma and died ten days later.

On 13 November 1982, Mancini met South Korean challenger Duk Koo Kim. Kim had to lose several pounds before the fight and was dehydrated. By fight time, Kim was already weakened; during the fourteen rounds of the fight, Kim sustained brain injuries that led to his death five days later. (Mancini went to the funeral in South Korea, but he fell into a deep depression afterward.)

Professional boxing continues to attract large audiences, at least for heavyweight bouts, in part because of the continued excitement generated by some of the sport's most successful and controversial characters, such as Mike Tyson, a fierce fighter who was twice convicted of date rape and bit off part of the ear of an opponent in a 1996 bout. Muhammed Ali, perhaps the greatest fighter who ever lived, is also the most recognized person on the planet, having brought boxing to Africa and become an ambassador for sports and humanitarian causes worldwide.

Boxing has also been the subject of several notable films including *On the Waterfront* (1954), in which organized crime's control of the unions is challenged by a former boxer whose career had been cut short because the mob had fixed one of his fights; *Rocky* (1976), a film that celebrates the success of a journeyman working-class Italian boxer named Rocky Balboa against incredible odds; and *Raging Bull* (1980), the story of Jake LaMotta, one of the most vicious punchers in the sport's history.

Alternately vilified by moral crusaders as a brutal, murderous, blood sport and celebrated by writers like Norman Mailer and Joyce Carol Oates as somehow more authentic in its violence, boxing remains a troubling masculinizing sport, one that is simultane-

ously hard to watch and from which it is also impossible to turn away.

Michael Kimmel

See also Stallone, Sylvester
Further Reading:
Gorn, Elliott. 1986. *The Manly Art: Bare-Knuckle Prize Fighting in America.* Ithaca, NY: Cornell University Press.
Kimmel, Michael. 1996. *Manhood in America.* New York: Free Press.
Oates, Joyce Carol. 1995. *On Boxing.* New York: Ecco Pren.

Boy Scouts

The Boy Scouts, an organized youth movement for boys, was created in the first decade of the twentieth century by men in England and in the United States in response to what they perceived as a "crisis" in white, middle-class masculinity. Lord Robert Baden-Powell, a military hero of the Boer War (1899–1902), created the movement by that name in 1908, but his organization and the Boy Scouts of America (BSA), founded in 1910, inherited philosophies, programs, and personnel from late-nineteenth-century organizations, such as the Young Men's Christian Association (YMCA). The BSA has been an enormously successful organization, especially among middle-class adolescents. On 4 April 2000, the BSA registered its 100 millionth member since its founding.

Many forces in the closing decades of the nineteenth century contributed to the sense that white, middle-class masculinity was in crisis. Social Darwinism suggested that one of the costs of modern, evolved society was a loss of men's connections with their more natural, primitive condition, and that the effect of modern society was to "soften" and otherwise feminize the male. The increasing split between public and privates spheres of life, and the increasing influence of women in the domestic sphere and in public school teaching, contributed to this sense that boys were being feminized. People also feared that urban living decreased the physical activity and fitness of boys and men; indeed, Lord

Baden-Powell created the Boy Scouts out of his experience with "unfit" men under his command. In the United States, increased immigration brought to city streets large numbers of unruly children in need of Americanization. Severe economic cycles in the 1880s and 1890s created enormous uncertainty in the lives of middle-class men and their families. The cumulative effect of these forces in the United States was to create a climate for the rise of movements and organizations meant to revitalize American youth. A fundamental principle of these movements was called "muscular Christianity," the notion that training the boy's body and his moral character amounted to the same project.

The men who founded the BSA borrowed heavily from Lord Baden-Powell's ideas, but they also "Americanized" the movement. Ernest Thomson Seton brought to the movement and to his writing of large sections of the first *Handbook for Boys* (1911) his experience creating the "Woodcraft Indians" (1903); Daniel Carter Beard brought ideas from his "Sons of Daniel Boone" (1905), based on pioneer life; and Edgard M. Robinson, John L. Alexander, and James E. West brought their organizational and program experiences working with the YMCA. The BSA obtained a charter from Congress in 1916, assuring the organization's claim to the name and positioning it to become the most powerful and widespread organization for socializing boys.

The BSA credits the "patrol idea" for the success of its programs. The patrol of eight boys is the primary friendship group for the boy in a larger "troop." The boy cooperates in projects with his patrol, often hikes and camps with them, and might have his first leadership experience in the patrol. Troops usually have sponsors, such as schools, religious congregations, or fraternal societies, which provide meeting space and other support (often financial). With few exceptions, leaders in the Boy Scouts are male. The Cub Scouts, created for boys eight to ten years of age (the Boy Scouts is for boys eleven to seventeen), follows the organizational idea of smaller 'dens' (with "den mothers") and a larger "pack," usually led by a male. The BSA has experimented with various coeducational programs for adolescent males and females aged fourteen through seventeen, but these programs always struggle with the competition from other activities that lure the high school teenager away from scouting.

In the BSA boys learn skills and demonstrate physical and mental competence to earn badges and ranks, including the pinnacle achievement, that of Eagle Scout. The BSA aims to train boys for leadership, and character training has always been a highly visible goal of the organization. The issue of "character training" brought the BSA into the public spotlight in the 1980s and 1990s, as the "culture wars" pitted social progressives and conservatives against each other. Conflicting understandings of masculinity were an issue in the culture wars, as forces similar to those at the end of the nineteenth century created another masculinity crisis at the end of the twentieth. By the 1980s the BSA was targeted by lawsuits concerning "the three Gs"—that is, God, girls, and gays. Atheists denied membership in the BSA claimed discrimination, as did girls and gay boys and men. Symptomatic of the masculinity crisis of the 1990s, the most highly visible court cases concerned the right of the BSA to exclude openly gay boys and men. With conflicting decisions from two state supreme courts (California and New Jersey), the United States Supreme Court announced on 28 June 2000 its split (5–4) decision affirming the right of the BSA, as a private organization, to exclude from membership those people whose values and behaviors conflict with the official philosophy and goals of the organization. The controversy continued in the wake of that decision, as local governments and charitable organizations (e.g., the United Way) struggled with conflicts between their own nondiscrimination rules and practices favoring local Boy Scout organizations. Meanwhile, Scouting for All and other social movement organizations worked to persuade the BSA to change its policies voluntarily. Many troops continue resisting into the 2000s the national BSA policies on matters of membership for atheists and gays, sometimes openly and sometimes covertly.

With about 4 million members in 2001, the BSA remains an important institution for the socialization of boys and young men. The 1990s saw a rise in newspaper, magazine, and television news stories about threats to boys or about boys as threats to others (e.g., the Columbine High School and similar shootings). Numerous advice books in the 1990s, such as William Pollack's *Real Boys* (1998), addressed parents, teachers, athletic coaches, Scoutmasters, social workers, counselors, and others who work with preadolescent and adolescent boys, offering analysis and advice about the modern crisis in American "boyhood." The BSA's 1990s recruiting slogan, "Character Counts," was part of its effort to join this public debate and to offer a solution based in traditional notions of manhood and masculinity.

Jay Mechling

See also Baden-Powell, Robert Stephenson Smyth; Thompson-Seton, Ernest

Further Reading:

Boy Scouts of America website. At http://www. bsa.scouting.org (cited 31 December 2001).

Hunter, James Davison. 1991. *Culture Wars: The Struggle to Define America.* New York: Basic Books.

———. 2000. *The Death of Character: Moral Education in an Age without Good or Evil.* New York: Basic Books.

Macleod, David I. 1983. *Building Character in the American Boy: The Boy Scouts, YMCA, and Their Forerunners, 1870–1920.* Madison, WI: University of Wisconsin Press.

Mechling, Jay. 2001. *Boy Scouts and the Making of American Youth.* Chicago: University of Chicago Press.

Pollack, William. 1998. *Real Boys: Rescuing Our Sons from the Myths of Boyhood.* New York: Holt.

Rosenthal, Michael. 1986. *The Character Factory: Baden-Powell and the Origins of the Boy Scout Movement.* New York: Pantheon Books.

Scouting for All website. At http://scoutingforall.org (cited 31 December 2001).

Boyhood

Boyhood is often romanticized as a time of carefree play, a happy time free of pressures and responsibilities. It may be, but it is also a time when young males come to understand the meaning of manhood and the expectations that they will live up to its "code." According to this code of masculinity, boys must learn:

1. To be independent and self-reliant.
2. To not express their emotions (particularly those that show vulnerability or their attachment to another person).
3. To be tough and aggressive.
4. To seek high social status.
5. To always be ready for sex.
6. To avoid all things "feminine" lest there be any confusion about their masculinity.
7. To reject homosexuality.

This is quite a demanding set of behaviors, at once stoic and heroic.

Although the code is waning, it still holds sway and, in fact, profoundly affects how our sons are raised. It is interesting that the code is more strongly endorsed by males than females and shows differential endorsement in different ethnocultural subgroups in our society. Nonetheless, we all get caught up in the code, whether we explicitly endorse it ourselves, carry it as a set of unexamined assumptions, or have it forced on us by others (e.g., our spouses, other children acting on their parents' views, teachers, coaches, or the culture at large). The net result is that it has a profound influence on the shaping of our boys' emotional lives.

From their earliest development, boys must confront emotionality. Although boys start out more emotionally expressive than girls, they wind up much less so due to their socialization by parents and peers. This emotional socialization process is aimed at curbing boys' expression and ultimately their awareness of both their caring and connecting emotions (such as affection, fondness, etc.) and their vulnerable emotions (like fear, sadness, etc.). However, anger and aggression are permitted and even encouraged.

One of the more interesting biological differences is that boys seem to be more emotional than girls at birth and remain so until at least one year of age. A review of twelve studies (eleven of which were of neonates just hours after birth) found that boys cry more often and more intensely, but that they also coo, gurgle, and smile more often, and that they fluctuate more rapidly between emotional states than girls. Another study found that infant boys were judged to be more emotionally expressive than were infant girls, even when the judges were misinformed about the infants' actual sex, thus controlling for the effects of gender-role stereotyping on the part of judges. Finally, boys remain more emotional than girls at least until six months of age, exhibiting more joy and anger, more positive vocalizations, fussiness, and crying, and more gestural signals directed towards the mother than girls (Cunningham and Shapiro 1984, cited in Brody and Hall 1993; Haviland and Malatesta 1981; Weinbeg 1992).

Despite this initial advantage in emotional expressivity, boys learn to tune out, suppress, and channel their emotions, whereas the emotional development of girls encourages their expressivity. These effects become evident with respect to verbal expression by two years of age and facial expression by six years. One study found that two-year-old females refer to feeling states more frequently than do two-year-old males. Another assessed the ability of mothers of four- to six-year-old boys and girls to accurately identify their child's emotional responses to a series of slides by observing their child's facial expressions on a TV monitor. The older the boy, the less expressive his face, and the harder it was for his mother to tell what he was feeling. This researcher found no such correlation among the girls: Their mothers were able to identify their emotions no matter what their age. The author concluded that between the ages of four and six "boys apparently inhibit

and mask their overt response to emotion to an increasing extent, while girls continue to respond relatively freely"(Buck 1977; Dunn, Bretherton, and Munn 1987).

What would account for this "crossover in emotional expression" such that boys start out more emotional than girls and wind up much less so? The socialization influences of mother, father, and peer group combine to result in the suppression and channeling of male needs and emotions and the encouragement of female emotionality. These influences are wrought through: (1) selective reinforcement, modeling, and direct teaching of desired behavior; (2) the different kinds of experiences that boys and girls have with parents and peers; and (3) punishment for breaking the code of masculinity.

In their children's infancy, mothers work harder to manage their more excitable and emotional males. They smile more when their sons are calm, thus reinforcing calm, inexpressive behavior. In fact, mothers may go to special lengths to ensure that their sons are contented. Mothers also control their own emotional expressivity to avoid upsetting their sons' more fragile emotional equilibrium. In contrast, mothers expose their infant daughters to a wider range of emotions than they do their sons.

In the toddler years, fathers take an active interest in their children. This begins in the thirteenth month of life, and from that point on fathers tend to interact with their toddler sons and daughters along gender-stereotyped lines. Fathers interact more with infant sons than they do with daughters. With older children, fathers engage in more verbal roughhousing with sons and tend to speak more about emotions with daughters. Fathers also express more disapproval to sons who violate the code of masculinity by engaging in doll play or expressing emotions such as neediness, vulnerability, and even attachment. Many adult men that I have counseled recall experiences in which their fathers made them feel deeply ashamed of themselves for expressing vulnerable emotions such as sadness or fear, or attachment emotions such as caring, warmth, or affection.

Both parents participate in the development of language for emotions, which is differentiated along the lines of gender. Parents discourage their sons from learning to express vulnerable emotions. And, while they encourage their daughters to express their vulnerable and attachment emotions, they discourage their expression of anger and aggression. It should be noted that females' language superiority also plays a role in their greater ability to express emotions verbally. One investigative team found that mothers used more emotion words when speaking with daughters than they did with sons. Another found that mothers spoke more about sadness with daughters than sons and only spoke about anger with sons. With daughters, mothers discussed the experience of the emotion, whereas with sons they discussed the causes and consequences of emotions, which would serve to help sons learn to control their emotions. A third study had parents "read" stories to their children using wordless books and videotaped and transcribed their conversations. Mothers talked about anger twice as frequently with sons as compared to daughters. Finally, another team of researchers found that school-aged sons expected their parents to react negatively to the expression of sadness, whereas school-aged daughters expected their mothers to react more positively to the expression of sadness than they would to anger (Brody and Hall 1993; Dunn et al. 1987; Fivush 1989; Fuchs and Thelen 1988; Greif et al. 1981).

Sex-segregated peer groups complete the job. Young girls typically play with one or two other girls, and their play consists of maintaining the relationship (by minimizing conflict and hostility and maximizing agreement and cooperation) and telling each other secrets, thus providing experiences that foster learning skills of empathy, emotional self-awareness, and emotional expressivity. In contrast, young boys typically play in larger groups in structured games—experiences in which

skills such as learning to play by the rules, teamwork, stoicism, toughness, and competition are honed. A study found that boys experience direct competition in their play half of the time, whereas girls experience it very infrequently (less than 1 percent of the time). Boy culture is also notoriously cruel to boys who violate male role norms, such as expressing vulnerable emotions, showing affection, or being unwilling to fight (Crombie and Desjardins 1993, cited in Brody 1994; Lever 1976; Maccoby 1990; Paley 1984).

Many adult men recall that their first experience with limitations on expressing caring emotions actually occurred in the context of their relationships with their fathers, for, in the typical postwar family, hugs and kisses between father and son came to an end by the time the boy was ready to enter school. In addition to whatever messages boys hear at home, they also get the message from their peers that it is not socially acceptable to be affectionate with their mothers (lest they be a "mama's boy"), girls (for fear of being teased by friends), or boys (where anything but a cool, buddy-type relationship with another boy can give rise to the dreaded accusation of homosexuality). Childhood experiences of this type set up powerful barriers to the overt expression of attachment and caring emotions, which thus get suppressed.

Through a similar process boys become ashamed of expressing vulnerable emotions such as fear, sadness, loneliness, or hurt, so that they lose touch with their ability to express these emotions as well. On the other hand boys are allowed to feel and become aware of emotions in the anger and rage part of the spectrum, as prescribed in the toughness dimension of the male code. As a result, males express anger more aggressively than do females. The aggressive expression of anger is, in fact, one of the very few ways boys are encouraged to express emotion, and as a consequence, the outlawed vulnerable emotions, such as hurt, disappointment, fear, and shame, get funneled into the anger channel. This has been called "the male emotional funnel system," the final common pathway for all those shameful vulnerable emotions that are too unmanly to express directly. Some boys learn to actively transform these vulnerable emotions into anger, rage, and aggression, as when a boy is pushed down on the play ground and knows that he is expected to come back up with a fist full of gravel rather than a face full of tears. This facility to transform vulnerable emotions into aggression is learned in boy culture and accounts for the fact that many adult men get angry when their feelings are hurt. It may also have played a role in school killings in the 1990s by adolescent boys in Jonesboro (Arkansas), Pearl (Mississippi), and Paducah (Kentucky).

These socialization experiences not only prevent boys from being able to express a wide band of the spectrum of human emotions, but also make them feel very ashamed of themselves for even having these emotions. Because aggression is encouraged, it becomes boys' only outlet and as a result becomes overdeveloped.

This creates a tremendous burden for boys who come to feel that parts of themselves are unacceptable and even shameful and that they dare not let others see these parts of themselves. Hence, boyhood socialization puts boys at odds with parts of themselves and cuts them off from other people, thus creating low self-esteem and a self-imposed isolation. Although this isolation is socially-sanctioned, it is also destructive because boys have many needs and feel many vulnerable and caring emotions. Thus boys must live a lie and learn to deaden themselves to it.

Ronald F. Levant

Further Reading:

Brody, Leslie. 1994. "Gender, Emotional Expression, and Parent-Child Boundaries." In *Emotion: Interdisciplinary Perspectives.* Edited by Robert Kavanaugh, Betty Zimmerberg-Glick, and Steven Fein. Mahwah, NJ: Lawrence Erlbaum.

Brody, Leslie, and Judith Hall. 1993. "Gender and Emotion." In *Handbook of Emotions.* Edited by Michael Lewis and J. M. Haviland. New York: Guilford.

Brooks, Gary R. 1995. *The Centerfold Syndrome.* San Francisco: Jossey-Bass.

Buck, Ross. 1977. "Non-Verbal Communication of Affect in Preschool Children: Relationships with Personality and Skin Conductance." *Journal of Personality and Social Psychology* 35, no. 4: 225–236.

Campbell, Anne. 1993. *Men, Women and Aggression.* New York: Basic Books.

Dunn, Judy, Inge Bretherton, and Penny Munn. 1987. "Conversations about Feeling States between Mothers and Their Children." *Developmental Psychology* 23: 132–139.

Fivush, Robyn. 1989. "Exploring Sex Differences in the Emotional Content of Mother Child Conversations about the Past." *Sex Roles* 20: 675–691.

Fuchs, Dayna, and Mark Thelen. 1988. "Children's Expected Interpersonal Consequences of Communicating Their Affective State and Reported Likelihood of Expression." *Child Development* 59: 1314–1322.

Garbarino, James. 1999. *Lost Boys: How Our Sons Turn Violent and How We Can Save Them.* New York: Free Press.

Gilmore, David D. 1990. *Manhood in the Making: Cultural Concepts of Masculinity.* New Haven, CT: Yale University Press.

Greif, Esther B., Mildred Alvarez, and Kathleen Ulman. 1981. "Recognizing Emotions in Other People: Sex Differences in Socialization." (Paper presented at meeting of the Society for Research in Child Development. April. Boston, MA).

Haviland, Jeannette J., and Carol Z. Malatesta. 1981. "The Development of Sex Differences in Nonverbal Signals: Fallacies, Facts, and Fantasies." In *Gender and Non-Verbal Behavior.* Edited by Clara Mayo and Nancy M. Henly. New York: Springer-Verlag.

Horne, Arthur M., and Mark S. Kiselica, eds. 1999. *Handbook of Counseling Boys and Adolescent Males.* Thousand Oaks, CA: Sage.

Kimmel, Michael S. 2000. *The Gendered Society.* New York: Oxford University Press.

Levant, Ronald F., and Gini Kopecky. 1995. *Masculinity Reconstructed.* New York: Dutton.

Levant, Ronald F., and William S. Pollack, eds. 1995. *A New Psychology of Men.* New York: Basic Books.

Lever, Janet. 1976. "Sex Differences in the Games Children Play." *Social Work* 23, no. 4: 78–87.

Maccoby, Eleanor. E. 1990. "Gender and Relationships: A Developmental Account." *American Psychologist* 45: 513–520.

Paley, Vivian G. 1984. *Boys and Girls: Superheroes in the Doll Corner.* Chicago: University of Chicago Press.

Pleck, Joseph H. 1981. *The Myth of Masculinity.* Cambridge, MA: MIT Press.

Pollack, William S. 1998. *Real Boys: Rescuing Our Sons from the Myths of Boyhood.* New York: Random House.

Weinberg, Martha K. 1992. "Sex Differences in 6-Month-Old Infants' Affect and Behavior: Impact on Maternal Caregiving." (Doctoral dissertation, University of Massachusetts).

Boys' Book

A tradition of adventure fiction that flourished throughout the nineteenth century in Great Britain and the United States has been termed the boys' book. Popular authors in this genre included R. M. Ballantyne, H. Rider Haggard, G. A. Henty, W. H. G. Kingston, Oliver Optic, Captain Mayne Reid, Gordon Stables, and Robert Louis Stevenson. Periodicals like *The Boys' Own Paper* also published additional stimulating tales; the Religious Tract Society and the Society for the Promotion of Christian Knowledge published adventure stories that were often given as prize books in schools for good behavior, attendance, or scholastic merit. In their plots and characters, these books encouraged the values of industry, godliness, pluck, bravery, patriotism, attention to duty, and loyalty.

Castaway tales in the tradition of Daniel Defoe's *Robinson Crusoe* (1719) spawned a host of imitators or "Robinsonades" like Johann Wyss's *Swiss Family Robinson* (1812), Fredrick Marryat's *Masterman Ready* (1841), and R. M. Ballantyne's *The Coral Island* (1858), which proved popular with child readers. Outwitting cannibals, learning to survive in the wild, subduing wildlife, reproducing civilization's amenities, learning to do without luxuries, and strengthening religious faith are common plot elements.

Adventures at sea aboard merchant ships, fishing vessels, or in the naval service formed another favorite boys' book genre. Hunting for enemies, treasure, or animals, Marryat's *Mr.* *Midshipman Easy* (1836), R. L. Stevenson's *Treasure Island* (1883), Rudyard Kipling's *Captains Courageous* (1897), and Jack London's *The Sea Wolf* (1904) are typical examples of this genre. Sea stories often included obligatory storms or encounters with enemies like pirates, smugglers, or other nations' navies, while demonstrating the improving influence that a ship's discipline had on a boy's character.

In addition to castaway and sea narratives, other favorites in this genre included tales of exploration like Ballantyne's *The Gorilla Hunters* (1861) or Arthur Conan Doyle's *The Lost World* (1912), narratives about the jungle wilderness like Kipling's *The Jungle Book* (1894) and Edgar Rice Burroughs's *Tarzan of the Apes* (1912), or stories of political-military intrigue that dealt with a soldier's life in the service of empire, such as G. A. Henty's *One of the 28th* (1890). In America James Fenimore Cooper's *Leatherstocking Tales* and London's Alaskan narratives *The Call of the Wild* (1903) and *White Fang* (1906) characterized the American frontier as a place of peril and excitement by depicting encounters with warlike Native Americans and dangerous wild animals.

Some boys' books hearkened to a romantic medieval English past in which chivalrous knights rode to the rescue; Sir Walter Scott's *Ivanhoe* (1819) is the most famous example, but Robert Louis Stevenson's *The Black Arrow* (1888), set during the War of the Roses, follows this model as well. School stories like Thomas Hughes's *Tom Brown's Schooldays* (1857) or Kipling's *Stalky & Co.* (1899) were also popular with boy readers, along with old favorites like the various translations of *The Arabian Nights*. The genre of the boys' book began to wane in the twentieth century, with works like William Golding's dour *The Lord of the Flies* (1954), which painted boy culture in a grim light. The gendered split in reading preferences began to disappear as a more generalized "children's literature" became institutionalized. Narratives like J. R. R. Tolkein's *The Hobbit* and *The Lord of the Rings,* and C. S. Lewis's *The Lion, The Witch, and the Wardrobe* (1950) and subsequent *Narnia*

Chronicles, however, demonstrate the evolution of the boys' book genre into fantasy and science fiction tales.

Megan A. Norcia

See also *Lord of the Flies*

Further Reading:

Bristow, Joseph. 1991. *Empire's Boys: Adventures in a Man's World.* London: Unwin Hyman.

Fraser, Robert. 1998. *The Victorian Quest Romance: Stevenson, Haggard, Kipling, and Conan Doyle.* Oxford: University Press of Mississippi.

Green, Martin. 1979. *Dreams of Adventure, Deeds of Empire.* London: Marboro Books.

Phillips, Richard. 1997. *Mapping Men and Empire.* London: Routledge.

Brando, Marlon (1924–)

Born in Omaha, Nebraska, Marlon Brando graduated from the Dramatic Workshop of the New School for Social Research, directed by German director Erwin Piscator. Brando owes a debt to director Elia Kazan, the co-founder of New York Actors' Studio, who hired the actor in 1947 for a stage production of *A Streetcar Named Desire.* Four years later, Kazan directed a film adaptation of Tennessee Williams's play, with Brando again, that was unforgettable (*A Streetcar Named Desire,* 1951). They worked together on two subsequent Kazan movies: *Viva Zapata* (1952) and *On the Waterfront* (1954), in which Brando played a young dock worker who becomes an informer to denounce a gang. Released during the McCarthy era, the film received awards and was highly praised.

As an actor, Brando displays the quintessential style of the formula taught at the New York Actors' Studio: sullen, introverted, rebellious, and savage. In the early 1950s, Brando brought a new type of "bad guy" to the screen, different from those played by the usual suspects of the day, such as Edward G. Robinson, Peter Lorre, or Humphrey Bogart. He was younger, handsomer, and instinctive, but didn't say long lines and didn't sustain long conversations, which were usual then in Hollywood movies. Brando could mumble and the producers accepted it as "natural."

Perhaps the most durable character played by Marlon Brando in his early career was *The Wild One* (L. Benedek, 1953). Here, Brando played a rebellious young bum, the leader of a gang in competition with another gang of delinquents. Even if the offenders are penalized at the end, they still dominate the small town, unpunished, during most of the film. The famous poster showing Brando on his motorcycle, wearing a black leather jacket, was the romantic inspiration for many generations of riders, even after Denis Hopper's *Easy Rider* (1969). From the early 1950s, a whole generation recognized itself in Brando; he was only eclipsed by James Dean. During the 1960s, Brando played in various genres, from westerns to drama, without much success. Even his presence *à contre emploi* in Charles Chaplin's *Countess from Hong Kong* (1966) was not the best choice, mainly because Brando didn't fit the role and couldn't play comedy.

The older Brando played Vito Corleone in the movie *The Godfather* (1972) by F. F. Coppola, but Bernardo Bertolucci got more visibility by deconstructing the Brando myth in the provocative *Last Tango in Paris* (1973). The story was a torrid love affair between a beautiful French woman and an old tormented widower, who both agreed not to mention their names or personal stories. The nude scenes were raw and scandalous: Brando asked for a body double for the scene when he had to sodomize the actress Maria Schneider.

For the last thirty years into the 2000s, Brando lives only by the legend created around his first movies. He definitely is a celebrity: People talk about his private life, his opinions, his personal myth, but no longer about his current artistic work. In any other country, he would have long been forgotten. His roles in *Missouri Breaks* (1976) and *Apocalypse Now!* (1979) are minimal but somewhat impressive. Maybe only five of the some forty films he played in are worth seeing again. Retrospectively, Brando needed a great director in order to give the best of himself. Nevertheless, he has inspired many generations of actors in his country, from James Dean and Steve McQueen to Dustin Hoffman and Robert De Niro.

Yves Laberge

Further Reading:

Frome, Shelley. 2001. *The Actors Studio: A History.* New York: McFarland.

Grobel, Lawrence. 1999. *Conversations with Brando.* Lanham, MD: Rowman and Littlefield.

Kazan, Elia. 1997. *Elia Kazan: A Life.* New York: Da Capo Press.

Thomson, David. 2003. *Marlon Brando.* New York, DK Publishing, A&E Biographies.

Bravado

As they live their lives, boys negotiate with the social customs, rules, and opportunities of their societies. They make choices about the direction of their lives within a framework of possibility and constraint, what they might achieve, and what they cannot imagine attempting. This framework varies by society and by historical period but, as Gilmore (1990) found, "pressured masculinity" has been the norm among vastly different societies. His research detailed how boys everywhere are confronted with a necessity to prove themselves worthy for manhood, in customs both formal and constant.

Among these pressures, boys confront ubiquitous violence and threat. In the United States, practically every boy experiences fighting and bullying; most experience both roles, as victim and as perpetrator (Gelles and Strauss 1988; Trickett and Schellenbach 1998; Bloom and Reichert 1998). As a result, many develop a studied, public attitude of toughness, a show of willingness to face danger and to take risks. This public face of bravado, understood as an "ostentatious display of courage or boldness" or "action intended to intimidate" (*Oxford English Dictionary* Online 2002) represents a common construction for boys' identities. Acting brave, representing oneself as unafraid, posturing threateningly, and other such "signifiers of masculinity" develop in the context

of boyhood, where "the capacity to commit violence is one of the most essentialized attributes of dominant forms of masculinity" (Mills 2001, 19). If courage is an inward reckoning, a determined decision to do what needs to be done, an attitude of bravado is an outward look, a style for being male. While such a public face may belie an inner uncertainty, even fear, as Canada (1998) has suggested, it can also offer protection from victimization and propel boys through situations that might otherwise be paralyzing.

Boyhood is confusing: At the same time as boys' lives can be dominated by pressuring norms, they also benefit from systems of gender relations that offer them privilege relative to the lives of girls. This "strange combination of power and powerlessness, privilege and pain" (Kaufman 1994, 142) seems designed to remind boys, in the manner of a carrot and stick, of the dangers they will face should they stray from the prescribed path for masculine identity. Whether or not a boy feels brave or inclined toward competition, risk taking, aggressive self-assertion, or dominance seeking, he comes to appreciate that the disavowal of such behaviors can marginalize him. And life at boyhood's margins can be hazardous. Boys learn, essentially, that there is no escape from their birthright as males. "Boyhood," writes sociologist Michael Kimmel in a recent introduction to a book on the subject, "is the entitlement to and anticipation of power" (Foster et al. 2001, 16).

Bravado, then, at what cost? On a personal level, boys, who may be biologically predisposed to risk taking, can lose judgement and become self-deluded amidst the incitements of performative masculinity. Research on differences in health outcomes have attributed higher mortality rates for males in nine of the ten top causes of death to "male socialization," particularly to the acceptance of violence and threat as part of life (Stillion 1995). In this sense, boys learn soldiering and sacrifice not from their genes but from social cues that are present at birth and define the bounds of imagination for being a boy. On an emotional level, boys learn to dissociate personal from public to the extent that they can exhibit what some theorists characterize as "alexithymia," so complete is the separation of behavior from sense of self (Levant 1995). Boys can become personally cut off from the very ability to recover from hurts or debrief from a personal trauma (Real 1997), and in relationships, deficits in expressive skills lie at the heart of many explanations of male dysfunction (Bergman 1995; Gottman 1999).

On a broader social level, the requirement that boys act with aggressiveness, dominance, and courage can contribute to the kind of social scripts that must be unlearned in violence-reduction programs in schools (Olweus 1993) and communities (Kivel 1992; Denborough 1996). Once boys' connections with a personal self, as well as their empathic bonds to others, are subordinated to social dictates of bravado, there is no real limit to what damage males can do (Garbarino 1999; Hearn 1998; Bowker 1998).

Michael C. Reichert

Further Reading:

Bergman, S. J. 1995. "Men's Psychological Development: A Relational Perspective. Pp. 69–91 in *A New Psychology of Men*. Edited by R. F. Levant and W. S. Pollack. New York: Basic Books.

Bloom, S. L., and M. Reichert. 1998. *Bearing Witness: Violence and Collective Responsibility*. New York: Haworth.

Bowker, L. F., ed. 1998. *Masculinities and Violence*. Thousand Oaks, CA: Sage.

Canada, G. 1998. *Reaching Up for Manhood*. Boston: Beacon Press.

Denborough, D. 1996. "Step by Step: Developing Respectful and Effective Ways of Working with Young Men to Reduce Violence." Pp. 91–117 in *Men's Ways of Being*. Edited by C. McLean, M. Carey, and C. White. Boulder, CO: Westview Press.

Foster, V., M. Kimmel, and C. Skelton. 2001. "'What about the Boys?': An Overview of the Debates." In *What about the Boys?* Edited by W. Martino and B. Meyenn. Buckingham, UK: Open University Press.

Garbarino, J. 1999. *Lost Boys*. New York: Free Press.

Gelles, R. J., and M. A. Strauss. 1988. *Intimate Violence*. New York: Touchstone.

Gilmore, D. G. 1990. *Manhood in the Making*. New Haven, CT: Yale University Press.

Gottman, J. M. 1999. *The Seven Principles for Making Marriage Work*. New York: Crown.

Hearn, J. 1998. *The Violences of Men*. London: Sage.

Kaufman, M. 1994. "Men, Feminism and Men's Contradictory Experiences of Power." Pp. 142–164 in *Theorizing Masculinities*. Edited by H. Brod and M. Kaufman. Thousand Oaks, CA: Sage.

Kivel, P. 1992. *Men's Work*. New York: Ballantine Books.

Levant, R. F. 1995. "Toward a Reconstruction of Masculinity." In *A New Psychology of Men*. Edited by R. F. Levant and W. S. Pollack. New York: Basic Books.

Mills, M. 2001. *Challenging Violence in Schools*. Buckingham, UK: Open University Press.

Olweus, D. 1993. *Bullying at School*. Oxford, UK: Blackwell.

Real, T. 1997. *I Don't Want to Talk about It*. New York: Fireside.

Stillion, J. M. 1995. "Premature Death among Males." Pp. 46–67 in D. Sabo and D. F. Gordon. *Men's Health and Illness*. Thousand Oaks, CA: Sage.

Trickett, P. K., and C. J. Schellenbach. 1998. *Violence against Children in the Family and the Community*. Washington, DC: American Psychological Association.

Breadwinner

The "breadwinner" in a family is the person who provides the bulk of the material resources for the family's survival. The notion of the breadwinner sometimes also entails more than simply providing material resources; it also implies more general protection of other family members, meeting family members' needs in a variety of ways. The breadwinner role is typically associated with men. Indeed, sociologist Jessie Bernard wrote about the male role as the "good provider"—equating maleness with breadwinning.

The breadwinner role became a distinct family role with the transition from subsistence to market economies. Economic production shifted from household based to market based. In the process, breadwinning became distinguished from homemaking. Breadwinning is paid work, done in the public sphere; homemaking is unpaid work relegated to the private sphere. Breadwinning is valued and respected, while homemaking is devalued.

Prior to the Industrial Revolution, families supported themselves through a wide variety of economic activities, involving most members of the family. Although some tasks were assigned to men and others to women, both men and women contributed to the sustenance of the family. Production was centered in or near the home, and everyone in the family was involved in some way or another. After the Industrial Revolution, economic production moved away from the home and into factories, shops, and then offices. The breadwinner role came to be held primarily by men, at least within middle- and upper-class families.

In societies at the turn of the twenty-first century, the traditional family image of a male breadwinner and a stay-at-home mother represents only a small minority of families. More often than not, men and women share breadwinning responsibilities, though they may not contribute equal financial amounts to the family. Increases in single parenthood have resulted in women becoming a growing proportion of breadwinners. Changes in breadwinner roles have been accompanied by change in conceptions of fatherhood, the division of household labor, and marital satisfaction.

Although societal demands for men to be "good providers" have shifted over the last decades of the twentieth century, there is still a great deal of pressure for men to fulfill the breadwinner expectations into the twenty-first. Being the breadwinner, or good provider, continues to be seen as the most important aspect of men's family responsibilities. Even with contemporary changes in family structure, the breadwinner role has tremendous consequences for men's perceptions of themselves both within the home and in the workplace. Lillian Rubin's (1994) work on the effects of deindustrialization on working-class families illustrates the centrality of breadwinning for men's sense of themselves as men. She quotes an unemployed machinist who says, "It's not just the income; you lose a lot more than that. . . . When you get laid off, it's like you lose a part of yourself" (quoted in Rubin 1994, 110). When wages are critical for enacting the breadwinning role, decreasing real wages make it difficult for men to feel as if they are doing what they should to provide for their families. And when employment is equated with masculinity, unemployment has significant ramifications for men's mental and physical health, as well as for relationships.

Beth Rushing

See also Family; Work

Further Reading:

Bernard, Jessie. 1981. "The Good Provider Role." *American Psychologist* 36: 1–12.

Christiansen, Shawn L., and Rob Palkovitz. 2001. "Why the 'Good Provider' Role Still Matters" *Journal of Family Issues* 22: 84–106.

Coltrane, Scott. 1996. *Family Man.* New York: Oxford University Press.

Faludi, Susan. 2000. *Stiffed: The Betrayal of the American Man.* New York: Perennial.

Rubin, Lillian B. 1994. *Families on the Fault Line.* New York: Harper.

Breastfeeding

Breastfeeding has been deemed the optimal form of infant feeding, yet goals for initiation and duration of breastfeeding set by the U.S. Department of Health and Human Services fail to be met in the twenty-first century, possibly due to the lack of inclusion of fathers. The infant-feeding decision should include both parents and be based on accurate information and good discussion within the couple relationship. Fathers want what is best for their children, but often sabotage breastfeeding when they witness the intimate relationship between mother and infant necessitated by this feeding method. Feelings of jealousy and exclusion are common and often lead the father to encourage termination of breastfeeding. Fathers need to be acknowledged for their key role in the infant-feeding decision, support of breastfeeding, and involvement in parenting, and should be included in education about the advantages of breastfeeding.

Fathers can play a key role in the decision to breastfeed. Men with positive attitudes toward breastfeeding support the initiation and continuation of breastfeeding. Unfortunately, many men lack information on the physiological and psychological benefits of breastfeeding to both the infant and mother. They may feel pushed away from their mates by the interloper at the breast, especially if the breasts have been an important aspect of the couple's intimate relationship. Feelings of jealousy may result in negative effects on the adult couple and father-infant relationships. Such negative feelings may result in the father urging the mother to terminate breastfeeding. Men who are knowledgeable about the benefits of breastfeeding and have positive attitudes toward breastfeeding during pregnancy may be surprised by their negative responses to the realities of breastfeeding: the demands on the mother's time and energy and resentment of the exclusivity of the mother-infant feeding relationship. Breastfeeding may become the scapegoat for the unanticipated realities of caring for a totally dependent infant.

Fathers and families benefit from preparation for the realities of the early stages of parenting. Babies need to be fed every few hours around the clock, regardless of feeding method. If couples do not continue to focus on their own relationship, each partner may resent the relationship of the other to the infant. Fathers benefit from learning that there are meaningful ways to interact with their babies other than feeding. Bottle feeding can interfere with or sabotage breastfeeding. Talking to, playing with, and singing to the baby are important ways for men to interact with their babies. Fathers should be encouraged to have time alone with the baby to develop feelings of confidence and competence as parents. Fathers

are often responsible for the bedtime ritual, including bathing the baby. Feeding the baby may be inaccurately perceived as the most important means of interacting with the baby.

It is helpful to guide men in ways to assist their breastfeeding mate and to help fathers understand the demands of breastfeeding on mothers; breastfeeding is challenging to both parents. Providing such information has been shown to be effective in increasing the rates and duration of breastfeeding, satisfaction with the early stages of parenting, and father involvement in caregiving.

Pamela Jordan

See also Childcare; Reproduction
Further Reading:
Bar-Yam, Naomi Bromberg, and Lori Darby. 1997. "Fathers and Breastfeeding: A Review of the Literature." *Journal of Human Lactation* 13, no. 1: 45–50.

Gamble, Diane, and Janice M. Morse. 1992. "Fathers of Breastfed Infants: Postponing and Types of Involvement." *Journal of Obstetric, Gynecologic, and Neonatal Nursing* 22, no. 4: 358–365.

Jordan, Pamela L., and Virginia R. Wall. 1990. "Breastfeeding and Fathers: Illuminating theDarker Side." *Birth* 17, no. 4: 210–213.

———. 1993. "Supporting the Father When an Infant is Breastfed." *Journal of Human Lactation* 9, no. 1: 31–34.

Bridegrooms

See Grooms

Brown, Charles Brockden (1771–1810)

Charles Brockden Brown is generally considered the first professional author in America. Born into a Quaker family, he studied and briefly practiced law before taking the daring and novel step of venturing not only into writing as a profession, but into imaginative writing, as opposed to the advocacy writing more established and widespread at the time. Writing was not a profession when Brown decided to pursue it; in early America, even the printing trade was a very risky business—expensive to supply and train for, and both legally and culturally very much in flux. Before about the 1830s, printers could not survive by their presses alone. In such a climate, it was virtually impossible to make a living as an author. Yet Brown was dedicated and highly industrious, publishing six novels between 1794 and 1799, editing or acting as the principle writer for several magazines of note, and producing numerous pamphlets, papers, and registers as well.

Brown's most famous novel is his third, *Wieland: or the Transformation* (1798). It is a story of insanity and divine retribution in which the hero's father dies by spontaneous combustion (this apparently the retribution of a higher power). Later, Weiland murders his family and himself. The novel, while at times uneven and improbable, is considered a landmark in the development of the gothic, particularly in its translation from European to American tastes.

In much of his fiction, Brown articulated a far-reaching vision of equality. In his second novel, *Alcuin* (1798), Brown offers a sustained argument for the rights of women. Brown's literary style lies between the epistolary novel popular in the early eighteenth century and the more formal narrative that emerged in the nineteenth. The first two sections of *Alcuin* contain dialogue between a young man (Alcuin) and Mrs. Carter, who lectures her young interlocutor about the position of women. Mrs. Carter claims that she disapproves of the system of marriage because "it renders the female a slave to the man. It enjoins and enforces submission on her part to the will of her husband. It includes a promise of implicit obedience and unalterable affection. Secondly, it leaves the woman destitute of property. Whatever she previously possesses, belongs absolutely to the man" (cited in Kimmel and Mosmiller 1992, 58–59).

In another telling exchange, part of an excerpt that later appeared in *The American*

Charles Brockden Brown (Library of Congress)

Magazine and Literary Register of May 1805, Brown takes up the broader question of women's political exclusion, touching on the total invisibility of women in the American public sphere. Alcuin asks Mrs. Carter about her political views. "Pray, Madam, are you a Foederalist?" he queries. The female speaker answers with the sarcasm of the unduly dispossessed:

"Surely," she replied, "you are in jest. What! Ask a woman, shallow and inexperienced, as all women are known to be, especially with regard to these topics, her opinion on any political question! While I am conscious of being an intelligent moral being; while I see myself denied, in so many cases, the exercise of my own discretion, incapable of separate property; subject in all periods of my life to the will of another, on whose bounty I am made to depend for food and shelter; when I see myself, in my relation to society, regarded merely as a beast, as an insect, passed over, in the distribution of public duties, as absolutely nothing . . . it is impossible I should assent to their opinion, so long as I am conscious of moving and willing. No, I am no Foederalist." (cited in Aronson 2002, 70)

After such critical interrogations of the system of sexual inequality within supposed democracy, Brown's final two sections of *Alcuin* are a late-eighteenth-century version of a guided fanstasy: Alcuin tries to image a world in which women are equal. In the end, forced by the strength of logic, Alcuin retreats, claiming his views on women are based on illogical prejudice, not reason.

Brown's advocacy of women's rights waned later in his career. But even his later novels, like *Ormand* (1799), *Edgar Huntly* (1799), as well as some parts of his first, *Arthur Mervyn* (1794), address themes of sexual politics and women's rights. In *Ormond,* young Constantia is reluctant to marry because, as her friend Sophia recounts it, "Now she was at least mistress of the product of her own labor. Her tasks were toilsome, but the profits, though slender, were sure, and she administered her little property in what manner she pleased. Marriage would annihilate this power. Henceforth she would be bereft even of personal freedom. So far from possessing property, she would become the property of another" (cited in Fleischmann 1983, 117).

Unlike many of his contemporaries, Brown was also sensitive to the consequences that the separation of spheres had for men's lives. Arthur Mervyn's world is one of "failed fathers and ruined families" (Fleischmann 1983, 137), and Edgar Huntly emerges as a pathetic young man who is so consumed with anxiety about his place in the public world of the competitive marketplace that he becomes, as Brown puts it, "a formidable engine of destruction" (Fleischmann 1983, 137). Surely, this is one of the first instances in American literature of a man's insecurity over his masculinity in the public sphere contributing to his propensity for violence.

Amy Aronson

See also John Neal

Further Reading:
Aronson, Amy Beth. 2002. *Taking Liberties: Early American Women's Magazines and Their Readers.* Westport, CT: Praeger.
Bennett, Maurice J. 1987. *An American Tradition: Three Studies: Charles Brockden Brown, Nathaniel Hawthorne, and Henry James.* New York: Garland.
Dunlop, William. 1977. *The Life of Charles Brockden Brown.* St. Clair Shores, MI: Scholarly Press.
Fleischmann, Fritz. 1983. *A Right Views the Subject: Feminism in the Works of Charles Brockden Brown and John Neal.* Erlangen, Germany: Palm and Ende.
Kimmel, Michael, and Thomas E. Mosmiller. 1992. *Against the Tide: Pro-Feminist Men in the United States 1776–1990.* Boston: Beacon Press.
Rosenthan, Bernard. 1975. *Critical Essays on Charles Brockden Brown.* Woodbridge, CT: G. K. Hall.
Watts, Steven. 1994. *The Romance of Real Life: Charles Brockden Brown and the Origins of American Culture.* Baltimore, MD: Johns Hopkins University Press.

Browning, Robert (1812–1889)

Together with Alfred Tennyson, Robert Browning is one of the major English poets of the Victorian era. His long artistic career, which includes drama as well as poetry, started with the publication of 'Pauline' (1833), which was followed by 'Paracelsus' (1835) and the longer 'Sordello' (1840). After this earlier phase in which his verse was permeated by the influence of the Romantics and especially of Shelley, Browning developed a distinct and mature poetic voice. In *Dramatic Lyrics* (1842), *Bells and Pomegranates* (1841–1846), and *Dramatic Romances and Lyrics* (1845) he became a master in the use of the dramatic monologue, a poetic genre in which a speaker, often a real or invented historical character, addresses the reader in the first person, revealing some striking trait of his or her personality. In 1845 Browning eloped with Elizabeth Barrett, probably the most famous woman poet of the age. The Brownings set up house in Italy where they would remain almost uninterruptedly until Elizabeth's death in 1861. In these years Browning published his acclaimed collections *Men and*

Women (1855) and *Dramatis Personae* (1864). The years 1868–1869 saw the creation of *The Ring and the Book*, Browning's most ambitious poetic experiment. Here, through twelve dramatic monologues, he relates the contrasting opinions of the characters involved in a famous seventeenth-century court case. Among Browning's later collections are *Red Cotton Night-Cap Country; or, Turf and Towers* (1873), *Pacchiarotto and How He Worked in Distemper, with Other Poems* (1876), *Dramatic Idyls* (1879), and *Dramatic Idyls: Second Series* (1880). The last book of his verse, *Asolando* (1889), was published on the day of his death.

Browning's verse is characterized by a marked dramatic quality and a vigorous and disjointed style that departed from the poetic conventions of his time. This, and the obscurity of which he was often accused, determined that Browning, who is now unanimously considered one of the most eminent voices in Victorian literature, enjoyed late and comparatively scant fame while still alive. In many of his lyrics Browning shows an interest in extreme states of consciousness, isolation, and psychosis, and in exploring the borderline that separates normality and pathology. He devised the epithet "madhouse cells" to define his lyrics dealing with these subjects. Many of Browning's poems, especially in *Men and Women,* deal with questions of gender and sexuality, the relations between the sexes, and love and marriage; they are celebrations of heterosexual desire based on healthy virility. Some of them expose the dangers of enforced celibacy and sexual repression, especially as encouraged by the Catholic faith. Browning is also interested in cases in which male sexual energy turns into a diseased or murderous force. The early "Porphyria's Lover," for instance, describes the murder of a woman by her lover caused by his desire to possess her fully and forever; the famous "My Last Duchess" tells of the paranoia of an Italian nobleman who had his wife shut up in a convent and possibly killed out of uncontrollable jealousy. Such poems, in which the man/narrator

Robert Browning (Library of Congress)

reenacts his crime in the act of retelling it, seem to plea for an aesthetic justification of extreme sexual violence, forcing the readers into uncomfortable moral positions

Stefano Evangelista

Further Reading:
Browning, Robert. 1981. *Robert Browning: The Poems.* Edited by John Pettigrew. Harmondsworth, UK: Penguin.

Dellamora, Richard. 1990. *Masculine Desire: The Sexual Politics of Victorian Aestheticism.* Chapel Hill, NC: University of North Carolina Press.

Maxwell, Catherine. 2001. *The Female Sublime from Milton to Swinburne: Bearing Blindness.* Manchester and New York: Manchester University Press.

Sussman, Herbert. 1995. *Victorian Masculinities: Manhood and Masculine Poetics in Early Victorian Literature and Art.* Cambridge and New York: Cambridge University Press.

Buddy Films

Buddy films offer a space for negotiating masculine crises incited by issues of class, race, and gender through the juxtaposition of two men of differing personalities and backgrounds and their evolving relationship. These differences are accepted over the course of their adventures as both men recognize that together they can face that which threatens their masculinity—whether women, the enemy, or the law. The genre has developed from comedy duos in the 1930s, to outlaws in the 1960s, to cop action heroes in the 1980s, to "sensitive males" and to male/female buddies in the 1990s. The continued popularity of the buddy myth is due to its adaptability to changing gender concerns. As a backlash against feminist empowerment, buddy narratives offer male movie-going audiences escapist fantasies of men rejecting women, marriage, and domesticity for the independence, adventure, and rewards of male bonding.

Buddy films originally focused on comedic male duos such as Laurel and Hardy in the 1930s, Bing Crosby and Bob Hope in the 1940s, Dean Martin and Jerry Lewis in the 1950s, and Walter Matthau and Jack Lemmon in the 1960s. However, with the impact of second-wave feminism and the resulting backlash of a developing men's movement in the late 1960s and 1970s, buddy films shifted from a comedic portrayal of male relationships to a serious contemplation of masculinity, for example *Midnight Cowboy* (1969) and *Dog Day Afternoon* (1975). Films like *Butch Cassidy and the Sundance Kid* (1969) and *Easy Rider* (1969) saw the fusion of the buddy narrative with counterculture outlaw heroes and social rebels, enjoying independence and freedom from the domestic restraints imposed by mainstream society and, especially, women. To punish women for their desire for equality, buddy films exclude them from the narrative by replacing the traditional romantic couple with a male buddy relationship and a narrative focus on masculine crisis.

By the 1980s outlaws became law enforcers and buddies became action heroes relishing physical violence and excessive firepower. The increasing equality of women by the 1980s, and its feared feminizing effect on

masculinity, incited a mythopoetic men's movement that promoted the rediscovery of men's masculinity. Just as the movement promoted the reclamation of traditional notions of masculinity, the buddy film celebrated male bonding in a resistance to feminist empowerment. The pumped-up bodies and hypermasculine physiques of the action buddy heroes emphasized sexual difference and masculinity as empowered when at its most manly. These films responded to the perceived threat of women with action, violence, and male bonding under extreme duress and, most importantly, with the absence of women from the narrative. In these films, female characters played a minimal role, being present only to assure audiences of the hero's heterosexuality. The message of these films was that there was no place for women in the man's world—a world defined by danger and violence. Their presence, and subsequent feminizing effect on masculinity, could bring about the downfall of the hero by inciting "soft" feelings and vulnerability. In *Lethal Weapon* (1987) it is Murtaugh's kidnapped daughter, and in *Die Hard* (1988) McClane's hostage wife, that put the heroes at a disadvantage with the enemy. Instead, it is the tough feelings inspired by the male bond that empowered the buddies to face and defeat their enemies.

Similarly, the gains of African Americans in the decade following the Civil Rights movement had an impact on the buddy film. The buddies were often of differing racial backgrounds, most notably Eddie Murphy and Nick Nolte in *48 Hrs* (1982) and Mel Gibson and Danny Glover in *Lethal Weapon*. These biracial buddy films tended to conform to white mainstream attitudes by placing the African American buddy in a subordinate position as trusty sidekick to the white hero. He tended to offer one of two stereotyped images of black masculinity as the embodiment either of black subculture in terms of attitude and style, for example Eddie Murphy in *48 Hrs,* or of the black middle-class as a domesticated and devoted family man, for example

Denzel Washington in *Philadelphia* (1993). Biracial buddy films explored issues of masculinity through the differing racial backgrounds of the two heroes, each man developing a mutual respect for the other because of his difference, not in spite of it.

The gratification of the biracial male bond is a myth that has pervaded American culture from Fenimore Cooper's *Leatherstocking Tales* (1823–1841), Herman Melville's *Moby Dick* (1851), and Mark Twain's *Huckleberry Finn* (1885). In these biracial buddy narratives, a "civilized" white man is initiated into the ways of the real world by a "savage" dark-skinned man—Hawkeye and Chingachoock, Ishmael and Queequeg, and Huck and Jim, respectively. In the 1980s biracial buddy film, this paradigm is reversed: The black man is over-civilized, feminized, and domesticated—and the "savage" white man helps him to rediscover his masculinity. As in the traditional form of the myth, the homosocial bonds forged between these heroes unite the black and white men against the repression of women and the law. These films presented racial difference; however, the white hero's ultimate acceptance of his black sidekick neutralized rather than explored issues of race.

The buddy films of the early 1990s explored the need for masculine sensitivity in order to experience true fulfillment. In films such as *City Slickers* (1991), *The Fisher King* (1991), and *The Shawshank Redemption* (1994), one buddy learns the value of sensitivity from the other and undergoes a conversion through the course of the film. Despite this focus on the male relationship in the early 1990s, the need for male bonding seemed to lessen as the decade wore on. Buddy films began to embrace and explore new kinds of buddy relationships: the female couple with Geena Davis and Susan Sarandon in *Thelma and Louise* (1991), the platonic couple with Julia Roberts and Denzel Washington in *The Pelican Brief* (1993), and the Asian/African American male couple with Jackie Chan and Chris Tucker in *Rush Hour* (1998). The African American buddy

saw a shift from being the sidekick of a white hero to having one of his own—often a woman—in films like *The Bone Collector* (1997) and *Kiss the Girls* (1997), or to being the equal partner of a white man in films like *Seven* (1995). These changing images of the buddy couple over the last decade reflect the ability of the genre to attract broader audiences with its dual protagonists, as well as the social gains made by women and ethnic men in American society

Philippa Gates

See also Action Television Series
Further Reading:

Ames, Christopher. 1992. "Restoring the Black Man's Lethal Weapon: Race and Sexuality in Contemporary Cop Films." *Journal of Popular Film and Television* 20, no. 3: 52–60.

Cohan, Steven, and Ina Rae Hark, eds. 1993. *Screening the Male: Exploring Masculinities in Hollywood Cinema.* London: Routledge.

———. 1997. *The Road Movie Book.* New York: Routledge.

Goldstein, Patrick. 2001. "The Big Picture— It's Still a Guy Thing: The Evolution of Buddy Movies." *The Los Angeles Times,* 9 October, "Calendar," at F1.

Guerrero, Ed. 1993. "The Black Image in Protective Custody: Hollywood's Biracial Buddy Films of the Eighties." Pp. 237–246 in *Black American Cinema.* Edited by Manthia Diawara. New York: Routledge.

Jeffords, Susan. 1994. *Hard Bodies: Hollywood Masculinity in the Reagan Era.* New Brunswick, NJ: Rutgers University Press.

King, Neal. 1999. *Heroes in Hard Times: Cop Action Movies in the U.S.* Philadelphia: Temple University Press.

Null, Gary. 1993. *Black Hollywood: From 1970 to Today.* New York: Citadel Press.

Tasker, Yvonne. 1993. *Spectacular Bodies: Gender, Genre and the Action Cinema.* London: Routledge.

Bukowski, Charles (1920–1994)

Charles Bukowski moved to the United Stated at the age of three and lived most of his life in southern California. His writings, performance readings, and the legends of his drinking, fighting, and other acting-out behaviors attracted an enormous "underground" readership from the mid-1960s until his death in 1994. He published his first short story in 1944 and he did not start writing poetry until he was thirty-five years old. Many of his forty-five published books have been translated, some into more than a dozen languages. At the time of his death he was earning over a million dollars a year in royalties from the German publications of his works alone. Bukowski's autobiographical screenplay for the feature film *Barfly* (1987), a story of his younger drinking years, is perhaps his best-known American work.

Two areas of Bukowski's writing relate most strongly to his importance to masculinity studies. Although the role of the outsider and loner is a constant theme in all of Bukowski's writings, his rejection of the "American dream" as related to a work ethic is an ongoing and important element in much of his work. Usually employed in marginal, low-paying jobs, Bukowski believed there was a critical unfairness in the very concept of selling time for wages. In spite of being a self-declared nonpolitical writer, Bukowski presented a consistent rejection of work for wages as in any way ennobling. This element in Bukowski, although he always denied affiliation with any philosophical school, nonetheless aligns him with a long American tradition dating back to at least the American Transcendentalists (Emerson and particularly Thoreau), through the beatnik and hippie movements of the 1950s to the 1960–1970s, on into the anarchist "punk" movement of the 1980s–1990s.

Bukowski's other area of interest to the study of masculinities is his presentation of male-female relationships. Reviled by feminists for his perceived "antifeminist" stance, Bukowski's writing often attempted to characterize, in frequently brutal, honest autobiographical terms, his failures at relationships with women. In poetry, short stories, and longer works of prose, Bukowski often portrayed men as victims of female power. His work, although often characterized as negative toward women, more often showed a self-deprecating confusion and frustration at his protagonists' powerlessness in intimate relationships with females. At the time of his death Bukowski was in a happy and successful marriage and was extremely close to his adult daughter.

Bukowski's contribution to American letters is more widely appreciated outside the United States, but his posthumous publications of poetry and letters continues to feed a large worldwide audience.

Terry Trueman

Bullying

See Boyhood; School Shootings

Bunuel, Luis (1900–1983)

Among the most original film directors of the twentieth century, Luis Bunuel was born in Calanda in the south of Spain on 22 February 1900. He studied along with poet Federico Garcia Lorca and Salvador Dali at the Institución Libre de Enseñanza in Madrid, in 1917 and 1925. He went to Paris in 1926, and in 1929 became a member of the Surrealist movement. Many of his films feature scenes charged with masculine desire toward a woman. In his first avant garde movie (coscripted with painter Salvador Dali), *Un chien andalou* (*An Andalousian Dog;* 1929), Bunuel shows a man who tries to touch a voluptuous woman but can't, because—for no reason known to the viewer—he has to pull two pianos linked with two bishops in order to reach the inaccessible object of his desire. In *L'Âge d'or* (*Golden Years;* 1930), a film that was banned for half a century, a man and a woman try to embrace each other in public, but they feel the reprobative reaction of the bourgeois institutions that surround them. This scheme is also recurrent in other famous movies such as *El* (1952), *Le Charme discret de la bourgeoisie* (*The Discrete Charm of the Bourgeoisie;* 1972), and *Cet obscur objet du désir*

(*That Obscure Object of Desire;* 1977), his last masterpiece.

In 1946 Bunuel emigrated to Mexico, although he directed his most famous movies in France during the 1960s. In Bunuel's movies, the man is a prisoner of his desire and limited by the social rules that stop him from behaving freely. This is true even in his adaptation of *The Adventures of Robinson Crusoe* (1950). In *El* (1952), a man thinks for a moment of sewing his wife's vagina closed, in order to be sure she will remain faithful. In *The Exterminating Angel* (1962), a group of friends can't leave the living room where they just had a party. For no apparent reason, they just feel they have to do as the others and stay all through the night. In *Le Charme discret de la bourgeoisie* (1972), a group of friends want to meet and have dinner together, but there is always something that stops the project: the restaurant is closed, some people are late, there is a war, etc. Also, many illicit affairs are suggested between some characters, but are postponed and can't take place. In his film *Le Fantôme de la liberté* (*The Phantom of Liberty;* 1974) a married couple want to make love without the knowledge of their guests. When the man tells his wife, "It's impossible, you scream too loud," they hide in their garden. But the guests, surprised by their absence, leave the party. They leave the house without knowing where their hosts live. In his final movie, *Cet obscur objet du désir* (*That Obscure Object of Desire;* 1977, inspired by a novel by Pierre Louys, *La femme et le pantin*), a duplicitous woman promises to give herself to a rich man but she always changes her mind at the last minute. In Bunuel's universe, there is always an element that stops the fulfillment of the man's desire.

In his autobiography, titled *My Last Sight,* Bunuel devoted a whole chapter to explaining his main obsessions. Insects, guns, and blind men fascinated him with a mixture of revulsion and attraction. Destructive love is his most frequent theme—passion makes a man like an animal; jealousy transforms love into something not far from murder.

Yves Laberge

Further Reading:

Bunuel, Luis. 1976/1993. *Là-bas.* With a preface by Jean-Claude Carrière. Paris: Éditions Écriture.

———. 1983. *My Last Sigh.* New York: Alfred A. Knopf.

———. 2000. *An Unspeakable Betrayal: Selected Writings of Luis Bunuel.* Berkeley: University of California Press.

Bunuel, Luis, and Salvador Dali. 1998. *L'Âge d'or.* Edited by Paul Hammond. Berkeley, CA: University of California Press.

Camacho, Enrique, and Manuel Rodriquez Blanco. *Buñuel, 100 añnos: es peligroso asomarse al interior.* 2001. New York: Instituto Cervantes, Museum of Modern Art.

Buonarroti, Michelangelo

See Michelangelo Buonarroti (1475–1564)

Burroughs, Edgar Rice (1875–1950)

Edgar Rice Burroughs was one of the most successful American writers of popular fiction in the twentieth century. Although his literary credentials never met lofty academic standards, he had an uncanny ability to tell an adventure story that grabbed and held a reader's attention. He especially animated the fantasies of his mainly male readership. Burroughs is best known for the romance and adventure stories of Tarzan, a male child born into English nobility who loses his parents and is subsequently raised by a tribe of African apes. *Tarzan of the Apes* first appeared as a magazine serial in 1912 and was published as a hardback book in 1914. Burroughs had a knack for creating larger-than-life characters in the Tarzan tales, science fiction adventures (John Carter of Mars), westerns, and seafaring stories that contributed to his commercial success and enduring presence in American popular culture. His books remain in print to this day and are among those most avidly prized by collectors.

Edgar Rice Burroughs was born in Chicago on 1 September 1875, the son of a successful businessman and former Civil War officer. Young Edgar attended military school but was denied admission into West Point. His plans for an army career were foiled by the discovery of a heart murmur. He married in early 1900 and, as a young husband and father, experienced difficulty earning a living. He moved from one job failure to another, from selling candy to hawking purported cures for alcoholism. Burroughs never found success in the business world, and at times he and his wife pawned or sold their belongings in order to survive. During these troubled times, his biographers believe, he escaped the dismal realities of work and economic failure through fantasy and writing. He sold his first story, *A Princess of Mars* (1912), to a pulp magazine publisher who paid him $400, a decent amount of money at the time. More serials followed, his readership mushroomed, the Tarzan books soared in popularity, and he became America's most successful pulp fiction writer for the next three decades. During the 1930s, Burroughs founded his own publishing company and spun the Tarzan character into advertising ventures, radio serials, and newspaper comics. Tarzan movies became a Hollywood staple during the 1930s and 1940s (although Burroughs disliked the way his strong, intelligent, morally astute, and emotionally complex literary hero was misrepresented on the silver screen).

Second-wave feminists could dispense with Burroughs as a purveyor of patriarchal swill. At first glance, Tarzan embodies traditional masculinity—he is strong, aggressive, ruthless in battle, goal oriented, and determined to climb to the top of the jungle hierarchy. His relationship with Jane fits into the dominance-submission model or the masculine-feminine binary (the famous movie line, "Me Tarzan, you Jane"). And mired in the Social Darwinism of his day, Burroughs often naturalizes Tarzan's ferocious individualism and masculine drives with homespun evolutionary biology. But there is more to Tarzan (and Burroughs) than meets the Second Wave eye; Tarzan accepts his vulnerability to injury and death. He finds refuge in the jungle from the injustice and violence of men and so-called civilization. Indeed, Tarzan is wary of men's depravity, skeptical of their claims to superiority. In Tarzan's view of men, white men are no different from black men, no more civilized than apes, and as cruel as jungle predators (Farmer 1972). In his heart and mind, Tarzan longs for human connection and community, but he does not find it in the world around him. His relationship with Jane is predicated on respect, fidelity, and fervent love. Nor is Jane a subservient wallflower. As her character evolves, she learns to hunt and track, to use weapons, and to climb and swing through the jungle foliage with athletic alacrity. Jane is more a partner to Tarzan than a patriarchal prop or feminine princess.

In summary, Edgar Rice Burroughs was a complex man and so are his male characters. Burroughs experienced economic failure and success. Chagrined but humble, he accepted the fact that he was a popular writer rather than a serious author. He distrusted bureaucracy and the business world but forged his way through it nonetheless. A quiet and seclusive man, he was a steadfast husband and father who led a basic domestic life while fantasizing great adventure in jungles, on the high seas, and in outer space. Although his male characters personified traditional masculinity, they were also self-reflective and emotionally driven. Romance was a constant theme in a Burroughs novel, and his male heroes swooned over the women they loved. Indeed, the Tarzan books can be described as romance novels for men, a pulp fiction vehicle for male readers to explore their passion and love for women as much as their longing to exemplify traditional manhood. It may be that the abiding popularity of the Tarzan character is partly owed to the fact that he combines traditional aspects of masculinity with a vision of a caring, rational man who longs to mold himself and the world around him in ways that patriarchal society has disallowed.

Don Sabo

Further Reading:
Farmer, Philip Jose. 1972. *Tarzan Alive*. New York: Doubleday.

Holtsmark, Erling B. 1981. *Tarzan and Tradition: Classical Myth in Popular Literature.* Westport, CT: Greenwood Press.

Lupoff, Richard A. 1965. *Edgar Rice Burroughs: Master of Adventure.* New York: Canaveral Press.

Porges, Irwin. 1975. *Edgar Rice Burroughs: The Man Who Created Tarzan.* Provo, UT: Brigham Young University Press.

Zeuschner, Robert B. 1996. *Edgar Rice Burroughs: The Exhaustive Scholar's and Collector's Descriptive Bibliography of American Periodical, Hardcover, Paperback, and Reprint Editions.* Jefferson, NC: McFarland and Company.

Butler, Rhett

Rhett Butler is an enduring icon of rogue masculinity from Margaret Mitchell's best-selling Civil War/Reconstruction novel (1936) and blockbuster movie (1939) *Gone with the Wind.* Because of the sympathetic treatment of the character in the novel and the charismatic performance by Clark Gable on screen, audiences have tended to overlook serious flaws in the character, including blockade running, gambling, drinking, support of the Ku Klux Klan, association with prostitutes, murder (in the book), and an inability to communicate with the woman he loves. Particularly in the movie, Rhett Butler is a personification of the active life, but he is "no gentleman," as he is continually reminded, living well outside the bounds of prevailing social rules.

Clark Gable as Rhett Butler (Library of Congress)

Rhett's character makes the transition from novel to film much more intact than his rival in Scarlett's affections, Ashley Wilkes (Molt 1990). Ashley is demoted from military hero to wimp, while Rhett retains both his good characteristics, as well as his bad. Many of Rhett's more serious flaws were softened in the film because of censorship (his continuous association with prostitutes is only hinted at); the efforts of the producer, David O. Selznick (who blurred the racial issues in the film); and the desire of the star, who wanted Rhett to be seen as a full-blown hero. Gable's role in defining the film presence of Rhett Butler has been well documented, especially the prolonged negotiations in convincing Gable to cry at Rhett's daughter's funeral, an acting option specifically prohibited by his contract (see Fisher 1993; and Harmetz, 1996).

One line of interpretation of the story and Rhett's character has been that, while the first part of the film presents an inaccurate glorification of antebellum Southern society, the second half reflects better the Depression-era South, during which the novel was written, than the Reconstruction South, in which it is set (see several essays in Harwell 1983; Rubin 1982; and Hanson 1991).

Hollywood made few Depression-era films about the Depression, but exported issues (drought, financial collapse, crime, relocation) into other eras.

A prickly episode in both the book and the film involves a confrontation between Rhett and Scarlett. Scarlett has, throughout the film, been romantically attracted to Ashley Wilkes. Ashley, never the man of action or directness, seems unable to tell her that not only does he not love her, but that he loves his wife. Scarlett is now married to Rhett, but she has been found in Ashley's arms. Rhett forces Scarlett to dress in red and wear rouge and sends her alone to a party. Scarlett is saved from humiliation by Ashley's wife, who is secure in her husband's affections. Rhett has spent the early evening with prostitutes and when Scarlett later comes down from her bedroom looking for a drink, he is drunk and angry that she has been spared the humiliation he planned. He threatens to crush her skull like a walnut but ends up carrying a reluctant Scarlett up the stairs. Although some reviewers of the film at its opening found this scene mildly disturbing, it has occasioned a great deal of criticism as the issue of rape within marriage has come to public consciousness.

A sequel of sorts to the original book, *Scarlett,* was published in 1991 by Alexandra Ripley and made into a successful television miniseries in 1994, which continued to chronicle the on-again, off-again relationships between Rhett and Scarlett. Rhett was portrayed by Timothy Dalton.

Ashton D. Trice
Samuel A. Holland

Further Reading:

Fisher, Joe. 1993. "Clark Gable's Balls: Real Men Never Lose Their Teeth." Pp. 124–147 in *You Tarzan: Masculinity, Movies and Men.* Edited by Pat Kirkhan and Janet Thumim. New York: St. Martin's Press.

Hanson, Elizabeth I. 1991. *Margaret Mitchell.* Boston: Twayne Publishers.

Harmetz, Aljean. 1996. *On the Road to Tara: The Making of* Gone with the Wind. New York: Harry N. Abrams.

Harwell, Richard, ed. 1983. *Gone with the Wind as Book and Film.* New York. Paragon House Publishers.

Molt, Cynthia Marylee. 1990. *Gone with the Wind on Film: A Complete Reference.* Jefferson, NC: McFarland.

Rubin, Louis D., Jr. 1982. *A Gallery of Southerners.* Baton Rouge: Louisiana State University Press.

Taylor, Helen. 1989. *Scarlett's Women: Gone With the Wind and its Female Fans.* London: Virago.

Trice, Ashton D., and Samuel A. Holland. 2001. *Heroes, Antiheroes, and Dolts: Portrayals of Masculinity in American Popular Films, 1921–1999.* Jefferson, NC: McFarland.

Vertrees, Alan David. 1997. *Selznick's Vision: Gone with the Wind and Hollywood Filmmaking.* Austin, TX: University of Texas Press.

Byron, George Gordon (1788–1824)

The Romantic poet Lord Byron, a bisexual man in homophobic early-nineteenth-century England, had a troubled relationship with masculinity. He formed the basis for the Byronic hero, a misunderstood young man whose moodiness women (and men) find irresistible. The Byronic hero always has a dark secret. In Byron's case, it was his sexual relationship with his half-sister Augusta, the rumors of which made him live in permanent exile in 1816. His bisexuality had to be kept secret in England, but he explored it openly during his tour of Greece and Turkey in 1810. In his elegiac poem "To Thyzra," one of his most popular works, Byron is addressing John Edleston, his choirboy lover at Cambridge. Although homosexual acts were common in all-male schools, it was expected that the boys would grow out of it and go on to marry. Sodomy was punishable by death in early nineteenth-century England, so Byron needed to be discreet. Byron was a victim of homophobic repression, but he also believed women to be inferior, which makes him a source for many critical debates. Although he has become the focus for queer theorists who address his bisexuality, some feminist theorists argue that the male Romantic poets integrate the feminine aspects of emotion in their work while still acting the part of the powerful male. This is surely applicable to Byron. He believed women to be incapable of rational thought, a common notion of the time but an idea Byron took to an extreme. To complicate matters further, Byron was sexually abused as a child by his Calvinist nanny, who mixed sexuality with threats of hellfire. This added to Byron's misogyny and sexual confusion.

It is usual to see Byron's poems as thinly veiled autobiography. Byron played up his outsider status as a way to keep people at a distance and to keep his secrets safe. *Childe Harold* and *Manfred* are poetic creations that helped to construct the Byronic hero. Although *Childe Harold* addresses imperialism, especially the reemergence of monarchies after the final defeat of Napoleon in 1815, and mocks arrogance of all stripes, there is a disturbing element of misogyny in the poem. Harold accuses women of being more attracted to money than love. Byron was suspicious of literary women, including Mary Shelley, another instance of his misogyny. He was also a ladies man who had liaisons with many women. Paradoxically, he was faithful to his last love, Teresa Guccioli. His physical deformity (it is still unknown whether Byron suffered from a clubfoot or some other disfigurement) made him overcompensate in areas of manly prowess. He boxed and famously swam the Hellespont (now called the Dardanelles), the narrow strait in northwestern Turkey connecting the Aegean Sea with the Marmara Sea. He was also very vain and went on punishing diets to stay attractive to men and women.

Byron's adventures in Turkey and Greece form the basis of *Don Juan,* which chronicles the adventures of the effeminate young Juan. The Turkish Canto (V) of *Don Juan* paints Juan in effeminate terms, especially when he has to dress like a harem member after being bought in a Turkish slave auction. Juan is androgynous, and therefore moves between binaries of male and female. However, Byron's unease with his own masculinity makes him fluctuate between upholding and subverting masculinity. Sultana Gulbeyaz is powerful enough to order the purchase of Juan for her own sexual pleasure, which places Juan in a traditionally female position. He reasserts his manliness by raping one of the sleeping harem women. Queer and feminist theory helps the reader to see that Byron's contradictory attitudes toward sexuality mean that he may not have fully accepted hegemonic masculine roles. Conversely, while Byron liked individual women, he thought they should not mix in society, reflecting a misogynist strain in gay male culture.

June Scudeler

See also "Byronic Hero"
Further Reading:

Crompton, Louis. 1985. *Byron and Greek Love: Homophobia in 19th-Century England.* Berkeley, CA: University of California Press.

Gilmour, Ian. 2002. *The Making of the Poets: Byron and Shelley in Their Time.* London: Chatto and Windus.

Gleckner, Robert F., ed. 1991. *Critical Essays on Lord Byron.* New York: Macmillan.

Grosskurth, Phyllis. 1997. *Byron, the Flawed Angel.* Toronto: Macfarlane, Walter and Ross.

McGann, Jerome J. 2002. *Byron and Romanticism.* New York: Cambridge University Press.

Mellor, Anne K. 1993. *Romanticism and Gender.* New York: Routledge.

"Byronic Hero"

The Romantic poet Lord Byron (1788–1824) gave rise to the Byronic hero, an archetype of masculinity, heterosexual desire, and, conversely, effeminacy, homosociality, and homosexuality.

On 10 March 1812, Byron awoke to find himself the most celebrated poet of the age, or of any age. The first two cantos of *Childe Harold's Pilgrimage,* introducing the prototype for future Byronic heroes, became an overnight best-seller and "Byromania," the contemporary rage for Byron and the Byronic, was born. It was not, however, the man or his work that inspired this "craze"—a term coined to describe Byron's unprecedented popularity—but the persona of the Byronic hero: Byron's significance as a writer was eclipsed by his fictional protagonists (Brewer 2001, 142).

The Byronic hero's suffering, isolation, and defiance of authority and conventional morality captured the deflated spirit of a generation who had witnessed the horrors of the French Revolution. But the figure's principal attraction was an irresistible sex appeal. In the oriental tales, the Byronic hero's passionate devotion to his beloved conveys a religious fervency: "Yes, it was love—unchangeable—unchanged,/ felt but for one from whom he never ranged" (*The Corsair,* ll. 287–288). It is testament to Byron's mercurial personality and the multifaceted Byronic "self" that he is both a lover noted for constancy and a libertine. The *British Critic* denounced *Don Juan* as "a manual of profligacy," and Byron's high-profile affairs compounded his image as a seducer (Rutherford 1970, 2). Byron's reputation became even more scandalous when Annabella Milbanke hinted at her estranged husband's incestuous relationship with his half-sister and homosexual encounters with Greek boys. Byron was ostracized and became an exile in Europe, yet his poetic reputation rose to new heights. According to William St. Clair's calculations, over 1.5 million people read *Don Juan* between 1819 and 1828 (Rutherford 1990, 18). Allusions to unnameable sexual "sins" heightened the mystique of the Byronic hero, and, in the guise of the vampire and the Regency rake, the thrill of Byronic passions retains its allure. The Byronic hero became part of the mythology of the age, and almost two centuries later continues to be a cultural phenomenon.

To some extent, the Byronic hero preceded Byron. As Peter Thorslev (1962) outlined, the Byronic hero resembled the Gothic villain, the noble outlaw, the child of nature, Satan, and Prometheus. What made the Byronic hero so successful was the combination of these characters. It is, however, worth remembering that Byron's fictional heroes are not uniform; where, for example, Childe Harold contemplates, the heroes of the orien-

tal tales act. It is this diversity within the "type" that enables the Byronic hero to epitomize both the effeminate poseur and a masculine ideal. Acknowledging this paradox, Carlyle described Byron as a "Sentimentalist and Power-man" (Rutherford 1970, 288). Byron attracted women—he claimed to have received enough letters from English ladies to fill a large volume—and men; according to Macaulay, "they learned his poems by heart, and did their best to write like him, and to look like him. Many of them practiced at the glass, in the hope of catching the curl of the upper lip, and the scowl of the brow, which appear in some of his portraits. A few discarded their neckcloths, in imitation of their great leader" (Rutherford 1970, 315–316). Elfenbein (1995) highlights how figures such as Bulwer-Lytton and Disraeli performed the role of the Byronic dandy to ensure their success in society: a controversial pose was cultivated for conservative ends.

Susan Wolfson (1991) argues that Byron's poetry inverts rather than reinforces gender stereotypes and focuses on homoeroticism in *Don Juan*. Jonathan David Gross (2001) identifies a gay narrator in the same poem and proceeds to discuss the political significance of this voice. The narrator's homoerotic engagement with the hero, Gross argues, reinforces the poem's endorsement of political and sexual liberty. Gross also situates Byron within a homosocial sphere in which his relations with women merely enhanced his prestige amongst other men. Similarly, Paul Cantor (1993) highlights the homosexuality in the oriental tales, arguing that the most passionate exchanges are between men. The heroines are only peripheral characters, pawns in a masculine world of violence and war.

Consequently, women writers have had a troubled yet fruitful relationship with Byron and his poetry. As Caroline Franklin (1992) has argued, Byron's rebelliousness appealed to women writers of the nineteenth century, while also representing a masculine type to oppose. From the fiction of Mary Shelley, Jane Austen, and Felicia Hemans, to the

Brontës and George Eliot, the egotism of the Byronic type is exposed and the hero is subsequently destroyed, redeemed, or domesticated. Ironically, it is largely through female revisions, and adaptations of their fiction, that Byron and his work retain a widespread appeal; Heathcliff and Rochester, for example, have become synonymous with the Byronic hero. As Atara Stein (2002) argues, the Byronic hero is as popular and pervasive—albeit in numerous guises—as it was in the early nineteenth century. In his study of Byronism, Samuel Chew predicted that Byron "was not, and he ha[d] never been, among those whom the world willingly lets die" (Chew 1924, 220).

Sarah Wootton

See also George Gordon, Lord Byron
Further Reading:

Brewer, William D., ed. 2001. *Contemporary Studies on Lord Byron.* Lewiston, ME: Edwin Mellen Press.

Cantor, Paul A. 1993. "Mary Shelley and the Taming of the Byronic Hero: 'Transformation' and 'The Deformed Transformed.'" Pp. 89–106 in *The Other Mary Shelley: Beyond Frankenstein.* Edited by Audrey A. Fisch, Anne K. Mellor, and Esther H. Schor. New York: Oxford University Press.

Chew, Samuel C. 1924. *Byron in England: His Fame and After-Fame.* London: John Murray.

Elfenbein, Andrew. 1995. *Byron and the Victorians.* Cambridge, UK: Cambridge University Press.

Franklin, Caroline. 1992. *Byron's Heroines.* Oxford, UK: Clarendon Press.

Gross, Jonathan David. 2001. "Epistolary Engagements: Byron, Annabella, and the Politics of 1813." Pp. 17–36 in *Contemporary Studies on Lord Byron.* Edited by William D. Brewer. Lewiston, ME: Edwin Mellen Press.

Rutherford, Andrew, ed. 1970. *Byron: The Critical Heritage.* London: Routledge and Kegan Paul.

———, ed. 1990. *Byron: Augustan and Romantic.* Basingstoke, UK: Macmillan.

Stein, Atara. Romantic Circles Praxis Series. "Immortals and Vampires and Ghosts, Oh My!: Byronic Heroes in Popular Culture." http://www.rc.umd.edu/praxis/contemporary/stein/stein.html (cited 8 April 2002).

Thorslev, Peter L., Jr. 1962. *The Byronic Hero: Types and Prototypes.* Minneapolis: University of Minnesota Press.

Wilson, Frances, ed. 1999. *Byromania: Portraits of the Artist in Nineteenth- and Twentieth-Century Culture.* Basingstoke, UK: Macmillan.

Wolfson, Susan. 1991. "'A Problem Few Dare Imitate': Sardanapalus and 'Effeminate Character.'" *ELH* 58: 867–902.

———. 1987. "'Their She Condition': Cross-Dressing and the Politics of Gender in Don Juan." *ELH* 54: 595–617.

C

Castration

Castration is the removal of or the interruption of the function of the gonads or reproductive glands (the testicles in the man and the ovaries in the woman). In regard to men and boys, a centuries-old tradition persists of castration as a cultural and religious practice, as a form of punishment and oppression, or as a surgical procedure.

During earlier centuries, in China and in the Middle East, boys and grown men were castrated for them to serve as harem guards or chamberlains. In the Middle Ages, castration was a widespread means of court-appointed punishment for felonies and rape. From the Christian tradition, cases of self-castration with a celibate intent are known. The church, however, did not accept such self-mutilation, expressly forbidding it in the sixteenth century. Nevertheless, with the spread of baroque music from the end of the sixteenth century into the eighteenth century, the Vatican tolerated that thousands of boys, chosen for the special quality of the castrato voice, were castrated before their change of voice to sing in church choirs and operas. In the course of the French period of the Enlightenment, castration was criticized as barbaric and inhuman by Voltaire and Rousseau and has, since, increasingly disap-

peared from the array of legitimate cultural practices. At the end of the nineteenth century, the development of the vasectomy as a method of male sterilization in which the function of the testicles is not impaired (as distinguished from castration) also contributed to the decline of castration as an acceptable cultural practice. Nowadays, castration as a cultural and religious practice occurs only in a small number of closely defined cultures (e.g., the followers of the goddess Bahucharji in Northern India) and continues likewise, to a limited degree, as a surgical measure for some cancers and in sex-change operations. In isolated cases, and under special legal conditions, voluntary castration or castration ordered by legal decree is still employed in a number of countries for cases of serious and repeated sexual offenses.

The consequences of castration differ, depending on the type of surgery and whether it was performed before or after the affected individual had reached puberty. In the prepubescent castrati of the baroque period (the "early castrati"), the testicles were removed by way of an incision in the groin, or they were left to deteriorate by surgical means. In the castration of postpubescent grown men intended to become eunuchs, as well as for punishment, in addition to the removal of the testicles, the penis sometimes was also amputated. This also applies to sex-change operations in which an artificial vagina is constructed following the removal of the penis and the testicles. In medical indications, a direct application of radiation is also used for the removal of the testicles.

The physical consequences of the castration in a man go back to the interruption of the function of the testicles and the discontinuation of testosterone production. If the surgery takes place before puberty, the age-related pubescent body development does not take place. As in the early castrati, the voice does not change, retaining the higher pitch of childhood. There is also a lack of body hair and no beard. In addition, a disposition toward the female body shape with rounded hips and distinctly marked breasts is frequently observed. Furthermore, many of the early castrati developed a height unusual for their day and, in part, displayed a tendency toward obesity. In postpubescent-castrated individuals, these physical consequences, to a large degree, do not occur, so that in a sex-change operation from male to female, surgical alterations must be supplemented with feminizing hormones like estrogen.

Depending on the type of castration and the age of the castrato, the surgery influences the sexual sensations and the sexual conduct of the affected individual. Although the ability to procreate is lost without exception, the ability to obtain an erection still often remains if the castration has been limited to the removal of the testicles only. From the early castrati of the baroque period it is known that some of them were capable of having only Platonic relationships, whereas others were ably to carry on an almost normal sexual life, though with a somewhat diminished libido. Sexual orientation in the sense of hetero- or homosexuality is not influenced by castration.

The psychic and social consequences of castration are complex and depend on the respective social and cultural context. In some cultures, castration was certainly associated with an attractive and, in some exceptional cases, even socially powerful position. Thus, in the Assyrian and Byzantine Empire as well as in China, eunuchs could aspire to become high-ranking military leaders. The castrati of the baroque period were, to some extent, celebrated and highly remunerated artists who also had a strong erotic effect on their audiences. But such privileged positions, which made it easier for the affected individuals to live with their limitations and to even be proud of them, were rather the exception. In most cultures castration had the meaning of emasculation in the sense of an incomplete or mutilated masculinity associated with a social devaluation and, on the part of the affected individual, with a subjective feeling of low self-esteem and humiliation. Not rarely did the castrati, due to their difference, become the target of attacks, ridicule, and humiliation by the public, particularly by men. Therefore, in the overwhelming majority of cases, the castration was forced upon the affected individuals and was attached to an underprivileged social position caused by poverty, slavery, imprisonment, or delinquency.

Yet, beyond the individual consequences of the affected individuals, castration, to this day, possesses a highly symbolic importance, whereby this symbolism, in contrast to the actual practice, does not refer to the testicles but instead to the penis or phallus as the synonym for masculinity and power. Not only in psychoanalysis alone but also in everyday thinking, the loss of power, leadership, authority, or ability is frequently interpreted as a symbolic castration.

Holger Brandes

See also Castration Anxiety; Contraception; Transsexualism

Further Reading:

Barbier, Patrick. 1989. *Histoire des Castrats*. Paris: B. Grasset.
———. 1994. *Farinelli le Castrat des Lumieres*. Paris: B. Grasset.
Taylor, Gary. 2000. *Castration. An Abbreviated History of Western Manhood*. New York: Routledge.

Castration Anxiety

Little is known about castration anxiety in connection with actual castration practices. Psychologically, as well as in everyday language, the term became important at the beginning of the twentieth century in reference to imaginary castration in the sense of anxiety about the loss of masculine power or autonomy or as symbolic emasculation. Castration anxiety gained central theoretical import for explaining the male psyche in the framework of psychoanalytical theorizing. Freud (1856–1939) claimed to have discovered infantile anxiety fantasies that may even operate unconsciously into adult life. This, on the one hand, he leads back to a sexual theory that children are able to understand anatomical sexual differences only by way of castration. On the other hand, Freud (1908) interprets castration anxiety as a reaction to masturbation being forbidden and the threats of punishment associated with this. These castration fantasies and anxieties he then links with the Oedipus legend (in Greek mythology Oedipus had the misfortune of killing his father and marrying his mother), and solidifies this by assuming a universal, culturally overlapping, and, lastly, hereditarily conditional "Oedipus complex" as the central phenomenon of psycho-sexual development in early childhood (1924).

According to Freud's opinion, the child passes through several developmental steps and experiences that come together in the Oedipal developmental phase during which the child become aware of the anatomical differences between the sexes. In the boy, this revolves entirely around his penis. First, the boy discovers his penis as the source of pleasurable feelings, which find expression in early masturbation and a libidinous, narcissistic preoccupation with the penis. His parents then react negatively to this pleasure-centered preoccupation with the penis, whereby their forbidding masturbation is accompanied by the threat of castration. This threat, according to Freud, has a decisive effect as the boy at this time becomes aware of the difference between his and the female genitals, interpreting these not merely as a differently structured, independent organ but solely in the sense of the "missing penis."

Moreover, the boy desires the place at his mother's side at this stage of development, thus finding himself in a competitive situation with his father. As the boy in this situation projects similarly destructive intentions onto his father as he himself experiences toward him while wooing his mother, the anxiety of being castrated by his father arises in him. Because of his narcissistic preoccupation with his penis, the boy finally gives up his mother as his love object. Instead he identifies himself with his father and in this identification he accepts his father's commands and ideas from which the "superego" springs forth as the normative inner authority of the psychic apparatus. Freud worked out his theoretical model by mainly referring to male development but claimed its basic validity for both sexes, insinuating that girls, instead of having castration anxiety, have fantasies about a castration they had supposedly suffered and develop "penis envy."

The critique of Freud's concept of castration anxiety essentially concentrates on two points. First, criticism focuses on the overimportance of the penis in Freud's understanding of castration (Taylor 2000) as well as on his interpretation of the infantile sexual theory. In this connection, the feminist corner also finds fault with Freud's developing his theory for the most part only in reference to male development and as such being unable to offer a convincing variant of a female Oedipus complex. A second, more fundamental point of the critique concerns the universality and the inevitability of castration anxiety and the Oedipus complex attached to it as insinuated by Freud. This finds its expression in the way he interprets this complex as biologically conditional and inherited, thereby tying the formation of the superego as a normative inner authority directly to this complex. Associated with this is also the critique that Freud underestimates the contributions of the interactions between the parents and the child that lead to the formation of the individual castration anxiety.

Although in his exemplary case study of "Little Hans" (1909), Freud describes this interactive side of castration anxiety, as the cause, however, he lastly brings it back to inner psychic instinctual dynamics and a universally operating and hereditarily conditional biological disposition. In today's post-Freudian psychoanalysis, the assumption of the existence of a universal castration anxiety has partially been dropped and replaced by the opinion that castration anxiety is a symptomatic expression of a specific and pathological development, and that boys who are exposed to the reactions of psychologically healthy parents do not suffer a significant degree of castration anxiety during the Oedipal phase (Kohut 1987). As a universal phenomenon, castration anxiety is increasingly being reduced to a metaphor for male anxiety about an alleged loss of power and autonomy, whereby, especially in the French tradition of Lacan, there is a pronounced differentiation made between the penis as the organ and the phallus as the symbol.

Holger Brandes

See also Castration; Erectile Dysfunction; Penis
Further Reading:

Green, André. 1990. *Le complexe de castration.* Paris: Presses Universitaires de France.
Freud, Sigmund. [1908] 1953–1974. "Über infantile Sexualtheorien" (About infantile sexual theory). S. 209–226 in *The Standard Edition of the Complete Psychological Works of Sigmund Freud.* Vol. 9. Edited by James Strachey. London: Hogarth Press.
———. [1909]. 1953–1974. "Analysis of a Phobia in a Five Year-Old ('Little Hans')." S. 5–147 in *Standard Edition.* Vol. 10. London: Hogarth Press.
———. [1924] 1953–1974. "Der Untergang des Ödipuskomplexes" (The decline of the Oedipus complex). S. 173–179 in *Standard Edition.* Vol. 19. London: Hogarth Press.
———. [1931] 1953–1974. "Female Sexuality." S. 225–243 in *Standard Edition.* Vol. 21. London: Hogarth Press.
Kohut, Heinz. 1987. *Wie heilt die Psychoanalyse?* Frankfurt/M., West Germany: Suhrkamp.
Taylor, Gary. 2000. *Castration. An Abbreviated History of Western Manhood.* New York: Routledge.
Ward, Ivan. 2003. *Castration: Ideas in Psychoanalysis.* Victoria, AU: Totem Books.

Cather, Willa Sibert (1876–1947)

Throughout her life, Willa Cather challenged traditional notions of gender identity, refusing the correlation of power to masculinity and weakness to femininity. She saw gender as a social construction, not a biological essence, and acted to undermine gender's repressive precepts. As a young child, Cather mounted elaborate dramas for family and friends with herself playing male roles. In adolescence, she baptized herself "William Cather, Jr.," claiming access to her masculine lineage. With her father's support, she attended college at the University of Nebraska where she started studies to become a surgeon, signing letters home with the appellation "William" and often dressing in men's clothes (O'Brien 1987, 11–16). Cather's maturation into adulthood, then, represented her individual struggle with social strictures placed on women through gender and compulsory heterosexuality. Her work as a major U.S. modernist and lesbian writer continued this battle by critiquing naturalized connections between masculinity and men, manhood, and power.

In her early novels, Cather disrupted masculinity's associations with male anatomy and with power by creating female characters that adopted masculine characteristics successfully, yet also claimed feminine identity, thus undermining casual dichotomous definitions of gender. The novel *O Pioneers!* (1915), for example, depicts Alexandra Bergson as a sexually desirable, feminine woman. Yet Alexandra takes over the family farm at her father's death (with his blessing) and improves the family's fortunes. She reveals a superior business sense by resisting conventional thinking even as her brothers complain about her womanly failings. Yet her success, a product of her fortitude and intelligence, exposes the traditionally masculine arena of business as easily accessible to women. Her adoption of a masculine position reveals the gender politics that discouraged women from entering the business world as well as depicts the successes that women could have in that arena. Cather's *My Ántonia* (1918) provides another example of a woman who flouts gender roles in the pursuit of family success. Ántonia Shimerda also becomes the titular head of her family upon the suicide of her father and in that role adopts many characteristics traditionally coded as masculine. She wears men's clothes, works a plow better than her male counterparts, and runs the family. Yet Ántonia also attracts men who want to marry her and seduce her, and she delights in traditionally feminine pursuits such as dancing and domestic work. Ántonia, then, disrupts the casual associations between gender, sex, and behavior challenged in the postwar era.

My Ántonia, however, also represents a shift in Cather's representations of masculinity. In creating Jim Burden, a narrator trapped in a romantic vision of the past, Cather attacks dominant masculinity's power to control representation and thus to conscript men and women into its service. Jim Burden consistently interprets the world around him in a romantic fashion, seeing Ántonia as the young girl of his past and not the grown woman who represents the nation's future for Cather. Burden's descriptions entrap Ántonia in a particular moment, seducing the reader into accepting his vision even as Cather reveals his romantic fallacy. Jim Burden represents a particularly idealized masculinity (often seen as heroic by other characters) that Cather critiques as a central determinant in the world's breaking in two.

Cather continues her critique in *One of Ours* (1922), her Pulitzer Prize-winning novel about Claude Wheeler, a young man who goes to war and dies because of a misguided romanticism that defined masculinity in terms of heroic sacrifice. This masculinity is not only futile, as the novel's women reveal in their postwar discussion of Claude's displaced nature, but also disembodied, replacing Claude's wounded body with the memory of his wholesome (though dead and therefore unavailable) body. Cather's critique reveals the strategies by which masculinity remained noncorporeal as part of its claim to universal ideals of national identity and citizenship. But Cather's critical project reaches its apex in *The Professor's House* (1925). Claude Wheeler's character is taken here by Tom Outland, the dead antagonist who, from beyond the grave, presents a disembodied, romantic masculine identity that the novel's other men must face. Outland causes dissent and conflict, and indoctrinates the professor to his worldview such that he almost dies in a near-fatal accident while sleeping underneath Outland's blanket. In each of her major postwar novels, then, Cather critiques masculine identity's fallacious romanticism and naturalized claims to power. Even her later novels, such as *Death Comes for the Archbishop* (1927) and *Shadows on the Rock* (1931), repudiated bifurcated visions of gender that demeaned women as incapable and constrained individual men to a singular vision of masculinity. As she advanced her career, Cather's novels and her actions continued to undermine static notions of gender that separated men and women unfairly.

David E. Magill

Further Reading:

Butler, Judith. 1993. *Bodies that Matter.* New York: Routledge.

Fryer, Judith. 1986. *Felicitous Space: The Imaginative Structures of Edith Wharton and Willa Cather.* Chapel Hill, NC: University of North Carolina Press.

Gelfant, Blanche. 1971. "The Forgotten Reaping-Hook: Sex in *My Ántonia.*" *American Literature* 43: 60–82.

Goldberg, Jonathan. 2001. *Willa Cather and Others.* Durham, NC: Duke University Press.

Lindemann, Marilee. 1999. *Willa Cather: Queering America.* New York: Columbia University Press.

Lucenti, Lisa Marie. 2000. "Willa Cather's *My Ántonia:* Haunting the Houses of Memory." *Twentieth Century Literature* 46: 193–215.

Nealon, Christopher. 1997. "Affect-Genealogy: Feeling and Affiliation in Willa Cather." *American Literature* 69: 5–37.

O'Brien, Sharon. 1987. *Willa Cather: The Emerging Voice*. New York: Oxford University Press.

Rosowski, Susan J. 1986. *The Voyage Perilous: Willa Cather's Romanticism*. Lincoln, NE: University of Nebraska Press.

Woodress, James. 1987. *Willa Cather: A Literary Life*. Lincoln, NE: University of Nebraska Press.

Cavalier Poets

"Cavalier" is the appellation of a group of poets in early seventeenth-century England: Thomas Carew (1595–1639), Richard Lovelace (1618–1658), and Sir John Suckling (1609–1641). Some critics and anthologists add Robert Herrick (1591–1674) and Edmund Waller (1606–1687), although their longer careers, extending well into the Restoration period, display significant differences in poetic evolution and interests from the former three. In their lyric poetry, the cavalier poets sang the mores and attitudes of the aristocratic circles of the court of Charles I (1625–1649). Theirs is the voice of the male royalist defense of king and country, as well as the light-hearted song of sexual desire and male inconstancy. Their compositions followed patterns employed in particular by major poets of the period such as Ben Jonson and John Donne, who in turn had adapted poetic forms from the classics (the love poetry of Ovid and Catullus, the wit and concision of Horace and Martial), to the extent that Jonson was greeted as the most Roman of English poets.

The career of Ben Jonson (1572–1637), a successful playwright and prolific masque writer, set a respected example for these courtly poets. His epigrams (short, occasional poems) celebrated the military ("strength of my country," he called them) and the qualities of the monarch: "Who would not be thy subject, James, t'obay/ A prince, that rules by example, more than sway?" (Epigram 35, to King James I). He also expressed his admiration and support for many members of the high aristocracy, like the famous patroness Lucy, Countess of Bedford. Among his most celebrated compositions is "To Penshurst," which describes the country house of the Sidney family as a well-ordered realm where the many qualities of its owners secures the well-being of all inhabitants, big or small. Jonson saw his role as fulfilling a social function at court by encouraging appreciation of true nobility and aristocratic charisma.

Thomas Carew's much shorter career was likewise associated with the court. He worked as secretary to several noblemen who served as ambassadors in Italy and the Netherlands, and in 1630 he was appointed gentleman of the Privy Chamber, a position close to the king. He followed Jonson's lead in many ways, even to the extent that he adopted the country house poem developed in "To Penshurst" in his own "To Saxham," the country house of Sir John Crofts. Similarly, Carew's description emphasizes the generous hospitality of the owners and presents the house as a haven for dwellers and strangers alike. However, Carew is perhaps best known for "The Rapture," a composition of sexual fulfillment in the mode of John Donne. There the speaker urges his beloved Celia to reject conventional notions of honor and join him in the pursuit of sexual pleasure in a paradisal setting where "the hated name/ Of husband, wife, lust, modest, chaste, or shame,/ Are vain and empty words, whose very sound/ Was never heard in the Elysian ground" (107–110).

Richard Lovelace participated in the king's campaigns in Scotland, was twice imprisoned and spent some time in exile due to his royalist politics. His best-known poems are compositions made on the occasion of his leaving for the war or written from prison and often addressed to his beloved Lucasta. In them the speaker expresses his admiration for the king and renews his commitment to his country: "I/ With shriller throat shall sing/ The sweetness, mercy, majesty,/ And glories of my King" ("To Althea. From Prison" 17–20). War is a mistress to be preferred over Lucasta, and rather than her body, the poet "with a stronger faith embrace[s]/ A sword, a horse, a shield" ("To Lucasta. Going to the Wars" 7–8).

Sir John Suckling shared Lovelace's royalist involvement, but his compositions have a lighter mood. In the song "Why So Pale and Wan, Fond Lover?" the speaker scorns the commitment of an unrequited lover and condemns the cruelty of the lady who tortures him, ending with an exasperated "The devil take her!" In "Out upon It!" the poet claims to be a miracle of constancy because he has loved "three whole days together" and may even remain faithful for three more.

Such an antiplatonic attitude is also characteristic of Robert Herrick and Edmund Waller, authors both of compositions praising sensual pleasures and celebrating the consummation of physical love. Herrick's "To the Virgins, to Make Much of Time" is an excellent example of the "carpe diem" motif of classical poetry, exhorting girls to "be not coy, but use your time" and enjoy life's joys while they are still young and beautiful. Waller's famous song "Go, Lovely Rose" expands the same motif by sending a rose to the cruel beloved, a vehicle to remind her that all beautiful things do nevertheless perish, and so she should be more receptive to her lover's desire. In "To Phyllis," the poet once more urges the woman not to delay "pleasures shorter than the day" (2). At other times, Waller uses royalist metaphors to define love concerns, as in "On a Girdle," where the woman's waist becomes both a kingdom and a crown, and the object of the speaker's most intense desires: "Give me but what this ribbon bound,/Take all the rest the sun goes round" (11–12).

Pilar Cuder-Domínguez

See also Wilmot, John, Second Earl of Rochester
Further Reading:
Corns, Thomas N. 1993. *The Cambridge Companion to English Poetry, Donne to Marvell.* Cambridge, UK: Cambridge University Press.

Harp, Richard, and Stanley Stewart, eds. 2000. *The Cambridge Companion to Ben Jonson.* Cambridge, UK: Cambridge University Press.

Maclean, Hugh, ed. 1974. *Ben Jonson and the Cavalier Poets: Authoritative Texts and Criticism.* New York: Norton.

Marcus, Leah. 1986. *The Politics of Mirth: Jonson, Herrick, Milton, Marvell, and the Defense of Old Holiday Pastimes.* Chicago: University of Chicago Press.

Miner, Earl. 1971. *The Cavalier Mode from Jonson to Cotton.* Princeton: Princeton University Press.

Parfitt, George. 1985. *English Poetry of the Seventeenth Century.* London: Longman.

Parry, Graham. 1985. *Seventeenth-Century Poetry: The Social Context.* London: Hutchinson.

Smuts, R. Malcolm. 1999. *Culture and Power in England, 1585–1685.* London: Macmillan.

Cervantes, Miguel de
See Don Quixote

Chandler, Raymond (1888–1959)

Raymond Thornton Chandler—American author and screenwriter—is considered a founder of the hard-boiled school of detective fiction and one of the greatest mystery writers of all time. The protagonist of Chandler's novels, Philip Marlowe, has become an icon of American hard-boiled masculinity, often associated with Humphrey Bogart's portrayal of him in *The Big Sleep* (1946), and infinitely copied as a model for the detective-hero. In his 1944 article "The Simple Art of Murder," Chandler wrote the famous line—"Down these mean streets a man must go who is not himself mean"—evoking his hero who was tough but never mean.

Chicago-born Chandler spent his youth in England, studying at Dulwich College in London and then working as a teacher and journalist before returning to the United States. During World War I, he served in the Canadian army and later the Royal Air Force. He worked for a petroleum company until the Great Depression and heavy drinking ended his career there, and then turned to writing full time at the age of forty-five.

Chandler began writing for pulps like *Black Mask* and *Dime Detective Magazine,* his first short story being "Blackmailers Don't Shoot" (1933). His first novel, *The Big Sleep* (1939), introduced his private-eye protagonist Philip Marlowe, the hero of all seven of his novels including *Farewell, My Lovely* (1940), *The Lady in the Lake* (1943), and *The Long Goodbye* (1953). Many of Chandler's novels were adapted into films including *Murder, My Sweet* (1945) starring Dick Powell, *The Big Sleep* (1946) starring Humphrey Bogart, *The Lady in the Lake* (1947) starring Robert Montgomery, *The Long Goodbye* (1973) starring Elliot Gould, and *Farewell, My Lovely* (1975) starring Robert Mitchum. Although Chandler wrote the original screenplay for *The Blue Dahlia* (1946), his major work in Hollywood was adapting other writers' novels, including the 1944 film of James M. Cain's *Double Indemnity* and the 1951 film of Patricia Highsmith's *Strangers on a Train.*

Chandler is remembered primarily for his hard-boiled detective-hero. Marlowe was a street-wise, tough-talking, and heavy-drinking private eye, but not a typical tough guy. He was an honest and romantic idealist who was college educated and had a penchant for classical music and chess. He was known by various names in Chandler's early stories—Carmody, Dalmas, Malvern, Mallory—before crystallizing as Marlowe, the name originating from the English sixteenth-century writer and suggesting a knightly hero. The figure of Marlowe had a powerful resonance for veterans returning from World War II as he embodied and worked through wartime trauma and postwar readjustment, especially in relation to independent women and changing gender roles. Marlowe was always attractive to but never manipulated by women, thus representing masculinity as manly but independent and never domesticated. He offered a template of the detective-hero as troubled but attractive, tough, and chivalrous, and he has been widely imitated—influencing even contemporary portrayals of hard-boiled heroes.

After the death of his wife of thirty years in 1954, Chandler began to drink more and write less, finally returning to England where he was surprised to find himself a celebrated writer. He died in 1959 from pneumonia, leaving an unfinished novel, *Poodle Springs,* and his legacy: Philip Marlowe.

Philippa Gates

See also Detectives; Gangster Films, Classic

Further Reading:
Clark, Al. 1996. *Raymond Chandler in Hollywood.* Los Angeles: Silman-James Press.
DeAndrea, William L. 1997. *Encyclopedia Mysteriosa: A Comprehensive Guide to the Art of Detection in Print, Film, Radio, and Television.* New York: Macmillan.
Hiney, Tom. 1997. *Raymond Chandler: A Biography.* New York: The Atlantic Monthly Press.
Luhr, William. 1982. *Raymond Chandler and Film.* New York: Frederick Ungar.
Phillips, Gene D. 2000. *Creatures of Darkness: Raymond Chandler, Detective Fiction, and Film Noir.* Lexington, KY: University Press of Kentucky.
Widdicombe, Toby. 2001. *A Reader's Guide to Raymond Chandler.* Westport, CT: Greenwood Press.
Wolfe, Peter. 1985. *Something More than Night: The Case of Raymond Chandler.* Bowling Green, OH: Bowling Green State University Popular Press.

Chaplin, Charlie (1889–1977)

Charles Spencer Chaplin, an English-born actor/director whose pantomimic art flourished along with the burgeoning film industry in Hollywood, crafted a character in the first year of his career, the Little Tramp ("Charlie"), whom he portrayed in more than seventy films and who became one of the most widely known and recognized icons of the common man ("everyman") in the twentieth century. The stark contrast between this film character, played as if he were an adolescent street urchin who is the embodiment of both nonconformity and tenaciousness, and the cunning, wealthy, and sexually predatory individual who Chaplin the man was alleged to be, makes him a figure of continued interest to scholars. In addition to the stark contrast between "Charlie" and Chaplin, he fascinates because he also repre-

Charlie Chaplin in The Circus *(Library of Congress)*

sents, in either guise, a masculinity tinged with the feminine in many respects. A consummate mimic, his particular expression of this art—his grace, agility, and balletic form—is often mistaken as evidence of effeminacy by moviegoers today, but only demonstrates his great range of ability. Able to attract men and women both on and off the screen, Chaplin also intrigues because of his obvious biological success, having wed four wives and produced his tenth child when in his seventies.

Chaplin gave all the credit for his pantomimic ability to his mother. Born in London in 1889, Chaplin was the son of two music hall performers and thereby destined for a life on the stage. Chaplin's father abandoned his family, including Chaplin's mother and older half-brother, when Charles was three, and so

he began a childhood fraught with poverty, insanity (his mother), and learning his craft under his mother's tutelage. It was in this atmosphere that Chaplin's mind began to create two characters that were to appear again and again in his films, the helpless (often sick or crippled) female and the tattered little "gentleman" who endures endless hardships to make her life better.

The Little Tramp character appeared for the first time in the film *Kid Auto Races at Venice* in 1914. Chaplin created the character as a compilation of contradictions—baggy pants/tight vest, floppy shoes/small derby hat—all gentlemen's clothes, but tattered ones. A subtler contradiction existed in "Charlie's" comportment. The Little Tramp was agile, lithe, and even delicate, but in this semblance of femininity, he projected an undeniable manliness. He was vulgar, tough, resourceful, and sometimes unbelievably strong. And, he never gave up. It was this unending pluck, combined with his ability to nurse an orphan child as in *The Kid* (1921) that made the character wildly popular. Chaplin's melding of comedy and pathos in his films after 1918 was not only groundbreaking in terms of cinematic art, but also presented an image of "man" to the public that they had not seen before. "Charlie" was the most mischievous of boys that carried around the heart and manipulativeness of the most sensitive of girls. He was not above either kicking his foe in the pants or outright flirting with him.

Off screen, Chaplin presented similar contradictions that worked to complicate the picture of masculinity as it was then known and understood. He remained a bachelor until the age of twenty-nine and then began a series of marriages to young girls, finally achieving a happy one with eighteen-year-old Oona O'Neill, daughter of Eugene O'Neill, whom he married at the age of fifty-four. This predatory nature was also to land him in court on two occasions besides the divorces: a Mann Act trial that he won and a paternity suit that he lost. His reputation was so notorious in this area, in fact, that Vladimir Nabokov's novel *Lolita* was inspired by it (Chaplin's second child-bride was Lillita McMurray). Part of his appeal to women was his "little lost boy" persona (emphasized by his physical diminutiveness) that brought out the desire to "comfort" him from his young lovers. Even men were not immune to this persona; in between his relationships with women, Chaplin always attracted the platonic companionship of young men who were motivated only by their desire to shield him from harm.

Chaplin's sexual predation, combined with his growing wealth and problematic political beliefs (the FBI wrongly believed him to be a communist) helped finally to dethrone him in terms of his honorary "everyman" status. Beginning in the 1930s, Chaplin began to give voice to his political and eco-nomic "theories" and although such vocalizations were heralded by the adoring intelligentsia, the average person, and especially the average American citizen, could not. With his film *The Great Dictator* in 1940, in which he both satirizes Hitler and proclaims his hopes for the world in a lengthy final speech, the public demoted Chaplin from icon to pariah. *The Great Dictator* was a popular film—Chaplin's greatest moneymaker, in fact. However, this was mostly due to the fact that it had been four years since his last film and that this was his first talkie. After seeing it, the public was displeased with its political agenda.

Although Chaplin hoped to divert attention from the lecherous and predatory character the media had constructed to his new life as loving husband and father, his film *Monsieur Verdoux* (1947) threw this plan off course and worked even further damage on his already shaky relationship with the American public. A dark comedy greatly admired by critics today, it was based on the French "bluebeard," Landru. Chaplin's Landru, Henri Verdoux, survives the ravages of the depression by wooing rich old women and murdering them for their money. With this film, the carefree Little Tramp was replaced by a scheming, maniacal murderer of women—a masculine predator. *Monsieur Verdoux* was booed on opening night and withdrawn from circulation within several weeks of its opening. Chaplin, man and film character, were *both* now predatory creatures endangering the sanctity of young women in the minds of the American moviegoing public. His last American film, *Limelight,* though a thoughtful attempt on Chaplin's part to repair this damage, failed to be released in the United States as scheduled in 1952. In fact, with production completed, Chaplin was in the process of traveling with his young family to London for the first time for the premiere there when he was informed a few hours outside of New York that his reentry permit to the United States had been revoked by U.S. attorney general McGranery. Chaplin chose to settle in and live out the remainder of his life in Switzerland, from which home base he completed two more films, both less successful than any of his silents. His long and happy marriage to Oona produced eight children, the last in 1962 when Chaplin was 73. He died early on Christmas Day in 1977 with his family at his side.

Lisa K. Stein

Further Reading:

Chaplin, Charles. 1964. *My Autobiography.* New York: Simon and Schuster.

Lynn, Kenneth S. 1997. *Charlie Chaplin and His Times.* New York: Simon and Schuster.

Maland, Charles. 1989. *Chaplin and American Culture: The Evolution of a Star Image.* Princeton, NJ: Princeton University Press.

Robinson, David. 1984. *Chaplin: The Mirror of Opinion.* London: Secker and Warburg.

———. 1985. *Chaplin: His Life and Art.* New York: McGraw-Hill.

Tyler, Parker. 1972. *Chaplin: Last of the Clowns.* New York: Horizon Press.

Chemical Dependency

Chemical dependency is a biological, psychological, and social disease. Due to its insidious, progressive, and debilitating nature, chemical dependency impacts several life areas: medical health; mental health; and social, occupational, interpersonal, family, and spiritual relationships. Its economic cost to society is staggering. In 1998, the National Institute on Drug Abuse (NIDA) reported that the consequence of chemical dependency (e.g., missed days at work, job loss, health problems, criminal behavior, dependence on the welfare system) was estimated at $97.7 billion, a figure that has been progressively increasing since the mid-1970s (Swan 1988). Needless to say, the traumatic nature of chemical dependency and its painful ramifications on loved ones, family members, and concerned friends are overwhelming.

Extensive empirical research on the biological, psychological, and social facets of the disease have been ongoing during the past six decades. Accumulating evidence suggests that the initiation, progression, consequences, and treatment of the disease may be different for men and women. To date, most of this research has focused on women, while there has been little research on men. This is surprising given recent statistics suggesting that men abuse alcohol more than women. For instance, the Hazelden Foundation reported in February 2000 that, "men are more likely to drink than women (59% vs. 45%), more likely to binge drink (23.2% vs. 8.6%), and more likely to drink heavily (9.7% vs. 2.4%)" (1). In a study examining parents' grief reactions following a perinatal loss (e.g., stillbirth, neonatal death, sudden infant death syndrome), mothers frequently cried and were depressed while fathers heavily abused alcohol as a way to medicate feelings, even up to thirty months following the loss (Vance, Boyle, Najman, and Thearle 1995). Furthermore, there is research evidence suggesting that men and women respond to chemical dependency treatment differently. In one study, men relapsed more frequently than women (32 percent versus 22 percent) because the former did not attend as many treatment sessions (7.9 sessions versus 10.9 sessions), suggesting that men may be reluctant to seek professional help (Fiorentine, Anglin, Gilrivas, and Taylor 1997). Therefore, the evidence suggests that men abuse alcohol, relapse at higher rates, and express more ambivalence about seeking professional help than women. Why might this gender difference exist?

One possible answer could involve masculinity. A historically neglected research area within chemical dependency, masculinity can significantly shape addictive thoughts, feelings, and behaviors. One study, for instance, found that components of the traditional male sex role perpetuated steroid abuse and dependence in male weight lifters (Khorrami and Franklin 2001). It is possible that these same components can affect chemical dependency to other mind- and mood-altering drugs. Specifically, masculinity could interact with the psychological and social facets of the disease.

Some traditional men socially construct their masculinity through chemical dependency, where excessive drug use is seen as masculine. These men often model their drug-using behavior after famous deceased men who were chemically dependent (e.g., James Dean, Jim Morrison, Kurt Cobain). Furthermore, traditional men may compete with one another to see who can use more of the drug within a specific period of time. Clearly, competition with others, one component of the traditional male sex role, significantly contributes to the progression of the disease.

Regarding chemical dependency treatment, some traditional men may have difficulty completing the first step of a traditional twelve-step recovery program. The first step involves admitting powerlessness over the drug, believing that there is no control over its use, and admitting that one is a drug addict. Socialized to strive for autonomy and independence, traditional men eschew dependence and helplessness. These components of the traditional male sex role may make true acceptance of the first step difficult.

Some traditional men believe that masculinity is defined by remaining strong, silent, and stoic during difficult times and situations. For these men, self-disclosure of ones feelings, vulnerabilities, and fears seldom occurs. This can cause problems in chemical dependency treatment groups, where sharing concerns and emotions with other group members is therapeutically important. Furthermore, these men may not self-disclose strong cravings and urges to use drugs (which is very common in early or beginning recovery), in order to avoid being perceived as weak, unable to handle problems, or helpless.

Traditional men in chemical dependency treatment programs may benefit from interacting with less traditional men, who are in middle-to-late stages of recovery. The latter could "sponsor" the former and could model novel, drug-free behaviors. These sponsors, for instance, could show that the expression of vulnerabilities, fears, and concerns is a natural part of the recovery process. Over time, it is possible that traditional men's definition of masculinity could be reconstructed in terms of sober living beliefs, thoughts, and coping skills.

Sam Khorrami
Anthony M. Rizzo

Further Reading:

"Current Trends in Substance Abuse." 2000. *Hazelden Foundation: Research Update* (February): 1–2.

Fiorentine, R., M. D. Anglin, V. Gilrivas, and E. Taylor. 1997. "Drug Treatment: Explaining the Gender Paradox." *Journal of Substance Abuse Treatment* 32, no. 6: 653–678.

Khorrami, S., and J. Franklin. 2001. "The Influence of Competition and Lack of Emotional Expression in Perpetuating Steroid Abuse and Dependence among Male Weightlifters." *International Journal of Men's Health* 1, no. 1: 119–133.

Swan, N. 1998. "Drug Abuse Cost to Society." *NIDA NOTES* 13, no. 4: 12.

Vance, J. C., F. M. Boyle, J. M. Najman, and M. J. Thearle. 1995. "Gender Differences in Parental Psychological Distress Following Perinatal Death or Sudden Infant Death Syndrome." *British Journal of Psychiatry* 167: 806–811.

Childcare

Men's roles in childcare have changed dramatically in modern history. In the preindustrial era men participated in the household production of the family and also shared in the emotional nurturance and care of their children. Although family chores were segregated along sex-based lines, there was still a collective sharing of tasks. For example, mothers educated the young children, while fathers generally took over this task as the children got older. Fathers, mothers, and children worked in the fields together for the family's survival. This time allowed fathers to be with their children. Time working together helped children develop skills for later employment and also allowed time for togetherness and teaching. The father in this period took major responsibility for moral and religious education, literacy education, and courtship and marriage making for his children. Fathers were also thought to be sensitive in perceiving the psychological needs of their children. Because of the abilities attributed to fathers during this period, fathers were likely to have the role of counseling their children on personal matters. Besides the sensitivity of the father to the psychological needs of children, fathers also demonstrated sensitivity and nurturance in the role of caregiver. An example of a father's nurturing behavior during this period might be a father who stayed up all night with his children whenever they became seriously ill. Another father might run barefoot all night long to find help for his sick child.

Industrialization reshaped the structure of American families as fathers were taken from the home to the factory and workplace. As the father entered the workplace, his family roles were taken over almost completely by the mother and replaced by his preoccupation with salary or wage labor. As fathers' roles in the home diminished, their abilities as parents were questioned. It is during the industrial age that terms like "the missing man," "the forgotten man," or the father as "almost invisible" were heard. Clergymen and others lamented that fathers had only limited roles to play in the family at this time. The roles left for fathers were as an audience, playmate, disciplinarian, and discussion leader. Of all these roles, father as provider took precedence.

Despite the "incompetent" father myth during this period, fathers expressed great interest and devotion to their children. Fathers made many sacrifices working and providing for the material needs of their families. Fathers also cherished the time they had with their children, typically on weekends, when they would play games, read stories, or simply talk with their children. Despite images of the "part-time" father, fathers were active in the physical, moral, and mental development of their children.

Fathers typically influenced children's physical development through the role of playmate. This role also was important in the emotional bond between fathers and children. Fathers also influenced their children's moral and mental development through giving advice and supporting the child's education through financial sacrifice and emotional support.

Though many fathers are still the primary providers of material necessities such as food, clothing, and shelter, mothers have increasingly entered the workforce and many now share the provider role with their husbands. When women are in the workforce, it is necessary for men to share more childcare with their wives. Not only have structural factors in society influenced fathers to be more involved in the daily care of children, changing cultural and societal images of the "good" father have also changed. This "new" style of fathering has been called "androgynous," "involved," or "highly participant" fatherhood. This new image of fatherhood emphasizes the father who is present at the birth of his children and is also involved in the daily care of his children from the time that they are infants. The "new" father is also sensitive to his children's needs and is equally involved with both his daughters and sons. Obviously, this image is an ideal, but it nonetheless represents many fathers and their involvement with their children in the United States in the dawning years of the twenty-first century.

Fathers who are affectionate with their children help them to develop positive sibling relationships. Children are more sure of themselves and feel in greater control of their lives when they have an involved and accessible father. These children also have higher cognitive ability and have less stereotypical gender beliefs about the roles that women and men should play in society. When fathers are active in their children's intellectual, social, and physical development, children are likely to have higher educational and occupational success when they become adults.

Fathers who spend time with their children and are available to meet their children's needs also have better relationships with their children. Children who have fathers who are involved with them have more self-control, self-esteem, and better social skills.

Fathers need active participation in childcare to perpetuate and further develop their parenting skills. At the birth of their children, many fathers show sensitive caretaking abilities such as touching, kissing, talking to, and feeding their infants. Fathers learn to care for their children much like any other job; parenting skills are acquired through participation and practice. Because mothers are on the job more, they acquire more parenting skills. Because fathers often spend less time with their children than mothers, over time they feel less confidence as parents and can become less sensitive to their children's needs. However, fathers who do participate actively in the care of the children gain the skills and confidence needed for sensitive care. Fathers who fail to involve themselves with their children, particularly in cases when they do not have custody, suffer from isolation, loneliness, and depression later on in life (Snarey 1994). It can be said that if fathers want the support and love of their children later in life, fathers must support and love their children while they are young.

Shawn Christianson

See also Fatherhood; Fathers, Cultural Representations of

Further Reading:

Demos, John. 1986. *Past, Present, and Personal: The Family and the Life Course in American History*. New York: Oxford University Press.

Hawkins, Alan J., and David C. Dollahite, eds. 1997. *Generative Fathering: Beyond Deficit Perspectives*. Thousand Oaks, CA: Sage Publications.

Lamb, Michael E., ed. 1997. *The Role of the Father in Child Development*. 3d ed. New York: Wiley.

Marsiglio, William, ed. 1995. *Fatherhood: Contemporary Theory, Research, and Social Policy*. Thousand Oaks, CA: Sage.

Popenoe, David. 1996. *Life without Father: Compelling New Evidence that Fatherhood and Marriage are Indispensable for the Good of Children and Society*. New York: The Free Press.

Snarey, John. 1994. *How Fathers Care for the Next Generation: A Four-Decade Study*. Cambridge, MA: Harvard University Press.

Childhood

Childhood is a period of tremendous development and growth, and also, according to most developmental psychologists, a period in which gender identity must be established so that the child can grow up to be a healthy man or woman. Our need to establish the gender identity of another person may even be more pressing than our need to establish it in ourselves.

When we see a newborn child, for example, we often immediately impose stereotypes about masculinity or femininity, assuming that the baby is gentle, nice, and delicate if it is a girl and sturdy, strong, and stable if it is a boy. The examples of differences that we believe are there are numerous, and we draw such conclusions despite the fact that those differences actually do not exist between newborn children of different sexes.

That we perceive newborn children in different ways has been established in a number of research studies. In a classic study, Rubin, Provenzano, and Luria (1974) interviewed couples of parents about their newborn children. The parents were asked to describe their children on a special form. Overall, the girls were judged as gentler, smaller, nicer, less attentive, and more delicate. The boys were judged as firmer, sturdier, more alert, stronger, and better coordinated. Actually the fifteen newborn girls and fifteen boys did not differ in length, weight, or Apgar scores, a test of basic body functions given shortly after birth. (Fathers were actually more insistent about these differences than were mothers.)

Furthermore, we treat infants differently when we think we know their sex. Will, Self, and Datan (1976) conducted a study in which some mothers encountered a six-month-old boy. Half of them were led to believe that he was a boy and half that he was a girl. The main result from this study was that the mothers could not differentiate between boys and girls at age six months. All the mothers also said that there were no differences in six-month-old boys' and girls' behavior. Still, they treated the child differently depending on what they thought his or her sex was.

Worth mentioning is also the study of Condry and Condry (1976). More than 200 persons saw a short videotape in which a nine-month-old child looked at different objects and reacted to them. From all the objects, the child chose to play with a jack-in-the-box. After a while the child started to cry. The observers were asked to explain why the child reacted that way. Half of them, who thought they saw a boy, said the reaction was one of anger. The other half, who thought they saw a girl, said that "she" became afraid.

These studies, as well as many more, show consistent patterns. Adults see differences between infant boys and girls that are not there. They treat infants differently depending on the infants' sex. And very often this differentiating, this *gendering*, goes on without the adult even being aware of it.

So, massive gendering influences are brought to bear even on infants. This process goes on as the child grows older, and old gendered patterns are reinforced through life. It is therefore no surprise that children very early show different behaviors depending on their sex. They have been gendered.

These studies reveal how children are affected by the outside world. This view can be completed with a view from developmental psychology. Modern theorists give a very similar picture of how the early development looks. While Freud thought he was observing cultural universals, Dinnerstein (1976), Chodorow (1978), and Bergman (1990) base their theories on the empirical observation of unequal childcare in the early years. Both girls and boys spend their first years very close to their mothers. In their theoretical appropriation of Freud, they argue that in the early period of a child's, life its mother represents everything the child needs: food,

warmth, love, and other feelings. This could, of course, also be expressed in other, more negative, terms: that the mother has complete power over the child in this period. From the child's point of view, the child and its mother constitute a whole, the child cannot see itself as separated from its mother. The assumption that the child sees its mother as the person it loves most in the world is fully justified.

In this early period it is difficult to believe that girls' and boys' conception of themselves should differ. We will never know how they regard themselves, so we assume that their views are the same. Eventually, the child begins to realize that its mother also has a life "outside" the child, that she has a life of her own, with her own wishes, which are sometimes in direct conflict with the child's.

In the eyes of the child the mother changes from being the most loved person in the world to taking up a double role—a role that is also infused with conflict for the child. The mother becomes the most loved person in the world and at the same time the most threatening and dangerous person.

This conflict—and it is indeed a conflict in the most profound psychological sense to see one and the same person as both the most loved and the most feared—is tackled in completely different ways by girls and boys. The solution of this conflict, of course, depends primarily on how the child is treated by people close to it.

A girl who sees her points of likeness with her mother will try to keep close to her mother and imitate her. In a way, she continues her close relationship with her mother. This relationship is already established when the girl becomes closer to her father, and it can be said that her relationship with her father is superimposed on her relationship with her mother.

When a boy discovers that he is different from his mother and that he resembles his father, he is forced to deny or quell his love of his mother. He must identify with his father and repudiate his mother. He is forced to define his own limits in order to solve the conflict between the two images of his mother —loving and threatening. He has to strengthen his masculinity and he does so by imitating his father and adjusting to the man's world, while suppressing his relationship with his mother.

The fact that many fathers are absent does not change this picture. Most children's lives include adult men who are close enough for the children to realize that men are different from women. Even if this image becomes stereotyped and/or blurred, the children still regard women and men as different.

To continue our description of the boy, it could be said that because his father is not particularly close to him, he will experience and define masculinity as everything his mother does not stand for. Thus masculinity will have no substance of its own—it becomes the negation of femininity.

With the separation from his mother as the starting point, and underlined by several other factors during his development, the boy will regard himself as separate and autonomous and having well-defined limits. In other words, the boy sees himself as independent.

The drawback may be that his detachment from his mother can lead to the boy developing a fear of entering into close relationships, not necessarily to the extent that he is unable to handle a close relationship, but rather that he develops a fear of entering into close relationships.

In any event, the break from his mother is traumatic for the little boy because he has been so close to her. With this repudiation and disidentification, boyhood has begun. He learns to devalue women as a demonstration of his successful separation from mother. He learns that he will have to act like his father and other boys to be accepted as a man. He learns that being a man has costs—in terms of emotional connection, intimacy, and dependency.

Gilligan (1982) also stresses the development for boys toward autonomy and inde-pendence. She says there is a clear line from the early separation from the mother via struggle for independence to autonomy. It is a central theme for boys to set up their own boundaries, to cut themselves off from others and in that way avoid close relationships.

Boys measure their progress during growth by what other men and boys do, think, and feel, and in this way they relate to the "male world" with its dominant features of efficiency and competitiveness.

Lars Jalmert

See also Boyhood

Further Reading:

Bergman, S. J. 1990. (Lecture at Stone Center, Wellesley College, Wellesley MA, 7 November. Also published in Sweden as "Ömsesidighet i relationer en utmaning för dagens män." *Kvinnovetenskaplig tidskrift* 1: 22–39, 1993.)

Chodorow, Nancy. 1978. *The Reproduction of Mothering: Psychoanalysis and the Sociology of Gender.* Berkeley, CA: University of California Press.

Condry, J., and S. Condry. 1976. "Sex Differences: A Study of the Eye of the Beholder." *Child Development* 47: 812–819.

Dinnerstein, Dorothy. 1976. *The Mermaid and the Minotaur.* New York: Harper and Row.

Gilligan, Carol. 1982. *In a Different Voice. Psychological Theory and Women's Development.* Cambridge, MA: Harvard University Press.

Rubin, J. Zick, F. J. Provenzano, and Zella Luria. 1974. "The Eye of the Beholder: Parents Views on Sex of Newborns." *American Journal of Orthopsychiatry* 44, no. 4: 512–519.

Will, J. A., P. A. Self, and Nancy Datan. 1976. "Maternal Behavior and Perceived Sex of Infant." *American Journal of Orthopsychiatry* 46: 135–139.

Childlessness

The childless man is best defined as a universal enigma. Challenging the widespread association between adult status and parenthood, preferably through reproduction, the man without progeny defies description almost everywhere. The story of childlessness and masculinity is not, however, a neatly ordered, clearly defined, thread of knowledge. Rather it is best described as one part of a two-part, mostly invisible history of humanity, emerging from myth and storytelling into the world of formal scholarship only recently. The small body of current knowledge suggests a unique transformation in adult development may be underway for both sexes.

Childless men often appear in mythology, folklore, biography, and literature as archetypes. These men are presented as idealized or demonized images, as saints, demons, fools, or romantic heroes. Implied rather than directly stated, their childlessness is evidenced in an absence of worldly concerns. Though familiar and popular, these men are not known to us as images of normal or fulfilled adults.

Cross-cultural gender studies find reproductive imperatives as an essential universal ingredient for achieving adult status for both sexes. For men, procreation and sexual potency are essential components of achieving manhood and social competence in most societies. A childless man, a man who does not pursue women or sex with the aim of reproduction, is a deviant, diminished, or highly suspicious man (Gilmore 1990, 32).

The emphasis on reproduction as a cornerstone of gender identity and adult status makes sense given the precarious nature of human life until recently. High rates of childlessness, although usually measured in terms of female fertility, have been regarded as indicators of extreme social strain and/or social decadence for both sexes. For example, historians have noted the manifest tolerance of voluntary childlessness during the latter days of the Roman empire (Kenkel 1966, 77). Anthropologist Nancy Scheper-Hughes's (2001) work in rural Ireland in the 1970s is a case study in the link between declining fertility and social malaise. Men who were not fathers were often unmarried or married in celibate unions. Like their female counterparts, they were remarkable to the anthropologist precisely because they were so unremarkable in their own community.

Similar trends can be found in early American history. In New England during the late nineteenth century, deliberate childlessness aroused attention (Calhoun 1919). The increase in the number of childless wives during the colonial period was viewed as an indicator of social decadence (Crum 1914).

Rates of childlessness rose to an all-time high during the Great Depression (May 1995, 81) and have been regarded as a tragedy and a sacrifice but also as an indicator of shifting opportunities for both sexes. Rates of childlessness among the Baby Boom generation (born between 1946 and 1964) are similar to those recorded during the Great Depression and are also believed to reflect similar although expanded constraints and opportunities (May 1995, 182). In other words, once an index of strained social conditions, childlessness has expanded its historical meaning in the early twenty-first century to include the opportunity for a renegotiation of gender roles for both sexes.

During the 1970s a literature emerged on involuntary childlessness. This research, growing in proportion to the size of the industry surrounding it, reflects a shift in thinking about causes of infertility as well the role reproduction plays in the human psyche. Until recently, men were excluded from consideration in the infertility picture because the problem was considered a female one. Now infertility is viewed as a couple's problem. Expert opinion suggests that women were blamed for infertility for millennia precisely because the idea was too humiliating for men to consider about themselves.

Between the 1960s and 1980s a small body of evidence emerged on the topic of chosen childlessness (Veevers 1979). Focused mainly on couples and women, this work largely ignores men. It is noteworthy though that as the idea of reproductive choice was gaining ground in the society at large, negative images of intentional childlessness marked the views others' held of both sexes choosing it (Houseknecht 1987, 385).

Motivated by the first male fertility study conducted by the United States Census

Bureau, Lunneborg published the first exploratory study of the motives and consequences of voluntary childlessness from a male perspective. Based on in-depth interviews with American and British men, the author found diverse motives for rejecting fatherhood, in the process challenging many myths about men and reproduction.

As part of an ongoing study of voluntarily childless women and couples, Clarke (2002) turned attention to men. Because diverse forms of childlessness are common features of societies like the United States (where such phenomena as increased life expectancy, reduced fertility, and delayed childbearing are also common), this exploratory work considers intentional childlessness of particular value in its ability to highlight the problems and promises of this transformed life cycle. Specifically, childless men offer clues to a unique shift in human development already underway in the ideas both sexes hold about what it means to be an adult. According to this view, this unique shift has several components, among them a psychological stance suggesting hidden difficulties both for human society and the scientific community.

The cornerstone of this unique shift is the interacting influence of changes in life expectancy and fertility. On average, humans have longer lives and fewer children than their counterparts in earlier generations. This means that both sexes have more of the life cycle about which relatively little is known (i.e., adulthood) and less of the universal mechanism for coping with it and giving it meaning (i.e., fertility, children). Reproduction and parenthood, universal lynchpins of gender, are diminishing as defining features of adulthood. Other threads of change are involved in this shift. A revolution in the world of work, sometimes called the Third Industrial Revolution, is another new challenge. Work, the way people's worth has been measured for the whole market era, is increasingly unstable. Revolutions in marriage, in the family, in childhood, and in the

timing and nature of life cycle transitions also overlap with work-related issues (Skolnick and Skolnick 2001). While new opportunities are involved in these changes, they also place considerable uncertainty and heavy demands for inventiveness in the lives of both sexes (Clarke 2002).

Clarke (2002) has placed these overlapping shifts in two related perspectives. The first places these previously described revolutions in the context of human history. Many believe that these revolutions are taking place at a unique time, a time comparable to other "watershed" periods when the long-term survival of a culture is at stake. Although perhaps more difficult for people to think about than the issues described earlier (e.g., marriage and family), matters of globalization, ecological sustainability, and questions of human rights are among the other pressing challenges confronting contemporary humanity.

In this view, the demands of current conditions can be appreciated from the metaphors used to described them (e.g., "the edge of history"). Deviant behavior (e.g., childlessness) under these circumstances can and often does serve important social functions, among them giving birth to new social forms that in time become the basis of social and cultural transformation. Childlessness as an example has been identified as one of fifteen ideas that could shake the world. It is viewed as having transformational potential because of the broad spectrum of social parenting associated with childlessness (in the past and in the present) and because of the willingness and ability of some (for a variety of reasons) to challenge strong social pressure to parent and act upon an acute and realistic awareness of an inability/unwillingness to parent.

The other perspective on the shift is a psychological one, addressing a discrepancy between reality and ideas for interpreting it. Though adults have more adulthood and more childlessness, ideas about adulthood appear to be largely restricted to reproduction and parenthood. This contradiction is masked by the widespread endorsement of ideas about reproductive choice and freedom that, according to research focused on the responses of other people to the childless decision, are not entirely what they seem to be. Rejection, anger, and hostility are not uncommon responses from other people to the childless decision. These responses also include challenges and suspicions about a broad range of emblems associated with adult identity, among them religious and ethnic commitments, competence, generosity, liking of children, love of parents, maturity, mental health and stability, patriotism, and commitment in relationships.

This line of research has interpreted these findings psychologically, suggesting that the idea of reproductive choice is largely mythic in nature. This myth appears as a broadly shared psychocultural mechanism for coping with anxiety and facilitating denial in the developmental shift. This reasoning suggests that the myth functions both as a mask covering anxiety about childlessness and the other changes linked with it and as a mechanism for denying the challenges involved in inventing a broader definition of adulthood for both sexes. The influence of this myth (in this view) is not limited to popular thinking but extends to influencing the place of childlessness in the workings of mainstream science (Clarke 2002).

Though various forms of childlessness are a distinctive feature of the life cycle in demographically mature societies, the subject of childlessness is conspicuously absent or dismissed as unimportant within the framework of mainstream science. As noted earlier, though a small body of knowledge on childlessness evolved in the late 1970s, the subject actually dwindled as a topic of interest as the phenomenon gained ground in the demographic realities of people's lives. In other words, the myth of reproductive choice, which makes choosing within a restricted range (e.g., alternatives leading to parenthood) seem to be the same as choosing between options (e.g.,

parenthood and childlessness) within an expanded range, renders childlessness invisible and silent. This psychological and cultural sleight-of-mind has been ascribed to what cultures do not want to know about themselves and more specifically what cultures do not want to know about gender.

The question of what is known about childless men depends upon where we look and whether we can see that which mythology renders invisible. As described earlier in this review, childless men are in fact quite common in biography, fiction, and mythology. Creating a life at the edge of human experience is for better and for worse the stuff of well-known lives (e.g., Jesus, Sherlock Holmes, Gregor Mendel). Even when men have been fathers, temporary or situational childlessness, the freedom from daily and direct demands of parenting, has played a prominent role in marking life conditions. Furthermore, childlessness of one kind or another is a silent and hidden variable in much contemporary research. As an organizing variable in human life, parenthood sets limits. For better and for worse, such limits are freer to vary under conditions of childlessness, which as already noted are in fact common.

In terms of formal research on childless men, it is instructive to keep in mind that involving men in reproductive research in general is relatively recent. Therefore, involving them in research on childlessness (other than the infertile trying to conceive question) is close to nonexistent. As such, research specifically focused on men and childlessness is best described as being at the descriptive, exploratory stages.

Childless men appear to represent a broad cross section of society: *Traditionals* tend to look back, rejecting the social system as it is and the modern secular worldview accompanying it. *Moderns,* representing the scope of the mainstream, generally accept the social system and its workings and the worldview that goes with it. *Cultural Creatives* look forward and in many ways away from the mainstream. Often critical of the social system, they are in many ways attempting to redefine it and go beyond it. These categories do not mean to imply distinct nonoverlapping concerns or a lack of diversity within groups, but rather value priorities for different groups of people at this time (Clarke 2002).

Childless men arrive at their decision in a variety of ways. Some (like some childless women) decide early in development, in childhood or adolescence. Other decisions are shared decisions between a man and his partner. Still others are decisions where a man who wanted children accepted his partner's wish to remain childless. Though people commonly believe that women encounter more derision than men for the childless decision, it may be that people simply respond differently but with similar sentiments. Though childless men do seem to feel (more than childless women) that others may suspect their decision masks some form of sexual dysfunction, they also encounter (like women) the restricted range of ideas others often hold about adulthood in the form of suspicions about immaturity and irresponsibility.

Men's reasons for initially considering childlessness and for maintaining commitment to the decision over time touch on virtually all the revolutions described in the previous section. In other words, many new adult demands require choosing between the traditional press of gender (e.g., being a breadwinner) and new realities (e.g., the revolution in work).

Among the more common reasons are those suggesting the potential for innovation in deviant approaches to novel circumstances. Although not the only source of motivation, work-related decisions are common. Childless men have both the freedom from work and the freedom to work and this comes through loud and clear in the admittedly small body of evidence (Lunneborg 1999; Clarke 2002). Work concerns include but are frequently not restricted to the economics of work. Among these stories are

those desiring meaningful work or the opportunity to pursue activities that may not earn income at all. Some decisions reflect the desire to reduce the priority of making money in their decisions about life in general.

Overlapping with work issues is often the quest for time. Time for personal development can be a strong source of motivation. Childless people often love learning for its own sake regardless of their own level of education or the social prestige associated with their occupation.

Other factors showing up somewhat less frequently point to the potential for innovation in nonetheless deviant responses to common life decisions. A desire to reduce stress or to address health-related concerns (mental and physical) is included here. The absence of a strong desire for children, a dislike of children, or a belief in being unable to bring to bear suitable conditions for parenting also shows up in men's decision making. In the specific areas of parenting, men sometimes express a desire to avoid repeating parental mistakes. Concerns about the state of childhood and children's lives also emerges in some men's narratives about their decisions. Existing caring obligations, sometimes of a longstanding nature, to one or more family members also play a role in childless decisions. Infertility, concerns about passing on inherited conditions, and the state of a partner's health show up as well. Some men include in their reasoning concerns about global conditions and the quality of life for young people in the future.

Like childless women, childless men do not usually appear to have just one reason for choosing not to parent, and also like childless women, reasons for maintaining the decision change over time. Unlike childless women though, who often cite the desire to have control over their lives as a reason for not having children, this does not appear to arise in the reasons given by childless men.

Though myth and popular wisdom insist that a primary motive in the male (any) life is reproduction and progeny, this issue hardly surfaces in present scholarship. While this apparent gap may be due to the limitations of a small body of knowledge, it may also be due to the workings of mainstream science.

Though reproduction as the primary (even sole) purpose of living things dominates popular and scientific thinking, this may not represent the complete picture of society in any species. Research has shown that sexuality and reproduction are far more variable throughout the animal kingdom, including our closest living relatives, than is usually suggested by either popular or scientific ideas. Nonreproducing adults are ever present in the social organization of many species. In primates, including ourselves, the social roles and functions of these are as a rule ignored.

Perhaps the reproductive motives of all species, including ourselves (homo sapiens), are more diverse and more malleable than we care to believe and perhaps those beliefs unwittingly shape what we believe we know and how we go about inquiring about reproduction and parenting.

Though the study of men and masculinity arose from the study of gender, both have generally ignored the possibility that, while helpful, common research paradigms (e.g., methods, indicators, sampling) may lack the validity of the past under current conditions. In this regard, the study of childless men and couples has been instructive in ferreting out other potentially fruitful procedures for studying gender issues (e.g., adult identity issues, creativity, social values, other species). These suggestions are based on assumptions that childlessness can be viewed as a social index of a world where men and women are being confronted by the burden and privilege of unprecedented choices in the task of reinventing the meaning of what it means to be an adult and in the process are redefining childhood as well (Clarke 2002).

While childlessness often conjures up images of immaturity, it can also be the ultimate existential challenge. To be without child, intentionally or otherwise, increases the likelihood of confronting the mixed blessing of an awareness of the human condition along with the task of coping with it and making meaning in spite of or because of it. Certainly, childlessness creates freedom from many social constraints, but it also poses the problem of having the freedom to invent, to work with ambiguity. Thus, a condition usually linked with the life of "mythic figures," where this essay began, is now in varying degrees the burden and the privilege of both sexes. What we learn about this depends a good deal upon what society wants to know about itself. At this writing, though childlessness is common, the childless man, like the childless woman, is mostly an enigma.

Paula K. Clarke

Further Reading:

Calhoun, Arthur W. 1919. *A Social History of the American Family from Colonial to Present Times.* Cleveland, OH: Arthur H. Clark.

Clarke, Paula K. 2002. "Intentionally Childless Men and the Procreative Imperative; Lessons from Lives in Times of Change." (Paper presented at the Thirty-Second Popular Culture Association and Twenty Fourth American Culture Association Annual Conference. Toronto: 14 March 2002.)

Crum, Frederick S. 1914. "The Decadence of the Native American Stock." *American Statistical Association Journal* 14 (September): 215–222.

Gilmore, David D. 1990. *Manhood in the Making: Cultural Concepts of Masculinity.* New Haven, CT: Yale University Press.

Houseknecht, Sharon K. 1987. "Voluntary Childlessness." Pp. 369–395 in *Handbook of Marriage and the Family.* Edited by Martin B. Sussman and Susan K. Steinmetz. New York: Plenum Press.

Kenkel, W. 1966. *The Family in Perspective.* New York: Appleton, Century, Crofts.

Lunneborg, Patricia. 1999. *The Chosen Lives of Childfree Men.* Westport, CT: Bergin and Garvey.

May, Elaine Tyler. 1995. *Barren in the Promised Land: Childless Americans and the Pursuit of Happiness.* Cambridge, MA: Harvard University Press.

Rutter, Virginia. 1996. "Who Stole Infertility?" *Psychology Today* (March/April): 46–68.

Scheper-Hughes, Nancy. 2001. *Saints, Scholars, and Schizophrenics: Mental Illness in Rural Ireland.* Berkeley, CA: University of California Press.

Veevers, Jean E. 1979. "Voluntary Childlessness: A Review of Issues and Evidence." *Marriage and Family Review* 2: 1–24.

China Boy

Gus Lee's autobiographical novel *China Boy* (1994) asks how a second-generation Chinese American male can attain manhood, as defined by post–World War II American society, without discarding his Chinese ethnicity. Set in the San Francisco Panhandle, this *Bildungsroman* dramatizes the gender issues and racism that problematize identity formation for Asian American males.

Lee's American-born protagonist, Kai, learns from his father, T. K. Ting, that authentic manhood is incompatible with Chinese ethnicity. Therefore, Ting wants his son to emulate his ideal man: an American soldier educated at West Point, the heroic "Major Henry Norman Schwarzhedd." In the words of Yichin Shen, "Ting equates ideal manhood with a gun and an army uniform" (7). Ting believes Americanization is essential to manliness because he has internalized what David L. Eng calls "the historical configuration of the Chinese American male as feminized and passive" (95).

In contrast to Ting, Kai's mother, Mahmee, symbolizes motherland China and dreams her son will become a peace-loving Chinese scholar and a second Mozart, bridging East and West. The clash in Kai's parents' values adumbrates the second-generation Chinese American male's dilemma: to assimilate or not to assimilate? Mahmee believes Kai should embrace both cultures, whereas T. K. Ting advocates complete assimilation, equating Chinese ethnicity with effeminate primitivism.

Chinese racial and gender stereotypes are, however, subverted, as well as reinforced by Lee's complex portraits of Kai's parents. Mahmee, in her youth, emerges as a rebellious intellectual, though devoted to her Chinese father. Her pacifism partly reflects Patricia Chu's description of "the Asian American mother as the would-be enforcer of misapplied 'Asian' values that threaten the autonomy, Americanness, and masculinity of their American-born sons." (61). But Mahmee herself also earns Kai's admiration as a heroic fighter who led her daughters across war-torn China. Moreover, she teaches Kai about legendary and historical Chinese warriors, counterbalancing his father's notions of Chinese masculinity.

At home Ting appears martial but passive, hot-tempered yet browbeaten. After Mahmee dies, Ting asserts his American manliness by marrying Edna McGurk, a white supremacist who resembles Marilyn Monroe and whose abuse of her stepchildren replicates the U.S. exclusion and oppression of Chinese. Shen says, "on a symbolic level, Edna is America, and the children of the Ting family are its unwanted stepchildren" (4). Ting, like a stereotypical emasculated Chinese male, submits to Edna's dominance. His failure to protect his children from her persecution impedes Kai's maturation and exacerbates his alienation from a society that marginalizes Asian Americans.

Lee portrays Ting as too weak to oppose Edna's fascism, let alone teach Kai how to fight like a man. That task befalls Kai's YMCA coaches, men of diverse ethnic backgrounds who transform him from a helpless victim to a manly pugilist. These surrogate fathers, all veterans of World War II and the boxing ring, exemplify transcendence of gender polarities by combining masculine strength with nurturance and sensitivity. Indeed, Kai's primary substitute father, Tony Barraza, repudiates Ting's masculine ideal of the soldier hero and condemns the brutality of war, even though Barraza himself is a decorated veteran.

The YMCA coaches, unlike Ting, understand that Kai cannot pass the test of his manhood until he begins to construct a Chinese American identity, emblematized by Mahmee's photo and Chinese calligraphy. *China Boy* ends by suggesting that the tension between American manhood and Chinese ethnicity can be overcome: Kai reconciles them by defeating two major symbols of American racism, his stepmother Edna and the neighborhood bully, Big Willie Mack. But, as Christine So notes, the humorous nature of Kai's victories reflects "the inherent anxiety lurking behind such a project" (152).

Margaret K. Schramm

See also Asian American Men's Studies

Further Reading:

Chin, Frank, Jeffrey Paul Chan, Lawson Fusao Inada, and Shawn Wong, eds. 1975. *Aiiieeee!: An Anthology of Asian American Writers.* Garden City, NY: Anchor.

Chu, Patricia P. 2000. *Assimilating Asians: Gendered Strategies of Authorship in Asian America.* Durham, NC: Duke University Press.

Eng, David L. 2001. *Racial Castration: Managing Masculinity in Asian America.* Durham, NC: Duke University Press.

Nguyen, Viet Thanh. 2000. "The Remasculinization of Chinese America: Race, Violence, and the Novel." *American Literary History* 12, nos. 1–2: 130–157.

Shen, Yichin. 2002. "The Site of Domestic Violence and the Altar of Phallic Sacrifice in Gus Lee's *China Boy.*" *College Literature* 29, no. 2: 99–113.

So, Christine. 1996. "Delivering the Punch Line: Racial Combat as Comedy in Gus Lee's *China Boy.*" *MELUS* 21, no. 4 (Winter): 141–155.

Circumcision

Circumcision is the surgical removal of the foreskin (prepuce) of the penis. The long-standing practice of circumcising newborns and older boys stands as an issue of distinct interest to men and women worldwide. Medical circumcision is currently practiced as an elective, prophylactic procedure on approximately two-thirds of boys born in the United States, most often as a matter of course and covered by health insurance. The present rate of circumcision in the United States is in sharp decline from a high of 85 percent in 1960. Infant circumcision rates in other countries range from 1 or 2 percent in Britain and New Zealand, to 18 percent in Australia and 25 percent in Canada. Circumcision is also practiced on older boys and adult males for medical, religious, and aesthetic reasons.

Although seldom performed before the nineteenth century, routine medical circumcision of newborn boys became the norm during the Victorian era, when it was believed to cure or prevent numerous "ills" including masturbation, promiscuity, headaches, bed-wetting, and insanity. While widely regarded as unnecessary surgery, there is some medical evidence to suggest the efficacy of circumcision, and there is much confusion about, and opposition to, parents' decisions to have their newborn sons circumcised.

Medical circumcision commonly occurs at the hospital on the first or second day after birth and prior to the mother and child being discharged. The procedure may be done by the child's pediatrician, the mother's obstetrician, or by another attending physician, with parents observing or not by their own choice. Several different methods are employed for the procedure according to the preference of the doctor, including surgical scissors, Gomco clamp, Plastibell, and a Mogen (shield) device. A topical or local anesthesia is frequently applied in the case of newborn circumcision, while adults undergoing the procedure may receive a general anesthetic.

Several medical conditions have been correlated with intact foreskins, including urinary tract infections (UTI), sexually transmitted disease (STD), and penile cancer, along with higher rates of cervical and uterine cancer in the female sexual partners of uncircumcised men. Between 2 and 8 percent of males not circumcised at birth ultimately require a circumcision later in life because of complications related to the retained foreskin. While the practice of circumcision remains widespread, a 1999 policy statement by the American Academy of Pediatrics (AAP) states that although "existing scientific evidence demonstrates potential medical benefits of newborn male circumcision," the AAP concludes that the "data are not sufficient to recommend routine neonatal circumcision" (Task Force on Circumcision, AAP 1999, 686). Their stance is shared by the American and Canadian Medical Associations, the American Cancer Society, and numerous other medical professional organizations.

Circumcision is currently practiced ritually by members of both the Jewish and Moslem faiths, and evidence of it can be traced to the ancient Semites through biblical references and Egyptian artifacts. Weiss and Harter (1998) suggest a 10,000-year history of circumcision found in evidence from Paleolithic-era cave drawings (19). Circumcision is the only surgery mentioned in the Hebrew Bible where God speaks to the aged Abraham, commanding Abraham to circumcise himself and "every man child among you that is eight days old shall be circumcised" including slaves and servants (Genesis 17:10–14). Abraham's son Isaac was the first Jew to be circumcised at eight days of age, and this practice continues today with a Jewish ceremony called *brit milah* meaning "covenant of circumcision." Most modern Jews fulfill the covenant by engaging the services of a specially trained *mohel* to perform the procedure, often in a loving ritual of welcome into the community of Jews that takes place in their own homes. Although still a small number, it is increasingly more common for Jewish parents to celebrate the birth of a son with a ceremony that eschews the actual circumcision, leaving their child uncut; it should be noted that by Jewish law, a boy does not need to be circumcised to be considered a Jew.

In Islamic tradition, Abraham circumcised his son Ishmael, a precursor to Muhammad, when Ishmael was age thirteen. Although the Muslim holy book, the Koran, does not require circumcision, the ritual is widely practiced throughout the Islamic civilization.

The decision of parents increasingly to not circumcise their newborn sons is based on personal beliefs and observations that align with the ambivalence of the medical community. Parents fear causing excessive pain and trauma to a defenseless infant, find no clear and compelling medical reason for excising the prepuce, and reject the oft-cited aesthetic argument that their son should look like his dad (assuming that the father is circumcised, and also that father and son will be comparing their penises).

These same sentiments are echoed, indeed championed, by several active, anticircumcision groups, including the National Organization of Circumcision Information Resource Centers (NOCIRC), the National Organization to Halt the Abuse and Routine Mutilation of Males (NOHARMM), and Doctors Opposing Circumcision (DOC). In addition, a nascent "foreskin reclamation" movement encourages men who are circumcised to stretch their remaining prepuce or elect reconstructive surgery to undo the infant circumcision over which they had no control.

Female circumcision is practiced in certain Islamic and Arab countries, as well as in Central African nations that have been influenced by Muslin culture. The practice takes many forms, from surgical removal of the clitoral hood to *clitoridectomy* (removal of part or all of the clitoris), and other extreme procedures that excise the vulva or sew shut most of the vaginal opening. While these procedures are widely considered to be misogynist in origin, the American medical community has seen a rise in female circumcision consistent with immigration from regions where it is traditionally practiced. A rider to the 1997 omnibus appropriations bill signed into law by President Bill Clinton outlawed the practice of genital mutilation in the United States for anyone under the age of eighteen.

Douglas M. Gertner

Thanks to Chuck Ault, Rabbi Stephen Booth, Fred Grossman, M.D., and Martin Koyle, M.D., for reviewing a draft of this entry.

Further Reading:

Bigelow, Jim. 1989. *Exploring Circumcision: History, Myths, Psychology, Restoration, Sexual Pleasure, and Human Rights.* Aptos, CA: Hourglass.

Boyd, Billy Ray. 1998. *Circumcision Exposed: Rethinking a Medical and Cultural Tradition.* Freedom, CA: Crossing Press.

Goldman, Ronald. 1997. *Circumcision: The Hidden Trauma.* Boston: Vanguard.

Gollaher, David. 2000. *Circumcision: A History of the World's Most Controversial Surgery.* New York: Basic Books.

Task Force on Circumcision, American Academy of Pediatrics. 1999. "Circumcision Policy Statement (RE9850)." *Pediatrics* 3 (19 March): 686–693.

Weiss, Gerald N., and Andrea W. Harter. 1998. *Circumcision: Frankly Speaking.* Fort Collins, CO: Wiser Publications.

Zoske, Joseph. 1998. "Male Circumcision: A Gender Perspective." *Journal of Men's Studies* 6, no. 2: 189–208.

The Citadel and the Virginia Military Institute (VMI)

The Citadel is the military college of South Carolina, located in Charleston, South Carolina. The Virginia Military Institute (VMI) is located in Lexington, Virginia. In the early 1990s these two schools became embroiled in major lawsuits involving the admission of women to their corps of cadets.

The Citadel was founded in 1842 initially to protect the city of Charleston from impending slave revolts, and VMI was founded three years earlier. Graduates of both schools served among the first Confederate soldiers in the Civil War; VMI students raced to the Battle of New Market, one of the first skirmishes of the war in Virginia, while Citadel students were the first to fire on the Star of the West, a steamship carrying supplies to Fort Sumter in Charleston harbor—the first shots fired in the war.

In 2003 the two schools are the only state-supported military institutions of higher learning in the United States (although other state universities, such as Texas A&M and Virginia Tech, have corps of cadets for their ROTC students.) About 20 percent of their graduates make the military a career; the rest leave soldiering to others after college.

In the early 1990s, VMI and the Citadel became lightning rods in gender politics when the Civil Rights Division of the U.S. Department of Justice brought a sex discrimination case against VMI, and a young female South Carolina high school student named Shannon Faulkner applied for admission to the Citadel. These two battles were fought on parallel tracks in federal district courts in both Charleston and Roanoke and were eventually joined when the Circuit Court of Appeals for the Fourth Circuit in Richmond heard both. Eventually, the VMI case (*United States v. Virginia,* 116 S.Ct. 2285) reached the Supreme Court, where a seven-to-one decision forced the school to admit women; Justice Clarence Thomas recused himself because his son had attended VMI. (The Citadel went coeducational the day after the VMI decision was reached.)

The suit by the Justice Department argued that the all-male admissions policy at VMI and the Citadel was a violation of the Fourteenth Amendment to the U.S. Constitution, which guarantees all citizens equal protection under the law. VMI and the Citadel countered by denying that they had violated such rights, claiming that, unlike race-based discrimination, their admission standards passed the criteria set forward by the Supreme Court that permitted discrimination against women.

In essence, the schools' defense centered on the unique educational methodology they employed to develop their vision of manhood—a code that included honor, integrity, and discipline, as well as blind obedience to authority, vicious hazing, and stupefying indoctrination, which was defended as necessary to instill the new corporatist values of the school. Both schools maintained a strict honor code, which proclaimed, "A Cadet does not lie, cheat, or steal or tolerate those who do."

The life of a first-year cadet was particularly harsh, and "rats" (VMI) and "knobs" (Citadel) were subjected to constant harassment, fierce scrutiny by upperclassmen for potential infractions, and rigid physical standards coupled with more relaxed academic standards. As Pat Conroy, a Citadel graduate and best-selling author wrote, in his novel *The Lords of Discipline,* which was based on his experiences as a Citadel cadet during the era of integration:

> We did not receive a college education at the Institute, we received an indoctrination, and all our courses were designed to make us malleable, unimaginative, uninquisitive citizens of the republic, impregnable to ideas—or thought—unsanctioned by authority.
>
> The entire design of our education at the Institute was the creation of the citizen soldier, a moral amphibian who could navigate both the civilian and military worlds with equal facility. It demanded limitless conformity from its sons, and we concurred blindly. We spent our four years as passionate true believers, catechists of our harsh and spiritually arctic milieu, studying, drilling, arguing in the barracks, cleaning our rooms, shining our shoes, writing on the latrine walls, writing papers, breaking down our rifles, and missing the point. The Institute was making us stupid; irretrievably, tragically, and infinitely stupid. (Conroy 1986, 80–81)

VMI and the Citadel took different tacks in arguing that their "adversative" educational methodology was unsuitable for women, and therefore not in violation of the Constitution. VMI claimed that women possessed neither the physical toughness nor the emotional wherewithal to withstand the brutality of the first-class system. The school claimed that there simply was no demand for a VMI-type education among women, and should they receive it, they would fail.

The Citadel conceded that there were, indeed, women who could perform adequately and might even seek the sort of education the Citadel provided. (They pointed to the successful gender integration at West Point and in the U.S. military as evidence.) However, they argued that what made the Citadel education special was the dramatic and intense bonding among the first-year cadets as a result of their shared experience of initiation. This fragile bonding would be upset by women's entry, and women would,

in effect, experience a sort of "Catch–22": The education they sought would disappear the moment they entered.

Although the district court in Virginia found in favor of VMI, the circuit court demanded that the state of Virginia develop an alternative that would provide for women an appropriate educational opportunity equal to that which VMI afforded men. VMI's remedial plan proposed the Virginia Women's Institute for Leadership (VWIL) at nearby Mary Baldwin College, a genteel all-women's college. The Citadel followed with a proposal for the South Carolina Institute for Leadership (SCIL) at Converse College.

The district court in Virginia approved VMI's plan, claiming that the differences between women and men demanded separate educational facilities and, while VMI "marched to the beat of a drum, and VWIL to the melody of a fife," they would arrive at the same end at the conclusion of their march. When the circuit court of appeals upheld VMI's remedial plan the stage was set for a showdown in the Supreme Court.

In Virginia and South Carolina these cases assumed proportions beyond the historical fates of two educational institutions. Newspaper editorials and articles cast this as yet another battle of the Civil War, a war fought because the federal government continually wanted to tell individual states what they may and may not do. And it was also seen as the last stand of a beleaguered masculinity, a time-tested and honorable traditional definition of masculinity that had been under assault by feminists, "new age" men, and emasculating federal bureaucrats. "Save the Males!" became the rallying cry among the schools' supporters and bumper stickers and banners bearing this slogan appeared all over the two states.

In 1996 the Supreme Court declared that VMI's remedial plan, VWIL, was "but a pale shadow" of VMI, and that it was based on false stereotypes about women and therefore was in violation of the Fourteenth Amendment's equal protection clause. Women were ordered admitted to VMI, and both schools went coeducational. Although Shannon Faulkner withdrew after only four days as a cadet in 1997, women have been successfully assimilated as cadets at both schools.

Michael Kimmel

See also Male Bonding; "Save the Males!"
Further Reading:
Baker, Gary. 1989. *Cadets in Gray.* Columbia, SC: Palmetto Bookworks.
Conroy, Pat. 1986. *The Lords of Discipline.* New York: Bantam.
Kimmel, Michael. 2000. "Saving the Males: The Sociological Implications of the Virginia Military Institute and the Citadel." *Gender & Society* 14, no. 4 (August): 494–516.

Civil War

See American Civil War

City Slickers

This 1991 film manages to combine a rowdy comedy with the heartfelt exploration of three urban men's midlife crisis. This precarious balance was created by director Ron Underwood, also responsible for the blue-collar action comedy *Tremors* (1990), and screenwriters Lowell Ganz and Babaloo Mandel, who found the comic potential of serious family issues in *Parenthood* (1989).

Billy Crystal plays Mitch, a radio sales manager who finds his work meaningless and, like Steve Martin in *Parenthood,* finds his wife Barbara and children more of a burden than a source of joy. To "find his smile," his wife orders him to join his two best friends for a dude ranch vacation. His friends are facing major midlife crises of their own: Phil Berquist (Daniel Stern) has long been bullied by his wife and father-in-law, who are now threatening him with divorce and unemployment; and Ed Furillo (Bruno Kirby) is a driven entrepreneur, who is struggling to remain faithful to his new bride, a lingerie model who wants to have a child. The dude ranch vacation is the latest in adventurous vacations that Ed has organized for the trio,

which Barbara categorizes as increasingly "desperate attempts to cling to your youth."

City Slickers also coincided with Hollywood's renewed interest in the mythos of the American West. Though the film may exploit the comic clash of urban and Western mentalities, the power of the West is treated with respect. Oscar-winning cinematographer Dean Semler gives *City Slicker*'s Western setting the same beauty he evoked in *Dances With Wolves.* The trail boss, Curly, who serves as mentor to Mitch, is played by Western veteran Jack Palance, who first appeared on screen in the classic *Shane* (1953). Though he is literally a "dying breed," Curly is more virile and alive than the midlife crisis trio (Palance demonstrated this point during his Oscar acceptance when he spontaneously did a set of one-arm push-ups). Curly brushes aside Mitch's self-created angst, challenging him to find his "one thing" that really matters: "everything else don't mean shit."

The dude ranch guests all belong to demographics that were previously excluded from Western mythology: Jews, Italian Americans, African Americans, and females. They individually assert their claim to this landscape by reenacting the "Yee-hah" scene from the classic film *Red River* (1948) at the beginning of the cattle drive. Like the title characters in *Thelma and Louise* (1991), these contemporary characters are attracted to the West because of its "promise of liberation and/or redemption, rebirth and reinvention" (Hoberman 1994, 52), a promise that is delivered through the challenge the three friends face in bringing in the herd alone.

The cattle drive might help the three men find their respective "one thing" and lead more emotionally fulfilling lives, but the two weeks remain a fantasy experience: These are urban men whose Western identification is sporadic and temporary. Though Mitch's conversation with Curly may be a "no bullshit" discussion of love and the meaning of life, the slickers bond over consumer trappings, like ice cream, baseball, and programming VCRs. The theme music from *The*

Magnificent Seven (1960) is used to score this film and its action, sometimes ironically, other times sincerely celebrating heroism. The film's popularity rests equally in its perfect comic timing and its resonance as a yuppie male fantasy.

Fred Pfeil includes *City Slickers* and its protagonist Mitch Robbins as part of the "Year of Living Sensitively," his name for a series of 1991 films that chronicle a man's harsh conversion to sensitivity: *Regarding Henry, The Doctor, The Fisher King,* and *Hook.* The protagonists of these films arrive at sensitivity only after their passage through significant trials and sufferings. The strategies of these films are related to the rhetoric of Robert Bly and the men's movement that peaked in the 1990s: These men blame their problems on contemporary capitalism, inadequate fathering, and overly strong women. The protagonists of this film must nearly die to grow emotionally. To survive their crises, they relegate women to the background in favor of male mentors. A major marker of their emotional development is their increased ability to nurture children, often, as in Mitch's case, acting as a mother. As in later films like *Kindergarten Cop* (1990), being a father surpasses the fulfillment of traditional heroic action. *City Slickers* was the third-highest-grossing film of 1991; the number one film, *Terminator 2,* also featured a motherly hero, who goes the next step by literally giving his life for his foster son.

Elizabeth Abele

See also Buddy Films; "Midlife Crisis"
Further Reading:

Dowell, Pat. 1995. "The Mythology of the Western: Hollywood Perspectives on Race and Gender in the Nineties." *Cineaste* 22, nos. 1–2: 6–10.
Ebert, Roger. 1991, June 7. Review. http://www.suntimes.com/ebert/ebert_revi ews/1991/06/653922.html (cited 27 August 2003).
Gehring, Wes D. 1999. *Parody as Film Genre: Never Give a Saga an Even Break.* Westport, CT: Greenwood.
Hoberman, J. 1994. "On How the West Was Lost." In *They Went Thataway: Redefining Film Genres.* Edited by Richard T. Jameson. San Francisco: Mercury.
Jeffords, Susan. 1994. *Hard Bodies: Hollywood Masculinity in the Reagan Era.* New Brunswick, NJ: Rutgers University Press.
Pfeil, Fred. 1995. *White Guys: Studies in Postmodern Domination and Difference.* London: Verso.

Classroom Dynamics

Classroom dynamics describes verbal exchanges between teachers and students during interactive instruction. One of the major organizing mechanisms of classroom dynamics is gender—both the gender of the teacher and the students, and the "gender" of the formal and informal curriculum. Many students report that they prefer active participation to passive listening. Research studies suggest that interactive teaching is an effective instructional strategy that can enhance academic achievement (Good and Brophy 2000). This finding raises fascinating questions, such as: Do all students prefer this interactive style? Do all students benefit equally? And, do all students enjoy equal access to the teacher's attention? Research findings suggest that the answer to all of these questions may very well be "no." For example, studies show that students sitting in the same classroom and being taught by the same teacher often experience significantly different educational environments. Studies analyzing classroom dynamics from grade school through graduate school document that male, white, and nondisabled students are likely to receive more teacher interactions than female, nonwhite, and disabled students. More active students also attract a higher level of teacher attention (Jones and Gerig 1994; Sadker and Sadker 1995; Montague and Rinaldi 2001).

Teachers are involved in as many as one thousand interactions with students a day, and are often unaware of gender inequities in these exchanges (Jackson 1968). Males receive more teacher attention—both positive and negative—than do females. Teachers ask males both more factual (lower-order) and thoughtful (higher-order) questions, give males more precise directions on how to accomplish tasks for themselves, and offer them more precise, clear feedback concerning the quality of their intellectual ideas. One reason boys get more teacher attention is that they demand it. Males are twice as likely as females to call out answers and questions (Sadker and Sadker 1995). Even when males do not call out on their own or even raise their hands, teachers are more likely to direct questions to males. Teachers not only direct higher-order, more difficult questions toward males more often than toward females, they also give them more precise and helpful feedback through praise, criticism, and remediation. The importance of active and direct teacher feedback has been well documented. Direct, precise, and frequent teacher attention is positively associated with student achievement (Johnson and Johnson 1999; Sadker and Sadker 1995).

Sometimes this extra teacher attention is welcome, but sometimes the spotlight is uncomfortable. Males are disciplined more harshly, more publicly, and more frequently than females, even when they violate the same rules. Parents of male elementary school students are contacted more frequently about their child's behavior or schoolwork than are parents of female students, and boys constitute 71 percent of school suspensions (U.S. Department of Education 2000).

Although males receive more teacher time and attention, females receive fewer academic contacts in class. They are less likely to be called upon by name, are asked fewer complex and abstract questions, receive less praise or constructive feedback, and are given less direction on how to do things for themselves. In short, girls are more likely to be invisible members of classrooms. Moreover, gender and race intersect to reveal inequitable interaction patterns. A three-year study of elementary and secondary schools found that white males are

most likely to be involved in classroom discussions, followed by males of color, and white females. Students least likely to receive teacher time and attention were females of color (Sadker and Sadker 1995).

Females and students of color receive fewer opportunities to share their ideas. Students who need more time to contribute to discussions—because they take more time to think through issues and questions, come from a cultural background that encourages a slower response, or for whom English is a new language—often become spectators to rapid classroom exchanges. When teachers allow their classroom dialogue to be dominated by a few animated students, they are abandoning one of their key educational responsibilities: the responsibility to include *all* their students in active learning.

There are several instructional methods designed to encourage more equitable and thoughtful classroom dialogue. For example, organizing students into smaller groups appeals to students who are reluctant to speak in front of the entire class. In cooperative learning classes, collaboration—rather than individual competition—is the social norm as students work together on tasks. For students from African American or Native American backgrounds, for many females, and even for shy males, this may be a more attractive and productive learning environment. But even smaller student grouping is not problem free, and inequities emerge. For instance, in cooperative learning groups, girls tend to assist both other girls and boys, while boys are more likely to help only other boys. In addition, boys often dominate the group, while girls are more reticent (Johnson and Johnson 1999). These challenges suggest the need for active teacher involvement in managing small-group learning.

Ineffective use of wait time also contributes to inequitable classroom dynamics. Research suggests that white male students, particularly high achievers, are more likely to be given adequate wait time—quiet time to respond to questions and to critically think about their answers—than are females and students of color (Rowe 1986). Not only do teachers give different amounts of wait time to different students, they also give themselves inadequate time to consider student answers. Teachers who wait three to five seconds before calling on a student can thoughtfully choose which students to call on, sending high-expectation messages that all students are expected to participate and that all students will receive enough time to develop thoughtful answers. Teachers also typically give themselves less than a second to consider and react to student responses. By waiting three to five seconds *after* a student speaks, teachers give themselves enough time to carefully respond and offer precise, quality feedback to all students. In fact, one benefit of extended wait times is an increase in the quality of student participation, even from students who were previously silent.

Studies on teacher effectiveness and student achievement indicate that the frequency and precision of teacher-student interactions may impact not only academic performance, but gender differences in adult behaviors as well (Altermatt, Jovanovic, and Perry 1998; Sadker and Sadker 1995).

Karen Zittleman and David Sadker

See also Coeducation; "What about the Boys?"
Further Reading:

Altermatt, Ellen, Jasna Jovanovic, and Michelle Perry. 1998. "Bias or Responsivity? Sex and Achievement-Level Effects on Teachers' Classroom Questioning Practices." *Journal of Educational Psychology* 90: 516–527.

Good, Thomas, and Jere Brophy. 2000. *Looking in Classrooms.* 8th ed. New York: Wesley Longman.

Jackson, Philip. 1968. *Life in Classrooms.* New York: Holt, Rinehart, and Winston.

Johnson, David, and Roger Johnson. 1999. *Learning Together and Alone: Cooperative, Competitive, and Individualistic Learning.* 5th ed. Boston: Allyn and Bacon.

Jones, Gail M., and Thomas M. Gerig. 1994. "Silent Sixth-Grade Students: Characteristics, Achievement, and Teacher Expectations." *The Elementary School Journal* 95: 169–182.

Montague, Marjorie, and Christine Rinaldi. 2001. "Classroom Dynamics and Children at Risk." *Learning Disability Quarterly* 24: 75–83.

Rowe, Mary Budd. 1986. "Wait Time: Slowing Down May Be a Way of Speeding Up!" *Journal of Teacher Education* 37: 43–50.

Sadker, Myra, and David Sadker. 1995. "Missing in Interaction." Pp. 42–76 in *Failing at Fairness: How America's Schools Cheat Girls.* New York: Touchstone.

———. 2003. "Questioning Skills." In *Classroom Teaching Skills.* 7th ed. Edited by James M. Cooper. Boston: Houghton Mifflin.

United States Department of Education, National Center for Education Statistics. 2000. *Trends in Educational Equity for Girls and Women.* Washington, DC: Office of Educational Research and Improvement.

Cleaver, (Leroy) Eldridge (1935–1998)

As the minister of information (or official spokesman) for the Black Panther Party during the 1960s, Eldridge Cleaver created and promoted a lethal mix of violent revolution and race/class critique. He espoused a particular black masculinity predicated on the rape of white women as a way to manifest his politics. Once considered one of the most important African American political activists, Cleaver wrote *Soul on Ice* (1968), which served as the philosophical foundation of the Black Power movement. Cleaver is widely credited as a cofounder of the Black Panther Party and with conceiving the slogan, "You're either part of the problem or part of the solution." However, many of his critics believe that Cleaver's call for socialism in America was overshadowed by his long-term struggle with drug addiction, multiple rape and burglary convictions, intense misogyny, and, later, his bizarre conversion to born-again Christianity and failed career in Republican politics. Nevertheless, *Soul on Ice* still survives as a seminal text about militant revolution and the Black Power movement.

Leroy Eldridge Cleaver was born in Wabbaseka, Arkansas, in 1935 and moved to

Eldridge Cleaver led a life of transformations: youthful years of crime and imprisonment, a decade as a famous African-American activist and writer, a period of exile, and recent years as an outspoken and conservative Christian. (Library of Congress)

Los Angeles as a teenager. By his eighteenth birthday, Cleaver was convicted for possession of marijuana and served a sentence at Soledad state prison. As a consequence of additional drug violations and rape convictions, he spent most of the 1950s and 1960s in other prisons in California. It was during these years that Cleaver wrote one of the most important books in the Black Power movement. *Soul on Ice* is a reflective confession of his life as a rapist and drug user, a thoughtful critique of segregation, religion, and patriotism in America, and an articulate argument for African Americans to gain influence in the U.S. economy and govern-

ment. *Soul on Ice* quickly became a bestseller and was named one of the top ten books of 1968 by the *New York Times*. In sum, *Soul on Ice* allowed Cleaver to share with his readers what it meant to be black in white America.

Despite the wide popularity of *Soul on Ice* even among white intellectuals and activists, most critics found Cleaver's unapologetic homophobia and ruthless attitude toward white women highly problematic. Cleaver attempted to explain how his violent rapes were a critique of the white race's standards of beauty, as well as retribution for centuries of slave owner rapes of slaves. Cleaver explained in an early chapter of *Soul on Ice* how he considered the rape of white women by black men as a politically justifiable act. Cleaver referred to the white woman as "the ogre" who was responsible for placing lust and desire in his heart and, as a result, compromising his otherwise valid critique of American capitalism. To destroy "the ogre," Cleaver explained how he "started out by practicing on black girls in the ghetto" and then proceeded to rape white women as "an insurrectionary act." He explained, "It delighted me that I was defying and trampling upon the white man's law defiling his women" (33). While in prison and as he began to write what would become *Soul on Ice,* Cleaver expressed remorse for his violent acts against white women, describing these acts as his "revolutionary sickness."

In a related, though utterly ridiculous platform, Cleaver advocated for establishing a system under the Civil Service Administration in which salaried white women would "minister to the needs of those prisoners who maintained a record of good behavior." He argued in *Soul on Ice* that the idea of conjugal visits was unjust because single prisoners, like Cleaver, "needed and deserved action just as married prisoners did" (25).

When Cleaver was released from prison in 1965, he moved to Oakland and helped found the Black Panthers, a militant, anti-establishment, black-nationalist group. Cleaver provided this organization an important critique of American capitalism based on his readings of Rousseau, Nechayev, Voltaire, and Marx. Cleaver envisioned the Black Panthers as providing the backbone that was missing from Martin Luther King's nonviolent movement. Along with Bobby Seale and Huey Newton, Cleaver worked for the Black Panther Party on issues related to police brutality, access to housing and education, and social and political justice. However, while some members of the Black Panther Party focused more on community concerns, such as health clinics and breakfast programs for school children, Cleaver's energy focused on fostering militant revolution.

In 1968 Cleaver was the presidential candidate for the Peace and Freedom Party. During this campaign, he was directly involved in a shootout in Oakland in which a seventeen-year-old member of the Black Panther Party was killed while in police custody. Three police officers were also wounded, and when a judge determined that Cleaver's role in this tragedy was considered a parole violation, Cleaver fled to Algeria instead of risking a return to prison. From 1968 to 1975 Cleaver lived in exile, though he continued his relationship with the Black Panther Party, serving as the head of the International Black Panther Party in Algeria and routinely visiting China, Uganda, Cuba, North Korea, Nigeria, France, and North Vietnam.

In the mid-1970s Cleaver suddenly became disenchanted with Marxism and arranged to return to the United States with the support of the FBI. Considered a "sellout" by many political activists, Cleaver agreed to a sentence of probation that involved community service and official renunciation of the Black Panthers and Maoism. To make matters worse for the activist black communities in the United States, Cleaver told reporters that he was treated fairly by the American judicial system upon his return. He also informed the press that he had become a born-again Christian. Many suspected that his political and religious views changed only to enable his return.

In 1978 Cleaver published *Soul on Fire,* a book in which he explained these religious and political conversions. Despite his claims that he was reformed, Cleaver continued to struggle with the American justice system; his addiction to crack cocaine was widely publicized, and he had little success in Republican politics, including a failed run for the GOP Senate nomination in California in 1986 based on a platform of "red fighting." Soon thereafter, *Rolling Stone* magazine reported that he was employed as a clothing designer with a line of men's pants, featuring a design that emphasized the genitals, which he called a "Cleaver sleeve." In 1994 Cleaver was again arrested for drug possession and burglary, but he managed to avoid prison this time due to a procedural error by the police during his arrest. Cleaver worked as a diversity consultant at University of La Verne in southern California until his death in 1998.

David Alan Sapp

See also Black Panthers; Malcolm X
Further Reading:

Cleaver, Eldridge. 1968. *Soul on Ice.* New York: Dell.
———. 1978. *Soul on Fire.* Nashville, TN: W Publishing Group.
Lockwood, Lee. 1970. *Conversation with Eldridge Cleaver: Algiers.* New York: McGraw-Hill.
Rout, Kathleen. 1991. *Eldridge Cleaver.* Boston: Twayne Publishers, United States Authors Series, vol. 583.

Clinton, William Jefferson (Bill) (1946–)

Bill Clinton was the forty-second president of the United States and the first Democrat to serve two consecutive terms (1993–2001) since Franklin D. Roosevelt. Born in August 1946, in Hope, Arkansas, he graduated from Georgetown University in 1968, went on to Oxford as a Rhodes scholar, and graduated from Yale Law School in 1973 (Kane 1993, 292). Clinton was elected governor of Arkansas in 1979 at only thirty-two years of age. He served one term, was reelected in 1982, and then again in 1984 and 1988 (Kane 1993, 294). Bill Clinton and his vice president, Al Gore, were the first elected officials of these high offices to have been born after World War II and heralded the rise of a new generation in American politics.

An idealist president whose 1992 campaign slogan pledged, "Putting People First," Clinton's legacy, despite his excellent economic record and welfare reforms, remains tarnished by scandals, including the congressional hearings of the Whitewater real estate venture, and a sexual harassment suit brought against him by Paula Jones dating

from his time as governor. Clinton's visible weaknesses problematize the symbolic meaning of the American presidency. This crisis can be located in the wider cultural anxiety over the disempowering of hegemonic masculinity and the rise of "angry white men" that characterized the decade. The perception of Clinton as a dishonest, weak, and morally compromised man culminated in the 1998 charges of sexual misconduct with a White House intern, Monica Lewinsky. As a result, Bill Clinton became the second president to be impeached by the House of Representatives on charges of perjury and obstruction of justice.

Dubbed the "Comeback Kid," Clinton exhibited resilience in a presidency that can be characterized by many such moments of crisis, loss, and recovery. His was a presidency defined by paradoxical themes: hope and disappointment, success and failure, discipline and chaos, idealism and reality. Clinton's presidency was dominated by public debate around questions of character, and these questions revealed much cultural anxiety regarding American ideals about both the presidency and dominant constructions of masculinity. Clinton's improper model of masculinity was used repeatedly as evidence of political inefficacy and unpresidential qualities. Clinton had a strong commitment to minority issues and, in putting together his first Cabinet, hoped to assemble a diverse membership that "looked like America." Four out of its eleven members were women. Among his election promises, women's issues were high on the agenda, including reproductive rights and childcare, which compounded the white male's sense of loss. Clinton's infidelities were greeted paradoxically. While this sort of behavior may be seen as proof of manhood, in the context of the idealized model of masculinity embodied by an American president, it became indicative of a lack of discipline and control and a weak moral character. The president is expected to be a better model of man than the average citizen. Further, it was the type of "sexual relations" in which Clinton and Lewinsky engaged that compromised his manhood.

Clinton was characterized as a racial and class outsider, his beginnings thought to be too Southern and too poor for respectability. Although Clinton's sexual appetites and weaknesses marked him as an undisciplined, feminized man, these charges of emasculation were compounded by his perceived draft dodging during the Vietnam War, and his "don't ask, don't tell" pledge to lift the ban on homosexuals in military service. His failure to tell the truth about the incident complicates the already "immoral" character that these acts reveal. Further debate focused on Clinton's doughy physique, on a body defined by raging hormones, appetites, and urges, constantly escaping its proper masculine and presidential borders. His undisciplined need for junk food and sex, his emotional, public displays of crying and feeling other people's pain, all weakened his status as the most powerful man in the world. In addition, Clinton's strategy in the Middle East, for example, characterized him as a negotiator and consensus seeker, not a man who played "hard ball." Clinton was trying to bring peace to the Middle East by acting as a go-between, facilitating discussions between Israel and Palestine, rather than laying down the law, telling them how it was going to be, or, like his predecessor and successor, going to war in the hope of bringing about change. In this context his diplomacy was seen as more feminine, less active, and less decisive.

Clinton's masculinity was most significantly marginalized and compromised from the beginning of his political career by the perceived masculinity of his wife, Hillary Rodham Clinton. The 1992 campaign ran on the promise that a vote for Bill Clinton was also a vote for Hillary: "two for the price of one." This equal partnership was the cause of much gender anxiety. The Clinton marriage enacted a real shift in gender roles and relations and did this on a national stage. Throughout her husband's career, Hillary underwent a number of "feminizing" makeovers

to soften her image. Although debate often trivialized her physical appearance, Hillary was ultimately punished for equally valuing her career and her family. Hillary did not know her place. During the 1992 campaign, debates about a woman's right to choose either family or career or some combination collided in the image of femininity presented by the future first lady. At the 1992 Republican National Convention, Hillary was condemned as a feminist symbol for all that was wrong with American family values.

Hillary represented a new model of first lady as a professional woman who was smart, opinionated, and ambitious. She did not immediately relinquish her own career or her own name and wanted to be involved in policy making and public debate. She did not vanish into the shadow of the president. When Bill Clinton named her the head of the ill-fated Task Force on National Health Reform, Hillary became the first presidential spouse to occupy a West Wing office. This visibility elicited strongly polarized reactions from the public. Although the women's movement saw her as an icon, critics saw her as an emasculator, or enabler, willing to ignore the president's flaws in her own pursuit of power.

Joanna L. Di Mattia

Further Reading:

Bartley, Robert L., et al. 1999. "Clinton, the Country, and the Political Culture: A Symposium." *Commentary* 107 (January): 20–42.

Bennett, William J. 1998. *The Death of Outrage: Bill Clinton and the Assault on American Ideals.* New York: The Free Press.

Burrell, Barbara. 1997. *Public Opinion, The First Ladyship, and Hillary Rodham Clinton.* New York: Garland Publishing.

Cultural Critique. Special Issue: The Politics of Impeachment 1999, no. 43.

Kane, Joseph Nathan. 1993. *Facts about the Presidents: A Compilation of Biographical and Historical Information.* 6th ed. New York: H. W. Wilson.

Klein, Joe. 2002. *The Natural: The Misunderstood Presidency of Bill Clinton.* New York: Random House.

Maraniss, David. 1995. *First in His Class: A Biography of Bill Clinton.* New York: Simon and Schuster.

Coeducation

Coeducation is the practice of teaching males and females together in mixed-sex schools or classrooms. While coeducation suggests a side-by-side, equitable educational experience, a long history of male-only education and the differential values and expectations that society places on males and females frequently creates dissimilar coeducational learning climates. Moreover, confusion persists in the relative effectiveness of coeducation and single-sex climates. Which milieu better supports academic achievement and psychological development? Which approach better prepares students to meet society's needs?

Education in colonial America was initially informal in nature. Young boys and girls were taught lessons in reading, values, manners, social graces, and vocational skills at home. This home-as-school phenomenon transferred to the dame school, where very young children were cared for in the home of a dame, or well-respected woman, as parents attended to work and other responsibilities. While both boys and girls were educated in dame schools, they received different instruction. Girls were taught basic homemaking skills and rarely learned even to sign their names, while boys received a stronger emphasis on academics, including writing and arithmetic. Beyond these dame schools, education was essentially a male monopoly. In New England, for example, the Puritans established the Massachusetts Law of 1647 that required every town of fifty or more families to provide a basic, albeit brief, education for their children. Although some towns did provide girls with one or two hours of instruction before or after the regular school day, girls most often were denied an education. It was not until the 1830s, with the development of the common school, that the ideas of universal schooling and coeducation took root.

Horace Mann, Massachusetts secretary of education, became the nation's leading advocate for the common school, today's public elementary school. Mann worked to end gender and race segregation, arguing that public coeducational schools would help develop the talents of all children, male and female, rich and poor, while creating a "common" American culture. In practical terms, he believed that educated workers would create a more productive economy. Mann's common school established the foundation for formal coeducation.

Secondary education—today's high school experience—remained an affluent, white male preserve from the fifteenth into the nineteenth century. The Latin grammar school, one of the oldest colonial secondary schools, prepared wealthy boys for college and the ministry with a curriculum that focused on classic European literature, mathematics, science, and modern languages. As colonial English grammar schools developed, the curriculum moved away from the classical Latin tradition to more practical studies. English grammar schools were viewed not as preparation for college, but as preparation for business careers and as a means of instilling social graces. Along with their curricular changes, some of these schools set another precedent by admitting white girls. For example, Boston's English Classical School was created in 1821 as a free secondary school for males and, in 1852, broke new ground by admitting females. The appearance of these public high schools ignited a heated coeducation debate. Defenders of coeducation argued that the presence of females would actually improve the behavior of rambunctious males, leading to more effective classroom instruction. Critics predicted that the tough academic exchanges and standards of all-male classroom discussion would soften in deference to women and that schools would be feminized. Despite the objections and obstacles confronting girls in coeducational settings, by 1900 they constituted 60 percent of the nation's high school population (Tyack and Hasnot 1990).

From the 1860s into the twentieth century, teaching faculties also experienced a gender revolution. As common schools proliferated, the shortage of male teachers became evident and schools increasingly hired women, who would be a cost-saving factor for school budgets, as women were often paid less than men. The Civil War accelerated the male exodus from teaching. By the early 1900s, women had become more than 85 percent of the nation's teachers, and critics now lamented the "women peril" (Tyack and Hasnot 1990). Pundits argued that schools had become a battleground between female teachers who were stressing decorum and conformity and free-spirited boys who were struggling to grow into the traditional male role. In this battle of the sexes, boys were considered the losers. This backlash was fanned by critics such as military leader Admiral F. E. Chadwick and President Theodore Roosevelt who declared that female teachers represented a threat to healthy male development and endangered national security.

To counter women's growing dominance on the faculty, efforts were made to retain male educators and protect boys from the female school climate. Administration, coaching, vocational education, and certain high school departments such as science and math became male bastions and created a male leadership hierarchy. The curriculum was also divided by traditional gender roles. In secondary schools across the country, girls were barred from shop and boys from home economics. Males also dominated the playing fields, because sports were thought to reduce the male dropout rate, toughen boys, and give unruly males an energy outlet. In the final analysis, many programs and subject areas became sex segregated, yet other subjects, like history or English, did not, while all existed under the auspices of coeducation. Why weren't single-sex schools created to respond to the sex-segregated enrollment patterns? The decisive argument was economic: Separate schools and programs for boys and girls were simply too costly, and taxpayers proved unwilling to pay the bill. By 1900, 98 percent of high schools were coeducational, and coeducation was all but universal in American elementary and secondary public schools (Tyack and Hasnot 1990).

The roots of collegiate coeducation reach back to 1837 when Oberlin became the first college to admit women and men, although female students were expected to do housekeeping chores and assume a secondary role to the male scholars. But it was the Civil War that opened wide the door to higher education for women. The enormous casualties suffered during that war denied colleges and universities their stream of potential male candidates. Without these male tuition dollars, colleges were forced to admit female students. Women frequently encountered a hostile campus reception, harassed by male students and ridiculed by professors. College women were accused of devaluing the worth of a university degree, and colleges responded to this threat in much the same ways that secondary schools had: They segregated the curriculum. Relegated to what was sometimes called the "Ladies Curriculum," women in coeducational institutions pursued careers in areas such as teacher training, social work, and home economics. Other institutions found a way to both accept women as students while rejecting coeducation. The Ivy League channeled women into newly created (and less prestigious) companion colleges. Radcliff, for example, not only provided women with an education, it also ensured that Harvard would remain a male bastion, which it did until the 1970s.

Many Ivy League scholars believed coeducation to be a bad idea. Harvard medical professor Dr. Edward Clarke published *Sex and Education* in 1873, arguing that coeducation was ruinous to women's health. His book advanced the idea that learning diverted blood destined for menstruation from the ovaries and toward the brain. According to Clarke, females would exhaust their reproductive energies trying to keep up with their male classmates, damaging their brains, and becoming candidates for mental problems. Women were being presented a choice: algebra or ovaries (Tyack and Hasnot 1990).

In 1972 Congress passed Title IX, an amendment to the Civil Rights Act of 1964, which prohibited sex discrimination in educational institutions, including most cases of single-sex segregation. Despite this law, de facto sex segregation continues. Secondary school vocational programs like cosmetology remain overwhelmingly female, while others, like computer specialties, remain predominantly male. At the college level, few women can be found in engineering, physics, chemistry, and computer science, while few men can be found in nursing, teaching, library science, or social work. In effect, even within coeducational schools, virtual "glass walls" often exist, channeling students into traditional career paths.

While many programs remain sex segregated, institutional coeducation has been an established practice in the United States for over a century. Only 1 percent of all students attend single-sex schools, most of which are private (Campbell and Sanders 2002). In public schools, legal and economic challenges have discouraged local efforts to offer single-sex education. However, the rise of school choice programs has revived the discussion of the merits of single-sex education. In 2002 the Bush administration authorized the expenditure of public monies on single-sex schools and classes, as well as a review of the Title IX limits on single-sex education.

Arguments favoring single-sex education are fueled by research on the disparate academic achievement in coeducational classrooms, where females often defer to males, are called on less frequently, receive less teacher attention, and are less likely to study mathematics and science. Males in coeducational settings receive lower grades, have a storied history of reading and writing difficulties, account for two-thirds of all students served in special education, and have a higher dropout rate, especially males of color. Many argue that boys and girls create sexual "distractions" from academic pursuits (Sadker and Sadker 1995).

Yet research on the effectiveness of single-sex schools remains inconclusive. Single-sex schools may provide boys with strong male role models, which some believe lowers dropout rates, truancy, and violence while improving academic achievement (Woody 2002). For females, single-sex education may improve academic performance and encourage exploration of nontraditional career paths (Campbell and Sanders 2002; Sadker and Sadker 1995). Opponents of single-sex education, however, note that separate often means unequal education. Some studies document how separating boys and girls can increase sex bias and stereotypes, even creating a culture of misogyny. Advocates of coeducation argue that the positive outcomes associated with single-sex schooling may reflect the more effective educational practices found in these schools rather than sex segregation. Small class size, student-centered instruction, skilled teachers, and strong parent involvement are more frequently found in single-sex environments, factors that, if transferred to coeducational classrooms and schools, might result in similarly positive academic outcomes (Black 1998; Campbell and Sanders 2002).

Karen Zittleman
David Sadker

See also Classroom Dynamics; "What About the Boys?"

Further Reading:

Black, Susan. 1998. "Boys and Girls Together." *American School Board Journal* 185: 30–33.

Campbell, Patricia, and Jo Sanders. 2002. "Challenging the System: Assumptions and Data behind the Push for Single-Sex Schooling." In *Gender in Policy and Practice: Perspectives on Single-Sex and Coeducational Schooling.* Edited by Amanda Datrow and Lea Hubbard. New York: Routledge.

Lasser, Carol, and Sondra J. Peacock, eds. 1987. *Educating Women and Men Together: Coeducation in a Changing World.* Urbana, IL: University of Illinois Press.

Riordan, Cornelious. 1990. *Girls and Boys in School: Together or Separate?* New York: Teachers College Press.

Sadker, Myra, and David Sadker. 1995. "Different Voices, Different Schools." Pp. 226–250 in *Failing at Fairness: How America's Schools Cheat Girls*. New York: Touchstone.

Tyack, David, and Elisabeth Hasnot. 1990. *Learning Together: A History of Coeducation in American Schools*. New Haven, CT: Yale University Press.

Woody, Elisabeth. 2002. "Constructions of Masculinity in California Singer Gender Academies." In *Gender in Policy and Practice: Perspectives on Single Sex and Coeducational Schooling*. Edited by Amanda Datrow and Lea Hubbard. New York: RoutledgeFalmer.

Cold War Masculinities

During the first decade of the Cold War (1947–1956), masculinity in the United States underwent a reorganization designed to ensure political and economic stability in the face of the threat of communist subversion. In an ideological shift that contributed directly to the economic expansion of the 1950s and 1960s, men were no longer encouraged to exert their independence from the domestic sphere but were expected to define themselves through their identities as consumers—an expectation hitherto limited mostly to women—and to take an active role in family life. Beginning with Philip Wylie, who in his 1942 bestselling book *Generation of Vipers* coined the term "momism" to describe women's allegedly pernicious influence over the domestic sphere, experts warned that unless fathers began to counteract the deleterious effects of overly protective mothers on the nation's children, the nation would succumb to communism. Moreover, as more and more middle-class men found employment in corporations, a new social type emerged, the "organization man," which further transformed masculinity. As sociologists C. Wright Mills, William Whyte, and David Riesman showed in now classic studies of this type, succeeding in a corporation required a different set of skills from those that traditionally defined masculinity. The independent, self-reliant entrepreneur who had embodied American manhood earlier in the twentieth century would never have survived in the corporate world. Instead, men with corporate jobs needed to fit in and to have "personality." Their success depended not on showing initiative or competing aggressively with other men but on getting along with their coworkers and pleasing those above them in the corporate hierarchy. Limited primarily to the white middle class, this model of masculinity gradually became hegemonic in the 1950s.

In many respects, this transformation merely represented a culmination of social and economic processes that could be traced to the late nineteenth century. As Mills showed in his highly influential study *White Collar*, published in 1951, the "organization man" didn't come into being spontaneously but had his roots in the shift from industrial to monopoly capitalism in the late nineteenth century. With this shift, corporations emerged as a major source of employment for middle-class men and required them to define themselves along the lines described above. But in other respects, the domestication of masculinity represented a genuinely new development in American society. To begin with, the government took several steps to ensure that the "organization man" became the dominant representative of American manhood. Signaling a retreat from the New Deal, which had included a commitment to public housing and mass transit, Congress passed legislation that all but enacted the domestication of masculinity into law. This legislation included the Servicemen's Readjustment Bill of 1944, popularly known as the GI Bill of Rights, which provided grants to returning veterans so they could receive vocational training or attend college. This legislation enabled an unprecedented expansion of the middle class, as the nearly 8 million veterans who received free college educations were able to enter the professional and managerial classes (Davis 1986, 181–230). Equally important was the Interstate Highway Act of 1956 that, in capitalizing the massive highway construction of the postwar period, spurred the growth of the suburbs by making them accessible to millions of Americans. Combined with a government-sponsored system of credit that included federally insured home loans and tax deductions for mortgages, this legislation didn't just encourage the domestication of masculinity, it subsidized it.

But men had an even more powerful incentive for consenting to the reorganization of masculinity. During the Cold War, the U.S. government actively promoted fears that there was no way to tell homosexuals apart from heterosexuals, and homophobia began to play a central role in the formation of American national identity. In 1950, after holding widely publicized hearings in which the chief officer of the District of Columbia vice squad testified that thousands of federal employees had been arrested on morals charges, many of them across from the White House in Lafayette Square, a notorious cruising venue, the Senate Appropriations Committee issued a virulently homophobic report in which it asserted that male and female homosexuals posed a serious threat to national security and should be expelled from government jobs. At the same time, the committee stressed that unless such employees already had a police record, it would be virtually impossible to expose them. Pointing to scientific findings disputing the stereotypes of the effeminate gay and the masculine lesbian, the report stated that homosexuals were virtually indistinguishable from heterosexuals: "Many male homosexuals are very masculine in their physical appearance and general demeanor, and many female homosexuals have every appearance of femininity in their outward behavior" (U.S. Senate, 2–3). In this way, the report linked homosexuals to the communists and fellow travelers who were then also being investigated by Congress. For if gays and lesbians couldn't be easily identified, then they too could infiltrate the government without being detected and subvert it from within by perverting "normal" employees. Because they had no distinguishing characteristics, the report claimed, "one homosexual can pollute a Government office" (U.S. Senate, 5).

The fear that gays and lesbians could escape detection by passing as straight can in part be traced to the Kinsey report on male sexuality, which despite the dry scientific manner in which it was written became an instant bestseller when it was published in 1948. Kinsey, who himself engaged in homosexual activity, hoped that the report would lead to greater tolerance of homosexuality by showing that it was widely practiced and thus was "normal." Fifty percent of the men interviewed by Kinsey and his colleagues admitted to feeling attracted to other men at various times in their lives, 37 percent had had at least one homosexual experience following adolescence, and 4 percent claimed that they were exclusively homosexual (D'Emilio 1982, 35). None of these men fit the stereotype of the effeminate homosexual, and the report concluded that "persons with homosexual histories are to be found in every age group, in every social level, in every conceivable occupation in cities and on farms, and in the most remote areas of the country" (quoted in D'Emilio 1982, 35). These findings suggested that sexual identities, rather than being fixed and immutable, could shift over time. Thus, instead of increasing tolerance of homosexuality, as Kinsey hoped, the report reinforced fears that gays could subvert the nation from within. For if sexual identities weren't fixed and immutable, then, despite how manly they were, straight men could be converted to homosexuality.

The emergence of the homosexual as the "enemy within" served a crucial ideological function by elevating issues of gender and sexual identity to the level of national security. Men who deviated from or refused to conform to the domestic model of masculinity risked being seen as un-American and thus as posing a threat to national security that was no less serious than the one allegedly posed by communists and fellow travelers. In this way, Cold War homophobia discouraged men from rejecting a form of masculinity that helped to consolidate and maintain the position of the United States as the leader of the so-called free world. As already indicated, the domestication of masculinity contributed directly to the postwar economic expansion. Between 1946 and 1951, expenditures on household furnishings and appliances rose 240 percent (May 1988, 5). By 1949 Americans had purchased 21.4 million automobiles, 20 million refrigerators, 5.5 million stoves, and 11.6 million televisions (May 1988, 5). Housing starts grew from 114,000 in 1944 to an all-time high of 1,692,000 in 1950 (May 1988, 6). By the mid-1950s, the increase in the gross national product was due almost entirely to consumer spending on durable goods and residential construction (May 1988, 6). It goes without saying that any resistance to the hegemony of the domestic model of masculinity would have disrupted this expansion of the economy. One of the purposes of Cold War homophobia was to prevent this from occurring by instilling in men the fear that they might be mistaken for being homosexual if they rejected the socially prescribed roles of breadwinner and homeowner. As a result, the United States had a distinct advantage in its ideological struggle with the Soviet Union, for it could point to the economic prosperity of the 1950s and 1960s as proof that capitalism was superior to socialism.

Despite the powerful incentives to conform, the reorganization of masculinity was widely contested. Precipitating what many social commentators perceived to be a crisis in masculinity, many middle-class men experienced the expectation that they would define themselves through their roles as breadwinners and homeowners as feminizing, and they struggled to create alternative masculinities that wouldn't expose them to the risk of being labeled homosexual. Some of these men registered their opposition by refusing to settle down

in the suburbs and raise a family. Although these men often pursued careers in corporations, they settled in urban areas where they could participate in the "swinging" lifestyle promoted by magazines such as *Playboy* and *Esquire*. Such magazines actively promoted consumerism, but they neither urged their readers to restrict their sexuality to the domestic sphere nor linked male consumption to fatherhood and homeownership. Other middle-class men fashioned an oppositional form of masculinity by combining aspects of the beat movement, rock and roll music, and African American and working-class cultures. Such men rejected the economic security provided by corporate jobs and formed the backbone of the New Left and counterculture of the 1960s. Middle-class gay men also developed an alternative masculinity—one meant to mark them as gay. Although the gay macho style is often thought to have emerged in the 1970s in the wake of the gay liberation movement, its roots lay in the 1950s. To mark their difference from the "organization man," these gay men developed a style of gender presentation that drew on working-class masculinities and that involved bodybuilding and the wearing of leather jackets and tight-fitting jeans and tee shirts. Actors such as Marlon Brando and James Dean, icons of rebellious masculinity in the 1950s, modeled themselves partly on these gay men. In so doing, they gave this distinctive style of masculinity wider currency, and it began to influence the look of straight masculinities and to lose its specifically gay meaning. Not surprisingly, this oppositional masculinity was considered to be even more threatening than other such masculinities, as it reinforced fears that gay men were indistinguishable from straight men.

Robert J. Corber

Further Reading:
Cohan, Steven. 1997. *Masked Men: Masculinity and the Movies in the Fifties.* Bloomington, IN: Indiana University Press.

Corber, Robert J. 1993. *In the Name of National Security: Hitchcock, Homophobia, and the Political Construction of Gender in Postwar America.* Durham, NC: Duke University Press.

———. 1997. *Homosexuality in Cold War America: Resistance and the Crisis of Masculinity.* Durham, NC: Duke University Press.

Davis, Mike. 1986. *Prisoners of the American Dream: Politics and Economy in the History of the U.S. Working Class.* London: Verso.

D'Emilio, John. 1982. *Sexual Politics, Sexual Communities: The Making of a Homosexual Minority in the United States, 1940–1970.* Chicago: University of Chicago Press.

Ehrenreich, Barbara. 1983. *The Hearts of Men: American Dreams and the Flight from Commitment.* Garden City, NJ: Doubleday.

Kuznick, Peter J., and James Gilbert, eds. 2001. *Rethinking Cold War Culture.* Washington, D.C.: Smithsonian Institution Press.

May, Elaine Tyler. 1988. *Homeward Bound: American Families in the Cold War Era.* New York: Basic Books.

Spigel, Lynn. 1992. *Make Room for TV: Television and the Family Ideal in Postwar America.* Chicago: University of Chicago Press.

U.S. Senate, 81st Cong., 2nd sess., Committee on Expenditures in Executive Departments. 1950. *The Employment of Homosexuals and Other Sex Perverts in Government.* Washington, D.C.: Government Printing Office.

Collins, William Wilkie (1824–1889)

The Victorian novelist and prolific writer of sensation and detective stories, Wilkie Collins engaged critically with the controversial issues of his time, exploring the changing definitions of normality and transgression. Whereas the significance of his representation of subversive women has been studied by feminist critics from the 1980s onwards, the importance of his transgressive male protagonists has only recently been brought to the fore. His novels reveal a shift from an ambiguous treatment of sensitive antiheroes in his early fiction to a new ideal of male sensibility that is critical of mid-Victorian ideologies of muscular Christianity.

Wilkie Collins was born on 8 January 1824 and died on 23 September 1889. He never married, but lived together conjugally with Caroline Graves and later also with Martha Rudd, who bore him three children. Dividing his time between his two families and partly living under an assumed name, Collins kept his double life secret from his readers. Bigamous arrangements, adultery, and the incongruities of the marriage laws in Victorian Britain, however, recur in his fiction as sensational plot devices. A bestselling author, Collins wrote twenty-seven novels, more than fifty short stories, and various plays. He is best remembered for his influential sensation novel, *The Woman in White* (1860), which shows the genre at its height, and *The Moonstone* (1868), the first full-length detective novel. His later works came to be known as his "mission" novels, as he deliberately set out to attack controversial issues such as inconsistent marriage laws in *Man and Wife* (1870), vivisection in *Heart and Science* (1883), custody law in *The Evil Genius* (1886), and phrenology in *The Legacy of Cain* (1888). *Blind Love,* his last novel, was completed by Walter Besant and published posthumously in 1890.

Collins's fiction has been criticized for its deliberately sensational exploitation of a gendered conceptualization of nervousness, insanity, and also sensation, and embraced for its sympathetic portrayal of transgressing (anti)heroines. Critics speak of a "case of feminization via the nerves" (Miller 1987, 115). At the other end of the spectrum, Lyn Pykett argues that in opening up the transgressive domain of the improper feminine, the sensation novel can function as a form of political activism (1992, 41). The ways in which the "abnormalities" of male protagonists complement the transgressions of these subversive women have now similarly become the subject of critical analysis (Oppenheim 1991, 149; Tuss 1992, 2; Wagner 2002, 483–486). The sensation novel is seen to engage anew with ideals of masculinity as it plays with definitions of health and sanity as well as gender boundaries. Wilkie Collins goes a step further in his later fiction by eschewing the mid-Victorian fashion of an energetic and muscular masculinity. Exposing the ideals of muscular Christianity, *Man and Wife* forms the turning point in his representation of male sensibilities. Collins's subsequent novels critically explore the changing definitions of masculinity, creating alternative heroes that anticipate the decadent, fin-de-siècle hero as typified by Oscar Wilde's Dorian Gray or E. M. Forster's men of artistic sensibilities.

Tamara S. Wagner

Further Reading:

Miller, D. A. 1987. "*Cage aux Folles:* Sensation and Gender in Wilkie Collins's *The Woman in White.*" Pp. 107–136 in *The Making of the Modern Body: Sexuality and Society in the Nineteenth Century.* Edited by Catherine Gallagher and Thomas Laqueur. Berkeley, CA: University of California Press.

Oppenheim, Janet. 1991. *"Shattered Nerves": Doctors, Patients, and Depression in Victorian England.* Oxford, UK: Oxford University Press.

Pykett, Lyn. 1992. *The "Improper" Feminine: The Women's Sensation Novel and the New Woman Writing.* London and New York: Routledge.

Smith, Nelson, and R. C. Terry, eds. 1995. *Wilkie Collins to the Forefront: Some Reassessments.* New York: AMS Press.

Tuss, Alex J. 1992. *The Inward Revolution: Troubled Young Men in Victorian Fiction, 1850–1880.* New York: Lang.

Wagner, Tamara S. 2002. "Overpowering Vitality: Nostalgia and Men of Sensibility in the Fiction of Wilkie Collins." *Modern Language Quarterly* 63, no. 4: 473–502.

Colonialism

"Colonialism" defines the political repercussions of one country's imposing its values, culture, and administration on another. Contemporary critics generally prefer this word to "imperialism," which designates the period of European expansion (roughly 1830–1914) following Britain's, France's, and, later, Spain's abolition of slavery in their colonies. "Colonialism" refers to diverse forms of appropriation and domination with a much longer history and therefore connects best with the study of gender. Linked etymologically to "culture" (via the root *colonia*—Latin for "settlement"), "colony" underscores powerful ties among policies of economic expansion, cultural domination, and long-standing assumptions about male—and white—superiority.

Western masculinity and homosexuality share a complex relation to this history, of which only a fraction can be outlined here. These terms are, indeed, so powerfully connected that some critics view them as inseparable, claiming that colonialism is an inevitable outgrowth of Western patriarchal structures. Yet although such claims have rhetorical force, they simplify the economic and political forces driving especially European colonialism, making widely different historical epochs appear self-identical by presenting them in a static, essentialist light. Although varied cultural arguments about masculinity certainly informed—and helped justify—colonial expansion, historians remind us that opposition to these arguments, stemming partly from a desire to end slavery, grew from the mid-nineteenth century among liberals such as John Stuart Mill and Herbert Spencer, as well as near contemporaries like J. C. Prichard, H. T. Buckle, T. H. Huxley, R. G. Latham, J. Lubbock, J. L. A. Quatrefages de Brau, Edward B. Tylor, and Theodor Waitz (Young 63). All these intellectuals argued for a more elastic and relativistic understanding of civilization and cultural tradition, in claims that helped propel twentieth-century opposition into powerful anticolonial positions.

Transhistorical arguments about colonialism and masculinity are not sustainable for other reasons, too. Careful study of many nineteenth-century works reveals a conflicted dynamic among even proponents of European colonialism and the cultural superiority of Caucasian men. Their letters, memoirs, and ethnography quite often highlight both aversion to indigenous people and erotic fascination for them, even just a few chapters apart. So, in his now-famous "Terminal Essay," added to his rendition of *The Arabian Nights* (1885–1888), Sir Richard Burton voiced his belief in the Sotadic Zone, in which pederasty allegedly is "popular and endemic, [and] held at the worst to be a mere peccadillo," but beyond which, in northern cultures, is "look[ed] upon with the liveliest disgust" (159). Burton wanted his admittedly suspect ethnography to challenge "an age saturated with cant and hypocrisy" (192). Nevertheless, he later used widely held arguments about male superiority to offset Victorian opposition to this cross-cultural assertion, writing that in Africa, "as all the world over, the male figure is notably superior, as amongst the lower animals, to that of the female" (192).

Like Burton, Paolo Ambrogetti, Claude Ancillon, A. Kocher, Henry Junod, H. Quedenfeldt, Georg Schweinfurth, and Herman Soyaux studied kinship, as well as male and female homosexuality, in many parts of the world, using their data to endorse sexological claims about British and European culture (Bleys, 145–206). Much of this ethnography strove either to vindicate or to clarify Britain's and Europe's rapacious colonial policies.

Within the empires themselves, many white men and some women devoted themselves to service and duty, sometimes using the empire to displace national laws and restrictions that late-Victorian society established at home to check miscegenation and homosexuality. A wealth of material on miscegenation and its alleged cultural effects appears in Robert Young's carefully argued book *Colonial Desire* (1995). The following paragraphs focus more on connections and divisions between masculinity and homosexuality, as these help explain the emergence of subcultures based at the time on sexual and cultural dissent.

Sir Roger Casement exemplifies a radical lineage of homosexual men and women in Africa: He endorsed the antislavery movement in the Belgian Congo, and later in Peru, while recording in his "Black Diaries" his many interracial affairs with the Congolese. Britain executed Casement in 1916 for his role in Ireland's Easter Rebellion. Yet Casement's radical politics and sexuality were atypical. In southern Africa, General Sir Hector Macdonald, Cecil Rhodes, Leander Starr Jameson (Rhodes's companion), Viscount Alfred Milner, Field Marshal Earl Kitchener, and Baron Robert Baden-Powell, among many others, greatly influenced Britain's colonial policies. Macdonald, who gained national recognition for his military service in the Sudan and the 1899 and 1900 Boer wars, shot himself in 1903 after he was caught having sex with four Sinhalese boys in Ceylon. The incident greatly influenced Britain's subsequent policies on interracial relations. Kitchener's power also derived from his brutal military policies in the Sudan, his reputation later tarnished by his handling of the Boer wars and ensuing military policies in India. Recent biographies of these men identify either love letters written to close male companions, claims of self-imposed chastity, or statements that successful colonial duty can obtain only from confirmed bachelorhood. Kitchener insisted that his "Band of Boys" be unmarried; his group of elite servicemen included Macdonald and Colonel Oswald Fitzgerald, Kitchener's companion for at least ten years who drowned with Kitchener in 1916 when the HMS *Hampshire* struck a mine during the First World War.

It is relatively easy to identify these men's emphasis on intense same-sex friendships and shared emphasis on masculinity as a way to avert scandal and public disgrace, but harder to assess the role and meaning of homosexual desire in Britain's and Europe's empires and thus to bridge the complex interpretive gap among colonial policies, ethnographic material, and contemporaneous literature by, among others, Rudyard Kipling, H. Rider Haggard, G. A. Henty, John Buchan, and A. E. W. Mason. Some, like Major General Frank M. Richardson, have sought to rehabilitate Rhodes and Kitchener as important representatives of gay history, using these and other men as proof that male homosexuals were vital components of Britain's imperial past. To be sure, the military reputation of both men—and their simultaneous resistance to marriage—makes their influence over Queen Victoria highly paradoxical (Kitchener was her "special favourite" from 1888 on). This paradox suggests that expressions of male and female homosexuality were more diverse in fin-de-siècle Britain and its empire than Britain's severe proscriptions against effeminacy in men imply; these proscriptions surfaced with considerable vehemence in Oscar Wilde's second trial in 1895.

The complexity of Rhodes's and Kitchener's political positions derives in part from their loyalty to Britain's Purity movement, which aimed to curb homosexuality, prostitution, vagrancy, abortion, and the availability of contraception in Britain and its colonies. That such men actively encouraged punishment for same-sex relations in Britain and its empire also suggests a complex connection to their own desire (much of which was either unpronounced or discussed in nonsexual terms) that surpasses hypocrisy and bad faith.

Ronald Hyam has used these and other examples to claim that Britain's empire represented a field of "sexual opportunities," and that men and women fled Britain to sustain same-sex friendships and relationships abroad. In his impressive study *Colonialism and Homosexuality* (2003), Robert Aldrich makes a similar point about other European empires (particularly the French and German), though those countries' proscriptions against colonial homosexuality and interracial contact never rivaled Britain's. Generally, such arguments about sexual opportunity tend not only to downplay the material factors involved in colonial administration and to risk painting the colonial past in nostalgic ways but also to simplify the complex interplay among homosexuality, masculinity, patriotic identification, and partial sublimation that appeared to sustain these people abroad. Such

arguments can also ignore the context of homosexuality in each colonized country, whose postcolonial conceptions of homosexuality owe much to British legislation remaining after these countries' independence (see Moodie 1998). Still, Hyam has usefully identified the impact on all but a few of Britain's colonies of Lord Crewe's 1909 circular on interracial heterosexual relationships: Crewe's circular aimed to prohibit sexual contact between (primarily) British men and indigenous women, but Hyam argues convincingly that the circular was also implicitly designed to restrict same-sex interracial contact.

Not surprisingly, many critics are ambivalent about viewing Macdonald, Kitchener, Rhodes, and other colonials as homosexual, seeing their military loyalty and racism as the logical culmination of white men's sexual tourism elsewhere—for instance, in North Africa, the Near East, and various Mediterranean resorts, including Capri. Considering the ethnographic material published between 1850 and 1920, such arguments are reasonable, yet the relation between colonialism and tourism is complex and not self-evident. Work on European tourism clarifies its importance for homosexual men and women, as well as for heterosexual men, suggesting that literature and culture produced at the time would not have flourished had the resorts not existed as places free of persecution and as imaginative foci for diverse sexual fantasies. Aldrich has assessed the importance of Capri for lesbians such as Romaine Brooks, Renèe Vivien, Checca Lloyd, and Kate and Saidee Wolcott-Perry. Andrè Gide's *The Immoralist* (1902) and Thomas Mann's *Death in Venice* (1912) also exemplify these fantasies, the former novel complicated by its protagonist's involvement with Tunisian boys in the context of France's colonial relation to North Africa.

Because in both novels the protagonists' homosexuality emerges only from their distance from France and Germany, respectively, and their encounters with boys they consider different, even exotic, it is easy to conflate these protagonists' perspectives on foreign countries and cultures with those of their their wider cultures. Some critics even dismiss these characters as merely sexual manifestations of their cultures. Yet such readings downplay the very homosexuality violently alienating these protagonists from their countries, as well as the authors' frequent contempt for the white male supremacist arguments that helped bring about their cultural estrangement. If applied to men such as T. E. Lawrence and Jean Genet, the above claims would misunderstand how both writers struggled to renounce their national origins and to identify with the colonized because of—among other things—a shared sexual attraction. General claims about sexual tourism implicitly frown on interracial desire as irrevocably compromised or even shaped by colonial policies. By contrast, other critics have begun to assess the differences in style and structure between, for example, adventure fiction and travel memoirs, the latter often clarifying an author's varied observations, shifting racial and gender loyalties, and sexual perspectives.

Overall, the difficulty facing scholars and historians of colonialism stems partly from conservative *and* radical dimensions of desire, regardless of object choice. Desire may confirm—and even derive from—unequal material conditions; it may also undermine them, leading to more democratic arrangements beyond the immediate logic of European racism and shared beliefs about male supremacy. When critics and readers idealize neither the desire nor the men and women who experienced and acted on it, a complex picture emerges that can sometimes help us disentangle masculinity from colonialism.

Christopher Lane

See also Apartheid; Ethnocentrism; Masculinities
Further Reading:

Aldrich, Robert. 2003. *Colonialism and Homosexuality.* New York: Routledge.
Ballhatchet, Kenneth. 1980. *Race, Sex and Class under the Raj: Imperial Attitudes and Policies and Their Critics, 1793–1905.* New York: St Martin's.

Bleys, Rudi C. 1995. *The Geography of Perversion: Male-to-Male Sexual Behavior outside the West and the Ethnographic Imagination, 1750–1918.* New York: New York University Press.
Boone, Joseph A. 1995. "Vacation Cruises; or, The Homoerotics of Orientalism," *PMLA* 110, no. 1: 89–107. Bristow, Joseph. 1991. *Empire Boys: Adventures in a Man's World.* London: HarperCollins.
Burton, Sir Richard. 1885. "Terminal Essay." Pp. 158–93 in *Sexual Heretics: Male Homosexuality in English Literature from 1850 to 1900.* Edited and compiled by Brian Reade. London: Routledge and Kegan Paul.
David, Deirdre. 1995. *Rule Britannia: Women, Empire, and Victorian Writing.* Ithaca, NY: Cornell University Press.
Hyam, Ronald. 1990. *Empire and Sexuality: The British Experience.* Manchester, UK: Manchester University Press.
Lane, Christopher. 1995. *The Ruling Passion: British Colonial Allegory and the Paradox of Homosexual Desire.* Durham, NC: Duke University Press.
McClintock, Ann. 1995. *Imperial Leather: Race, Gender, and Sexuality in the Colonial Conquest.* New York: Routledge.
Moodie, T. Dunbar. 1998. "Migrancy and Male Sexuality on the South African Gold Mines." *Journal of Southern African Studies* 14: 228–256.
Richardson, Frank M. 1981. *Mars without Venus: A Study of Some Homosexual Generals.* Edinburgh, UK: William Blackwood.
Royle, Trevor. 1985. *The Kitchener Enigma.* London: Michael Joseph.
Sawyer, Roger, ed. 1984. *Roger Casement's Diaries, 1910: The Black and White.* New York: Random House.
Young, Robert J. C. 1995. *Colonial Desire: Hybridity in Theory, Culture and Race.* New York: Routledge.

Columbine

On 20 April 1999, two students, Eric Harris, eighteen, and Dylan Klebold, seventeen, brought guns to Columbine High School, in Littleton, Colorado. They proceeded to kill twelve students and a teacher before committing suicide. The nation's deadliest in a series of school shootings in the 1990s, the Columbine shooting received unprecedented media coverage. The term *Columbine* quickly became synonymous with school shootings and school violence in the United States. The Columbine shooting sparked national debate on the subjects of gun control, media violence, and school safety. Columbine prompted much of the search for trends among the numerous school shootings during the 1990s in such communities as Jonesboro (Arkansas), West Paducah (Kentucky), and Pearl (Mississippi). The severity of the shooting at Columbine High School, prompted U.S. schools to adopt "zero tolerance" policies under which administrators take any kind of student threat seriously. The term *Columbine effect* describes these sweeping changes in school environments, the installation of metal detectors and security cameras in schools, and the enforcement of zero-tolerance policies. Under these policies, students across the country faced suspension and expulsion for bringing to school any object that could be used as a weapon, for writing violent stories, or for making threats to students or faculty. The fact that adolescents Harris and Klebold were able to obtain an arsenal of guns for the shooting induced a national debate on gun control targeting the accessibility of guns for youth, responsible gun use, and gun culture in the United States.

Similar to other school shooters of the 1990s, Eric Harris and Dylan Klebold did not fit traditional notions of juvenile delinquents. In the year before the shooting, they were arrested for breaking into a car, and consequently completed their juvenile diversion program with glowing reviews from court officers who cited their intelligence and willingness to follow rules as likely to lead to future success in school. Harris and Klebold lacked any history of troubled behavior at school and teachers considered them excellent students. Because Harris and Klebold played violent video games, watched violent films, and idolized fictional characters who were violent and powerful, the Columbine shootings fueled a national debate on the influence of violence in the entertainment industry.

After the shooting in Littleton, Colorado, the media searched for explanations in the lives of Harris and Klebold, and began to describe the two as "outcasts" in their school who were taunted and alienated from their classmates. Consequently, bullying became an issue of concern for parents, educators, and academics. The fact that Columbine and other school shootings have been committed by boys has yet to induce a national debate concerning expectations of masculinity in the United States. In the aftermath of the shooting, scholars have sought to understand Columbine and other incidents of school violence within the context of school culture and bullying, and within our accepted culture of masculinity and violence.

Sociologists have found that when bullying occurs in schools where gender dichotomies are pervasive in the classroom and in social hierarchies, it is comprised of direct attacks on masculinities not valued by the dominate peer culture. In their analysis of school social structure, Wooden and Blazak note that "jocks" (athletically inclined boys) largely occupy the powerful position at the top of the hierarchy and as such, function as school bullies to students like Harris and Klebold who belonged to the bottom of the hierarchy. Scholars Gilligan (1996), Garbarino (1999), and Pollack (1998) have explored how such repeated attacks on masculinity are internalized as feelings of shame in young men. As indicated by Garbarino, young men such as Harris and Klebold learn to cope with shame through the code of violent masculinity, and frequently violence is seen to be the only option left for young men to cope with constant affronts on their masculinity. Finally, Kimmel theorizes that school shooters like Harris and Klebold are actually gender conformists, using male violence as a means to prove successful masculinity.

Wendy M. Christensen

See also School Shootings

Further Reading:

Garbarino, James. 1999. *Lost Boys: Why Our Sons Turn Violent and How We Can Save Them.* The Free Press.

Gilligan, James. 1996. *Violence: Reflections on a National Epidemic.* New York: Vintage Books.

Kimmel, Michael S. 1994. "Masculinity as Homophobia." In *Reconstructing Gender: A Multicultural Anthology,* edited by E. Disch. Boston, MA: McGraw Hill.

———. 2000. *The Gendered Society.* New York: Oxford Press.

———. 2001. "Manhood and Violence: The Deadliest Equation." *Newsday* (August): 41.

Pollack, William. 1998. *Real Boys: Rescuing Our Sons from the Myths of Boyhood.* New York: Henry Holt.

Condom Use

Male latex condoms, when used correctly and consistently, are highly effective at preventing the transmission of HIV and other sexually transmitted diseases (STDs) (Centers for Disease Control and Prevention 2001b; Davis and Weller, 1999). Yet, condom use remains a politically contentious public health issue. Although the Centers for Disease Control and Prevention (CDC) had long touted condoms as a "highly effective" means of preventing HIV infection, the federal agency reversed course in 2002 with a revised condom use fact sheet. The updated fact sheet states that "no protective method is 100 percent effective, and condom use cannot guarantee absolute protection against any STD" (CDC 2002). Critics have charged that the CDC's decision to minimize the effectiveness of condoms and promote abstinence and monogamy reflect the Bush Administration's desires to privilege politics over public health (Clymer 2002; Meckler 2002). Despite debates over the effectiveness of condoms, most researchers agree that "human factors" rather than condoms themselves are the greatest barrier to STD prevention (Center for AIDS Prevention Studies 1996). That is, factors such as inconsistent condom use, condom slippage, or breakage account for a greater proportion of STD transmission than the correct and consistent use of condoms.

Beyond the mechanics of condom use lies another reality: Condom use is a gender issue with different meanings and consequences for men and women (Amaro 1995; Campbell 1995). Amaro (1995), a leading theorist on issues of gender, power and HIV/AIDS, has posited that condom use is a distinctly different behavior for men than it is for women: "for men, the behavior is wearing the condom; for women, the behavior is persuading the male partner to wear a condom or, in some cases, deciding not to have sex when the male partner refuses to wear a condom" (440). Feminist scholars have also opined that it is impossible to discuss condom use in heterosexual relationships without acknowledging issues of power; namely that sex typically occurs in contexts in which men have greater power than women (Amaro 1995; Marin and Gomez 1997). At one end of the power continuum is the use of nonaggressive persuasion to garner a woman's consent for sex with or without a condom; at the other extreme is male violence (or the threat of it) in response to a female partners' request for condoms (Beadnell, Baker, Morrison, and Knox 2000; Suarez-Al-Adam, Raffaelli, and O'Leary 2000).

The HIV/AIDS epidemic in the U.S. has prompted an unprecedented increase in condom use (Catania et al. 1995). This rise however has not been consistent over time or among groups. For example, condom use declines for heterosexually active men as they get older, as well as for men involved in long-term relationships (Alan Guttmacher Institute 2002; Anderson, Wilson, Doll, Jones, and Barker 1999; Sonenstein and Stryker 1997). Moreover, recent surges in STDs among men who have sex with men (MSM) have prompted AIDS activists and public health officials to confront the disturbing reality that condom use has also diminished dramatically among MSM (CDC 1999; *LA Syphilis Cases Grow* 2002). (Note: Sexual behavior is often incongruent with sexual identity [e.g., heterosexual, gay, bisexual]. Terms such as *men who have sex with men* [vs. gay or bisexual] and *heterosexually active men* [vs. heterosexual] are more accurate descriptors of men's sexual experiences.) The CDC speculates that many MSM's perceptions about the effectiveness of antiretroviral therapy may explain the increase in STDs.

National study data indicate that condom use also varies by relationship status. People are far more likely to report using condoms with casual partners (62%) than steady partners (19%) (Anderson et al. 1999). National studies also indicate that condom use is higher among those with casual or multiple sex partners and those who are black, male, and younger (Anderson et al. 1999; Pleck, Sonenstein, and Ku 1991; Tanfer, Grady, Klepinger, and Billy 1993). The sex of sexual partners also influences reasons for condom use. Among heterosexually active men, STD prevention and/or contraception are the main reasons for condom use (Anderson et al. 1999; Tanfer et al. 1993). By contrast, STD prevention is the primary reason for MSM's condom use, compared with just 8 percent of heterosexually active men (Tanfer et al. 1993). Men's reasons for not using condoms are more numerous. Heterosexually active men's most frequently cited reasons for condom non-use include: reduced sexual sensation, interference with sexual performance, discomfort using condoms, or embarrassment at buying or putting a condom on in front of a partner (AGI 2002; Sonenstein and Stryker 1997).

Some empirical studies with heterosexually active men have linked lack of condom use to traditional masculine ideologies (Noar and Morokoff 2002; Pleck, Sonenstein, and Ku 1993). Pleck et al. (1993) found that black, white, and Latino adolescent males with more traditionally masculine ideologies were more likely to have had more sexual partners in the past year, more negative attitudes toward condoms, and less consistent condom use. Although MSMs express many of the same reasons for condom non-use as do heterosexually active men, there are important differences. Specifically, MSMs also cite their sense of fatalism about contracting

HIV and their loss of control during sexual situations (Dilley et al. 2002).

A growing body of HIV researchers are calling upon other HIV researchers and theorists to incorporate a focus on social inequality (e.g., poverty, racism, heterosexism) into their understanding of men's HIV risk (AGI 2002; Diaz 1998; Whitehead 1997). Indeed, Latino and African American men, particularly those who are poor, are disproportionately represented in cases of HIV/AIDS among men in the United States (AGI 2002; CDC 2001b).

The correct and consistent use of condoms remains an essential step in preventing the transmission of HIV and other STDs. Accordingly, many HIV activists and researchers have asserted that U.S. public health officials, condom marketers, and advertisers must promote condoms more effectively. They recommend several avenues through which this promotion can occur: social marketing efforts such as public health campaigns; television and other mass media advertising; and increased availability of condoms in settings such as schools, community-based organizations, and bars (CAPS 1996; Sonenstein and Stryker 1997). The current political climate about condom use in the United States suggests however that propositions for public health officials to enhance the promotion of condom use are, at least for the foreseeable future, untenable.

Lisa Bowleg

See also AIDS; Risk Behaviours, Sexual; Safer Sex; Sexually Transmitted Infections

Further Reading:

Alan Guttmacher Institute (AGI). 2002. *In Their Own Right: Addressing the Sexual and Reproductive Health Needs of American Men.* Washington, DC: Alan Guttmacher Institute.

Amaro, H. 1995. "Love, Sex, and Power: Considering Women's Realities in HIV Prevention." *American Psychologist* 50, no. 6: 437–447.

Anderson, J. E., R. Wilson, L. Doll, T. S. Jones, and P. Barker. 1999. "Condom Use and HIV Risk Behaviors Among US Adults." *Family Planning Perspectives* 31, no. 1: 24–28.

Beadnell, B., S. A. Baker, D. M. Morrison, and K. Knox. 2000. "HIV/STD Risk Factors for

Women with Violent Male Partners." *Sex Roles* 42, no. 7–8: 661–689.

Campbell, C. A. 1995. "Male Gender Roles and Sexuality: Implications for Women's AIDS Risk and Prevention." *Social Science Medicine* 41, no. 2: 197–210.

Catania, J. A., D. Binson, M. Dolcini, R. Stall, K. H. Choi, L. M. Pollack, et al. 1995. "Risk Factors for HIV and Other Sexually Transmitted Diseases and Prevention Practices among US Heterosexual Adults: Changes from 1990–1992. *American Journal of Public Health* 85, no. 11: 1492–1499.

Center for AIDS Prevention Studies (CAPS). 1996. *Do Condoms Work?* http://www.caps.ucsf. edu/condtext.html (cited 7 July 2002).

Centers for Disease Control and Prevention. 1999. "Increases in Unsafe Sex and Rectal Gonorrhea among Men Who Have Sex with Men." San Francisco, California 1994–1997. 48, no. 3: 45–48.

———. 2001a. *Fact Sheet: Condoms and Their Use in Preventing HIV Infection.* http:///www.cdc.gov /hiv/pubs/facts/condoms.html.

———. 2001b. HIV/AIDS Surveillance Report. 13, no. 2.

———. 2002. *Fact Sheet for Public Health Personnel: Male Latex Condoms and Sexually Transmitted Diseases.* http://www.cdc.gov/hiv/pubs/ facts/condoms.pdf (cited 20 December 2002).

Clymer, A. 2002. *U.S. Revises Sex Information, and a Fight Goes on.* http://www.nytimes.com/ 2002/12/27/politics/27ABOR.html (cited 28 December 2002).

Davis, K. R., and S. C. Weller. 1999. "The Effectiveness of Condoms in Reducing Heterosexual Transmission of HIV." *Family Planning Perspectives* 31, no. 6: 272–279.

Diaz, R. M. 1998. *Latino Gay Men and HIV: Culture, Sexuality and Risk Behavior.* New York: Routledge.

Dilley, J. W., W. McFarland, W. J. Woods, J. Sabatino, T. Lihatsh, B. Adler, et al. 2002. "Thoughts Associated with Unprotected Anal Intercourse among Men at High Risk in San Francisco 1997–1999." *Psychology and Health* 17, no. 2.

LA Syphilis Cases Grow amid Calls for Education. 2002. http://story.news.yahoo.com/ news?tmpl=story2&cid=571&ncid=751&e=3 &u=/nm/20021227/hl_nm/la_syphilis_dc (cited 28 December 2002).

Marin, B. V., and C. A. Gomez. 1997. "Latino Culture and Sex: Implications for HIV Prevention. Pp. 73–93 in J. G. Garcia and M. C. Zea, eds. *Psychological Interventions and Research with Latino Populations.* Needham Heights, MA: Allyn & Bacon.

Meckler, L. 2002. *CDC Fact Sheet Not Promoting Condom Use.* http://www.washingtonpost. com/wp-dyn/articles/A8652–2002 Dec18.html (cited 20 December 2002).

Noar, S. M., and P. J. Morokoff. 2002. "The Relationship between Masculinity Ideology, Condom Attitudes, and Condom Use Stage of Change: A Structural Equation Modeling Approach." *International Journal of Men's Health* 1, no. 1: 43–58.

Pleck, J. H., F. L. Sonenstein, and L. C. Ku. 1991. "Adolescent Males' Condom Use: Relationships between Perceived Cost-Benefits and Consistency." *Journal of Marriage and the Family* 53, no. 3: 733–745.

———. 1993. "Masculinity Ideology: Its Impact on Adolescent Males' Heterosexual Relationships." *Journal of Social Issues* 49, no. 3: 11–29.

Sonenstein, F. L., and J. Stryker. 1997. *Why Some Men Don't Use Condoms: Male Attitudes about Condoms and Other Contraceptives.* Menlo Park, CA: Henry J. Kaiser Family Foundation.

Suarez-Al-Adam, M., M. Raffaelli, and A. O'Leary. 2000. "Influence of Abuse and Partner Hypermasculinity on the Sexual Behavior of Latinas." *AIDS Education and Prevention* 12, no. 3: 263–274.

Tanfer, K., W. R. Grady, D. H. Klepinger, and J. O. Billy. 1993. "Condom Use among U.S. Men, 1991." *Family Planning Perspectives* 25, no. 2: 61–66.

Whitehead, T. L. 1997. "Urban Low-Income African American Men, HIV/AIDS, and Gender Identity." *Medical Anthropology Quarterly* 11, no. 4: 411–447.

Consciousness Raising

Men's consciousness-raising (CR) groups developed in the 1970s, as men became aware of the emotional and physical costs of traditional male roles. Using the benefits of small group dynamics, men were interested in looking at ways to increase their awareness of how their actions affected women, children, families (of whatever configuration), and other men.

The major catalyst for the development of CR groups was the advent of Second

Wave feminism in the mid-1960s. Women began to examine how the patriarchal structure negatively affected their lives and joined together to form the women's movement. This had a definite impact on the husbands, partners, and other men in their lives. As a result, those men were very strongly encouraged and/or shamed into looking at their own issues, their own actions that perpetuated the patriarchal social structure, and how this impacted their own lives as men, as well as the lives of the women with whom they were in relationships, be it intimate, platonic, or having other relational aspects. Here's how one man described his experience:

> Ann came back from the women's Pennsylvania weekend meeting high on the togetherness, strength, and beauty that she and many of the other women felt there. They had rapped together, played ball together, walked together, danced together, argued together, *felt* together. At homes afterwards, watching and listening to her and to friends of ours who were at the meeting, I could see how beautiful an experience the weekend was, how connected the women got, how strong and good the feelings were. And I could also know that I never had, and maybe never would, experience such beautiful human feelings. And I don't believe this is a personal hang-up of mine alone, but is a problem common to *all* men, even supposedly liberated hip-left men [emphasis in the original].
>
> My weekend, in contrast, was spent in unacknowledged, fearful anticipation of what changes the weekend might put Ann through. You see, there's no doubt in my mind at all that women are more in touch with their humanity than men. After all, women's qualities—responsiveness to others, sensitivity, compassion, patience, subtlety, intuitive conceptualizing, etc.—are exactly the ones our future utopian society would foster and flourish on; while the male qualities—self-interest,

> competitiveness, aggression, force, rigid thinking, etc.—are precisely our enemies and what we are struggling to eliminate. The pressing question is whether we men can ever in our lifetime regain our humanity. Also, I think today's women are crazy to continue messing around with men the way they have been, and in fact it seems they are becoming more and more unwilling to do so. It must be a terrific drain on their energy—always having to be responsible for someone else, always mothering someone along, and just getting ignored, used, and shit on as a result. Whereas when they direct their keener sensitivity, insight, and energies toward themselves and other women—toward people who can really understand, respond to, and support each other—the result is genuine growth, development, and good feelings.
>
> Anyway, self-pity was not an adequate response. I knew I had better get on the ball and do something about me right now. Right now I see that I have to push myself more and more to expose and risk my feelings before other people and also probably get into another encounter/consciousness raising group. Perhaps ideally that would be with other men similarly aware of their sexism and committed to struggling against it. However, a three or four month stint about a year ago in a male anti-sexist group did little for any of us, and we occasionally used it to support some oppressive tendencies. In any case, new forms of struggle are desperately needed, and it is the responsibility of men conscious of their male chauvinism to develop these and to seriously put them into effect for more and more men. The women's movement will probably be much help to us through our observing it and to some extent, when possible, experiencing their revolutionary struggle, letting it be an indication to us of the direction in which we go. (Snodgrass 1971, 7, 8, and 10)

In this quote are elements of the impact of the women's movement along with the need for a group to support one's rising consciousness and to assist in getting in touch with feelings that are contrary to the way in which men are socialized in this culture.

Why a men's group? "[F]or many men the John Wayne image of success is not enough. The success of the women's liberation movement has prodded many men to question and examine their own lives and the traditional roles expected of them as men" (Krebs 1980, 3). A men's group is simply a group of men who get together on a regular basis to deal with issues relating to being men in today's society:

> A men's support group helps men share common feelings, concerns, and experiences. Support groups often help with problem solving in an individual's life and provide encouragement and personal support that we often need in difficult situations or in our work toward change.
>
> A men's consciousness raising (c.r.) group fills the functions of a support group with an additional quality. It introduces new ideas on men's issues to group participants so as to foster an exchange of viewpoints and information among the group members. A men's c.r. group aims at expanding the group's understanding and awareness of sex role issues. It serves as a base for men to change their attitudes, beliefs, and behaviors in ways they deem valuable. Though c.r. groups may prove more challenging than a support group, they also offer more excitement and potential for individual growth than other group experiences. (Krebs 1980, 8)

Today men's support and CR groups differ politically—some oppose and some support feminism, for example—but all develop at least one of these four areas: 1) self-discovery; 2) consciousness raising; 3) sexuality and intimacy; or 4) parenting. Each of these roughly corresponds to a different branch of the men's movement.

Since the 1970s, CR activities—particularly where they include looking at men's

sexism, homophobia, and racism—have evolved into the National Organization for Changing Men, which is now the National Organization for Men Against Sexism (NO-MAS). At the other end of the continuum of the men's movement in the early 2000s is Warren Farrell and the National Coalition for Free Men, in what would be classified as the men's rights branch of the movement.

Most CR and support groups in the 2000s take place within the general framework of the mythopoetic men's movement. Some are open men's support groups, sometimes called drop-in groups. Others are closed, which mean they have a fixed membership, which may temporarily open up to add new members and then close again (Barton 2000). The most common type of a closed mythopoetic men's support group in the early 2000s, which is growing worldwide, is the ManKind Project's I-Group, with I-Groups in Australia, Canada, France, Germany, New Zealand, South Africa, Sweden, the United Kingdom, and the United States. (See The ManKind Project.) The gateway to the activities of the ManKind Project is through its New Warrior Training Adventure, an initiatory weekend for men.

Edward Read Barton

See also The ManKind Project

Further Reading:

Barton, Edward Read. 2000. "Parallels between Mythopoetic Men's Work/Men's Peer Mutual Support Groups and Selected Feminist Theories." Pp. 3–20 in *Mythopoetic Perspectives of Men's Healing Work: An Anthology for Therapists and Others.* Edited by Edward Read Barton. Westport, CT: Bergin and Garvey.

Karsk, Roger, and Bill Thomas. 1987. *Working with Men's Groups.* Duluth, MN: Whole Person Press.

Krebs, Tony. 1980. *Facilitators Manual for Men's Consciousness Raising and Support Groups.* 3d ed. Seattle, WA: Metropolitan YMCA Seattle Men's Programs Unit.

Snodgrass, Jon, et al., eds. 1971. *Unbecoming Men: Men's Consciousness-Raising Group Writes on Oppression and Themselves.* Washington, NJ: Times Change Press.

Contemporary Literature by Women

With the emergence of more contemporary female authors, a noticeable change has occurred in terms of the workings of masculinity within these authors' texts. More and more, this fiction penned by women is concerned with the workings of women's lives and intricate characterizations of such women, while masculinity (and even male characters, for that matter) seems to fall by the wayside and become of lesser importance. In other words, instead of masculine male characters, the norm becomes female characters who "come into their own," with male characters being, for the most part, ancillary.

Faye Weldon's *The Life and Loves of a She-Devil* (1983) is a novel that presents masculinity as a force that must be destroyed for a woman to thrive. The novel's protagonist, Ruth, trapped in an unfulfilling role as a housewife, reinvents herself and becomes a wealthy, powerful figure—one modeled after her husband's current love interest. One aspect that makes the protagonist unhappy is her dwindling relationship with her husband, Bobbo. While on route to becoming an empowered woman, Ruth destroys her husband's career and becomes a catalyst for getting him sent to prison for crimes that he did not commit. Years later, the protagonist, totally physically transformed, takes back her husband so as to torture him.

Jeanette Winterson's fiction is often cited for its lack of prominent male characters, the most notable example probably being *Boating for Beginners* (1997), which is an account of several woman who survive the biblical deluge. Of Winterson's male characters, one of importance is the minister from *Oranges Are Not the Only Fruit* (1997), who is responsible for a cruel exorcism performed upon the young female protagonist. However, he remains a secondary character; instead, the book centers upon the protagonist's relationship with her mother. The soldier Henri from *The Passion* (1987) and the explorer Jordan from *Sexing the Cherry* (1989) are two of Winterson's male protagonists, but neither character is particularly masculine, and neither comes to a particularly happy end. Henri commits a gruesome murder, is incarcerated, and is eventually revealed to be content within his own insanity. Jordan, on the other hand, never recovers from his unrequited love.

A. S. Byatt's fiction, too, is primarily woman centered. *The Game* (1990) considers the relationship between sisters. *Possession* (1990) traces in part the love affair between a man and woman, but the pivotal graveyard scene at the climax of the novel highlights the importance of the female scholar, Beatrice Nest. *Still Life* (1997), *The Virgin in the Garden* (1978), and *Babel Tower* (1996) consider the lives of the Potter family, but the primary character of interest is the daughter, Frederica. When masculinity rears its head, though, the head is ugly indeed. In *Still Life,* Byatt presents Lucas Simmonds, a science teacher and a pedophile who suffers a nervous breakdown and dramatically goes mad, covering himself, Ophelia-style, with water plants. In *Babel Tower,* Frederica leaves her abusive husband, Nigel Reiver, who abuses her by calling her a bitch and pulling her hair, punching her in the ribs, and—giving a "great whoop of laughter"—throwing an axe at her. Frederica wins the battle with her husband by obtaining a divorce and custody of their son, Leo. Finally, in *The Biographer's Tale* (2000), the masculinity of Phineas G. Nanson is only observable when contrasted to the homosexuality of Erik and Christophe. Thus, masculinity becomes equated with heterosexuality.

Margaret Atwood's Booker Prize–winning *The Blind Assassin* (2000) is another novel that considers the life of a family; again, though, this novel is primarily concerned with the lives and deaths of the sisters Iris and Laura Chase. *Cat's Eye* (1998) considers the childhood and adulthood of the fictional Canadian artist, Elaine Risley. *Alias Grace* (1997) and *The Robber Bride* (1998) consider the evolutions of relationships among women. In *The Edible Woman* (1969), Marian McAlpin finds herself trapped within the confines of a patriarchal system (via her fiancé, Peter) and gradually loses her ability to eat a growing number of foods; ironically, she finds the strength to battle this system from the androgynous, enigmatic Duncan.

Masculinity is much more a factor in *The Handmaid's Tale* (1986), in which women have been stripped of their rights and privileges in a world dominated almost exclusively by men. The anonymous female narrator is tasked with regularly copulating with a high-ranking male official in an attempt to bear him a child. Women who fail to provide children for such men (often older and perhaps impotent) are exiled. Thus, men are shown to be in possession of most power in this society; although women do maintain some lower positions of leadership, even the highest-ranking woman is subservient to the lowest man.

Toni Morrison uses masculinity to show its inclination for destruction. Whereas *Sula* (1973) primarily considers the relationship between two women, Sula and Nel, in *Paradise* (1999), Morrison considers the lives of a group of women who live together within a large house. The women form their own happy family, but this family is destroyed, and one of the woman is executed, by angry and suspicious men. In *Beloved* (1987), African American men, such as Paul D., are emasculated when forced to live in unsafe conditions and by being forced to provide oral sex for the white prisoner guards. Paul D. becomes empowered and regains his manhood by escaping with his fellow prisoners, eventually settling down with Sethe, another former slave. *Song of Solomon* (1997) traces the warring masculinities of Milkman and Guitar, a battle that eventually ends in death. Both characters possess much strength, but the nature of masculinity is such that it seeks to destroy competing masculinities.

W. S. Hampl

Further Reading:

Atwood, Margaret. 1969. *The Edible Woman.* New York: Bantam, 1996.

———. 1986. *The Handmaid's Tale.* New York: Doubleday.

———. 2000. *The Blind Assassin.* New York: Doubleday.

Byatt, A. S. 1978. *The Virgin in the Garden.* New York: Vintage, 1992.

———. 1990. *Possession: A Romance.* New York: Random House.

———. 1996. *Babel Tower.* New York: Random House.

———. 2000.

The Biographer's Tale. London: Chatto and Windus.

Morrison, Toni. 1983. *Sula.* New York: Random House.

———. 1987. *Beloved.* New York: Plume.

———. 1997. *Song of Solomon.* New York: Random House.

———. 1999. *Paradise.* New York: Plume.

Weldon, Fay. 1983. *The Life and Loves of a She-Devil.* New York: Ballantine Books.

Winterson, Jeanette. 1987. *The Passion.* New York: Vintage.

———. 1989. *Sexing the Cherry.* New York: Vintage, 1991.

Contraception

For decades, the idea of increasing men's participation in birth control or family planning has received attention, mainly linked to promoting vasectomy or condoms. (The early term used for contraception, *birth control,* eventually gave way to *family planning.* The term *reproductive health,* introduced at the International Conference on Population and Development [ICPD], which incorporates contraception, sexually transmitted diseases including HIV/AIDs, and other concerns, has now become the preferred language.) Only recently has a gender analysis been applied to the issue of "male involvement" in this field. This has come about due to a shift from a top-down, population control, demographic mentality to one concerned with meeting people's reproductive health needs and also to the fact that HIV/AIDS threatens men as well as women. The breakthrough Programme of Action resulting from the 1994 United Nations International Conference on Population and Development (ICPD) urges "gender equality in all spheres of life" and specifically calls for an increase in males' responsibility for their sexual and reproductive behavior (ICPD paragraph 4.25).

Although the reproductive health of individuals is largely dependent upon a relational act occurring between two people, family planning programs from their beginnings in the 1950s and 1960s were established to serve primarily women clients. Sociologists have attributed the origin of single-sex services to the development of the oral pill, which could be delivered to women relatively inexpensively in stand-alone clinics or through social marketing, pharmacies, or door-to-door delivery. Not until the 1990s did the recognition that more than 70 percent of HIV infections occur as a result of heterosexual sex (Piot 2001) lead to a greater scrutiny of women's ability to control the timing and circumstances under which sex takes place. Many providers added men to their reproductive health services because women made it known that they were powerless to use contraception or negotiate condom use to protect themselves from a sexually transmitted disease without the involvement of male partners.

Historically, however, the predominant means of preventing births were four methods used by men. The oldest of these, coitus interruptus (or "withdrawal"), was known to at least three ancient religious traditions and was responsible for the fertility decline that took place in Europe in the nineteenth century. It is still used by 35 million people to control fertility. Nearly as many couples rely on periodic abstinence (or the "rhythm" method). In both cases, the methods are free of cost and side effects, but have a high failure rate in preventing pregnancy. The condom has prevented births for more than 250 years, but the AIDS epidemic has broadened its importance as a means to prevent transmission of HIV (Ringheim 1996). The condom (either male or female) is the only method that provides "dual protection" from both pregnancy and disease. Critics of the male condom argue that it reduces sexual pleasure and in some cultures, where maleness is associated with the quality and quantity of semen, both women and men are reluctant to "waste" semen by using condoms (Gupta, Joshi, and Crook 2001). Vasectomy is a century-old method that is reliable, safe, and inexpensive, but requires minor surgery and is, for all practical purposes, a permanent end to fertility. It is used by about 7 percent of the world's contracepting couples, as compared to a third of married contracepting couples who rely on female sterilization (Ringheim 1996).

Whether as a consequence of the less desirable contraceptive options available to men after the pill was developed or an increased unwillingness of men to share the burden of contraceptive drawbacks, the responsibility for contraception is now primarily borne by women. In the early 2000s, 74 percent of global contraceptive use was of methods used by women. In addition to the oral pill and sterilization or tubal ligation, these methods include the intrauterine device (IUD), hormonal injections or implants, and barrier methods such as the diaphragm and cervical cap.

Encouraging greater gender equity in contraceptive practices is one goal of the efforts to involve men as partners in family planning and reproductive health. The method mix, or percent distribution of each method's contribution to total use, can indicate the extent of gender balance in contraceptive responsibility within a country or program. For example, there are only three countries in the world, and none in the developing world, where the number of vasectomies equals or exceeds the number of female sterilizations, despite the fact that vasectomy is easier, safer, and less expensive. In India, the ratio of thirty-five female sterilizations to one vasectomy suggests that the program is heavily biased toward female responsibility for contraception.

The inherent gender issues in contraception include the fact that pregnancy occurs as a result of a sexual act between men and women, yet women alone bear the physical manifestation of failure to (successfully) contracept. The fact that only one sex can become pregnant has affected contraceptive development for decades. Women have been viewed as having greater self-interest in avoiding unwanted pregnancy than men. Some believe that this has fostered less attention to the development of a viable noncoital dependent, nonsurgical method for men. Other scientists have found that the daily production of sperm is a more formidable challenge to contraceptive interruption than the once-a-month release of the egg. In any case, funds for the development of a method for men that would be comparable in effectiveness and acceptability to the female pill have been extremely limited since the pill became widely available in the 1960s.

A handful of international researchers have continued to pursue the development of a hormonal method for men. In 2003 prototypes are in clinical trial in several countries and a product is anticipated within seven to ten years. Research has also been conducted on whether, once men have a comparable option, they will share responsibility for contraception more equitably with women. Surveys have found that men would be far more willing to share contraceptive responsibility more equitably if methods for men didn't involve surgery, a permanent end to fertility, or loss of pleasure. In clinical trials of hormonal methods for men, male participants often had female partners who suffered serious side effects from the methods available to women. When men said they wanted to "help out" by joining the trial, their female partners sometimes resented the idea that men were "helping" with a responsibility that they felt should be equally shared (Ringheim 1996). Some women said they wouldn't trust the male partner to correctly and consistently use a male method. These findings indicate a range of gender issues that must be addressed if power in sexual relations and contraceptive responsibility is ever to be truly shared.

The existence of particular contraceptive technologies that are dependent on use by women or men is clearly set into a context of socially constructed gender roles and male-female power dynamics. Beyond the technology of contraceptive methods, these human components have a major influence on a sexually active person's ability to successfully prevent unwanted pregnancy and to avoid contracting and spreading sexually transmitted disease. Male behavior influenced by masculinity stereotypes is both directly and indirectly linked to the use of birth control methods through a number of mechanisms.

Besides men's own practice of contraception, another issue of men's participation in reproductive health is their support, or lack of it, for their women partners' use of contraceptive methods. Although decisions about contraception are often considered female business, a man often influences the contraceptive use of the woman (or women) with whom he has sexual relations, by forbidding her to seek contraception, refusing to pay any expense involved, indicating his preferences about the choice of a method, etc. Simply aiming at increasing "male involvement" or the use of male-dependent contraceptives should not be seen as an automatic or an unqualified step forward, especially when it means diminished control or autonomy for women (Helzner 1996).

There are several levels at which gender imbalances can affect contraception programs and their clients, and where gender analysis can be useful. First, *institutions* can address masculinity stereotypes within their own structures, including the composition by sex of each level of staff, the attitudes of staff members, the counseling and medical practices of providers, and the content of educational materials. Providers are members of the societies in which they live, and not immune to gender bias or stereotypes. When counseling male-female couples together, providers may direct attention to the male partner and exclude the female partner from the discussion (Kim et al. 2000). They may feel that men should not be asked to deal with whatever minimal reduction of sensation might occur with condom use. Providers and male clients alike may place a greater value on the health of men and share the belief that it is unnecessary to impose on men a procedure that women can undergo in their place (Ringheim 2002). Providers may share their clients' biases against vasectomy and can convey to clients that vasectomy is less safe and causes impotence and weakness.

Second, *individuals,* regardless of age, face gender-role expectations. For example, risk taking is often a feature of young men's lives, and having unprotected sex is one arena where this may play out. As male and female clients select a contraceptive method, they can be offered an opportunity to consider the effect of dominant gender roles in their own lives. Taking risks or being placed at risk of a sexually transmitted disease or pregnancy by a partner's behavior, should, in addition to one's medical background, factor into the contraceptive decision-making process. A dominant, hegemonic model of masculinity not only affects men's own sexuality and contraceptive use, but also the way they view women's roles in this area. When pleasure and performance are the key criteria by which men judge the world of contraception and reproductive health, and if women are not accorded the same recognition of their sexual health, then a "double standard" exists.

Judith Helzner
Karin Ringheim

See also Condom Use

Further Reading:

Cohen, Sylvie I., and Michele Burger. 2000. "Partnering: A New Approach to Sexual and Reproductive Health." *United Nations Population Fund* Technical Paper No. 3. New York: United Nations Population Fund.

Drennan, Megan. 1998. "New Perspectives on Men's Participation." *Population Reports,* Series J, no. 46. Baltimore, MD: Johns Hopkins University School of Public Health, Population Information Program.

Gupta, Pawan, Anuradha Joshi, and Barbara Crook. 2003. "Gender and Social Justice." Pp. 31–51 in *Three Case Studies.* Washington, DC: Interagency Gender Working Group.

Helzner, Judith F. 1996. "Men's Involvement in Family Planning." *Reproductive Health Matters* 7: 146–154.

Piot, Peter. 2001. "World AIDS Campaign: Men Key to Reducing HIV/AIDS. New Campaign Targets Widely Held Beliefs about Masculinity." News release. Melbourne: UNAIDS.

Ringheim, Karin. 1996. "Whither Methods for Men? Emerging Gender Issues in Contraception." *Reproductive Health Matters* 7: 79–89.

———. 2002. "When the Client Is Male: Client-Provider Interaction, from a Gender Perspective." *International Family Planning Perspectives* 28, no. 3: 170–175.

"Cool Pose"

Cool pose is a term that describes the posture and affective displays of black men. Initially identified by psychologists Richard Majors and Janet Mancini Billson, "cool pose" is a defensive strategy, a coping mechanism to deal with the emasculations of racism. As they describe it:

Of all the strategies embraced by black males to cope with oppression and marginality, the creation of the cool pose is perhaps the most unique. Presenting to the world an emotionless, fearless, and aloof front counters the low sense of inner control, lack of inner strength, absence of stability, damaged pride, shattered confidence, and fragile social competence that come from living on the edge of society.

For some black males, cool pose represents a fundamental structuring of the psyche—the cool mask belies the rage held in check beneath the surface. For others it is the adoption of a uniquely creative style that serves as a sign of belonging and stature. Black males have learned to use posing and posturing to communicate power, toughness, detachment, and style: that is to say, self. They have developed a "third eye" that reads interpersonal situations with a special acuity. They have cultivated a keen sense of what to say, and how and when to say it, in order to avoid punishment and pain and to embellish their life chances.

Since their first days as slaves in this and other countries, African American males have discovered that masking behavior is a supremely useful device. During slavery, black males were masters of cool. Now cool pose has become an integral thread in the fabric of black-black and black-white relationships. It has been exported out of the ghetto and into the lives of middle-class black males. Cool has long blended into jazz and other black music that belongs to all of American society, indeed, the world. And cool has influenced mainstream culture through entertainment, sports, clothing, and the media.

As with most coping strategies, cool pose helps individuals adapt to environmental conditions and neutralize stress. Humans, like other animals, struggle for existence within the context of their social and physical environment. As Darwin pointed out in his theory of evolution, those who survive have found strategies that help them cope with their particular environment. Cool pose is such a strategy for many black males. Wilkinson and Taylor indicate that playing it cool has been a defense for blacks against exploitation. Sometimes being cool may be automatic and unconscious; other times it may be a conscious and deliberate facade. In either case, being cool helps maintain a balance between the black male's inner life and his social environment.

The cool front of black masculinity is crucial for preservation of pride, dignity, and respect. It is also a way for the black male to express bitterness, anger, and distrust toward the dominant society. Cool pose works to keep whites off balance and puzzled about the black man's true feelings.

Being cool enhances the black man's pride and character, helps him cope with conflict and anxiety, and paves an avenue for expressiveness in sports, entertainment, rap talking, break dancing, and street cool. It is part of daily life.

Cool pose furnishes the black male with a sense of control, inner strength, balance, stability, confidence, and security. It also reflects these qualities. Cool helps him deal with the closed doors and negative images of himself that he must confront on a daily basis. It may represent one of the riches untapped areas for understanding black male behavior today.

Richard Majors
Reprinted by permission of John Wiley and Sons.
© 1992 by John Wiley and Sons.

See also Black Masculinities; Machismo
Further Reading:
Majors, Richard, and Janet Mancini Billson. 1992. *Cool Pose: The Dilemma of Black Masculinity.* New York: John Wiley.

Cooper, James Fenimore (1789–1851)

One of America's first successful novelists, Cooper's most notable works—the five *Leatherstocking* novels—capture as well as criticize the pioneering spirit of the early- to mid-nineteenth century. Cooper entered the literary scene when America was badly in need of popular "homegrown" authors who could combat England's lingering cultural influence (McWilliams 1995, 7). In Natty Bumppo, Cooper created a self-reliant hero who owes nothing to society, a man upon whose frontier instincts and thirst for adventure reflect an ideology that contrasts with the superficial nature of the white settlers' preoccupations and forms a basis for Cooper's social criticism (Franklin 1982, 34).

Cooper, the twelfth of thirteen children, was born in Burlington, New Jersey, but in 1790 his family moved to Lake Otsego in upstate New York and founded the Cooperstown settlement. A string of financial and personal disasters left a thirty-one-year-old Cooper badly in need of steady income, and—according to a famous family story—Cooper's career as a novelist arose from simple frustration. Exasperated with the novel he was reading aloud, Cooper threw it aside and exclaimed, "I could write you a better book than that myself!" (quoted in Ringe 1988, 1). His first novel, *Precaution* (1820), was a novel of morals and manners in the English tradition, but many of his subsequent novels were more significant for their synthesis of fiction and American history. Thanks mostly to the *Leatherstocking* novels, Cooper was internationally recognized as America's "national novelist" at the time of his death.

A complex interplay between masculinity, morality, and nature lies at the heart of the *Leatherstocking* novels. One quickly realizes that the men of Cooper's world must adapt their behavior to the environment in order to survive. White men, however, have failed to adapt to the wilderness. In the *Last of the Mohicans* (1826), entire armies of English and French are swallowed by the forest only to emerge as scattered remnants (Ringe 1988, 43). With the exception of Hawkeye (aka Natty Bumppo), whites can only exert power from the safety of their forts and roads or by eliminating the wilderness altogether through settlement, partitioning, or deforestation. Cooper's sweeping descriptions of the landscape, however, communicate how tenuous a fort's grip on the frontier really is; these "outposts of civilization" are easily enveloped by the ever-encroaching wilderness (Ringe 1988, 153).

Cooper imbues Hawkeye with a certain moral practicality that other white men lack. During a Huron attack in the *Last of the Mohicans,* Hawkeye chastises himself for, at Duncan Heyward's request, wasting his last bullet in an act of mercy toward a dying Huron warrior. Heyward advocates this course of action because he, an English officer, is expected by his peers to live up to certain standards of male behavior that Hawkeye later regrets indulging: "[W]hat mattered it," Hawkeye muses, "whether he struck the rock living or dead?" (Cooper 1983, 75). Hawkeye's philosophy makes

sense in the wilderness, where the European concept of honorable surrender at Fort William Henry only leads to their massacre at the hands of the Hurons. The "civilized" behavior expected of European men is incompatible with the demands of survival in Cooper's wilderness. In the *Pathfinder* (1840), Mabel is incredulous at Scotsman McNab's reluctance to retreat into a blockhouse. Exclaims McNab, "We are broadsword men, and love to stand foot to foot with the foe . . . this American mode of fighting will destroy the reputation of His Majesty's army" (quoted in Franklin 1982, 67). McNab pays a high price for this attitude: He is promptly shot by an Indian hidden nearby. Natty Bumppo, unlike McNab and most other whites, has jettisoned European baggage that equates masculinity with facing one's enemy face to face on a traditional battlefield. He realizes that preventive killing, sabotage, and other guerilla warfare tactics are preferable to a straight fight if they increase one's odds of survival.

In writing the *Leatherstocking* novels, especially the *Last of the Mohicans,* Cooper drew parallels between the patriarchal warrior cultures of the American Indians and ancient Greeks. Like Homer's *Iliad,* the *Last of the Mohicans* climaxes in single combat between Chingachgook and Magua reminiscent of that between Achilles and Hector. Both novels also end with speeches that, although they attempt to process the significance of the events that have transpired, only succeed in deconstructing male power. Conquering the frontier and waging war demands male heroism, but those who demonstrate these qualities are eventually destroyed. The spiritually broken patriarchs whose speeches comprise the conclusion of the *Last of the Mohicans* don't speak of a bright future; instead, they lament the emptiness that follows bloodshed.

Natty Bumppo's own status as a mythical hero is checked by the historical forces at work against him; the inexorable march of westward expansion ensures that he will never be able to live in peace. Even in the *Deerslayer* (1841), a chronicle of Natty's earliest exploits, the frontier incursions of Judge Cooper (*The Pioneers*, 1823) and other, later enemies are expunged only to be replaced by Tom Hutter and Harry March. These two white men foreshadow the approaching civilization that will destroy Natty over the span of Cooper's five epic novels (Franklin 1982, 107).

James Fenimore Cooper was a gifted author whose *Leatherstocking* novels provided a fledgling nation with pioneering heroes and frontier adventures. Through Natty Bumppo, Cooper explored not only the conflicts between man and frontier that dominated the national consciousness but also the morality of that frontier. His writing career may have stemmed from mere dissatisfaction, but he was a better author than even he himself believed.

Forrest K. Lehman

See also Buddy Films; Frontier
Further Reading:

Clark, Robert, ed. 1985. *James Fenimore Cooper: New Critical Essays.* London: Vision Press.

Cooper, James Fenimore. [1826] 1983. *Last of the Mohicans.* Albany: State University of New York Press.

Fields, Wayne, ed. 1979. *James Fenimore Cooper: A Collection of Critical Essays.* Englewood Cliffs, NJ: Prentice-Hall.

Franklin, Wayne. 1982. *The New World of James Fenimore Cooper.* Chicago: University of Chicago Press.

Kelly, William P. 1983. *Plotting America's Past: Fenimore Cooper and the Leatherstocking Tales.* Carbondale, IL: Southern Illinois University Press.

McWilliams, John. 1972. *Political Justice in a Republic: James Fenimore Cooper's America.* Berkeley, CA: University of California Press.

———. 1995. *The Last of the Mohicans: Civil Savagery and Savage Civility.* New York: Twayne.

Railton, Stephen. 1978. *Fenimore Cooper: A Study of His Life and Imagination.* Princeton, NJ: Princeton University Press.

Rans, Geoffrey. 1991. *Cooper's Leatherstocking Tales: A Secular Reading.* Chapel Hill, NC: University of North Carolina Press.

Ringe, Donald. 1988. *James Fenimore Cooper.* Boston: Twayne.

Taylor, Alan. 1995. *William Cooper's Town: Power and Persuasion on the Frontier of the Early American Republic.* New York: Knopf.

Cop Films

The hero of the cop action film offers moviegoing audiences a potent image of American masculity as tough, independent, and victorious in the face of a society that is dominated by crime. The cop action hero may be an average guy just doing his job, but he is also a fantasy of indestructible masculinity embodying a wisecracking defiance of villainous criminals and law-enforcement bureaucracy alike. The first cop films were the police procedurals of the late 1940s and 1950s that focused on the organized nature of the police force and the scientific methods of investigation available to them. The cop shifted from being an average figure just doing his duty in the late 1940s to a violent and vigilante cop in the 1970s. In the 1980s the vengeful vigilante cop became a wisecracking action hero; however, in the 1990s, an emphasis on brains over brawn saw the arrival of a cop hero more dependent on his intellect than his firepower. The cop remains a popular hero offering moviegoing audiences a figure that works through issues of class, gender, and race as well as embodying an idealization of law-enforcement and masculine heroism in American culture.

Until the 1940s the policeman tended to be portrayed as a bumbling or inefficient figure who stood at the sidelines while the amateur sleuth or private eye solved the case. The police detective emerged as a hero in the mid-1940s in a reflection of the professionalization of real-life law enforcement and of national security concerns incited by the Cold War. The police procedural, most notably the radio and television series *Dragnet,* presented audiences with detailed scenes of the methods employed by the law to combat crime including ballistics tests, tracking, surveillance, and forensic technologies. The police detective represented an idealized image of masculinity as organized, methodical, and driven by duty. The procedural hero ignored the disillusionment and paranoia of the Cold War period and instead offered a hero that was effective and committed to eradicating crime but was sterile and conservative. The procedural in its original form all but disappeared by the late 1950s; however, its legacy is introducing the cop as an American hero, a trend that continues today.

The conservative image of masculinity and law enforcement embodied by the procedural detective was eradicated by the arrival of the vigilante cop film in the late 1960s. The abolition of film censorship in 1968 allowed for more violent and controversial heroes. *Bullitt* (1968), *Coogan's Bluff* (1968), *The French Connection* (1971), and *Dirty Harry* (1971) introduced the tough and often angry hero who annihilated crime at any cost, even to the extent of ignoring or even breaking the law to get the job done. In a period when President Nixon's hard-line politics on crime and the widespread loss of confidence in law enforcement were dominating the American psyche, and the vigilante cop film presented an image of masculinity that was tough, independent, violent, and successful in the war against crime.

The 1970s began a trend whereby the dominance of white, middle-class, middle-aged masculinity was gradually called into question following the Civil Rights movement and second-wave feminism. By the 1980s, the privileges that men had enjoyed and taken for granted were regarded as unearned advantages and hegemonic masculinity found its position in society challenged. The cop action film, as a central genre of the 1980s and 1990s, can be seen as a backlash to this challenge, offering a space for the expression and fictional resolution of problems of race, class, gender, and crime that overwhelmed American masculinity. The advances in terms of opportunities for African Americans in society posed a seeming threat to the dominance of white masculinity. The biracial cop film of the 1980s negated the

threat of this empowerment with the black buddy being placed in a subordinate role to the white cop hero and helping in the fight against crime that threatened white America, for example *48 Hrs* (1982) starring Nick Nolte and Eddie Murphy.

Just as the empowerment of African Americans posed an inferred threat to dominant masculinity, so too did the emerging equality of women result in the fear of a potential loss of male power. The cop action film offered an antidote to the perceived female threat with an emphasis on the hero's body as muscular, manly, and spectacular. The male body became the hero's most effective weapon in the fight against crime and injustice and, thus, compounded issues of sexual difference. Cop action films revelled in scenes of action and violence with the male body at the center engaged in fistfights, kickboxing, car chases, and gunplay. The cop action hero, like John McClane in *Die Hard* (1988) and Martin Riggs in *Lethal Weapon* (1987), followed in the tradition of the vigilante cop but also the male rampage hero like Rambo, and represented an idealized image of American masculinity as violent, independent, muscular, and victorious. The cop action hero as an icon of American masculinity did not betray his emotions—an emasculating and effeminate weakness. Instead, he expressed himself through wisecracking quips and physical violence, with his body as the site upon which masculine crisis could be expressed and resolved. The body of the cop action hero was a spectacle of hypermasculinity but was not marked explicitly as an erotic object because of the homoeroticism that might imply for the heterosexual male audience. Rather than his body being spectacular in passivity, like that of the on-screen woman, the male body was most often only shown stripped off when in action, offering an ideal to emulate for the film's predominantly heterosexually male audience. However, recent scholarship suggests he also presented an erotic appeal for female and gay spectators. For example, Jean-Claude Van

Damme produced an erotically charged persona and achieved a sex symbol status by the early 1990s (he was number one of *National Enquirer*'s "Top Ten Sexiest Men in the World"), most likely the result of mainstream cinema's need to exploit the star's appeal to the broadest audience base possible.

The 1980s also saw an emphasis on the hero's relationship to other men and, thus, the genre frequently crossed over into the buddy film genre. Whereas most Hollywood films stress the relationship between the hero and a love interest, the cop action film replaced the woman with another man for a contemplation of male bonding in the face of danger. Romance was pushed to the side and masculine concerns were brought to the fore. As buddy narratives, these films focused on the relationship between two men and the contrast of their often opposing types of masculinity. Films like *Tango and Cash* (1989) explored the issues of clashing background and class, whereas films like *Beverly Hills Cop* (1984) explored the juxtaposition of different races. These films stress the overcoming of these differences in order for masculinity to successfully defeat the common enemy and preserve the values of American society. Issues of class and race may have be explored in these films through the clash and resolution of the heroes' differences; however, these films have been criticized for simplifying important issues, especially race, and reducing them to narrative tropes to create dramatic effect rather than truly addressing them as important issues in American society.

The 1990s saw a gradual reduction in the number of cop action films as a result of changing social attitudes toward masculinity over the last decade of the twentieth century. Ideals of masculinity shifted from ones embodying brawn and violence to ones embracing intelligence and vulnerability. In the early 1990s a new sensitive type of masculinity emerged to replace the retributive masculinity of the 1980s as an ideal. The working-class cop as action hero came to be replaced by a new kind of police detective that was middle-class, well-educated, and employed his/her skills of observation and deduction, rather than firepower, to solve the crime. This shift from violent to vulnerable masculinities is evident in the new roles that former action stars began to portray. Bruce Willis abandoned guns and wisecracks in favor of more sensitive roles in films like in *Mercury Rising* (1998) and *The Sixth Sense* (1999), and Clint Eastwood gave up his vigilante roles to play more mature and intellectual heroes in films like *In the Line of Fire* (1993), *True Crime* (1999), and *Bloodwork* (2002).

Just as cop action heroes came to be replaced by thinking, more sleuth-like detectives, so, too, has the definition of the American hero undergone change. With an emphasis on the intellect rather than the body, the cop hero no longer is defined only as white, muscular, and male. New detective figures have arrived since the early 1990s including female, African American, and older detectives. For decades cop action films reveled in narratives of masculine empowerment for male moviegoing audiences, exploring and attempting to resolve issues of race, class, and gender; however, shifts in social conceptions of masculinity and femininity have brought about new permutations in the genre and the kinds of heroes that preserve American society.

Philippa Gates

See also Action TV Series; Detectives; "Dirty Harry"; Gangster Films, Classic; Gangster Films, Contemporary

Further Reading:
Clarke, Eric, and Mathew Henson. 1996. "Hot Damme! Reflections on Gay Publicity." Pp. 131–150 in *Boys: Masculinities in Contemporary Culture*. Edited by Paul Smith. Cultural Studies Series. Boulder, CO: Westview Press.
Fuchs, Cynthia. 1993. "The Buddy Politic." Pp. 194–210 in *Screening the Male: Exploring Masculinities in Hollywood Cinema*. Edited by Steven Cohan and Ina Rae Hark. London: Routledge.
Inciardi, James A., and Juliet L. Dee. 1987. "From Keystone Cops to *Miami Vice*: Images of Policing

in American Popular Culture." *Journal of Popular Culture* 21, no. 2: 84–102.

Jeffords, Susan. 1994. *Hard Bodies: Hollywood Masculinity in the Reagan Era.* New Brunswick, NJ: Rutgers University Press.

Lehman, Peter. 1993. *Running Scared: Masculinity and the Representation of the Male Body.* Culture and the Moving Image. Philadelphia: Temple University Press.

King, Neal. 1999. *Heroes in Hard Times: Cop Action Movies in the U.S.* Philadelphia: Temple University Press.

Pfeil, Fred. 1995. *White Guys: Studies in Postmodern Domination and Difference.* London: Verso.

Rafter, Nicole. 2000. *Shots in the Mirror: Crime Films and Society.* New York: Oxford University Press.

Reiner, Robert. 1985. "Keystone to Kojak: The Hollywood Cop." Pp. 195–220 in *Cinema, Politics, and Society in America.* 2d ed. Edited by Philip Davies and Brian Neve. Manchester, UK: Manchester University Press.

Studlar, Gaylyn. 2001. "Cruise-ing into the Millennium: Performative Masculinity, Stardom, and the All-American Boy's Body." Pp. 171–183 in *Ladies and Gentlemen, Boys and Girls: Gender in Film at the End of the Twentieth Century.* Edited by Murray Pomerance. Albany, NY: SUNY Press.

Tasker, Yvonne. 1993. *Spectacular Bodies: Gender, Genre and the Action Cinema.* London: Routledge.

Couvade

Couvade is the term for a set of ritual practices engaged in by putative fathers surrounding pregnancy and birth in widely scattered regions of the world. The term originated with E. B. Tylor, one of anthropology's founders, who noted in 1865 many societies where new fathers deviate from normal activities. Sometimes interpreted as reflecting male envy for aspects of women's natural role, *couvade* is derived from the French verb couver, to brood or hatch. It originally described a custom once practiced in Europe, particularly the Basque region, in which the husband of a woman giving birth took her place in bed and was taken care of by attendants (Menget 1982, 194). This was said to distract the attention of evil spirits from the real mother and child.

The classic understanding of the couvade is found in the *Dictionary of Anthropology*: "The imitation by the father of many of the concomitants of childbirth, around the time of his wife's parturition; it is also called men's childbed. The father may retire to bed, go into seclusion, and observe some taboos and restrictions in order to help the child" (cited in Munroe, Munroe, and Whiting 1973, 30).

However, most of the practices that are called couvade cross-culturally have little to do with imitating childbirth. Typical ethnographic descriptions include practicing food taboos, being secluded along with the mother and infant for a period following birth, and not engaging in certain activities such as hunting. Local explanations for these practices often stress the connection between father and child, but do not hint that the father is imitating a woman's role.

Some cross-cultural researchers (Munroe, Munroe, and Whiting 1973) have accepted the idea that food and activity avoidances are tantamount to imitating childbirth and proposed a psychodynamic interpretation of couvade as a practice found in cultures where men have a psychological need to imitate women. Where social arrangements are such that boys have a "primary identification" with mothers that is not resolved in the transition to adulthood (as indicated by the absence of harsh initiation rituals at puberty), couvade is found with greater statistical frequency than in other societies. Boys identify with mothers, according to these authors, where men have "low salience" for children, as indicated by matrilocal residence and mother-child sleeping arrangements.

A critique of the psychodynamic approach is that it connects one social pattern with another through a totally hypothesized chain of psychological causality, with no reference to what is said about the cultural meanings of the behaviors in question. Further, in reanalyzing the cross-cultural sample used by the Munroes and Whiting, Broude (1988) found that couvade is positively associated with presence of fathers in the lives of children and also has other correlates that run counter to their hypotheses.

In the Lowland South America cultural region, both matrilocal residence and couvade practices are especially common. However, many ethnographic accounts from the region show men highly involved in the care of children (Kloos 1971; Maybury-Lewis 1974). According to Peter Kloos, Maroni River Carib (Surinam) "parental roles are relatively balanced" (Kloos 1971). Of course, male childcare itself might be seen by some as further evidence of men imitating women's role.

Other views of the couvade deny the existence of special behaviors of fathers at the time of birth that can be separated from generalized systems of magical practices with more general internal logics (Riviere 1974; Menget 1982; Broude 1988). P. G. Riviere (1974) explains the beliefs of the Trio and Waiwai of the Brazil-Guyana-Surinam border area. As both parents contribute to the physical essence of a child, so they both contribute to its spiritual essence. Before and after birth, soul-matter is channeled to the soul of the child through those of the parents. What parents do affects their spiritual states, hence that of the child. Until the child's soul is fixed, it follows around those of the parents and is highly vulnerable, and could be frightened away by vigorous activity or certain sights. Thus it is best if both parents stay close to the child (Riviere 1974). This means that the father is unable to carry out his side of the sexual division of labor (hunting) and lies with the child in the hammock while his wife continues her normal activity of processing manioc. This custom could have looked to early explorers like something akin to the reported Basque custom: the father taking it easy as if *he* were the one who had given birth.

Anthropological consensus at the turn of the millennium is that couvade as it exists ethnographically is very different from what it is commonly believed to be. Although men engaging in couvade practices are making important symbolic statements about their spiritual connection to their children, close ethnographic scrutiny of such practices shows little trace of men imitating childbirth. Still, popular accounts and websites (based on no actual observation) commonly portray vast numbers of "primitive" societies where men suffer morning sickness and scream in agony while their wives are in labor. And there actually exists in Euro-American societies the psychological phenomenon of "couvade syndrome" in which expectant fathers experience indigestion, nausea, increased or decreased appetite, bowel irregularity, toothache, backache, and other symptoms (Trethowan and Conlon 1965, 61–62). Perhaps belief in the classically described couvade dies so hard because it validates the experiences of men in contemporary societies.

Regina Smith Oboler

Further Reading:

Broude, Gwen J. 1988. "Rethinking the Couvade: Cross-Cultural Evidence." *American Anthropologist* 90: 902–911.

Kloos, Peter. 1971. *The Maroni River Carib in Surinam.* Assen, Netherlands: Van Gorcum.

Maybury-Lewis, David. 1974. *Akwe-Shavante Society.* New York: Oxford University Press.

Menget, Patrick. 1982. "Time of Birth, Time of Being: The Couvade." In *Between Belief and Transgression.* Edited by M. Izard and P. Smith. Chicago: University of Chicago Press.

Metraux, Alfred. 1963. "The Couvade." In *Handbook of South American Indians, Vol. 5: The Comparative Ethnology of South American Indians.* New York: Cooper Square Publishers.

Munroe, Robert L., Ruth H. Munroe, and John W. M. Whiting. 1973. "The Couvade: A Psychological Analysis." *Ethos* 1: 30–74.

Rival, Laura. 1998. "Androgynous Parents and Guest Children: The Huaorani Couvade." *Journal of the Royal Anthropological Institute* 4: 619–642.

Riviere, Peter G. 1974. "The Couvade: A Problem Reborn." *Man* 9: 423–435.

Trethowan, William H., and M. F. Conlon. 1965. "The Couvade Syndrome." *British Journal of Psychiatry* 111: 57–66.

Tylor, E. B. 1865. *Researches into the Early History of Mankind and the Development of Civilization.* London: J. Murray.

Cowboys

The cowboy is among the most enduring symbols of American masculinity. The cowboy is emblematic of a strong, hard, ruggedly independent masculinity that settled the West, conquered Indians, tamed a hostile land, and ensured the spread of American democracy from sea to sea. From his origins in the middle of the nineteenth century, through his valorization in the westerns at the turn of the century, to his iconic status as the very embodiment of American masculinity, the cowboy has endured as the noble denizen of the untamed frontier. He is America's contribution to the world's stock of mythic heroes.

The cowboy was not always a hero. In the 1860s and 1870s, he was called a "herder" and appeared in public prints and writing as a rough, uncouth, shaggy, and dirty man, whose behavior was violent, barbarous, and rowdy. Writing in 1875, Laura Winthrop Johnson saw no glamour in these "rough men with shaggy hair and wild staring eyes, in butternut trousers stuffed into great rough boots" (cited in Smith 1950, 122). But around 1882, a cowboy named Buck Taylor at the First Wild West Show captured the attention of a writer, Prentiss Ingraham. The Wild West Show was a re-creation of the West in the form of a traveling circus. Organized by Buffalo Bill Cody, the show depicted the conquest and taming of the Wild West. When Ingraham wrote a fictional biography of Taylor in 1887, later expanded into a series of dime novels, the new heroic cowboy had been invented.

By 1887, the great cattle drives that were his home had ended, and the "big die up" of the winter of 1886–1887 had bankrupted many cattle outfits and so altered ranch life that the cowboy was "less a knight errant and more a hired man on horseback" (Stegner, in Vorpahl 1972, ix). In fiction, though, the cowboy was all guts and glory. The cowboy thus emerged in literature at the same moment of his disappearance, his transformation from an independent artisan on the range to a wage worker in a new industry of cattle ranching.

As a mythic creation, the cowboy was fierce and brave, willing to venture into unknown territory, a "negligent, irrepressible wilderness," and tame it for women, children, and emasculated civilized men. As soon as the environment had been subdued, it was time to move on, unconstrained by the demands of civilized life, unhampered by clinging women, whining children, and uncaring bosses and managers. His is a freedom that cannot be "bounded by the fences of a too weak and timid conventionalism," as Harold Wright put it in his western novel *When a Man's a Man* (1916) (cited in Gerzon 1983, 77). Civilization, women, family—all were constraints on the cowboy's freedom. To the cowboy, civilization "meant responsibility, meant law, meant fences and homesteads, and water rights and fee-simple land ownership, meant women" (in Vorpahl, 1972, ix). Don't fence him in.

The cowboy was also a man of impeccable natural ethics, whose faith in natural law and natural right is eclipsed only by the astonishing fury with which he demands rigid adherence to them. He is a man of action—"grim [and] lean, . . . of few topics, and not many words concerning these." He moves in a world of men, in which daring, bravery, and skill are his constant companions. He lives by physical strength and rational calculation; his compassion is social and generalized, but he forms no lasting emotional bonds with any single person. He lives alone, a "hermited horseman," out on the range, settling the West.

But, of course, he no longer exists—and perhaps he did only in the pages of the western, the new literary genre heralded by the publication of Owen Wister's novel *The Virginian* in 1902. In this novel, more than any other single work, the myth of the cowboy was created.

In Wister's effete eastern eyes, the cowboy was everything that he was not. He was manly, a natural aristocrat, a "natural nobleman, formed not by civilization and its institutions but the spontaneous influence of the land working on an innate goodness." He is a "handsome, ungrammatical son of the soil," who, having mastered his apprenticeship, was not the master of the crafts of riding, roping, and killing. His were the tried and true artisanal values of the earlier century: "self-discipline, unswerving purpose; the exercise of knowledge, skill, ingenuity, and excellent judgment; and a capacity to continue in the face of total exhaustion and overwhelming odds." He is a free man in a free country, embodying republican virtue and autonomy (in Vorpahl 1972, 81, 93, 94).

In myth, if not in reality, he was also white. To Wister, the west was "manly, egalitarian, self-reliant and Aryan" although the first three of those qualities are what attracted many freed slaves to the West in the years after the Civil War. As William Loren Katz shows, the myth of the cowboy flourished for white easterners; the reality of the cowboy as wage worker of the range was the life for an increasing number of black men.

In the twentieth century, the cowboy was the most famous American mythic hero, returning to popularity during periods of complacent conformity. In the 1950s, the high water mark of the western, the cowboy was the featured hero in most Hollywood movies and television shows. By the turn of the twenty-first century, he remained potent, enshrined as the Marlboro man, but was also affectionately seen as an anachronism, once heroic perhaps, but now "Woody" to the new generation's hero, "Buzz Lightyear" in the Disney/Pixar *Toy Story* series.

Michael Kimmel

See also *City Slickers*; Marlboro Man; Rodeo; Wayne, John; Wister, Owen
Further Reading:
Gerzon, Mark. 1983. *A Choice of Heroes*. Boston: Houghton, Mifflin.
Kimmel, Michael. 1996. *Manhood in America: A Cultural History*. New York: The Free Press.

Vorpahl, Ben Merchant, ed. 1972. *My Dear Wister: The Frederic Remington–Owen Wister Letters*. Palo Alto: American West Publishing.

Custody

See Divorce; Fathers, Non-Residential; Single Fathers

Cyberculture

The fluid identity politics of cyberculture allow the binary categories of male/female and masculinity/femininity to be destabilized. A dominant strand of cybercultural studies has been cyberfeminism. Cyberfeminism employs the metaphor of the cyborg—as first articulated by Donna Haraway in 1985—to reposition notions of gender, sex, and identity in our technoculture. This critique of both sexual politics and technology disturbs the Enlightenment paradigms of man/technology and woman/nature. This disruption has resulted in a deconstruction of these paradigms, rather than a reversal of them. Masculinity can no longer be identified as a viable category within cyberculture as it offers the opportunity of divorcing the performance of masculinity from the body. Cyberculture, a recent phenomenon in the history of technology, exists within any computer-generated and computer-sustained virtual reality. It includes spaces as diverse as the Internet, biomedical technologies, and interactive digital entertainment. Moreover, cyberculture is also predicated upon an individual's relationship with cybernetic technology as the human-machine interface occupies an essential position in the cybercultural debates. The questions at the core of these debates are as follows: Are computers extensions of our identities? Have we become cyborgs?

The computer—that central component of cyberculture—has a history stretching further back than the last twenty years of the twentieth century. In 1833 Charles Babbage designed a steam-powered "analytical engine." Never built, the design promised a machine that might undertake the intellectual functions of the human brain. Forerunners of the contemporary computer include the Hollerith punch-card machine (devised to expedite the U.S. census of 1890) and Colossus (developed by British intelligence to decode encrypted German communications in World War II). Although the size of computers decreased in the 1950s and 1960s, they still retained intellectual identities as calculators. However, on 13 August 1981, the personal computer was put on the market. Less than two years later, the computer was *Time* magazine's "Man of the Year." The launch of the IBM Personal Computer in 1981 and the Apple Macintosh in 1984 were successful marketing strategies that brought the computer into personal and domestic spaces. The Internet, which was originally a network intended to guarantee military communications during the Cold War, exploded during the 1990s, becoming a global network. These cybertechnologies are embedded in our lives and cyberculture is concerned with the kinds of relationships we have with these technologies.

These technologies opened up spaces in which we can engage in bodily pleasures and interactions by getting rid of our actual body in cyberspace. The term *cyberspace* was coined by William Gibson in *Neuromancer* (1984): "Cyberspace. A consensual hallucination experienced daily by billions of legitimate operators. A graphic representation of data abstracted from the banks of every computer in the human system. Unthinkable complexity. Lines of light ranged in the nonspace of the mind, clusters and constellations of date" (51). The possibilities of a degendered space have been explored by many on the Internet. One of the most famous cases is that of Sandford Lewin. He signed on to a discussion on CompuServe in 1984 under the gender-neutral term of "Dr." and found that other members assumed he was a woman. He then created the online character of Julie Graham, a disabled bisexual atheist.

Eventually he found the demands of Graham's personality too much and tried to kill her off. Lewin's performance as Graham was discovered by Graham's friends, sparking a debate about gender, identity, and cyberculture that is still ongoing. Sex, in cyberculture, is a choice rather than a fact. Sex and gender differences can be explored online without fear of censure as we "cyberdrag." Such cross-gendered performances emphasis the attributive nature of the sex-gender binary.

The Enlightenment paradigm of men/technology still has a powerful resonance in popular culture. Male users of the Internet attempt to separate themselves from the nerd stereotype, the result of anxiety deriving from an overinvolvement with the soft technologies of information. Men supposedly derive power and status from their involvement with cyberculture, to which the cowboy image of the hacker, and much of the cyberpunk genre, attests. Moreover, the techno-cultural embodiments of Hollywood still employ notions of technology as the domain of male power, for example, the *Terminator* films (1984; 1991; 2003) or *The Matrix* trilogy. Sadie Plant has pointed up the ways in which masculinity and technology interact:

> This phallic quest has always played a major role in the development and popularization of visual techniques. Sex has found its way into all the digital media—CD-ROMs, Usenet, E-mail, bulletin boards, floppy disks, the World Wide Web—and both hardwares and softwares are sexualized. Much of this activity is clearly designed to reproduce and amplify the most cliched associations with straight male sex. Disks are sucked into the dark recesses of welcoming vaginal slits, console cowboys jack into cyberspace, and virtual sex has been defined as "teledildonics." Here are more simulations of the feminine, digital dreamgirls who cannot answer back, pixeled puppets with no strings attached, fantasy figures who do as they are told. (1997, 181)

Cyberfeminism is predicated upon critiquing the masculine-orientated machines and "boys'" toys. It seeks to transcend these sorts of configurations, attempting to find ways in which women can access the virtual world without the intermediary of the man/technology binary. Cyberculture has moved from military and business discourses—traditional male domains—to domestic spaces, disrupting a male hold on technology. This can only serve to emphasize the degendering of cyberculture, moving toward a postgender space.

The cyborg is an exemplar of this movement. The human/machine interface is a space in which Enlightenment notions of embodiment must be abandoned as we are redefined as information-processing entities. The metaphor of the cyborg enables us to think through our relationship with technology. We spend much of our time connected to or working with machines. Are we cyborgic when we drive a car? When we exercise at the gym? These are two activities that have been traditionally regarded as deeply gendered. If we can describe the body in these activities as cyborgic then we are moving beyond the male/female binary to a postgendered space. The cyborg metaphor troubles the boundaries of human and machine as well as male and female. The decentering power of cyberspace has allowed the subject to disappear into a hyperreality of reproduction and representation. In cyberculture, identity is performed, as is the body. As we rebuild ourselves incessantly, gender, and even sex, are no longer conceived of as essential.

Stacy Gillis

See also Cyberspace
Further Reading:

Bell, David, and Barbara Kennedy, eds. 2000. *The Cybercultures Reader.* London: Routledge.

Gibson, William. 1984. *Neuromancer.* London: Victor Gollancz.

Gillis, Stacy. 2001. "Cybercriticism." Pp. 202–216 in *Introducing Theory at the 21st Century.* Edited by Julian Wolfreys. Edinburgh, UK: Edinburgh University Press.

Haraway, Donna. 1991. *Simians, Cyborgs and Women: The Reinvention of Nature.* New York: Routledge.

Hayles, N. Katherine. 1999. *How We Became Posthuman: Virtual Bodies in Cybernetics, Literature, and Informatics.* Chicago: University of Chicago Press.

Ludlow, Peter, ed. 1996. *High Noon on the Electronic Frontier: Conceptual Issues in Cyberspace.* Cambridge, MA: MIT Press.

Plant, Sadie. 1997. *Zeros + Ones: Digital Women and the New Technoculture.* London: Fourth Estate.

Stone, Allucquère Rosanne. 1995. *The War of Desire and Technology at the Close of the Mechanical Age.* Cambridge: MIT Press.

Turkle, Sherry. 1996. *Life on the Screen: Identity in the Age of the Internet.* London: Weidenfeld & Nicolson.

Cyberporn

See Pornography and New Media

Cyberspace

In its most common current usage, cyberspace refers to the Internet and the World Wide Web. Cyberspace metaphorically denotes the social and informational connections created by computers. People are said to be "in cyberspace" when they engage in such activities as browsing the World Wide Web, writing email, chatting with others through text online, etc. From its inception, the Internet has been dominated by male participants, and many online subcultures continue to reflect a masculine bias.

The term *cyberspace* was coined by the science fiction writer William Gibson in 1984 in his depictions of a future world in which people immersed themselves in graphical representations of the information contained in computers. Gibson is one of a group of writers whose science fiction style became known in the mid-1980s as "cyberpunk." Beyond supplying terminology that describes cyberspace and online activities, this genre has influenced aspects of online culture as well. Usually dystopic, violent, and dark, cyberpunk fiction tends to denigrate the body (sometimes referred to as "meat" or "wetware") and valorize computer skills. To the mostly male underground and outlaw heroes featured in the genre, skill and intimacy with computers matters more than skill and intimacy with people. This cyberspace ethos, with its emphasis on skills and technology associated with masculinity, is echoed in many online subcultures, especially those associated with hackers.

The Internet, and its military-funded predecessor Arpanet, preexisted cyberpunk and the term *cyberspace*, with the first links on Arpanet going up in 1969. Arpanet was developed in hopes of providing communications redundancy for the military in case of nuclear attack, as well as to give researchers in diverse locations remote access to supercomputers. Ironically, from the beginning the largest use of the Internet has been email and other forms of interpersonal communication rather than the more "instrumental" uses envisioned by Arpanet's founders.

The earliest users on Arpanet and later the early Internet consisted primarily of a limited group of academics, and government and military personnel mostly from computer science and related technical and scientific fields. The computer science field in general is heavily male dominated (Spertus 1991). Thus, not surprisingly, most people on the Internet in its early years were white, middle-class, college-educated men. Taking advantage of the Internet's capability to connect people with others with similar interests in remote geographical locations, these early users established the first online forums and communities. The norms and patterns of behavior in these forums were based on values reflecting the identities and backgrounds of the mostly male users.

Internet newcomers found themselves in an established social environment with particular expectations and assumptions about behavior and identity. Early popular press accounts often described the Internet as a "new frontier," emphasizing its rough mores and the occasional lawlessness of hackers. Media accounts of life online continue to be dominated by stories about predators, identity thieves, and other dangers. Although these popular media accounts often exaggerate the dangers of online interaction, the dominant mode of discourse in many online forums can feel much more comfortable to men than to women. Aggressive communication styles such as "flaming" (vituperative personal attacks through email or other forms of online posts), though excoriated in some contexts, are celebrated in others. Even as the numbers of women participants have increased, men still often dominate online discussions (Herring 1995).

Several famous online incidents demonstrate some of the tensions between the mostly male early users of the Internet and the increasing numbers of women newcomers. In 1993 America On Line (AOL) first connected its users to the Internet, where many of them accessed the Internet bulletin-board service known as Usenet. Usenet allowed thousands of users to post and read messages about topics of mutual interest. Many of the more experienced Internet users disdained this flood of newcomers, who, in addition to generally being less experienced with computers, included a much higher percentage of women.

One group of young, brash, computer-savvy habitues of the Usenet group alt.tasteless decided to stage an invasion—tellingly dubbed a virtual "panty raid"—of the group rec.pets.cats. Rec.pets.cats had a much higher percentage of women and new users than many other Usenet groups. The alt.tasteless members began posting gross messages about cat abuse and mutilation, often hidden behind fake email addresses and deceptive subject headings. Within months, rec.pets.cats became all but useless for its original purpose, and many new users had been chased from the Internet (Quittner 1994).

In another infamous online incident, a participant on a mud (a form of online chat space) known as LambdaMOO staged a "virtual rape" of several other participants by forcing their online characters to perform sexual and self-mutilating acts (Dibbell 1998). In both cases, these incidents resulted in offline as well as online consequences, including charges of harassment and participants having their online accounts cut off.

In the 2000s, the incidence of spam (widely distributed unwanted email) has increased, with much of that spam consisting of information about pornographic websites. More than half of Internet users have received such pornographic spam, and the numbers of people who find this a problem is increasing. One report states that the number of Internet users finding pornographic spam a problem increased from 33 percent in 2000 to 44 percent in 2001 (Horrigan and Rainee 2002). Given the content of most online pornography, this phenomenon is likely to be more problematic for women than for men.

As the Internet quickly grew, its demographics became more diverse. However, the number of women did not come close to equaling that of men until the early 2000s. Currently, approximately 50 percent of online participants are women. However, a higher percentage of men in the United States are online than of women (because there are more women in the United States). Men still engage in a broader range of activities online. On average, they are more likely to use the web to search for hobby, news, and financial information, and are more likely to purchase things online (Rainie and Packel 2001). Women surpass men in the use of the web to find health information and make greater use of email to maintain kin relationships (Rainie and Packel 2001; Boneva et. al. 2001).

As the numbers of women online have grown, many women have found useful connections and resources on the Internet. Women have established websites celebrating their technological interests and providing mutual support, such as www.nrrdgrrls.org (no longer an active site). Other sites, such as the Center for Women and Information Technology (http://www.umbc.edu/cwit/), provide a wide range of information of interest to feminists and academic women. In the late 1990s and early 2000s, mainstream media providers also began establishing sites geared toward women consumers, such as Oxygen Media's www.oxygen.com.

Lori Kendall

See also Cyberculture

Further Reading:

Boneva, Bonka, et. al. 2001. "Using E-mail for Personal Relationships." *American Behavioral Scientist* 45, no. 3 (November): 530–549.

Dibbell, Julian. 1999. "A Rape in Cyberspace." Pp. 14–23 in *My Tiny Life*. New York: Owl Books. Available online at *http://www.levity.com/julian/bungle.html*.

Gibson, William. 1984. *Neuromancer*. New York: Ace Books.

Herring, Susan, with Deborah Johnson and Tamra DiBenedetto. 1995. "'This Discussion is Going Too Far!' Male Resistance to Female Participation on the Internet." Pp. 67–96 in *Gender Articulated: Language and the Socially Constructed Self*. Edited by Mary Bucholtz and Kira Hall. New York: Routledge.

Horrigan, John, and Lee Rainie, principal authors. 2002. "Getting Serious Online." Report of the Pew Internet and American Life Project, 3 March 2002. At *http://www.pewinternet.org/reports/toc.asp?Report=55*.

Quittner, Josh. 1994. "The War between alt.tasteless and rec.pets.cats." *Wired* 2.04 (May). At *http://www.wired.com/wired/archive/2.05/alt.tasteless_pr.html*.

Rainie, Lee, and Dan Packel, principal authors. 2001. "More Online, Doing More." Report of the Pew Internet and American Life Project, 18 February 2001. At *http://www.pewinternet.org/reports/toc.asp?Report=30*.

Spertus, Ellen. 1991. "Why Are There So Few Female Computer Scientists?" At *http://www.mills.edu/ACAD_INFO/MCS/SPERTUS/Gender/pap/pap.html*.

Sterling, Bruce. 1993. "Short History of the Internet." Available online at numerous locations, including http://www.forthnet.gr/forthnet/isoc/short.history.of.internet.

D

Dads and Daughters

Dads and Daughters (DADs) is the national education and advocacy nonprofit organization for fathers and daughters. Through a variety of methods, DADs provides tools to help strengthens father-daughter relationships and help transform the pervasive cultural messages that value daughters more for how they look than for who they are.

Dads and Daughters was formed in 1999 by father, activist, and businessman Michael Kieschnick. Kieschnick was motivated by the immense negative cultural pressures on his daughter and recognition of the unique influence fathers can have on daughters and the larger culture. Hence, Dads and Daughters combines practical support for fathers in their family relationships with organized public activism.

For example, DADs members sent letters and emails that persuaded the Campbell's Soup Company to stop airing a TV spot marketing soup to preadolescent girls as a diet aid and convinced Chattem, Inc. to pull a "Sun-In" ad (in *Teen People*) that read: "4 out of 5 girls you hate ask for it by name. Stop hating them. Start being them. With Sun-In." Much of this monthly member activism draws public attention to marketing efforts that undermine girls' (and often boys') well-being. Periodically, DADs' actions also draw attention to marketing that supports girls and good father-daughter relationships. For example, DADs gave a national award to Chevy Trucks for its television spot portraying a father's lifelong, active involvement in his daughter's sports participation.

Dads and Daughters publishes the national newsletter *Daughters,* with a circulation of approximately 100,000. DADs uses *Daughters,* an extensive website (www.dadsanddaughters.org) and a biweekly Email Update to educate members and others interested in raising healthy, confident girls. Parents, educators, social service agencies, and policymakers use its "Ten Tips for Dads of Daughters" extensively.

Dads and Daughters presents workshops on fathering, girls' development, activism, and media around North America. The group also produces regularly published op-ed and opinion pieces and hosts an online discussion group for fathers with daughters. Media outlets frequently call on DADs for comment about issues in these areas. DADs's first executive director, Joe Kelly, is author of the book *Dads and Daughters* (2002).

DADs has also developed a pilot program for the YMCA of the United States called "Fathers and Daughters Growing Together." It brings together girls ages ten to fourteen and their fathers or father-figures for weekly sessions addressing communication, trust, and a variety of issues facing daughters and fathers. The program culminates with a weekend retreat for participants.

Dads and Daughters is a membership-based nonprofit organization; most members live in the United States, with a handful in other countries. The organization is a founding member of Stop Commercial Exploitation of Children and the National Eating Disorders Coalition for Research, Policy and Action. The Dads and Daughters national office is in Duluth, Minnesota.

Joe Kelly

Further Reading:

Dads and Daughters. Contact address. PO Box 3458, Duluth, MN 55803; Telephone 1.888.824.DADS; Dads and Daughters website at http://dadsanddaughters.org.

Kelly, Joe. 2002. *Dads and Daughters.* New York: Broadway Books/Random House.

Dance

Men have danced in most cultures throughout history. Anthropologists such as Polhemus (1993) have argued that different forms of dance are an "expression of the cultural system within which they are found" (8). Thus, knowledge about the ways in which men do and do not dance within a particular culture can inform our understanding of its social norms, particularly how men's bodies are supposed to look and move, the relative status of men compared with women, and the nature of relationships within and between the sexes.

There is enormous diversity of form and function in the dance that men do, as well as in the ways masculinity has been expressed through dance in different cultural locations.

Dancing has regularly been viewed as "unmanly," particularly, although not exclusively, in Western countries during the last two hundred years or so. This is most clearly the case with ballet and its twentieth-century offshoots, modern (and later postmodern), and contemporary dance. Burt (1995) argues that ballet dancing, an activity that prior to the turn of nineteenth century had been associated with European royalty and nobility, fell afoul of early Victorian bourgeois sensibilities and was seen as the antithesis of the soberly dressed, industrious, and emotionally controlled public image of middle-class masculinity. This suspicion of male dancers was, if anything, even more pronounced in non-European Western countries such as the United States, Australia, and New Zealand. Here, "manliness" had become increasingly linked to notions of the "rugged," outdoor life of the frontier and a rejection of what white colonial society tended to see as fey and cloistered European culture.

According to Burt, the suspicion that male ballet dancers were not only "unmanly" but also homosexual developed later, probably during the final decades of the nineteenth century as Victorian society increasingly demonized and pathologized those who failed to conform to prevailing gender stereotypes.

The exceptions to these developments seem to have been in Russia and Holland where ballet remained under royal patronage and did not suffer the same loss of prestige as elsewhere in Europe. And indeed, it was not until the Russian entrepreneur Serge Diaghilev brought his company, the Ballet Russes, to France and England in the second decade of the twentieth century that the male ballet dancer reemerged as a focal point of the art form. The Ballet Russes' various line-ups produced many of ballet's most celebrated names, in particular the prodigiously talented Vaslav Nijinsky. Nijinsky is considered by some to have been the greatest male ballet dancer of all time and is regularly credited as being the catalyst for the eventual rejuvenation of Western ballet in general, and male dancing in particular.

In the United States, the project of making male dancing on the public stage respectable is most closely associated with the modern dance pioneer Ted Shawn. Shawn's career spanned most of the first half of the twentieth century and, through his choreography and numerous speeches and publications, was devoted to showing that dance was not for "sissies."

Other scholars have sought to understand the social significance of Western society's discomfort with men who dance (for examples see Flintoff 1991; Gard 2001). As with many areas of gender scholarship, most of this work has followed in the footsteps of pioneering feminist research and the relatively recent proliferation of philosophical and sociological interest in "the body." Therefore, rather than suggesting that men have been discriminated against by stereotypes that discourage them from dancing, this work has focused on the ways in which attitudes toward dancing male bodies reflect social arrangements that privilege men over women and straight men over gay men. These scholars argue that, as an activity commonly associated with girls and women, dancing by males has the potential to disrupt and contradict taken-for-granted ideas about men's bodies as necessarily different or physically superior to women's bodies. This work, in turn, connects more generally with feminist-inspired research that sees masculinity as something that, rather than preordained and unchanging, is performed by men in order to avoid accusations of effeminacy or homosexuality. Gard's research (2001), for example, shows how some boys often reject dancing altogether, not just ballet, because of the risk of ridicule or homophobic abuse.

Michael Gard

Further Reading:

Burt, Ramsay. 1995. *The Male Dancer: Bodies, Spectacle, Sexualities.* London: Routledge.

Flintoff, Anne. 1991. "Dance, Masculinity and Teacher Education." *British Journal of Physical Education* (Winter): 31–35.

Gard, Michael. 2001. "'I Like Smashing People, and I Like Getting Smashed Myself': Addressing Issues of Masculinity in Physical Education and Sport." Pp. 222–235 in *What about the Boys?: Issues of Masculinity in Schools.* Edited by Wayne Martino and Bob Meyenn. Buckingham, UK: Open University Press.

Polhemus, Ted. 1993. "Dance, Gender and Culture." Pp. 3–15 in *Dance, Gender and Culture.* Edited by Helen Thomas. London: Macmillan.

Dance, Hollywood

Dancing in Hollywood is a predominantly female activity, and is seen as such by the majority of viewers. For a male movie star to dance without having his masculinity questioned he must take his body off display by subverting the male gaze and purposely establish his heterosexuality. Today, when a Hollywood male star dances he must also perform demonstrations of masculinity to appease perceived challenges to established masculine ideology arising from the feminist movement and gay liberation. Although almost every major male star has danced on film, from Clark Gable in *Idiot's Delight* (1939), to Marlon Brando in *Guys and Dolls* (1955), to Richard Gere in *Chicago* (2002), only a handful have managed to successfully establish a masculine identity and flourish as male Hollywood dancers.

The two most successful Hollywood male dancers, Fred Astaire (1899–1987) and Gene Kelly (1912–1996), established their identities at a time when men's patriarchal role in Western culture had not yet been seriously questioned. Also, they danced in an era—the mid-1920s to the early 1950s—when America's demand for musical entertainment was at its height, and Hollywood was producing musicals at a staggering rate.

In his first films, Fred Astaire set up his image as a suave, happy-go-lucky capitalist about town, who could just happen to tap up a storm. Fondly remembered for his partnering with Ginger Rogers and other starlets, Astaire adopted the duet form to demonstrate his' preference for the opposite sex. In these duets the female is clearly a prize to be won and shown off. Astaire leads her, lifts her, and hardly ever takes his eyes off of her, and she hardly ever looks at him directly. Moreover, the film makes the duet seem like part of a courting ritual in which Astaire triumphs with his suave, sophisticated dancing.

Astaire's first fully produced solo on a Broadway-type set came in *Top Hat* (1935) and is now considered his signature piece. In this production Astaire dances with a chorus of men, all dressed exactly like him, which has the effect of homogenizing his masculinity and making him appear like another one of the boys. Astaire challenges the male chorus to keep up with his dancing, but he is clearly the superior dancer and the chorus soon leaves, defeated. Astaire's solo follows and is as much about miming the intrigue of being followed by something unseen, and seemingly dangerous, as it is about Astaire's virtuoso tapping. Giving the indication of a plot within the solo keeps the audience from "interpreting" Astaire's movement. Also, because Astaire was a very talented tap dancer, he was able to use the diversion of tapping difficult sequences to keep his body from being objectified; it is hard to imagine that Astaire would have found the same success as an interpretive ballet dancer as he did as a tap dancer. Toward the end of Astaire's solo sequence in *Top Hat,* the male chorus returns and Astaire, using his taps to make the sound of a machine gun and his cane as the gun, proceeds to shoot each of the chorus members. Once all of the chorus members have fallen, the curtain closes and Astaire takes a solo bow for an audience made up entirely of men dressed exactly like Astaire and the fallen chorus members; it is a final image that establishes that Astaire's dancing is an acceptable activity for such a talented man.

In "Feminizing the Song and Dance Man: Fred Astaire and the Spectacle of Masculinity in the Hollywood Musical," Steven Cohan (1993) writes primarily about Astaire's integrated musicals of the 1950s and establishes a clear argument for the star's spectacle that stops the show's narrative and feminizes his performance. Cohan maintains that Astaire comes through the complexity of feminiza-

tion, in part, by performing his danced sequences as instruction for his female costars, in his varied roles of teacher, director, lover, and eventually as himself, Fred Astaire—the patriarch, the dancer, the star.

Gene Kelly followed in Astaire's steps and established himself as a major dancer in Hollywood's mega-musicals of the 1940s and 1950s. An engaging performer and talented dancer, Kelly had the advantage of having a compact, muscular body that kept his dance movements within the sphere of acceptable masculine activity. Watching Kelly dance, one feels that, unlike the females in his choreography, Kelly never fully lengthens his limbs or extends his gestures and that this limitation gives him the appearance of an athlete, an image that he cultivated with his publicized wish to be a baseball player.

Although other male dancers such as Ray Bolger (1904–1987), Donald O'Connor (b. 1925), Bob Fosse (1927–1987) and Gregory Hines (1946–2003) found acceptance and success as dancers, Astaire and Kelly remain the most successful and most loved dancers Hollywood has produced.

John Travolta scored a major hit with his dancing in *Saturday Night Fever* (1977), but instead of subverting the male gaze, as Astaire and Kelly did, Travolta invited the audience, men and woman, to look at his body and imagine their own scenarios. Travolta's conscious, aggressive objectification coincided with the growing need to define masculine sexuality in ways that would be seen as different from the sexuality of the "other": women and gay men. Portraying a young, popular, misunderstood, male stud on the prowl for sexual conquests and the meaning of life, Travolta's fantastical character touched the lives of many young men who identified with him and who imitated him on disco floors across North America.

Patrick Swayze's chiseled body, bedroom eyes, and pelvic thrusts brought erotic dancing to a new level of acceptability in *Dirty Dancing* (1987). A trained ballet dancer, Swayze never repeated his success as a dancer on-screen, but focused instead on action films, melodramas, romances, and one film in which he played a drag queen, which all but ended his career.

Successful films of the late twentieth and early twenty-first centuries to include men dancing, *The Full Monty* (1997) and *Billy Elliot* (2000), were produced in Britain and both include politically correct homosexual subplots. But neither film allows the male star to dance without clearly establishing his heterosexual, masculine identity. Hollywood has yet to produce films of men dancing with sensitivity, expression, and passion as either an alternative to established masculine ideals, or as an example of the diversity in North America's male population.

Darcey Callison

Further Reading:
Burt, Ramsay. 1995. *The Male Dancer: Bodies, Spectacles, Sexualities.* New York: Routledge.
Callison, Darcey. 2001. "Astaire's Feet and Travolta's Pelvis: Maintaining the Boy Code." *Torquere: Canada's Journal of Gay and Lesbian Studies* 3: 40–56.
Cohan, Steven. 1993. "Feminizing the Song and Dance Man: Fred Astaire and the Spectacle of Masculinity in the Hollywood Musical." Pp. 46–69 in *Screening the Male: Exploring Masculinities in Hollywood Cinema.* Edited by Steven Cohen and Ina Rae Hark. New York and London: Routledge.

Dance, Theatrical

The Western theatrical male dancer held distinction and respect in the baroque era (1650–1750), fell to near-oblivion in the romantic era (the mid-1800s), and has experienced a partial rise in the last century. Homophobic anxieties and an unwillingness to place the male body on display for the enjoyment and interpretation of an audience still keep boys and men out of dance classes.

The height of the male dancer's prestige was reached in France during the reign of Louis XIV (1638–1715), who used dance as a means of controlling his kingdom's ambitious noblemen. The ability to dance with poise, expression, and precision was inte-grally connected with one's ability to rise in rank at court and therefore had a great impact on one's economic potential. Practiced daily at court, as was fencing and horsemanship, dancing was considered a reflection of true nature and a man's innate quality as a nobleman, business partner, and lover. When viewing reconstructions of baroque dances, it is easy for a contemporary masculine sensibility to view the baroque dancer's gestures as artificial and/or unmanly. But these baroque gestures were expected, refined, and developed by noblemen who were competing with each other to impress the king and other nobles with their ability to effortlessly dance complicated sequences.

Louis XIV, the first real dance star, was by all accounts a very talented dancer. In theatrical spectacles, Louis danced the role of the god who arrives from the clouds to restore peace and harmony to the world of the ballet and metaphorically to France. One of Louis's first roles, as a boy-king, was that of the Sun God in *Ballet de la Nuit* (1653). This image of Louis became the symbol for his reign as the Sun King.

Initially, noblemen danced all the ballet roles, male and female, but as the choreography grew more demanding, professional dancers replaced the nobles, and women began to perform. After Louis's death, ballet was transferred to the professional theaters in Paris, and women appeared regularly. Male dancers like Auguste Vestris (1760–1842) were stars and made contributions to the advancement of ballet's movement vocabulary. But ballet was swiftly becoming a peep show where women exposed their legs. By the romantic era (early 1800s) male dancers had all but been driven from the stage, and women often danced the male roles.

The male dancer received serious attention in the Danish ballet of August Bournonville (1805–1889), but he was to achieve real progress at the turn of the century in the Imperial Russian Ballet under the directorship of Marius Petipa (1818–1910). Russian peasants brought their young boys to audition for the Imperial School of Ballet, and if he was lucky enough to be accepted, the boy and his family would be provided for. This was an inviting alternative to the difficult life of farming or joining the army.

One of the most intriguing male dancers to come from Russia was Vaslov Nijinsky (1889–1950). As a dancer, Nijinsky apparently lost himself in each of the roles he danced and at the same time possessed a spectacular physical technique. Critics writing about Nijinsky's jumping described him as seemingly staying in the air and landing when he wanted to. Eventually diagnosed as a schizophrenic, his career ended swiftly. For many he is a homosexual icon for his genius and the misunderstanding he endured during his brief but brilliant career.

In the last half of the twentieth century, Rudolf Nureyev (1938–1993) and Mikhail Baryshnikov (1948–), who both trained at the Russian Imperial School of Ballet, awakened an interest in the potential of the male dancer. Nureyev defected from Russia in 1961 and brought his dancing to the forefront of the ballet world. In 1974, Mikhail Baryshnikov defected and brought the spectacle of machismo to ballet. He became a superstar, touring the world like a rock star.

The black theatrical male dancer had to overcome many of the same obstacles mentioned in this article. However, he also needed to navigate a labyrinth of racism that emanated from dance audiences, historians, and critics. Basically, the black male's dance body was seen as a location of "primitivism" that, it was thought, could not embody Western ideals of classical perfection. This racist notion prevailed in ballet establishment until the Civil Rights movement and the publication of such articles as Joann Kealiino-homoku's "An Anthropologist Looks at Ballet as a Form of Ethnic Dance" (1970). Denied access to traditional white ballet companies, in the 1930s, 1940s, and 1950s, black male dancers performed in companies created for and by black dance artists such as Aubrey

Hitchens (1906–1969). These companies were short-lived, but provided an opportunity for black dancers to perform and for audiences to see them expressing their physicality outside of racial stereotypes. Arthur Mitchell (b. 1934) danced for the New York City Ballet in the 1950s and 1960s, and was the first black man to reach the level of principal dancer in an American ballet company. When New York City Ballet's cofounder and artistic director, George Balanchine (1904–1983), partnered Mitchell with a white woman in the 1950s, it was an artistic triumph and a strong political statement. In 1968 Mitchell founded the Dance Theatre of Harlem as a reaction to the assassination of Martin Luther King Jr. and his desire to fight for the place of the black dancer in ballet.

Modern dance originated at the turn of the century and is viewed as primarily the invention of some very talented and powerful women: Martha Graham (1894–1991), Doris Humphrey (1895–1958), and others. The lack of male inclusion may not have been from lack of desire, but from the social and cultural expectations placed on men at the turn of the century. However, in spite of cultural challenges, many male dancers/choreographers did contribute to the development of modern dance, including Ted Shawn (1891–1972), Charles Weidman (1901–1975), Eric Hawkins (1901–1945), José Limón (1908–1972), and Merce Cunningham (b. 1919), to mention a few. In his book, *One Thousand and One Night Stands* (1979), Ted Shawn recalls the remark of a friend that epitomizes the challenges males dancers experienced: "Dancing may be alright for aborigines and Russians but it is hardly a suitable career for red-blooded American male" (11). In his book, Shawn recounts his life as a dancer and his travels across America with an all-male dance troop wanting to prove that men *do* dance.

In 1958, Alvin Ailey (1931–1989) formed The Alvin Ailey American Dance Theatre and produced many successful choreographies reflecting on his experience and heritage as an African American. Bill T. Jones (b. 1952) formed a company with his partner Arnie Zane (1947–1988) and continues to create works that question traditional masculine ideals and racial bias, and that challenge the image of the male dancer as a sleek muscular object of desire. Neither Ailey nor Jones denies the sexuality imposed on the black male body, and both have choreographed within the context of the black body's sensuality, at the same time deconstructing racial perceptions and revealing the full potential of the dancer's artistic personality.

The codes of behavior William Pollack outlines in his book *Real Boys* apply equally to Broadway male dancers who, unlike their female colleagues, often include choreography and directing to refine their image as in-control males. For example, Bob Fosse (1927–1987), Tommy Tune (1939–), Gregory Hines (1946–2003), and Savion Glover (1973–) have each had successful careers as dancers and choreographers.

In the late 1960s, Steve Paxton (b. 1939) initiated a dance form called Contact Improvisation. It was based on principles from the martial arts and the spontaneous effects of gravity and balance. Now an integral part of a dancer's training, Contact Improvisation has found success with young men who find this form of contact dance challenging and athletic.

Today, men remain vastly outnumbered in dance classes. Although professional athletes such as hockey and basketball players are often required to take ballet in order to increase their coordination and range of movement, the value of dance as an activity for men remains overshadowed by the perception that dance is the domain of women. Challenging this perception, Matthew Bourne's male *Swan Lake* (1995) had a successful run in London's West End and on Broadway. DV8 choreographer Lloyd Newson's *Dead Dreams of Monochrome Men* (1989) and *Enter Achilles* (1995) are successful choreographies that deal with issues of male violence, bonding, and redemption.

Most of Bill T. Jones's choreography explores alternative views of masculinity, including his autobiographical work *Last Night on Earth* (1995). Choreographer/dancer Mark Morris's *Dido and Aeneas* (1989) and *The Hard Nut* (1991) are wonderful examples of dancers being used for their talent, without regard for conventional gender expectations.

Darcey Callison

Further Reading:

Burt, Ramsay. 1995. *The Male Dancer: Bodies, Spectacles, Sexualities.* New York: Routledge.

DeFrantz, Thomas. 2001. "Simmering Passivity: The Black Male Body in Concert Dance" Pp. 342–349 in *Moving History/Dancing Cultures: A Dance History Reader.* Edited by Ann Dils and Ann Cooper Albright. Middletown, CT: Wesleyan University Press.

Cohen. Sarah R. 2000. *Art, Dance, and the Body in French Culture of the Ancien Régime.* Cambridge UK: Cambridge University Press.

Desmond, Jane C., ed. 2001. *Dance Desires: Choreographing Sexualities On and Off Stage.* Madison, WI: The University of Wisconsin Press.

Pollock, William. 1998. *Real Boys.* New York: Henry Holt.

Shawn, Ted. 1979. *One Thousand and One Night Stands.* New York: Da Capo Press.

Dante
[Dante Alighieri] (1265–1321)

In the realm of literary studies, the medieval Florentine Dante Alighieri was one of the first writers to praise, defend, and compose in the vernacular language. Because Dante considered the lyrical vernacular to be the perfect medium for conveying and depicting all forms of human expressions, his critical works focused and expounded upon the similarities between the quest for physical and spiritual love and that for knowledge. In fact, by writing in his own voice and employing the literary theme of the journey, Dante not only expressed his personal views regarding religion and philosophy, but he also introduced that the struggle for self-recognition and self-confirmation takes place when both

Dante, 1265–1321 (Perry-Castaneda Library)

men and women interact. In other words, the quest for the self proved to be intricately tied to religious and philosophical debates, as well as early literary notions of femininity and masculinity.

In one of his earliest works, *La Vita nuova (The new life)*, composed somewhere between 1292 and 1294, Dante uniquely combines and juxtaposes prose and poetry as he writes about his search for happiness, his love for Beatrice, and his renouncement for his youthful misdeeds. In these thirty-one poems, Dante borrows from the Roman author Ovid the classical metaphor for love—whose pursuit, conquest, and maintenance uses similar language to that of war for its description—in order to express both his spiritual quest for a Christian love and his quest for a physical love with Beatrice. In his literary description of passion, virtue, intoxication, a lover's gaze, and all the various movements of love that later poets like Petrarca, Ronsard, and Shakespeare imitated, Dante sets forth foundational metaphors to de-

scribe the role of and interchange between men and women in love. For example, by speaking of the power of a love in Beatrice's eyes (*Ne li occhi porta la mia donna Amore; In my lady's eyes the power of love is created*) (Ch. XXI), Dante not only points to the eyes as vehicles through which a woman communicates her ardor but also through which a man is brought to life. While some critics would single out the obvious power struggle between the beholder and the beloved, what is so innovative about Dante's poetics is that he complicates the gender roles; Dante is both beholder and beloved. This tangled embrace of opposing positions of authority is related to the troubadours, the medieval wandering minstrels who performed in court. In their songs, the troubadours would depict this reversal of roles because it was an integral component to a courtly love relationship and to a man's public identity and position within the court. The triumphant troubadour, like Dante, would simultaneously claim to be at the mercy of his beloved's love and pledge his love for his king. Because his amorous concern was then directly related to his public standing at court, the successful poet like Dante would send his poems to men occupying political and powerful positions of authority in order to be publicly judged worthy. And since Dante's concern is centered more on the development of the self and its possible inscription, the intriguing characteristics of early gender roles are truly more complex and ambiguous, especially if they were meant for a public validation by men. After all, in *La Vita nuova,* as in most troubadour poetry, it is the man who undertakes and is altered by the journey for a woman's love, thus situating the quest as a trial for masculinity.

Amongst his other admired works that explore a man's journey for knowledge and love are the *De vulgari eloquentia (On Eloquence in the Vernacular), Convivio (Banquet),* and the celebrated *Commedia (Divine Comedy).* This latter work was composed from 1307 to 1321 while he was in political exile from

Florence, and it most skillfully presents Dante's vision of how together the vernacular and a narrative storytelling structure can convey the drama of one man's journey to God. Divided into three parts—*Inferno, Purgatorio,* and *Paradiso*—and made up of 100 cantos, Dante presents two first-person singular personalities undergoing this experience—Dante the pilgrim and Dante the poet. As the self is bifurcated in this process of the poet remembering and the pilgrim wandering, both nevertheless require the assistance of guides to reach the indescribable realm of God's glory. One important guide is the same Beatrice from *La Vita nuova* who aids the pilgrim in *Paradiso* just before he encounters the Virgin Mary who will facilitate Dante's gaze of the celestial glory. As he reaches this visual ascent to God and dares to write about it in the vernacular, Dante introduces to the literary world one of the early models of subjectivity, couched in a discourse of what it meant to be a man in pursuit of love.

Nhora Lucía Serrano

Further Reading:

Auerbach, Erich. 1961. *Dante: Poet of the Secular World.* Translated by Ralph Manheim. Chicago: Chicago University Press.

Freccero, John. 1986. *Dante: The Poetics of Conversion.* Edited by R. Jacoff. Cambridge, MA: Harvard University Press.

Kirkpatrick, Robin. 1990. "Dante's Beatrice and the Politics of Singularity." *Texas Studies in Literature and Language* 32, no. 1: 101–119.

Martinez, Ronald L. 1998. "Mourning Beatrice: The Rhetoric of Threnody in the *Vita nuova.*" *Modern Language Notes* 113: 1–29.

Mazzotta, Giuseppe. 1986. "The Light of Venus and the Poetry of Dante: *Vita nuova* and *Inferno* XXVII." Pp. 189–204 in *Modern Critical Views: Dante.* Edited by H. Bloom. New York: Chelsea.

Menocal, Maria Rosa. 1991. *Writing in Dante's Cult of Truth: From Borges to Boccaccio.* Durham, NC: Duke University Press.

Vickers, Nancy J. 1989. "Widowed Words: Dante, Petrarch, and the Metaphors of Mourning." Pp. 97–108 in *Discourses of Authority in Medieval and Renaissance Literature.* Edited by K. Brownlee and W. Stephens. Hanover, NH: University Press of New England.

Darwinism

Darwinism refers to the principles of organic evolution set out by Charles Darwin and more specifically to the popularization of his concepts in the late nineteenth and early twentieth centuries and the application of his ideas to social theory and human relations. Darwinism provided new perspectives on men's place in nature, relations between men and women, and competition between groups and individuals. Darwinism contributed directly to concepts of masculinity, arguing that men arose from animals rather than a moment of divine creation, that men and women had evolved differently, and that competition is crucial to the progress and maintenance of men and society. Darwinism thus problematized static views of relations between sexes and races, but helped define a normative masculinity that emphasized men's competition and their pursuit of heterosexual reproductive sex and that justified the interests of white middle- and upper-class men.

Darwin argued in *On the Origin of Species* (1859) that different species, rather than the result of individual moments of divine creation of the realization of eternal types, instead were mutable forms that changed over time with natural selective pressures—survival and reproduction—acting on randomly occurring variation in characters. Darwin's account of organic evolution by natural selection challenged prevalent religious and philosophical conceptions of humans' and in particular men's place in the universe. From a Darwinian perspective, human bodies are not divinely created but instead arise from the same process as other animals. Moreover, the mutability of species suggests that humans actually arise from some prior, less complex form, contradicting biblical accounts of Eden and the Fall. Finally, Darwinism suggested that women were not derivative of men—that Eve was created of Adam—destabilizing existing gender hierarchies based on biblical accounts of creation.

As revolutionary as Darwin's theories were, Darwinism nonetheless naturalized many of the race and gender relations of the late nineteenth and early twentieth centuries. Darwinism suggested the possibility that different racial groups represented different stages of evolution, reinscribing existing racial hierarchies. Darwinian theory explains general differences between sexes as a result of sexual selection, or mate choice. Darwinists used the general parameters of sexual selection to argue, for example, that men were more evolved intellectually than women, or that men and women had evolved for different roles—men for competition and work outside the home, women for child care and homemaking. Such arguments, which essentialize "man" and "woman," were often used to bolster the status quo, limiting women's educational opportunities and political rights and justifying men's sexual needs and pleasures. In response, women Darwinian theorists tended to emphasize complementarity between the sexes and the possibility of equivalence with difference, rather than a hierarchy of genders.

The most direct effect of Darwinian thought was realized in social Darwinism, which suggested that the selective pressures of competition in the natural world could explain relations between human individuals and societies. Social Darwinism emphasized the importance of competition between individuals, and in particular between men, in the progress and maintenance of society. Darwinism was used to diagnose social pathologies of nonnormative manhood, such as alcoholism, homosexuality, and suicide, as the product of the malfunctioning of natural selection in the context of modern society. Homosexuality in particular was condemned by many social Darwinists because of its nonreproductive "corruption" of reproductive functions. Social Darwinism has been seen as part of the justification for the rise of capitalism and increasing class inequality. However, recent historical work suggests that social Darwinism explains little of American male entrepreneurialism, which instead was rooted in Christian and Enlightenment ideals

of struggle against evil. Eugenics in the United States, closely linked to fears of propertied families of the dilution of racial stock by unfettered immigration, drew upon Darwinian concepts of blended inheritance to argue for the limitation of reproduction of biologically and morally degenerate groups. Charles Davenport, an American scientist and social theorist, is most directly associated with a negative eugenics of racial purifying though means such as sterilization, rather than the positive eugenics of better breeding espoused in England by figures such as Sir Francis Galton.

Reactions to Darwinism varied in the United States largely by region and religious denomination, with Protestantism in the South connected with the most concerted resistance to Darwinian thought. Southern Protestantism at the time held a model of masculinity grounded in the superiority of white men over both women and other races. Such a model depended on the unchanging relation of men with women. However, Catholic skepticism for eugenics movements prompted by Darwinism did exist, linked to arguments against artificial birth control methods and emphasizing men's fertility rather than control over their reproduction. Conservative Protestants and Catholics condemned Darwinism as a materialist philosophy that denied the divine creation of humans, preferring a model of masculinity associating men in particular with the divine.

Literary and philosophical works have been associated with Darwinism, including the anxiety about men's place in the world it has provoked and the explanations for competition it has engendered. Evolutionary thinking greatly influenced the work of social theorists that were to have profound influences on concepts of masculinity. Karl Marx saw shifts from less to more complex societies and economic regimes as evolutionary progressions, and as economic man (*Homo economicus*), or man realized through his alteration of and interaction with the external world, as the result of evolution. Friedrich Engels, Marx's collaborator, based his trajectory of societies characterized by matriarchal to patriarchal relations in part on Darwinian principles. Sigmund Freud directly used Darwinian thought in *Civilization and Its Discontents,* describing tension in the human psyche between sexual instincts and the need to socialize those instincts, and explaining particular human psychological problems in modern society as caused by constraints of civilization on men's and women's natural tendencies. Works of gothic fiction by authors such as Robert Louis Stevenson, Charlotte Brönte, Bram Stoker, and Mary Shelley have been associated with Darwinism—such works depict men who, rather than scientifically controlling the natural world, are instead subject to its laws. The best example is in Stevenson's *Dr. Jekyll and Mr. Hyde,* in which a scientist, experimenting with releasing his human potential, instead unleashes an inner beast, an animal that is his antithesis while at the same time containing some of his most human and masculine characteristics—strength, cunning, and sexual appetite. In the twentieth century, John Updike's *Rabbit* series evokes the concept of corporate Darwinism, emphasizing the importance of competition in the creation of the American businessman.

Darwinian thought continues to influence social theory, most directly in the fields of sociobiology and behavioral ecology, which attempt to explain human behaviors, reproductive and otherwise, as the result of selective pressures realized in ecological context. Sociobiologists such as E. O. Wilson have argued that different reproductive strategies pursued by men and women in different contexts give rise to other aspects of social organization. However, feminist evolutionary theorists have pointed out that sociobiology continues to overgeneralize male and female as categories, to reify existing gender roles, and to emphasize biological givens rather than potentials.

Matthew Dudgeon

See also Evolution

Further Reading:
Bannister, Robert C. 1979. *Social Darwinism: Science and Myth in Anglo-American Social Thought.* Philadelphia: Temple University Press.
Conkin, Paul Keith. 1998. *When All the Gods Trembled: Darwinism, Scopes, and American Intellectuals.* Lanham, MD: Rowman and Littlefield Publishers.
Haraway, Donna J. 1991. *Simians, Cyborgs, and Women: The Reinvention of Nature.* New York: Routledge.
Hawkins, Mike. 1997. *Social Darwinism in European and American Thought, 1860–1945: Nature as Model and Nature as Threat.* New York: Cambridge University Press.
Hendershot, Cyndy. 1998. *The Animal Within: Masculinity and the Gothic.* Ann Arbor: University of Michigan Press.
Horner, Carl S. 1992. *The Boy Inside the American Businessman: Corporate Darwinism in Twentieth-Century American Literature.* Lanham, MD: University Press of America.
Kaye, Howard L. 1997. *The Social Meaning of Modern Biology: From Social Darwinism to Sociobiology.* New Brunswick, NJ: Transaction Paper.
Numbers, Ronald L. 1998. *Darwinism Comes to America.* Cambridge, MA: Harvard University Press.
Numbers, Ronald L., and John Stenhouse. 1999. *Disseminating Darwinism: The Role of Place, Race, Religion, and Gender.* New York: Cambridge University Press.
Roberts, Jon H. 1987. *Darwinism and the Divine in America: Protestant Intellectuals and Organic Evolution, 1859–1900, History of American Thought and Culture.* Madison: University of Wisconsin Press.

Date Rape

Rape is sexual penetration without consent. Approximately 25 percent of U.S. women are the victims of actual or attempted rape at some point in their lives. Although the stereotypical rapist is the deranged man who springs from hiding and attacks a woman somewhere outdoors, in actuality the victim knows the attacker in more than three-quarters of rapes. Koss estimated that men rape or attempt to rape about 50 out of every 1,000 college women in any given year. About 8 percent of college men report having forced a woman to have sexual intercourse against her will on at least one occasion (Koss, Gidycz, and Wisniewski 1987), and the sexual victimization of males is much more frequent than is generally believed (Scarce 1997). Sexual assault perpetrators are male over 99 percent of the time.

A common occurrence of sexual assault is a rape that takes place in the context of a date in which the man wants to have sex and the woman does not. In most of these date rapes, the perpetrator and/or victim have been drinking alcohol. However, alcohol does not cause rape, as many men drink heavily and never commit sexual assault. Perpetrators often use alcohol to subdue their victims, summon the nerve to commit the attack, and/or to deny their responsibility for the attack ("I was drunk and didn't know what I was doing."). When an attack occurs during a time when both the victim and the perpetrator had been drinking, the tendency is to attribute less blame to the man and more to the woman than if both were sober (Kilmartin 2001).

Despite beliefs to the contrary, date rapes are rarely a product of miscommunication. Rather they are acts of violence in which the perpetrator often systematically isolates and subdues his victim. Rapes are also never the result of a failure to control one's sexual feelings; people can control their behavior even when highly aroused. Rapists usually plan their attacks, and they often have to masturbate and/or force the victim into oral sex in order to get an erection. They frequently have difficulty remembering whether or not they had orgasms during the rape (Groth 1979).

Sexual assault is a product of three conditions: the perpetrator's pathology, the decision to attack, and a social-cultural context in which men are encouraged to see themselves as different from and better than women (Kilmartin 2001). With regard to the first condition, Lisak (1997) cites fourteen

studies demonstrating that hypermasculine characteristics such as adversarial sexual beliefs and negative attitudes toward women are strongly connected to sexualized violence. Therefore, sexual assault can be conceptualized as overconformity rather than deviance. Sexually aggressive men tend to view a date as a kind of competition in which their goal is to obtain sex and the woman's goal is to obtain affection and/or get them to spend money on her (Hall 1990). Date rapists also show high levels of hostility toward women, beliefs that women like to be forced into sex, underlying anger and power motivations, dominance as a motive for sexual interactions, and hypermasculinity. They invariably express bitter feelings and clear disappointments toward their fathers, whom they describ emotionally distant and sometimes as physically violent (Lisak 1991).

The second condition is the decision of the perpetrator. Regardless of his pathology, a perpetrator makes a conscious decision to rape, and he is responsible for his behavior. These decisions are influenced by the third condition of rape, the social and cultural support for the behavior. Lacking an internal sense of positive masculinity, rape-prone men often join hypermasculine peer groups that are aggressive and misogynist (Koss and Dinero 1988). Theorists argue that some fraternities (Sanday 1996) and some athletic teams (O'Sullivan 1991) serve this function on college campuses.

In a participant-observer study of high-risk and low-risk fraternities, Boswell and Spade (1996) found that the latter were characterized by friendly atmospheres and relaxed social interactions between men and women. In contrast, high-risk fraternities had significantly greater separation of the sexes, more crude sexual behavior and open hostility toward women at parties, and negative social sanctions for fraternity members who developed long-term relationships with women. The message that these fraternities send to their members is that women are only for sex and that they are worthy of contempt. In these high-risk fraternities, members often collude in attacks and in efforts to thwart investigations of rapes by their fraternity brothers.

These findings echo the conclusions of anthropological studies that link violence against women to social and physical separation of the sexes and to low levels of women's social power (Sanday 1996). On a societal level, rape is a product of the male social domination of women. Anthropologist Peggy Sanday (1981) reported that rape is virtually nonexistent in forty-four nonpatriarchal societies.

Solutions to the problem of rape can involve a variety of strategies, including law enforcement, rehabilitative interventions, rendering environments less conducive to rape, educating potential victims, and changing the destructive aspects of traditional masculinity. In service of the latter goal, several men's antirape groups such as Men Can Stop Rape (MSR) and the National Organization for Men Against Sexism (NOMAS) challenge the rape-tolerant aspects of the culture. Because the incidence of date rape on college campuses and universities is alarmingly high, many schools engage in programmatic efforts to decrease violence against women. As the twenty-first century begins there has been an increase in programs designed specifically for men with a variety of goals, including sensitizing men to the negative consequences of sexual violence for the perpetrator; facilitating empathy for victims of sexual assault; educating men about the rape-supporting aspects of socialization, culture, and patriarchy; and helping men understand the role of male peer support in sexual assault.

Efforts to address the rape-supportive aspects of peer cultures are especially hopeful, as they address the behavior of all men, not just perpetrators, and address what men can do about the problem that goes beyond merely refraining from the behavior. Most young men do not realize that they contribute to a rape-supportive social atmo-sphere when they fail to confront other men's sexist attitudes and behavior, and programming can help men to acquire the knowledge, attitudes, and skills to do so (Kilmartin 2001). Although most college men are uncomfortable with sexism, they overestimate other men's comfort. Preliminary evidence suggests that correcting this cognitive distortion may be the first step in helping men to challenge sexism (Berkowitz 1997).

These efforts specifically to address sexual assault can also be accompanied by educational interventions that help men understand themselves as gendered beings, develop positive relationship skills, and change the destructive aspects of masculinity. Men's gender awareness and change should contribute to an improvement in the specific problem of sexual assault, the general problem of men's violence, and a number of other quality-of-life issues for men, such as physical health, relationship satisfaction, and mental health.

There is a growing awareness of the problem of male-on-male sexual assault, which victimizes as many as one in eight men in the United States. Most rapes of males are committed by heterosexual men against children or against homosexual men (King 1992). Funk (1997) describes being gang-raped by a group of men who attacked him because he spoke in support of feminist causes. He views this event as an example of the use of coercive sexuality to maintain masculine privilege, similar to its function in sexual assaults on women. Male rape survivors experience similar psychological responses as female survivors, but have access to even fewer resources for treatment and support.

Date rape is a common form of patriarchal domination that occurs behind closed doors. Like all gender-based violence, it has cultural origins that interact with the characteristics of individual men to produce the problematic behavior. The fact that rape shows striking cross-cultural variations is evidence that it is embedded in the social meanings attached to gender. Therefore, solutions must be broad in scope, encompassing economic, educational, legal, and social activist strategies.

Chris Kilmartin

See also Sexual Assault Prevention
Further Reading:
Berkowitz, Alan D. 1997. "Effective Sexual Assault Prevention Programming: Meeting the Needs of Men and Women." (Paper presented at the Seventh International Conference on Sexual Assault and Harassment on Campus, Orlando, Florida, October).

Boswell, A. Ayres, and Joan Z. Spade. 1996. "Fraternities and Collegiate Rape Culture: Why Are Some Fraternities More Dangerous Places for Women?" *Gender & Society* 10, no. 2: 133–147.

Funk, Rus E. 1997. "Men Who Are Raped: A Profeminist Perspective." Pp. 221–231 in *Male on Male Rape: The Hidden Toll of Stigma and Shame.* Edited by M. Scarce. New York: Plenum.

Groth, A. Nicholas 1979. *Men Who Rape: The Psychology of the Offender.* New York: Plenum.

Hall, Gordon C. N. 1990. "Prediction of Sexual Aggression." *Clinical Psychology Review* 10: 229–246.

Kilmartin, Christopher T. 2001. *Sexual Assault in Context: Teaching College Men about Gender.* Holmes Beach, FL: Learning Publications.

King, Michael B. 1992. "Male Sexual Assault in the Community." Pp. 3–12 in *Male Victims of Sexual Assault.* Edited by G. C. Mezey and M. B. King. New York: Oxford University Press.

Koss, Mary P. 1983. "The Scope of Rape: Implications for the Clinical Treatment of Victims." *The Clinical Psychologist* 36: 88–91.

Koss, Mary P., and T. E. Dinero. 1988. "Predictors of Sexual Aggression among a National Sample of Male College Students." Pp. 133–147 in *Human Sexual Aggression: Current Perspectives.* Edited by R. A. Prentky and V. L. Quinsey. New York: New York Academy of Sciences.

Koss, Mary P., C. A. Gidycz, and N. Wisniewski. 1987. "The Scope of Rape: Incidence and Prevalence of Sexual Aggression and Victimization in a National Sample of Higher Education Students." *Journal of Consulting and Clinical Psychology* 55: 162–170.

Lisak, David. 1991. "Sexual Aggression, Masculinity, and Fathers." *Signs* 16: 238–262.

———. 1997. "Male Gender Socialization and the Perpetuation of Sexual Abuse." Pp. 156–177 in *Men and Sex.* Edited by R. F. Levant and G. R. Brooks. New York: Wiley.

O'Sullivan, Christine S. 1991. "Acquaintance Gang Rape on Campus." Pp. 140–156 in *Acquaintance Rape: The Hidden Crime.* Edited by A. Parrot and L. Bechofer. New York: Wiley.

Sanday, Peggy Reeves. 1981. "The Socio-Cultural Context of Rape: A Cross-Cultural Study." *Journal of Social Issues,* 37: 5–27.

———. 1996. *A Woman Scorned: Acquaintance Rape on Trial.* New York: Doubleday.

Scarce, Michal. 1997. *Male on Male Rape: The Hidden Toll of Stigma and Shame.* New York: Plenum.

Deadbeat Dads

A deadbeat dad is a father who does not comply with child support obligations following separation or divorce. The term *deadbeat* connotes dereliction not only of financial obligations but of social and moral responsibilities as well. Definitions of *deadbeat* range from the relatively neutral notion of one who avoids payment of debts to the more antiquated characterization of "a worthless sponging idler" (Barber 2001). In the interest of gender neutrality, the term deadbeat parents is sometimes used in the media to indicate that mothers may be noncompliant with child support as well. The term *deadbeat dad* does, however, reflect the reality that fathers overwhelmingly constitute the large body of separated or divorced parents who are obligated to pay support, based on their relatively higher incomes, and therefore make up the vast majority of parents who do not comply with child support obligations. The popularization in North America of the concept of deadbeat dads in recent decades reflects social discourses that justify shifting attitudes in law and public policy toward child support. These attitudes hold parents—and fathers in particular—responsible for the economic well-being of their children, whatever the state of the marital or parent-child relationships. An accompanying stance is that support recipients (usually custodial or resident mothers) should not prevent children from seeing their fathers, whether or not child support is being paid. The principle behind these theoretically complementary expectations is to serve "the best interests of the child."

The increasing visibility of paternal child support as a social issue is a product of the convergence of several historical and social processes. Primary among these are the tendency—as the twentieth century progressed—for mothers to seek and be awarded custody, the increase in divorce rates (especially in the latter half of the twentieth century), the linking in the 1980s of nonsupport with high rates of poverty among single mothers and children, and the rising interest in various disciplines in the role of fatherhood from the 1960s onward. The women's movement and feminist activism raised awareness of how women and children are disadvantageously positioned in divorce; the growing men's rights movement countered with an analysis of the disadvantages to men.

Interest in fathers' reasons for nonpayment was fueled by a number of motivations. One was to find a solution to the problem of nonsupport within the traditional framework of the father-led family, with the father continuing as provider. Another was growing interest in new perspectives on men's experiences of parenthood, life-span development, and relationships in general. New analyses of gender roles, especially within the family, fostered different kinds of inquiry into the meaning of fatherhood to men and the changes to the fathering role and identity through marital separation.

Research into noncompliance patterns have yielded mixed results. Some studies have found that inability to pay is the main reason for nonsupport, or inconsistent or incomplete support. Others have found unwillingness, or more complex relationships between support levels and such factors as relative attenuation of the father-child relationship, the preseparation parenting relationship, the existence of a new partner or family for either spouse, the quality of the relationship with the former spouse, and the father's psychological well-being or identity, among other reasons for nonsup-port. Some fathers reject the role of provider when the marital relationship comes undone, especially if their access to the children is limited.

Other researchers have examined broader social conditions that might explain the extent of noncompliance, arguing that such a common phenomenon cannot be a matter of individual subjective experiences. Some of these studies blamed the problem of noncompliance on weak and inconsistent social policies, arguing that only stronger enforcement can remedy the problem. In this analysis, psychological links between support default and limited access to children are rejected.

The current emphasis in North American social policy on aggressive enforcement of child support is a relatively recent historical development, triggered by the research indicating that court decisions and lack of enforcement were the causes of the problem. It is an approach that reflects both concern about the effects of widespread poverty for women and children and about the strain on government coffers of providing financial support when fathers do not pay. The introduction of new enforcement measures in the 1980s and 1990s was accompanied by formal separation of support issues from issues of custody or access. Sometimes, they were introduced against a backdrop of government-sponsored media campaigns designed to shame fathers and increase public disapproval of nonsupport. Subsequently, some efforts have been made to accommodate the sensibilities of fathers in the framing of legislation and policy related to custody, access, and support. In some North American jurisdictions, collection of child support has been privatized. Aggressive enforcement has ameliorated the problem to some degree, but has by no means solved it. There is evidence to suggest that payment often remains more a matter of will than of being subject to authority.

Responses to the trend of enforcement and its failure as a solution have become increasingly polarized. Child support has been compared on one hand to taxation without representation for fathers and on the other hand has been characterized as leaving the welfare of families in the hands of individuals whose sense of responsibility to them may be minimal.

There are many different views of and structures for child support throughout the world. They vary according to such factors as prevailing cultural norms and values, dominant welfare, gender and legal ideologies, resources, legal infrastructure, and political issues.

Deena Mandell

See also Fathers, Nonresidential; Divorce

Further Reading:
Arendell, Terry. 1995. *Fathers and Divorce.* Thousand Oaks, CA: Sage.
Barber, Katherine, ed. 2001. *Canadian Oxford Dictionary.* Toronto, Canada: Oxford University Press.
Bertoia, Carl, and Janice Drakich. 1995. "The Fathers' Rights Movement: Contradictions in Rhetoric and Practice." Pp. 230–253 in *Fatherhood: Contemporary Theory, Research and Social Policy.* Edited by William Marsiglio. Thousand Oaks, CA: Sage.
Kahn, Alfred J., and Sheila B. Kamerman, eds. 1988. *Child Support: From Debt Collection to Social Policy.* Newbury Park, CA: Sage.
Kruk, Edward. 1993. *Divorce and Disengagement: Patterns of Fatherhood within and beyond Marriage.* Halifax, NS, Canada: Fernwood.
Lupton, Deborah, and Lesley Barclay. 1997. *Constructing Fatherhood: Discourses and Experiences.* London: Sage.
Mandell, Deena. 2002. *Deadbeat Dads: Subjectivity and Social Construction.* Toronto, Canada: University of Toronto Press.

Dean, James (1931–1955)

James Dean was a Hollywood actor who, along with Marlon Brando, popularized a tough-but-tender version of masculinity in the 1950s teenage rebel genre. After starring in three major films in a two-year period, Dean's career was curtailed when he was killed in a car crash at the age of twenty-four in 1955. His premature death precipitated deep, heartfelt emotional responses from his loyal community of fans, along with rumors and inquiries regarding his sexual orientation. Fans' commemorative activities and public speculations continue into the twenty-first century.

Born in rural Indiana in 1931, Dean was raised by his aunt and uncle after his mother's death from cancer and his father's relocation to California. In New York during the early 1950s he trained briefly at the Actor's Studio, made several television appearances, and performed in a Broadway stage version of *The Immoralist* before Elia Kazan "discovered" the actor and offered him the part of the "bad" son Cal Trask in the film version of *East of Eden* (1954). Dean developed the persona of the alienated teenage antihero as Jim Stark in Nicholas Ray's *Rebel without a Cause* (1955), a Warner Brothers project that capitalized upon the then-current national controversy surrounding juvenile delinquency. The actor's fatal car crash occurred near Salinas, California, shortly after he finished filming his final scenes as outcast-turned-millionaire Jett Rink in George Stevens's *Giant,* which was released in 1956. The *James Dean Story,* a Warner Brothers biopic directed by Robert Altman, appeared in theaters in 1957.

During Dean's brief film career, Warner Brothers press releases described him as a brooding, insecure, vulnerable, country-born actor alienated by the superficiality of Hollywood, asserting Dean's authenticity by strategically noting the similarities between his on-screen roles and his off-screen, "private" persona. Popular film reviews and fan magazine articles reinforced the public's sense of Dean's genuine and unaffected qualities, building his image as a man who lacked—yet craved—the comfort of others. Instrumental to Dean's sexual appeal was the fact that his alienation and vulnerability were promoted as the attributes of an accessible form of masculinity, one distinct from the tough-guy image that several other male stars of the era embodied. With Dean, vulnerability became a sign of strength.

After his death, the star's vulnerability was extended to human mortality. Warner

Brothers publicists, *Photoplay* journalists, and devoted fan communities across the country used various strategies to confront the senselessness of the actor's sudden death. Some reports rewrote the actor's life story such that death became the tragic yet inevitable outcome of an alienated childhood and adolescence. Using a Freudian psychology popularized in the 1950s, other reports used the early death of Dean's biological mother as evidence to account for his purported lack of fulfillment, speculating upon how Dean's personal life might have developed had he not died young. The large number of women whom Dean purportedly "dated" in Hollywood provided sufficient material for such speculations. In the context of his associations with rebellion and vulnerability, however, the fact that the actor was uncommitted in a relationship at the time of his death soon opened up questions regarding his sexual orientation, fueled by close friends' public suggestions that Dean had been sexually intimate with men.

If this negotiation of a celebrity's sexuality was shaped by cultural prohibitions limiting public discourse on homosexuality in the 1950s, the Gay Rights movement resurrected the issue of Dean's sexuality in the early 1970s. The actor became a central figure in the movement's political struggle over sexual identity, foregrounding the matter of whether engaging in a homosexual act necessarily constitutes homosexual identity and whether sexuality itself is fluid or stable. Dean thus became a figure who struggled in vain to maintain his homosexual identity in the midst of a repressive American culture. The numerous book-length biographies of the star released in the 1970s openly treated the "problem" of Dean's sexuality, and in the book *The Real James Dean* (1975), biographer John Gilmore spoke from firsthand experience as one of Dean's male lovers. Some argued that his same-sex encounters were only tactical maneuvers for career advancement; others protested that Dean was exclusively gay, and that any denial of this fact disavowed a formative aspect of his experience as a man.

Following trends in popular sexual discourse that became popular in the 1990s, a more recent set of Dean biographies pose a third possibility—that Dean was bisexual. Yet the case of Donald Spoto's biography *Rebel* (1996) describes this bisexuality as a symptom of indecisiveness brought about by the constraints of mid-century American culture. Earlier accounts of Dean's alienation often centered upon his conflicted search for a lost maternal figure, but in *Boulevard of Broken Dreams* (1994) Paul Alexander finds Dean contemplating or acting upon sexual relations with almost every man he encounters, in a compulsive search for father substitutes.

Michael DeAngelis

Further Reading:

Alexander, Paul. 1994. *Boulevard of Broken Dreams: The Life, Times, and Legend of James Dean*. New York: Viking.

Babuscio, Jack. 1975. "James Dean—A Gay Riddle." *Gay News* 79: 17–18.

Bast, William. 1956. *James Dean: A Biography*. New York: Ballantine Books.

Cohan, Steven. 1997. *Masked Men: Masculinity and the Movies in the Fifties*. Bloomington, IN: Indiana University Press.

Dalton, David, ed. 1991. *James Dean Revealed!* New York: Delta Books.

DeAngelis, Michael. 2001. *Gay Fandom and Crossover Stardom: James Dean, Mel Gibson, and Keanu Reeves*. Durham, NC: Duke University Press.

d'Emilio, John. 1983. *Sexual Politics, Sexual Communities*. Chicago: University of Chicago Press.

Gilmore, John. 1975. *The Real James Dean*. New York: Pyramid Books.

Spoto, Donald. 1996. *Rebel: The Life and Legend of James Dean*. New York: Harper-Collins.

Death of a Salesman

Playwright Arthur Miller undertook an examination of masculinity, aging, work, and family in his brilliantly insightful 1949 play, *Death of a Salesman*. Protagonist Willy Loman is a salesman in the twilight of his career who is performing poorly in his job and thus becoming an economic liability for his employer.

Willy's self-esteem is almost completely invested in fulfilling the traditional masculine provider role. He defends against his feelings of vulnerability by attempting to convince himself that his troubles are temporary and the future is bright. Fantasized conversations with his successful and adventurous brother Ben serve to remind Willy that he is a financial (masculine) failure. Ben says, "When I was seventeen I walked into the jungle, and when I was twenty-one I walked out. And by God I was rich."

Like many men of his era, Willy Loman believes that financial success is the barometer of masculinity and self-worth, and so he is tortured by the feeling that his life has been wasted because of his lack of courage and ingenuity. Adding to his difficulties are the career failures of his two sons, Biff and Happy. Willy is racked with guilt about a brief extramarital affair that Biff discovered, which appears to have been a trigger for Biff's dropping out of high school and never fulfilling his (and Willy's) dream of becoming a college football star. Willy attempts to deal with his own feelings of failure by alternately criticizing his sons' lack of industry and encouraging them to share his delusions about a successful future. Occasionally Biff challenges his father's defensiveness, but the result for Willy is deepening despair and panic.

These feelings come to a head when Willy is fired because of his lack of productivity. Because he has a substantial life insurance policy, he begins to believe that suicide is his only remaining means for fulfilling the provider role and escaping from his pain. He fantasizes about his funeral, believing that hundreds of people will come from miles around to mourn his passing.

Because of his profound feelings of failure, loss, helplessness, hopelessness, and worthlessness, Willy finally commits suicide in an intentional car accident, ironically in the same week of the final payment on the family house. Although Willy was an ade-quate provider for many years and was able to purchase a home, thus somewhat successful in the traditional masculine cultural paradigm, he felt completely emasculated at the loss of his status as a worker. He failed to find other aspects of his self-concept to replace this identity and could not live vicariously through his sons. Willy's standards of masculinity demanded that he become rich and powerful, a level of success that he never began to approach, and so he felt that his only alternative was to make what he considered to be a graceful exit. *Death of a Salesman* is the tragedy of an ordinary man who would rather die than be considered unmasculine.

Chris Kilmartin

Further Reading:

Miller, Arthur. [1949] 1998. *Death of a Salesman.* New York: Penguin USA.

Democracy

Democracy invites equality. Democratic theorists, citizens, activists, commentators, critics, and politicians speak about equal rights, equal respect, equal opportunity, equal results, equal influence, equal participation, and equal representation in government. Although societies rarely achieve egalitarian ideals, democratic discourses on equality are important. They popularize and legitimize the efforts of oppressed peoples to claim a greater share of liberty, prosperity, and self-government.

By contrast, discourses on masculinities spotlight inequality. Hegemonic masculinity requires subordinated masculinities. The virtues of manhood are articulated in opposition to youthful passions, female vices, and slavelike dependency. Talk about masculinities usually emphasizes competition and comparative performance. Boys excel at mind games or physical contests in competition with other boys. Young men achieve manhood by performing in the bedroom, marketplace, and battlefield. Older men risk

losing other men's respect when they lose independence, income, and importance.

Even the most egalitarian masculinities reproduce and reinforce male hierarchies. Fraternal organizations that bind men together often have intricate tests and rituals that place members at different levels of distinction and on different tiers of authority. Fraternities of battle that unite armed men against common enemies usually appear within the context of hierarchical military institutions that distinguish men by rank, uniform, and command structure. And nearly always, the price of male bonding is the exclusion and subordination of women. If democracy justifies equality, masculinities reward inequality. What happens when democracy and masculinities mix?

Consider the American founding. The leaders of the American Revolution faced the challenge of mobilizing large numbers of young men to risk their health, lives, and family prosperity in a struggle against the most powerful military force in the world, the British army and navy. Popular writers such as Thomas Paine and politicians such as John Adams regularly issued promises of greater liberty and equality to entice young men to enlist in the cause and endure self-sacrifice to gain national independence. When the Revolution ended, radical democrats lost their audience in respectable society as politicians warned that too much equality endangered the stability of the new nation. It was one thing to promise greater democratic equality to mobilize men for battle but quite another to implement democratic equality once the battle was over.

For most founders, the problem with democratic equality was that it threatened to empower lower-class men whose passions, impulses, and interests disposed them to vice and disorder. The founders also feared that democratic talk undermined the authority of those well-bred, highly educated gentlemen whose reason, civility, and civic virtue qualified them for leadership. The political problem was that the Revolution set loose demo-

cratic forces that could not be reversed. Those who explicitly opposed democracy (e.g., Adams) risked their public lives; those who embraced democratic rhetoric (e.g., Jefferson) invigorated their public lives. The challenge for political survivors was to embrace democratic rhetoric but simultaneously exclude disorderly men from power and legitimize the authority of "natural aristocrats."

In part, the founders addressed this challenge by counteracting democratic forces with an informal "grammar of manhood" that degraded some men, afforded respect and dignity to others, and elevated a few to high-status roles. The most egalitarian political norms, rules, and institutions could be neutralized by men's tendency to rate and rank each other and sort themselves out according to shifting norms of manhood. America's fearful founders discovered that the demons of democracy could be tamed by masculine inequalities. How? In post-Revolution America, ministers and magistrates assaulted the manhood of young, unpropertied, unattached males who left their parents homes only to engage in frontier violence or urban vice. Their mobility and vagrancy, indebtedness and irresponsibility, marginal racial or immigrant status, criminal associations and activity, and deviance from masculine norms effectively excluded them from participation in public life and made them vulnerable to official action and criminal sanction. In general, the founding generation reserved citizenship and public participation for settled, married men whose property holdings testified to their manly independence and whose patriarchal family responsibilities (which included governing and provisioning dependents) guaranteed their sobriety, productivity, and patriotism.

Still, manly citizenship and manly leadership were two different things. Most founders did not believe that salt-of-the-earth farmers and average family men were up to the task of governing a new nation that suffered from internal instability and external threats. They believed that America needed as leaders and legislators men of exceptional civic virtue, those they called "the better sort." And during historic times, such as their own, they felt that the new nation was desperate for that truly rare soul—that "man among men"—who disdained popularity, asserted the prerogative to rule without law or against law, and willingly sacrificed his own interests for the public good. Democratic rhetoric demanded equality but masculinities kept the rogue powerless, the farmer industrious, and George Washington at the helm.

Does this analysis suggest that democracy and masculinities are always at cross-purposes? Democracy demands equality among men and women, but masculinities regularly devalue women's attributes and women themselves. Democracy demands equality among men, but masculinities reward differences among men and then rank them. It is likely that democracy and masculinities will remain at odds until some masculinities become inclusive of women and reward equality among men and women.

Mark E. Kann

Further Reading:

Connell, Robert W. 1987. *Gender and Power: Society, the Person and Sexual Politics.* Stanford, CA: Stanford University Press.

Kann, Mark E. 1998. *A Republic of Men: The American Founders, Gendered Language, and Patriarchal Politics.* New York: New York University Press.

Kimmel, Michael S. 1996. *Manhood in America: A Cultural History.* New York: Free Press.

Rotundo, E. Anthony. 1993. *American Manhood: Transformations in Masculinity from the Revolution to the Modern Era.* New York: Basic Books.

Depression

An estimated 11 million Americans suffer each year with depression. The combined effect of lost productivity and medical expense due to the disorder costs the United States over 47 billion dollars per year—a toll comparable with heart disease. And yet the condition goes mostly undiagnosed. Somewhere between 60 to 80 percent of depressed people never get help. The silence about depression is particularly heartbreaking because its treatment has a high success rate. Estimates in the early 2000s are that between 80 and 90 percent of depressed patients find relief with proper treatment (see Real 1997).

Until the 1990s it was thought that depression was largely a woman's disease—with women estimated as depressed at rates about twice that of men. A number of sociologists and mental health professionals, however, have begun to question the conventional wisdom—claiming that depression in men is underreported, underdiagnosed, and, most important, misunderstood. According to this view, male depression represents nothing less than a hidden epidemic affecting millions of men and their families.

The first reason why male depression remains "hidden" is shame. While depression is not experienced by women as unwomanly, unfortunately many men experience depression as unmanly. In the stoic code, men are not supposed to be either too emotional or two vulnerable, and a depressed man is both—a man "brought down" by letting his feelings "get the better of him." Depression itself can be described as a shame state. The depressed man generally feels worthless, "not as good as," or inadequate. The discrepancy between the state of depression and traditionally defined masculinity sets up compound depression; the man feels ashamed about feeling ashamed, depressed about feeling depressed. And he hides his condition from others. These same forces render those around men less willing to recognize and confront the condition; spouses report feeling that doing so further humiliates an already fragile-seeming person, and doctors, even trained mental health professionals, have been shown repeatedly to underdiagnose the disorder in men.

There is another reason, however, that accounts for the lack of recognition of depression in men. Many researchers have come to believe that men express depression differently from women. While many men exhibit the same symptoms as women, a perhaps even greater number do not. These men, unlike most women, attempt to ward off the depression through defensive patterns of self-medication, withdrawal, and acting out. They suffer from what might be called "covert" depression. In covert depression one does not see the symptoms of depression itself but rather the desperate measures men employ to escape it. While not all problem drinkers or ragers have an undiagnosed depressive condition at their core, many do.

Currently there is no category in psychiatric nomenclature for a covert or a specifically male form of depression, although there have been proposals for change. For now, someone suffering from this disorder would be diagnosed, if they were fortunate enough to be understood, as a patient with a "dual diagnosis": depression and alcoholism, depression and antisocial behavior. While self-medication with substances might be uncovered, it would be unlikely, unfortunately, that self-medication through activities (what addictions experts call process addictions) would be correctly diagnosed. Process addictions include such activities as sex addiction, workaholism, gambling, risk taking, and, some argue, rage.

The best treatment for covert depression requires a two-pronged approach in which the defenses are treated, per se, and then the underlying depression. First, the man is brought into sobriety with regard to the substances or actions that have been serving him as self-medication, and then the underlying depression rises, with little clinical assistance, to the surface. The cure for a covert depression is an overt depression.

Understanding the unique characteristics of male depression demands—as well as an appreciation of its manifestation—a grasp of its etiology. Just as many men express depression differently from women, so too, the causes of the disorder are different. While there is no doubt that most depressions have a biological base, the injuries to men and women culturally differ. The core wound to most women in treatment is some form of disempowerment and the healing course is one of reempowerment. The core wound to most men in treatment is not disempowerment but disconnection. Depressed men are universally men who are cut off—from their own feelings; from their wants and needs; from sensitivity to, and even connection with, others. The healing work for most men follows a course of reconnection. While medication is a critical adjunct to treatment, and while all but the most mildly depressed men should consider a trial of medication, pills alone serve as a foundation for the psychological work, not its replacement. The most lasting cure for depression in men is intimacy.

Terrence Real

See also Anger.; Suicide
Further Reading:

Gilligan, Carol. 2002. *The Birth of Pleasure.* New York: Alfred A. Knopf.

Lynch, John, and Christopher T. Kilmartin. 1999. *The Pain behind the Mask: Overcoming Masculine Depression.* New York: Haworth.

Mellody, Pia. 2003. *Facing Codependence.* San Francisco: Harper.

Real, Terrence. 1997. *I Don't Want to Talk about It: Overcoming the Secret Legacy of Male Depression.* New York: Scribner.

———. 2002. *How Can I Get Through to You? Closing the Intimacy Gap between Men and Women.* New York: Hyperion.

Rosen, Laura Epstein, with Xavier F. Amador. 1997. *When Someone You Love Is Depressed: How to Help Your Loved One without Losing Yourself.* New York: Fireside.

Silverstein, Olga. 1994. *The Courage to Raise Good Men.* New York: Viking Press.

Detectives

The detective has been a popular and pervasive image of American masculinity—one that articulates manliness, perseverance, and heroism. Despite the proliferation of female detectives, especially in the last decade, the detective hero has been predominantly male. The detective narrative follows the detective's investigation of a crime and, itself, offers an investigation of the hero's masculinity as it is tested and proved through his solving of the case. The detective genre has remained popular because of its adaptability to social change, evolving from the classical to the hard-boiled then to the police procedural and, most recently, to the criminalist narrative. Detective heroes offer audiences models of an ideal manhood but they also reflect changing social attitudes toward masculinity.

Edgar Allan Poe is generally regarded as the creator of the fictional detective with the introduction of his sleuth C. Auguste Dupin in 1841; however, it was not until Sir Arthur Conan Doyle's Sherlock Holmes in the late nineteenth century that the classical detective, or sleuth, achieved widespread popularity. Holmes remains the most famous fictional detective and also one of the most recognized names—real or fictional—in the world. With his international appeal, it is not surprising that Holmes is one of the most popular detectives with over 200 films and television shows being centered on his character. The sleuth has been portrayed by more actors than any other character in the history of cinema. Like Poe's Dupin, Holmes solves mysteries through observation and logical deduction in a reflection of Victorian ideals of manhood. The golden age of the classical detective story occurred between the two world wars, mainly in Britain, with the novels of authors such as Agatha Cristie and Dorothy Sayers.

In the 1920s and 1930s, American detective fiction saw a shift from the gentleman sleuth to the hard-boiled private eye. Conceptions of masculinity in American society at this time included an increasing emphasis on physicality, toughness, and sexuality, and a corresponding shift occurred in the fictional representations of masculinity. Prohibition and the spread of organized crime in society marked the end of the classical detective as an effective solution to fic-

tional crime. The sleuth, with his superior skills of deduction, was replaced by the tough but troubled hard-boiled detective who relied on violence and street smarts to get the job done. The hard-boiled detective can be regarded as the adaptation of the British sleuth to the environment and concerns of urban American society and was popularized by writers like Raymond Chandler and Dashiell Hammett. Many of the hard-boiled novels were adapted to the screen in the 1930s; however, the heroes of Hollywood's detective series were less violent and troubled than their literary counterparts and instead tended to be portrayed as suave, erudite gentlemen like the Falcon and the Thin Man.

In the 1940s and 1950s, however, the hard-boiled detective came to the screen as the hero of film noir. Film noir is generally regarded as the genre or film style that began with *The Maltese Falcon* (1941) and ended with *Touch of Evil* (1958) and that was visually, as well as morally, dark. The films were set in the seedy underbelly of American society and followed a general progression from protagonists with questionable morals in the early 1940s like Sam Spade in *The Maltese Falcon* to border-line criminals in the late 1950s like Mike Hammer in *Kiss Me Deadly* (1955). Veterans returning from World War II struggled with feelings of displacement: American society had changed in their absence and upon their return they faced unemployment, changing gender roles, alienation, and often disablement. Film noir presented audiences with traumatized but tough heroes that could express and work through society's postwar disillusionment.

The advent of organized crime incited a restructuring of law enforcement to a more organized level, and the appearance of the police procedural narrative in detective fiction of the 1940s can be seen as a reflection of this professionalization of real-life crime detection. American society in the late 1940s and 1950s was dominated by concerns raised by the Cold War and organized crime, and these fears were reflected in the detective genre with the emergence of the police detective as hero in procedurals like *The Naked City* (1948) and television's *Dragnet*. With new technologies in surveillance and forensics as well as the power of an organized force at his disposal, the police detective offered the assurance that law enforcement was equipped to neutralize the threat of organized and international crime. The police detective represented a man whose duty to serve and protect came before his personal desires and goals. The procedural was not enduring as a genre, with the exception of television's *Columbo*, which has run since 1967; however, its hero—the police detective—has remained the norm for the detective genre.

The assurances of the procedural paled in the face of social insecurity in the late 1960s and 1970s. President Nixon's hard-line politics regarding crime, the failure of the Vietnam experience, internal disturbance, social unrest, and the loss of confidence in the police undermined this image of masculinity as competent and empowered. Instead, a violent and vigilante cop appeared—epitomized by Clint Eastwood's Harry Callahan in *Dirty Harry* (1971)—as the antidote to burgeoning crime. The vigilante cop hero represented violent, independent, and defiant masculinity that could annihilate crime when the bureaucracy of law enforcement made the police seem impotent.

The impact of second-wave feminism had thrown social conceptions of masculinity into flux by the 1980s and led to conflicting conceptions of positive masculinity in the media. The "new man" materialized, for example in television's *Magnum P.I.*, who embodied a somewhat feminized type of masculinity: He was sensitive, romantic, and fashion conscious. Simultaneously, however, the "retributive man"—the successor of the vigilante cop—was popular, such as John McClane in *Die Hard* (1988). The action cop with his emphasis on physicality and violence embodied hypermasculity and emerged in part as a backlash to the newer, more feminized images of masculity that pervaded the media, especially fashion magazines.

Since the early 1990s, a shift has taken place in the type of masculinity that society deems admirable—from the appreciation of physical masculinity to that of masculinity defined as intellectual and vulnerable—and it has prompted a similar shift in the representation of masculinity in the media. There has been a return to a thinking detective—a criminalist—not dissimilar to the first sleuths of the detective genre. Originating in the fiction of authors such as Thomas Harris and Patricia Cornwell, the criminalist—or forensic detective—has flourished on the big and small screens. Criminalists such as Detective Somerset of *Seven* (1995) and Agent Clarice Starling of *Silence of the Lambs* (1991) and *Hannibal* (2001) have thrived in film, while Gil Grissom of America's *C.S.I.: Criminal Scene Investigation*, Sam Ryan of Britain's *Silent Witness*, and Dominic DaVinci of Canada's *DaVinci's Inquest* are evidence of the criminalist's success on television. Criminalists employ observation, forensic science, and profiling rather than firepower and violence to solve cases and to track serial killers. With this emphasis on intelligence over muscularity and the reliance on weapons, new kinds of detective heroes have emerged, including women, older, and ethnic detectives.

Just as the heroes of the genre have altered over time, so too have the kinds of crime they have fought. The classical detective story was distinguished by nonviolent crime, like theft, or distinctly bloodless crime, like murder by poison or asphyxiation. However, with film noir, murder was taken out of the drawing room and onto the city streets, where guns and violence became characteristic elements of crime. As descendants of the frontier hero, the vigilante and action cops blew away criminals with increasing firepower and escalating bloodshed. In opposition to white, heterosexual, masculine heroes, criminals were independent women (*Black Widow*, 1987), black men (*Sudden Impact*, 1983), homosexual men (*The Silence of the Lambs*), and lesbians (*Basic

Instinct, 1992). More recently, the villain is the serial killer (*Seven*), and the criminalist uses science rather than violence to hunt him. However, this is merely a displacement of masculine violence and backlash from action heroes to serial killers who rape, mutilate, torture, and kill mainly women in a brutal spectacle of gore. Thus, the shifting representation of detective heroes and the crimes they investigate can be seen as occurring in conjunction with broader social change. The icon of the detective has begun, and will continue, to evolve beyond the traditional white male action hero and offers audiences assuring images of masculinity, and more recently femininity, that can bring a halt to crime.

Philippa Gates

Further Reading:

Delamater, Jerome, and Ruth Prigozy, eds. 1988. *The Detective in American Fiction, Film, and Television.* Westport, CT: Greenwood Press.

Everson, William K. 1980. *The Detective in Film.* Secaucus, NJ: Citadel Press.

Jeffords, Susan. 1994. *Hard Bodies: Hollywood Masculinity in the Reagan Era.* New Brunswick, NJ: Rutgers University Press.

King, Neal. 1999. *Heroes in Hard Times: Cop Action Movies in the U.S.* Philadelphia: Temple University Press.

Krutnik, Frank. 1991. *In a Lonely Street: Film Noir, Genre, Masculinity.* London: Routledge.

Lehman, David. 2000. *The Perfect Murder: A Study in Detection.* Ann Arbor, MI: University ofMichigan Press.

Mandel, Ernest. 1984. *Delightful Murder: A Social History of the Crime Story.* London: Pluto Press.

Naremore, James. 1998. *More than Night: Film Noir in its Contexts.* Berkeley, CA: University of California Press.

Parish, James Robert, and Michael R. Pitts. 1990. *The Great Detective Pictures.* Metuchen, NJ: Scarecrow Press.

Reiner, Robert. 1985. *The Politics of the Police.* Brighton, UK: Wheatsheaf Books.

Dickens, Charles (1812–1870)

The novels of Victorian writer Charles Dickens provide a rich field for the study of gender and masculinity in the emerging middle classes in the nineteenth century. His abiding interest in the condition of children in Victorian England and portraits of gentlemen and aspiring gentlemen give insight into the constructions of gender in a rapidly changing, newly industrialized England. An examination of his work reveals a deepening consideration of the psychology of self-definition and identity, and the influence of social norms on identity. Dickens does not always endorse or accept Victorian ideals of identity and class unequivocally, and he often gives the reader a character that resists or somehow subverts expectations of gender and class. However, the presence and power of those social conventions and ideals are always apparent. Dickens was the author of fifteen novels, some of them among the most well known in English literature. He was also a magazine publisher and editor, an energetic public reader of his own work, and author of countless periodical articles and short stories.

Charles Dickens was born on 7 February 1812, at Portsmouth to John and Elizabeth Dickens. He was the eldest of eight children and his relatively untroubled childhood was abruptly changed in 1824 when the family fortunes took a turn for the worse and his father, a naval pay clerk, was jailed in the Marshalsea debtor's prison in London, which was later to become the setting for *Little Dorrit* (1855). The young, sensitive Dickens was forced to work at Warren's Shoeblacking Factory, labeling bottles. This experience seems to have been the single most formative experience of the novelist's childhood, and one that, in later life, he recalled with great bitterness. Many readers and critics of Dickens trace his lifelong interest in the treatment of children in Victorian England to this experience, and it is his interest in children and the development of character and identity that holds the most interest for gender studies.

Dickens is concerned with what happens to these boy children as they grow into society. His novels examine the "lower reaches of the middle class in its most anxious phase of self-definition" (Gilmour 1981, 106). Perhaps because of his own middle-class roots, Dickens was fascinated with the question of what constituted a gentleman and the nature of manly, as well as womanly, virtue. Dickens contributes significantly to the ongoing conversation about societal expectations of men and the conflicting pressures on them to behave in a prescribed manner. More specifically, Dickens focused particularly on the difficulties of rising in class to become a gentleman (Gilmour, 1981, 103) in a society that saw a decline in the influence of the aristocracy that corresponded with a rise in the influence of business and the man of commerce. The novelist is less interested in the somewhat vexed position of the traditional ruling class of men and more interested in the difficulties of the middle-class man's definition of self. *Great Expectations* (1860) is Dickens's most notable examination of this subject, but in every Dickens novel, there is a man who must weigh the value of honor and decency against material success and the expectations of class.

The idealized characterization of very young male Victorian children was a feminized one (Robson 2001, 5), that is suggestive of Paul Dombey in *Dombey and Son* (1846). Further, the Romantic ideal of childhood innocence was tempered by a countervailing Evangelical perspective that called for a wary vigilance over the child to ensure the greatest chance for redemption (Robson 2001, 7). Dickens gives the reader a tragicomic example of these competing ideologies, and the hypocrisy they can engender, in *Bleak House* (1851). The evangelical Reverend Chadband "eloquently" preaches to—or rather at—the pathetic orphan Jo. Chadband is shown to be ridiculous and cruel by the omniscient narrator for his inability to see the suffering child that is right before him. These sometimes conflicting notions of the child were amplified when the boy grew to understand what was expected of him as a man. As middle-class Victorian boys entered adolescence, they left behind a gentle, ideal

Charles Dickens, 1876 (Illustrated London News Group)

ized childhood and prepared to make their way in the world as men of business, law clerks, and schoolmasters. Dickens's novels are particularly suited to a study of attitudes surrounding these occupations and to a study of the pressures that young men felt as they assumed both domestic and imperial responsibilities.

Dickens's first novel was initially published in monthly serials in 1836 and 1837. *The Pickwick Papers* was a commercial success, describing in humorous detail the (mis)adventures of an older gentleman and his group of companions. As Dickens's career progressed, his novels fall into three broad categories; these categories usually, though not always, follow a chronological development. Many of Dickens's early novels are concerned with the coming of age of a male protagonist, often orphaned or at least badly parented. *Oliver Twist* (1837), *David Copperfield* (1849), and *Great Expectations* (1860) are among the more familiar titles of this type. These novels have at their heart the personal progress of the hero. Other novels such as *Dombey and Son* (1846), *Bleak*

House (1851), and *Little Dorrit* (1855) combine the personal with the social in that a personal story of love and family unfolds against the richly textured, public backdrop of Victorian England's industrial, urban landscape. In *Hard Times* (1854), *A Tale of Two Cities* (1859), and Dickens's last completed novel, *Our Mutual Friend* (1864), the attitudes and concerns of society are placed in the foreground. Although rich in character and subplot, these novels have as their primary focus public and systemic, rather than private and individual, concerns. Dickens becomes increasingly convinced that the making of an identity is irrevocably bound up in systems and institutions, and the study of those Victorian systems and institutions becomes critical to his, and our, understanding of "manliness."

One of Dickens's more eccentric patriarchs, John Jarndyce, notes early in *Bleak House* that the universe makes an "indifferent parent," and the novelist is hard on selfish or self-serving parents, even as he endorses a faith in the natural goodness and dignity of the child. It is the "universe," left unmanaged and unchallenged, that perverts and damages the child. Good and manly qualities like compassion, protectiveness, and generosity, incipient in the male child, can all too quickly lapse into meanness and greed unless nurtured by a kind and loving parent or surrogate. Further, that loving adult is by no means necessarily female. Dickens provides the reader with adult men who are among the most nurturing and loving of his creations. Jarndyce of *Bleak House* and the blacksmith Joe Gargery of *Great Expectations* are but two examples of men whose decency is at least in part defined by their willingness and ability to care for and nurture children.

Dickens died on 9 June 1870, after suffering a stroke at his home at Gad's Hill. His final novel, *The Mystery of Edwin Drood,* was unfinished at the time of his death.

Anita R. Rose

Further Reading:

Ackroyd, Peter, 1990. *Dickens.* New York: Harper Collins.

Adams, James E., 1995. *Dandies and Desert Saints: Styles of Victorian Masculinity.* Ithaca, NY: Cornell University Press.

Kaplan, Fred. 1990. *Dickens: A Biography.* New York: Avon.

Gilmour, Robin. 1981. *The Idea of the Gentleman in the Victorian Novel.* London: George Allen & Unwin.

Hall, Donald, ed. 1994. *Muscular Christianity: Embodying the Victorian Age.* New York: Cambridge University Press.

Miller, Andrew H. 1995. *Novels behind Glass: Commodity Culture and Victorian Narrative.* New York: Cambridge University Press.

Robson, Catherine. 2001. *Men in Wonderland: The Lost Girlhood of the Victorian Gentleman.* Princeton, NJ: Princeton University Press.

Tosh, John. 1999. *A Man's Place: Masculinity and the Middle-Class Home in Victorian England.* New Haven, CT: Yale University Press.

"Dirty Harry"

A character played by Clint Eastwood in a series of cop action films in the 1970s and 1980s, Dirty Harry was a fantasy of cool, commanding, and spiteful male anger. *Dirty Harry,* the 1971 movie directed by Don Siegel that introduced the eponymous character, brought white male backlash against the women's, gay liberation, civil rights, and antiwar movements front and center in American popular culture. The film gave Eastwood his most unforgettably iconographic role, and it bears a political message specific to the polarized Nixon era. Harry Callahan is a tough cop chasing a murderer, but he finds his hands tied by laws that protect the rights of the accused and by politicians willing to acquiesce to the demands of criminal blackmailers. The churlish and politically pointed anger of *Dirty Harry* caused *New Yorker* critic Pauline Kael to charge that "this action genre has always had a fascist potential and it has finally surfaced" (Kael 1972, 388). Kael's "fascist" accusation stuck, and Eastwood would spend years defending himself from it. Eventually he would rethink the ideas that made the "Harry" films open to such attacks.

Like fascist art, *Dirty Harry* does indulge the desire for an overpowering force that obliterates inequities by means of sheer size and strength. On the other hand, Harry encounters not the compliant, adoring throngs that would await a fascist dictator, but a weak and ragtag scattering of individual and "feminized" concerns. This explains why the film displays such irritation toward ordinary people who get in Harry's way. Moreover, Harry scarcely embodies a wish for state power—quite the opposite. The character, in specifically American fashion, manages to appear antiauthoritarian and authoritarian at once. A working-class hero, Harry chafes at an authoritarian structure based on law that has taken power out of the hands of the enforcers. If the law prevents Harry from searching the prime suspect's home without a warrant, "then the law's crazy." Harry fights and resists a creeping feminization in sixties-era American society. When femininity refuses its patriarchal role in the "veneration of the phallus," which, according to feminist theorist Luce Irigaray, cares only "about keeping the phallic emblem out of the dirt" (Irigaray 1974, 117), when it seeks instead to project its values onto the patriarchal realms of law and enforcement, then it must be shunned and abandoned. Hence *Dirty Harry* opens with the gold emblem of a police badge and ends with that same badge being flung in the dirt by Harry, who feels that it has betrayed him, the last real man.

As the social polarities in America changed without disappearing after Vietnam, the later "Harry" films blunted the polemics while sharpening the formula. The films were known for acid taglines (e.g., "Do I feel lucky?"; "A man's got to know his limitations"; and "Make my day"); gaudy, violent setpieces early in the action, before the plots get going in earnest; and minority cop partners who start out fending off Harry's antagonism and end up admiring him. The films, like Eastwood's movies in other genres, display a growing preoccupation with racial is-

sues. The treatment of race starts out a clever tit-for-tat that allows the films to be racist and tolerantly "colorblind" at once and evolves into a somewhat more complex treatment of race relations. Ditto Harry's relations to women; in *The Enforcer* (1976), he even accepts a female partner, and in *Sudden Impact* (1983) he allows a rape victim to wreak vengeance outside the law. As Eastwood as director moved into increasingly revisionist territory late in his career, rueful shades of Harry and his ideology are strewn through his work.

Dennis Bingham

See also Cop Films; Eastwood, Clint
Further Reading:
Irigaray, Luce. 1974. *Speculum of the Other Woman.* Translated by Gillian C. Gill. Ithaca, NY: Cornell University Press.
Kael, Pauline. 1972. "Saint Cop." Pp. 385–388 in *Deeper into Movies.* Boston: Little, Brown.

Disco

Disco is a European/American popular dance music of the period ranging from approximately the early 1970s to the early 1980s. The use of recorded music (as opposed to live bands) in social dance settings—often a result of economic imperatives—dates from the early to mid-twentieth century, discotheques (the term related to the French *bibliothèque*) having become popular fixtures in such urban centers as Paris (Regine's) and New York (Electric Circus). However, the emergence of what has come to be known as *disco*—a term that may be seen as encompassing not only music but a range of styles, behaviors, and spaces (dance movements, fashions, discos, etc.) is inextricably tied to a largely (but not exclusively) black and/or Latino gay culture in New York City. It is perhaps this linkage of a popular cultural production with a nonwhite, nonheterosexual population that has been responsible for the invectives slathered upon disco. From the widespread epithet "Disco Sucks" (often emblazoned upon bumper stickers or T-shirts, for example) to the mass destruction of disco records at Chicago's Comiskey Park in 1979 organized by DJ Steve Dahl, critiques of disco, although ostensibly based upon aesthetic criteria, were frequently underscored with an air of homophobia. Despite the commercialization and "heterosexualiztion" of disco—due, in part, to the film *Saturday Night Fever* (1977) with its straight, male (and antigay) protagonist Tony Manero (John Travolta)—in the late 1970s, disco remained for many a sign of sexual (and racial) "otherness." An examination of the ways in which disco challenged stereotypical notions of masculinity is instructive in pointing out the contingent nature of all such gender constructions, as well as the crucial role of popular culture in both bolstering and engendering such constructions. Although disco enjoyed popularity internationally, this article deals mainly its manifestations in the United States.

Disco's emergence in the 1970s was concurrent with an era of great social upheaval—not only the Vietnam War, the Watergate scandal, and a lingering economic recession, but also the assertion of a right to social equality and social space by previously marginalized groups (as evidenced, for example, by the black power and gay liberation movements and the Stonewall Riots) (Brewster and Broughton 1999). As Byers (1995) notes, it is exactly in such times of "uncertainty" that those in power—here, patriarchal power—may find it necessary to attack the imagined locus of such "subversion" (see also Jeffords 1989). Thus, the increased social visibility of a racially mixed, homosexual culture (in such seminal discos as The Loft or The Gallery), as well as the increasingly important role played by such a group in the dissemination of a cultural production (and thus the shaping of popular musical taste) made disco a convenient target. It can hardly be a coincidence that the greatest calumnies hurled at disco were concomitant with its apogee of popularity in the late 1970s. Disco, it seems, might have remained

acceptable had it only "known its place." And while racism was certainly a factor in the antipathy towards this syncretic music (which drew upon such styles as funk, Philly soul, and European electronic music), it is worth noting that the negative response to disco could be found emanating from both black and white communities.

Disco's challenge to masculine power was not, however, confined to its very existence as a putative "gay music." Rather, the challenges were inherent in the forms of the music itself, as well as the actions of the dancers/listeners who were integral to its very existence. Krasnow (1993), for example, states that disco, through its use of both recording technology and the role of the disc jockey, problematized the idea of "authorship" so prevalent in the aesthetics and discourses of rock music—a symbol par excellence of a certain type of masculinity and masculine control of artistic form (see also Laski 1993). Furthermore, Hughes (1994), focusing on the omnipresent beat in disco—a beat which "penetrates" the dancer/listener—sees the constant, foregrounded rhythmic aspect of the music as engendering a type of "discipline," one which "disturbs the very foundations of conventional constructions of masculine selfhood," and requires an embracing of "the traditional role of slave" (151).

Indeed, the relationship of disco and pleasures of the body (rather than an enjoyment of textual or harmonic narratives, virtuosic musical spectacle, or intellectual stimulation) contributed to its "feminization," insofar as this bolstered the Cartesian binary of the "rational male" and "feeling female" (cf. Bordo 1986). Certainly many of the most popular disco songs served as invocations to revel in bodily sensation, either through dance (Earth, Wind and Fire and the Emotions' "Boogie Wonderland"; Heatwave's "Boogie Nights"; The Brothers Johnson's "Stomp"; Peaches and Herb's "Shake Your Groove Thing") or, whether through explicit or allusive imagery, sexual enjoyment (Andrea True Connection's "More, More,

More"; Musique's "Push, Push in the Bush"; S.O.S Band's "Take Your Time [Do It Right]"; Foxy's "Get Off"). Dyer notes that the eroticism in disco, however, stands in direct opposition to the phallic, thrusting quality of rock; it is rather an eroticism of the entire body, one that produces joy through open-ended repetition. Although by the late 1970s disco had become a widespread commercial success, moving out of an almost exclusively gay milieu (and into such famous locations as Studio 54 or Le Jardin), the hedonistic and erotic components remained constant, further problematizing notions of stereotypical masculinity. By compelling the dancer to perform the sensual (rather than simply viewing it from a "safe" physical and psychological distance, as in rock), disco blurred the lines between audience and performer (cf. Krasnow 1993), putting the male in the stereotypically feminine position of the sensual/sexual object. If, as Brett (1994) suggests, music and homosexuality are linked by dint of having been viewed at various times as "dangerous" (and deviant), then disco made such linked dangers—viewed here as a sensuality antithetical to constructions of the "thinking" male—a lived reality.

Stereotypical constructions of the masculine were further roiled by the appropriation of certain semiotic codes within the (gay) disco: for example, the hypermasculine appearance of the 1970s gay "clone," and the almost cartoonlike "masculine" characters of the Village People (as well as the textual allusions to masculinity in such songs as their "Macho Man," "YMCA," and "In The Navy," and Macho's "I'm a Man"). If gay men had appropriated symbolic, visual codes of masculinity, then how to reconcile this with "real" masculinity? (On this, see also Healey 1994). However, after disco's demise, "masculinity" was once again enlisted in an attempt to bring legitimacy to dance music. According to Straw (1993; see also Straw 1997), the purging of the sexual and the sensual (in favor of a political militancy), the foregrounding of technology (electronic tex-

tures serving as references to a mechanized, bureaucratic society), and the stance of connoisseurship vis-à-vis the music, served to "purge" the music of its "vulgar" appeal to the body, situating it instead in relation to the "thinking subject." Indeed, the recent genres of Filter Disco (a filter being an electronic device that affects the timbre of a voice or instrument) and IDM (Intelligent Dance Music) seem to support this contention. However, both technology and the role of the musical connoisseur were integral elements of disco (embodied, for example, in the role of the DJ), yet failed to mark disco with the imprimatur of masculinity. Additionally, such attributes may, in fact, be enlisted by both gay and straight audiences/actors in their constructions of musical gendering (Amico 2001), indicating the role of the discursive rather than the essential in the production of gendered meaning (see also Scott 1993).

Stephen Amico

See also Dance

Further Reading:

Amico, Stephen. 2001. "'I Want Muscles': House Music, Homosexuality and Masculine Signification." *Popular Music* 20, no. 3: 359–378.

Bordo, Susan. 1986. "The Cartesian Masculinization of Thought." *Signs* 11, no. 3: 439–456.

Brett, Philip. 1994. "Musicality, Essentialism and the Closet." Pp. 9–26 in *Queering the Pitch: The New Gay and Lesbian Musicology.* Edited by Philip Brett, et al. New York: Routledge.

Brewster, Bill, and Frank Broughton. 1999. *Last Night a DJ Saved My Life: The History of the Disc Jockey.* New York: Grove.

Byers, Thomas. 1995. "Terminating the Postmodern: Masculinity and Pomophobia." *Modern Fiction Studies* 41, no. 1: 5–33.

Dyer, Richard. 1995. "In Defense of Disco." Pp. 407–415 in *Out in Culture: Gay, Lesbian and Queer Essays on Popular Culture.* Edited by Cory Creekmur and Alexander Doty. Durham, NC: Duke University Press.

François, Anne-Lise. 1995. "Fakin' It/Makin' It: Falsetto's Bid for Transcendence in 1970s Disco Highs." *Perspectives of New Music* 33, nos. 1–2: 442–457.

Haden-Guest, Anthony. 1997. *The Last Party: Studio 54, Disco and the Culture of the Night.* New York: William Morrow.

Healey, Murray. 1994. "The Mark of a Man: Masculine Identities and the Art of Macho Drag." *Critical Quarterly* (Critically Queer issue) 35, no. 1: 86–93.

Hughes, Walter. 1994. "In the Empire of the Beat: Discipline and Disco." Pp. 147–157 in *Microphone Fiends: Youth Music and Culture.* Edited by Andrew Ross and Tricia Rose. New York: Routledge.

Jeffords, Susan. 1989. *The Remasculinization of America: Gender and the Vietnam War.* Bloomington, IN: Indiana University Press.

Jones, Alan, and Jussi Kantonen. 1999. *Saturday Night Forever: The Story of Disco.* Chicago: A Cappella.

Krasnow, Carolyn. 1993. "Fear and Loathing in the 70s: Race, Sexuality and Disco." *Stanford Humanities Review* 3, no. 2: 37–45.

Laski, Alexander. 1993. "The Politics of Dancing: Gay Disco Music and Postmodernism." Pp. 110–131 in *The Last Post: Music after Modernism.* Edited by Simon Miller (*Music and Society* Series). Manchester, UK: Manchester University Press.

Scott, Derek. 1993. "Sexuality and Musical Style from Monteverdi to Mae West." Pp. 132–149 in *Music after Modernism.* Edited by Simon Miller (*Music and Society* Series). Manchester, UK: Manchester University Press.

Straw, Will. 1993. "The Booth, the Floor and the Wall: Dance Music and the Fear of Falling." Pp. 249–254 in *Popular Music: Style and Identity.* Edited by Will Straw et al. Montreal, Canada: The Centre for Research on Canadian Cultural Industries and Institutions.

———. 1997. "Sizing Up Record Collections: Gender and Connoisseurship in Rock Music Culture." Pp. 3–16 in *Sexing the Groove: Gender and Popular Music.* Edited by Sheila Whiteley. London, New York: Routledge.

Disney, Walt(er) E. (1901–1966)

Walt Disney used his male, Midwestern (he was born in Merceline, Missouri) character-istics—which included the ability to think things out, steady entrepreneurship, and a wish to display the true values of life—to build an enormously successful career in a field once dominated mostly by itinerant artists, half-hearted attempts to produce newspaper humor, and sensation-breeding "penny-dreadfuls." Indeed, Disney elevated the lowly cartoon into a true art form, teaching life's lessons to everyone, and he did this by taking firm control of his vision and transforming his dreams into amazing reality.

Walt began early to recognize his interest in cartoon art. "[H]e made his first drawings [in childhood] of a whiskered rabbit waving frantically to another concealed in the grass" (Mosley 1990, 28). Early on he began to see animals as more than just animals, and he retained this ability into adulthood. And, he gave them personalities. Unfortunately, he was not suited to the realities of the farm where he lived as a boy: He once saw his brother Roy shoot a rabbit with an air gun and then have to kill it with a "rabbit-punch" and never forgot it. His disdain for the negative side of rural life greatly influenced the choice of his life's work. Disney would later include his childhood experiences and observations in his cartoons. Disney's profession was not one that was commonly chosen by men. As early as Walt's youth, he saw that "women were regarded as adorable, but fallible creatures and men were the ones who never let you down" (Mosley 1990, 133). However, his later experiences brought a realization of the sad human condition and gave him more of an impetus to show something that would mitigate it. Disney felt that the fairy tale "Snow White and the Seven Dwarfs" was perfect for him because it presented "a folklore plot that touched the hearts of human beings everywhere" (Thomas 1994, 130). (It should be remembered that men [the Grimm brothers] originally told the story of Snow White, but Disney made it more attractive to children by his animal personalities, so that his lesson "love conquers evil and death" was more palatable to the kids.) In another instance, Disney returned to America after a European trip with children's books with pictures of "little people, bees, and small insects" in a "quaint" atmosphere (Thomas 1994, 132).

Walt Disney (Library of Congress)

Disney decided to continue to experiment with incorporating people, animals, and insects in a single story. Disney thus gave human attributes to all his characters, even the bugs. He felt that audiences would better accept his ideas by this device.

Working with Disney and his brother was Ubbe "Ub" Iwerks. Disney shared many experiences with Iwerks, beginning in 1919 when they began work with the Kansas City Film Ad. Later, Disney started his own Laugh-O-Gram business. These were film short cartoons distributed in theatres. Disney soon began his own Laugh-O-Grams company with Ub Iwerks. Unfortunately, Laugh-O-Grams went bankrupt. So, Disney relocated to California to work with his brother, Roy. It was here in California that he and Roy started their own animation studio, called The Disney Brother's Studio. Disney wanted the company name to be changed to Walt Disney Studio. Disney would take the management end of the business and Roy would deal with the finances. The change proved beneficial and successful. Disney took charge over his interests.

Disney also learned early that he had to have control over virtually all aspects of his creations. Because he lacked this control he lost one of his most promising characters— Oswald the Rabbit. Oswald the Rabbit was created after Disney's *Alice Comedies* came to an end. He relocated to the West, where he and his brother began their own animation studio. They became acquainted with Charles Mintz, who was a New York–based film distributor (Gross, www.mr-moody.com). After suggesting that he create a character for his studio, he created Oswald the Lucky Rabbit. His rabbit was considered a success. Disney decided that with Oswald the Rabbit's success, he deserved more money. However, while in New York, Disney inadvertently discovered that Oswald's likeness was being used to sell various products. Disney requested more money for the success of his creation, but after numerous offers, Mintz offered less pay and reminded Disney that when he signed his contract with Mintz, he lost all rights. Oswald the Rabbit belonged to the Mintz family. Not only did Disney lose Oswald the Lucky Rabbit, but several of the animators who worked with Disney went with Mintz. At this juncture, Disney reminded Mintz that what just occurred could turn against him. Since he was not able to create another rabbit for the public, he decided to create another cartoon character.

Perhaps Disney's most famous character was Mickey Mouse. He vowed to make a virtual household word of this character, thus demonstrating the quality of male ambition even in his first works. In 1928, Disney created Mickey based on a mouse that had been discovered in his Kansas City office. Originally, Mickey Mouse was named Mortimer Mouse. Disney's wife, Lilly, thought he looked more like a Mickey instead of a Mortimer. Everyone agreed that the name Mortimer did not portray a character who stood up for the weak. With the help of Ub Iwerks, who gave the mouse a working personality and supplied the voice of Mickey, the mouse was born.

Disney's new character did not receive an enthusiastic reaction in his first cartoon, *Plane Crazy* (taken from the Lindbergh transatlantic flight). To avoid the problems that previously had occurred with Oswald the Lucky Rabbit, on May 21, 1928, Disney patented the name "Mickey Mouse." The critics did not seem to warm up to Mickey, and one of the problems was that there was no sound. It was not until *Steamboat Willie,* when sound was introduced, that Mickey was accepted by critics and the public. (This movie was one of the first that had a soundtrack.) Disney believed in his character and he did not give up on promoting Mickey.

One person who instilled insurmountable knowledge in Disney was Charlie Chaplin. Not only did he give Disney sound advice, he also was instrumental in providing a prop for Mickey Mouse's character—the Little Tramp. With the Little Tramp, Disney could show the mischievous side of Mickey, but also the innocent and optimistic side. Upon meeting Charlie Chaplin, Disney took his advice: To "protect your independence you've got to own every [thing] you make" (Thomas 1994, 114). Disney followed this dictate for the remainder of his life. Following Chaplin's advice paid off throughout his lifetime. On January 16, 1936, Director Rene Clair was reported by the *New York Journal* as saying, "The reason (Charlie Chaplin and Walt Disney) were considered 'outstanding figures in the movies' was . . . they act as their own producer, director, and even attend to their own stories and musical scores" (in Finch 1995, 85). As a matter of fact, in a lecture on

March 13, 1936, in Tulsa, Thornton Wilder was quoted as saying, "The two presiding geniuses of the movies are Walt Disney and Charlie Chaplin" (Finch 1995, 85). Yet another expression of praise of Disney was from Mary Pickford, who said, "There is only one Walt Disney. . . . He is the greatest producer the industry has ever turned out" (Finch 1995, 85). His genius didn't stop with just Mickey Mouse.

Walt Disney discovered that his movies were becoming quite a success with audiences of all ages. In the 1940s, he decided to create live-action movies with real actors interacting with cartoon characters. Again, Disney's vision was correct. One of his books from childhood was *Uncle Remus*. This book metamorphosed into the movie *Song of the South*. As a matter of fact, the song in the movie, *Zip-a-dee-doo-dah*, won an Oscar for best song in 1946. Financially, *Song of the South* did very well; however, Disney didn't realize how expensive it was to hire real actors. Money was not a big concentration for him; he left that to his brother. Three of the most recognized movies in the 1940s were *Pinocchio* (1940), *Fantasia* (1940), and *Bambi* (1942). In the 1950s, Disney devoted time to animated films such as *Cinderella* (1950), *Alice in Wonderland* (1951), *Peter Pan* (1953), *Lady and the Tramp* (1955), and *Sleeping Beauty* (1959), to name a few. In 1964, the movie *Mary Poppins* was released and considered "the biggest commercial success that Studio would enjoy during Walt Disney's lifetime" (Finch 1995, 368). The last film Disney was involved in was *The Jungle Book* (1966). Before Disney's death, he approved the movie *The Aristocats*. It has been noted that Disney's "greatest contribution . . . was the genius he brought to the art of animation" (Finch 1995, 357). He found pleasure in bringing laughter to his audiences.

This laughter was not evident in Disney's trips to various amusement parks. Discouraged by existing amusement parks on outings with his family, Disney envisioned Disneyland Park, to be located in Southern California. He wanted to build a place where families could go and enjoy themselves together. Another reason for his creation was his love of trains. Disney wanted to have a park that incorporated "vintage trains defining the perimeter of the Park . . . a reproduction of a small Midwestern town" (Finch 1995, 396). In 1952, plans began with the organization of a committee—the WED—whose job was to create the theme park. This committee later changed its name to WDI—Walt Disney Imagineers—and they were supplemental in the creation of Walt Disney World and the EPCOT Center.

Initially, the majority of finances for Disneyland Park were provided by Disney himself, owing to the skeptical reception of his latest idea by financial backers and even his brother Roy. However, in 1954, Disney received a financial break when ABC purchased more than a third of the shares of Disneyland, Inc., and Disney, in return, provided ABC with a show (titled *Disneyland*) (Finch 1995, 396). When other financial investors heard about the plans for the park, they wanted to play a financial role.

On July 17, 1955, Disney opened his theme park to the public. The reception of the park was immediate and Disney had a success on his hands. One of the successes of Disneyland was in creating togetherness, where children, as well as adults, could enjoy the park. He wanted to have a park that was a place where "the ideals, the dreams, and the hard facts that have created America . . . will be a source of joy and inspiration to all the world" (Finch 1995, 404). These words are placed on a plaque in Town Square in Disneyland.

In 1955, The Mickey Mouse Club originated with children who had no theatrical experience ever. He wanted realism in his show by having children who had talent, but were children nevertheless. These participants were labeled "Mouseketeers." These children would be appearing in a one-hour show. The show met with great success and one of his most famous "Mouseketeers" was Annette Funicello. The Mickey Mouse Club was successful for the first two seasons; however, the third season was fraught with corporative problems, predominantly commercials.

After settling problems with ABC and the demise of the Mickey Mouse Club, Disney decided to purchase ABC's shares in Disneyland. With this move, he had creative freedom and control over his enterprises. He and his brother decided to approach NBC and their idea of using color in their television shows. On September 24, 1961, *Walt Disney's Wonderful World of Color* debuted including "Ludwig Von Drake, lecturing on how the Disney cartoons moved from silent to sound and from black-and-white to color" (Thomas 1994, 287). Once again, Disney's vision proved successful.

Disney utilized a concept that he became interested in in the 1940s, Audio-Animatronics. Using the idea of clock's movement and an Ebsen puppet (a 9-inch replica of Buddy Ebsen) promoted the idea of having figures in 3-D to create real figures. He wanted these figures to have sound and authenticity in movement. He was able to present his latest invention to the 1964 New York World's Fair. Their exhibits were such a success that they were added to Disneyland Park and Disney World.

Disney and his brother realized the paramount importance of creating yet another theme park and this time having it on the East Coast. This time, the park would be named Walt Disney World. Money was no problem because everyone watched the success of Disneyland. Unfortunately, Walt Disney was not able to see his latest dream come true. Therefore, his brother Roy made sure that Walt's dream would come to fruition. On October 23, 1971, Disney World opened its gates. Sadly, on December 21, 1971, Roy Disney died.

From the beginning, Disney envisioned a "special place," where people would congregate as a "community." This is the vision of the Experimental Prototype Community of Tomorrow or EPCOT Center. "It's like the city of tomorrow ought to be" (Thomas 1994, 349). There was one addition to EPCOT and that was the monorail. It was not until October 1982 that the EPCOT Center opened, years after Disney's death. Author Ray Bradbury stated that "the influence of Walt Disney would be felt for centuries to come" (Thomas 1994, 359).

When Roy Disney passed away, the Disney Company remained vital and strong with the help of his son Roy O. Disney. He saw success in Michael Eisner (chair of the Walt Disney Company), Frank Wells (financial strategist), and Jeffrey Katzenberg (chair of Walt Disney Pictures and animation). With Roy Disney's influence and control, on September 24, 1984, Eisner and Wells were now responsible for the success and survival of the Walt Disney Company.

Disney wanted to keep male and female roles traditional. For some, the success of the Disney Company shows how both roles have a "constrained set of gender expectations that are proposed over and over" (Shields 2002, 2). However, the "fairy tale" at the heart of all Disney creations "reveal[ed] a gendered world structured under patriarchy" (Shields 2002, 3). Therefore, what worked during the 1950s would not be deemed as effective today.

Despite the problems encountered with the characters of Disney today, there was one thing that was never forgotten when producing and distributing Disney's cartoons, television shows, and movies, and that was quality. If the producers and the executives of the companies did not see quality in the product, it was not introduced to the public. They did accept societal changes and addressed them; however, they remained totally committed to Disney's visions. In 1983, the Walt Disney Company started the Disney Channel. Then, in 1984, the executives made the decision to have movies for children with the Walt Disney Studio and then entertainment for adolescent and adult audiences with Touchstone. In 1984, *Splash!,* the first Disney feature for adults, was distributed by Touchstone.

In 1985, Disney World introduced a new addition to the park, Disney-MGM Studio, a replica of Grauman's Chinese Theatre. Not only was there an emphasis on entertainment, but Eisner provided an educational program with the Disney Institute.

In 1988, in keeping with the style of *Mary Poppins,* Disney produced the live-action movie *Who Framed Roger Rabbit.* In 1992, following the success of Disneyland Tokyo, EuroDisney opened in France with Disneyland Paris. In 1993, Disney bought Miramax, which produced *The Crying Game* and *The Piano.*

Controversy seems to be at the core of the Disney Company and their audience's views of gender stereotypes and the company exhibiting little or no moral values. Disney's attempt to keep up with the changes occurring in the late twentieth century brought the company right into yet another issue. The newsletter of the Plainfield Christian Church, *Salt and Light* reported that on October 13, 1995, Disney offered health insurance to the domestic partners of gay and lesbian employees. The newsletter also explained how the Disney Company was instrumental in promoting "Gay Day in the Magic Kingdom." Originally, "Gay Day" was one day when gays, communicating on an e-mail message board, made plans to spend a day at Disney World. Since 1991, Gay Day has been occurring at Disney World. Currently, Gay Day has grown to include not just Disney World, but other Florida theme parks as well.

Disney promoted teachings and family values through his visions, which included characters (Mickey Mouse), theme parks (Disneyland/Disney World), exhibits (Disneylandia), television shows (*The Mickey Mouse Club*) and films (*Snow White* [1937]). Thus, Walt Disney created a world using the new technique of Technicolor and fantasy in his films and audio animatronics in his theme park exhibits. But, in his life and in his business dealings, he was a down-to-earth, no-nonsense controlling entity. Thus, did he reflect several of the "masculine" qualities of modern men: vision, seeing beyond everyday life, but mixed with strength of character enough to lead all his enterprises. Disney's life would not be complete without urban legends that have maintained a vigil throughout the years. One legend that has been passed down is the idea that he is "frozen" cryogenically. This claim is false. Unknowingly, this story has aided in his popularity, but it's definitely a rumor. He was interested in the technique, but not enough to have himself frozen and brought back. Walt Disney was cremated. Disney was an animator, but not someone who wanted to experience re-animation.

Another rumor is that Disney was gay. Disney was not gay. He was a product of his times and found men to be trustworthy and reliable. Women were considered the inferior sex. His marriage was very stable and despite his difficult mood swings, bouts with depression, and obsessions, his wife was right there for him. Disney had a temper, that is obvious, but at the same time, he knew what he wanted and he went after it passionately. His staff could always tell when Disney was in the building by his incessant smoker's cough. When he was in a bad mood, he was referred to as the "Grouching Bear." He was obsessed, focused, myopic, and a perfectionist. At the same time, he was caring and traditional in his thinking, always wanting to spread laughter and fantasy.

The legacy of Walt Disney involves his contribution to the world. His genius was in his creations of characters that would live forever. He was able, through his cartoon characters, movies, and theme parks, to invite everyone, young or old, and from every country, to be children and remain children at heart.

Karen E. Holleran

Further Reading:

Adinolfi, Anthony. 2002. "Animation: A Lost Art Form." At *http://www.bandaranimation.com/lostart.html* (cited 24 October 2002).

Bauck, Andy. 2000. "This Mouse Roars: Disney and the Power of Children's Entertainment." At http://www.washingtonfreepress.org/17/Disney.html (cited 28 August 2003).

Branom, Mike. 2003. "Fabulous! Disney Prepares for 13th Annual Gay Days." At http://www.inoohr.org/disney13thannual.htm (cited 27 August 2003).

Chew, Robin. "Walt Disney: American Animator and Film Producer." At http://www.lucidcafe.com/library/95dec/disney.html (cited 30 August 2002).

Finch, Christopher. 1995. *The Art of Walt Disney: From Mickey Mouse to the Magical Kingdom.* New York: Harry N. Abrams.

Greene, Katherine, and Richard Greene. "A Cartoon Menagerie 1923-1933." At Disney.go.com/disneyatoz.waltdisney (cited 27 August 2003).

Gross, David. 2003. "Charles Mintz (1896–1940)." At http://www.mr-moody.com/goldenboy/whoswho/mintz (cited 19 August 2003).

Johnson, Paul. 2002. "Walt Disney and His Influence on the Mass Media." At http://www.lib.niu.edu/ipo/ihy930354.html (cited 5 November 2002).

Maio, Kathy. 2002. "Women, Race and Culture in Disney's Movies." At http://www2.gol.com/users/bobkeim/Disney/diswomen.html (cited 22 October 2002).

Marling, Karal Ann. 1994. *As Seen on TV: The Visual Culture of Everyday Life in the 1950s.* Cambridge, MA: Harvard University Press.

Mickelson, Barbara, and David P. "History of 'Frozen Disney' Rumor." At http://www.snopes.com/disney/waltdisn/frozen.htm (cited 8 August 2003).

Mosley, Leonard. 1990. *Disney's World.* Lanham, MD: Scarborough House.

Plainfield Christian Church—CIM. "Is Disney Still Family Friendly?" 1995. *Salt & Light* 3, no. 11 (November): 1–2.

Polsson, Ken. 2002. "Chronology of Walt Disney." At http://www.islandnet.com/~kpolsson/disnehis/ (cited 30 August 2002).

Shields, Vickie Rutledge. 2002. "From Disney to Calvin Klein: The Implications of Sense-Making for Gendered Audience Reception of Entertainment and Advertising." At http://communication.sbs.ohio-state.edu/sense-making/meet/m99vshields.html (cited 5 November 2002).

Sherman, Richard. 2002. "Gender through Disney's Eyes." At http://www.units.muohio.edu/psybersite/disney/disneygender.shtml (cited 5 November 2002).

Thomas, Bob. 1994. *Walt Disney: An American Original.* New York: Hyperion.

Toan, Debbie. "Walt Disney." Pp. 35–63 in *Houdini / Walt Disney.* West Haven, CT: Pendulum Press.

"Walt's Story: Episode 1." At http://disney.go.com/disneyatoz/waltdisney/maincollection/waltsstoryepisode01.html (cited 30 August 2002).

Divorce

Few social phenomena evoke greater public concern than divorce. Divorces, which have doubled in the United States since 1966 and tripled since 1950 (U.S. Department of Health and Human Services), have been blamed for such social ills as juvenile delinquency and substance abuse, adolescent pregnancy and suicide, and declining academic achievement. In fact, the surge in the divorce rate in the 1960s and 1970s was not the unprecedented phenomenon that many assumed. Divorce rates in the United States have been climbing fairly steadily since the 1860s, reflecting long-term shifts in the nature of marriage, women's roles, and expectations of personal fulfillment. The growing number of divorces also partly reflected a decrease in the incidence of desertions and marital separations.

Nor has divorce had all the negative consequences attributed to it. Conflict-riven marriages seem to have more detrimental effects on children than divorce. Divorce's one indisputable effect is declining income for the divorced mother and her children, which, in turn, often results in shifts in neighborhoods and schools, exacerbating divorce's stresses. Despite recent efforts to better enforce child support payments, the United States has failed to adapt institutionally to the fact that a near majority of children now spend part of their childhood in a single-parent home.

Divorce is not a new phenomenon. Most ancient and many non-Western societies permitted easy divorce. The early Christian church was unique in embracing the doctrine of marital indissolubility. During the early modern era, however, many Catholic and especially Protestant reformers favored divorce as a way to punish moral wrongdoing, such as adultery. During the Reformation, most Protestant countries, with the notable exception of England, liberalized access to divorce. The goal of much early divorce legislation was punitive; in most instances neither spouse was allowed to remarry.

In the late eighteenth century, access to divorce with a right to remarry increased. The French Revolution witnessed the first experiments in no-fault divorce. The American Revolution not only provided ideological justification for divorce from patriarchal tyranny, it also encouraged the substitution of judicial for legislative divorce. In the 1830s, a number of states allowed judges to grant divorces on any grounds deemed appropriate. The federal system meant that divorce statutes varied widely; it also encouraged liberalization of divorce laws, as some states, including Indiana and later Nevada, competed to attract divorcing couples. In the late nineteenth century, recognition that the United States had the Western world's highest divorce rates led reformers to restrict the grounds for divorce. Nevertheless, divorce rates steadily mounted, as jurists interpreted statutes allowing divorce on grounds of physical cruelty to encompass mental cruelty. By the 1920s, 200,000 divorces were taking place in the United States each year.

Divorce remained disreputable well into the twentieth century even in the United States, and most Europeans were unable to obtain divorces until after World War II. A surge in divorces followed the war, but a steep rise only began in the 1960s, which encouraged enactment of no-fault divorce laws to reduce divorce's stigma, produce less adversarial proceedings, and eliminate the connivance that frequently accompanied divorce suits.

A low divorce rate in the past does not necessarily mean that marriages were happier then. Marriage was an economic necessity and mutual love was not considered an essential element. Families were interdependent economic units, and almost all unmarried women lived in extreme poverty, forcing many to foster out their children. The threat of physical violence or witchcraft prosecutions and a lack of economic and residential options forced women to tolerate unhappy marriages. Increased opportunities for wage labor, longer life spans, and an emphasis on the individual as opposed to the family as a corporate unit were essential elements in the spread of divorce.

It is important to distinguish divorce, a legal process that only became common in Western societies in the nineteenth century, from marital breakdown, which occurs in all societies. Although marriage partners in the past probably had lower expectations of marital happiness, there also existed escape hatches from miserable marriages, including desertion, separation, concubinage, and bigamy. In early modern England, the complexities of the marriage process under ecclesiastical and civil law (including rules about parental consent) allowed some partners to terminate marriages. One of the most striking folk customs was "wife sale," described in Thomas Hardy's *The Mayor of Casterbridge*. A woman, wearing a halter, was led to a marketplace where she was "sold" for a small, symbolic sum to another man.

Historically, divorce has been a woman's weapon; most petitioners have been female. Therefore, legislative efforts to reduce the incidence of divorce have tended to restrict women's ability to exit unhappy marriages. Still, divorce and women's interests are not identical, and today divorce usually results in an immediate drop in the woman's income. Partly, this is due to inadequate child support awards and men's failure to pay, as well as women's willingness to bargain child support for child custody.

The high divorce rates in the early twenty-first century do not necessarily signal, as some fear, a declining commitment to marriage. Even as alternatives to marriage have grown more feasible, marital expectations have also risen. Precisely because contemporaries attach a higher valuation to emotional and sexual fulfillment than their predecessors, they are less likely to tolerate loveless or abusive marriages.

Steven Mintz

See also Childcare; Deadbeat Dads; Fathers, Nonresidential

Further Reading:

Basch, Norma. 1999. *Framing American Divorce: From the Revolutionary Generation to the Victorians.* Berkeley, CA: University of California Press.

Bumpass, Larry. 1999. "The Changing Contexts of Parenting in the United States." http://parenthood. library.wisc.edu/bumpass/bumpass.html.

Chused, Richard H. 1994. *Private Acts in Public Places: A Social History of Divorce in the Formative Era of the American Family.* Philadelphia: University of Pennsylvania Press.

DiFonzo, J. Herbie. 1997. *Beneath the Fault Line: The Popular and Legal Culture of Divorce in Twentieth-Century America.* Charlottesville, VA: University Press of Virginia.

Griswold, Robert L. 1982. *Family and Divorce in California, 1850–1890: Victorian Illusions and Everyday Realities.* Albany, NY: State University of New York Press.

Halem, Lynne Carol. 1980. *Divorce Reform: Changing Legal and Social Perspectives.* New York: Free Press.

Hartog, Hendrik. 2000. *Man and Wife in America: A History.* Cambridge, MA: Harvard University Press.

Hetherington, E. Mavis, and John Kelly. 2002. *For Better or for Worse: Divorce Reconsidered.* New York: W. W. Norton.

"Increased Cohabitation Changing Children's Family Settings." September 2002. http://www.nichd.nih.gov/about/cpr/dbs/pubs/ti13.pdf.

May, Elaine Tyler. 1980. *Great Expectations: Marriage And Divorce in Post-Victorian America.* Chicago: University of Chicago Press.

Phillips, Roderick. 1988. *Putting Asunder: A History of Divorce in Western Society.* Cambridge, UK: Cambridge University Press.

Riley, Glenda. 1991. *Divorce: An American Tradition.* New York: Oxford University Press.

Stone, Lawrence. 1990. *Road to Divorce: England 1530–1987.* Oxford, UK: Oxford University Press.

U.S. Department of Health and Human Services, National Center for Health Statistics. http://www.cdc.gov/nchs.

U.S. Department of Health, Education, and Welfare. 1973. "100 Years of Marriage and Divorce Statistics in the United States, 1867–1967." National Vital Statistics System, series 21, no. 24. http://www.cdc.gov/nchs/data/series/sr_21/sr21_024.pdf.

Dogs

Dogs have come to be seen not merely as pets, but as props to project their owners' gender identities and personalities. Among men, dogs are linked specifically to their masculine gender identities (Hirschman 1994; Sanders 1990). Men interact with and describe their dogs in traditionally masculine ways. Regardless of the dogs' specific breed or size, men typically describe their dogs using traditional masculine characteristics. It therefore matters less which type of dog a man owns than that he simply has a dog—rather than another type of animal, especially a cat—as a pet. Because dogs are essentially extensions of the owners' selves, masculine dogs give an impression of masculine owners. Dogs are therefore used as gender displays for their owners.

To begin with, simply being in the presence of a pet makes one appear more approachable to outsiders (Sanders 1999). Dogs facilitate social interaction among unacquainted persons in public places (Robins, Sanders, and Cahill 1991). People are more likely to approach someone with a dog and initiate conversation and other interactions than they are with uncanine-accompanied persons. Thus, dogs have a "positive impact on the owner's social identity" (Sanders 1999, 7). However, dog ownership has additional consequences to individuals' identities, specifically their gender identities.

Because gender identities are at least partially socially constructed, they must constantly be established and reaffirmed to outsiders, as well as to oneself. Additionally, individuals often use cultural objects as "props" or use their relationships with others as a display of gender identity (West and Zimmerman 1987). As such, there is evidence that men use dogs to "do" gender and to display their masculinities.

Dogs can act as an extension of the self (Hirschman 1994; Ramirez 2001). Dogs act to "demonstrate features of owners' identities" (Sanders 1999, 6). Dogs become props that are decorative additions to the self. They were once the symbol of upper-class status and a sign of wealth (Sanders 1999; Hirschman 1994). While owning a purebred or expensive pet can be a visible sign of wealth and high social class standing (Hirschman 1994, 617), dogs also characterize one's gender identity. Dogs represent an "appropriate masculine image" and therefore reinforce masculinity in male owners (Hirschman 1994, 621). This is especially apparent with men who own dogs of larger breeds or of aggressive natures (Hirschman 1994; Sanders 1990). However, almost any size or type of dog will accomplish the display of masculinity in the owner. Small dogs can affirm masculinity in their owners by the owners' drawing attention away from the dog's size, while focusing on the dog's attitude and personality (Ramirez 2002). It is suitable for men to own small dogs, so long as their dogs have a tough demeanor. To date, there is no research on gay men's dog ownership practices. While it may be that they construct the relationship differently than do straight men, research has yet to uncover this.

Additionally, men characterize their dogs in ways consistent with their own personal (and typically traditional) masculine gender identities. The aspect of the relationship most valued by men is related to the activities in which they participate with their dogs, such as jogging, training, or other forms of play as opposed to the companionship itself that female owners value (Ramirez 2002). In doing so, the owners highlight the activities that they themselves enjoy the most as well.

These activities are traditionally masculine pursuits. Men see their dogs as workout partners or, in some cases, as athletes. Again, by highlighting these physical and traditionally masculine roles, dogs reaffirm the athleticism or outdoorsy traditions of men. Other men use their dogs more directly to showcase their masculinities. Men describe their dogs as "similar" or "exactly like" themselves (Ramirez 2002). Having an "outdoorsy" dog makes the owner be seen as "outdoorsy" as well. In cases such as these, dogs are a reflection of the owner's self. In general, men's descriptions of their dogs are descriptions of themselves (Ramirez 2001). Men essentially project their identities onto their dogs to maintain traditional notions of masculinity.

Other domesticated animals, however, can threaten masculinity. Men distance themselves from "less masculine" animals, cats in particular. They are seen as "too feminine" by male dog owners and are therefore seen as a handicap to their masculinities. While this is a generalization and many masculine men own pets other than dogs, the dog-preference tendencies among some men may be the result of a few factors. First, dogs are more easily controlled and trainable than are cats. As control is often symbolic of hegemonic masculinity, dogs may allow men to project a more masculine identity than other pets would. Secondly, relationships with dogs are often characterized as having a greater physical dimension. Similarly to cultural conceptions of friendships among men, men's relationships with dogs are often centered on activity rather than intimacy. Additionally, men—especially in relationships in which there is a power imbalance, as is the case with pets—have the power to impose meaning on their pets' behaviors and personalities to better reflect an appropriate masculine image onto themselves (Ramirez 2002).

Unlike other traditional props (e.g., cars and clothing) that typically signify social status, dogs can display more internal, unobservable, and intangible qualities, such as being stoic, independent, or adventurous. As such, dogs are the ideal backdrop for the elusive concept of masculinities. Men's characterizations of their dogs show that these men use their dogs as symbols of their gender identities. While women tend to characterize their dogs as nurturing, maternal, respectful, and even flirtatious, men most often describe their dogs, regardless of breed or size, as active, energetic, tough, and "adventure oriented" (Ramirez 2002). Dogs reinforce the sense of masculinities the owners believe they personify. No longer just "man's best friend," the dog of today is man's best signifier of masculinity.

Michael Ramirez

Further Reading:

Hirschman, Elizabeth C. 1994. "Consumers and Their Animal Companions." *Journal of Consumer Research* 20: 616–632.

Ramirez, Michael. 2001. "Identity Work among Dog Owners." (Master's thesis, Department of Sociology, University of Georgia).

———. 2002. "Dog Ownership as a Gender Display." (Unpublished manuscript, Department of Sociology, University of Georgia).

Robins, Douglas M., Clinton R. Sanders, and Spencer E. Cahill. 1991. "Dogs and Their People: Pet-Facilitated Interaction in a Public Setting." *Journal of Contemporary Ethnography* 20: 3–25.

Sanders, Clinton R. 1990. "The Animal 'Other': Self Definition, Social Identity and Companion Animals." *Advances in Consumer Research* 17: 662–668.

———. 1999. *Understanding Dogs: Living and Working with Canine Companions.* Philadelphia: Temple University Press.

West, Candace, and Don H. Zimmerman. 1987. "Doing Gender." *Gender & Society* 1: 125–151.

Domestic Violence

Investigations of domestic violence reveal significant relationships between interpersonal violence, masculinity, and gendered power relations. One in five women and one in fourteen men has been physically assaulted by a current or former intimate partner in their lifetimes (Tjaden and Thoennes 2000, 25–26). Men's physical violence against women is accompanied by a range of other coercive and controlling behaviors. Domestic violence is both an expression of men's power over women and children and a means through which that power is maintained. Men too are subject to domestic violence at the hands of female and male sexual partners, ex-partners, and other family members. Yet there is no "gender symmetry" in domestic violence; there are important differences between men's and women's typical patterns of victimization; and domestic violence represents only a small proportion of the violence to which men are subject.

Domestic violence was first placed on the public agenda through the activism of the women's movements. The term *domestic violence* refers to interpersonal violence enacted in domestic settings, family relationships, and intimate relationships, and is most readily applied to violence by a man to his wife, or female sexual partner or ex-partner. However, *domestic violence* is used also to denote violence between same-sex sexual partners, among family members (including siblings and parent-child violence either way), and by women against male partners. Three other terms commonly applied to some or all of these forms of violence are *family violence, men's violence against women,* and *intimate violence,* while newer terms include *relationship violence* and *partner violence.* Each of the six terms excludes some forms of violence, is accompanied by certain theoretical and political claims, and is subject to shifting meanings in the context of both academic and popular understandings.

Focusing on domestic violence, many definitions center on violence between sexual partners or ex-partners, excluding parent-child, sibling-sibling, and adolescent-parent violence (Macdonald 1998, 10). "Domestic" violence often takes place in nondomestic settings, such as when young women experience dating violence in a boyfriend's car or other semipublic place. Definitions of domestic violence or partner violence may exclude violence in relationships where the sexual partners have neither married nor cohabited (Jasinski and Williams 1998, x). Domestic violence is often understood as distinct from sexual violence, but the two often are intertwined in violence against women by male partners or ex-partners. While the phrase "family violence" more clearly includes violence against children and between family members, its utility is affected by how one understands the term "family" (Macdonald 1998, 12–13). Some feminists criticize both the terms *domestic violence* and *family violence* for deflecting attention from the sex of the likely perpetrator (male), likely victim (female), and the gendered character of the violence (Maynard and Winn 1997, 180). Yet the alternative phrase *men's violence against women* excludes violence against children or men and by women. The names chosen to describe and explain forms of interpersonal violence will never perfectly contain the phenomenon (Macdonald 1998, 36), and any act of naming involves methodological, theoretical, and political choices.

The word *violence* refers in the first instance to any "act carried out with the intention or perceived intention of causing physical pain or injury to another person" (Gelles 1997, 14). It may be tempting therefore to define domestic violence in terms of the presence of physically violent behavior by an individual to another person with whom they have or have had a sexual, intimate, or familial relationship. This approach is adopted by one school within domestic violence research, "family conflict" studies, in which domestic violence is measured using a tool titled the Conflict Tactics Scale (CTS). The CTS asks one partner in a relationship whether, in the last year, he or she or his or her spouse has ever committed any of a range of violent acts toward the other such as hit with a fist or an object, slapped, shaken, or kicked.

In one sense, any physical aggression between sexual partners or ex-partners rightly can be named domestic violence, as this communicates the message that such violence is unacceptable. However, this definition can obscure important variations in the meaning, consequences, and context of violent behaviors in relationships. Some heterosexual relationships suffer from occasional outbursts of violence by either husbands or wives during conflicts, what Johnson (1995) terms "common couple violence" (284–285). Here, the violence is relatively minor, both partners practice it, it is expressive in meaning, it tends not to escalate over time, and injuries are rare. In situations of "patriarchal terrorism" on the other hand, one partner (usually the man) uses violence and other controlling tactics to assert power and authority or to restore them when they are perceived to be breaking down. The violence is more severe, it is asymmetrical, it is instrumental in meaning, it tends to escalate, and injuries are more likely.

In the typical situation of male-to-female domestic violence, the man's physical aggression is accompanied by a wide range of other abusive, controlling, and harmful behaviors. He threatens his partner with the use of violence against her or their children, sexually assaults her, and intimidates her with frightening gestures, destruction of property, and showing weapons. He isolates her and monitors her behavior, which increases his control, increases her emotional dependence on him, and makes it easier to perpetrate and hide physical abuse. He practices insults, mind games, and emotional manipulation such that the victim's self-esteem is undermined and she feels she has no other options outside the relationship. Finally, he minimizes and denies the extent of his violent behavior, disavows responsibility for his actions, and blames the victim for the abuse (Gamache 1990, 74–79). Such efforts, while certainly not always successful, make it more likely that the woman will follow his rules and even act against her own best interests.

Recognition of such patterns informs some feminist authors' argument that domestic violence or intimate partner abuse can be best understood as chronic behavior that is characterized not by the episodes of physical violence that punctuate the relationship but by the emotional and psychological abuse that the perpetrator uses to maintain control over his or her partner. In fact, many female victims report that the physical violence they suffer is less damaging than the relentless psychological abuse that cripples and isolates them.

Why do some men use violence against women? Feminist scholarship rejects traditional explanations in terms of the actions of "sick" or "deviant" individuals, in which men's violence is pathologized and individualized (Maynard and Winn 1997, 182–184). Instead, domestic violence is seen to be perpetrated by normal men in normal families. In fact, men's violence against women is "normalized" in some contexts, in that it is the expression of violence-supportive cultural values, gendered power relations, and gender roles.

Feminist scholarship also rejects victim-blaming accounts in which women are said to "provoke" or "precipitate" violence against them by their actions, inaction, dress, or other characteristics. Instead, responsibility for violent behavior rests with the perpetrator. Feminist discussions are critical of accounts of domestic violence in terms of men's uncontrollable rage and failure to "manage their anger," pointing to the fact that men who abuse their partners choose with great care where, when, and how they will be violent (Pringle 1995, 101).

Feminist explanations of domestic violence have centered on male dominance, patriarchal ideologies of male supremacy and entitlement, and constructions of masculinity as aggressive and sexist. However, there is a growing emphasis on multivariate explanations, in which it is assumed that men's violence against women is "a multifaceted phenomenon grounded in an interplay among personal, situational, and sociocultural factors" (Heise 1998, 263–264). While such frameworks doc-

ument empirical relationships at multiple levels of the social order between the organization of masculinity and violence, they also begin to integrate biological, psychological, and interactional risk factors for domestic violence, synthesizing what has been a fragmented literature (O'Neil and Harway 1999, 220–230).

Violence against women is more likely in cultures in which manhood is culturally defined as linked to dominance, toughness, or male honor. In contexts where "being a man" involves aggressiveness, the repression of empathy, and a sense of entitlement to power, those men who are violent are acting out the dictates of what it means to be a "normal" male. Men with more traditional, rigid, and hostile gender-role attitudes are more likely to practice marital violence (O'Neil and Harway 1999, 192; Heise 1998, 278). Further predictors of domestic violence include a male sense of ownership of women, cultural approval for physical punishment of women, and the condoning of violence as a means to settle interpersonal disputes.

At the level of social networks and communities, social isolation is both a cause and a consequence of domestic violence, with higher rates of violence in contexts where family and community members do not intervene, husband-wife relations are seen as private, and women have poor family and friendship networks. Poverty increases the risk of abuse by providing fodder for relationship disagreements, making it harder for women to leave, and involving crowding, hopelessness, and stress (Heise 1998, 273–277). Especially among young men, attachment to male peers who encourage and legitimate woman abuse is a significant predictor of domestic violence (Heise 1998, 277).

At the level of the immediate context in which domestic violence takes place, there are further relationships between masculinity, power, and domestic violence. Cross-culturally, male economic and decision-making dominance in the family is one of the strongest predictors of societies showing high levels of violence against women (Heise 1998, 270–271). Wife abuse is more likely in couples with a clearly dominant husband and in societies in which men control the wealth, especially the fruits of family labor (Heise 1998, 271).

Domestic violence is also shaped by race, class, sexuality, and other social divisions. The lives of female victims who are poor, of color, lesbian, disabled, or in prostitution are seen as less "valuable" or "innocent" than the lives of women who are privileged, white, heterosexual, and so on (Russo 2001, 11–12). In turn, male perpetrators are more likely to be held accountable and criminalized if they are poor or men of color. Media and public discourses represent domestic violence by black men in terms of the interrelations of violence, blackness, and criminality, while white men's crimes are depicted as individual and unique (Russo 2001, 147–162). Histories of colonization, marginalization, and the disintegration of family and community structures shape interpersonal violence in general and domestic violence in particular in indigenous communities and ethnic group families (Sanchez-Hucles and Dutton 1999). Racism and classism are the context for the greater scrutiny, control, and criminalization by the police and the criminal justice and welfare systems to which poor people and people of color are subjected, and limit the ability and willingness of individuals and communities to report or respond to domestic violence.

Debates regarding the "gender symmetry" of domestic violence are an important focus of recent scholarship. Crime victimization studies (based on large-scale aggregate data from household and crime surveys and police statistics) find that men assault their partners and ex-partners at rates several times the rate at which women assault theirs and female victims greatly outnumber male victims (Tjaden and Thoennes 2000, 25–26). On the other hand, family conflict studies measuring aggressive behavior in married

and cohabiting couples find gender symmetries in the use of violence (Archer 2000).

The contrast between these findings is the product of differing samples and particularly of different definitions and measurements of domestic violence. The claim that domestic violence is gender-symmetrical is supported primarily by studies using the Conflict Tactics Scale (CTS). Yet the CTS is widely criticized for not eliciting information about the intensity, context, or meaning of the violent act, ignoring who initiates the violence, assuming that violence is used expressively (e.g. in anger) and not instrumentally (to "do" power or control), omitting violent acts such as sexual abuse, stalking, and intimate homicide, ignoring the history of violence in the relationship, neglecting the question of who is injured, relying on only one partner's reports despite poor interspousal reliability, and omitting incidents after separation and divorce, which is a time of increased danger for women.

Comparative data from Canada and Australia further illuminate both apparent gender symmetries and actual asymmetries in experiences of domestic violence. While the Canadian General Social Survey found that 7 to 8 percent of both women and men experienced some form of family violence, both this and a recent Australian study also documented that women were far more likely than men to be subjected to frequent, prolonged, and extreme violence, to sustain injuries, to fear for their lives, and to be sexually assaulted (Kimmel 2001, 19; Bagshaw et al. 2000). The Australian study noted, too, that men subjected to domestic violence by women rarely experience postseparation violence and have more financial and social independence. Female perpetrators of domestic violence are less likely and less able than male perpetrators to use nonphysical tactics to maintain control over their partners (Swan and Snow 2002, 291–292). As with female victims of domestic violence, research among male victims finds that forms of emotional, verbal, and psychological abuse are perceived to be at least as harmful as physical violence (Hines and Malley-Morrison 2001).

Women's physical violence towards intimate male partners is largely in self-defense, according to studies among female perpetrators (DeKeseredy et al. 1997; Hamberger et al. 1994; Swan and Snow 2002, 301) and men presenting to hospital emergency departments with injuries inflicted by their female partners (Muelleman and Burgess 1998, 866). On the other hand, women's intimate violence can also be motivated by efforts to show anger and other feelings, and a desire for attention or retaliation for emotional hurt, jealousy, and control (Hamberger et al. 1994), and CTS-based studies find significant proportions of couples characterized by female-only violence (Hines and Malley-Morrison 2001, 78–80). It is inadequate to explain women's violence simply in terms of their own oppression and powerlessness, and naive to assume that women are immune from using violence to gain or maintain power in relationships (Russo 2001, 16–19).

Some authors argue that men are likely to underestimate and underreport their subjection to domestic violence by women, because admitting such vulnerability is emasculating (George 1994, 149; Stockdale 1998, 63). There is no evidence, however, that male victims are more likely to underreport than female victims. In fact, men tend to overestimate their partner's violence and underestimate their own, while women do the reverse (Kimmel 2001, 10–11).

Men are victims of domestic violence also in gay male relationships, and such violence has distinctive dynamics in the context of a homophobic society (Vickers 1996). Theorizations of domestic violence in gay male relationships tend to draw on frameworks for understanding men's domestic violence against women, stressing the similarities between gay and heterosexual male batterers. For Cruz (2000, 77–79) and Island and Lettelier (1991, 50–51), gay men's abusive behavior is an expression of the social intertwining of masculinity with aggressive domination, in which men "doing gender" means enacting power, toughness, domination, and control.

Further shifts in recent scholarship include the theorization of the agency of and strategies of management and resistance used by women living with domestic violence, more complex typologies of perpetrators, and greater attention to the ways in which criminal justice systems and other institutions do and should respond to domestic violence.

Michael Flood

See also Batterer Intervention Programs; Battering; White Ribbon Campaign; "Wife Beaters"

Further Reading:

Archer, John. 2000. "Sex Differences in Aggression between Heterosexual Partners: A Meta-Analytic Review." *Psychological Bulletin* 126, no. 5: 651–680.

Bagshaw, Dale, Donna Chung, Murray Couch, Sandra Lilburn, and Ben Wadham. 2000. *Reshaping Responses to Domestic Violence.* Canberra, Australia: Office for the Status of Women, Department of Prime Minister and Cabinet.

Cruz, J. Michael. 2000. "Gay Male Domestic Violence and the Pursuit of Masculinity." Pp. 66–82 in *Gay Masculinities.* Edited by Peter M. Nardi. Thousand Oaks, CA: Sage.

DeKeseredy, Walter S., Daniel G. Saunders, Martin D. Schwartz, and Shahid Alvi. 1997. "Meanings and Motives for Women's Use of Violence in Canadian College Dating Relationships: Results from a National Survey." *Sociological Spectrum* 17, no. 2: 199–222.

Gamache, Denise. 1990. "Domination and Control: The Social Context of Dating Violence." Pp. 68–83 in *Dating Violence: Young Women in Danger.* Edited by Barrie Levy. Seattle, WA: Seal Press.

Gelles, Richard J. 1997. *Intimate Violence in Families.* 3d ed. Thousand Oaks, CA: Sage.

George, Malcolm J. 1994. "Riding the Donkey Backwards: Men as the Unacceptable Victims of Marital Violence." *Journal of Men's Studies* 3, no. 2: 137–159.

Hamberger, L. Kevin, Jeffrey M. Lohr, and Dennis Bonge. 1994. "Intended Function of Domestic Violence Is Different for Arrested Male and Female Perpetrators." *Family Violence and Sexual Assault Bulletin* 10, no. 3–4: 40–44.

Heise, Lori L. 1998. "Violence against Women: An Integrated, Ecological Framework." *Violence Against Women* 4, no. 3: 262–283.

Hines, Denise A., and Kathleen Malley-Morrison. 2001. "Psychological Effects of Partner Abuse against Men: A Neglected Research Area." *Psychology of Men & Masculinity* 2, no. 2: 75–85.

Island, David, and Patrick Lettelier. 1991. *Men Who Beat the Men Who Love Them: Battered Gay Men and Domestic Violence.* New York: Harrington Park Press.

Jasinski, Jana L., and Linda M. Williams, eds. 1998. *Partner Violence: A Comprehensive Review of 20 Years of Research.* Thousand Oaks, CA: Sage.

Johnson, Michael P. 1995. "Patriarchal Terrorism and Common Couple Violence: Two Forms of Violence against Women." *Journal of Marriage and the Family* 57, no. 2: 283–294.

Kimmel, Michael S. 2001. "Gender Symmetry in Male Victims of Domestic Violence: A Substantive and Methodological Research Review." *Violence against Women* 8, no. 11 (November): 1332–1364.

Macdonald, Helen. 1998. *What's in a Name? Definitions and Domestic Violence.* Melbourne, Australia: Domestic Violence and Incest Resource Centre.

Maynard, Mary, and Jan Winn. 1997. "Women, Violence and Male Power." Pp. 175–197 in *Introducing Women's Studies: Feminist Theory and Practice.* 2d ed. Edited by Diane Richardson and Victoria Robinson. New York: New York University Press.

Muelleman, Robert L., and Patricia Burgess. 1998. "Male Victims of Domestic Violence and Their History of Perpetrating Violence." *Academic Emergency Medicine* 5: 866–870.

O'Neil, James, and Michele Harway. 1999. "Revised Multivariate Model Explaining Risk Factors for Violence against Women: Theoretical Propositions, New Hypotheses, and Proactive Recommendations." Pp. 207–241 in *What Causes Men's Violence against Women?* Edited by Michele Harway and James O'Neil. Thousand Oaks, CA: Sage.

Pringle, Keith. 1995. *Men, Masculinities and Social Welfare.* London: UCL Press.

Russo, Ann. 2001. *Taking Back Our Lives: A Call to Action for the Violence against Women Movement.* New York: Routledge.

Sanchez-Hucles, Janis, and Mary Ann Dutton. 1999. "The Interaction between Societal Violence and Domestic Violence: Racial and Cultural Factors." Pp. 183–203 in *What Causes Men's Violence against Women?.* Edited by Michele Harway and James O'Neil. Thousand Oaks, CA: Sage.

Stockdale, Graham L. 1998. "Men's Accounts of Domestic Violence." (Masters thesis, Faculty of Health and Behavioural Sciences, School of Nutrition and Public Health, Deakin University, Melbourne, Australia).

Swan, Suzanne C., and David L. Snow. 2002. "A Typology of Women's Use of Violence in Intimate Relationships." *Violence against Women* 8, no. 3: 286–319.

Tjaden, Patricia, and Nancy Thoennes. 2000. *Full Report of the Prevalence, Incidence, and Consequences of Violence against Women: Findings from the National Violence against Women Survey.* Washington, DC: National Institute of Justice, U.S. Department of Justice.

Vickers, Lee. 1996. "The Second Closet: Domestic Violence in Lesbian and Gay Relationships: A Western Australian Perspective," *Murdoch University Electronic Journal of Law* 3. At http://www.murdoch.edu.au/elaw/issues/v3n4/vickers.html (cited 13 May 2002).

Don Juanism

A "Don Juan" is a man who feels a compulsion to find, seduce, and abandon a woman, usually within the shortest period of time possible, often as little as an hour or two. Such men report feeling distracted from other activities by the need to plan and complete this action within the time at their disposal. Although sexual attraction may play some part in the selection process, many report that almost any woman will do. It is not unusual for Don Juans to keep a count or even a detailed record of "conquests." Perhaps this is because they are so emotionally numb that, unless the act has been recorded, *it* (and they) will feel unreal. Women who "cut" sometimes describe a similar feeling. Most Don Juans say that, even if there was sexual pleasure at first, eventually the entire process is experienced as a tiresome chore.

In describing what they call "sex addiction," Earle and Crowe (1989) list what they see as common attributes of all addicts, sexual or otherwise. These include:

- a tendency to hold low opinions of themselves and to focus on their deficiencies;

- distorted or unrealistic beliefs about themselves, and their own and others' behavior;
- a desire to escape from or suppress unpleasant emotions;
- difficulty coping with stress;
- at least one powerful memory of an intense high that reduced stress, and an ever-present desire to re-capture the euphoric feeling; and
- refusal to admit that they have a problem.

This description is useful in understanding Don Juanism. As opposed to the casual wom-anizer, the Don Juan feels continually com-pelled to perform his act, usually experi-ences a letdown following a "success," and then craves still another adventure. Don Juans have a need for excessive admiration, a lack of empathy, and a tendency to be ex-ploitative. Given these qualities, it may be helpful to think of Don Juanism as a type of narcissistic personality disorder. Like most personality-disordered patients, the Don Juan is particularly treatment resistant. He tends to feel comfortable enough with his own behavior, and sees the concern of others as "their problem."

Don Juans usually perceive their mar-riages as satisfying, and have no wish to di-vorce. Their prognosis is therefore very poor, with one exception: Because they value their marriages they fear that discov-ery of their behavior will lead to divorce. This creates enough anxiety to propel them towards therapy. Such therapy is best ac-complished with a twofold approach: There must be intense individual therapy for the Don Juan, in which narcissistic issues and their relationship to acting-out behavior are fully explored. As the Don Juan's individual treatment yields results, parallel couples' sessions are also advisable. A systems-trained therapist should conduct both therapies.

Don-David Lusterman

Further Reading:

Earle, Ralph, and George Crow. 1989. *Lonely All the Time: Recognizing, Understanding and Overcoming Sex Addiction, for Addicts and Codependents.* New York: Pocketbooks.

Lusterman, Don-David. 1997. "Repetitive Infidelity, Womanizing and Don Juanism." Pp. 26–44 in *Men and Sex: New Psychological Perspectives.* Edited by Ronald F. Levant and Gary R. Brooks. New York: John Wiley and Sons.

Don Quixote

Alonso Quixano from Argamasilla, a town in the Spanish province of La Mancha, is better known as one of the most famous and beloved literary characters of all time—Don Quixote. Dreamt up by the Spaniard Miguel de Cervantes Saavedra for his novel *El Ingenioso Hidalgo Don Quixote de la Mancha* (1605—part I, and 1615—part II), the char-acter of Don Quixote strives to view reality through the lens of a chivalric romance. In keeping with the values of sixteenth-century Iberian society that embraced the medieval chivalric code of conduct—honor, loyalty, and service to king and country through mil-itary prowess, and the public performance of these good deeds plus ridding the world of monsters in order to be worthy of a woman's love—Don Quixote comported himself like a chivalrous knight from King Arthur's court, the socially acceptable behavior for men in Cervantes's day. However, not pos-sessing the socially acceptable age, physique, or even the economic background to be the masculine and mythical knight, the character of Don Quixote distorts and questions early modern society's assumptions of what it means to be a male hero. This perversion of the "Western European man of distinguished valor" is accomplished through parody and satire, because Cervantes is reacting against an antiquated notion of masculinity and cri-tiquing society's blindness to the evolving role of the man in a changing world. In fact, *Don Quixote* as a whole offers a social commentary on the large number of popular chivalric romances that followed and imitated Ariosto's *Orlando furioso* (1532) and Rodríguez de Montalvo's *Amadís de Gaula* (1508), and which preserved and advocated generalized and stereotypical notions of gender—the woman silently resides in the private and domestic space while the man communicatively marches in a public and legal space. Yet it is through Don Quixote and his adventures that Cervantes presents to the literary world a new type of protagonist who can be both loved and mocked, a modern antihero who laughs at outdated gender characteristics.

This critique is taken even further with the inclusion of the faithful squire Sancho Panza, the realist counterpoint character to Don Quixote's idealistic social deviation. Together they undertake adventures in which Sancho points out the folly and danger of Don Quixote's chivalry and physically suffers along with his master the mishaps and punishments that their chivalrous actions invite. Most importantly though, Sancho reminds Don Quixote of his unsuitability to be a hero in a world where chivalry is dead and there is no longer any social code of honor for men. In other words, both Don Quixote and Sancho Panza are the driving forces in a picaresque romance whose masterful narrative storytelling is the result of a dialogue between two friends with opposing opinions who help to define each other's masculinity. In fact, their loyal companionship also ushers in the modern idea of a "buddy relationship," in which men who engage with polemical ideas of philosophy and social behavior are able to interact with each other in a nonthreatening and character-building way. Thus, Sancho Panza's realistic warnings and Don Quixote's idealistic attempts to be a knight living out a chivalric romance together point to a slowly shifting definition of masculinity and early modern society's inability at times to accommodate this evolving role of literature, men, and masculine friendships.

A scene from Don Quixote, *Miguel de Cervantes's great tale of adventure. Spain's most celebrated author, Cervantes published this tale of the adventures of an ailing knight and his faithful sidekick in 1605. (Library of Congress)*

From a literary perspective, the poor retired gentleman who transforms himself into Don Quixote and deviates from society's norms for basic male behavior by knighting himself and by engaging in ridiculous adventures seemingly advocates the Platonic argument that literature is potentially dangerous for men and a male republic. In fact, at the beginning of the novel, Don Quixote's deviant behavior is neatly explained as madness instigated by his excessive reading of chivalric romances. Yet, some scholars believe that in his attempts to manage his life as if he were "The Knight of the Sorrowful Countenance," Don Quixote's literary madness brings to light these questions: How can literature serve as a lens for deciphering reality if that reality has been altered? And what, if any, is the role of the hero anymore? These questions not only affected and inspired the development of the novel, but they also challenged how gender roles and specifically masculinity were to be praised, described, and illustrated in both literature and in early modern society.

Considering that the end of the sixteenth century and the beginning of the seventeenth century were the age of pirates, shifting cartographies, encounters with indigenous peoples, and continuous New World discoveries, it is no wonder that romance as a genre, the hero as a concept, and the European man as the center of the universe were brought under scrutiny. In this unsettling and burgeoning new age, there was a need for stable axes of social definition. In this light, *Don Quixote* could be considered as suggesting that early modern society presented men with only two choices for social behavior and self-definition. In other words, the modern knight who strolled through society was either Don Quixote's realist companion Sancho Panza who lacks education and is unable to read or the idealist Don Quixote himself who lacks societal common sense and misreads the world. But it is through his most famous adventures—mistaking a group of windmills for giants, erroneously freeing a chain gang of criminals, and interrupting a meeting of lovers—that Don Quixote not only confuses fact with fiction, but delivers his strongest criticism of the social and literary conventions of the day. Man was no longer the "Renaissance" individual around whom the world revolved. Instead, man and his masculinity were decentered, unmasked, and redefined by satire and realism, other male

companionship, and the oceans to the west. In fact, for some literary scholars *Don Quixote* foreshadows Daniel Defoe's *Robinson Crusoe* (1719) where the lost man at sea has a "buddy friendship" with Friday, an island savage, and together they redefine masculinity in the age of high seas adventures. It is in fact Cervantes who first points to the social instability and already shifting boundaries of masculinity in the early modern period that were underway with the adventurous character of Don Quixote.

Nhora Lucía Serrano

Further Reading:

Castillo, David R. 2001. *(A)wry Views: Anamorphosis, Cervantes, and the Early Picaresque*. West Lafayette, IN: Purdue University Press.

Castro, Américo. 1987. *El pensamiento de Cervantes*. Barcelona, Spain: Editorial Crítica.

Cervantes, Miguel de. 1999. *Don Quijote: A New Translation, Backgrounds and Contexts, Criticism*. Translated by Burton Raffel. New York: W. W. Norton.

Fuentes, Carlos. 1976. *Don Quixote: Or, the Critique of Reading*. Austin, TX: Institute of Latin American Studies, University of Texas.

Hutchinson, Steven. 1992. *Cervantine Journeys*. Madison, WI: University of Wisconsin Press.

Mariscal, George. 1991. *Contradictory Subjects: Quevedo, Cervantes, and Seventeenth-Century Spanish Culture*. Ithaca, NY: Cornell University Press.

Spadaccini, Nicholas, and Jenaro Talens. 1993. *Through the Shattering Glass: Cervantes and the Self-Made World*. Minneapolis, MN: University of Minnesota Press.

Douglass, Frederick

See Slave Narratives; Southern Writers

Drag

See Stonewall Riots; Transvestism

Drug Abuse

See Chemical Dependency

E

Eastwood, Clint (1930–)

An American film star for four decades, the California-born Eastwood first fashioned his screen persona for Italian director Sergio Leone in ironic, sadistic European Westerns, the earliest of which, *Fistful of Dollars,* became a surprise box-office sensation in Europe. From 1968 on, Eastwood starred in American films, often under his own direction, as a glinting, omnipotent, and amoral rendition of the strong, silent, masculine archetype of American Westerns. For the Vietnam period and beyond, he became the new John Wayne, with a postmodern bent. Eastwood's persona was a pastiche of masculine codes—lean, tall, laconic, soft-spoken to the point where he speaks only to snarl out vague threats, an enforcer of a strongly subjective form of justice for a moral system in sad decline—one last, persistent strong male in an antiheroic and feminized world. Eastwood was an ahistorical fantasy figure for a Euro-American media culture increasingly forgetful of its history and presumptuous about its myths. Unlike all earlier stars of Westerns and war films, Eastwood made no attempt to create characters who might have inhabited a recognizable past. John Wayne himself wrote to Eastwood to protest the depiction of frontier settlers in *High Plains*

Drifter (1973) as vindictive, cowardly exploiters, saying "That isn't what the West was all about. That isn't the American people who settled this country" (Biskind 1993, 59).

Far from being an agent of progress for white pioneers, Leone's Eastwood (whose character, famously, was so archetypal as not to require a name) was a trickster whose main virtues lay in not being (all) bad and certainly in not being ugly. For Don Siegel in *Coogan's Bluff* (1968) and *Dirty Harry,* he was a contemporary figure who begrudgingly rescued from heinous criminals a society he regarded with sneering contempt. Under Eastwood's own direction, at least until the end of the 1970s, the figure was a mixture of both, an avenging man meting out punishment for personal, not social, wrongs. Always articulating the Eastwood protagonist was a camera and editing style in which Eastwood's physical frame, in its imposing substantiality, was contradicted by spectator positioning that appeared to look through Eastwood, thereby establishing the centrality of the gaze and the desire of a spectator assumed as potently, scopically male.

Attempts to take the Eastwood persona in a different direction occurred early. Eastwood and Don Siegel made *The Beguiled* (1971) almost a year before their definitive

Clint Eastwood in For a Few Dollars More
(Bettmann/Corbis)

collaboration on *Dirty Harry.* A fascinatingly peculiar male Gothic set during the Civil War, *The Beguiled* features Eastwood against type as a lying, predatory Union soldier who finds himself behind enemy lines, injured, and taking refuge in a girls' boarding school. The Eastwood character here was not only lecherous and dishonest but vulnerable. For his leering treachery, he is first symbolically castrated (the women amputate his gangrened leg) and finally killed. The releasing studio, Universal, had no idea how to sell a film in which Eastwood was not the all-powerful hero—assuming such a project could have been sold—and the film failed. Not for almost ten (very profitable) years would Eastwood again try to deconstruct the powerful male fantasy of this star's persona. But beginning in 1980, when Eastwood was fifty years old, he made career revisionism his project, alternating safe, reaffirmative projects like *Any Which Way You Can* (1980) and *Sudden Impact* (the fourth *Dirty Harry* sequel, 1983) with movies like *Bronco Billy* (1980), a comedy parodying Eastwood's indomitable image, *Honky Tonk Man* (1982), a male tearjerker casting Eastwood as a down-and-out country singer during the Great Depression, and *Tightrope* (1984), an atypical Eastwood cop film that suggests that an unconscious attraction toward violence to women dwells within authoritative white masculinity.

With a star persona as inflected by gender, race, and class politics as Eastwood's, career renovation meant ideological revisionism. *Tightrope* in particular attracted the attention of gender critics, with major articles by Christine Holmlund (1986) and Judith Mayne (1987). By the 1990s, Eastwood had become the poster boy for the academic thesis that masculinity is a construction replete with ruptures and contradictions. Eastwood helped this project along by continuing to produce, direct, and star in films that threw his once-monolithically omnipotent persona into increasingly troubled waters. In *White Hunter, Black Heart* (1990) Eastwood played "bad boy" director John Huston in a film that turned out to be less about Huston making *The African Queen* (or not making it, as Peter Viertel, who wrote his 1953 novel based on the experience of working on the script with Huston) and more about a powerful and irresponsible white male who uses his power as an opportunity for self-indulgent and destructive macho gamesmanship.

Unforgiven (1992) brought Eastwood's persona full-circle. He plays a reformed Western gunfighter—a term that, in this film, is a euphemism for "mass murderer"—who, with his Christian wife dead, is tempted into the life of a bounty hunter (like Leone's Man with No Name) and falls by degrees back into the mentality of a bloodthirsty killer. *Unforgiven* reverses most of the meanings of earlier Eastwood films. The vengeful identification figure is now a psychopath. Weakness now applies to men who give into their violent impulses, not to those who look for alternatives to violence. The authoritarian Dirty Harry figure is reimagined as Sheriff Little Bill Daggett (Gene Hackman), a tyrant who runs his town as a police state, cozying

up to the troublemakers in town and minimizing the complaints of female victims of
violence. Where Dirty Harry and his
Western counterparts had undeniable criminals to hunt, Will Munny (Eastwood) and his
fellow bounty hunters search for their prey
on the basis of rumors and anecdotes, the
truth being considerably less certain than in
the seventies films where, if the goodness of
the Eastwood hero was not always clear-cut
(giving the strong point-of-view positioning
with the protagonist an air of danger and
nonconformity), the evil of the villains was
always beyond doubt. Moreover, where the
seventies films allowed identification with a
kind of transcendental phallocentrism,
Unforgiven debunked the equation of gun and
phallus. Significantly, *Unforgiven* was made
from a script written by David Webb Peoples
in 1976. (Peoples, in the documentary accompanying the 2002 DVD, says he wrote
it after watching *Taxi Driver* [1976], a film
that refers to *Dirty Harry* and deconstructs
Eastwood-style messianic vigilantism.) Eastwood thus returns to his definitive period,
the 1970s, and makes the very kind of damn-
ing revisionist film that ran diametrically
counter to the films with which he made his
reputation then.

Eastwood's films since *Unforgiven* have
continued to revise his unforgiving persona,
venturing into such new territories as sympathy for the criminal (*A Perfect World,* 1993),
romantic melodrama (*The Bridges of Madison
County,* 1995), and aging and illness (*Space
Cowboys,* 2000; *Blood Work,* 2002). Eastwood's
new fascination with his own frailty and
mortality reached a point where "Go ahead.
Make my day" (*Sudden Impact,* 1983) gave
way to "I've got to go home and take my
pills" (in *Blood Work*). Nonetheless, despite the
inevitable harmlessness that time, age, and
honors award to a star as durable as
Eastwood, the monolithic harshness of his
original persona made an indelible mark
upon international images of masculinity in
the postmodern age.

Dennis Bingham

See also "Dirty Harry"
Further Reading:
Beard, William. 2000. *Persistence of Double Vision:
    Essays on Clint Eastwood.* Edmonton: University
    of Alberta Press.
Bingham, Dennis. 1994. *Acting Male: Masculinities
    in the Films of James Stewart, Jack Nicholson, and
    Clint Eastwood.* New Brunswick, NJ: Rutgers
    University Press.
Biskind, Peter. 1993. "Any Which Way He Can."
    Premiere (April): 52–60.
Holmlund, Christine. 1986. "Sexuality and Power
    in Male Doppelgänger Cinema: The Case of
    Clint Eastwood's *Tightrope.*" *Cinema Journal* 26,
    no. 1: 31–41.
———. 2002. "The Aging Clint." In *Impossible
    Bodies: Femininity and Masculinity at the Movies.*
    London and New York: Routledge.
Mayne, Judith. 1987. "Walking the *Tightrope* of
    Feminism and Male Desire." In *Men in Feminism.*
    London and New York: Routledge.
Schickel, Richard. 1996. *Clint Eastwood: A
    Biography.* New York: Alfred A. Knopf.
Smith, Paul. 1993. *Clint Eastwood: A Cultural
    Production.* Minneapolis: University of
    Minnesota Press.

Eating Disorders

Until the last decades of the twentieth century, conventional wisdom has held that only
women suffer with eating disorders such as
anorexia and bulimia nervosa. Although
health professionals and academics are finding increasingly that men are also susceptible, the general public is still largely unaware. As a result, there is little information
to help health professionals deal adequately
with eating disorders when they occur in
men. Although the clinical literature on
women's eating disorders is a good place to
begin, emerging research (Drummond
1999, 2002; Pope et al. 2000) is identifying
specific issues for men.

Although the anorexic male and female
both display excessively lean physiques, and
bulimics both binge and purge with intense
regularity, there are differences linked to
gender, to the ways in which masculinity and
femininity are constructed and represented
(Drummond 2002). First, there are the

undisputed gender issues that affect men's health in general.

Men are largely reticent to seek assistance for any health condition for fear of appearing weak, out of control, or somehow failed as a man. With eating disorders specifically, men confront additional and particular concerns. Eating disorders are commonly regarded as feminine illnesses. Fear of ridicule or embarrassment therefore disincline men to seek assistance (Drummond 1999, 2002; Pope et al. 2000). Further, eating disorders are mental illnesses, which are also widely considered to be feminine conditions. The growing literature on masculinity and men's health suggests that it will be a significant challenge to conquer these conceptions and get men to seek health care interventions when they need them.

For men, the links among sport, physical activity, and the body may be explanatory factors in the incidence and also the potential severity of eating disorders. Evidence coming to light indicates that men use physical activity and sport as a primary means of weight loss and they often couple these activities with food restriction or dietary restraint. Thus, men can often legitimize or mask eating-disordered, body-obsessed behaviors through the use of normalized physical activity. By claiming to be a "marathon runner" or "triathlete," men can create an ideal facade behind which to hide deviant— and dangerous—behaviors. As Pope et al. (2000) have identified, it is not only endurance athletes, but also bodybuilders who display excessively controlling body behaviors (see also Klein 1993).

A related issue is competition, which may be another important factor in male eating disorders. Men are encouraged to compete with each other from an early age, across a range of activities. Because competition becomes such a normal way of operating in the world for men, eating disorders can themselves become the focus of competition. These competitions can take place among others, as with weight loss, for example; with family members, as expressed in terms of defiance; and also with oneself in relation to living up to individual and personal expectations and standards (Drummond 1999, 2002).

Treatment options that include placing eating disordered patients with one another in order to provide unity and a sense of belonging therefore may need to be adjusted or changed when it comes to treating male patients. In fact, current and past male sufferers of anorexia and bulimia nervosa have voiced highly critical opinions of being "lumped" in with female eating-disordered patients. Men claim to have needs different from women and therefore to require different alternatives (Drummond 1999, 2002).

In the early twenty-first century, men are beginning to share in the commercialization and commodification of the body that has helped make women susceptible to body-based obsessions for some time. A number of factors help determine whether these obsessions lead to serious illnesses such as anorexia and bulimia nervosa. However, it cannot be questioned that the male body is being placed under greater scrutiny and perfectionist pressure than ever before. Contemporary advertising markets the male body as an object of envy for both males and females. This is not to say that advertising causes male body obsession and subsequent eating disorders. But it does help normalize an ideal of the masculine physique, which is strong, defined, athletic in appearance, devoid of fat, and nearly impossible to attain. The onslaught of such media images needs to be addressed, much in the same way that women's body-image and eating disorders have been theorized and acted upon over the past three decades of the twentieth century. Plus, high quality research across a broad spectrum of approaches, from qualitative, to quantitative, to sociocultural, to biomedical, to psychological is urgently required.

Murray Drummond

See also "Adonis Complex"; Anabolic and Androgenic Steroids; Bodybuilding, Contemporary

Further Reading:

Drummond, Murray. 1999. "Life as a Male 'Anorexic.'" *Australian Journal of Primary Health Interchange* 5, no. 2: 80–89.

———. 2002. "Men, Body Image and Eating Disorders." *International Journal of Men's Health* 1, no. 1.

Klein, A. 1993. "Little Big Men. Bodybuilding Subculture and Gender Construction." Albany, NY: The State University of New York Press.

McCreary, D., and D. Sasse. 2000. "An Exploration of the Drive for Muscularity in Adolescent Boys and Girls." *Journal of American College Health* 48: 297–304.

Pope, H., K. Phillips, and R. Olivardia. 2000. *The Adonis Complex. The Secret Crisis of Male Body Obsession.* New York: Free Press.

Effeminacy

Effeminacy can refer to any person or thing that is expected to be masculine that is instead feminine. Frequently used in a misogynistic manner to chastise men for not being sufficiently "manly," the concept of effeminacy is predicated upon a belief in distinct gender-based identities. According to the *Oxford English Dictionary,* to be effeminate has meant "womanish, enervated, feeble, self-indulgent, voluptuous, unbecomingly delicate or over-refined" (82). However, the less common, more positive, sense of effeminate as "gentle, tender, [or] compassionate" (82) is also noted. Despite the fact that the negative interpretation of effeminacy has been dominant in Western culture, there have also been persistent countermovements that celebrate effeminacy as a sign of culture, refinement, and sensibility. In sexual terms, effeminacy became the stereotypical attribute of the passive partner in homosexual couplings after the Oscar Wilde trial of 1895. Previously, excessive heterosexual desire or masturbation were cited as equally likely causes of effeminacy. In general, the label of effeminacy has had less to do with censuring any one particular sexual act than with ensuring the continuation of power structures based on the maintenance of clearly demarcated male and female social roles. By drawing attention to the way gender is performed, effeminacy reveals the unavoidable instability at the heart of all performances of masculinity.

The idea that to be effeminate is to forfeit mastery can be seen in the works of Shakespeare (Sinfield 1994, 27). John Ford, also writing in the seventeenth century, highlighted the illegitimacy of Perkin Warbeck's claim to the throne by emphasizing the pretender's effeminate characteristics (Howard 1988, 272). Effeminacy, according to these writers, prevents a man from properly wielding power because strict self-discipline—including the strict regulation of one's sexual desires—is a prerequisite for the idealized autonomous manhood that was supposed to uphold the power of the nation. Later in the seventeenth century, "the fop" and "the rake" were both accused of effeminacy because their sexual behaviors "disturb[ed] the hierarchies of family, inheritance, alliance and property" (Sinfield 1994, 37). The fop was considered to be effeminate because of his inability to dominate women, while the rake was considered to be effeminate because his excessive love of women could lead to adultery.

Similarly, in the eighteenth century, sexual behavior believed to be antisocial, like masturbation or sodomy, was labeled effeminate (Sharrock 1997, 411). Although Carter (1997) argues that effeminacy implied asexuality more commonly than sodomy, he concurs that effeminacy was used to label any gendered activity deemed socially deviant (432). Effeminacy was believed to be antisocial because it was associated with a worldview that privileged the rights of the individual above the requirements of the state (Bristow 1995, 4–5). As Sharrock (1997) puts it, "the health or disease of the body and body politic is seen to be dependent upon the man's being able to 'perform' his part well" (422). Effeminacy was seen as a general sign of the aristocracy, although the men who attended "molly-houses"—eighteenth-century clubs for effeminate, cross-dressing gay men—were primarily from the lower and the middle classes. The association of effeminacy and the upper class was used to criticize the aristocracy as a whole, but it also served as a justification for those that believed effeminacy "embodied aspirations towards refinement, sensitivity, and taste" (Sinfield 1994, 52).

In a similar way, Oscar Wilde's gender performance in the late nineteenth century was viewed by contemporary decadent writers as furthering the cause of "oppositional identities that involved differences in gender behavior, sexual practice, and literary strategies" (Hamilton 1999, 69). However, after Oscar Wilde was imprisoned for his sexual activities, the opposing view of his gender performance as "individualistic and anti-social" (Bristow 1995, 10) gained strength. Effeminacy, in the public mind, became strongly linked to a specifically gay identity. As Bristow points out, post-1885 gay writers have all had to come to terms with the stereotype of the effeminate gay man. Although some authors, like E. M. Forster, have carefully distanced themselves from the stereotype, other writers, like Ronald Firbank, have developed a "camp aesthetic" that celebrates effeminate behavior (Bristow 1995, 12).

Despite the modern association of effeminacy with homosexuality, earlier definitions continue to exist that see effeminacy as a problem because the needs of the state may be neglected as effeminate men are too busy pleasing, or identifying with, women. The "cute and accessible 'boys'" of twentieth-century boy bands like the Backstreet Boys have been labeled effeminate by virtue of their careful pandering to a vast fan base of young girls (Wald 2002, 10). In response to charges of effeminacy following the release of a video that directly addressed their female audience, the Backstreet Boys attempted to bolster the image of their masculinity by producing a video that showed them deliberately ignoring sexy women as they pursued a futuristic military campaign (Wald 2002, 18–19). Effeminacy continues to be used to disparage those who do not conform to gender stereotypes, although it has also been knowingly embraced in order to subvert both gender norms and larger societal institutions and belief systems that insist that all men are cut from the same—masculine—cloth.

Holly Crumpton

See also Homophobia; Wimp
Further Reading:
Bristow, Joseph. 1995. *Effeminate England: Homoerotic Writing after 1885.* New York: Columbia University Press.
Carter, Philip. 1997. "An 'Effeminate' or 'Efficient' Nation? Masculinity and Eighteenth-Century Social Documentary." *Textual Practice* 11, no. 3: 429–443.
Hamilton, Lisa. 1999. "New Women and 'Old' Men: Gendering Degeneration." Pp. 62–80 in *Women and British Aestheticism.* Edited by Talia Schaffer and Kathy Alexis. Charlottsville: University Press of Virginia.
Howard, Jean. 1988. "'Effeminately Dolent': Gender and Legitimacy in Ford's Perkin Warbeck." Pp. 261–277 in *John Ford Critical Revisions.* Edited by Michael Neill. Cambridge, UK: Cambridge University Press.
Sharrock, Catherine. 1997. "Reviewing 'the Spirit of Man-hood': Sodomy, Masturbation and the Body (Politic) in Eighteenth-Century England." *Textual Practice* 11, no. 3: 417–428.
Sinfield, Alan. 1994. *The Wilde Century: Effeminacy, Oscar Wilde and the Queer Moment.* New York: Cassell.
Spear, Gary. 1993. "Shakespeare's 'Manly' Parts: Masculinity and Effeminacy in *Troilus and Cressida.*" *Shakespeare Quarterly* 44, no. 4: 409–422.
Wald, Gayle. 2002. "'I Want It that Way': Teenybopper Music and the Girling of Boy Bands." *Genders* 35: 1–22.

Eliot, George [Marian Evans] (1819–1880)

Widely acknowledged by her contemporaries as well as by more modern critics as one of the preeminent writers of the nineteenth century, George Eliot is the pseudonym of Marian Evans, a British writer best known for her realist novels of provincial life. Although she did not begin her career as a novelist until she was thirty-seven, she was already deeply involved in the literary world as a translator, freelance writer, and editor. Her break with the Christian faith, as well as her intimate relationship with the married intellectual and writer George Henry Lewes (who actively supported Eliot's literary career), ostracized her from her family and mainstream Victorian society. Her first work, *Scenes of Clerical Life* (1857), met with an appreciative audience and *Adam Bede* (1859), her second work, was hailed as a masterpiece. Forced to reveal her identity because of rumors that the obscure Joseph Liggins was actually George Eliot, she paid the price for her loss of anonymity. Although the reviews of her next work, *The Mill on the Floss* (1860), generally acknowledged the literary merit of the novel, objections were made to the supposedly dubious morality of this new work despite the fact that the infanticide in *Adam Bede* had passed without comment.

Relying on careful research and meticulous observation, Eliot was committed to producing fiction as true to life as possible. Eliot herself asserted that "I undertake to exhibit nothing as it should be" (Perkin 1990, 22). Instead, Eliot, an inspiration to Henry James, chose to focus on the complexities of the individual psyche. Rejecting the notion that women feel while men think, Eliot insisted that the ability to suspend judgement and respond to the failings and sorrows of others with compassion is an indispensable virtue for men as well as women. Although her works emphasize the importance of individual morality, the slipperiness of Eliot's overall political view has fostered ongoing debates about the ideological content of her work.

Reacting against sentimental pastoralism, Eliot tries to represent English peasants as they actually were. However, despite her willingness to represent the thoughts, feelings, and struggles of the lower class, her description of the injustices suffered by the urban poor in *Felix Holt, the Radical* (1866) does not lead her to advocate for any abrupt change to the status quo. Likewise, her representation of the middle-class man of busi-

George Eliot (Library of Congress)

ness does not consistently valorize middle-class ideals. Although *Adam Bede* has been read as a tale about the triumph of middle-class values as Adam rises from dedicated worker to small business owner (Homans 1993, 156), these same values are shown to be blinders that prevent Tom Tulliver from understanding his unconventional sister Maggie in *The Mill on the Floss*. Furthermore, instead of describing the middle class as a monolithic force of unanimously held opinions, *Middlemarch* (1873–1874) documents intraclass struggle amongst various subgroups of the bourgeoisie. Turning to the upper class, Eliot critiques examples of unfeeling aristocratic masculinity that casually tramples on the rights of those, particularly women, with less power. However, Arthur Donnithorne's seduction of a country girl in *Adam Bede* or Henleigh Grandcourt's pleasure in dominating all within his reach in *Daniel Deronda* (1876) are shown to be the personal failings of individuals who are not living up to the responsibilities that come with power, rather than an indictment of class distinctions in the first place.

Eliot's hesitation in life as well as in fiction to uncritically support any one political position does not mean that she was unaware of how society shapes the individual. Tom Tulliver begins *The Mill on the Floss* as a sensitive boy, but he is warped by his classical education (Beer 1986, 79–80). Similarly, in *Silas Marner* (1861), before he becomes the loving guardian of a lost little girl, Silas's affections are stunted by an inhospitable community. In *Romola* (1862–1863), her only novel set outside of England, Eliot shows how marriage laws prevent Romola from protecting the library left to her by her father (Beer 1994, 445). Thus, education, community, and marriage are all shown as part of the social web that can corrupt or destroy the individual who would stand apart from the crowd.

Eliot's interest in men as men, rather than as symbolic representatives of ideological positions, is clearest in her representation of clergymen. The extent to which Eliot does not value clergymen according to their adherence to a particular doctrine is highlighted by her sympathetic portrayal of Jewish spiritual leaders in England in her last novel *Daniel Deronda*. Eliot's fictional clerics, regardless of their specific creed, are frequently shown to be sources of wisdom and comfort in their communities when they can overcome their doctrinal prejudices and reach out to others regardless of gender, class, or religion (Perlis 1989, 105).

Holly Crumpton

Further Reading:

Beer, Gillian. 1986. *George Eliot*. Bloomington, IN: Indiana University Press.

———. 1994. "George Eliot and the Novel of Ideas." Pp. 429–455 in *The Columbia History of the British Novel*. Edited by John Richetti. New York: Columbia University Press.

Booth, Alison. 1992. "Not All Men Are Selfish and Cruel: *Felix Holt* as a Feminist Novel." Pp. 143–160 in *Gender and Discourse in Victorian Literature*. Edited by Anthony H. Harrison and Beverly Taylor. DeKalb, IL: Northern Illinois University Press.

Homans, Margaret. 1993. "Dinah's Blush, Maggie's Arm: Class, Gender, and Sexuality in George Eliot's Early Novels." *Victorian Studies* 36, no. 2: 155–178.

Levine, George, ed. 2001. *The Cambridge Companion to George Eliot*. Cambridge, UK: Cambridge University Press.

McCaw, Neil. 2000. "'Slugs and Snails and Puppy Dogs' Tails'? George Eliot, Masculinity and the (Ir)religion of Nationalism." Pp. 149–163 in *Masculinity and Spirituality in Victorian Culture*. Edited by Andrew Bradstock, Sean Gill, Anne Hogan, and Sue Morgan. New York: St. Martin's Press.

Perkin, J. Russell. 1990. *A Reception-History of George Eliot's Fiction*. Ann Arbor, MI: UMI Research Press.

Perlis, Alan D. 1989. *A Return to the Primal Self: Identity in the Fiction of George Eliot*. Vol. 71, Series 4, of *English Language and Literature*. New York: Peter Lang.

Reed, John R. 2001. "Soldier Boy: Forming Masculinity in *Adam Bede*." *Studies in the Novel* 33, no. 3: 268–284.

Ellison, Ralph

See *Invisible Man*

Elvis

See Presley, Elvis

Eminem [Marshall Mathers] (1972–)

When white rapper Eminem shot to controversial prominence in 1999, he was rehearsing a familiar formula in the history of pop culture: the charismatic "bad boy," or masculinity as transgression. Discovered by one of the founders of "gangsta rap," Dr. Dre, Eminem (Marshall Mathers) often hilariously combines the hyperbolic aggression of that genre with a deliberate assault on his critics and the notions of political correctness he ascribes to them. Thus, the outcry that arose in response to the misogyny and homophobia of Eminem's lyrics only played into his strategy, increasing his popularity among teens themselves encountering similar voices of regulation at home and school. As a white male in an art form wholly identified with black experience, Eminem shows an allegiance to the realist and confrontational aspects of the "gangsta" ethos, yet it would be a stretch to call him a gangster rapper.

Indeed, in some ways, Eminem looks like a critic of the genre, especially in the way he often satirizes masculine identity. His real cultural precursors were not, as his critics assume, Dre, or Ice-T, but those obnoxious poets of white middle-class "ill," the Beastie Boys. Eminem's self-deprecations, absurdist imagery, and narratives of violence dramatize not the phallic dominance of the black gangster, but the antibourgeois artiness of the white cultural provocateur, a tradition more commonly associated with rock artists like Mick Jagger, Lou Reed, and Elvis Presley—though borrowers all from black musical traditions.

Eminem "keeps it real" by turning his admission of this fact into a boast in "Without Me": "Though I'm not the first king of controversy/ I am the worst thing since Elvis Presley/ to do black music so selfishly/ And use it to get myself wealthy." Thus disarming his critics, Eminem performs his own ironic form of dominance. But in songs of hard times like "Rock Bottom," this mastery has a strange attribute: it is the dominance of the downtrodden, the wronged man—perhaps the ultimate borrowing for this blue-eyed rapper—for whom no doors were closed due to race or sex, the stance of marginality and masculine victimization.

This alternation between victimhood and dominance is perhaps Eminem's most striking trait. David Savran (1998) identifies the fantasy of the white male as victim as an ascendant one in American culture, but notes how this fantasy is a false gesture. These kind of representations, Savran argues, "characteristically conclude with an almost magical restitution of phallic power" (37). Thus it is with Eminem, for the masculine persona that emerges from his albums is the perse-

Eminem performs during the 45th Annual Grammy Awards at Madison Square Garden, 23 February 2003, in New York. Eminem won a Grammy for Best Rap Album for The Eminem Show. *(AFP/Corbis)*

cuted white man triumphant—and with a vengeance. Though Eminem has been criticized for the venomous homophobia and misogyny of his diction, these complaints have been weakened by respondents pointing to the complexities of his narrative voice and his studied provocativeness. But Eminem's cultural power is not in his epithets, but the way he makes a particular version of masculinity—smart but smarting, victimized but itself aggressively victimizing—appealing to teens. If, as feminists, we wish to be heard by the teens who pay to hear Eminem "keep it real," we should start by analyzing the context and constructed nature of that reality.

Todd Onderdonk

See also Rap

Further Reading:

Docherty, Neil. 1999. "The Merchants of Cool." Videocassette. PBS Video. Available at http://www.pbs.org/wgbh/pages/frontline/shows/cool (accessed 27 July 2003).

Christgau, Robert. 2001. "Missing the Point of the Many Masks." At http://events.calendar live.com/top/1,1419,L-LATimes-Grammys–0!ArticleDetail–22014,00.html (accessed 7 November 2002).

Kim, Richard. 2001. "Eminem—Bad Rap?" *The Nation* 272, no. 9 (5 March): 4.

Morgan, Joan. 1999. *When Chickenheads Come Home to Roost: My Life as a Hip-Hop Feminist.* New York: Simon and Schuster.

Rose, Tricia. 1994. *Black Noise: Rap Music and Black Culture in Contemporary America.* Hanover, NH: Wesleyan University Press.

Savran, David. 1998. *Taking It Like A Man: White Masculinity, Masochism, and Contemporary Culture.* Princeton, NJ: Princeton University Press.

Environment

In the late nineteenth century, John Muir gathered followers as a proponent of the spiritual and aesthetic values of nature preservation. When his campaigns roused opposition, Muir's rivals often sought to dismiss him as an "innocent nature lover." In the first decade of the twentieth century, Muir and Robert Underwood Johnson fought unsuccessfully against the damming of Hetch Hetchy Valley, then part of Yosemite National Park. Johnson complained that preservationists were up against "so-called practical men" and "the materialistic idea that there must be something wrong about a man" who loves beauty. James Phelan, the leading proponent of the dam, dismissed Muir as a "poetical gentleman" who would "sacrifice his own family for the sake of beauty" (Fox 1981, 142).

The progressive conservation movement also surfaced in the early 1900s. Resource managers and government officials addressed problems of scarcity with "scientific management" of resources. From 1898 to 1910, Gifford Pinchot headed the U.S. Forest Service and became the target for westerners skeptical of forest reserves. In 1907 western senators, concerned that the withdrawal of land from settlement would restrict the region's development, took the floor of Congress to halt additional withdrawals. Senator Charles W. Fulton of Oregon declared that the Forest Service was "composed of dreamers and theorists" who were no longer part of the everyday world where "real men are at work." Critics also denounced the Forest Service's staff as effeminate "dudes and invalids" (Lukas 1997, 623–624). Congress passed legislation to prevent more forest reserves in 1907, but President Theodore Roosevelt added 16 million acres to the reserves at Pinchot's urging before signing the legislation.

Roosevelt identified himself with both utilitarian conservation and nature preservation, establishing five national parks and fifty-one wildlife refuges. Roosevelt touted rugged outdoors activities and "the strenuous life" of the "frontier" as ways to regain the lost manliness of bygone American frontiersmen. By promoting "vigorous, manly out-of-door sports, such as mountaineering, big-game hunting" and riding, Roosevelt voiced a widespread concern about "overcivilization," effeminacy and physical weakness. Even Muir expressed concern about "overcivilization" and developed a pride in his efforts to face the dangers of the wild. As the Sierra Club's president, Muir led the "High Trip," the club's annual hike to the remote areas of the Sierra Nevada. Historian Hal K. Rothman notes that although a few women were present on the High Trip, the "predominant tone" of the club's signature event was "male—and aggressively so" (Rothman 2000, 24).

Muir and other preservationists were heartened by Roosevelt's interest in national parks, but they were not so taken with Roosevelt's hunting heroics. Roosevelt organized the Boone and Crockett Club, a society of sportsmen who had killed at least three species of North American big game "in fair chase." At one point Muir reportedly remarked, "Mr. Roosevelt, when are you going to get beyond the boyishness of killing things?" (Strong 1988, 103).

In response to the Great Depression of the 1930s, one of President Franklin Roosevelt's first New Deal relief projects was the Civilian Conservation Corps (CCC). The CCC was designed to provide work for some of the millions of unemployed urban young men (women were excluded from the program) and to advance the work of conservation and reforestation on federal and state lands. The young men lived in military-style barracks and did hard physical work planting trees, building reservoirs, developing parks, and improving agricultural irrigation. Agents of the Soil Conservation Service, another New Deal agency, located sand dunes and worked to recreate ground cover and crops. Historian Hal K. Rothman writes, "some residents likened them to the Cavalry of the Old West, whose troops arrived at the last possible moment to rescue individuals and communities in distress" (Rothman 2000, 81).

In 1935 Aldo Leopold joined with others to found the Wilderness Society, an organization devoted to expanding and protecting the nation's wilderness areas. Leopold wanted wilderness areas preserved for the study of well-balanced biotic communities, not as hunting or recreational grounds. A collection of Leopold's essays was published in 1949, the year after his death, as *A Sand County Almanac*. It later became the bible of the environmental movement of the 1960s and 1970s. In the final section of his book, Leopold likens "man's relation to land and to the animals and plants which grow upon it" to Odysseus's domination and disposal of his slave girls. "Land, like Odysseus's slave-girls, is still property" (Leopold 1949, 237–243).

In the 1960s and 1970s, ecofeminists made more explicit connections between the domination of women and the exploitation of the environment. Ynestra King, an early proponent, argued that "'nature friendly' and 'woman respectful' political transformation require one another" (1994). By contending

that male-dominated society is accountable for the domination and exploitation of both women and of nature, ecofeminists brought together feminist and environmental thought. Some ecofeminists celebrated what they saw as a universal relationship between women and nature, often pointing to women's reproductive role as the tie that binds women to nature. Some ecofeminists also maintained that there was once a harmonious, precolonial golden age during which women exercised political and social power. The development of a male-dominated society disrupted this harmony between humankind and nature. Anthropologists, historians, and others have critiqued the notion of a universal link between women and nature, arguing instead that power relations are particular to certain times, places, and social relations.

New legislation passed in the 1970s gave environmental organizations the opportunity to advance their causes through litigation, but some grassroots organizations decided to forgo lawsuits to hold protests and publicity campaigns. Historian Ted Steinberg notes that the "largely white, male-dominated big green organizations" made law and legislation their focus, while working-class women and people of color led grassroots community activist groups. This divide was not missed by critics, who called protestors "overemotional" women and "hysterical housewives" (Steinberg 2002, 253–255).

In 1980, Dave Foreman, an ex-Marine and Wilderness Society staffer, along with several others, started Earth First! to take direct action by sabotaging projects they considered to be environmentally destructive. Their tactics of blockading logging roads, spiking trees, and damaging machinery became known variously as "ecotage," "ecoterrorism," and "monkywrenching." Sometimes calling themselves "ecowarriors," Earth First!ers made militancy a core part of their tactics and criticized environmentalists in such organizations as the Sierra Club for being too passive. Foreman argued, "it is time to act heroically," but he also stressed that ecotage is sabotage, not terrorism. Ecotage peaked in the early 1990s and waned later in that decade as many people involved in the movement came to believe that ecotage ostracized people rather than advancing environmental causes. Yet at the time of this writing, the Earth First! website still asks, "Are you tired of namby-pamby environmental groups?"

Elizabeth Cafer

See also Farming; Frontier; Roosevelt, Theodore; Thoreau, Henry David

Further Reading:

Foreman, Dave. 1987. *Ecodefense: A Field Guide to Monkeywrenching.* 2d ed. Tucson, AZ: N. Ludd.

Fox, Stephen. 1981. *John Muir and His Legacy.* Boston: Little, Brown.

Hays, Samuel P. 1959. *Conservation and the Gospel of Efficiency: The Progressive Conservation Movement, 1890-1920.* New York: Atheneum.

King, Ynestra. 1994. "Ecofeminism in International Context." In *Women, Politics and Environmental Action: An International Symposium.* Edited by Barbara Welling Hall. Moscow, Russia, 1–3 June.

Leopold, Aldo. 1949. *A Sand County Almanac, and Sketches Here and There.* Illus. by Charles W. Schwartz. New York: Oxford University Press.

Lukas, J. Anthony. 1997. *Big Trouble: A Murder in a Small Western Town Sets Off a Struggle for the Soul of America.* New York: Touchstone.

Merchant, Carolyn. 1995. *Earthcare: Women and the Environment.* New York: Routledge.

Rothman, Hal K. 2000. *Saving the Planet the American Response to the Environment in the Twentieth Century.* Chicago: Ivan R. Dee.

Steinberg, Theodore. 2002. *Down to Earth: Nature's Role in American History.* New York: Oxford University Press.

Strong, Douglas H. 1988. *Dreamers and Defenders: American Conservationists.* Lincoln: University of Nebraska Press.

"Why Earth First?" 1998. *Earth First! Journal* (20 May). http://www.earthfirstjournal.org/efj/primer/WhyEF!.html (accessed 25 July 2003).

Erectile Dysfunction

Erectile dysfunction (ED) is the term that popular and medical literatures currently use to describe problems with getting a man's penis stiff enough to accomplish penetration of a sexual partner. Most of the time it refers to persistent problems with vaginal penetration in heterosexual intercourse. In the early 1990s, ED replaced the term *impotence,* as the latter was thought to be vague and stigmatizing because it signified general weakness or incapacity and wasn't limited to sexuality. Although medical and psychological research and popular media uncritically present ED as an established disease with ever-improving diagnostic and treatment management, social science and gender studies focus on how ED discourse is used in constructions of contemporary masculinity and to maintain the coital imperative in sexual (erotic) conduct.

From the perspective of those interested in masculinity, ED medicalizes a specific sexual act that has come to be seen as synonymous with manhood itself. Vaginal intercourse with ejaculation is the act that allows men to participate in reproduction, and feminists have argued that a culture in which intercourse is the sexual act *sine qua non* is a patriarchal culture that uses the sexual situation to celebrate men. The manhood being celebrated is one of achievement, where masculinity is at stake during every encounter and its success only temporarily affirmed by each successful erection. Erectile dysfunction equates a specific failed activity—penetration—with generalized failed manhood. "I'm not a man," the ED sufferer often says.

To hear men say that ED is "a fate worse than death" is to realize how the performance of intercourse is a symbolic accomplishment that, despite a culture of contraception and low birthrates, has become the centerpiece of contemporary masculinity and an irreplaceable element of many men's self-esteem.

Throughout the 1980s and 1990s, health and science media produced a steady stream of reports on new physiological research on ED, focusing public discussion of sexual problems on men's genital function. Although ED is usually presented in both media and professional writings as well-established biomedical science, in fact, the scientific discussion lacks precision. Surprisingly, it is impossible to find a specific or precise definition of normal erection in the biomedical literature. Penile erection is simply assumed to be the condition of the penis becoming erect. But penises come in many ages, shapes, and sizes, and it isn't clear how erect an "adequate erection" is, or for precisely how long a good erection should last.

By contrast, it is easier to find a definition of ED than sunshine in the tropics. Here is the definition that appears in the American Psychiatric Association's official list of disorders:

> The essential feature of Male Erectile Disorder is a persistent or recurrent inability to attain, or to maintain until completion of the sexual activity, an adequate erection. The disturbance must cause marked distress or interpersonal difficulty. There are different patterns of erectile dysfunction. Some individuals will report the inability to obtain any erection from the outset of a sexual experience. Others will complain of first experiencing an adequate erection and then losing tumescence when attempting penetration. Still others will report they have an erection that is sufficiently firm for penetration but that they then lose tumescence before or during thrusting. (APA 1994, 502)

Notice that subjective sexual arousal, excitement, and pleasure are absent from this definition. Erectile dysfunction is purely a matter of mechanical performance. This emphasis on performance is consistent with broader trends toward standardization and rationalization of human social behavior and the medicalization of deviance. Note also that there is no mention of situational context, sexual orientation, or a sexual partner in this definition, despite the obvious fact that penetration depends as much on the (sexual, physiological, and psychological) condition of the sexual partner as on the

hardness of a man's penis. And note again that, although the definition of ED is based on "an adequate erection," nowhere is that specific entity defined.

Tremendous numbers of popular and self-help books, websites, and medical publications are devoted to the subject of ED. Many of them are commercial enterprises that promote particular products to treat ED. But even noncommercial sexuality education books and websites approach the subject within a biomedical framework by assuming that erection is a physical function of the penis in the way that heartbeat is a function of the heart or urine production is a function of the kidney. Erectile dysfunction, then, within this medical model, becomes a failure of the penis to perform in its biologically ordained way, and constitutes a health problem comparable to any other organ abnormality. This is an essentialist perspective that assumes erection is a biological, rather than cultural, concept. Outside the medical model, however, the analogies between erection and bodily functions appear more limited, as there are no partners or specific behaviors involved in heartbeat and urine production, and these functions are not subject to the kind of shifts in cultural meaning we see with erections.

Books and research studies on ED usually begin with the anatomy and physiology of the penis and mechanisms of erection. The following one is from a chapter with 228 references in a 700-plus-page tome on ED and illustrates the high end of complex biomedical rhetoric: "Normal erectile function requires the involvement and coordination of multiple regulatory systems and is thus subject to the influence of psychological, hormonal, neurological, vascular and cavernosal factors [cavernosal spaces are tiny areas in the penis that fill with blood during erection]. An alteration in any of these factors may be sufficient to cause ED, but in many cases a combination of several factors is involved" (deTejada et al. 2000, 80).

In other words, erection is a highly complex physical event and parts can malfunction individually or in combination. Following this sort of general opening statement, advanced scientific texts invariably go on to reveal that many details of penile anatomy and erectile physiology are not known.

Controversies persist over issues such as which nerve transmitter chemicals cause the smooth muscles comprising the penile artery walls to contract thereby admitting more blood, or exactly how this blood-trapping process ends, causing the erection to subside. Because the ultimate facts about erection remain unknown, precise causes of ED in an individual are usually not specifiable. However, as in many situations of medicalization, the technical vocabulary and atmosphere of the clinic or doctor's consulting room intimidates most people from realizing the limits of the biomedical perspective. Medical mystification makes ED seem more universal, standardized, and precise than it actually is.

How many men have ED? One might imagine it would be simple to question a statistically valid sample and produce a numerical answer to this question. In fact, although there are many casual or convenience surveys of ED, often consisting of men who happen to come to a particular clinic or doctor during a given period of time, only two American studies claim to be statistically representative.

One of these surveys seems to approach erectile dysfunction as a subjective condition. In addition to taking several physiological measures and obtaining information about difficulties with intercourse, this survey asked a representative sample of 1,709 men living in Massachusetts in the late 1980s one question about their erections. Survey participants were instructed on how to define impotence, and what seemed at first a general inquiry about "sexual activity" quickly became one about "sexual intercourse":

Impotence means not being able to get and keep an erection that is rigid enough for satis-

factory sexual activity. How would you describe yourself?

Not impotent (always able to get and keep an erection good enough for sexual intercourse),

Minimally impotent (usually able to get and keep . . .),

Moderately impotent (sometimes able to get and keep . . .),

Completely impotent (never able to get and keep . . .).

(Derby, Araujo, Joannes, Feldman, and McKinlay 2000, 199)

When results of the survey were published, answers were often divided into only two categories: "no erectile dysfunction" and "erectile dysfunction." Collapsing categories in this way produces high population estimates of the prevalence of erectile dysfunction. Remember that the American Psychiatric Association diagnosis required that "The disturbance must cause *marked* distress or interpersonal difficulty" (1994, 502, emphasis added).

Yet nothing in this Massachusetts epidemiological survey asks about distress associated with any of the four categories of self-defined impotence. It is assumed that men who are not always "able to get and keep an erection that is rigid enough for satisfactory sexual activity" are automatically distressed about this. Once this is assumed, the groups of completely, moderately, and minimally impotent men can all be said to have ED.

By contrast, Dutch and Japanese surveys of the early 2000s explicitly asked not only about the frequency of intercourse problems, but about the degree of distress the men experienced. Surveys in both countries found that "most men have a low level of concern about their dysfunction" (Blanker et al. 2001, 766). The inflation of prevalence statistics for ED is one reason why the topic is so prominent. Any medical issue that is said to affect half the population seems like a major public health problem. However, as with the definition of ED, the science behind the epidemiology of ED is not as secure as one might expect.

Essays by sexually active Americans over sixty years of age demonstrate how age-related changes in erectile function challenge the coital imperative (Blank 2000). Many older people remain sexually active and interested by pursuing medical treatment of ED and other age-related changes in genital function. Many others, however, change the choreography of their sexual encounters so that penile penetration is not required and orgasm is more optional than mandatory. Accurate sex information or trial-and-error learning teaches that stimulating a soft penis can produce pleasure, and that orgasm can occur without a hard erection. Much of the changed sexual choreography in later years focuses on whole-body as well as genital pleasure, emotional intimacy as well as physical intensity, and on playfulness and creativity more than an orgasmic goal orientation. This challenge to the coital imperative seems more acceptable when competitive masculinity is no longer a primary psychological issue.

One trend to watch is how the medicalization of women's sexual problems under the rubric of "female sexual dysfunction" is imitating the genital performance focus of ED and how this trend is being promoted by commercial forces developing drugs for women that mimic Viagra, the first pill for ED.

Leonore Tiefer

See also Penis; Viagra

Further Reading:

American Psychiatric Association (APA). 1994. *Diagnostic and Statistical Manual of Mental Disorders.* 4th ed. Washington, DC: APA.

Blank, Joani, ed. 2000. *Still Doing It: Women and Men over 60 Write about Their Sexuality.* San Francisco: Down There Press.

Blanker, M. H., J. L. H. Ruud Bosch, F. P. M. J. Groeneveld, A. M. Bohnen, A. Prins, S. Thomas, and W. C. J. Hop. 2001. "Erectile and Ejaculatory Dysfunction in a Community Based Sample of Men 50 to 78 Years Old: Prevalence, Concern and Relation to Sexual Activity." *Urology* 57: 763–768.

Derby, C. A., A. B. Araujo, C. B. Joannes, H. A. Feldman, and J. B. McKinlay. 2000.

"Measurement of Erectile Dysfunction in Population-Based Studies: The Use of a Single Question Self-Assessment in the Massachusetts Male Aging Study." *International Journal of Impotence Research* 12: 197–204.

de Tejada, I. S., N. G. Cadavid, J. Heaton, H. Hedlund, A. Nehra, R. S. Pickard, U. Simonsen, and W. Steers. 2000. "Anatomy, Physiology and Pathophysiology of Erectile Function." Pp. 65–102 in *Erectile Dysfunction.* Edited by A. Jardin, G. Wagner, S. Khoury, F. Giuliano, H. Padma-Nathan, and R. Rosen. Plymouth, UK: Health Publication, Ltd.

Friedman, David. M. 2001. *A Mind of Its Own: A Cultural History of the Penis.* New York: The Free Press.

Tiefer, Leonore. 1995. *Sex is Not a Natural Act, and Other Essays.* Boulder, CO: Westview Press.

Ethnocentrism

Ethnocentrism is a diffuse hostility against members of other ethnic groups implying the feeling of ethnic superiority (Rieker 1997, 13). There are different degrees of ethnocentrism. It may range from nationalism to hostility against foreigners, or from racism to xenophobia, which is defined as an irrational assumption that the "out-group" might take material goods or positions that should be reserved for the "in-group." Ethnocentrists believe in a hierarchy of races, cultures, religions, and sexes, at which they are the top. They also favor violent solutions and have a contempt for modern democracy.

Various approaches have tried to explain the emergence of ethnocentrism. From the perspective of ethnology, ethnocentrism stems from the failure of the individual to achieve the ethnic identity that provides a feeling of "security" within an ethnic community and also in relationship to people from other ethnic backgrounds. Ethnocentrists do not feel "safe" in their social environment, but constantly fear they are being "threatened" by the out-group (Erdheim 1993, 163, 166). The "strangeness" of the out-groups is socially constructed (e.g., "Blacks are . . . ," "Turks are . . . ," "Women are . . . ," etc.) and transferred to any other "inferior" group in society.

Sociological explanations see the roots of ethnocentrism in the development of the authoritarian character in the socialization process (see Adorno 1950). More recent studies focus on the consequences of modernization (Bacher 2001, 335). According to this view, ethnocentric individuals feel that they cannot meet the demands of modern society and so they construct "scapegoats." They accept violence as a means of receiving attention, knowing that violent acts hit the "weak" side of the society they detest. At the same time, they get the feeling of societal approval, especially when public debate and media coverage focus on anti-immigrant discourse or a policy against asylum seekers (Fekete 2001). Such approaches help to understand the phenomenon of ethnocentrism, but no single explanation seems to be satisfactory.

Looking at the number of crimes committed against members of ethnic minorities, it is evident that the majority of offenders are young men. A study of 1,400 cases in Germany revealed that 96 percent of the violent acts had in fact been committed by men (Jaschke 2001, 177). This must not lead to the conclusion that ethnocentrism is only a typical male attitude. In surveys, nearly the same number of women expressed ethnocentric views as did men, often expressing support for the traditional role of women in society (Birsl 1993). Like men, women also hold "the others" responsible for their personal and economic problems. The reason for the high level of male participation in crimes with a racist undertone may be seen in the fact that generally more crimes are committed by the cohorts of younger men. Physical violence is also an "accepted" behavior among boys, aimed at gaining "habitual security" within the in-group and in confrontation with the out-group (Meuser 2002, 1–3). A considerable number of boys have internalized that habit and exclude others, for example, homosexuals, weaker men, and women, from their own confined "world."

The classical explanation of male ethnocentrism looks at the family background. A correlation exists between father dominance in traditional families and ethnocentric attitudes as part of the "authoritarian character." Boys tend to justify their fathers' authoritarian education and even aggressiveness and build up a reservoir of aggressive behavior patterns that they then act out against weaker individuals. It is not important for the emergence of ethnocentrism that the fathers are ethnocentrists themselves. Ethnocentrists can be found in families with extreme "left" and extreme "right" tendencies (Rieker 1997, 185 [referring to a study by Hennig 1982]). It is characteristic of the families of ethnocentrists that emotional links between the family members are minimal or lacking. In such families the feeling of belonging together is often expressed by a certain amount of hostility against the outside world. This attitude of excluding others becomes a pattern of orientation among boys. Unstable emotional relationships are responsible for the low level of self-esteem in boys. This is usually compensated for by aggressiveness. Often mothers encourage dominant behavior of boys ("Walk like a man!") as part of traditional male socialization (Rieker 1997, 175). Evidence also suggests that ethnocentric views of mothers are transmitted to boys over a long period (Urban 1998, 287), whereas the influence of fathers decreases at the time of puberty (Urban 1998, 290).

In contrast to public opinion, ethnocentric males do not stem from typical problem families (Koopmans 2001, 475), but problems in the family have a certain effect on the emergence of ethnocentrism. Unfavorable emotional conditions during and after a parental divorce may draw boys closer to ethnocentric orientations (Rieker 1997, 142). They often feel burdened by new emotional dependency on them by their mothers ("Now you are my little man!"). Divorced mothers also tend to transfer a negative image of men, which boys use for excluding other "inferior" men. More authoritarian ed-

ucation may occur in families after divorce (Rieker 1997, 139), which also promotes the development of an "authoritarian character." The increasing number of boys who grow up without fathers in single-parent families have to be watched carefully (Rieker 1997, 191 [referring to a study by Montau in 1995]). They seem to find violent peer groups very attractive. There is, however, no clear evidence of any influence of peer groups on ethnocentrism. This is due to the fact that many ethnocentric peer groups appear spontaneously and have no persistent influence on the individual, although they provide emotional security by excluding all "others" from their community.

Long-term research on the development of ethnocentrism during a life span is sparse. When confronted with the risks of modernization, including unemployment and poverty, men may experience their ethnocentrism and xenophobia increasing with age (Rieker 1997, 30). Many ethnocentric males have found that they are not able to play the traditional male role as the breadwinner of the family, and consequently they blame "others" for that. No research has been done to examine the effect the presence of a life partner has on ethnocentric attitudes in men (Rieker 1997, 231). However, it appears that men's participation in violent acts against persons of other ethnic backgrounds declines after marriage.

Various attempts to reduce ethnocentrism have been made in the field of education. No single measure has proved to be effective. Perhaps in the future, the findings in men's studies may provide a basis for further educational approaches.

Hans-Günther Tappe

See also Race, Biological Asumptions of; Race, Conceptions of; White Supremacy; Whiteness

Further Reading:
Adorno, Theodor W., et al. 1950/1969. *The Authoritarian Personality.* New York: Norton.
Bacher, Johannes. 2001. "In which Social Contexts Do Juveniles Learn Ethnocentrism?" *Kölner Zeitschrift für Soziologie und Sozialpsychologie* 2: 334–349.
Birsl, Ursula. 1993. "Right-Wing Extremism Is No Male-Specific Phenomenon." *Frankfurter Rundschau,* (27 November): 16.
Erdheim, Mario. 1993. "On Ethnic Identity." Pp. 163–183 in *Xenophobia and Hostility against Foreigners.* Edited by Mechthild Jansen and Ulrike Prokop. Basel, Germany: Stroemfeld.
Fekete, Liz. 2001. "The Emergence of Xeno-Racism." *Race & Class* 43, no. 2: 23–40.
Hennig, Eike. 1982. "Neo-Nazi Militancy and Right-Wing Extremism among Youths." *Aus Politik und Zeitgeschichte* 32: 23–37.
Jaschke, Hans-Gerd. 2001. *Right-Wing Extremism and Hostility Against Foreigners.* Wiesbaden, Germany: Westdeutscher Verlag.
Koopmans, Ruud. 2001. "Right-Wing Extremism and Xenophobia in Germany." *Leviathan* 4: 469–483.
Meuser, Michael. 2002. "Doing Masculinity—Understanding the Logics of Male Violence." (Paper presented at the interdisciplinary conference AIM Gender, Stuttgart, Germany. 9 November 2002.
Reiker, Peter. 1997. *Ethnocentrism in Young Men: Xenophobia and Nationalism and the Conditions of Their Socialisation.* Weinheim: Juventa.
Urban, Dieter. 1998. "Transmissions of Anti-Foreigner Attitudes from Parents to Children." *Zeitschrift für Soziologie* 4: 276–296.

Eugenics

Eugenics was a doctrine that presumed certain people were "unfit" and thereby presumed that only *some* people—for our purposes here, men—were "fit."

Eugenicists believed that qualities such as intelligence and morality were inherited and that society needed to take steps to produce desirable offspring. Eugenics originated in 1865 in Britain when Francis Galton first published his theory that one's reputation and talent relied on inherited ability. In the beginning of the twentieth century, the biologist Charles B. Davenport began the American eugenics movement by appropriating Galton's ideas and merging them with Gregor Mendel's gene theory. Eugenicists advocated "negative eugenics," the attempt to prevent the proliferation of undesirables, and "positive eugenics," the attempt to promote the proliferation of desirables (Kevles 1995, 85). Eugenics differed greatly from another popular theory, Social Darwinism, in that supporters of the latter believed that natural processes would automatically take care of the "unfit." Eugenicists, on the other hand, believed that those natural processes were not working to their fullest extent and that too many of the unfit were surviving in large numbers. This popular belief culminated in the organization of the American Eugenics Society, founded in 1923. The Great Depression, however, would see the biggest expansion of the eugenics movement in America's history. By the middle of the 1930s, approximately 20,000 legal sterilizations had been performed in the United States (Kevles 1995, 112).

It was also at this time that American masculinity was most in crisis. As men were losing work and, thus, their status as "breadwinners," the crisis over a traditional notion of masculinity was woven through the cultural fabric of America. In the wake of World War I and the economic upheaval of 1929, men during the 1930s had no real means to prove their manhood. The eugenics movement complicated matters because now there were thousands of men who appeared "unfit" due to the fact that they were out of work. With so many men who were poor and needy, how could one identify the "truly" genetically unfit? Also, another question cropped up: If there are genetically "unfit" men, then what does that assumption say about masculinity *in general?*

In response, there emerged a broad and multileveled effort to save this highly esteemed gender position. In 1933, for instance, President Franklin D Roosevelt launched the Civilian Conservation Corps (CCC) to provide employment to young, unmarried men. Each man received $30 a month and sent $25 home to his family. This program proved instrumental in giving men a chance to be "men" again. In his article "Conserving the Youth" (1997), Patrick Clancy argues that a major goal of the CCC was to reshape the gendered fabric of America as the program "reinforced the traditional role of the man as the family breadwin-

ner" (10). Or, as one man who was enrolled in the CCC put it: "'They sure made a man out of ya'" (Terkel 1986, 58). In another effort to boost traditional notions of masculinity, a member of the American Eugenics Society, Lewis Terman, published a seminal study about gender entitled *Sex and Personality: Studies in Masculinity and Femininity* in 1936. In this text, Terman and Catherine Cox Miles introduced a way to quantifiably measure and prove one's masculinity and femininity through the "M-F Test." In his preface to Miles's earlier volume on genius, Terman wrote that the founder of eugenics, Francis Galton, was a genius (1926). In their book about gender, Terman and Miles undoubtedly allowed eugenic biases to creep in. In an era when the bodybuilder Charles Atlas told men how to look buff, the Depression-era's fascination with masculinity was immense. However, the disparity between a "god" like Atlas and a poor migrant worker loomed large. Most men were not gods, but were indeed transient workers in the fields and factories of America.

The fusion of masculinity and eugenics became a subtext in Depression-era literature and film. For example, William Faulkner's *The Sound and the Fury* (1929) interrogates readers' fears about the lustful nature of a feebleminded man like Benjy. And, in the film *Frankenstein* (1931), the monster is a product of 1930s fears of the eugenically unfit rather than the benevolent, intelligent creature that Mary Shelley created. In the film the monster has a "criminal brain." Like Faulkner's Benjy, he is a feebleminded, animalistic, and masculine creature that does not know its own strength. The viewer sits on the edge of his or her seat as the monster comes eerily close to the virginal, blond-haired Elizabeth in her white wedding gown. Luckily, she is spared from this dangerous masculine presence. Similarly, John Steinbeck's Lennie (*Of Mice and Men*, 1937) is a feebleminded man who does not fit society's definition of manliness. Steinbeck, therefore, pairs him with

George—a strong-willed and intelligent field hand who *does* fit society's definition. Steinbeck chooses to stabilize classic masculinity by differentiating it from the "unfit" masculinity that was tarnishing the reputation of men during the 1930s. As Michael Kimmel has noted, certain men were depicted in American culture to let other men "feel more manly" (195). And, George admits this himself. Traveling with Lennie has "[m]ade me seem God damn smart alongside of him." In the end, he is the one who kills Lennie when Lennie kills Curley's wife. The execution serves as a symbolic gesture about the power of traditional masculinity, especially so as George walks off with Slim, the most macho character in the book. Slim tells George that it was okay to kill Lennie because men have to take control: "A guy got to sometimes."

Although many historians note that the popularity of American eugenics waned with the start of World War II and the news of Hitler's atrocities, American eugenics did not disappear completely at the end of the Depression. It may no longer be called "eugenics," but such a doctrine certainly exists in American culture into the early twenty-first century. In 1994, Richard Herrnstein and Charles Murray published *The Bell Curve* in which they argued that welfare dependency was the effect of an inherited subnormal intelligence and that the government was encouraging unfit women to procreate. More recently, Pat Buchanan's *The Death of the West* (2002) argues that civilization is threatened by "immigrant invasions" and that the "wrong" types of people are procreating while the "right" types of people are having fewer babies. In regard to technological discoveries, Daniel Kevles (1995) argues that "the specter of eugenics hovers over virtually all contemporary developments in human genetics" (ix). For example, Kevles argues that gene manipulation could become eugenically charged because it "could discriminate against socially costly or devalued groups and individuals" (1995, x). Indeed, it

has. Gay men have most recently been the targets of eugenic theories and policies. As recently as 2002, the Food and Drug Administration (FDA) has considered regulations that would prohibit men who have had sex with other men in the past five years from being anonymous sperm donors. Also, gay men who have chosen a specific woman with whom to have a child would need to have their sperm frozen and tested for HIV after six months. Generally, however, only one in six men have sperm that could survive such a process (Pampalone 2002). A coalition of gay activists and gay-friendly sperm banks argue that the FDA's proposed regulations come close to eliminating the possibility of gay men having biological children and that the regulations would be a "program of mass sterilization by regulation" (Gay Sperm Bank 1999). It is clear, then, that further research needs to be done in regard to present-day genetic theories and society's conception of worthy and unworthy fathers, or worthy and unworthy masculinity.

Sarah C. Holmes

See also Race, Biological Assumptions of; Race, Conceptions of; Terman, Lewis

Further Reading:

Buchanan, Patrick J. 2002. *The Death of the West: How Dying Populations and Immigrant Invasions Imperil Our Country and Civilization.* New York: St. Martin's Press.

Clancy, Patrick. 1997. "Conserving the Youth: The Civilian Conservation Corps Experiences in the Shenandoah National Park." *Virginia Magazine of History and Biography* 105, no. 4: 1–20.

"Eugenics Watch." At *http://www.africa2000 .com/ENDX/aenames.htm* (cited 3 October 2002).

Faulkner, William. 1929. *The Sound and the Fury.* New York: Jonathan Cape and Harrison Smith.

Gay Sperm Bank, "Back to Basters." *http://www.gayspermbank.com/ frontLA.htm* (cited 28 May 1999).

Herrnstein, Richard, and Charles Murray. 1994. *The Bell Curve: Intelligence and Class Structure in American Life.* New York: Free Press.

Kevles, Daniel. 1995. *In the Name of Eugenics: Genetics and the Uses of Human Heredity.* Cambridge, MA: Harvard University Press.

Pampalone, Tanya. 2002. "Gay Sperm Donations Could Soon Be Illegal." *San Francisco Examiner,* 11 February.

Steinbeck, John. 1975. *Of Mice and Men.* New York: Bantam, 1937.

Terkel, Studs. 1970/1986. *Hard Times: An Oral History of the Great Depression.* New York: Pantheon-Random.

Terman, Lewis M. 1926. Preface to *Genetic Studies of Genius,* by Catherine Cox Miles. Vol. 2. Stanford, CA: Stanford University Press.

Terman, Lewis M., and Catherine Cox Miles. 1936. *Sex and Personality: Studies in Masculinity and Femininity.* New York: Russell and Russell.

Whale, James. 1931. *Frankenstein.* Universal Studios.

Evans, Marian

See Eliot, George

Evolution

Evolution refers to a general theory accounting for change in biological species over time and has been used to explain different traits and behaviors exhibited by males and females in sexual species, including humans. Evolutionary theory has been used to provide novel explanations of numerous characteristics of men and masculinity in general, as well as differences between men and between men and women, primarily thorough selective pressures on the sexes that lead to different reproductive strategies. Evolutionary theory, when applied to humans, has been criticized for reifying the categories of "man" and "woman," for emphasizing reproductive behaviors over others, and for naturalizing sex differences that may have more social or cultural explanations. However, given the central place of evolutionary theory in modern biology, it remains a powerful tool for explaining many sex differences.

Evolutionary theory suggests that individuals exhibit physical and behavioral traits, or adaptations, that have evolved over time to optimize reproductive success within the context of the organism's environment. Evolution occurs through a combination of random variation in genes and differential representation of those genes in succeeding generations due to natural selection. Natural selective pressures on novel traits are described as somatic (growth, development, and maintenance of the body) and reproductive (optimization of the number of offspring in succeeding generations).

In sexual species, genetic material from two individuals, male and female, is combined to produce new members of the species, allowing for distinct selective pressures on sexes that over time produces differences between them, or sexual dimorphism. Those selective pressures act differently on males and females because of the different ways in which males and females of most sexual species reproduce and invest in offspring. In placental mammals, females gestate, give birth, and lactate, such that their reproduction requires greater somatic investment from them relative to males. Moreover, gestation time and litter size set a biological upper limit to the number of offspring a female can produce.

Mammalian males, however, tend to a lower initial somatic investment in offspring and fewer biological limits on the number of offspring they produce in a lifetime. Thus males and females of mammalian species tend to pursue different reproductive strategies that tend to resolve into recognizable mating patterns. Males, because of their lower initial somatic investment, are predicted in general to invest less in any particular reproductive opportunity than females, and more in achieving multiple reproductive opportunities. Females are predicted to spend more time in guaranteeing offspring survival during development through direct caregiving. Males may therefore spend more time either actively seeking reproductive opportunities or in securing resources that may guarantee those reproductive opportunities and offspring survival. Male reproductive strategies have thus generally been characterized as "Cads," seekers of reproductive opportunities, and "Dads," investors in offspring.

These different reproductive strategies in turn lead to sexual competition both be-

tween members of the same sex and between the two sexes. Sexual competition between males depends heavily on environmental context. For example, if resources in
the environment are scarce but easily
guarded by single males, then sexual dimorphism may evolve such that males are larger
than females, males may mate with several
females and guard a cluster of resources and
those mates from other males. However,
where resources are evenly distributed in the
environment and not easily defensible, males
and females may show very little sexual dimorphism, and males and females may mate
exclusively in lifelong pairbonds. Males may
compete directly, through aggressive displays
or violence, or they may compete indirectly,
through sneaking copulations with females
or through sperm competition.

Studies of primates, especially of great
apes, provide the most important and ger-
mane models for comparison with human reproductive and mating patterns. Primates
exhibit a wide range of mating strategies that
have been generally characterized as monogamous, polygamous, solitary, multimale mul-
tifemale, and plural. Monogamous primates
such as the gibbon tend to show little sexual
dimorphism, pair bonding, and high paternal
investment in offspring. Polygamous primates such as the gorilla exhibit high sexual
dimorphism, single-male mulifemale
harems, and limited direct paternal investment in offspring. Solitary primates such as
the orangutan tend not to aggregate, with females living with children and males living
alone, with males and females coming together only to mate, and with male
orangutans occasionally forcing females to
copulate through rape. Multimale multife-
male groups such as chimpanzees and bono-
bos, or pygmy chimps, show several mating
strategies, including male and female coalitions and copulations with multiple partners
by both males and females. Humans exhibit a
plural mating strategy, including all of those
listed above as well polyandry, in which single females mate with multiple males. All of

Author, natural historian, geologist, and botanist
Charles Darwin formulated and popularized the
controversial theory of evolution in the mid-nineteenth
century and published On the Origin of Species in
1859. (Library of Congress)

these mating strategies are flexible, however,
and change with environmental context.

In the case of human evolution, the general
parameters for mammalian sexual production, along with examples of reproductive and
mating strategies from primate groups, have
been used to explain human traits, including
differences in male and female physical and
behavioral characteristics. On average, for example, human males tend to be about 20 percent larger than human females, intermediate
between the over 50 percent difference in
body size in gorillas and the relatively minimal
dimorphism in gibbons. Other biological differences between human males and females
explained by evolutionary theory include differences in body fat and muscle patterning and
skeletal development related to reproduction,
timing of puberty and reproductive senes-

cence, and complements of sexual steroidal hormones. Human males tend to have higher relative muscle and lower relative fat content than females, they tend to mature more slowly and longer (delaying reproductive investment for somatic investment as growth), they do not experience a punctuated menopause, and they tend to exhibit lower levels of estrogens and higher levels of testosterone and its derivatives. Such biological differences do not lead directly to specific differences in behaviors between sexes. However, because of the success of evolutionary theory in explaining behaviors of other animals, including other primates, in environmental context (a branch of evolutionary theory called behavioral ecology), evolutionary theory has also been applied to human behaviors. These attempts have focused mainly on explaining: (1) the evolution of human reproductive strategies and mating patterns, (2) the current expression of those strategies and patterns, and (3) the relation of these patterns to broader sociopolitical patterns of organization. They extend to many behaviors deemed male and female, such as aggressive behavior (including violence and murder), same-sex coalitions, range and display of emotion, differences in cognitive abilities and psychological dispositions, use of styles of makeup and clothing, and homosexuality.

The plurality of human mating patterns has only recently been recognized, with prior attempts aimed at explaining a single human reproductive strategy or mating pattern leading to generalizations about evolutionary history. The once-popular "man the hunter" model of human evolution related the development of human cognition, language, and complex social ordering to selective pressures on early humans to form male coalitions for collective hunting of large game. This explanation used baboon models, whose social groups exhibit strict dominance hierarchies and male aggression, for early human societies based on similar environments in the African savannah. Feminist primatologists have pointed out that baboon

models may be very inappropriate given the large time divergence in simian and human evolution. Moreover, the "man the hunter" model relied heavily on current sexual mores and stereotypes, such as male aggression and dominance, and underestimated the importance of female contributions, such as selection of cooperative males for mating and female technological innovation. Feminist evolutionary theorists have given a more active role to early human females in the evolution of human mating strategies, suggesting for example that menstruation, hidden ovulation, and relatively continuous female sexual receptivity (relative to other great apes such as chimps) may be a particularly human strategy for the confusion of paternity, such that males in multimale groups will be more likely to invest generally in female offspring and minimize aggression toward those offspring. Other feminist theorists have more generally challenged evolutionary theory as a grand metanarrative that historically centers men and de-centers women by placing emphasis on reproduction and other biological, ahistorical forces to naturalize gender differences and inequalities. Moreover, they argue that evolutionary theory tends to universalize the categories "male" and "female" rather than looking at differences between men and women.

One branch of evolutionary theory, evolutionary psychology, has sought to explain differences in gendered behavior among humans using the parameters of evolutionary theory. These explanations often suggest that the majority of human evolution over the past million years took place in a relatively similar environment, or the Environment of Evolutionary Adaptation (EEA), such that: 1) current human environments are very different from the EEA, and 2) human psychological proclivities evolved for adaptation to the EEA rather than current environments. Evolutionary psychologists base many of the differences in observed patterns in human male and female sexual and reproductive strategies on adaptations to the EEA rather than current environmental conditions. For example, a tendency to rape females by males may have once improved reproductive fitness, but under current circumstances of law enforcement and incarceration may no longer do so. Examples of such explanations include women's use of makeup (lipstick, blush) as a way to exhibit health, youth, and fecundity, a male preference for characteristics of proportionately narrow waists and wide hips in women as fecundity markers, male proclivities to violence and aggression as related to resources and mate competition, male desires for multiple partners and frequent copulations and women's choosiness in partner selection as seeking to maximize reproductive success based on different patterns of paternal investment. Such evolutionary theorizing is ultimately only testable against the predicted outcome of reproductive success, and many of the claims of evolutionary psychologists have been challenged as reifying cultural constructions of masculinity and femininity, or of providing insight into tendencies rather than behavioral outcomes.

Matthew R. Dudgeon

See also Darwinism

Further Reading:

Betzig, Laura L., Monique Borgerhoff Mulder, and Paul Turke. 1988. *Human Reproductive Behavior: A Darwinian Perspective.* Cambridge, UK: Cambridge University Press.

LeCroy, Dori, and Peter Moller. 2000. "Evolutionary Perspectives on Human Reproductive Behavior." *Annals of the New York Academy of Sciences.* Vol. 907. New York: New York Academy of Sciences.

Ridley, Mark. 1994. *Evolution.* New York: Oxford University Press.

Wood, James W. 1994. *Dynamics of Human Reproduction: Biology, Biometry, Demography, Foundations of Human Behavior.* New York: Aldine de Gruter.

Evolutionary Psychology

Like sociobiology, evolutionary psychology explores physiological sources of and/or contributions to human behavior and cultural phenomena. Evolutionary psychologists focus on the brain as an information-processing system that, in response to natural and sexual selection pressures early in human evolution, has adaptively developed function-specific structures and circuitry that result in demonstrably predictable—though varied—situation-specific behaviors by humans of any culture or era.

Researchers in evolutionary psychology seek to uncover cognitive mechanisms that have evolved in the human brain to guide humans' mental analyses and basic responses to given situations. These cognitive mechanisms are generally not tied to conscious awareness; the information-processing mechanisms in the brain function without an individual purposely setting the process in motion or being aware of it. Furthermore, evolutionary psychologists note, the circuitry that our brains developed hundreds of thousands of years ago may produce behavioral tendencies that, in modern environments, may be neither necessary nor adaptive.

Evolutionary psychology traces its earliest roots to nineteenth-century writings on evolution, especially Charles Darwin's *The Descent of Man, and Selection in Relation to Sex* (1871), and William James's *Principles of Psychology* (1890). James asserted that although humans see themselves as creatures of reason—in comparison to instinct-driven animals—human intelligence and behaviors are actually the result of our species' many evolutionarily developed, brain-centered instincts. The field's modern foundations rest on twentieth-century rethinkings of evolutionary theory, particularly George C. Williams's *Adaptation and Natural Selection* (1966), Harvard biologist E. O. Wilson's *Sociobiology: The New Synthesis* (1975) and *Human Nature* (1978), and Donald Symons's *The Evolution of Human Sexuality* (1979). Psychologists E. E. Maccoby and C. N. Jacklin's *The Psychology of Sex Differences* (1974) also had a major impact. Although Maccoby and Jacklin cautioned against attributing male/female differences solely to biology, their critical review of more than

2,000 studies on psychological gender differences concluded that while most were insignificant, there was consistent evidence of "well established" female-male differences in regard to males' greater aggressiveness and superior spatial and mathematical abilities, and females' stronger verbal ability (findings challenged and/or modified by later evolutionary psychologists [see Barkow, et al., 1992]). Current evolutionary psychology is also heavily influenced by Richard Dawkins's *The Selfish Gene* (1976, 1989), which argues that the human body is a "survival machine" for its genes, which direct its evolution to ensure the genes' replication.

Pivotal in the discussion of male and female differences is a focus on the evolutionary process of "sexual selection," the ways organisms evolve to maximize reproductive success. The process of sexual selection adaptation is viewed as potentially explaining differing male-female mating behaviors (e.g., regarding mate selection, frequency of sexual encounters, number of sexual partners, competition for mates); parenting patterns (e.g., commitment to young, stepchild abuse); and other gender-based predispositions and capabilities (e.g., altruism, cooperation, linguistic abilities, family and kinship relations). Human mental, emotional, and behavioral responses, according to evolutionary psychologists, developed due to the adaptive value those responses had in producing and ensuring survival of healthy offspring. Both males and females, they hypothesize, have mental processing structures that, for example, lead us to seek clear-skinned, symmetrically featured, smiling mates—these features being subconsciously recognized signs of possible mates' health and cooperative potential. Some evolutionary psychologists also assert that males are naturally drawn to young women with somewhat exaggerated waist-hip ratios and large breasts because these are indicators of reproductive potential, while females will be drawn to tall, muscular males with plentiful resources (in twenty-first-century terms, money, prestigious careers, etc.) because these are indicators of both healthy genetic strains and ability to provide well for offspring. Such traits are termed "honest signs" of fitness that allow selection of the best mate.

Although females and males both invest in the survival of their offspring, evolutionary psychologists assert that the form and degree of that investment often differs because of the physiology of human sexual reproduction. Termed "parental investment," this hypothesis refers to a combination of factors related to females "investing" greater physical resources and energies than do males in production of gametes (ova are considerably larger than sperm), and in gestation, childbirth, lactation, and rearing of offspring. The resulting adaptations may account for gender differences we see today. The stronger female response of tenderness and protection toward individuals of extreme youth, for example, can be explained as triggered by cognitive mechanisms in females that evolved in relation to their greater "parental investment."

A key component of sexual selection is "female choice." The human reproductive process allows a female to produce a maximum of roughly twenty offspring in a lifetime, while the number of offspring a male can produce is limited only by his access to females. Therefore, evolutionary psychologists state, there is competition among males for the chance to mate, and female choice of mating partners is a significant selection pressure. As a result, males have evolved both a drive to mate more frequently and traits that make them more successful competitors for females. Such traits include desirable physical features, behaviors (e.g., aggression, courtship displays), and skills (e.g., hunting food, fighting). Another posited result of reproductive process differences is that Pleistocene males became predisposed to engaging in risky behaviors because by so doing they demonstrated to females and competitors their strength and prowess. Dubbed the "handicap principle" by Amotz Zahdvi (1997), these behaviors were triggered in situations in which the potential reproductive advantage outweighed the risk.

Another significant aspect of sexual selection is the individual's ability to ensure that she or he is expending energies on her or his own genetic offspring. Among our Pleistocene ancestors, although women invested considerable time and energy gestating, breast-feeding, and caring for offspring, the payoff was that females were guaranteed the children they were investing so much in were genetically theirs. The early human male, however, had no way of knowing whose child a female was bearing (since both ovulation and conception, the evolutionary psychologists say, are hidden in humans), nor whether the mother would prove successful at rearing the child. Thus, some researchers hypothesize, while a female strove to hold the attention of one or more males to father and help support her offspring, males developed a built-in "powerful craving" (Buss and Malamuth 1996, 16) for frequent sexual encounters with multiple women and a less fully developed commitment to parenting. This same cognitive mechanism, they add, can be seen at work in men and women today, in studies on attitudes toward marital infidelity that indicate that women are more likely to be greatly concerned with whether their husband has formed a new emotional tie (indicating greater likelihood of his providing support to the other woman), while men are more concerned about sexual infidelity itself.

Feminist and masculinity studies scholars from the natural and social sciences (and other fields) present strong critiques of evolutionary psychology, stating that the label and field itself is simply a move to avoid the stigma of sociobiology—often termed sexist and racist by its critics—while retaining the same biases and scientifically questionable assumptions and methodologies (Rose and Rose 2000). Evolutionary psychology and its practitioners are charged with disingenuousness in regard to the political agendas inherent in their work. Critiques of evolutionary psychology's science center on five primary areas:

1. reductionism (e.g., seeing the individual gene as determinant of evolutionary adaptations; reducing the mind to a mechanical model);
2. mistaking physiological enabling features (e.g., DNA) for causative agents in human emotions, skills, behaviors, and social systems;
3. application of existing (particularly Western) gender roles and stereotypes in formulating hypotheses about early humans, as well as in designing studies and interpreting data, often resulting in circular logic;
4. questionable use of nonhuman (e.g., primate, duck, insect) studies to explain human behaviors;
5. linguistic slippage both in applying to animals terms relating to human experiences that carry complex socio-historic meanings (e.g., "rape," "homosexuality," "fidelity") and in the lack of consistent definitions for key concepts (e.g., "aggression," "competition," "nurturance"), including differential definitions when applying terms to similar male and female behaviors.

Elizabeth Renfro

Further Reading:
Barkow, Jerome, Leda Cosmides, and John Tooby, eds. 1992. *The Adapted Mind: Evolutionary Psychology and the Generation of Culture.* New York: Oxford University Press.
Barash, David. 2001. *Revolutionary Biology: The New, Gene-Centered View of Life.* New Brunswick, NJ: Transaction.
Buss, David M., and Neil M. Malamuth, eds. 1996. *Sex, Power, Conflict: Evolutionary and Feminist Perspectives.* Oxford, UK: Oxford University Press.
Dawkins, Richard. 1976, 1989. *The Selfish Gene.* Oxford, UK: Oxford University Press.
Rose, Hilary, and Steven Rose, eds. 2000. *Alas, Poor Darwin: Arguments against Evolutionary Psychology.* New York: Harmony Books.

Expectant Fatherhood

Despite the fact that approximately 90 percent of married couples in the United States become parents, there has been comparatively little study or documentation of the experience of the transition to fatherhood (Cowan and Cowan 2000). Couples often discuss having a baby at some point, and then the father is surprised to learn his partner has made a unilateral decision on the timing of conception and is pregnant. This typically begins a journey on which the father is along for the ride, experiencing pregnancy vicariously through his mate and being perceived primarily as a support person and breadwinner. Men tend to be involved as parents to the extent they are allowed or invited to be by the mother. Fathers are very important to family stability and child development. Men are demonstrating increasing interest in playing more active roles in childbearing and parenting.

Men lag behind women in their developing sense of being a parent. Fathers depend on the changing body and behavior of their mates to reinforce the reality of the pregnancy. Typically, the pregnancy and baby are not completely real to the father until well after birth, when the baby enters the father's living space and life (Jordan 1990). This gives women a head start on parenting and involvement with the baby.

Many men attend childbirth preparation classes with their partners, but often resent being relegated to the role of coach, rather than being acknowledged as a parent. During labor and birth, fathers search for an appropriate role to enact. Some take on the role of coach, while others are teammates, and still others are merely witnesses (Chapman 1991). During labor, fathers often feel helpless in their inability to alleviate their partner's pain or speed the process. They also fear for their mate's safety and survival. The actual birth of their baby is an intensely emotional experience (Chandler and Field 1997).

Men often have little prior experience with infants and also believe their mates have instinctual and innate parenting abilities. Mothers characteristically assume the role of primary caregiver with the father relegated to the role of assistant or support person. Fathers lack role models for parenting. They want to be more active and involved than their own fathers were; yet they lack role models, guidance, or support to achieve this goal. Over the transition to fatherhood, men labor to incorporate the role of father into their identity and to be perceived by others as an important part of childbearing and parenting. Friends, family, coworkers, the baby, and his mate play key roles in recognizing and acknowledging the man in his new role of father (Jordan 1990). Fathers continue to evolve as more active participants in caregiving and parenting.

Pamela Jordan

See also Fatherhood

Further Reading:

Brott, Armin A. 1997. *The New Father.* New York: Abbeville Press.

Brott, Armin A., and Jennifer Ash. 1995. *The Expectant Father.* New York: Abbeville Press.

Chapman, Linda. 1991. "Searching: Expectant Fathers' Experiences during Labor and Birth." *Journal of Perinatal and Neonatal Nursing* 4, no. 4: 21–29.

Chandler, Susan, and Peggy Anne Field. 1997. "Becoming a Father: First-Time Fathers' Experience of Labor and Delivery." *Journal of Nurse-Midwifery* 42, no. 1: 17–24.

Cowan, Carolyn Pape, and Philip A. Cowan. 2000. *When Partners Become Parents.* Mahwah, NJ: Lawrence Erlbaum.

Jordan, Pamela L. 1990. "Laboring for Relevance: Expectant and New Fatherhood." *Nursing Research* 39, no. 1: 11–16.

Extramarital Sex

See Husbands

F

Family

The family is a primary social group and a social institution that organizes interpersonal and intergenerational relationships and reproduces gender ideals and inequalities. As a primary social group, the family is a collection of individuals who recognize each other as family members and interact in socially prescribed ways with regard to sexual intimacy, emotional expression, domestic labor, and the rearing of children. As a social institution, the family allocates resources and links individuals to society through shared values, norms, and statuses. Families reproduce gender relations by assigning different rights, duties, and expectations to husbands and sons and wives and daughters. Families often concentrate wealth in male household heads, exercise control over female sexuality, allocate housework and emotional labor to females, and socialize boys and girls to occupy different positions in future families and in society.

The United States Census Bureau defines a family as two or more persons related by birth, marriage, or adoption who live together as one household. Other family definitions focus on love, support, and commitment rather than living arrangements, legal status, or biological relationship. Debates about what constitutes a "real" family have become more complex as divorce, remarriage, same-sex marriage, nonmarital birth, cohabitation, childlessness, adoption, surrogacy, and other kinship practices have gained social acceptance. Debates about family definitions and family values often focus on men's and women's "proper" roles in families, and tend to emerge during periods of rapid social change (Coontz 1992; Stacey 1996). Changes in economic, political, and social conditions promote shifts in family ideals, family composition, and family practices, and studying such changes provides insight into the social organization of gender.

Women have been primary caretakers of children in all cultures, but men's participation in family labor has varied from virtually no direct involvement to active participation in all aspects of children's routine care, feeding, instruction, and discipline. Anthropologists have identified two general patterns of men's family involvement in the small-scale societies representing most of human history—one intimate and the other aloof. In the intimate pattern, men eat and sleep with their wives and children, talk with them during evening meals, attend births, and participate actively in infant care. In the contrasting aloof pattern, men often eat and sleep apart from women, spend their leisure time in the company of other men, stay away during births, and seldom help with childcare. Research shows that about half of the world's known societies have exhibited close father-child relationships. Compared to societies with distant fathers, those with involved fathers are more likely to be peaceful and to afford women opportunities to act independently, control property, and be public leaders. Distant-father societies, in contrast, are more likely to encourage violent competition among men, exclude women from leadership, and demand deference from wives (Coltrane 1996; Hewlett 1991).

As technological advances promoted the accumulation of wealth and the development of complex societal systems over the long sweep of history, men's family relationships remained embedded in patterns of production and property ownership. Different cultural, linguistic, and legal conceptions of families developed reflecting these economic and power relations. In ancient Greece, "family" (*oikos*) referred to the household economy—including the land, house, and servants belonging to the male household head. In ancient Rome, the term for "family" derived from *famulus,* meaning "servant," and *familia,* meaning "the man's domestic property." In medieval Europe, the male family head not only exercised rights over wife and children, but peasants who lived on feudal estates were considered part of the lord's "family," and he was called their "father" (pater), even though they were not related to him by blood. In seventeenth- and eighteenth-century Europe and America, men's family involvements continued to be shaped by productive activities. Because men's work as farmers, artisans, and tradesmen occurred in family households, most fathers were a visible presence, introducing sons to farming or craft work and overseeing others' work. The preindustrial family home was thus a system of control, as well as a center of production, and both functions reinforced the father's authority and shaped family relation-

ships. Though mothers provided most direct care for infants and young children, men tended to be active in the training and tutoring of children, so much so that most parental advice was addressed to fathers (Griswold 1993).

When market economies took over from home-based production in the nineteenth and twentieth centuries, the father's position as head of household and moral instructor of children was slowly transformed. Men were increasingly called upon to seek employment outside the home and their direct contact with family members declined. As the wage-labor economy developed, men's occupational achievement outside the household took on stronger moral overtones and men came to be seen as fulfilling their family and civic duty not by teaching and interacting with their children as before, but by supporting the family financially. The ideal of separate gender spheres developed—work for him and home for her. Middle- and upper-class women wore tight corsets symbolizing their incapacity and making it impossible to perform hard labor. As images of the ideal white, middle-class woman became more fragile, images of the ideal white, middle-class man shifted toward rugged individualism. Because men's and women's underlying physical and emotional capacities changed little during this era, scholars suggest that the real cause of the development of separate spheres ideology was increased competition between them for jobs (Coontz 1992; Kimmel 1996).

Marriage laws have also encouraged gender difference and male privilege. The common law doctrine of coverture, which essentially made the wife not only the property of, but also the person of the husband, was only officially abandoned in the mid-nineteenth century. The ideal of a wife giving up her identity to her husband continues to pervade the symbolic meaning of marriage, illustrated by women adopting the surname of husbands when they marry. Following Roman and English common law traditions, until the 1970s, marriage contracts in the United States also made the husband the legal head of the household and held the wife responsible for domestic services and childcare. Similarly, legal precedents allowed husbands to "physically chastise" their wives, with abusive husbands often protected by family privacy ideals and governmental neglect (Collier 1995). Most marriage laws now treat husbands and wives similarly, but in some states, married women still lose legal rights to control property or enter into legal contracts on the same basis as men or unmarried women.

Although individuals are socialized in many different contexts throughout life, the family is the primary initial socialization agent for children. Modern parents transmit gender-laden assumptions and values, often determining the sex of their child before birth so that they can plan for gender-appropriate nurseries and wardrobes. Boys are housed in blue or red rooms outfitted with sports and adventure paraphernalia; girls in pink nurseries with dolls and soft things to cuddle. Newborn boys are dressed in blue and given gifts of tiny jeans and bold-colored outfits, whereas girls are outfitted in pink-ruffled pastel ensembles. Parents and others use gender stereotypes to assess a baby's personality, behavior, and potential, and interact with infants based on these preconceptions. For example, research shows that parents (particularly fathers) tend to react to infant boys by encouraging activity and more whole-body stimulation and to girls with more verbalization, interpersonal stimulation, and nurturance.

Gender-differentiated treatment continues as children grow, reinforced through toys (trucks, sports equipment, and toy guns for boys; dolls, tea sets, and toy stoves for girls), as well as expectations for behavior that result in praise and reinforcement for gender-appropriate behavior and reprimand and punishment for gender-inappropriate behavior. Parents tend to actively discourage displays of emotion in boys by pressuring them

not to cry or otherwise express their feelings, whereas girls are not only encouraged to express their emotions, but are also taught to pay attention to the feelings of others. Throughout childhood, fathers tend to enforce these gender stereotypes more than mothers, especially in sons. Children thus come to see the world in gender-polarized ways, preparing them to recreate a world in which boys and men and girls and women are not only different, but polar opposites (Bem 1993; Coltrane 1998).

Boys are raised to expect mothers to wait on and nurture them, and girls to help mothers perform repetitive family work. By associating masculinity with "anything not feminine" and associating femininity with family and domesticity, boys and men are defined as figuratively outside families. Boys are expected to reject their mothers and leave their families to achieve manhood, but are later expected to come back to domesticity by creating and leading families of their own. Having internalized independent masculine ideals and subsequently experienced valorization of them in all-male peer groups, young men often find themselves "force-fitting" their masculinity into "feminine" family life. Rather than participating in families through caring, nurturing, and serving, men generally try instead to mold families to conform to their own sense of masculine entitlement, expecting that their wives will care for and serve them. Primarily as a result of such care and attention, men tend to benefit more from marriage than women, doing less housework and reporting greater marital satisfaction, less depression, and fewer mental health problems than married women (Coltrane 1998).

The ideal of separate spheres, coupled with labor-market inequities, has encouraged a vision of men as breadwinners and women as homemakers. This gendered division of labor shapes marital relations, parenting practices, and emotional relationships in families. Although women's labor-force participation has increased dramatically in recent decades, mothers still do most of the family work, including scheduling and managing children's activities and monitoring their social and emotional lives. Fathers, in contrast, often remain on the sidelines of family life, serving as helpers, playmates, and occasional disciplinarians. The resulting emotional distance between fathers and children is increasingly seen as a problem, insofar as popular cultural ideals now expect even breadwinner fathers to be emotionally connected to their children (Coltrane 1996; Townsend 2002).

More American couples are attempting to share breadwinning and homemaking, and such practices are becoming more common in all ethnic groups, class levels, and geographic regions. Although the average American husband still does only about half as much family work as his wife, absolute levels of involvement have increased, and the expectations for fathers to be involved with their children have increased substantially. When men participate in the nurturing and supportive activities that serve children, they are also more likely to share in childcare and home maintenance activities. In contrast, when men enact fatherhood based on masculine recreation or family headship, they share less domestic labor with wives. In an estimated 20 percent of two-parent families in the United States, men are almost as involved as mothers interacting with and being available to their children (Coltrane 1998). When fathers share childcare and housework with their partners, mothers escape total responsibility for family work, evaluate the division of labor as more fair, are less depressed, and enjoy higher levels of marital satisfaction. When men regularly care for young children, they emphasize verbal interaction, notice and use more subtle emotional cues, and treat sons and daughters similarly rather than focusing on play, giving orders, and sex typing children as traditional fathers do. Regular care by fathers encourages less gender stereotyping among young adult children and promotes independence in daughters and emotional sensitivity in sons (Coltrane 1996).

Further changes in men's family involvements are likely to be driven by women's increasing independence. Ironically, women's enhanced economic position also makes them able to form families and raise children without men. In the future, men will be less able to rely on superior earnings and institutionalized privilege to maintain family connections and will be expected to care for and serve family members in new ways. Some will not sustain family commitments, some will maintain them through breadwinning, and others will maintain them through equal partnerships and direct caregiving. Diversity in men's family involvement is thus likely to be a hallmark of the future.

Scott Coltrane

Further Reading:
Bem, Sandra Lipsitz. 1993. *The Lenses of Gender.* New Haven, CT: Yale University Press.
Collier, Richard. 1995. *Masculinity, Law and the Family.* London: Routledge.
Coltrane, Scott. 1996. *Family Man: Fatherhood, Housework and Gender Equity.* New York: Oxford University Press.
———. 1998. *Gender and Families.* Newbury Park, CA: Pine Forge/Sage.
Coontz, Stephanie. 1992. *The Way We Never Were: American Families and the Nostalgia Trap.* New York: BasicBooks.
Griswold, Richard L. 1993. *Fatherhood in America: A History.* New York: Basic Books.
Hewlett, Barry S. 1991. *Intimate Fathers.* Ann Arbor, MI: University of Michigan Press.
Kimmel, Michael. 1996. *Manhood in America: A Cultural History.* New York: Free Press.
Stacey, Judith. 1996. *In the Name of the Family: Rethinking Family Values in the Postmodern Age.* Boston, MA: Beacon.
Townsend, Nicholas. 2002. *The Package Deal: Marriage, Work, and Fatherhood in Men's Lives.* Philadelphia: Temple University Press.

Farming

At some point in their upbringing, most children in the English-speaking world still encounter this old and innocent little ditty:

> *The farmer in the dell, the farmer in the dell*
> *Hi-ho the dairy-o, the farmer in the dell*

Some never learn any more of the song than that. Which is perhaps just as well, for by the time we reach the second verse, "The Farmer in the Dell" is no longer so innocent.

The farmer takes a wife, the farmer takes a wife
Hi-ho the dairy-o, the farmer takes a wife . . .

This verse sings not only of masculine possession of the feminine—the "taking" of a wife—but also of an old cultural presumption about farming: that farmers are men. Like so much else, farming is culturally gendered.

At first sight, it may appear that there is ample empirical evidence to substantiate the presumption that farmers are men. For instance, in reviewing U.S. Census of Agriculture data one may find that an overwhelming majority of farmers are male and also find similar figures in censuses conducted around the world, in rich countries and poor. But central to these figures is the determination of what counts as "farming," and how census forms are set up. Despite industrialization, farming remains a largely heterosexual family-based endeavor, even in the rich countries. Why, then, do census forms presume that there is "a" farmer in a farm family, and not a farm couple? Are the tasks of family life—cooking, cleaning, childcare—any less central to the success of a "family farm" than the tasks of the field and barn? Moreover, in addition to taking on most of the work in the home, most farm women also do at least some of the work in the field and the barn, as well as doing much, if not most, of the increasing amount of paperwork farming requires. In many poor countries, women actually do the majority of farm and barn labor, including the heavy physical labor of planting, weeding, and harvesting (Boserup 1989 [1970]).

In the early 2000s social scientists have begun to study the construction of the cultural association of men and farming. Campbell and Bell (2000) suggest that there are two broad, and interacting, forms of this construction: the *masculine rural* and the *rural masculine*. The *masculine rural* refers to the creation of ideas of masculinity within rural spaces, as in the idea of the farming man, the mining man, and the logging man. The *rural masculine* refers to how rural spaces themselves help to construct ideas of masculinity everywhere, as in the billboard image of the Marlboro man or the pick-up truck in the suburban driveway.

But these constructions are not accidental. Gender ideas are created and recreated in social interaction. Masculinity is a social performance both witnessed and shaped by institutions of family, economy, religion, education, media, and politics. For example, Bell (2000) found that ideas of sexual orientation in rural masculinity are constructed and reinforced by the media. In rural Iowa, Peter et al. (2000) found that the institutions of the family and the structures of performance within agriculture help form and recreate masculine farm identity that had implications in the types of agricultural practices farmers adopt, and decision-making practices on the farm and within the family. Moreover, Peter et al. (2000) argue that particular types of rural masculinities manifest within both conventional and alternative agricultural arenas. Campbell (2000) makes the argument that rural masculinity in New Zealand pubs reproduces a pub(lic) masculinity with its own rituals and socially constructed behaviors. Meares (1997) showed how quality-of-life issues on the farm in Minnesota are socially constructed along with gender identity and the spirituality of the male farmer.

Some studies of rural masculinities show how gender identity is linked to power and influence. For instance, Kimmel and Ferber (2000) explain how the ideologies of right-wing militia groups and ideologies of masculinities are interwoven. They argue that right-wing militia groups in the United States tend to be men's movements that reinforce a traditional, masculine identity. Woodward (2000) examines how military training is also the construction of rural masculine identity. Liepens (2000) explains that agriculture-based masculinities in Australia and New Zealand are constructed and maintained by agricultural organizations and the media. Little and Jones (2000) link rural masculinity and rural policy issues.

The link between gender and power in farming is not inevitable, however. Alternative structures of performance for social interaction can provide the cultural space for more egalitarian solutions to gender relations in farming. For instance, many sustainable agriculture groups have a more open and dialogue-based organizational style and likewise exhibit far more gender equity than conventional farm organizations (Bell et al. 2003; Peter et al. 2000). Future studies may further the understanding of the social support mechanisms necessary for not just constructing but reconstructing masculinities in rural areas. In this light, conjuring up alternative cultural symbols of farming identity may have the next generation singing different versions of old folk songs and promoting a better understanding of the interdependence of everyone in the food system.

Gregory Peter
Michael M. Bell

Further Reading:
Bell, David. 2000. "Farm Boys and Wild Men: Rurality, Masculinity, and Homosexuality." *Rural Sociology* 65: 547–561.
Bell, Michael, with Susan Jarnagin, Gregory Peter, and Donna Bauer. 2003. *Farming for Us All: Practical Agriculture and the Cultivation of Sustainability.* College Station, PA: Pennsylvania State University Press.
Boserup, Ester. 1989 (1970). *Woman's Role in Economic Development.* London: Earthscan.
Brandth, Berit. 1995. "Rural Masculinity in Transition: Gender Images in Tractor Advertisements." *Journal of Rural Studies* 11: 123–133.
Campbell, Hugh. 2000. "The Glass Phallus: Pub(lic) Masculinity and Drinking in Rural New Zealand." *Rural Sociology* 65: 562–581.
Campbell, Hugh, and Michael M. Bell. 2000. "The Question of Rural Masculinities." *Rural Sociology* 65: 532–546.
Kimmel, Michael, and Abby Ferber. 2000. "'White Men Are This Nation': Right-Wing Militias and the Restoration of Rural American Masculinity." *Rural Sociology* 65: 582–604.
Law, Robin, Hugh Campbell, and John Dolan, eds. 1999. *Masculinities in Aotearoa/New Zealand.* Palmerston North, NZ: Dunmore Press.
Liepins, Ruth. 2000. "Making Men: The Construction and Representation of Agriculture-Based Masculinities in Australia and New Zealand." *Rural Sociology* 65: 605–620.
Little, Jo, and O. Jones. 2000. "Masculinity, Gender, and Rural Policy." *Rural Sociology* 65: 621–639.
Meares, Alison. 1997. "Making the Transition from Conventional to Sustainable Agriculture: Gender, Social Movement Participation and Quality of Life on the Family Farm." *Rural Sociology* 62: 21–47.
Peter, Gregory, Michael Bell, Susan Jarnagin, and Donna Bauer. 2000. "Coming Back across the Fence: Masculinity and the Transition to Sustainable Agriculture." *Rural Sociology* 65: 215–233.
Stolen, Kristi A. 1995. "The Gentle Exercise of Male Power in Rural Argentina." *Identities: Global Studies in Culture and Power* 2: 385–406.
Woodward, Rachel. 2000. "Warrior Heroes and Little Green Men: Soldiers, Military Training, and the Construction of Rural Masculinities." *Rural Sociology* 65: 640–657.

Fassbinder, Rainer Werner (1945–1982)

Although he gained world fame for his stunning "portraits de femmes," such as in *The Bitter Tears of Petra von Kant* (1972), *Fontane Effi Briest* (1974), *The Marriage of Maria Braun* (1979), *Lili Marleen* (1980), and *Lola* (1981), German filmmaker Rainer Werner Fassbinder created the most intimate and penetrating movies about the masculine identity.

Born on 31 May 1945 in Bad Wörishofen, near München, (West) Germany, Rainer Werner Fassbinder always said he was born in 1946, to distance himself from Germany during World War II. After a few years in drama schools, he directed his first feature film, *Love Is Colder than Death* (1969), a title that could be used for all his subsequent works. In all his movies, treason is present and love is complicated or discredited.

One of the early themes of Fassbinder's movies was alienation through work: *Why Does Herr R. Run Amok?* (1969), *The Merchant of the Four Seasons* (1971), and *Eight Hours Are Not a Day* (1973) all show a worker who gives all his energy to earn his living and can't engage in any other activities—except drinking. His provocative movie *Fox and his Friends* (1974) shows that some homosexuals can abuse other gay men, just because some are younger and more naive. Here, Fassbinder illustrates the class differences between the young worker (played by Fassbinder himself) who is introduced into a more snobbish milieu. In melodramatic films such as *I Only Want You to Love Me* (1975), *Mother Kusters Goes to Heaven* (1975), and *Lili Marleen* (1980), Fassbinder introduces his favorite theme: the weaker man dominated by others, especially women. This is also true in *Bremer Freiheit* (1973) and specially *The Marriage of Maria Braun* (1979), when a widow from World War II becomes a powerful assistant in a big German company, around 1950. This gendered dilemma culminates in his movie titled *In the Year of the Thirteen Moons* (1978), when a man changes his sex to seduce the man with whom he is in love, hoping that he will be more attractive as a woman. Even his ultimate masterpiece, *Veronika Voss* (1982), shows an actress destroyed by another woman (her doctor), and the man in love with her can't succeed while trying to free her from drug dependence.

In many Fassbinder movies, heterosexual love becomes impossible. In *The Marriage of Maria Braun* (1979) and *Lili Marleen* (1980), the heroine is separated from the man she loves because of the war. In *Chinese Roulette* (1976), both illicit couples are just too immature to hold a normal relationship.

In his fifteen-hour feature film, *Berlin Alexanderplatz* (1980), adapted from Alfred Döblin's book, Fassbinder illustrates a theme taken from the German expressionist era: a man who cannot face his freedom. When Franz Biberkopf gets out of jail, he just doesn't know where to go and puts his hands on his ears and screams like the figure in Edward Munch's famous painting. In other films—such as *Despair* (1977) (from Vladimir Nabokov's novel), the central character feels the presence of his double, and therefore can't stand his attractive wife anymore. Fassbinder's last film, *Querelle* (1982), is taken from Jean Genet's *Querelle de Brest*. It is a dark universe inhabited only by men, where the only female character (played by Jeanne Moreau) sings Oscar Wilde's poem, "Each Man Kills the Thing He Loves." But Fassbinder always said *Querelle* was more a film about the quest for identity, not about homosexuality (Schidor 1982, 10). This comment could apply to all his movies.

Yves Laberge

Further Reading:
Elsaesser, Thomas. 1996. *Fassbinder's Germany: History, Identity, Subject.* Amsterdam, The Netherlands: Amsterdam University Press.
Schidor, Dieter. 1982. *Rainer Werner Fassbinder tourne Querelle.* Paris: Persona.
Shattuc, Jane. 1995. *Television, Tabloids, and Tears: Fassbinder and Popular Culture.* Minneapolis, MN: University of Minnesota Press.
Watson, Wallace Steadman. 1996. *Understanding Rainer Werner Fassbinder: Film as Private and Public Art.* Columbia, SC: University of South Carolina Press.

Fatherhood

Social scientists have studied a wide range of topics related to fatherhood in the latter decades of the twentieth and early years of the twenty-first centuries. Although psychologists took the early lead in this field, anthropologists, economists, historians, legal scholars, sociologists, and others have increasingly made important contributions to understanding the social and cultural context for fathering and how fathers' involvement is related to outcomes for children and men.

Some scholars have dealt explicitly with how men's experiences as fathers are intertwined with gender issues (Marsiglio and Pleck, forthcoming). Fathering can be studied in connection to dominant as well as alternative constructions of masculinities that give meaning to men's everyday lives in diverse situations. However, much of the scholarship on fatherhood has not been guided directly by a gender lens or concern about masculinities in particular.

To do so requires confronting several debates. First, are fathers, as men, uniquely equipped with characteristics that differentiate their parenting styles and contributions to children from those of mothers (see also Parke, forthcoming)? The debate is often couched in terms of "essentialist" and "social constructionist" approaches to fatherhood. Two of the main points underlying the essentialist position are that gender differences in parenting are universal and biologically based, and fathers' uniquely masculine form of parenting significantly improves developmental outcomes for children, especially sons (see Silverstein and Auerbach 1999). Evidence suggests that gender-differentiated child rearing is far less universal than often thought. Fathers' level of involvement relative to mothers varies significantly across world societies, although men, on average, are harder to motivate to be caregivers in various types of societies. Once motivated, they can be as effective in their parenting as mothers. Further, fathers around the world are likely to have "similar concerns about the safety, health, and tradeoffs between spending time with their children and doing things that attract and keep women (e.g., working to increase status, prestige or wealth)" (Hewlett 1992, xv).

Second, how does the style of men's fathering contribute to gendered inequalities in the context of committed relationships involving marriage or cohabitation as well as nonresident relationships? A number of studies in the 1980s and 1990s have consistently shown that compared to mothers, coresident fathers spend considerably less time actively involved in face-to-face interaction (engagement) with their children or being accessible to them (Pleck 1997). The good news is that the relative (compared to mothers) and absolute time these fathers spend engaged with or accessible to their children has increased

since the 1970s (Pleck 1997). For nonresident fathers, the picture is less rosy. Overall, these fathers have relatively low rates of involvement in their children's lives, fathers become increasingly less involved as children age, and there is no evidence that nonresident fathers in general have become more involved in recent years (Marsiglio, Amato, Day, and Lamb 2000). As expected, fathers with joint legal custody are more involved than those without. Debates are heated as to whether these low rates are due primarily to women's "gatekeeping" or fathers' genuine lack of interest.

Third, how does fathering vary with age, race or ethnicity, socioeconomic status, and sexual orientation? These contexts create different opportunities and obstacles for fathers involving expectations about men presenting a masculine image. Young males are often at a disadvantage because they are unlikely to possess the parenting and interpersonal skills needed to be effective fathers. Men of color, especially African Americans, face a number of problems as fathers, too. Most notably they tend to represent a high-risk population that, when compared to whites, have a high rate of unemployment, imprisonment, poor access to health care, a shorter life span, less education, and are more likely to be victims of fatal crimes. Though accentuated for African Americans, having or not having money can shape how men of any race feel about themselves as fathers and affect their ability to negotiate their involvement with their children. Being poor restricts fathers' options and is most damaging to those fathers who do not live with their children. With money comes power, and with power men are better positioned to manage their paternal identities, fathering experiences, and family arrangements to display their masculinity. Finally, gay fathers often must battle societal stereotypes that emphasize how the badge of masculinity is based on heterosexual fatherhood. Although the data are limited, some evidence suggests that when compared to heterosexual fathers, gay fathers are more nurturing and less traditional in their parenting (Bigner and Jacobsen 1992).

With these questions to consider, we might address the theoretical, methodological, and substantive issues. A number of theorists have wrestled with how to conceptualize fatherhood and father involvement. Gender issues sometimes affect the way frameworks are developed and interpreted. For example, how concerns about gender equity within domestic life or the value of fathers' breadwinning are factored into the frameworks has implications for how fathers are studied and evaluated.

Researchers have examined the linkages between dimensions of the father-child relationship and developmental outcomes among children and fathers. Most of this research has focused on how aspects of father involvement influence minor children's lives. This involvement has been measured typically in terms of one-on-one engagement activities, financial support, and visitation. The latter two have been particularly relevant to studies of nonresident fathers. Far less is known about how minor children affect fathers and little is known about how older fathers affect their adult children. Some evidence suggests that fathers who are positively involved with children when the children are young are more likely to become invested in their communities when they reach midlife (Snarey 1993).

Researchers have become more attentive to how structural features of men's lives as fathers are related to the processes of fathering. Many of the analyses of fathers' involvement consider fathers in different demographic circumstances including two-parent and single-parent households, nonresident arrangements, and stepfamilies. Although much of this research does not use a gender lens, the gendered social order affects how fathers' lives are structured and how they define and negotiate their involvement with children.

Although conclusions must be tempered because of numerous methodological concerns, most studies of fathers in two-parent households show that positive father involvement is related to desirable child outcomes such as academic success, lower levels of behavioral and emotional problems, and positive social behaviors (social competence, popularity, size of support networks) (Marsiglio, Amato, Day, and Lamb 2000). Nonresident fathers can also enhance their children's lives, largely by providing authoritative parenting (providing emotional support, monitoring children's behavior, and noncoercive disciplining) within the context of cooperative relations between the birth parents. Because such arrangements are not typical, nonresident fathers face an uphill battle in their parenting efforts.

Future fatherhood research should use a critical gender perspective. The politics of gender continue to be heated when attention turns to the longtime debate about whether biological factors should be considered when studying fathers' behaviors. With recent technological advances, researchers now are able to examine in more rigorous ways social, behavioral, and biological processes, including fathers' potentially unique ways of interacting with children. Though studying social and cultural factors is likely to provide more penetrating and broader insights about men's complex experiences as fathers, researchers would be remiss to discourage explorations of the "possible" biosocial dimensions of fathering (parenting).

A compelling line of inquiry involves identifying why some males are more likely than others to embrace a "nurturing" father model. Additional research also is need to better understand how changing structural, cultural, social, and psychological factors influence how fathers' negotiate their contributions to parenting and domestic labor as well as their "agreements" about child custody, support, and visitation.

How are fathers' interactions with their children shaped by their involvement in different gendered organizational and social contexts? Prime sites to purse this question include several social movements, such as

Promise Keepers and fathers' rights groups in which gendered ideologies of family life are prominently featured, as well as group counseling sessions for violent men. Other viable research settings are those flavored by a distinctive masculine culture (e.g., military, law enforcement, prison). How do fathers, as men, manage their impressions to others inside various organizational and social settings that transcend the typical family/household setting? Exploring father involvement in these types of contexts frames fathering as a socially constructed performance, implicating how the gender order both supports and discourages fathers' involvement. Further, scholars should continue to address the complex realities of contemporary men's lives. These realities include: the diverse and dynamic ways men move in and out of relationships/households involving children; how gendered social structures (e.g., work, prison) and processes (e.g., negotiating childcare or visitation) within and outside of a family context influence men's involvement with their children; and how fathers' resources, perceptions, and ways of interacting with their children may change over the duration of fathers' and children's shared life courses. Central to this line of inquiry are men's roles as stepfathers. Prevailing sociodemographic patterns ensure that large numbers of men will continue to face the opportunities and struggles associated with being fatherly toward other men's children.

For those planning to journey deeper into the fatherhood literature and consider these and related questions, it is advisable to be mindful of how knowledge about fathering is produced, disseminated, and evaluated. Research and policy issues subject to the most vigorous debate focus on: whether (and how) fathers matter to their children in unique and meaningful ways, the presumed positive value of marriage in fathers' lives, nonresident fathers' financial and interpersonal commitments to their children, and the potential danger that stepfathers may pose for their stepchildren. Those studying or debating

these issues sometimes practice gender politics and swear allegiance to various brands of feminism, family and/or religious values, theoretical perspectives, or modes of scientific inquiry. Stakeholders most effective in framing the key issues and paradigms in the minds of the research community, the general public, and policymakers shape the types of questions researchers ask, the way research is conducted, and how research is presented, interpreted, and used by researchers, policymakers, social service professionals, and the general public alike. Thus, becoming familiar intimately with this literature bolsters one's appreciation for how the gender-related and ideological struggles among the knowledge producers can confound research and political agendas within the field itself.

William Marsiglio

See also Expectant Fatherhood; Fatherhood Responsibility Movement; Fathers, Cultural Representation of; Fathers, Gay; Fathers, Nonresidential; Fathers' Rights; Paternity; Perinatal Loss

Further Reading:

Arendell, Terry. 1995. *Fathers & Divorce.* Thousand Oaks, CA: Sage.

Bigner, J. J., and R. B. Jacobsen. 1992. "Adult Responses to Child Behavior and Attitudes toward Fathering: Gay and Non-Gay Fathers." *Journal of Homosexuality* 23: 99–112.

Blankenhorn, David. 1995. *Fatherless America: Confronting Our Most Urgent Social Problem.* New York: Basic Books.

Booth, Alan, and Ann C. Crouter. 1998. *Men in Families: When Do They Get Involved? What Difference Does It Make?* Mahwah, NJ: Lawrence Erlbaum.

Braver, S. L., and D. O'Connell. 1998. *Divorced Dads: Shattering the Myths.* New York: Tarcher/Putnam.

Coltrane, S. 1996. *Family Man: Fatherhood, Housework, and Gender Equity.* New York: Oxford University Press.

Daniels, C. R. 1998. *Lost Fathers: The Politics of Fatherlessness in America.* New York: St. Martin's Press.

Day, R. D., and M. E. Lamb. In press. *Measuring and Conceptualizing Paternal Involvement.* Mahwah, NJ: Lawrence Erlbaum.

Dowd, N. E. 2000. *Redefining Fatherhood.* New York: New York University Press.

Federal Interagency Forum and Child and Family Statistics. 1998. *Nurturing Fatherhood: Improving Data and Research on Male Fertility, Family Formation, and Fatherhood.* Washington, DC: U.S. Government.

Gerson, K. 1993. *No Man's Land: Men's Changing Commitments to Family and Work.* New York: Basic Books.

Griswold, R. L. 1993. *Fatherhood in America: A History.* New York: Basic Books.

Hawkins, A. J., and D. C. Dollahite. 1997. *Generative Fathering: Beyond Deficit Perspectives.* Thousand Oaks, CA: Sage.

Hewlett, B. S. 1992. *Father-Child Relations: Cultural and Biosocial Contexts.* New York: Aldine de Gruyter.

Hobson, B., and D. Morgan. In press. *Making Men into Fathers: Men, Masculinities, and the Social Politics of Fatherhood.* Cambridge, UK: Cambridge University Press.

Kiselica, M. A. 1995. *Multicultural Counseling with Teenage Fathers: A Practical Guide.* Thousand Oaks, CA: Sage.

Lamb, M. E. 1987. *The Fathers' Role: Cross-Cultural Perspectives.* Hillsdale, NJ: Lawrence Erlbaum.

————. 1997. *The Role of the Father in Child Development.* 3d ed. New York: John Wiley and Sons.

LaRossa, R. 1997. *The Modernization of Fatherhood: A Social and Political History.* Chicago: University of Chicago Press.

Lerman, R. I., and T. J. Ooms. 1993. *Young Unwed Fathers: Changing Roles and Emerging Policies.* Philadelphia: Temple University Press.

Lupton, D., and L. Barclay. 1997. *Constructing Fatherhood: Discourses and Experiences.* Thousand Oaks, CA: Sage.

Marsiglio, William. 1995. *Fatherhood: Contemporary Theory, Research, and Social Policy.* Thousand Oaks, CA: Sage.

————. 1998. *Procreative Man.* New York: New York University Press.

Marsiglio, William, Paul Amato, Randal D. Day, and Michael E. Lamb. 2000. "Scholarship on Fatherhood in the 1990s and beyond." *Journal of Marriage and the Family* 62: 1173–1191.

Marsiglio, William, and Joseph H. Pleck. Forthcoming. "Fatherhood and Masculinities." In *The Handbook of Studies on Men and Masculinities.* Edited by R. W. Connell, J. Hearn, and M. Kimmel. Thousand Oaks, CA: Sage.

Parke, Ross D. In press. "Fathers and Families." Pp. 27–33 in *Handbook of Parenting.* 2d ed. Edited by M. Bornstein. Hillsdale, NJ: Lawrence Erlbaum.

Parke, Ross D., and Armin Brott. 1999. *Throwaway Dads: The Myths and Barriers That Keep Men from Being the Fathers They Want to Be.* Boston: Houghton Mifflin Company.

Peters, H. Elizabeth, Gary W. Peterson, S. K. Steinmetz, and R. D. Day. 2000. *Fatherhood: Research, Interventions and Policies.* New York: Haworth Press.

Pleck, Joseph H. 1997. "Paternal Involvement: Levels, Sources, and Consequences." Pp. 123–167 and 325–332 in *The Role of the Father in Child Development.* 3d ed. Edited by M. E. Lamb. New York: John Wiley and Sons.

Popenoe, David. 1996. *Life without Father.* New York: Free Press.

Silverstein, Louise B., and Carl F. Auerbach. 1999. "Deconstructing the Essential Father." *American Psychologist* 6: 397–407.

Snarey, John. 1993. *How Fathers Care for the Next Generation: A Four-Decade Study.* Cambridge, MA: Harvard University Press.

van Dongen, Miriam C. P., Gerard A. B. Frinking, and Menno J. G. Jacobs. 1995. *Changing Fatherhood: An Interdisciplinary Perspective.* Amsterdam, The Netherlands: Thesis Publishers.

Fatherhood Responsibility Movement

The Fatherhood Responsibility Movement (FRM) mobilized in the United States at the beginning of the 1990s as a strategic alliance between a wide range of men's groups with a mutual interest in increased funding and activities around fatherhood. The FRM consists of a network of local and national organizations, such as the National Fatherhood Initiative, the Institute for Responsible Fatherhood and Family Revitalization, the National Practitioners Network for Fathers and Families, and the National Center for Strategic Non Profit Planning and Community Leadership. Since 1994 the FRM has run highly visible public campaigns; expanded the field of research, policy, and programs around fatherhood; and influenced a number of federal initiatives. These include former Vice President Al Gore's "Father to Father Initiative" in 1994; congressional, mayoral, and presidential task forces since 1997; the

"Fathers Count Act of 1999" (H.R. 3073); and the "Responsible Fatherhood Act of 2000" (H.R. 4671). Rallying around politically mainstream concerns about fathers' importance to the family and child well-being, the FRM portrays itself as bipartisan and "beyond politics." Well-known political actors from both conservative and liberal organizations represent the movement, such as National Fatherhood Initiative's Wade Horn (who became the assistant secretary for family support in 2001), conservative author David Blankenhorn, and Ronald Mincy from the Ford Foundation. Despite presenting a unified image in joint campaigns that seek to bridge competing constituencies of men, the actors within the FRM diverge into mainly two wings. The "fragile families" wing generally emphasizes structural and economic issues from the perspectives of low-income and minority men. Representatives of fragile families fathers primarily construct masculinity politics with reference to *other men*, i.e., white, middle-class men. In contrast, the "promarriage" wing is mainly concerned with cultural and moral processes from a generalized white, heterosexual male perspective and primarily casts masculinity in binary relation to notions of *femininity*, while seeking to reinforce notions of gender difference.

Promarriage representatives within the FRM view parental gender difference, cemented in marriage, as central to responsible fatherhood. In contrast, fragile families organizations are more concerned about the constraints of unemployment, poverty, and racism on fatherhood responsibility and seek to encourage "team parenting"—which does not necessarily presuppose marriage—in order for children to have both biological parents in their lives. Whereas marriage and individual moral obligations are central within the promarriage wing, struggles for equal opportunity in work and education are crucial within the fragile families wing of the Fatherhood Responsibility Movement. In fragile families representatives' view, opportunity structures within the labor market

are key to men's standing on the "marriage market" and their likelihood for long-term involvement as fathers. Subsequently, from a fragile families–oriented perspective, it makes more sense to focus on fathers' *financial* conditions for family involvement than their *moral* commitment to marriage. In contrast, marriage proponents might acknowledge the relevance of employment for certain populations of fathers, but do not bring this up as a primary issue. As opposed to confronting racial and socioeconomic inequalities, marriage proponents call for a confrontation with "culture," casting "radical" feminist and liberal "family relativism" and "androgyny advocacy" as their main opponents.

Despite internal tensions, the FRM converges in certain grievances, presumptions, and practices. Men's marginalization in "the family" is a central grievance within the FRM. According to FRM representatives, the social and governmental definition of the family has increasingly come to mean "mother and child" as a result of feminist claims, the changing demographics of family formation, and (white, middle-class) women's increased independence from men as primary breadwinners. Due to the increasingly expendable positions of fathers in families, the FRM claims that parenting itself has been feminized by increasingly being associated with motherhood. While expressing support for liberal feminist principles, the FRM commonly responds to men's changing positions in families by a set of masculinizing practices. Both fragile families–oriented and promarriage-oriented fatherhood programs use a set of "masculine" discourses and practices in order to deal with parenting in ways that appeal to men in framing fathering outside the feminizing influence of domesticity. For instance, both fragile families– and promarriage-oriented fatherhood programs use religion and sport as unifying "male" grounds across racial and socioeconomic divisions. By masculinizing fatherhood through contested images of men as, for instance, moral leaders or coaches to their families, the FRM asserts that fathers parent in specifically male ways and thus are indispensable for the well-being of children, family, and society. Simultaneously, religion and sport are used as tools for bonding and competition in all-male fatherhood programs while constituting arenas for contesting the boundaries of masculinities. Although the FRM constitutes a response to feminist mobilizations, its competing constituencies of men are far from unitary in their approach to gender politics. Whereas the fragile families wing extends into civil rights struggles and strategically seeks dialogue with women's groups involved in family policy, marriage proponents overlap with the so-called marriage movement and the Promise Keepers in adversarial relation to what they call "radical feminism."

Despite diverging approaches to racialized and gendered relations within the FRM, representatives share some fundamental presumptions about male sexuality in which definitions of masculinity are inseparable from notions of male heterosexuality. Within the FRM, male heterosexuality is perceived as innately "promiscuous" while differentiating masculinity from women and gay men. Fatherhood programs are occupied with men's perceived inability to control their innate heterosexual urges so as to not have more children than they are able or willing to father. Thus, the FRM boils down to an effort to control men's sexuality through marriage or "team parenting" as key to fatherhood responsibility and social order. Subsequently, the same "indispensable" traits that make men male in this view also constitute a central problem within the FRM. Here, the FRM runs into a dilemma that has haunted U.S. discussions around "new fatherhood" for centuries: how do you *domesticate masculinity* into fatherhood and at the same time *masculinize domesticity?* The FRM's contradictory attempts to virilize *and* control the maleness of fatherhood is emerging in both

adversarial and nonadversarial response to feminist politics while crystallizing racial and socioeconomic asymmetries between men.

See also Promise Keepers
Further Reading:

Daniels, Cynthia R., ed. 1998. *Lost Fathers: the Politics of Fatherlessness in America.* New York: St. Martin's Press.

Gavanas, Anna. 2001. *Masculinizing Fatherhood: Sexuality, Marriage and Race in the U.S. Fatherhood Responsibility Movement.* Stockholm, Sweden: Stockholm University Doctoral Dissertation.

———. 2001. "The Fatherhood Responsibility Movement: The Centrality of Marriage, Work and Male Sexuality in Reconstructions of Masculinity and Fatherhood." In *Making Men into Fathers. Men, Masculinities and the Social Politics of Fatherhood.* Edited by Barbara Hobson. London: Cambridge University Press.

Griswold, Robert L. 1993. *Fatherhood in America.* New York: Basic Books.

Horn, Wade F., David Blankenhorn, and Mitchell B. Pearlstein, eds. 1999. *The Fatherhood Movement: A Call to Action.* New York: Lexington Books.

Kimmel, Michael S. 1996. *Manhood in America: A Cultural History.* New York: Free Press.

Levine, James A., and Edward W. Pitt. 1995. *New Expectations: Community Strategies for Responsible Fatherhood.* New York: Families and Work Institute.

Stacey, Judith. 1996. *In the Name of the Family: Rethinking Family Values in the Postmodern Age.* Boston: Beacon Press.

———. 1998. "Dada-ism in the 1990's: Getting Past Baby Talk about Fatherlessness." In *Lost Fathers: the Politics of Fatherlessness in America.* Edited by Cynthia R. Daniels. New York: St. Martin's Press.

Fathers, Cultural Representations of

Cultural representations of fathers are socially constructed symbols that signify, connote, or refer to fathers or fatherhood. These representations or "cultural objects" (Griswold 1994) include language forms, iconography, prescriptive guidelines, and fictional and nonfictional stories. Paternal representations may offer clues to the degree to which fathers are valued and the formal and informal scripts they are expected to follow. However, deciphering the clues can be a challenge.

A recurring question in the popular press is whether the print and electronic media portray fathers differently, and specifically more negatively, than they do mothers. In the 1920s, it was said that "even a superficial acquaintance with contemporary publications discloses that contemptuous jests about father are the mainstay of our humoristic literature" (Murphy 1925, 127). In the 1940s, radio was singled out for "regal[ing] the kiddies with a whole string of programs in which father is the comedy relief" (Yoder 1948, 28). And from the 1950s to the present, the television industry has been criticized, off and on, for making "a fool out of Dad" (Gale 1957, 35; see also Dart 1999). Some have said that the reason behind the characterizations is that society does not value fathers as much as it does mothers, or at least does not value fathers as much it did "before" (i.e., in some nostalgic past). Linking cultural representations to societal-level values is anything but a simple process, however, because symbols can be interpreted in a variety of ways. Consider, for example, the empirical finding that, in the 1920s, fathers were significantly more likely than mothers to be depicted as incompetent in *Saturday Evening Post* cartoons (LaRossa, Gordon, Wilson, Bairan, and Jaret 1991). Does the gender disparity in the comic representations necessarily mean that fathers were unappreciated in the 1920s? In all likelihood, no. The intended target of the male cartoonists, drawing for a socially conservative magazine, may not have been fatherhood, per se, but the early twentieth-century feminist movement, which had worked diligently to promote the idea that fathers should be more active inside the home. Depicting men as incompetent when disciplining or caring for children could have been the cartoonists' way of saying that, as far as they were concerned, the "modern" fathers of the 1920s had lost their patriarchal bearings and would do well to return to their former (authoritarian and domestically aloof) selves. (For evidence of a similar pattern in the 1960s, see LaRossa, Jaret, Gadgil, and Wynn 2000.)

It is also important to note the socioeconomic bias in fatherhood satire. The television shows that portray dad as "a fool" almost always have been working-class comedies (Cantor 1990, Glennon and Butsch 1982). *The Life of Riley* (1949–1958), *The Flintstones* (1960–1966), *All in the Family* (1971–1983), *Sanford and Son* (1972–1977), *Married with Children* (1987–1997), and *The Simpsons* (1989–) are vivid illustrations. Middle-class family sitcoms, on the other hand, have tended to portray fathers in a positive light. A number of long-running middle-class comedies—to include *Father Knows Best* (1954–1963), *Leave it to Beaver* (1957–1963), *The Donna Reed Show* (1958–1966), *The Andy Griffith Show* (1960–1968), *My Three Sons* (1960–1972), and *The Cosby Show* (1984–1992), to name a few—featured father figures who were surefooted and wise. Thus, even within a fairly narrow genre (TV sitcoms), cultural representations of fathers can vary.

Prescriptions on how to be a father also are important cultural representations. The most talked-about prescriptions are embedded within childcare/rearing texts. In the first edition of *The Common Sense Book of Baby and Child Care* (hereafter *Baby and Child Care* [1946]), Dr. Benjamin Spock counseled that it was possible to be both "a warm father and a real man" (15). He also said that fathers should get involved "right from the start" (15). We might be tempted to think that Spock was encouraging fathers and mothers to be equally committed cocaregivers, but reading further we see that he was not proposing anything of the sort: "Of course, I don't mean that the father has to give just as many bottles or change just as many diapers as the mother. But it's fine for him to do these things occasionally" (Spock 1946, 15). Offering a prescription in one paragraph and then seemingly blunting that prescription in the next paragraph may have confused some parents, but most fathers and mothers probably navigated through the book just fine. Research indicates that cultural representations typically offer a repertoire or storehouse of conflicting symbols. Confronted with an assortment of ideas, people will pick and choose, or "shop," for chunks of text that suit their strategic interests (Swidler 2001). A father who wanted to limit his childcare thus could use Spock's disclaimer to justify why it was appropriate for him to change diapers only "occasionally." A mother who wanted a more active partner might accentuate the statement that fathers should be involved "right from the start."

If divergence can exist within a single text, we should not be surprised to see divergence across many texts. Hence, books and articles about superinvolved dads can appear on the same shelf as books and articles about abusive and deadbeat dads. "Good dad, bad dad" discourse and debate are not new. Similar concerns about fathers can be found in early twentieth-century texts, and the gender politics fueling those concerns were as real then as they are now (LaRossa 1997). In the main, culture is not explicit or unequivocal but "fluid, contradictory, and a site for struggle" (Cragin and Simonds 1999). Essentially, the culture of fatherhood can only be understood within a political context.

Fatherhood scripts also can serve as a basis for documenting trends. Frequently, childcare/rearing texts are examined over a period of time to determine whether and how scripts have changed. As in all historical studies, the starting point of an investigation influences what is reported. For example, because of the enormous popularity of *Baby and Child Care,* the first edition of Spock's manual is sometimes compared to later editions of the manual, as well as to other new childcare/rearing texts, to demonstrate how much fatherhood prescriptions have become more expansive in recent years (e.g., see Gibbs 1993). What is generally assumed is that *Baby and Child Care* was an improvement over its predecessors, making it an appropriate benchmark to begin a historical analysis. If we look closely at the childcare/rearing texts

published in the late 1930s and early 1940s, however, we see that a few of them encouraged *higher* levels of father involvement than did *Baby and Child Care*. Thus, Spock's manual was, in some ways, a step backward from the modernization of fatherhood evident in the prewar era (LaRossa 1997, 194). It is helpful in this regard to remember that cultural representations almost never shift in a linear way, but ebb and flow in the wake of major societal-transforming events (e.g., industrialization, economic depression, war). Over time, fatherhood images fluctuate.

Ralph LaRossa

See also Deadbeat Dads; Family; Fatherhood;
  Fatherhood Responsibility Movement; Fathers'
  Rights

Further Reading:

Cantor, Muriel G. 1990. "Prime-Time Fathers: A
  Study in Continuity and Change." *Critical
  Studies in Mass Communication* 7: 275–285.

Cragin, Becca, and Wendy Simonds. 1999. "The
  Study of Gender in Culture: Feminist
  Studies/Cultural Studies." Pp. 195–212 in
  Handbook of the Sociology of Gender. Edited by
  Janet Saltzman Chafetz. New York: Kluwer
  Academic/Plenum Publishers.

Dart, Bob. 1999. "Prime-Time TV Lacks Good
  Dads, Group Says: Fatherhood Watchdogs Rate
  Network Shows." *Atlanta Journal and
  Constitution* (March 3): C6.

Gale, Bill. 1957. "TV Makes a Fool Out of Dad."
  American Mercury 84: 35–39.

Gibbs, Nancy R. 1993. "Bringing up Father." *Time*
  (June 28): 53–61.

Glennon Lynda M., and Richard Butsch. 1982.
  "The Family as Portrayed on Television,
  1946–1978." Pp. 264–271 in *Television and
  Behavior: Ten Years of Scientific Progress and
  Implications for the Eighties, Vol. II, Technical
  Reviews.* Rockville, MD: National Institutes of
  Health, U.S. Department of Health and
  Human Services.

Griswold, Wendy. 1994. *Cultures and Societies in a
  Changing World.* Thousand Oaks, CA: Pine Forge
  Press.

LaRossa, Ralph. 1997. *The Modernization of
  Fatherhood: A Social and Political History.* Chicago:
  University of Chicago Press.

LaRossa, Ralph, Betty Anne Gordon, Ronald Jay
  Wilson, Annette Bairan, and Charles Jaret.
  1991. "The Fluctuating Image of the 20th
  Century American Father." *Journal of Marriage
  and Family* 53: 987–997.

LaRossa, Ralph, Charles Jaret, Malati Gadgil, and G. Robert Wynn. 2000. "The Changing Culture of Fatherhood in Comic-Strip Families: A Six Decade Analysis." *Journal of Marriage and the Family* 62: 375–387.

Murphy, Merle Farmer. 1925. "Poor Dad." *The Independent* 114: 127–129.

Spock, Benjamin. 1946. *The Common Sense Book of Baby and Child Care*. New York: Duell, Sloan, and Pearce.

Swidler, Ann. 2001. *Talk of Love: How Culture Matters*. Chicago: University of Chicago Press.

Yoder, Robert M. 1948. "Don't Shoot Father— Save Him for Laughs." *Saturday Evening Post* (August 14): 28, 92.

Fathers, Gay

Gay fathers come from a variety of parenting backgrounds. The gay father of the 1960s and 1970s emerged from a traditional heterosexual marriage, uncovering and revealing his gay identity after having followed a traditional societal male role. Advances in reproductive technology, as well as changing legal practices, have expanded options for gay men through donor insemination, surrogacy, and both single and coparent adoption and foster care.

Biological gay fathers have likely always existed. The social revolutions of the latter part of the twentieth century with the ensuing complex changes in the definition of masculinity influenced the organizational emergence of these individuals. Feminism explored traditional role structure and alternative radical cultures and permitted greater experimentation of hetero/homo/bisexuality among both men and women.

The myths popularly ascribed to gay fathers are explored in research studies: disturbed parental relationship myth (in their own childhood); machismo myth (more masculine than other gay men); germ myth (children will become gay); harassment/exposure myth (societal disapproval feared by children); molestation myth (will abuse their own children); sex fiend myth (sexual gratification is primary life force); smoke screen myth (procreate to avoid detection); compensation myth (parenting replaces homosexual desire); identification myth (fathering identified with feminine roles of mother and wife); and the sick myth (therapy can convert them to heterosexuals) (Barret and Robinson 1990, 27–50).

Homophobia in its most common manifestations projects a number of stereotypes of gay men. First, they are unstable and irresponsible. As such, they are sexually perverted and engage in sexual acts in the presence of children. If they form a gay couple, in addition to being unstable, roles are societally structured into exaggerated gender roles; every gay couple therefore is composed of two individuals with male and female role identities, further delineated typically as a "top" and a "bottom." These stereotypes have little validity.

Until recently, gay fathers were most commonly described as marrying and parenting in order to hide their sexual orientation and their sexuality. The homophobia cited above is further projected on stereotypes of children of gay parents. Not surprisingly most gay parents are born in heterosexual marriages. The contagiousness of sexual identity and orientation to the children is the most commonly held stereotype. Children raised by gay fathers will be confused in gender identity and are likely to become homosexuals. Children will be harmed witnessing affectionate behavior between same-sex partners; these same children will be marked psychologically, socially stigmatized for having lived with a gay father. These are the stereotypes not confirmed in research studies.

Research studies indicate no differences among children raised by heterosexual and homosexual fathers in their psychological profiles. The gay fathers, often because of society's homophobia, tend to teach problem-solving skills more often; they are more attentive, and provide more assistance and recreation to their children. These gay fathers have learned to survive in an alternative life style. They encourage their children to be autonomous and self-aware in the world around them (Barret and Robinson 1990).

Perhaps because of their sensitivity to society, gay fathers in research studies appear to be more strict and consistent in setting boundaries, rules, and regulations. They know the two worlds in which their children live. They also, because of their own particular role status, tend to be more sensitive and responsive to their child's perceived needs. Gay fathers require that children develop stronger cognitive skills, perhaps to defend themselves as well as their fathers. Fathers who are gay respond to their own internalized homophobia. The combined roles of gay man and father may produce a strange feeling of guilt that actually makes them more conscientious parents. They are sensitive to the perceived role of difference that shines the spotlight on them. As gay masculinity is different, gay fathers may, according to the research studies, see themselves as less conventional and more androgynous (Barret and Robinson 1990).

Children respond positively to society's emerging portraits of masculinity as their gay fathers have taught them to be more accepting of difference and its manifestation in the human experience. Studies indicate that children raised by gay parents are less likely to conform to traditional gender roles and more likely to choose less traditional sex-assigned standards and jobs. They also tend to be more open on sexuality and more likely to express sexuality at an earlier age. Children of divorced gay fathers seem to be less likely to blame themselves for the breakup of the marriage since the father's sexuality is clearly the rationale (Barret and Robinson 1990). Violation of gender stereotypes seems to contribute positively among the children of gay fathers to the development of mature and healthy individuals. The American Academy of Pediatrics in a recent study (2002) has concluded that children's optimal development seems to be influenced more by the nature of the relationship and the interaction within the family than by the particular structural form it assumes, heterosexual or homosexual.

Traditional notions of masculinity confront two societal images when faced with a gay father: the father and the gay man. Each carries its own cultural stereotype. The gay man is perceived as weak, irresponsible, and effeminate. The father is seen as strong, duty bound, and masculine. The gay father has already faced numerous challenges to his own identity adjustment: acceptance of self as well as acceptance by his children and by the gay community. He has seemingly confronted the enigma and the oxymoron of the gay father—gay, indicating homosexuality, and father, indicating heterosexuality. As a result, the gay father tends to create a nurturing parenting style, blending traditional maternal and paternal traits. In his willingness to confront the paradox, he presents an intact identity of homosexual orientation and father. His circumstances, whether biological or chosen through adoption, surrogacy, or foster care blends to produce a nonconforming gender role.

Until recently, gay fathers were most commonly described as marrying and parenting to hide their sexual identity and their sexuality. These perceptions contributed to the macho, compensatory identification and smoke screen myths previously cited. The option of gay fatherhood by choice broadens the panorama.

Traditionally, a man being both gay and a father has been perceived as a contradiction in masculine identity. Homosexuality was viewed as a negative, perhaps effeminate, pathway for a man, while marriage, heterosexuality, and fatherhood were considered appropriate fulfillment of one's masculinity and gender-role structure. Gay fathers, capable of heterosexual sex, were assumed to be more masculine than other gay men. Research findings do not support this myth. In fact, the studies indicate that gay men (fathers as well as nonfathers) tend to conform less to traditional male and female role structures (Barret and Robinson 1990). Sexual behavior and sex-role differentiation appear to be unrelated phenomena that develop out of distinctive experiences. Thus, masculinity within both gay and straight lifestyles presents itself in a wide range of expectations and manifestations. The concept of a loving parent does not restrict itself to a given sexual identity label, be it heterosexual or homosexual. When faced with society's negative perspective on gay identity, some men did marry as a smoke screen, hoping that marriage and perhaps subsequent paternity would replace homosexual desire.

The earliest account of a gay fathers' sociopolitical movement comes from San Francisco, where in 1975 a group of gay fathers, mostly hippies, marched with children, lovers, and others in the Gay Freedom Day parade. In the next several years, such organizations had spread to New York and other metropolitan areas, and articles had appeared in such journals as *Gay Sunshine* and *The Body Politic*. The Gay Fathers Coalition flourished in the 1980s, extending throughout the United States and Canada. Annual national meetings were held and the organizational mission changed as the common interests of gays and lesbians merged. In 1987 the Gay Fathers Coalition International (GFCI) became the Gay and Lesbian Parents Coalition International (GLPCI), and in 1998 the GLPCI became Family Pride Incorporated, a group for the multiple manifestations of parenting.

Advances in reproductive technology offered new family planning options for gay men. They could be anonymous or identified sperm donors to known or unknown mothers. In 1996 a gay donor wrote a legal contract specifying that he would accept no financial obligation in rearing the child conceived with his sperm. Nevertheless, a number of gay fathers have chosen to maintain relationships with their children conceived through these techniques. Recent legal challenges to access and to visitation rights have reduced the number of known donors. The Food and Drug Administration (FDA) has proposed guidelines that prohibit any man who has had sexual relations with another man in the last five years from becoming an anonymous sperm donor. However, private agencies such as Hello Baby and Prospective Queer Parents continue to offer donor insemination.

Surrogacy has provided a number of gay fathers, single or in couples, with another legal option. Foster parenting, a temporary but often long-term placement, has become a common experience, particularly with difficult-to-place children. Gay men who wish to become fathers provide a family environment for a child, often removed from a problematic home. Numerous states now encourage gay and lesbian couples to pursue foster parent training, thereby incorporating them into the placement process.

Adoption has provided another alternative to nonbiological gay fathers, and often to the gay couple. Single-parent adoption was traditionally less problematic. In 1999, because of the complex varieties of child custody concerns involving children in gay and lesbian relationships, a coalition of gay civil rights organizations led by Gay and Lesbian Advocates and Defenders (GLAD) wrote a set of guidelines for child custody matters in same-sex relationships.

The gay father has emerged in recent years first as a political movement stimulated by feminism and later further encouraged by the gay rights' and men's movements. Biological advances in reproductive technology, surrogacy, adoption, and foster care have created more opportunities for gay men to parent. Gay fathers are a visible presence in post-Stonewall American life.

John C. Miller

See also Fatherhood; Fathers, Nonresidential; Homophobia; Homosexuality

Further Reading:

Barret, Robert L., and Bryan E. Robinson. 1990. *Gay Fathers.* Lexington, MA: Lexington Books.

Green, Jesse. 1999. *The Velveteen Father.* New York: Villard Books.

Lynch, Michael. 1978. "Forgotten Fathers." *The Body Politic* (April): 1.

Miller, John C. 2001. "My Daddy Loves Your Daddy: A Gay Father Encounters a Social

Movement." Pp. 221–230 in *Queer Families, Queer Politics: Challenging Culture and the State.* Edited by Mary Bernstein and Renate Reimann. New York: Columbia University Press.

Savage, Dan. 2000. *The Kid (What Happened after My Boyfriend and I Decided to Go Get Pregnant): An Adoption Story.* New York: Plume.

Fathers, Nonresidential

The rise in single motherhood, child poverty, and noncustodial parenting have made the paternal roles, functions, and behaviors of nonresidential fathers a paramount concern among social workers, scholars, and policy analysts. This population of fathers is difficult to describe with a single term. Indeed, they differ by race, economic class, education level, and religious background. Most research on fathering remains based on studies of white, middle-class divorced males, and never married, low-income, adolescent fathers. We still know very little about the parenthood experiences of nonresidential fathers from varying racial and ethnic backgrounds, age groups, marital statuses, and economic classes. We know even less about how they understand their role as parents and negotiate the care of their children.

Paternal nonresidential status may be due to any number of circumstances, including divorce, marital separation, never-married births, and male institutionalization and incarceration. In the 1960s, 90 percent of children in the United States lived with two parents. By 2002, the rate was less than one-half. From 1980 to 2000 alone, the rate of children in two-parent homes dropped from 76.7 to 69.1 percent. Of those residing with both a mother and a father, 9 percent lived with a step- and biological parent, usually the mother. At the beginning of the twenty-first century, approximately one-third of all children were born to unmarried parents. These rates are more pronounced among some racial and ethnic minority groups—70 percent and 40 percent for African Americans

and Hispanics, respectively. Such trends are expected to escalate in the decades to come.

Most men experience fatherhood, and research suggests that they are quite interested in being parents. In spite of this, definitions of masculine and paternal roles are generally based on their *nonfamilial* roles: As husbands and fathers, they are foremost expected to be paid workers and economic providers. In the early twenty-first century—regardless of racial, ethnic, and class differences—even residential fathers remain on the periphery of family interaction. Primary childcare responsibilities tend to fall to mothers, even when fathers are present, and many women work full-time outside the home. In the event of divorce, many fathers maintain moderate and consistent levels of involvement with their children, though a sharp drop in contact tends to follow. The longer they have been divorced, the further fathers seem to withdraw.

Research suggests that never-married fathers experience similar patterns. Their paternal disengagement may fall into one of three categories: passive, active, or resistant. In the passive form, fathers may not seek to distance themselves from children, but the time between visits nonetheless increases. Their withdrawal may be a means of managing the emotional distress they feel at the end of visits. In cases of active disengagement, never-married nonresidential fathers may decide to devote more attention to new relationships and children. Others may choose to withdraw from their children's lives because they feel ill prepared or unable to provide appropriate paternal care. Finally, resistant disengagement may occur as a by-product of conflict between fathers and the mothers of their children, who prove unwilling to negotiate visitation. An increasing number of nonresidential fathers are resistively disengaged due to incarceration. In 1991 there were 770,000 children with a father in prison. Since then the number of men in prison has grown from 675,000 to well over 1 million. The number of children who live without them has predictably also skyrocketed. Approximately 40 percent of children who live in homes without their fathers have not seen them in the past year.

For many reasons, nonresidential fathers may often find themselves further out on the familial periphery than their residential counterparts. Still, the primary and most unambiguous role society requires of these fathers is that of economic provider, and most social policy targets them for formal child support payments. The Family Support Act in 1988 required states to strengthen efforts in identifying the paternity of "fatherless" children so that those fathers could be held accountable. The Personal Responsibility, Work, Opportunity, and Reconciliation Act of 1996 also requires mothers to identify their children's fathers and assist agencies in securing child support payments. As part of this federal push for child support, the National Directory of New Hires was launched in 1997 to track fathers across state lines and withhold wages to meet child support.

There is some evidence that these measures have produced results. The rate of custodial mothers reporting the receipt of payments rose 30 percent from 1993 to 1997. Yet, middle-income, white, divorced single mothers tend to benefit more than never-married parents, who are disproportionately poor and of color. Divorced mothers are better able to readily establish their children's paternity, and divorced men are typically employed. Children of never-married parents are more likely to have fathers who are tenuously employed or out of the work force altogether.

Given this, rates of nonpayment are higher for African American and Latino males for example, than for European American fathers. Men of color experience a disproportionate level of poverty and incarceration, and report having great difficulties meeting their own daily needs, let alone those of family members. Demanding support payments from these fathers does little to bring their children out of poverty. Most custodial mothers and nonresidential fathers agree that

fathers have a financial obligation to their children. Regardless of their relationships with fathers, it seems that most mothers would like to see consistent economic support from children's fathers. But perhaps equally important, they would like for fathers to spend more time and engage in more activities with their children. Similarly, many fathers, even those already involved with their children, express a desire for more paternal involvement.

Wanting to do more, however, and actually doing so are very different. Joint custody and other forms of visitation set by a court are often a nonissue for many never-married fathers, particularly those who are low income. This population of dads is less likely than divorced fathers to pursue custody, less likely to afford custody-related court costs or physical custody, less likely to be readily identified as fathers, and less likely to have any legal tie to their offspring. Though more inclusive notions of fatherhood have been advanced for fathers overall, it appears that the ability for nonresidential fathers to put them into practice is particularly difficult. Social policy attempting to address the emotional, social, and economic well-being of children has, to date, been largely ineffective. There are perennial problems with attempts to connect fathers to their children's lives based on traditional breadwinner ideals and assumptions of fatherhood. Increased rates of divorce and nonmarital births, coupled with deindustrialization, massive layoffs, and a rise in temporary, part-time employment means that many fathers are less able to meet either the social or economic demands of fathering.

Despite calls for more social and economic involvement, a mounting number of men work in environments that inhibit their ability to balance work and family. A large number of jobs available in the early twenty-first century do not offer wages and benefits (e.g., flexible work schedules, family leave, and paid vacations) that contribute to the time fathers could give to their children. Some studies of African

American working-class and low-income, never-married, nonresidential fathers suggest that this population may be developing a notion of fatherhood that contrasts sharply with that of the dominant culture. Their definition makes paternal social and emotional support primary (e.g., role modeling, discipline, and moral development), while deemphasizing the role of economic provider. This modification seems an adaptation to the tenuous social and economic position black men have experienced. The findings also demonstrate men's ability to modify, define, and voice their own vision of fatherhood in the context of their economic and social circumstances. For many men, the provision of nurturance, love, and affection may be priceless aspects of fatherhood—particularly when the financial role is difficult to obtain. Government-sponsored father initiatives and programs, increased child poverty within single-mother households, and other familial trends are certain to spur further research on a fatherhood form destined to become the norm.

Jennifer Hamer

See also Divorce; Fathers, Cultural Representations of

Further Reading:

Arendell, T. 1995. *Fathers and Divorce*. Thousand Oaks, CA: Sage.

Dowd, N. E. 2000. *Redefining Fatherhood*. New York: New York University Press.

Furstenberg, F. F., K. W. Sherwood, and M. L. Sherwood. 1992. *Daddies and Fathers: Men Who Do for Their Children and Men Who Don't*. New York: Man power Demonstration Research Corporation.

Fragile Families and Child Well-Being Study. 2002. Bendheim-Thoman Center for Research on Child Well-being, Princeton University. At http://crcw.princeton.edu.

Hamer, J. 2001. *What It Means to Be Daddy: Fatherhood for Black Men Living away from Their Children*. New York: Columbia University Press.

Horn, Wade F., David D. Blankenhorn, and Mitchell B. Pearlstein, eds. 1999. *The Fatherhood Movement: A Call to Action*. New York: Lexington Books.

Lawson, E. J., and A. Thompson. 1999. *Black Men and Divorce*. London: Sage.

Marsiglio, W., P. Amato, R. D. Day, and M. E. Lamb. 2000. "Scholarship on Fatherhood in the 1990s and Beyond." *Journal of Marriage and the Family* 62: 1173–1191.

Popenoe, D. 1996. *Life without Father*. New York: Free Press.

Fathers' Rights

In the 1970s fathers' rights groups formed across the Western world as part of the Men's Rights movement in response to Second Wave feminism as well as men's changing legal and financial conditions. For instance, in North America, Australia, Britain, France, and Holland, fathers' rights organizations have successfully advocated for joint custody statutes in the name of "gender neutrality" and also sought to impact divorce, child support, and visitation legislation. Fathers' rights organizations like the American Fathers Coalition and the U.K. Families Need Fathers protest legal reforms that they believe strip men of their property, resources, and rights while marginalizing fathers in the family. Fathers' rights advocates make demands on behalf of divorced fathers who feel discriminated against in terms of legal and social recognition and have experienced a loss in authority relative to their previous situations as married and custodial fathers. These fathers seek joint custody rights regardless of the extent of their involvement as caretakers before and after divorce, and they generally claim that women benefit from divorce laws at men's expense.

Fathers' rights organizations mainly represent white, heterosexual, and middle- or working-class men, and legitimize their claims by co-opting feminist and civil rights rhetoric of gender equality and rights. Reducing the politics of parenthood to individualized interpersonal relations, fathers' rights organizations focus on men's feelings of *powerlessness* and *victimhood,* regardless of their constituencies' relative and aggregate positions as groups. Furthermore, most fathers' rights advocates are personally involved in postdivorce battles and frequently use individualized horror stories to make angry cases about the injustices suffered by men, cast as victims of biased court systems and vindictive ex-wives.

Fathers' increased rights to access, decision making, and property impact the economic and legal conditions of mothers, some of whom are potentially at risk of domestic violence. Despite the frequent use of "equal rights" and "children's best interest" rhetoric within fathers' rights discourse, custody of children may be a power resource in familial relations. A father's legal relationship with his children has power implications for his relationship with the children's mother. However, some fathers' rights advocates accuse women of using false allegations of sexual or physical abuse as a weapon in custody and visitation battles.

Rather than seeking sole custody for fathers, fathers' rights organizations seek liberal access to their children and often presume that mothers are primarily responsible for everyday childcare. Joint custody legislation thus has little to do with the actual distribution of childcare work between parents, and may refer to a wide set of mandatory, optional, or preferred arrangements. Because women are generally more likely than men to have low-paying jobs and put their careers on hold as a result of childcare responsibilities, the "gender neutral" language of joint custody masks asymmetric financial constraints and bargaining positions of mothers and fathers. Nevertheless, fathers' rights organizations seek to minimize child support obligations on behalf of fathers and link these concerns to custody issues by arguing that fathers should have liberal access to the children for whom they are paying. Moreover, many fathers' rights advocates express concerns about ex-wives' expenditures and activities. Thus, regardless of the actual socioeconomic positions of mothers as compared to fathers, and regardless of who carries the burdens of primary caretaking, fathers' rights advocates may argue that ex-wives deny them "equal participation" in childcare while receiving outrageous amounts of child support.

On the one hand, the fathers' rights movement unites around the grievance that the legal system disregards fathers' equal rights to nurture their children. On the other hand, certain strains of fathers' rights rhetoric is less concerned with shared parenting responsibilities than with the control of property, children, and ex-wives' mobility. While there are many common features among fathers' rights organizations nationally and internationally, advocates range between liberal and conservative approaches to various strands of feminism. Liberal fathers' rights advocates express support for most liberal feminist principles of shared childcare and relatively flexible parental relations. In contrast, conservative fathers' rights advocates explicitly approach "radical" feminism as the enemy and promote patriarchal notions of gender difference in parenting. Thus, within the fathers' rights movement, there is a combination of fathers who express a desire to be involved in the everyday caretaking of their children, as well as seeking to assert control and authority in opposition to feminist claims and/or the wishes of their ex-wives.

Anna Gavanas

Further Reading:

Arendell, Terry. 1995. *Fathers & Divorce.* Thousand Oaks, CA, London, and New Delhi: Sage.

Bertoia, Carl, and Jane Drakich. 1993. "The Fathers' Rights Movement: Contradictions in Rhetoric and Practice." *Journal of Family Issues* 14, no 4.

Collier, Richard. 1995. *Masculinity, Law and the Family.* London and New York: Routledge.

———. 1996. "Coming Together?: Post-heterosexuality, Masculine Crisis and the New Men's Movement." *Feminist Legal Studies* IV, no 1.

Coltrane, Scott, and Neal Hickman. 1992. "The Rhetoric of Rights and Needs: Moral Discourse in the Reform of Child Custody and Child Support Laws." *Social Problems* 12, no 3.

Dowd, Nancy. 2000. *Redefining Fatherhood.* New York: New York University Press.

Fineman, Martha. 1995. *The Neutered Mother, the Sexual Family and Other Twentieth Century Tragedies.* New York and London: Routledge.

Messner, Michael A. 1997. *Politics of Masculinities: Men in Movements.* Thousand Oaks, CA: Sage.

Pollock, Scarlet, and Jo Sutton. 1985. "Father's Rights, Women's Losses." *Women's International Forum* 8, no. 6: 593–599.

Smart, Carol, and Selma Sevenhuijsen, eds. 1989. *Child Custody and the Politics of Gender.* London and New York: Routledge.

Ullrich, Vivienne. 1986. "Equal but Not Equal—A Feminist Perspective on Family Law." *Women's Studies International Forum* 9, no 1: 41–48.

Williams, Gwyneth, and Rhys Williams. 1995. "'All We Want Is Equality': Rhetorical Framing in the Fathers' Rights Movement." In *Images of Issues. Typifying Contemporary Social Problems.* Edited by Joel Best. New York: Aldine De Gruyter.

Faulkner, William (1897–1962)

The novels and short stories of William Faulkner are intensely aware of gender. This is in part because they are usually set in the American South. But just as much so because Faulkner himself was keenly aware of the artifice of gender, that it is a social construct—though no less a reality for this fact.

Faulkner was born in New Albany, Mississippi, on 25 September 1897. He grew up slight of stature among big men and, if one includes his ancestors, men bigger than life. As biographers such as Frederick Karl have noted, Faulkner created myths about himself, and some of these myths revealed his insecurities as a man among men. One such myth included tales of his exploits in the Canadian Royal Air Force. Through art and artifice, Faulkner transcended the limitations he imagined in his own masculinity. When he died in 1962, he left behind him a substantial body of fiction, suffused with an interest in gender, particularly as it is defined in the American South.

In the South as described in Faulkner's imaginary Yoknapatawpha County, masculinity is inseparable from the idea of gentility. The masculine ideal in white society was that of the Southern gentleman, the feminine ideal being that of the Southern belle. In Faulkner's fiction there is no Rhett Butler, but there is a Colonel Sartoris, who keeps reappearing in works like *The Unvanquished* (1938) and the short story "A Rose for Emily" (1930). And then there are those who are trying to achieve gentleman status, like Thomas Sutpen, who can't seem to separate himself from his past, and those like Abner Snopes, who admires Colonel Sartoris but has no hope of becoming a well-heeled gentleman.

Masculinity and class intertwine to create some of the most powerful scenes in Faulkner's work. The upper classes wield their privilege and the men of the lower classes react, sometimes violently, to the assault they perceive as intensely personal. In *Absalom, Absalom!* (1936), the overseer Wash fawns over his "gentleman" employer Sutpen, until Sutpen takes sexual advantage of Wash's granddaughter. Wash is reminded by this betrayal that he is not master, but manservant—really less than a man, because no family member and certainly no property are free from the invasion of the master, Sutpen. The betrayal, strongly associated with emasculation in the form of Sutpen in the cabin with horsewhip in hand (and the refrain "they sho' ain't whupped us yet, Kernel") drives Wash to retaliate, not with his own horsewhip but with an implement of his own social realm, a scythe.

One image looms large on the masculine horizon of Faulkner's works and that is the Southern gentleman as horseman. Whether in *Absalom, Absalom!* with Sutpen, or in "A Rose for Emily," as the father standing next to his daughter, Miss Emily, with horsewhip in hand, this association between the gentleman and his horse connects in a unique way the social ideal and the sexual ideal.

Insofar as masculinity is associated with social class, so it is associated with race. To play victim to a man of superior class is one thing, but to be at the behest of his servant strikes at the very core of one's manhood. Several of the most powerful scenes in Faulkner's work depict a white man of lowly station being chastised by the black servant of a man of position and influence. One such incident occurs in "Barn Burning" (1939), when Abner Snopes is forbidden entry to the DeSpain house by a black female servant. Similarly, Wash is forbidden entry to Sutpen's mansion by his black female servant. These incidents touch the core of manhood for the poor white man, as one of the narrow threads on which he hangs his self-esteem is his supreme confidence that at least he is white.

The South of Faulkner's imagination is filled with ghosts, and one such ghost is that of masculinity. Like so much in this fictional realm, masculinity, too, is a thing of the past. Try as they might, the men of the literary present cannot muster the potency in sex, politics, or war to compete with the men of yesteryear. So Faulkner conjures in our imaginations the forebears of the Compson family in *The Sound and the Fury* (1929): Quentin II, a one-time governor of Mississippi, and Jason II, Civil War brigadier general. Neither can Gail Hightower in the novel *Light in August* (1932) possibly compete with his lusty grandfather, a one-time cavalryman in the Civil War. Contrast the ancestors with their progeny: Hightower, an emasculated recluse, and the cynical philosopher and alcoholic Jason Compson Sr. Masculinity here participates in a general Faulknerian theme, that the present cannot compete with the past because the past can be embellished by the imagination. Once safely dead, the heroes of the past can become much bigger than they were in life, just as deeds of the past loom larger than the seemingly petty activities of the present.

This failure of the masculine is arguably Faulkner's way to overturn the masculine ideal of the Southern gentleman, for social status, while it fuels the ideal, is also masculinity's undoing; in social refinement lie the seeds of delicacy and effeteness. Quentin Compson cannot manage his sexual frustration that involves his sister Caddy, and he commits suicide. Gail Hightower, accused of sexual abnormality by his community, turns to a life of complete social and sexual retirement. Both characters become the impotent branches of once vital family trees.

Southern womanhood can be another means of masculinity's undoing in the Faulkner's South. Because the Southern lady is an essential part of the Southern gentleman's self-concept, to this extent she holds power over him. One humorous example of this power occurs in the short story "A Rose for Emily," when the town's Board of Aldermen show up at Emily Grierson's doorstep to collect taxes. Miss Emily shrewdly invokes the image of the long dead Colonel Sartoris who, she reminds them, said Miss Emily's father would owe no taxes. Before they can dispute her, Miss Emily shows them to the door. As much as the invoking of a hero now dead, it is Miss Emily's status as a white woman of station in the South that "vanquished" the men "horse and foot."

Kelly Cannon

Further Reading:

Clarke, Deborah. 2001. "Humorously Masculine—Or Humor as Masculinity—*Light in August*." *Faulkner Journal* 17, no. 1: 19–36.

Dews, Carlos L. 1999–2000. "Why I Can't Read Faulkner: Reading and Resisting Southern White Masculinity." *Faulkner Journal* 15, no. 1–2: 185–197.

Gray, Richard. 1994. *The Life of William Faulkner*. Oxford, UK: Blackwell.

Halden, Judith. 1982. "Sexual Ambiguities in *Light in August*." *Studies in American Fiction* 10, no. 2: 209–216.

Karl, Frederick R. 1989. *William Faulkner: American Writer*. New York: Weidenfeld & Nicholson.

Kartiganer, Donald M., and Ann J. Abadie. 1991. *Faulkner and Psychology: Faulkner and Yoknapatawpha, 1991*. Jackson: University Press of Mississippi.

———. 1994. *Faulkner and Gender: Faulkner and Yoknapatawpha*. Jackson, MS: University Press of Mississippi.

Polk, Noel. 2000–2001. "Testing Masculinity in the Snopes Trilogy." *Faulkner Journal* 16, no. 1: 3–22.

Fellini, Federico (1920–1993)

The films of Federico Fellini are sublime demonstrations of ethical questions and moral contradictions in the soul of a modern Catholic man, living in Italy after World War II. From 1951 to 1957, Fellini's first movies

Fellini by a poster for La Dolce Vita *(David Lees / Corbis)* were influenced by Neo-realism and therefore showed a sad, realistic universe with men portrayed as abusive liars and crooks (*The White Sheik*, 1952; *Il Bidone*, 1955; *The Nights of Cabiria*, 1957). In opposition, women were often seen as innocent and optimistic (*La Strada*, 1954; *The Nights of Cabiria*). That genuine feminine character was often played by Fellini's own wife, Giulietta Mesina (1920–1994). The conceptual transition and stylistic rupture from the early films appears in *La Dolce Vita* (1960), Fellini's first of five films with actor Marcello Mastroianni (1924–1996), considered as his alter ego. From the 1960s until the ultimate *La Voce della Luna* (1990), the director created a baroque and dreamlike world populated with phantasms, daydreams, and oneiric visions, exposed in a deconstructive narrative. All Fellini's obsessions were now apparent: anguish and guilt about forbidden free love, the illusions of art, the pangs of death.

In his films, Fellini's main interrogations and hesitations are linked with his own dilemmas; confronting his sexual desires were his Catholic strict morals and the limits of marriage. This is already clear in *8½* (*Otto e Mezzo*, 1963), but also in a very symbolic scene from *Amarcord* (1973), when a single man suddenly isolates himself in a tree and desperately asks for a woman ("I want a woman!"), and again in *Casanova* (1976), where sexual intercourse is only shown as an entertaining physical performance. In some of Fellini's films, an unbelievable superwoman character appears—very big, tall, long-haired, with monumental breasts—who serves as a clandestine erotic icon for fascinated boys or young teenagers. The memory of this evil feminine character is present in various ways in *8½, Amarcord, Casanova,* and to a lesser degree with the beautiful, lovely blond character played by the sculptural Anita Ekberg in *La Dolce Vita* (1960) and *Intervista* (1987). A nice sculptural woman also reappears in *The City of Women* (1980). Now and then, after conflicts and disputes with either a wife or a mistress, we sometimes see an oneiric, peaceful scene where a man (or a man as a young boy) is surrounded exclusively by gentle, docile, willing women, as in *8½, Amarcord, Casanova,* and *The City of Women*.

Even if childhood is seen by Fellini as a possible nostalgic refuge, not many characters in his films are fathers or parents: In *Il Bidone*, the crook is ashamed because his honest and respectable daughter, now an adult, realizes that her beloved father is a failure. In a dream from *8½*, Guido imagines his old father in his grave, unable to give any advice or even to explain what is happening to him. Since his childhood, Guido's distant mother has always been ashamed of her unfaithful sons; she is the unnamed source of the guilt that Guido often feels. The family in *Amarcord* is distressful. The rebellion against authority is evident in *8½* (the old naked bishop), but also in *Prova d'Orchestra* (1978), when the musicians expel their director, and also in the strange *And the Ship Goes On* (*E la Nave Va*, 1982). Psychoanalysis finds a fertile ground in Fellini's universe, where fathers are contested and women venerated.

Yves Laberge

Further Reading:

Fellini, Federico. 1987. *8½*. Directed by Federico Fellini. (Rutgers Films In Print), Vol. 7. New Brunswick, NJ: Rutgers University Press.

———. 1990. *Comments on Film*. Carbondale, IL: Southern Illinois University Press.

———. 1996. *Fellini on Fellini* (Directors on Directors Series). Cambridge, MA: Da Capo Press.

Fellini, Federico, and Inga Karetnikova. 1997. *Fellini's Casanova*. Chicago: Reed Elsevier.

"Female Masculinity"

The social construction of gender in the last century was so successful that we still presume that femininity is an expression of and by women and that masculinity is the social, cultural, and political expression of male embodiment. In the realm of masculinity studies, it has been particularly hard to unlink masculinity from men and so the concept of "female masculinity" crucially reminds us that "masculinity" is not just another word for "men." But, in general it seems to be easier in contemporary European American cultures to accept that men have a feminine side than to recognize that many women may make serious investments in their masculinities.

The term *female masculinity* stages several different kinds of interventions into contemporary gender theory and practice: First, it refuses the authentication of masculinity through maleness and maleness alone, and it names a deliberately counterfeit masculinity that undermines the currency of maleness. Second, it offers an alternative mode of masculinity that clearly detaches misogyny from maleness and social power from masculinity. Third, female masculinity may be an embodied assault upon compulsory heterosexuality, and it offers one powerful model of what "inauthentic" masculinity can look like, how it produces and deploys desire, and what new social, sexual, and political relations it can foster.

Scholarship on female masculinity is very recent, but the contemporary formulations of manhood as "in crisis" ensures that people will need to look for alternative models of masculine subjectivities. Female masculinity provides the raw material for considering such alternatives.

Explorations of the meanings and histories of masculinity in women take feminist analyses of the social construction of gender to their logical limit. In a binary gender system, quite obviously, some gendered subjects are going to cross-identify, and, rather than simply see these people as contrary at best or pathological at worst, we should recognize gender-variant people as part and parcel of dichotomous gendering. Furthermore, in our histories and theories of gender identity, we need to account for the impact of variant gendering.

We tend to associate female masculinity with lesbianism and we assume that masculinity in women is a sign of sexual orientation rather than a class or racial marker. The association between gender and sexual variance stems from early twentieth-century sexological accounts of "deviance." Studies by Havelock Ellis and others provided a heterosexual framework for sexual response by coupling same-sex desire with cross-gender identification. This convenient packaging of gender variance represented female masculinity as an expression of desire rather than as a socially conditioned form of embodiment. There is no essential relation between lesbianism and female masculinity, although female masculinity is an important component of some lesbian gendering. Female masculinity is as likely to be a product of class or work and it plays a large role in the gendering of racial identities, given that white femininity is established in a racist society as a gender ideal.

Judith Halberstam

See also Effeminacy; Transgenderism
Further Reading:
Butler, Judith. 1993. "The Lesbian Phallus and the Morphological Imaginary." Pp. 57–92 in *Bodies that Matter: On the Discursive Limits of "Sex."* New York: Routledge.
Davis, Madelaine, and Elizabeth L. Kennedy. 1993. *Boots of Leather, Slippers of Gold: The History of a Lesbian Community.* New York: Routledge.
Halberstam, Judith. 1998. *Female Masculinity.* Durham, NC: Duke University Press.
Newton, Esther. 2000. "Mythic Mannish Lesbian: Radclyffe Hall and the New Woman." Pp. 176–188 in *Margaret Mead Made Me Gay: Personal Essays, Public Ideas.* Durham, NC: Duke University Press.
Rubin, Gayle. 1992. "Of Catamites and Kings: Reflections on Butch, Gender and Boundaries." Pp. 466–843 in *The Persistent Desire: Femme-Butch Reader.* Edited by Joan Nestle. New York: Alyson.

Feminism

See Antifeminism; Feminist Theory; Gender Equality; Postfeminism; Second Wave Women's Movement

Vandana Shiva, chairperson of the antiglobalization U.S.-Indian Navdanya Foundation, answers questions 1 September 2002 during a press conference on the sideline of the World Summit on Sustainable Development in Johannesburg. Scores of world leaders or their representatives, many of them feminists, were in Johannesburg on the eve of a top-level debate on the world's future, crowning the ten-day Earth Summit. (AFP/Corbis)

Feminist Theory

The set of ideas that describe and seek to explain the subordination of women to men, the differences between men and women, the internalization and institutionalization of these differences, the representation of these differences in culture and ideology, the advantages of alternative gender arrangements, and the most effective means for improving women's lives and achieving a more equitable society.

Feminist theorists agree that contemporary gender arrangements are socially constructed and can be changed for the better. Some favor a world entirely without gender, in which people's reproductive anatomy will have no correlation with their personalities, desires, relationships, or social roles. Then the gender labels "masculinity" and "femininity," defined as the characteristics typically attributed to and differently valued in biological males and females, would become meaningless. Most feminists wish to reduce the importance of gender in determining individuals' opportunities and shaping social institutions. Some favor androgyny, in which both men and women will share the best characteristics now considered typical of each sex, like rationality and courage in men and empathy and tact in women. Others claim that masculinities and femininities can exist in a better future but be freed from differential social rewards. Most feminist theories agree that the subordination of women is inevitably and complexly linked to other harmful inequalities, for example, those of racial and class hierarchies, age divisions, and institutionalized heterosexuality. Feminist theories have inspired and continue to inform gender theory, queer theory, and masculinity studies.

Current feminist theories hold that gender is relational, so that the social categories and representations of men and women, and of masculinity and femininity, are defined in terms of each other; thus women and femininity are traditionally seen as opposites to men and masculinity. Masculinities and femininities are also defined by men among men, by women among women, and through contrasts between men and women with the divine, natural, animal, and mechanical. Since the Second Wave of the Women's Liberation Movement beginning in the late 1960s, feminists have believed that "the personal is political," meaning that even apparently individual or trivial matters, like which toys children play with or when women diet, are shaped by society's ideas about masculinity and femininity and by gendered institutions like the family, the state, religion, and the media. Feminists share a concern that their theories enable individual and institutional practices and social movements designed to improve women's conditions. They also tend to believe that all ideas, including their own, are shaped by the social positions or standpoints of those who hold them.

In recent years, three main types of objection have been lodged against feminist theories. The first type comes from what feminists usually see as a conservative backlash designed to erase women's social gains and reinvigorate male power. It rejects the major premises of feminist theory that women are unfairly disadvantaged in relation to men and that this disadvantage is changeable. It argues, for example, that women's longer lifespan proves that now women enjoy a privileged status over men, or that if men and women are legally equal, remaining disparities in income, occupations, and characters are the result of women's nature and preferences, not social bias. Since the 1990s, arguments for the desirability and inevitability of

traditional gender have often appealed to science, hypothesizing, for example, that sexual orientation is genetically determined or that male aggression and female monogamy are psychological inheritances of evolution. Feminist theorists argue, in response, that scientific views are themselves influenced by gender bias and that societies can act to reinforce or reduce apparently natural differences.

In contrast to their resistance to such conservative views, feminists have modified their theories in response to two other kinds of theories, those of feminists of color and poststructuralists or postmodernists. Feminists of color argued that the category of "women," as used by mainstream feminists, implicitly described only white, middle-class women and so excluded others, for instance, by positing women's problems as those of restless, educated housewives rather than as those of exploited laborers in other women's homes. Many feminist theories now centrally consider the situation of the disadvantaged women of color and address the intersections of racial, class, national, and linguistic inequalities. Postmodernist thinkers, who are skeptical of all comprehensive explanatory theories, dispute the very categories of "women" and "men" for naively accepting the division of people into two and only two genders. They also accuse many earlier feminist theories of "essentialism," meaning the belief that women and men are naturally different.

Many terms are used to describe and categorize feminist theories, but no nomenclature is universally accepted. The following brief sketch merely outlines some of these categories.

Prior to formal movements for women's emancipation or suffrage, many women felt that they were unfairly treated as inferior to men, even when they enjoyed the privileges of high social status or even education. They argued against women's social disadvantages and against false and demeaning views of women and femininity in comparison with false and inflated views of men and masculinity. Before organized feminism, individual thinkers defended women against misogynistic aspersions that connected women more than men with sin, vice, embodiment, intemperate sexuality, emotion, animality, and forces of nature, and they defended women's rights to speak, write, and represent themselves in public affairs rather than to be rendered silent, invisible, marginalized, and irrelevant. They also challenged the sexual double standard that divided women into many sinful Eves and a few sanctified Marys.

Feminism as a formal movement is a daughter of the Enlightenment, with its ideals of liberty, equality, and fraternity. Women sought liberty from traditional family, religious, legal, and other customary inhibitions on their talents and capacities, and they pursued equality in education and occupational choice, and the recognition of loyal bonds among women. Inspired by the ideals of the Rights of Man, Mary Wollstonecraft argued in "A Vindication of the Rights of Woman" (1792) that women were as capable of reason as men and that their deficiencies resulted from inadequate educations, not from nature.

Feminist theory in the United States grew up in conflicted relationship with American Enlightenment ideals and racist institutions. Many nineteenth-century U.S. feminists were abolitionists. Several were also Quakers who believed in the spiritual equality of all people. The Seneca Falls Declaration (1848) revised the United States Declaration of Independence to "hold these truths to be self-evident: that all men and women are created equal" and therefore that women should have voting, education, and property rights equal with men's. In France, Simone de Beauvoir modified existentialism to describe women as *The Second Sex* (1949), created by social behaviors and ideas, not by eternal nature: "One is not born, but rather becomes, a woman," she wrote, asserting that "Woman" was created as the negative and special case of normative "Man" (1). United States feminism after World War II,

like that in the nineteenth century, arose in relation to a civil rights movement for African Americans. Liberal feminists like Betty Friedan and the National Organization for Women (founded in 1966) believed changing laws and educating people against old prejudices could remedy discrimination against women, and they valued male allies in their campaigns.

Differentiated from these "equality" or "rights" feminist theories for some categorizers are the theories of "difference" or "gynocentric" feminisms. Instead of wishing women to become more like the normative rational male citizen, "cultural" feminists, one branch of "difference" feminists, value the traditional traits of women, and they criticize supposedly rational masculine social structures as instead repressive, violent, and dehumanizing. Especially important in the 1970s and 1980s, these theories inspired women's cultural institutions like magazines, publishing houses, music festivals, university women's studies programs, battered women's shelters, goddess-centered religious groups, and women-run health and abortion clinics. One crucial practice was "consciousness raising," usually in small, leaderless groups, in which women shared life stories and theorized on the basis of the "authority of experience." Women academics and writers also developed cultural feminist theories. Dorothy Dinnerstein (1976) argued that universal mother-dominated child rearing made all infants fearful of adult female power and so explained misogyny, while Nancy Chodorow (1978) thought female mothering created nurturant and empathic girls but competitive and autonomous boys; thus sexism could be cured if men shared equally with women in child care. In 1980 Adrienne Rich argued in "Compulsory Heterosexuality and Lesbian Existence" that despite social insistence on the inevitability of women's relationships with men, all women "exist on a lesbian continuum" in relation to love for and identification with other women. Carol Gilligan (1982) argued that women's "different voice" of an interdependent "ethics of care" should not be held inferior to masculine rights discourses.

Although some cultural feminists derived their theories from Freudian and object relations psychology, feminists like Luce Irigiray who were influenced by French psychoanalyst Jacques Lacan critiqued a "phallogocentric" culture that took its values from masculine social and linguistic power. Hélene Cixous (1975) suggested that the experimental writing style of *écriture féminine,* which could be written by men or women, could disrupt conventional society .

Although liberal feminist views are the most widely held today, many people identify feminism particularly with radical feminist theories. These theories stress women's oppression under patriarchies throughout history and across cultures rather than women's positive traits. They are sometimes grouped with cultural feminism under the rubric "difference feminism" or labeled "victim feminism" by their opponents. Theologian Mary Daly (1987) rejected patriarchal religions dependent on a Father God and sought to remake patriarchal language through a new "Wickedary." Legal theorist Catharine MacKinnon (1987) defined "feminism unmodified" as an attack on all male dominance and on all the ways women are restricted, violated, and objectified. She describes femininity as equivalent to women's "rape-ability," while seeing masculinity as constituted through eroticized violence. She and her allies effectively framed laws criminalizing sexual harassment and sought to ban all pornography as a violation of women's human rights. For Andrea Dworkin, heterosexual intercourse invades women's integrity and the only principled position for people with penises is what John Stoltenberg calls "Refusing to be a Man" (Stoltenberg 1989).

Women of color have been prominent thinkers throughout the U.S. women's movement, often in dialogue with both white feminists and men of their own communities. The Combahee River Collective sought "the development of integrated analysis and practice based upon the fact that the major systems of oppression are interlocking," yet they also defended theorizing a radical "identity politics" based on their own position as black lesbian feminists (1977). bell hooks (1984) points out both the common racist oppressions suffered by men and women in impoverished communities of color and the race-specific terms in which gender is always constructed, for example, in the demasculinization of African American men who cannot achieve breadwinner status. Yet feminists of color also deplore sexism and resist patriarchal nationalisms. Novelist Alice Walker (1983) popularized the term "womanism" for a feminism that celebrated women within a whole black community, and Patricia Hill Collins (1999) defined "Black feminist thought" through a "standpoint of and for Black women" (1999). Chicana, Native American, and Asian American theorists also emphasize the specificity of their religious, cultural, and linguistic traditions and the interlocking oppressions they suffer from racism, classism, sexism, and heterosexism.

Global feminist theorists like Gayatri Spivak, Uma Narayan, and Vandana Shiva have addressed the problems of attempting to speak for the world's least privileged women. They articulate indigenous feminisms and resist the view that arguments for women's rights enforce Western imperialism. Many of these feminists use Marxist and other materialist concepts that emphasize the exploitation of women of color, class differences among women, and the injustices of the global marketplace and international sex trade. Global and other materialist feminist theories are likely to situate most men as potential brothers and allies against common oppressions. Ecofeminist theories analyze the harmful effects of cultural analogies between women and nature; they deplore masculinist anthropocentrism and seek a more harmonious relationship between people and the environment.

The foregoing theories are all feminist in seeking to end sexist inequities and to improve women's lives. Poststructuralist and queer theorists, however, question feminism's fundamental gender categories. They emphasize the power of cultural representations and note the exclusions created by all categories, especially binary divisions like those between men and women and heterosexuality and homosexuality. In *Gender Trouble* (1990), philosopher Judith Butler claimed that gender is created by repeated performances, like ways of walking, rather than arising from biology, and that the two sexes are not biological facts but social categories based on heterosexual premises. For these theorists, the constraints on women are created less by individual men than by pervasive linguistic, social, and cultural structures, and they are likely to see themselves as allies, especially of homosexual men. Poststructuralist feminists also champion transgender and queer theories. For example, Judith Halberstam (1998) records the varieties of "female masculinity" that denaturalize the identification of masculinity with male bodies.

Judith Kegan Gardiner

Further Reading:

Beauvoir, Simone de. 1968. *The Second Sex.* Trans. and ed. by H. M. Parshley. New York: Bantam Books.

Butler, Judith. 1990. *Gender Trouble: Feminism and the Subversion of Identity.* New York: Routledge.

Chodorow, Nancy J. 1978. *The Reproduction of Mothering: Psychoanalysis and the Sociology of Gender.* Berkeley and Los Angeles: University of California Press.

Collins, Patricia Hill. 1999. "Moving beyond Gender: Intersectionality and Scientific Knowledge." Pp. 261–284 in *Revisioning Gender.* Ed. by Myra Marx Ferree, Judith Lorber, and Beth B. Hess. Thousand Oaks, CA: Sage Publications.

Daly, Mary, with Jane Caputi. 1987. *Webster's First New Intergalactic Wickedary of the English Language.* Boston: Beacon Press.

Dinnerstein, Dorothy. 1976. *The Mermaid and the Minotaur: Sexual Arrangements and Human Malaise.* New York: Harper and Row.

Gardiner, Judith Kegan, ed. 2002. *Masculinity Studies and Feminist Theories: New Perspectives.* New York: Columbia University Press.

Gilligan, Carol. 1982. *In a Different Voice: Psychological Theory and Women's Development.* Cambridge, MA: Harvard University Press.

Halberstam, Judith. 1998. *Female Masculinity.* Durham and London: Duke University Press.

hooks, bell. 1984. *Feminist Theory: From Margin to Center.* Boston: South End Press.

Kolmar, Wendy, and Frances Bartkowski, eds. 2000. *Feminist Theory: A Reader.* Mountain View, CA: Mayfield.

MacKinnon, Catharine. 1987. *Feminism Unmodified.* Cambridge, MA: Harvard University Press.

Meyers, Diana Tietjens, ed. 1997. *Feminist Social Thought: A Reader.* New York: Routledge.

Nicholson, Linda, ed. 1997. *The Second Wave: A Reader in Feminist Theory.* New York: Routledge.

Price, Janet, and Margrit Shildrick. 1999. *Feminist Theory and the Body: A Reader.* New York: Routledge, 1999.

Stoltenberg, John. 1989. *Refusing to Be a Man: Essays on Sex and Justice.* Portland: Breitenbush Books.

Tong, Rosemarie Putnam. 1998. *Feminist Thought: A More Comprehensive Introduction.* Boulder, CO: Westview.

Fight Club

Fight Club, a novel written by Chuck Palahniuk, published in 1996, explores the struggle for masculine identity in late twentieth-century America. The novel was adapted for the screen, and the film version was released in 1999. In the novel/film, an unnamed protagonist is dissatisfied with his life and attempts to build a new identity through the creation of an underground, bare-knuckle boxing club, known as Fight Club. For the protagonist and the other men in the exclusively male group, Fight Club provides temporary relief from lives in which they feel they are powerless. The participants believe that their frustration will vanish if they can revive a primal masculinity that has been lost.

In *Fight Club,* the protagonist first attempts to find relief for his insomnia and depression by attending a number of support groups for the chronically and terminally ill; there he finds the meaningful human contact lacking in his daily life, although he is not ill himself. The presence of another faker, a woman, de-

Still from Fight Club *with Brad Pitt and Edward Norton (Corbis Sygma)*

stroys his new-found peace of mind, and he and another character, Tyler Durden, begin Fight Club.

Fight Club serves its members in a number of ways. First, Fight Club offers participants intimacy with others, as did the support groups for the protagonist. However, in Fight Club, this intimacy is solely with other men, and, as in military units and sport teams, the men of Fight Club are free to come together without facing accusations of homosexuality because of the aggressive and violent nature of the group. The exclusion of women from the group may also allow the men greater freedom to act without fear of judgment. In addition, the men of Fight Club believe that, through pain and violence, they are reviving a lost element of their masculine identity. Americans saw a similar attitude ex-

pressed in the mythopoetic men's movement, which was inspired by Robert Bly's book, *Iron John* (1990). Although violence was not the primary vehicle for finding this lost masculinity, the movement was still criticized for its presumption of essential male and female characteristics.

Eventually, Fight Club evolves into Project Mayhem, a splinter group bent on urban terrorism. Project Mayhem members blame much of the loss of their masculinity on American consumerism, and the targets of their attacks are symbols of consumer culture such as franchise coffee shops, corporate art, and the buildings that house the records of the major credit card companies. The goal is to erase the debt record and presumably bring about greater equality; however, Project Mayhem quickly becomes another

Huckleberry Finn by Kemble (Library of Congress)

film for its violent content. Audience reaction was lukewarm. However, word of mouth spread, and the film developed a cult following, particularly among young men. On the Internet, a large number of websites have been devoted to the film; many offer advice on starting one's own Fight Club as well as suggesting terrorist acts similar to those perpetrated by Project Mayhem. The existence of these web pages as well as the overall popularity of the film/novel suggests that many American men see themselves as engaged in the identity struggle depicted by both.

Brenda J. Duge

Further Reading:
Faludi, Susan. 1999. *Stiffed: The Betrayal of the American Man.* New York: William Marrow.
———. 1999. "It's 'Thelma and Louise' for Guys." *Time* 17: 89.
Fight Club (film). 1999. Directed by David Fincher. Twentieth Century Fox.
Kimmel, Michael S., and Michael Kaufman. 1994. "Weekend Warriors: The New Men's Movement." Pp. 259–288 in *Theorizing Masculinities.* Edited by Harry Brod and Michael Kaufman. Thousand Oaks: Sage.
Palahniuk, Chuck. 1996. *Fight Club.* New York: Norton.
Pleck, Joseph. 1995. "Men's Power with Women, Other Men, and Society: A Men's Movement Analysis." Pp. 5–12 in *Men's Lives.* Edited by Michael S. Kimmel and Michael A. Messner. Boston: Allyn and Bacon.
Taubin, Amy. 1999. "So Good It Hurts." *Film Comment* 11: 16–19.

ideology controlling the men and isolating them from women. Upon joining Project Mayhem, the men must offer up all individuality and conform to a militaristic type of organization. Lacking personhood and therefore also lacking personal responsibility, members of the group find the violence Project Mayhem enacts escalating to a dangerous level. The group uses intimidation and violence to dominate others who might disagree, and the type of social control that the men had originally been reacting against is reinstated. The men must adhere to the rules of the group, and all who might oppose are to be silenced, often through threats of castration. Eventually, the protagonist realizes his creation has become dangerous and will not provide the stable masculine identity for which he has been searching.

Initial critical reaction to the novel was good; however, many critics later blasted the

Finn, Huckleberry

In the *Adventures of Huckleberry Finn,* Huck Finn moved from his position as Tom Sawyer's sidekick to a markedly different version of the good "bad boy," bringing a complexity to the stereotype that continues to resonate. After *The Adventures of Tom Sawyer,* Mark Twain turned over the narration to Huck Finn, who also narrated the less-famous sequels *Tom Sawyer Abroad* (1894) and *Tom Sawyer, Detective* (1896). With Huck, Twain created a specifically American voice that is always naive and hopeful, without the bemused cynicism of Sawyer or Twain. Leslie

Fiedler (1982) writes: "the memory of all the boy that Twain was or dreamed himself afterward is Tom; the memory of all he was not and only wished he dared to aspire to be is Huck" (277). Huck may not be presentable to society, but he always holds onto his "sound heart."

The *Adventures of Huckleberry Finn* continued Mark Twain's presentation of lively, appealing boys who failed to follow the precepts of more moralistic juvenile literature. However, in this novel, Twain more directly confronts the veiled hypocrisy of the age and furthers his attempts to depict a range of American characters across race and class. On the one hand, this frankness led to the novel being quickly banned by the Concord Public Library, right after its publication, as well as discomfort in contemporary classrooms and libraries. On the other hand, it was his most commercially successful novel and has been hailed by authors such as William Dean Howells, William Faulkner, and Norman Mailer. Ernest Hemingway famously called it the "one book" from which all American literature came (in Hutchinson 1999, 80, 83).

Unlike the sunny Hannibal (Missouri) of *Sawyer,* Huck's adventure is a largely gothic tale, haunted by men's hostility and the violent secrets of their past. He escapes his drunken father, choosing instead to share the terror of Jim's bondage and escape down the wide river. Huck's merger with Jim and the river reflects the elemental nature of Huck's experience. The river is a major force in the novel, with Lionel Trilling (in Hutchinson 1999, 95) describing it as an ambivalent and awesome deity, that nonetheless fosters goodness in those like Jim and Huck who willingly serve it. Huck's serious wrestlings with his conscience, poignant yet amusing parts of the novel, move him from a simple innocent boy to an American Hamlet or Whitman's I in "Song of Myself."

Huck is likewise a remarkable figure for his compassionate partnership with Jim. Ralph Ellison (in Hutchinson 1999, 86) notes that the character of Jim avoids stereotypes, with fully developed good and bad points: "after Twain's compelling image of black and white fraternity, the Negro generally disappears from fiction as a rounded human being." Fiedler sees Huck and Jim's relationship as the prime example of American literature's favored pairing of the white hero with the dark friend: "chaste male love as the ultimate emotional experience, the eternal adolescence of classic American literature" (1982, 182). However, unlike the unconditional acceptance by Queequeg and Chingachgook, Jim challenges Huck, with Huck's moral sense growing directly out of his intimate friendship with the escaped slave.

Similarly, Huck's discomfort with society and his refusal to grow up is markedly different from Tom Sawyer. Huck is less afraid of responsibility than of the moral compromises or the callousness that is presented as the norm for respectable men. He appreciates the nurturing care of women, particularly during his stay with the Wilks sisters, but he feels unworthy because he cannot live up to society's yardstick. He is therefore doomed to follow his "sound heart" and remove himself. Huck and Jim buy into Tom's overly elaborate escape plan, both because of their infinite patience to endure their fates as well as their expectations that society will continually invent arbitrary trials. He may threaten to "light out for the territories" at the end of the novel—yet the sequels still find him in Hannibal, following the tyrannical Tom, trying to find a way that he can be connected to the community. Huck Finn clings to the hope promised by American democracy, which may offer freedom to good and bad alike, yet believing that in the end there is more good than bad in us in the final equation.

In the final section, it is essential that Tom Sawyer appear (practically deus ex machina) and take control of the narrative, allowing Huck to give up role of hero and move into the background that he prefers. For Huck to end the novel in charge, he would have to "grow up" and learn to maneuver in society.

Huck instead weakly vows to "light out for the territories," even though it is a landscape that is collapsing. The *Adventures of Huckleberry Finn* chronicles Huck's heroic attempts to find a freedom where his "sound heart" can beat without compromise. Although other American literary heroes choose isolation to escape emotional entanglements, Huck seeks for an integrity in relationships that society, so far, has failed to provide.

Elizabeth Abele

See also Sawyer, Tom

Further Reading:

Cope, Virginia H. 1995. "Mark Twain's *Huckleberry Finn:* Text, Illustrations, and Early Reviews." *Mark Twain in His Times.* Electronic Text Center, University of Virginia. At *http://etext.lib.virginia.edu/twain/ huckfinn.html* (cited 29 September 2002).

Fiedler, Leslie. 1982. *Love and Death in the American Novel.* 3d ed. New York: Stein and Day.

Fishkin, Shelley Fisher. 1993. *Was Huck Black? Mark Twain and African-American Voices.* New York: Oxford University Press.

Hutchinson, Stuart. 1999. *Mark Twain, Tom Sawyer and Huckleberry Finn.* New York: Columbia University Press.

Railton, Stephen. 1996. "Adventures of Huckleberry Finn." *Mark Twain in His Times.* Electronic Text Center, University of Virginia. At http://etext .lib.virginia.edu/railton/huckfinn/huchompg. html (cited 27 July 2003).

First World War Literature

In Western culture, war has always been one of the main ways in which the sexes are divided and gender expectations enforced. Although such preeminent signs of masculinity as leadership, physical prowess, competitiveness, and courage can also be encouraged and displayed by women through sports or exploration, nation-states particularly require these characteristics of men through military training. Literature plays a major role in establishing the connection between war and manliness through its constructions of heroism. Militarist values, which promote certain ideas of masculinity and femininity, are disseminated through war literature both as entertainment and as education. Classic war texts primarily address men and all perpetuate the idea that "war is men's business" (women should "keep the home fires burning"). However, World War I provoked a crisis in the ideology of heroism demonstrated by personal combat. On the battlefields of the western front, technological advances led to mass carnage. Heroism came to seem futile because death was random and individual acts irrelevant. Furthermore, modern weapons of destruction can be as easily wielded or activated by women as by men. The "fracture in Western culture" created by World War I was widely manifested in imaginative literature. By the end of the century, theorists were explicating how war literature interrogated the costs of militarized masculinity. These ranged from the patriarchal imposition of heterosexuality, and the stresses of repressed femininity and same-sex desire, to the racist conceptions of white masculinity that underpinned imperialism.

Thus World War I holds a special position in the literature of the English-speaking countries that took part, but it functions differently in the various cultures, especially with regard to masculinity. If for Australia and New Zealand it meant a coming of age for colonial manhood, in the Caribbean and India, experience in the British army led directly to the independence movements (as shown in Mulk Raj Anand's *Across the Black Waters* [1940]). Similarly in the United States, World War I gave birth to the "New Negro" of the Harlem Renaissance (illustrated in plays like Alice Dunbar Nelson's *Mine Eyes Have Seen* [1918] and Mary Burrill's *The Aftermath* [1919]). In Northern Ireland, the battle of the Somme continues to be celebrated by Unionists (see plays by Christina Reid and Frank MacGuinness), whereas in the south the war was the opportunity for the 1916 Easter Rising (as remembered in texts including Sean O'Casey's *The Plough and the Stars* and Yeats's poetry). While the men of previously subordinated communities took pride in their wartime role, the massive casualties were a blow to imperialist hubris. High modernist texts showed other British and American men as physically and psychically wounded by the war: As Malcom Bradbury has observed, the emasculated war survivor is a prominent trope in modernist writing. (Examples include D. H. Lawrence's *Lady Chatterley's Lover,* Hemingway's *The Sun Also Rises,* Ford Maddox Ford's *A Man Could Stand Up,* Woolf's *Mrs. Dalloway,* T. S. Eliot's *The Wasteland,* Mansfield's *The Fly,* and O'Casey's *The Silver Tassie.*) Although Sandra Gilbert and Susan Gubar argue in *No Man's Land* (1989) that this trope was the result of a male crisis of self-confidence due to the New Woman's increased power, that view is challenged by the traumatized heroines of war writing by women (such as H. D.'s *Bid Me to Live,* Vera Brittain's *Testament of Youth,* and Helen Zenna Smith's *Not So Quiet . . .*). It seems more significant that all these writers were noncombatants.

A resurgence of interest in Great War literature took place during the 1960s, when the fiftieth anniversary was accentuated by CND and the Vietnam War. Writing produced by combatants (the so-called trench poets), particularly fictionalized autobiographies by Robert Graves, Siegfried Sassoon, Edmund Blunden, and Richard Aldington, and the poetry of Wilfred Owen, Isaac Rosenberg, David Jones, and Siegfried Sassoon were republished. Antiwar positions were promoted by Benjamin Britten's *War Requiem* and Theatre Workshop's *Oh What a Lovely War I,* which stressed the mass slaughter. Such imaginative works paralleled the complex analysis of World War I propaganda by literary critics. Stanley Cooperman (1967) and Peter Buitenhuis demonstrated government control of the aggressive ideology that inspired men to enlist. However, as Paul Fussell (1975) argued, by the early 1970s wider social change facilitated new treatments of war and war literature. Alterations in the laws on homosexuality and censorship redefined obscenity. By referring to particular World War I writers, particularly

Sassoon and Owen, authors could initiate an examination of previously taboo subjects.

Once it became possible to acknowledge the homosexuality of Sassoon and Owen openly, the homoerotic nature of their poetry could also be examined. Because they were decorated war heroes whose courage was unquestionable, they became icons of a masculine homosexuality that challenged previous stereotypes of the effeminate "pansy" and contributed to gay pride. From the 1980s interest also grew in the relation between madness and writing, due to developments in psychoanalytic literary analysis. Connections between "shell shock," war trauma, and repression were recognized in Elaine Showalter's *The Female Malady* (1986). Graves, Sassoon, and Owen had written war poetry as therapy while being treated by a Freudian psychoanalyst, W. H. Rivers, at Craiglochart Mental Hospital during the war. Showalter provided ways of discussing the complex interrelation between male bonding, traumatic illness, and the crisis over masculinity provoked by the war. The repression of emotion and the nature of close comradeship had been tackled obliquely in contemporary novels by Woolf and Rebecca West, and more recently in Susan Hill's *Strange Meeting* and Jennifer Johnston's *How Many Miles to Babylon?* The new openness about such matters is reflected in Frank MacGuinness's play, *Observe the Sons of Ulster Marching as to War.* The most thoroughgoing, outspoken exploration of war neurosis and masculine anxiety in imaginative literature is Pat Barker's novel trilogy: *Regeneration, The Eye in the Door,* and *The Ghost Road.* Their impact was increased by Gillies MacKinnon's feature film: *Regeneration* (1997). This emphasizes Barker's investigation of male wretchedness, patriarchal relations, and the role of the psychoanalyst as surrogate father. Julia Kristeva's theoretical work *On Horror* informed the film's imagery, so that it responds to the novel's connection of war with the abject. This treatment of war and obscenity compares with Thomas Pynchon's approach to the Great War in *Gravity's Rainbow.*

Two late twentieth-century analyses related World War I literature to texts from other wars. Graham Dawson's *Soldier Heroes* (1994) related war fiction to the genre of adventure stories for boys. He demonstrated the prevalence of imperial ideology in tales of British heroes and the ways in which men internalize these discourses of masculinity. Taking stories about T. E. Lawrence and the film *Lawrence of Arabia* (1962) as central, he was concerned to dissect military racism and xenophobia. Joanna Bourke's *An Intimate History of Killing* (1999) took letters, diaries, and memoirs from participants in both World Wars and from the Vietnam War to produce a radically different view of the war veteran from either the traumatized victim or the noble hero. She revealed that normal civilians were prepared by popular "narratives of pleasure" to become enthusiastic killers, never so intensely alive as when committing atrocities. This thesis is born out by certain World War I literary texts that are usually disregarded, novellas by working-class soldiers: James Hanley's *The German Prisoner* (1930) and Liam O'Flaherty's *The Alien Skull* (1924) and *Return of the Brute* (1929).

Claire Tylee

Further Reading:

Cooperman, Stanley. 1999. *World War I and the American Novel.* Baltimore, MD: Johns Hopkins University Press.

Fussell, Paul. 1975. *The Great War and Modern Memory.*

Fitzgerald, F. [Francis] Scott (1896–1940)

One of the most brilliant authors of American literature, F. Scott Fitzgerald dramatizes in his texts the triumphs as well as the tragedies of the men of his generation. In an effort to escape the anxiety generated by the aftermath of the Great War, Fitzgerald's male characters take refuge in the euphoria and the glamour of the Roaring Twenties, and seek to affirm their troubled, gendered selves in a romanticized construction of masculinity that contemplates women as a threat to their manhood.

Fitzgerald's men often fall prey to the feeling of loss of ethical values and the rise of materialistic aims that characterized the years of the Jazz Age. Confused by the rapid changes that the new century had brought along, F. Scott Fitzgerald, like the rest of the male authors of the Lost Generation, "wrote stories they thought as disclosing the secret truth about the century with which they had been born and with which they identified" (Minter 1996, 83). Naming themselves "prophets of the age," these authors—young survivors of the war— felt like "refugees of a general wreck, yet their prospects as artists were boundless" (Minter 82).

Most of Fitzgerald's fiction, critics agree, is intensely autobiographical, providing clues to the understanding of his male creations. The writer, who epitomized the glamorous contradictions of his generation, portrays the experiences of the lives of those men who, like himself, had become spokesmen for the "beautiful and the damned." Born in the Midwest, the son of an unsuccessful manufacturer (Fitzgerald's male characters will be haunted by their lack of economic wealth), the writer was stricken with social ambitions that were nurtured by his mother, a woman who—like most of Fitzgerald's main female characters—had aristocratic pretensions. While at camp in Alabama, Scott—like his most famous character, Jay Gatsby—fell intensely in love with a beautiful Southern and wealthy young woman. Her name was Zelda Sayre. After the war, and carrying the unaccepted draft of *This Side of Paradise* (based on a story initially titled "The Boy Who Killed His Mother"), Fitzgerald moved to New York to work in an advertising agency to earn enough money to marry his dream girl. Yet Zelda—like Rosaline in *This Side of Paradise* (1920)—broke off their engagement for fear of poverty. Back in his hometown, St. Paul, Minnesota, Fitzgerald rewrote his manuscript, which became a success in 1920. Zelda reconsidered the engagement and, eight days after its publication, married him in St. Patrick's Cathedral in New York.

Success, glamour, incessant parties, travels, money, and scandalous behavior characterized the life of the Fitzgeralds (and that of his main characters), turning them into the magnificent couple of the Magnificent Twenties. Yet, glory, fame, and money soon faded away. Financial instability brought family tensions. Drunken excesses, infidelities, and Zelda's internments in Switzerland to be treated for schizophrenia, drove the couple into permanent emotional bankruptcy—a theme that would be recurrent in Fitzgerald's fiction. The young writer died of a heart attack in 1940 after having explored the spiritual malaise of his time in *The Crack-Up* (1945) and leaving his impressive novel *The Last Tycoon* (1941) unfinished. In 1948, Zelda died in a fire that burned the Highland Hospital where she had practically resided for the past twelve years.

In a modern time that had substituted materialism for idealism, Fitzgerald's male protagonists try to uphold romantic values to give meaning to their lives. However, in spite of their efforts, they are distressed characters with a doomed destiny. "The central tragedy of the Fitzgerald hero," observes David Fedo (1980), "is that the ideals he holds concerning women (and life) are corroded and finally destroyed; a kind of romantic eagerness is gradually replaced by waste, and then by despair of death" (27). This is precisely Amory Blaine's fate in the writer's first and largely autobiographical novel, *This Side of Paradise* (1920). Blaine, a romantic egotist alienated by a world in the process of enormous changes, feels for the first time an unselfish love for Rosaline. Yet, when his wealth is diminished by his mother's death, he is abandoned by his romance girl, who marries another man, believing she will be unhappy without money. Rosaline's refusal is reminiscent of the adolescent Fitzgerald's first failed infatuation with Ginevra, a girl who "embodied his ideal of wealth and social position" and whose father's remark seems to have

been: "poor boys should never think of marrying rich girls" (Pelzer 2000, 3).

The theme "poor boy in search of the golden girl" is recurrent in Fitzgerald's prose. Amory Blaine, Dick Diver in *Tender Is the Night* (1934), and Jay Gatsby are characters who "do not rightfully belong in the world of privilege. Yet they aspire to it, not for materialistic reasons, but as a confirmation of their self-conceived destiny and their sustained visions" (Pelzer 2000, 30).

Anthony Patch in *The Beautiful and the Damned* (1922) is disinherited by Old Adam Patch when the latter intrudes on Anthony's drunken party. Left with no money, the young Patch discovers that he is unsuited to the business world (like Fitzgerald), and that there is nothing worth doing except to write. Unable to fulfill his desire and captured by Gloria's beauty, he marries her, only to discover that his new wife is an irresponsible woman, who ridicules his romantic ideals and is eager to spend her beauty and her youth the best way she can. The novel chronicles the decline in which the couple "fall prey to the perverse necessities of wealth and style and of the sad degradations of moral carelessness" (Pelzer 2000, 23). Similarly, Jay Gatsby, the hero of *The Great Gatsby* (1926), is destroyed by his romantic idealism in his search for the golden girl, Daisy, whose voice is "full of money." In *Tender Is the Night* (1934), Fitzgerald, affected by Zelda's depressive condition, seems to identify with Dick Diver. A distinguished psychiatrist, Dick falls in love and marries his wealthy and beautiful patient, Nicole Warren, who is treated for schizophrenia due to an incestuous relationship with her father. Having practically abandoned his job to live on the Riviera to attend Nicole, Dick feels enslaved by his wife's fortune. He goes finally to ruin when he is abandoned by *La Belle Dame sans Merci* who, having survived her illness, leaves him for another man.

Fitzgerald's women protagonists are often portrayed as spoiled human beings, pampered by their wealth, self-absorbed, possessors of an extraordinary beauty, careless, irresponsible, and more than anything, showing cruel behavior toward their male partners. "Fitzgerald," as critic Sarah B. Fryer (1984) says, "shows little sympathy for his female characters" (157). The vision of women as destroyers of men is recurrent in the writer's pages. "The notion that women are predators, that they are capable of destroying even the men they want most, becomes a central idea in nearly all of Fitzgerald's fiction" (Fedo 1980, 27). To further uncover the autobiographical thread in his fiction, it might be noted that Fitzgerald himself confessed to his daughter Scottie that "I decided to marry your mother after all, even though I knew she was spoiled and it meant no good to me. I was sorry immediately [that] I had married her" (cited in Fedo 1980, 26).

However, women in Fitzgerald's fiction are less fully developed characters than the male heroes and they seem to be there just to embody the men's (frustrated) desires. As Aldrich (1989) points out, "[f]or the irony is that Fitzgerald, the incessant brooder of women and Woman, was not particularly good at rendering full or convincing women characters in his long fiction" (152). Moreover, to the same confusion that affected the men in the world of the twenties (the absence of ethical values, a sense of fragmentation, sterility, and cultural emptiness) women had to add "American society's transition from a strict patriarchy to a greater degree of equality between the sexes. As Fitzgerald presents romantic relationships, he demonstrates a seemingly perpetual power struggle between men and women" (Fryer 1989, 2658).

Fitzgerald's men are portrayed as frail, insecure, with lost aspirations and defeated hopes, trying to grasp a dream (somewhere) to give meaning to their existence. Yet, their romantic egotism, based on a self-centered and fragile sense of manhood, drives them to project their hopeful desires onto a fixed "Other"—Woman, whose physical beauty (and wealth) signifies, according to their male gaze, the virginal and untainted land of America the beautiful. The "idealized" (and therefore unreal) woman fails them, just as America—a dream country constructed by masculinist ethics in which women had little public participation—had failed them. Fitzgerald's male characters' inability to explore their own maladjustments in relation to the dehumanizing values of the time, drives them to place the responsibility on women. Seeing that their imagined female counterparts are unable to fulfill their imagined expectations, they demonize them and consider them the cause of their own failures.

A traditionally constructed masculine legacy informs Fitzgerald's main character in his—considered to be—finest novel, *The Great Gatsby* (1926). Gatsby, who represents the quintessential nature of the American self-made man, is individualistic, self-absorbed, and unrelational to anyone or any place. Having "repudiated his former self, with its ancestry" (Lewis 1995, 197), Gatsby "sprang from his Platonic conception of himself." Such a conception bears the mark of the competitive values of wealth and success that defined the twenties and that find their ultimate expression in the men that serve as Gatsby's models. Having rejected his unsuccessful parents ("his imagination had never really accepted them as his parents at all"), Gatsby, "quick and extravagantly ambitious," sets out to sea with Dan Cody, a rich and unethical playboy "who 1/4 brought back to the Eastern seaboard the savage violence of the frontier brothel and saloon" (74). Their homosocial relationship is interrupted by Ella Kaye, a female journalist and Cody's occasional lover. Her presence not only interferes with their intimate male bonding, but Ella is held responsible for Dan Cody's death. It is Dan Cody's portrait that Gatsby keeps in his bedroom, as homage to the man who gave him a "singularly appropriate education" as well as a reminder of the "menace" that women represent to men and to men's friendship. Daisy herself (a product—like Gatsby—of his male fantasy), becomes objectified within Gatsby's "romantic" space of desire. Being "the phallic woman with a phallus of gold" (Fiedler 1982, 313), Daisy is there to confirm Fitzgerald's vision of women as predators.

David Fedo's (1980) argument that Fitzgerald's men are "morally weak, sent adrift by morally weaker women" (28) lends further support to the idea that Fitzgerald's men appear to be incapable of self-reflection in order to re-create a responsible manhood that they feel is under threat. Trying to solve their sense of dislocation in the "adoration of pure womanhood" (Fiedler 1982, 313) seems to be as escapist as looking—as Gatsby does—for a pristine dream located in the nation's past. For the American Dream, based on the male ethics of colonization and the genocide of the natives, has proved to be anything but innocent.

Àngels Carabí

Further Reading:
Aldrich, Elizabeth Kasper. 1989. "The Most Poetical Topic in the World: Women in the Novels of F. Scott Fitzgerald." Pp. 131–156 in *Scott Fitzgerald: The Promises of Life*. Edited by A. Robert Lee. London and New York: Vision Press and St. Martin's Press.

Bruccoli, Matthew J. 1993. *Some Sort of Epic Grandeur: The Life of F. Scott Fitzgerald*. New York: Carroll and Graft.

Decker, Jeffrey Louis. 1994. "Gatsby's Pristine Dream. The Diminishment of the Self-Made Man in the Tribal Twenties." *Novel* 28, no. 1: 52–71.

Fedo, David. 1980. "Women in the Fiction of F. Scott Fitzgerald." *Forum* 21, no. 2: 26–33.

Fiedler, Leslie. 1960/1982. *Love and Death in the American Novel*. New York: Penguin.

Fraser, Keith. 1984 "Another Reading of *The Great Gatsby*." Pp. 140–153 in *Critical Essays on F. Scott Fitzgerald's* The Great Gatsby. Edited by Scott Donaldson. Boston, MA: G. K. Hall.

Fryer, Sarah Beebe. 1984. "Beneath the Mask: The Plight of Daisy Buchanan." Pp. 153–166 in *Critical Essays on F. Scott Fitzgerald's* The Great Gatsby. Edited by Scott Donaldson. Boston, MA: G. K. Hall.

———. 1988. "Fitzgerald's New Women: Harbingers of Change." *DAI* 49, no. 9: 2658, sec. A: 1989.

Lewis, R. W. B. 1995. *The American Adam: Innocence, Tragedy and Tradition in the Nineteenth Century*.

Chicago and London: The University of Chicago Press.

Minter, David. 1996. *A Cultural History of the American Novel: Henry James to William Faulkner*. Cambridge, MA: Cambridge University Press, 1994.

Mizener, Arthur. 1972. *Scott Fitzgerald*. London: Thames and Hudson, 1987.

Pelzer, Linda C. 2000. *A Student Companion to F. Scott Fitzgerald*. Westport, CT: Greenwood Press.

Snyder, Katherine. 1999. *Bachelors, Manhood, and the Novel 1850–1925*. Cambridge, UK: Cambridge University Press.

Football

Vince Lombardi, one of American football's legendary coaches once said, "I firmly believe that any man's finest hour—his greatest fulfillment to all he holds dear is that moment when he has worked his heart out in a good cause and lies exhausted on the field of battle—victorious" (epigraph to film *Any Given Sunday,* 2000). This quote depicts football as a battle, in which a man's "finest hour" is defined by violent, bloody conflict. Embedded within the quote is the notion of degree. The harder the man slays his enemy, the greater his "fulfillment to all he holds dear." The quote leaves the reader with the idea that the harder the man battles, the more masculine he becomes to others (and possibly to himself).

A novice to the game of football may conceptualize it as a dangerous, violent sport with parallels to battle and war. Many football spectators can readily identify with the competitive, physical, and rough aspects of the sport. Some fans may enjoy only these elements of the game.

Historically, football embodied the darker side of masculinity. Beginning with President Theodore Roosevelt, football was hailed as a man's sport (Nelson Parcells 2000). The misogynist roots of the sport were sometimes expressed in terms of male violence against and domination of women. Date rape, domestic violence, and extramarital affairs symbolize the "off the field" behavior of some football athletes. The sport reinforced the objectification of women through its use of cheerleaders. That is, cheerleaders, who were often dressed provocatively, symbolized women as dumb sex-objects. Unfortunately, these negative masculine traits were rationalized by society through a biological essentialism framework (i.e., "boys will be boys").

Despite this history, football embodies both positive and negative qualities of masculinity. Male-to-male competition is an example of the former. While male-to-male emotional intimacy and friendship are the lesser known aspects of the sport, some football players and fans illustrate these positive masculine traits.

Regarding football players, competition is seen both between teams and within teams. The former occurs when one football team plays against another. The latter occurs when members of a particular team compete against each other for starting roles, playing time, and prestige.

During football games, masculinity is defined, in part, by how hard one player can hit and tackle another. As part of the game, football players take physical risks that are potentially life-threatening (Nelson Parcells 1988). Concussions, broken bones, head injuries, and punctured lungs are just a few consequences of the game. Playing football is an example of the unsafe and potentially harmful behaviors that men perform in order to define their masculinity. Courtenay (2000) discussed other dangerous and neglectful behaviors of men—not having annual medical examinations, a failure to eat healthy, not taking multivitamins and mineral supplements, and engaging in unsafe sexual practices.

To hit competitors even harder (and be considered even more manly) than their teammates, most football players participate in strength-training programs to enhance athletic performance. To this end, many football players seriously begin lifting weights to gain strength and lean muscle mass. Unfortunately, many abuse anabolic-androgenic steroids, often leading to dependence (Khorrami 2000; Khorrami and Franklin

2002), rendering chemical dependency treatment difficult (Khorrami 2003).

Football players also exhibit an unusual level of warmth and compassion toward one another. During games, it is common to observe players giving each other "high fives," embracing and hugging, and even kissing each other's cheek when a good play occurs. In *The Final Season*, coach Bill Nelson Parcells (2000) wrote:

> When you have a good team, the guys like one another, interact with one another as families, go to one another's houses for dinner, build strong friendships and wonderful bonds. . . . This special bond happens because there is such a heavy physical price to pay in this game. Players need one another, and they know it. And they respect one another because of what they go through together doing this job. They also pull a lot of practical jokes—no one is safe from the locker room antics. (70–71)

Regarding football fans, male-to-male intimacy and friendship is often defined within the context of the sport. While watching a televised game, for instance, many fans share the emotional vicissitudes of the game. Many male football fans give one another "high fives" and even embrace after a good play. They may look disgusted, yell, and scream after a bad play. The act of watching and cheering for a particular team fosters male-to-male bonding and intimacy. Often, male-to-male friendships initially develop around the sport. That is, two men may begin a friendship by talking about a football team, certain players, and current rumors around the league.

While enjoying televised football games, some men may simultaneously play fantasy football. This is a computer game (although many play "online") in which a player takes the part of the owner, general manager, and coach of a "fantasy" professional football team. Men may become friends if their fantasy teams play against one another or if their teams are in the same league. This gives the men a commonly shared experience through which a friendship can be built. Although this form of dialogue may seem impoverished in terms of content, it is contextually rich. It can represent the entry into a deeper, more meaningful friendship.

Football fans who attend the game may exhibit even more heightened levels of intimacy. Before the game, it is common that men get together and participate in a "tailgate party" in the parking lot of the football stadium. During this party, men discuss the upcoming game and barbecue (and eat) various foods. For these men, the upcoming football game represents a socially acceptable forum where male-to-male bonding can occur.

Sam Khorrami

Tracy L. Colsen

See also Baseball; Basketball, Physical Culture

Further Reading:

Courtenay, William H. 2000. "Engendering Health: A Social Constructionist Examination of Men's Health Beliefs and Behaviors." *Psychology of Men and Masculinity* 1, no. 1: 4–15.

Khorrami, Sam. 2003. "The Role of Masculinity in the Treatment of Chemically Dependent Men." *The Society for the Psychological Study of Men and Masculinity Bulletin* 7, no. 4: 10–11.

———. 2000. "Risk-Factors and Early-Warning Signs of Steroid Abuse in Male Weightlifters." *Michigan Psychologist* 25, no. 1: 2.

Khorrami, Sam, and J. Franklin. 2002. "The Influence of Competition and Lack of Emotional Expression in Perpetuating Steroid Abuse and Dependence in Male Weightlifters." *International Journal of Men's Health* 1, no. 1: 119–133.

Nelson Parcells, Bill. 2000. *The Final Season*. New York: HarperCollins.

Ford, Richard (1944–)

Richard Ford is an American writer who has devoted much of his fiction to portraying the alienation of the white, heterosexual, working-class man in contemporary America. From a men's studies perspective, his fiction becomes relevant, therefore, for two main reasons. First, it concerns itself with a large (and hegemonic) group of American men.

Second, it recurrently explores, and denounces, the detrimental effects of late capitalism on the working-class man.

In Richard Ford's fiction, masculinity proves both an important and subversive object of analysis. However, the writer himself has always insisted that he does not regard gender itself as a determining factor for his fiction. On one occasion, Ford commented, for instance, that his "assumption as a person who writes about moral issues is that women and men are alike," adding that "the differences that are perhaps inspired by gender are subterior to what is more important to me—how men and women treat other people, how they act in ways that bring about consequences in others' lives" (Majeski 2002, 3).

On the other hand, what might have prevented many scholars from analyzing men and masculinities in Ford's fiction is his works' supposedly conservative—and, therefore, uninteresting—sexual politics. Vivian Gornick argues, for instance, that, in terms of sexual politics, Raymond Carver, Andre Dubus, and Richard Ford are "Hemingway's three successors" (1990, 32). Insisting further, she complains about the "extraordinarily fixed nature" of male-female relationships from Hemingway to Ford, arguing that Ford's narrator "invariably subscribes to an idea of manhood that hasn't changed in half a century" (1990, 1, 31).

Even though Ford seems convinced that many things are "beyond gender" (Majeski 2002, 4), any reader of his novels will immediately realize that, indeed, all his narrators and protagonists to date have been men. From Robard Hewes and Sam Newel, the two main voices in *A Piece of My Heart* (1976), Ford's first novel, to Harry Quinn, the Vietnam veteran of *The Ultimate Good Luck* (1981), to sixteen-year-old Joe Brinson in *Wildlife* (1990), to Frank Bascombe, the narrator and protagonist of both *The Sportswriter* (1986) and *Independence Day* (1995), Ford's novels typically concern themselves with first-person male narrators and protagonists. And this also applies to most of his short stories. For instance, the defining viewpoints in "The Womanizer," "Occidentals," and "Jealousy," the three stories included in *Women with Men* (1997), are men: Martin Austin, Charley Matthews, and Larry, respectively. On the other hand, first-person male narrators also tell eight of the ten stories included in *Rock Springs* (1987). And, in fact, "Empire" and "Fireworks," the only two stories told in the third-person, also seem to "attain intimacy and intensity," as John Wideman rightly notes, "by being reflected tightly, exclusively through a single [male] consciousness in each story," Sims in the former, and Eddie Starling in the latter. As Wideman concludes, in *Rock Springs* "all the voices are male. All white. All approximately 25 to 40 years old. Predictably, they speak about gaining, losing or holding on to manhood" (1987, 1). So it seems clear that, in its recurrent interest in exploring the dynamics of masculinity, Ford's fiction, despite the author's claims to the contrary, is inevitably gendered.

Though obviously gendered, Ford's fiction is *not* sexually conservative. Indeed, his representation of male characters proves both complex and innovative. Even if Ford's literary men are usually drawn to "sex, violence, crime and sports" (Wideman 1987, 4), their behavior seldom reaffirms their masculinity. Indeed, rather than as supermen, Ford's male characters are best described as intrinsically alienated men. As Michiko Kakutani rightly suggests: "Mr. Ford's fictional world is hardly a brave frontier where heroes can test their mettle against nature. Rather, it's another contemporary outpost of rootlessness and alienation, a place where families come apart and love drifts away" (1987, 28).

In Ford's fiction, these feelings of "rootlessness and alienation" are often linked to the working-class man's exploitation by the late capitalist system. This may be illustrated, for instance, through *The Sportswriter* and *Independence Day,* Ford's two major works to date. Even though several critics, and Ford himself, have described Frank Bascombe, the novel's protagonist, as a "happy" man, stressing his positive acceptance of occasional sor-

row, it still seems undeniable that he is "deceptively amiable, easy going and sweet natured." Indeed, careful textual analysis reveals that Bascombe is a "damaged man" who has "retreated into cushioned, dreamy detachment to avoid grief and disappointment." After all, one should not forget that the difficulties of creating fiction have led Frank to abandon a promising career as a novelist and short-story writer for the simpler and more immediate gratifications of sportswriting, regularly paid money, and suburban life in New Jersey (Clemons, quoted in *Contemporary Authors* 2000, 84). So even if Bascombe claims to be happy doing office work, *The Sportswriter* is, in fact, a book about a man's thwarted desires and, therefore, "a devastating chronicle of contemporary alienation" (Kakutani 1986, 21)

Independence Day, Ford's sequel to *The Sportswriter,* keeps exploring Bascombe's alienation as a working-class man. In this novel, Bascombe is no longer a sportswriter, but a real estate agent in New Jersey. Though he has got a new job, he still is incapable of— or unwilling to—write fiction, which is what he really likes, and so he is "sunk deep into a morass of spiritual lethargy" (Kakutani quoted in *Contemporary Authors* 2000, 85), or what he calls the "Existence period." Significantly, Bascombe, who finally surrenders to American capitalism, becomes symbolic of (a large part of) American society. As Kakutani puts it: "Not only does Mr. Ford do a finely nuanced job of delineating Frank's state of mind (his doubts and disillusionments, and his awareness of those doubts and disillusionments), but he also moves beyond Frank, to provide a portrait of a time and a place, of a middle-class community caught on the margins of change and reeling, like Frank, from the wages of loss and disappointment and fear" (quoted in *Contemporary Authors* 2000, 85).

The oppression undergone by the working-class man within the late capitalist system is perhaps nowhere better expressed than in *Rock Springs*. Indeed, Ford peoples this collection of short stories with men who have lost their jobs, who seldom have enough money to get by, and who often become drunkards and/or criminals as a result. As Jeffrey J. Folks explains, most characters in *Rock Springs* "are victims of a harsh, unforgiving economic system, and their condition is intimately connected with internal colonialism and with their status at the bottom of that system" (2000, 151).

So it appears that in Ford's fiction masculine alienation is often linked to the oppression undergone by the working-class man within the late American capitalist system, which can even render him incapable of emotional commitment. In this sense, Folks contends, for example, that in *Rock Springs* many characters find "it difficult to enter a long-term relationship," as they are "frequently out of work and waiting for better times which may require geographical removal" (2000, 151). Even so, Ford has repeatedly argued that only love, or what he calls "affection," can help us overcome, even if only partially and temporarily, the feelings of alienation, individualism, and disengagement that so often characterize masculinities and gender relations in the late capitalist era. Insisting further, Ford has even suggested that one way of looking for "affection" is through language and literature. Though imperfect, language and literature, Ford contends, may indeed help us bridge the gap—or, to borrow Emerson's words, the "infinite remoteness"—that separates us all. In the writer's own words:

It's what Emerson in his essay on friendship (interestingly enough) calls the "infinite remoteness" that underlies us all. But . . . [the] predicament is a seminal one; that is, what it inseminates is an attempt to console that remote condition. If loneliness is the disease, then the story is the cure. To be able to tell a story . . . is in itself an act of consolation. Even to come to the act of articulating . . . is itself an act of acceptance, an act of some optimism, again in that Sartrean sense that to write about the darkest human possibility is

itself an act of optimism because it proves that those things can be thought about (quoted in Walker 1999, 141).

So even if "spare and grim on the surface" (Walker 2000, 132), Ford's fiction may not be irreducibly pessimistic and hopeless. For one thing, the recurrent images of masculine alienation and despair in his works are sometimes "illumined," even if only briefly, "by the flare of meaningful connection between one character and another" (Walker 2000, 132). For another, most of his works are told by first-person male narrators who articulate a story and are, therefore, in Ford's view at least, "act[s] of consolation." Clearly, such an act is political in itself. After all, literature, as an ideologically charged cultural commodity, can and should make one ponder the (gendered) politics of representation. Thus, in (re)presenting working-class masculinities in contemporary America, Ford opens up possibilities for a critical evaluation of the late capitalist system and its detrimental social effects on the working-class man.

Jose M. Armengol

Further Reading:
Contemporary Authors. New Revision Series. Vol. 86. 2000. New York: Gale Research.
Folks, Jeffrey J. 2000. "Richard Ford's Postmodern Cowboys." Pp. 141–156 in *Perspectives on Richard Ford.* Edited by Huey Guagliardo. Jackson, MS: University Press of Mississippi.
Gornick, Vivian. 1990. "Tenderhearted Men: Lonesome, Sad and Blue." *New York Times Book Review* natl. ed., sec. 7 (16 September): 1.
Kakutani, Michiko. 1986. Review of *The Sportswriter,* by Richard Ford. *New York Times Book Review* sec. C (26 February): 21.
———. 1987. "Books of the Times." Review of *Rock Springs,* by Richard Ford. *New York Times Book Review* sec. C (16 September): 28.
Leder, Priscilla. 2000. "Men with Women: Gender Relations in Richard Ford's *Rock Springs.*" Pp. 97–120 in *Perspectives on Richard Ford.* Edited by Huey Guagliardo. Jackson, MS: University Press of Mississippi.
Majeski, Sophie, "Interview with Richard Ford." At http://www.salon.com/weekly/interview960 708.html (cited 25 August 2002).

Walker, Elinor Ann. 1999. "An Interview with Richard Ford." *South Carolina Review* 31, no. 2: 128–143.

———. 2000. *Richard Ford.* New York: Twayne.

Weber, Bruce. 1988. "Richard Ford's Uncommon Characters." *The New York Times Magazine* (10 April): 50.

Wideman, John. 1987. "Love and Truth: Use with Caution." Review of *Rock Springs*, by Richard Ford. *New York Times Book Review* (20 September): 1.

Frankenstein; or the Modern Prometheus (1818)

Often hailed as the first work of science fiction, this novel by Mary Wollstonecraft Godwin Shelley is now cited as a foundational text in fields as diverse as literature, feminist studies, ecopolitics, medical ethics, and epistemology.

Frankenstein was begun in 1816 as part of a ghost-story writing contest, and it was completed at Shelley's husband's behest. When first published anonymously, the novel was widely assumed to have been written by a man, given its focus on "serious" issues, such as science and ethics, and its participation in radical politics, implied by its dedication to William Godwin, a leading radical writer and Shelley's own father. Shelley's introduction to the 1831 edition of her book described the composition process, articulated the concerns central to her narrative's development, and, belatedly, claimed for herself authorship of the novel quickly becoming one of the bestsellers of its time.

Shelley's novel tells the story of Victor Frankenstein, a young, dreamy student who falls prey to the arts of alchemy, and who devotes himself to the reanimation of a being stitched together from parts of sundry corpses—a being he imagines will worship him as its creator. Having "birthed" the Creature, as Shelley regularly calls him, Frankenstein turns away from it in horror; the Creature wreaks vengeance, often inadvertently, in response to its abandonment.

The Creature seeks only to appeal to its creator for mercy and love, and he asks his maker to create a female companion, promising that the couple will then forever depart the company of man. Although Frankenstein does begin such a creation, he finally rips the unfinished female form asunder, unleashing the Creature's wrath and leading to his attenuated and torturous pursuit of his creator. The novel culminates with Frankenstein's death aboard a ship captained by Robert Walton (Frankenstein's double) and, thereafter, the Creature's floating out into the black sea on a raft of ice.

Shelley's novel is often noted for its contribution to feminist critiques of masculinity and male subjectivity. Focusing on a work-centered, narcissistic, naively destructive creator, *Frankenstein* exposes the dangers of such aspects of masculinity recognized and encouraged by Western culture throughout the eighteenth, nineteenth, and twentieth centuries. Victor Frankenstein's arrogance and myopia are often singled out as aspects of masculinity that urge a rethinking of cultural values, particularly as these are assigned to men. Overtaking the privilege and process of gestation and birth for himself, Frankenstein's project implies the biological uselessness of women, and the eponymous character's repeated compromisings of the safety of those nearest to him align such an exclusion of women with the lack of fellow-feeling, with the absence of the potential for true and meaningful relationships, that is part and parcel of the sort of masculinity Shelley's novel examines. Without women, the novel seems to warn, creation devolves into destruction, love into hatred, progress into annihilation. Such are the concerns that Shelley brings to her work from the thought and practice of her mother, Mary Wollstonecraft, the leading eighteenth-century feminist writer, and such are the terms that inform feminist readings of Shelley's novel, many of which point to *Frankenstein* as a parable of the dangers of phallocentrism, because the problems that beset the Creature and his victims stem back to the *ur*-Man, Frankenstein himself.

Scientists and medical practitioners find in *Frankenstein* disquisitions on the limits of their disciplines, as well as warnings about the dangers of abusing their "godlike" powers. Practitioners of ecopolitics read the novel as advocating a respect for nature, and as counterpoising the spoils of the city and society to the unvarnished pleasures of rural family life and simple love. Students of literature and epistemology cite the novel as a demonstration of the importance of narrative, of storytelling, for it is in the desire to explain oneself, to understand one's place in culture, and to find appreciation and affirmation as a member of the human race that the novel's hopes—and fears—take shape.

Countless films and stage adaptations of the novel abound, although the cultural place of *Frankenstein* grows ever more complicated by a persistent and increasingly entrenched misreading: The novel's hero, the Creature, is routinely misunderstood as some sort of Halloween ghoul and is often assumed to be the character named "Frankenstein," whereas Shelley ties that moniker not to the Creature but to its creator, not to a heroic embodiment of a better future, but to a selfish and destructive embodiment of traditional, oppressive orders, of inequity, bias, and destruction.

Samuel Lyndon Gladden

Further Reading:
Bennett, Betty T. 1988. *Mary Wollstonecraft Shelley: An Introduction.* Baltimore, MD: Johns Hopkins University Press.
Gilbert, Sandra M., and Susan Gubar. 1979. *The Madwoman in the Attic: The Woman Writer and the Nineteenth-Century Literary Imagination.* New Haven, CT: Yale University Press.
Mellor, Anne K. 1988. *Mary Shelley: Her Life, Her Fiction, Her Monsters.* New York: Routledge.
Poovey, Mary. 1978. *The Proper Lady and the Woman Writer.* Chicago: University of Chicago University Press.
Shelley, Mary. 1818/1996. *Frankenstein. or, The Modern Prometheus.* Edited by J. Paul Hunter. New York: W. W. Norton.
St. Clair, William. 1989. *The Godwins and the Shelleys: The Biography of a Family.* New York: W. W. Norton.
Sunstein, Emily W. 1989. *Mary Shelley: Romance and Reality.* Boston: Little, Brown.
Veeder, William. 1986. *Mary Shelley and Frankenstein: The Fate of Androgyny.* Chicago: University of Chicago Press.

Fraternities

A fraternity is an exclusive, ritualized group of male university or college students and graduates whose primary goal is to provide an organized social life for its members (Sanua 2000). The word *fraternity* comes from the Latin word *Frater,* which means "brother." The modern fraternity is a distinctively American creation with roots in the revolutionary period. Fraternities are traditionally secretive and ritualized organizations that have developed an extensive culture made up of traditions borrowed from Greek, Roman, Christian, and Masonic sources, including the adoption of Greek letter names that hold special meaning for the members (Sanua 2000). Each fraternity is governed by its national organization, but its daily functioning is the responsibility of the individual chapters. Historically, fraternities have been the domain of the white, upper classes, barring membership to others, although it is now illegal for fraternities to discriminate against minority groups, and the history and current structure of the mainstream fraternity system has fostered the development of fraternities whose members have traditionally been excluded from fraternity life. Although variations among fraternities exist, they have often shared similar problems. In particular, fraternities have often been criticized for the creation of a culture that promotes a limited view of masculinity, hostility toward women, and male peer support endorsing sexual aggression.

The first fraternity, Phi Beta Kappa, was founded in 1776 at the College of William and Mary. Although today Phi Beta Kappa is primarily a scholarship society, it was originally founded to serve the social and literary needs of male members. Beginning in the 1820s, additional fraternities began to form on collegiate campuses to serve the social, recreational, and extracurricular needs of male students. These fraternities quickly developed a complex and extensive ritualized culture, including secretive meetings of members. To provide members with a formal meeting place as well as a place to eat and live, fraternity houses were built starting in the late 1860s. To fill these new houses, fraternities adopted pledge classes as a means for obtaining members. These pledge classes were groups of new recruits who were required to a complete a trial membership period before becoming full members of the fraternity (Martin and Hummer 1989). Fraternities saw their peak during the 1920s when fraternity membership was the key to collegiate social status as well as success in later political and social endeavors (Sanua 2000). After World War II, when colleges began to open their doors to a greater variety of students, fraternities responded in kind, and by the 1960s fraternities could not legally limit membership based on religion or race. Although fraternities experienced a boom in membership in the postwar years, by the late 1960s and early 1970s the fraternity system lost support as college radicalism gained prominence and the fraternity system came to be seen as part of the oppressive establishment. Although some of this sentiment still exists, fraternities through the 1980s and 1990s have regained some of their strength as the country has grown more conservative (Sanua 2000).

As noted, mainstream fraternities were closed until the mid-twentieth century to many minority groups including blacks, Asians, Latinos, Jews, Roman Catholics, and homosexuals. In light of these historic legal restrictions and the continuing cultural exclusion of certain groups, a variety of alternative fraternities have formed (Sanua 2000). For example, the first intercollegiate Greek-letter fraternity established by and for

African Americans was Alpha Phi Alpha, founded at Cornell University in 1906. It initially served as a support and study group for black students who faced racial prejudice on the campus and in the surrounding town. The formation of other black fraternities followed, all being established at historically black Howard University (Kimbrough 1995). Today, there are four national African American fraternities, all of which have served as a means for black students to advance their educational, social, and community service goals. However, these same fraternities have been placed at the forefront of the controversy over fraternity hazing. Although hazing has been found in many different fraternities, black Greek-letter fraternities have endured the most publicized cases and have been associated most with the issue of hazing (Jones 1999; Nuwer 1999).

The first fraternity for Jewish men was Zeta Beta Tau, founded at the Jewish Theological Seminary in 1898. As with blacks, these Jewish fraternities served as a haven against educational, residential, and occupational discrimination. In the first half of the twentieth century, these fraternities provided Jewish men with educational and social support against the anti-Semitism found on college campuses, but by the late 1960s much of the insularity and strength of these organizations had disappeared. This was a result of laws forbidding publicly supported educational institutions from discriminating based on race and religion and the more open attitude of traditional fraternities toward Jewish members. Today, there are five fraternities that identify themselves as being Jewish, although there are often non-Jewish men initiated into the organization (Sanua 2000).

Given the heterosexist nature of traditional fraternities, the first national gay fraternity, Delta Lambda Phi, was founded in October 1986 in Washington, D.C. Delta Lambda Phi does not discriminate based on sexual orientation, therefore providing a social alternative to college men. Although

Delta Lambda Phi is modeled after traditional fraternities with its focus on brotherhood and ritual, it does prohibit hazing and focuses on diversity. The situation of Delta Lambda Phi is complex, considering it is modeled after one of the most traditional, heterosexist cultures in straight society, and yet its goal is to accommodate the experience of gay and bisexual men. The result has been a lack of acceptance by both communities and various attempts by the organization to gain legitimacy.

Although fraternities represent a significant presence on many college campuses, a degree of negative attention has been focused on the nature of fraternity life. Beyond being elitist organizations, fraternities have been criticized for high alcohol consumption, hazing, and the reproduction of a culture of oppression and misogyny (Martin and Hummer 1989; Nuwer 1999). Research (Martin and Hummer 1989; Boswell and Spade 1996) has focused on how fraternities encourage a limited view of masculinity, which emphasizes hyper-heterosexuality, competition, the use of alcohol and drugs, and the objectification of women. The essence of fraternity culture supports the notion of women as sexual objects, whether in the form of representations of women's sexuality or as targets of sexual aggression. This behavior has become normative and rarely gains the attention of either inside or outside governing bodies (Martin and Hummer 1989). The most documented outcome of this condition is the high numbers of sexual assault cases occurring in fraternity houses and perpetrated by fraternity members (Martin and Hummer 1989; Boswell and Spade 1996; Humphrey and Kahn 2000).

Alexandra B. Berkowitz

See also Fraternities, Modern; Male Bonding
Further Reading:
Boeringer, Scot B., Constance L. Shehan, and Ronald L. Akers. 1991. "Social Contexts and Social Learning in Sexual Coercion and Aggression: Assessing the Contribution of Fraternity Membership." *Family Relations* 40: 58–64.
Boswell, A. Ayres, and Joan Z. Spade. 1996. "Fraternities and Collegiate Rape Culture: Why Are Some Fraternities More Dangerous Places for Women?" *Gender and Society* 10 (April): 133–147.
Cross, Lawrence, Jr. 2000. *The Divine Nine: The History of African American Fraternities and Sororities.* New York: Kensington.
Fox, Elaine, Charles Hodge, and Walter Ward. 1987. "A Comparison of Attitudes Held by Black and White Fraternity Members." *Journal of Negro Education* 56 (Autumn): 521–534.
Humphrey, Stephen E., and Arnold S. Kahn. 2000. "Fraternities, Athletic Teams, and Rape." *Journal of Interpersonal Violence* 15, no. 12: 1313–1322.
Jones, Ricky L. 1999. "The Hegemonic Struggle and Domination in Black Greek-Letter Fraternities." *Challenge—A Journal of Research on African American Men* 10, no. 1: 1–33.
Kimbrough, Walter M. 1995. "Self-Assessment, Participation, and Value of Leadership Skills, Activities, and Experiences for Black Students Relative to Their Membership in Historically Black Fraternities and Sororities." *Journal of Negro Education* 64 (Winter): 63–74.
Martin, Patricia Yancey, and Robert A. Hummer. 1989. "Fraternities and Rape on Campus." *Gender and Society* 3 (December): 457–473.
Nuwer, Hank. 1990. *Broken Pledges: The Deadly Rite of Hazing.* Atlanta, GA: Longstreet.
———. 1999. *Wrongs of Passage: Fraternities, Sororities, Hazing, and Binge Drinking.* Bloomington, IN: Indiana University Press.
Pike, Gary R., and Jerry W. Askew. 1990. "The Impact of Fraternity or Sorority Membership on Academic Involvement and Learning Outcomes." *NASPA Journal* 28, no. 1: 13–19.
Sanua, Marianne R. 2000. "Jewish College Fraternities in the United States, 1895–1968: An Overview." *Journal of American Ethnic History* 19, no. 2: 3–43.

Fraternities, Modern

Social fraternities are collegiate organizations characterized by Greek-letter names and secret rites and rituals. Fraternities are usually all male and adopt familial language to create group unity, describing members as "brothers." Fraternities are important elements of masculinity, not just because they are comprised of men, but also because they are in the business of "making men," as indicated by the historic and contemporary fraternity mottos "The fraternity makes men" and "Be men."

Men "rush" fraternities, seeking to be selected to the "pledge class" or "line" of a particular organization; those who successfully pledge are initiated as full members. While most fraternities explicitly prohibit hazing, pledge periods are often characterized by psychological and physical abuse and humiliation that can lead to injuries and fatalities (Nuwer 1990). While most fraternities that haze pledges do so in a wide variety of ways, severely beating pledges appears to be more common in predominantly black fraternities, while alcohol-related abuse disproportionately plagues predominantly white fraternities. Pledging is intended to bond potential members to each other and to the organization. The process breaks down the individual and reconstructs him as a man in the fraternity's image. Black fraternity members, in particular, use specific language to reflect this concept. Pledges often refer to initiation day as the day they were "made," with initiating members claiming of their initiates: "I made him" (Jones 2000).

Pledges accept hazing and desire fraternity membership for many reasons. Members describe fraternities as providing a family-like setting of close friends where they learn mutual trust and support, mediating an impersonal student environment. Fraternities sponsor social and service events and maintain a high level of status on campus, often dominating the top positions of student government, service organizations, and intramural sports. Members also enjoy future rewards, as alumni contacts provide career-enhancing networking opportunities.

Fraternities are defined by a dynamic of exclusion. Fraternities are prestige ranked, to a great extent, by the socioeconomic class or the social status of their members. The well-known fraternities also remain racially and ethnically segregated into white, black, and Jewish organizations, although newer and less prestigious fraternities, such as the national gay fraternity, are more likely to be racially integrated (Yeung and Stombler 2000). Under Title IX, fraternities are also permitted to exclude women from full membership. Women's participation as quasi members is limited to "little sister" or "sweetheart" programs, where they serve as hostesses or boosters for the brothers. Little sisters generally value the social aspects of association with a fraternity, although some object that fraternity men exploit them for their physical and emotional labor and their sexuality (Stombler and Padavic 1997).

Critical researchers charge that by constructing and reaffirming traditional gender relations, college fraternities actively create gender inequality (Stombler and Martin 1994). Fraternities tend to support a narrow conceptualization of masculinity comprising "competition, athleticism, dominance, winning, conflict, wealth, material possessions, willingness to drink alcohol, and sexual prowess vis-à-vis women" (Martin and Hummer 1989, 460), with black fraternity members also stressing the ability to withstand physical punishment as a sign of manhood. Fraternities have actively discouraged gay men from participating, in part because of a desire to preserve a "macho" image. Through boundary maintenance dynamics, fraternities reflect, reproduce, and often magnify society's race, class, gender, and sexual-orientation boundaries.

Researchers have explored connections between fraternity membership and sexually aggressive behavior toward women. Qualitative studies of predominantly white fraternities (e.g., Martin and Hummer 1989; Sanday 1990; Stombler and Martin 1994) describe a fraternity context where structure, culture, and the nature of rushing and pledging encourage sexual aggressiveness. Alcohol use and pressure to have sex with women, create a "party rape" culture where alcohol is wielded as a "weapon against sexual reluctance" (Koss and Cleveland 1996; Martin and Hummer 1989, 464). However, fraternities and their members are not equal in their propensity to construct such a culture or engage in sexual exploitation or assault (Humphrey and Khan 2000). Much depends on their traditions, guiding ideologies, relative levels of prestige, and interpersonal dynamics. Some fraternity men have sought to change fraternity culture, attending rape prevention programs and reflecting upon what it means to be a man. In the process, they have changed how they treat both women and the men whose versions of masculinity do not fit the historic fraternity model.

Mindy Stombler

Further Reading:

Humphrey, Stephen E., and Arnold S. Kahn. 2000. "Fraternities, Athletic Teams, and Rape: Importance of Identification with a Risky Group." *Journal of Interpersonal Violence* 15, no. 2: 1313–1322.

Jones, Ricky L. 2000. "The Historical Significance of Sacrificial Ritual: Understanding Violence in the Modern Black Fraternity Pledge Process." *Western Journal of Black Studies* 24, no. 2: 112–124.

Koss, Mary P., and Hobart H. Cleveland III. 1996. "Athletic Participation, Fraternity Membership, and Date Rape." *Violence Against Women* 2, no. 2: 180–190.

Martin, Patricia Yancey, and Robert A. Hummer. 1989. "Fraternities and Rape on Campus." *Gender & Society* 3, no. 4: 457–473.

Nuwer, Hank. 1990. *Broken Pledges: The Deadly Right of Hazing.* Atlanta: Longstreet.

Sanday, Peggy Reeves. 1990. *Fraternity Gang Rape: Sex, Brotherhood, and Privilege on Campus.* New York: New York University Press.

Stombler, Mindy, and Irene Padavic. 1997. "Sister Acts: Resisting Men's Domination in Black and White Fraternity Little Sister Programs." *Social Problems* 44, no. 2: 257–275.

Stombler, Mindy and Patricia Y. Martin. 1994. "Bringing Women In, Keeping Women Down." *Journal of Contemporary Ethnography* 23, no. 2: 150–184.

Yeung, King-to, and Mindy Stombler. 2000. "Gay and Greek: The Identity Paradox of Gay Franternities." *Social Problems* 47, no. 1: 134–152.

Freud, Sigmund (1856–1939)

Sigmund Freud was the founder of psychoanalysis, whose prolific works provide interesting and controversial frameworks for the

Sigmund Freud devised the therapy for mental disorders known as psychoanalysis, which involves uncovering repressed psychological traumas so that the patient can confront and overcome them. Though the specifics of many of his theories no longer command the wide acceptance they once did, the general framework for psychotherapy that he created has exercised an enormous influence on the theory and practice of psychology. (Library of Congress)

understanding of men and masculinity. Psychoanalysis proposes that adult personality is a product of the displacement of early instinctual (mainly sexual and aggressive) energy in an effort to compromise between the demands of these biological instincts and the requirements of society. The central task is to gratify one's instinctual needs in a socially acceptable way—to deal with the inevitable struggle between biological urges (as represented by the *id*) and the social demands of parents (as represented by the *superego*). The *ego* mediates between these two forces.

The psychoanalytic ideal is a paragon of positive masculinity as defined in Western culture: the person who can love and work.

Destructive masculinity (e.g., violence, philandering, self-absorption) can be conceptualized as being the result of poor superego development or poor ego strength. If the id is not controlled by the ego and superego, the person gives vent to sexual and aggressive impulses without restraint. One psychoanalytic conceptualization of the violent criminal is that he or she has a poorly developed ego and/or superego. About 90 percent of violent crimes in the United States are committed by males (Jacobs, Siegal, and Quiram 1997), suggesting that some aspects of the culture may encourage men to retain id domination, a problem of faulty childhood socialization.

According to Freud, the development of a strong superego depends critically on a son's identification with his father. If the father is absent, emotionally distant, or overly punitive, the identification is weakened. If the father approves of destructively masculine behaviors such as dominance over women or violence and/or punishes the son for behaving in culturally defined feminine ways, the son can develop a punitive superego that causes him to feel unworthy when he acts in ways that are defined as unmasculine.

Freud proposed that sex differences emerge in the phallic stage, which begins around age three, when the child experiences unconscious sexual desires for the other-sex parent and perceives the same-sex parent as a rival. Freud called this love triangle the "Oedipus conflict." During this time, the boy unconsciously fears that his father will punish him for his desire by cutting off his penis (castration anxiety). Therefore, he abdicates these sexual feelings for his mother and displaces them on to psychologically safer objects, such as female playmates. The son forms a psychological identification with his father, allowing him to feel less threatened and to experience romantic feelings for his mother vicariously. This is a critical step in superego development, as the son begins to internalize the father's values and characteristics.

Freud believed that girls in this stage of psychosexual development experience themselves as castrated males and suffer from "penis envy." He has been roundly criticized for this view of women. Karen Horney (1932) argued that women are envious of men's social power, not their penises. Hare-Mustin and Maracek (1990) noted Freud's sexism in his characterization of women's bodies as *not having* a penis rather than as *having* the female external genitalia (32, emphasis original).

Theoretically, the Oedipal crisis sets up later patterns in a man's relationships with women. Fine (1987) theorized that parents who punish a son's sexual expression toward his mother too harshly can cause a psychological rift between sex and affection, resulting in the "Madonna/Whore complex," in which the man denigrates women with whom he is sexual and has trouble feeling sexual toward women he loves. If a father is harsh and punitive with his son, the son grows up with a poor sense of internal masculinity. He may act in aggressive or misogynistic ways to defend against these unacceptable feelings.

Critics of Freud disagreed with his conceptualization of sexual instinct as the primary determinant of personality. Believing that the parent-child attachment is primarily social rather than sexual, Hartley (1959), and later Chodorow (1978) proposed that, because both boys and girls spend a great deal of time with their mothers and relatively little time with their fathers during early childhood identity development, girls tend to define themselves through the process of attachment. Conversely, boys form their identities through the process of separation, thus requiring a son to dis-identify with his mother. At a societal level, this need for opposition in the identification process results in the social definition of masculinity as antifemininity.

The catalyst for Freud's construction of the Oedipus conflict was his patient "Dora," who came into analysis at age eighteen complaining of migraine headaches and depression. She reported that, at age fourteen, a close friend of her father ("Herr K.") had kissed her against her will, and that she felt traumatized by this incident and had told her parents about it. Herr K. told Dora's father that this incident never took place, and her father believed him. Freud came to believe that Dora's memory of this incident was actually a fantasy (Freud 1905/1963). Hare-Mustin and Maracek (1990) point out that this reframing of Dora's experience was a victim-blaming example of the privileging of men's perspectives over women's and justified the marginalization of women.

Freud's opinion of human nature is largely pessimistic, a view of people as primitive animals who must be controlled through socialization and strike an uneasy compromise between the antithetical demands of biology and society. He has been widely criticized for contributing to cultural misogyny. Although it would seem unfair to hold historical figures to contemporary standards, the negative impact of traditional psychoanalytic theory on women's lives is undeniable. On the positive side, Freud's theories have provided a rich perspective for gender theory and research.

Christopher Kilmartin

See also Hall, G. Stanley; Penis; Phallus

Further Reading:
Chodorow, Nancy. 1978. *The Reproduction of Mothering: Psychoanalysis and the Sociology of Gender.* Berkeley, CA: University of California Press.
Fine, Reuben. 1987. *The Forgotten Man: Understanding the Male Psyche.* New York: Haworth.
Freud, Sigmund. 1905/1963. *Dora: An Analysis of a Case of Hysteria.* New York: Collier.
Hare-Mustin, Rachel T., and Jeanne Maracek. 1990. "Gender and the Meaning of Difference: Postmodernism and Psychology." Pp. 22–64 in *Making a Difference: Psychology and the Construction of Gender.* Edited by R. T. Hare-Mustin and J. Maracek. New Haven, CT: Yale University Press.
Hartley, Ruth E. 1959. "Sex Role Pressures and the Socialization of the Male Child." *Psychological Reports* 5: 457–468.
Horney, Karen. 1932. "The Dread of Women: Observations on a Specific Difference in the Dread Felt by Men and Women Respectively for the Opposite Sex." *International Journal of Psychoanalysis* 13: 348–360.
Jacobs, Nancy R., Mark A. Siegal, and Jacquelyn Quiram, eds. 1997. *Prisons and Jails: A Deterrent to Crime?* Wylie, TX: Information Plus.

Friendship

Throughout history, male-dominated images characterize the ideal of friendship. Women were incapable of "true friendship," but men's friendships were like "souls mingling and blending with each other so completely that they efface the seam that joined them," as Michel de Montaigne wrote in his sixteenth-century essay, *Of Friendship.* Stories, poems, and essays exalted men's heroic friendships, such as the one between Achilles and Patroklos in Homer's *Iliad.* Upon hearing about Patroklos's death, Achilles poured black ashes over his head and face, tore at his hair, and sighed heavily. He lamented that recent accomplishments bring little pleasure "since my dear companion has perished, Patroklos, whom I loved beyond all other companions, as well as my own life" (1951, 377).

These heroic friendships provoked an intensity of intimacy between men that, by the mid- to late nineteenth century, were often indistinguishable from the language and images of love relationships. These friendships could be erotic but not necessarily sexual because a certain degree of affectionate desire was allowed. However, as same-sex relationships began to be defined in pathological terms in the scientific and legal literature by the end of the nineteenth century, labels of perversion (as well as the newly created medical word "homosexual") were applied to same-sex romantic friendships.

The concept of friendship between men once included a range of erotic, sexual, and platonic possibilities. But as issues related to homosexuality, masculinity, and sexuality in the post-Freudian era became part of the public discourse, men's friendships in particular became more limited in scope. Romantic friendships, especially for men, were less visible and less of a topic to be discussed in poems and literature. True friendship, in the early twentieth century and continuing to this day, would be seen as something only women were capable of experiencing. The ideal form of friendship is now typically described with more "female" language: intimacy, trust, caring, disclosing, and nurturing.

Most academic research on friendship (Fehr 1996) supports the idea that men's friendships, in general, exhibit instrumental, "side-by-side" interactions, while women's friendships demonstrate expressive, "face-to-face" styles of intimacy. Women are much more likely to spend time with friends, share feelings, confide, and disclose intimate details of their lives, while men look for friends to share activities, interests, and sports. Men's friendships are less intimate, self-disclosing, and physically affectionate than women's, and men tend not to focus on the friendship relationship itself as a topic of conversation. Men use less intimate touch, sit further apart from their male friends, and spend less time with friends, especially less time on the telephone, compared with women.

In addition, men have fewer numbers of supportive relationships and receive less help from supporters when compared with women; women provide more emotional support compared to men. Men rate the meaningfulness of and satisfaction with their same-sex friendships lower than women do, while men view their cross-gender friendships as closer and more intimate than their same-gender ones compared with women who see their same-gender ones as closer.

However, studies are uncovering greater diversity within categories of gender, linked to such characteristics as race, class, and sexual orientation. Not all men interact with friends in the same way. For example, studies on social class show that financial circumstances affect people's interests and abilities to engage in certain kinds of activities. The kind of work people do and how it is organized constrain or contribute to friendship formation. Working-class friendships tend to be limited to the workplace; friends are rarely invited into the home. Middle-class friendship styles tend to emphasize the relationship over the setting and stress reciprocity. Class-related resources become salient in the development and maintenance of friendships and reciprocity.

Differences in men's friendships can also be attributed to sexual orientation. For most gay men and lesbians, friendships are inextricably part of their narrative histories and coming-out stories. Their friendships take on political power as they challenge the constraints imposed by the culture's social institutions of family, marriage, and sexuality. Friendships can turn into social movements when they provide the power and identity that are often minimized in gay men's lives by the dominant culture. They become the mechanisms for learning about gay identity and cultures, for entering gay communities, for organizing into resistance groups, and for maintaining personal identities within an otherwise nonsupportive social environment.

Gay men's friendships illustrate the complex ways people structure their lives in terms of sexual attraction, intimacy, and gender roles. The stories gay men tell about making friends are similar to the kinds of narratives they often tell about meeting their romantic partners. The intensity of first meetings, the emotional connections around identity, the sharing of feelings and personal fears, and the physical attractions are all components of the "how-we-became-friends" stories, just as they are parts of the "how-I-met-my-partner" narratives. Attraction and sexuality are inextricably linked to friendship formation among gay men in ways that do not typically play out among same-sex heterosexual male friendships.

In a study of gay men's friendship (Nardi 1999), almost 80 percent of the gay men surveyed described their one *best* friend (not a casual or close friend) who was not a current lover, as being of the same gender and sexual orientation as themselves; about 4 percent of gay men reported having a best friend who was a lesbian. About 11 percent of the gay men described their best friend as a heterosexual or bisexual woman. For the respondents who said their best friend was of the same gender and sexual orientation, almost 60 percent of the gay men said they were sexually involved with their best friend in the past, although only 17 percent described their best friend as their ex-romantic partner. Around 76 percent responded that they had ever had sex with their close gay male friends, and 63 percent with their casual gay male friends. The numbers were higher when they were asked if they had ever been sexually *attracted* to their friends.

Attraction and sexuality as elements of friendship among gay men raise issues central to the construction of masculinity for all men in our American culture. The types of interactions among gay men challenge the ways we think about friendship, as well as the meaning of gender and sexuality in contemporary American society. Questions are introduced about whether heterosexual men who bond with each other in some powerful way (such as the recurrent stories one hears about wartime friendships or sees in numerous male buddy movies) also feel erotic attraction and what the implications are for the construction of their masculinities.

Studying friendships among men in today's society reveals much about how a culture limits concepts of masculinity. Rather than look at friendship formation as something explainable solely in terms of gender roles or personality theories or some species-specific genetic code differences between men and women, consider how different locations in the economic, occupational, and related power spheres can lead to different kinds of interpersonal interactions and the enactment of gender.

People meet people in specific social contexts, such as work, school, neighborhood, and recreational organizations. Often, access to these situations is constrained by certain requirements, such as age, education, race, class, gender, and sexual orientation. Further-

more, these social contexts reflect the definitions of masculinity differing groups bring to the setting, thereby structuring the ways men can interact with one another. So what may appear to be a "problem" with men's friendships can be viewed instead as a function of the constraints imposed by the social institutions and their definitions of masculinity. How men bond in all-male military settings as opposed to more open environments as found in universities, for example, reflects these institutions' constructions of what is considered masculine.

Friendship is an essential component of people's lives. It is with friends that we get to test our boundaries, find identity, and learn to express intimacy and commitment. Friendship between men, however, is controlled by definitions of masculinity. For some, such as gay men, friendship can be a powerful means of solidifying identity and building communities. For others, close friendships with other men provide a process to overcome the constraints of the culture's limitations and seek the intimacy once characteristic of the heroic friendships of the past.

Peter M. Nardi

See also Friendship, Gay-Straight; Homophobia; Intimacy
Further Reading:
Allan, Graham. 1989. *Friendship: Developing a Sociological Perspective.* Boulder, CO: Westview.
Fehr, Beverly. 1996. *Friendship Processes.* Thousand Oaks, CA: Sage.
Fischer, Claude S. 1982. *To Dwell Among Friends: Personal Networks in Town and City.* Chicago: University of Chicago Press.
Friedman, Marilyn. 1993. *What Are Friends For? Feminist Perspectives on Personal Relationships and Moral Theory.* Ithaca, NY: Cornell University Press.
Homer. 1951. *The Iliad of Homer.* Trans. by Richmond Lattimore. Chicago: University of Chicago Press.
Nardi, Peter M., ed. 1992. *Men's Friendships.* Newbury Park, CA: Sage.
Nardi, Peter M. 1999. *Gay Men's Friendships: Invincible Communities.* Chicago: University of Chicago Press.
Rotundo, E. Anthony. 1993. *American Manhood: Transformations in Masculinity from the Revolution to the Modern Era.* New York: Basic Books.

Rubin, Lillian. 1985. *Just Friends: The Role of Friendship in our Lives.* New York: Harper & Row.

Friendship, Gay-Straight

The cultural ideal of masculinity requires that men compete with other men, reject effeminacy, and express heterosexual desire. Heterosexuality has become the most important way that men signify being masculine. By showing they are heterosexual, men can claim to be more powerful and valuable than at least one last group of people: gay men. Research has well established that men's attitudes toward male homosexuals are much more negative than women's attitudes. Heterosexual men often desire more social distance from gay men. Such intolerance is evidenced by their negative reactions to gays in the U.S. military and in the increasing number of hate crimes, predominately committed by heterosexual men against gay men (U.S. Department of Justice 2001).

Homophobia refers to a fear of, or discomfort with, nonheterosexual people, while heterosexism refers to beliefs that nonheterosexual people are inferior to heterosexual people and to the behaviors that create or reproduce heterosexual privilege. Homophobia is perhaps the last legally and socially acceptable form of discrimination. Although laws in the United States prohibit sexist and racist behavior, as a society Americans still promote heterosexism. In the United States, it is socially acceptable and legally legitimate for heterosexuals to subordinate homosexuals and to deny them the privileges that heterosexuals take for granted. Examples of subordination include the denial of marital and adoption rights, lack of protection against employment and housing discrimination, lack of survivor benefits to homosexual partners in employer retirement and health care plans, and institutional policies to reject and demean known homosexuals such as in the U.S. military, various religious denominations, and the Boy Scouts of America.

Straight men experience much pressure from each other to oppress gay men, while gay men have many reasons to fear and despise straight men. Straight and gay men who take the risk to be friends put other men's evaluations of them, their self-esteem, and their identities at risk. Friendships between gay and straight men offer insight on gender, inequality, and social change. By understanding men who act progressively with other men, we may learn how to similarly motivate other men.

Most gay men's close friends are other gay men and most straight men's closest friends are straight men, although they are often more confiding in their girlfriends and wives. Most gay and straight men believe they are too different to be friends. Most gay and straight men who are friends are casual friends. They spend little time together, often only interacting at work, and avoid emotional intimacy. They carry on their friendship by ignoring and hiding their sexual differences. Most gay men in these friendships refrain from showing or talking about homosexuality. Only the straight men share the more personal aspects of their lives. Most same-gender, cross-sexual male friendships are inconsequential in both men's lives. These friends may accept each other's sexuality, but they do not respect it.

Close friendships rarely occur between gay and straight men. In these friendships, both men express their sexuality in front of each other, but no more or less than they would with their same-sexual friends. They spend time together often, frequently with both men's partners, friends, and families. Both men share emotional intimacy and trust with one another. Both men accept and respect each other's sexuality. Their friendship plays a significant role in both men's lives.

A 1999 study of friendships between gay and straight men revealed that men's gender identities, and the resulting balance of power, determine the dynamics of their relationships (Price 1999). Men who enact traditional gender identities tend to have great difficulty being friends with men of a different sexuality. These straight men value and enact traditional masculinity, devaluing femininity and homosexuality. These gay men enact traditional femininity and many are just beginning to accept their sexuality, and they express gay language, mannerisms, and desire determinedly. In friendships between traditional straight men and gay men, the straight men demand their gay friends' deference. In contrast, the gay men demand acceptance.

Men who enact contemporary masculinities—neither traditionally masculine nor feminine—tend to share casual same-gender, cross-sexual friendships. Having a straight male friend makes these gay men feel part of the mainstream. To maintain this token membership, the gay men let the straight men set the terms of the friendship. Meanwhile, the straight men think of their gay friend "as a human being, not as a gay man." On the surface this sounds admirable, but it reveals that while the straight men accept their friends' sexuality, they do not respect it. The straight men feel sorry for their friends' plight in life, viewing it as a "condition" to endure.

Men who enact behaviors associated with both men and women tend to have close same-gender, cross-sexual friendships. None of these men believe stereotypes about gay or straight men. None think homosexuality is a psychological or biological disorder, or immoral. Because of their egalitarian values and beliefs about gender and sexuality, these men are able to be close friends with a man with a different sexual preference. These friends have moved beyond the heterosexism and homophobia that divide most gay and straight men, but they cannot escape the world around them. They experience resistance and pressure to act like more conventional gay and straight men from their partners, family, and friends.

Jammie Price

See also Friendship; Intimacy
Further Reading:

Connell, Robert W. 1987. *Gender and Power.* Stanford, CA: Stanford University Press.

————. 1992. "A Very Straight Gay: Masculinity, Homosexual Experience, and the Dynamics of Gender." *American Sociological Review* 57: 735–751.

Herek, Gregory M. 1987. "On Heterosexual Masculinity: Some Psychological Consequences of the Social Construction of Gender and Sexuality. Pp. 68–82 in *Changing Men: New Directions in Research on Men and Masculinity.* Edited by Michael Kimmel. Thousand Oaks, CA: Sage.

Lehne, Gregory K. 1989. "Homophobia among Men: Supporting and Defining the Male Role." Pp. 416–429 in *Men's Lives.* Edited by Michael Kimmel and Michael Messner. New York: MacMillan.

Nardi, Peter M. 1992. *Men's Friendships.* Thousand Oaks, CA: Sage.

————. 1992. "That's What Friends Are For: Friends as Family in the Gay and Lesbian Community" in *Modern Homosexualities: Fragments of Lesbian and Gay Experience.* Edited by Ken Plummer. New York: Routledge.

Nardi, Peter M., and Drury Sherrod. 1990. "Friendship Survey: The Results." *Out/Look* 2, no. 4: 86.

————. 1994. "Friendships in the Lives of Gay Men and Lesbians." *Journal of Social and Personal Relationships* 11: 185–199.

Patton, Clarence. 2002. *Anti-Lesbian, Gay, Bisexual, and Transgender Violence in 2001.* New York: National Coalition of Anti-Violence Programs.

Price, Jammie. 1999. *Navigating Differences: Friendships between Gay and Straight Men.* New York: Haworth.

Sherrod, Drury. 1987. "The Bonds of Men: Problems and Possibilities in Close Male Relationships." Pp. 213–239 in *The Making of Masculinities: The New Men's Studies.* Edited by H. Brod. Boston: Allen and Unwin.

U.S. Department of Justice. 2001. *Hate Crime Statistics.* Washington, DC: U.S. Department of Justice.

Frontier

The great outdoors, the tonic freshness of the open sky, the open plains and untamed wilderness—these have been among the highest values of American masculinity since the middle of the nineteenth century. The frontier provided a safety valve, a respite from the emasculating city, and a way to demonstrate and prove masculinity. The great historian Frederick Jackson Turner argued in 1898 that it was the frontier that defined American history; both in reality and in fantasy, the frontier was also what defined American masculinity.

In the middle of the nineteenth century, the frontier held promise for American men. "Go west young man, and grow up with the country!" wrote Horace Greeley in 1837. And they followed in droves. Turner argued that the western frontier "offered an exit into a free life and greater well-being among the bounties of nature, in the midst of resources that demanded manly exertion and that gave in return the chance for indefinite ascent on the scale of social advance" (Turner 1947, 92).

Turner had argued that the frontier had given American democracy its distinct character, freeing it from European convention, and enabling the "self-made man" to create himself and chart his own destiny. Others also championed the frontier as a safety valve that forestalled working-class rebellion, siphoning off potentially rebellious young men whose economic futures were stymied. Geographic mobility replaced economic and social mobility.

By the end of the century, though, Turner and others mourned the frontier's passing. A 1906 article in the *North American Review* noted that

> The old cabins and dugouts are replaced by modern dwellings. The great ranges are fast passing into orderly farms, where cultivated crops take the place of wild grasses. Steadily is man's rational selection directing the selection of nature. Even the cowboy, the essential creation of Western conditions, is rapidly passing away. Like the buffalo, he has had his place in the drama of civilization. The Indian of the plain must yield to civilization or pass away. . . . Pioneers of the old school are giving place to a young and vigorous group of men of intellect, will and ceaseless activity, who are turning the light of scientific discovery on plain and mountain. (cited in Worster 1992, 174)

As the frontier closed, it was instantly reborn as myth. Scores of writers, many of them effete Easterners, celebrated the revitalizing powers of frontier life. At the turn of the twentieth century, writers such as Owen Wister, Zane Grey, and artists like Frederick Remington extolled frontier virtues and hardy manhood. Clever entrepreneurs founded western frontier theme parks, called "dude ranches" where urban weaklings could go to regain their vitality and virility. In 1902 novelist Frank Norris lamented that "the frontier has become conscious of itself, acts the part of the Eastern visitor" (cited in Kimmel 1996, 399).

One of the frontier's main boosters was Theodore Roosevelt, who championed the "strenuous life" of vigorous manhood, of the outdoors, sports, and war. Roosevelt himself had been "cured" of early childhood asthma at a North Dakota dude ranch, and he both celebrated the masculinity of the frontier and developed environmental legislation to create the national parks system to preserve some remnant of the rapidly passing frontier.

Historian Richard Slotkin has traced the development of the "frontier fable" as a defining myth of American culture:

> The protagonist is usually represented as having marginal connections to the Metropolis and its culture. He is a poor and uneducated borderer or an orphan lacking the parental tie to anchor him to the Metropolis and is generally disinclined to learn from book culture when the book of nature is free to read before him. His going to the wilderness breaks or attenuates the Metropolitan tie, but it gives him access to something far more important than anything the Metropolis contains—the wisdom, morality, power, and freedom of Nature in its pure wild form. (Slotkin 1985, 374)

Unfortunately, Slotkin notes, the frontier also involves the retrieval of masculinity through an orgy of sanctimonious and self-justifying violence.

By the end of the twentieth century, the frontier became a symbolic recreation (in both meanings)—either as a Hollywood creation in films such as *City Slickers* (1991) and as a mythopoetic retreat to the woods, where men could rediscover their deep manhood, or "warrior."

The word "frontier" continues to resonate for American men, from John F. Kennedy's "New Frontier" to *Star Trek*'s declaration that space is "the final frontier." We have always believed that manhood lies at the edge of civilization, away from the emasculating seductions of urban lassitude, soul-deadening bureaucratic office work, and, of course, women.

Michael Kimmel

See also *City Slickers;* Cowboys; Grey, Zane; Parkman, Francis; Wister, Owen

Further Reading:

Kimmel, Michael. 1996. *Manhood in America: A Cultural History.* New York: The Free Press.

Slotkin, Richard. 1973. *Regeneration through Violence: The Mythology of the American Frontier, 1600–1860.* New York: Atheneum.

———. 1985. *The Fatal Environment: The Myth of the Frontier in the Age of Industrialization.* New York: Atheneum.

———. 1992. *Gunfighter Nation: The Myth of the Frontier in Twentieth Century America.* New York: Atheneum.

Turner, Frederick Jackson. 1893/1947. *The Frontier in American History.* New York: Holt, Rinehart and Winston.

Worster, Donald. 1992. *Under Western Skies: Nature and History in the American West.* New York: Oxford University Press.

G

Gangs

The gang has always been an arena for the acting out of gender. Most gangs today are unsupervised peer groups, but many have been institutionalized in urban ghettoes, barrios, and prisons. Male gang members typically display an aggressive masculinity expressing values of respect and honor, and condoning violence as a means to settle disputes. The gang also promotes a traditional, subservient femininity, but for girls, membership can also be a sign of gender-role rebellion. Like all of us, male and female gangsters "do gender" in a globalized world of uncertainty.

The mass media have held a fascination for the gangster and helped shape the public's understanding. From early films of the James Cagney "tough guy" in the 1930s through the romanticized *West Side Story* (1961) to films like *Boyz 'n the Hood* (1991) being a gang member has meant being "macho," or masculine. In the global era, this stereotype has been diffused across the planet, leading to such anomalies as the discovery of "Crips" (a notorious gang originating in Los Angeles) in the Netherlands.

The classic social science studies on gangs, however, spent little time analyzing gender. For Frederic Thrasher (1927), the father of gang research, the industrial era gang was a way to work out the masculine anxieties of immigrant boys, who were yearning to be free of the traditional bonds of their "old world" parents. For Albert Cohen (1955) the gang was the antithesis of femininity, masculine by definition, a rebellious assertion of working-class maleness in a modernizing world. Lewis Yablonsky (1966), Short and Strodtbeck (1965), Cloward and Ohlin (1960), and Malcolm Klein (1971), in their influential mid-century works, all described a quintessentially male group process and ignored female gangs.

Walter Miller (1958) argued that gang life essentially meant conforming to male lower-class "focal concerns" of "trouble," "toughness," "smartness," "excitement," "fate," and "autonomy." Miller found that male gang members rejected identification with their mothers through a compulsive concern for masculinity. On the other hand, Joan Moore's (1991) study of East Los Angeles gangs saw barrio life as full of "machismo," but also marriage, courtship, adjusting to the life after prison, and the search for a conventional life. Moore's barrio is populated by both male and female gangs, boyfriends, girlfriends, work, church, and families. The gang for Moore has practical and symbolic meaning, fulfilling functions of protection, solidarity, and, for some, becoming an alternative family.

Only a few later studies look specifically at issues of masculinity. James Messerschmidt (1993) explored how street gangs protect "turf" and wage street warfare "based on idealized notions of hegemonic masculinity" (111). Majors and Billson (1992) point out that the "cool pose" of African American youth "is designed to both render the black male visible and to empower him; it eases the worry and pain of blocked opportunities" (5). The black gang member, Robert Staples (1982) says, is reacting to an "internal colonialism," which has delegitimized authority and makes the masculine ethic of success a cultural imperative. Hagedorn (1998) compares male gang boys to "frat boys" and constructs a "typology of gang masculinities." All these studies stress the complex interaction of gender and social structures, and find that gang masculinities resemble mainstream notions of what it is to be a man more than deviant conceptions of hypermasculinity.

Immigration has always been strongly related to gangs, and in the United States in the early 2000s there are more Latino than African American or white gang members. In the last decade of the twentieth century, Vietnamese and Chinese gangs have spread across the country. For immigrants, the gang often resembles its classic form as a mechanism for male adjustment. However, the existence of organized gangs like the Tongs or Latin Kings, or prison gangs like La Eme, often divert the activities of adolescents into adult-run drug businesses and other criminal activities.

An enduring U.S. ghetto has meant enduring gangs. Los Angles and Chicago have both seen gang organizations continue for more than half a century, and gangs in most cities have lasted for more than twenty years. The globalization of the economy has given added importance to the informal sector, and many U.S. gangs have become little more than drug-selling enterprises. The war on drugs and high rates of incarceration have moved gangs into the prisons and helped institutionalize their organization on the streets.

Although the popular image of the gang member is inevitably male, female gangs have always been "present but invisible" (Chesney-Lind and Hagedorn 1999). Like males, girls in gangs vary in their conception of their gender. Although some female gang members are viciously victimized and exploited by males, others are rebellious and independent, challenging gender roles. Despite popular beliefs that violence among girls is increasing, girls remain much less violent than boys, with no signs of significant changes in the "violence gender gap." Gang life, and particularly the drug game, is male dominated and dangerous to female drug customers and gang members alike.

Violence remains strongly related to males settling disputes of honor and business, but the global era has introduced new patterns of gang activity and violence. Manuel Castells (1997) points out that shrinking the world to a communal level is a widespread and often violent response to globalization. In U.S. ghettos, he argues that a "resistance identity" has formed, consisting of a masculine and violent "culture of urgency" exemplified by drug-dealing gangs (1997, 64). Bourgois (1995) calls this a life "in search of respect," vividly describing the frustration and rage of young men humiliated by joblessness and demeaning low-wage work.

Gangs exist in most poor urban areas, but copycat groups have sprouted in suburbia and small towns. Some gangs today have become politicized and a few have been reported to have launched a struggle against "male chauvinism." However the culture of the gang remains one of aggressive male dominance, hustling for survival, and lower-class solidarity.

John M. Hagedorn

Further Reading:

Bourgois, Phillipe. 1995. *In Search of Respect: Selling Crack in El Barrio.* Cambridge, UK. Cambridge University Press.

Castells, Manuel. 1997. *The Information Age: Economy, Society, and Culture.* Vol. 2: *The Power of Identity.* Malden, MA: Blackwell.

Chesney-Lind, Meda, and John M. Hagedorn, eds. 1999. *Female Gangs in America: Essays on Girls, Gangs, and Gender.* Chicago. Lakeview Press.

Cloward, Richard, and Lloyd Ohlin. 1960. *Delinquency and Opportunity.* Glencoe, IL: Free Press.

Cohen, Albert. 1955. *Delinquent Boys.* Glencoe, IL: Free Press.

Hagedorn, John M. 1998. "Frat Boys, Bossmen, Studs, and Gentlemen: A Typology of Gang Masculinities." Pp 152–167 in *Masculinities and Violence.* Edited by Lee Bower. Thousand Oaks, CA: Sage.

Klein, Malcolm. 1971. *Street Gangs and Street Workers.* Englewood Cliffs, NJ: Prentice Hall.

Majors, Richard, and Janet Mancini Billson. 1992. *Cool Pose: The Dilemmas of Black Manhood in America.* New York: Simon and Schuster.

Messerschmidt, James W. 1993. *Masculinities and Crime: Critique and Reconceptualization of Theory.* Totowa, NJ: Rowman and Littlefield.

Miller, Walter. 1958. "Lower-Class Culture as a Generating Milieu of Gang Delinquency." *Journal of Social Issues* 14: 5–19.

Moore, Joan W. 1991. *Going Down to the Barrio: Homeboys and Homegirls in Change.* Philadelphia: Temple University Press.

Short, James F., and Fred L. Strodtbeck. 1965. *Group Process and Gang Delinquency.* Chicago: University of Chicago Press.

Staples, Robert. 1982. *Black Masculinity: The Black Man's Role in American Society.* San Francisco: BlackScholar Press.

Thrasher, Frederic. 1927. *The Gang.* Chicago: University of Chicago Press.

Yablonsky, Lewis. 1966. *The Violent Gang.* New York: MacMillan.

Gangster Films, Classic

Gangster movies, a Hollywood film genre of the 1930s, popularized a new and controversial image of masculinity. The figure of the gangster embodied a code of manliness that was hard-boiled, ruthless, and violent. Despite being a criminal and (typically) belonging to an ethnic minority group, the gangster exaggerated qualities of ideal American masculinity, particularly ambition. Gangster movies dramatize the arbitrariness and violence of masculine authority, and explore the negative side of the American dream—the drive to succeed at any cost.

Although gangster movies appeared during the silent era, they came of age with sound technology. Gun shots, car chases, and staccato dialogue became staple elements of the genre's tough, urban style. Three "classic" films—Mervyn LeRoy's *Little Caesar* (1930), starring Edward G. Robinson; William Wellman's *The Public Enemy* (1931), starring James Cagney; and Howard Hawks's *Scarface* (1932), starring Paul Muni—established the popularity and profitability of the gangster formula. This formula allowed the studios, especially Warner Brothers, to capitalize on public fascination with real-life criminals, including the bank robber John Dillinger and Chicago organized-crime boss Al Capone. Yet gangster movies also fueled a controversy over the threat Hollywood posed to American values. Although gangster movies ostensibly illustrated the moral that "crime doesn't pay" by depicting the rise and fall of their protagonists, the gangster appealed to the masses. His struggle against a tough world resonated with Depression-era audiences. Given the unpopularity of Prohibition, the gangster-bootlegger could be celebrated as an outlaw-hero. But he was too selfish, and too violent, to sustain such romantic constructions. He offered male viewers a negative role model. Censorship battles culminated with a moratorium on gangster film production in 1935 (Munby 1996, 104). Banished but not forgotten, the gangster movie paved the way for the detective film and film noir.

Gangster movies depict contradictions inherent in American ideals of manliness. The American gangster film offers a negative version of the Horatio Alger story and parodies myths of the self-made man (Brill 1984, 12). Robert Warshow attributed the genre's appeal to its cathartic condemnation of the American obsession with success. "The gangster," he argued, expresses "that part of the American psyche which rejects the . . . demands of modern life [and] 'Americanism' itself" (Warshow 1948, 130). Watching the gangster's inevitable fall assuages a collective guilt about the ruthlessness of American am-

James Cagney pushes a grapefruit into Mae Clarke's face in a scene from Public Enemy. *(Bettmann/Corbis)*

bition: "The gangster is doomed because he is under the obligation to succeed, not because the means he employs are unlawful. In the deeper layers of the modern consciousness, *all* means are unlawful, every attempt to succeed is an act of aggression, leaving one alone and guilty and defenseless among enemies: one is *punished* for success" (Warshow 1948, 133). The gangster suffers for having—in excess—the same qualities of the ideal American man: competitiveness, drive, and ambition.

Masculinity and gender studies have focused on both "classic" and later gangster movies (including Francis Ford Coppola's *Godfather* [1972] trilogy, Arthur Penn's *Bonnie and Clyde* [1967], and John Woo's Hong Kong films [1968–1992]). The gangster's hyperbolic masculinity draws attention to manliness as a social role rather than a biological essence. Insofar as "masculinity frequently derives considerable social and sexual power from being represented as castrated and wounded," the gangster movie reinforces,

even as it questions, fantasies of male dominance (Sandell 1996, 27; see also Silverman 1992). At the same time, the figure of the gangster highlights ways in which gender roles intersect with discourses of class, race/ethnicity, and sexual orientation. The figure of the gangster inverts the benefits of American masculinity by locating them within the body of an ethnic outsider. "Gangsters 'want in'—they want to 'go legit'—yet find themselves always positioned on the outside looking in"; by dramatizing the injustices their protagonists encounter, classic gangster movies challenged racial and ethnic exclusion (Munby 1996, 102). In captivating vernacular voices, cinematic gangsters questioned "ethnic and class inequality and the terms of cultural acceptance" (Munby 1996, 104).

Gangster movies insist on, but expose, the slipperiness of distinctions between homosocial and homoerotic male bonds. "The normative constructions of the gangster-crime genre" allow homosexual "play," but compensate for that play "by defining heroic masculinity in terms of a fundamental . . . homophobia" (Grossman 2000, 238). Gangster movies locate male bonds at the center of both the rigid codes of masculine behavior that their protagonists embody and the outbreaks of anarchic and sadistic violence that erupt when bonds are broken. In *The Public Enemy,* Tom Powers (Cagney) goes on a killing spree when his partner/friend is murdered. In such instances, the gangster's hypermasculinity—his toughness and misogyny—may compensate for socially inadmissible desires that make him vulnerable.

Pearl James

See also Gangster Films, Contemporary
Further Reading:

Bergman, Andrew. 1972. *We're in the Money: Depression America and its Films.* New York: Harper and Row.

Brill, Lesley. 1984. "Growing Up Gangster: *Little Caesar, The Public Enemy,* and the American Dream." Pp. 11–22 in *Hollywood: Réflexions sur l'écran.* Edited by Daniel Royot. Aix-en-Provence, France: Université de Provence.

Cohan, Steven, and Ina Rae Hark, eds. 1993. *Screening the Male: Exploring Masculinities in Hollywood Cinema.* New York: Routledge.

Grossman, Andrew. 2000. "Homosexual Men (and Lesbian Men) in a Heterosexual Genre: Three Gangster Films From Hong Kong." *Journal of Homosexuality* 39, no. 3/4: 237–271.

Karpf, Stephen Louis. 1973. *The Gangster Film: Emergence, Variation and Decay of a Genre: 1930–1940.* New York: Arno Press.

Munby, Jonathan. 1996. "*Manhattan Melodrama*'s 'Art of the Weak': Telling History from the Other Side in the 1930s Talking Gangster Film." *Journal of American Studies* 30, no. 1: 101–118.

———. 1999. *Public Enemies, Public Heroes: Screening the Gangster from* Little Caesar *to* Touch of Evil. Chicago: University of Chicago Press.

Ruth, David E. 1996. *Inventing the Public Enemy: The Gangster in American Culture, 1918–1934.* Chicago: University of Chicago Press.

Sandell, Jillian. 1996. "Reinventing Masculinity: The Spectacle of Male Intimacy in the Films of John Woo." *Film-Quarterly* 49, no. 4: 23–34.

Silverman, Kaja. 1992. *Male Subjectivity at the Margins.* New York: Routledge.

Warshow, Robert. 1948/1979. "The Gangster as Tragic Hero." Pp. 127–134 in *The Immediate Experience.* Edited by Robert Warshaw, Stanley Cavell, and Sherry Abel. New York: Atheneum.

Wood, Robin. 1986. *Hollywood from Vietnam to Reagan.* New York: Columbia University Press.

Gangster Films, Contemporary

Hollywood gangster movies center on male antiheroes from subordinated ethnic groups who use violence to climb their neighborhood hierarchies, rising quite high in some cases before falling, chasing criminal versions of the American Dream the whole way. The combination of social constraints (racism, intensive policing) and their own extravagant masculine aggression dooms these antiheroes to death or despondency. Women serve as wives and mistresses over whom the men kill each other, but mostly stay to the sidelines. The genre trains its focus on the manhood of conquered peoples, struggling, with violent rage, to climb political and economic walls built to lock them out. Well-known Hollywood cycles date from the 1930s (stars such as James Cagney, Paul Muni, and Edward G. Robinson), the 1970s (*The Godfather* series and the many low-budget crime films in the blaxploitation and Italian-American modes), and the 1990s (such Martin Scorcese operas as *Goodfellas* [1990] and *Casino* [1995], the neo-blaxploitation 'hood films such as *New Jack City* [1991] and *Menace II Society* [1993], and the Hong Kong "triad" films such as *A Better Tomorrow* [1986]).

Off screen, these genres have drawn fire for their unflattering depictions of the warrior males of minority groups (most often of Italian, Irish, and African American descent), and for their presumed power to inspire young men to imitate their doomed heroes. Depression-era Hollywood production proceeded under restrictive moral codes demanding that punishment of main characters be filmed with discretion, and caused public outcry over the corruption of British and U.S. youth. The 1990s 'hood movies, connected to the "gangsta rap" against which crusaders had already raised alarms, drew the same objection—that young men would find the brutal social climbing seductive no matter how inevitable the punishment of their heroes. Viewers can find pleasure in the company of these anti-heroes on their short-lived but glorious flights to the tops of economic food chains, and then follow the cautionary tales to their conclusions as these men pay the price for using violence as their means to American dreams.

Close analyses of these movies have revealed depths of homoeroticism and feminine weakness beneath the superficial machismo. Men grow possessive of each other in movies such as *Donnie Brasco* and *Best Seller* (1987). Parodies lampoon the emotional dysfunction, sending powerful men to psychiatrists for help managing stress (*Analyze This* [2001], *Mad Dog and Glory* [1993], the television series *The Sopranos* [2001–]). The most operatic stories (such as in the remake of *Scarface* [1983], or those of the Joe Pesci characters in *Goodfellas* and *Casino*) feature more hysterically brutal men, who die by bloody violence. Throughout, women remain sexual objects and voices of reason. Antiheroes lust after them and shoot each other in fits of jealous rage; a few women turn into choruses of virtue, counseling the men to wise up before they die. Few of the men listen, and the women remain marginal to the main action.

Neal King

See also Gangster Films, Classic
Further Reading:
King, Neal. 1999. *Heroes in Hard Times: Cop Action Movies in the U.S.* Philadelphia: Temple University Press.
Munby, Jonathan. 1999. *Public Enemies, Public Heroes: Screening the Gangster from* Little Caesar *to* Touch of Evil. Chicago: University of Chicago Press.
Rafter, Nicole. 2000. *Shots in the Mirror: Crime Films and Society.* London: Oxford University Press.
Shadoian, Jack. 2001. *Dreams and Dead Ends: The American Gangster / Crime Film.* London: Oxford University Press.

Gatsby, Jay

Jay Gatsby, the protagonist of F. Scott Fitzgerald's 1925 novel, *The Great Gatsby,* appears to be the quintessential American male hero. He is a powerful business man with shady connections, drives a glamorous car (evoking the American trope of the automobile as symbol of virility), and pursues the beautiful, privileged Daisy Fay Buchanan—despite the fact that she is married to a son of wealth and privilege. His idiosyncratic addressing of men as "old sport," a self-conscious invocation of fraternal amiability, belies discomfort with this persona. As the novel progresses, the reader learns that Gatsby (née James Gatz) is quite literally the self-made man celebrated in American legend. Tracing Gatsby's self-creation back to a Midwestern boyhood, narrator Nick Carraway illuminates the process by which Gatsby accumulates his wealth and power—an element of which is masculinity itself. Fitzgerald's interrogation of the ways in which patriarchal capitalism constructs gender and sexuality through systems of homosocial exchange reveals a deep ambivalence about the world of men.

Both Gatsby's and the author's own relationships with men are central to the novel. The crucial relationship of the novel is Nick's with Gatsby. Nick is compelled by loyalty and guilt to relate Gatsby's story, the heart of which is his relationship with mentors, frontiersman Dan Cody and gangster Meyer Wolfsheim—embodiments of American myths of violent masculinities shaped by capitalism and associated with imperialism, colonialism, and domination. Fitzgerald's own mentor, Sigourney Fay, who died in 1919, pervades the novel both in appearance and in name. The novel's profound ambivalence about the possibility of authentic, intimate male friendship untainted by power, particularly the power dynamics at work in the "mentoring" relationship, is apparent in Gatsby's and Nick's differing attitudes toward Cody, whom Gatsby calls his "best friend"—echoing the author's own comment on the

Catholic priest Fay—but whose photograph on Gatsby's dresser Nick sees as a "token of forgotten violence" (Fitzgerald 99, 173).

Nick understands the machinations of homosocial exchange because he works in stocks and bonds. His "volumes on banking and credit and investment securities," he claims, contain "shining secrets that only Midas and Morgan and Mæcenas knew" (7–8). In a patriarchal capitalist economy, wealth and power pass from father to son; the only way poor, powerless men can gain access into the system, then, is through the patronage of rich, powerful, and childless men. The reference to Mæcenas, along with allusions to Trimalchio, evoke a history of male "bonds" that highlights connections between modern mentoring and ancient traditions involving explicit slavery and overt homosexuality (which are deliberately constructed as implicit and covert throughout the novel). A self-described "bonds man," Nick is uniquely suited to tell this story of "connections" (a pervasive word in the novel), a story that reveals the underlying relationship between stocks and bonds, male bonding, and the bondage of slavery.

As a poor and powerless young man, James Gatz identifies and sympathizes with, but ultimately dislikes, women; by seventeen, he was "contemptuous [of women . . .] because they were hysterical about things that in his overwhelming self-absorption he took for granted" (104–105). In other words, he accepts that power is conferred by gender, wealth, and age, and that the powerful objectify and exploit the powerless—that human beings are themselves treated as "bonds," or "trade," on the basis of their gender, poverty, or youth. At seventeen, then, he changes his name to Jay Gatsby and offers himself to Cody, whom he serves "in a vague personal capacity" aboard his yacht until Cody's death five years later (106). When Cody's will is overturned and the money he left Gatsby awarded to a woman instead, Gatsby recognizes that patriarchal capitalism demands that wealth pass from man to man *through*

women. Wolfsheim later voices the way patriarchal capitalism makes heterosexuality compulsory when he refers to Gatsby as "the kind of man you'd like to take home and introduce to your mother and sister" (76–77).

Following his first mentor's death, Gatsby's process of acculturation through male societies and social institutions parallels Fitzgerald's own: After leaving Fay's tutelage at the Newman School, Fitzgerald attended Princeton, served in the army, and later married the beautiful, privileged Zelda; following Cody's death, Gatsby serves in the military and attends Oxford, hoping ultimately to marry Daisy Fay. Participation in male societies and social institutions such as education and the military are often perceived as opportunities for ambitious young men to rise in social class. Nick's tenuous friendship with Tom Buchanan is bolstered by their common membership in an elite fraternal organization, a "Senior Society," at Yale (11); in the same way, Nick's friendship with Gatsby is strengthened by their common military service during war. Yet despite the fact that both are from the Midwest, attended elite schools, and served in the military, Gatsby is rich while Nick is not. The difference, the novel suggests, is that Gatsby allows himself to be "mentored," while Nick repeatedly resists such "connections."

Gatsby's becoming a heterosexual man in a patriarchal capitalist economy is itself an element of the "corruption" alluded to throughout the novel. When Gatsby meets debutante Daisy Fay, the two forge a heterosocial alliance—their engagement represents an evasion of a patriarchal capitalist system in which they both are objectified and exploited, treated as bonds. When he resurfaces in her life, asking her to leave Tom and marry him, Daisy cries at the sight of the silk shirts in his wardrobe, symbols of his newly acquired status, realizing the extent to which he has become that which she originally sought to evade by marrying him.

Maggie Gordon

See also Fitzgerald, F. [Francis] Scott
Further Reading:
Fitzgerald, F. Scott. [1925] 1995. *The Great Gatsby.*
    New York: Scribner.
———. 2000. *Trimalchio: An Early Version of The
    Great Gatsby.* Edited by James L. W. West III.
    New York: Cambridge University Press.
Kerr, Frances. 1996. "Feeling 'Half Feminine':
    Modernism and the Politics of Emotion in *The
    Great Gatsby.*" *American Literature* 68, no. 2
    (June): 405–431.
Sipiora, Phillip. 1991. "Vampires of the Heart:
    Gender Trouble in *The Great Gatsby.*" Pp.
    199–220 in *The Aching Hearth: Family Violence in
    Life and Literature.* Edited by Sara Munson Deats
    and Lagretta Tallent Lenker. New York: Plenum
    Press.
Wasiolek, Edward. 1992. "The Sexual Drama of
    Nick and Gatsby." *The International Fiction
    Review* 19, no. 1: 14–22.

Gay Liberation Movement

The gay liberation movement refers to a relatively brief period in the history of organizing to benefit people with same-sex desire. Although there is disagreement about the start of the movement, most scholars understand the Stonewall Riots, the bar raid turned riot in New York City that occurred in late June 1969, as the event that led to a very different lesbian and gay politics as compared to the accommodationist, and narrowly conceived civil rights politics of the lesbian and gay organizations of the 1950s and 1960s (see Stonewall Riots). Rather than relying on sympathetic allies for support or the staid and respectful statements against discrimination by the Mattachine Society (the organization for gay men founded in 1951) and the Daughters of Bilitis (the organization for lesbians founded in 1955), the gay liberation movement employed highly visible and confrontational tactics, both to highlight pervasive heterosexism and antigay discrimination and to proclaim a public gay identity. This period of the movement lasted until around 1973 or 1974 as the national political culture turned conservative and as internal conflicts divided the movement

along gender and ideological lines. The subsequent period of gay politics focused on organization building; on pursuing antidiscrimination ordinances and legislation at the city and state levels; and on consolidating a commercialized, primarily gay white male subculture and a lesbian feminist political community.

The chief organizational expression of the gay liberation movement was the Gay Liberation Front (GLF) that started in New York City about four weeks after the Stonewall Riots and quickly spread to many cities across the country. Although some of the new liberationist thinking was already taking root in San Francisco and among some lesbian feminists in the women's movement, the three days of rioting in late June 1969 captured the imagination of thousands of people who then flocked into new organizations, came out of the closet, and lent their support to many of the activities and actions of the GLF.

One of the notable features of the gay liberation era was the explicit attention paid to the relationship between sex, gender, and sexuality. Heavily influenced by the radical feminist movement of the late 1960s, gay liberationist men and women were among the first to examine how a system of rigidly structured sex roles were built into all social institutions in American society and how this system contributed to gay oppression. Gay liberationist tracts traced how the threat of homosexuality was used to enforce rigid definitions of masculinity and femininity and how, in turn, these rigid definitions of gender prevented a more fluid, polymorphous understanding of sexuality. In this way, the gay liberation movement refused the dominant discourses that assumed that biological females would embody normative femininity and that a key feature of femininity is the sexual desire for conventionally gendered (i.e., masculine), conventionally sexualized (i.e., heterosexual) men.

In addition, these same tracts extended the emerging feminist analysis of sexism to include *hetero*sexism: an analysis of how the structure of many social institutions assumes and serves to enforce heterosexuality. In these ways, the gay liberation movement differed dramatically from its homophile predecessors by critiquing rather than seeking entrance to American society. It also laid the groundwork for a similar concept, heteronormativity, that captured the imagination of the queer movement in the 1990s. Heteronormativity stressed the ways in which the heterosexual/homosexual binary was inscribed in a variety of social discourses from literary texts to the institutions of the family, science, and medicine. It also emphasized the subtle and powerful ways in which heterosexual dominance became internalized in the development of modern identities.

Despite the gay liberationist critique of the dominant culture's normative alignment of sex, gender, and sexuality, the movement was never quite able to escape the power of this dominant discourse. Even as some men in the gay liberation movement linked the support for the Vietnam War to a language of dominant masculinity and rejected these norms of masculinity as guidelines for living their lives, others adopted a conventionally gendered language of resistance. Always characterized as passive and effeminate, many gay men, for example, participated in the hypermasculinized form of resistance typical of many movements in the late 1960s and early 1970s. Some have suggested that part of the appeal of the Black Panther Party (BPP), for example, to the men of the gay liberation movement was the hypermasculine discourse of the movement and the erotic power that many of the male leaders of the party held for gay liberationist men.

Women in the gay liberation movement were faced with a somewhat different dilemma. The response by some lesbians to the critique of sex roles and the analysis of heterosexism was to see any gender style as complicity with the patriarchy. Thus, one important expression of same-sex desire common among working-class women, butch/femme roles, was seen as mimicking hetero-sexual models and thus inherently oppressive. As an alternative, lesbians at this time subscribed to the notion of androgyny: the idea that women and men could transcend the oppressive nature of gender in their relationships, dress, and sensibility and, thereby, become genderless. This response served to alienate many butch/femme women who also experienced the force of homophobia and heterosexism in their lives.

Another feature of the gay liberation movement that both distinguishes it from its homophile predecessors and resurfaces in subsequent analyses of lesbian and gay politics is the notion of gay and lesbian identity.

Unlike the homophile movement that embraced a medicalized definition of the homosexual as a distinct type of person, the gay liberation movement talked about the fluidity of sexual roles and tried to broaden the culture's understanding of sexuality beyond sexual object choice to encompass a broader array of aims, objects, and desires. This fluidity was linked directly to another discourse of gay liberation that differs dramatically from the earlier sexual politics of the homophiles. Adamant about taking "the sex out of homosexual," both the Mattachine Society and the Daughters of Bilitis deplored the sexual subculture and promoted a sexual politics of respectability. If only homosexuals were accepted as equal participants in American society, the homophiles argued, this furtive and unsavory activity would be unnecessary. The gay liberation movement, by contrast, embraced and extended the sexual liberalism of the 1960s counterculture and equated the adoption of a gay identity to being "sexually free." Sexual liberation, however, did not primarily mean unfettered, guilt-free gay sex nor did it serve as an endorsement of the sexual subculture. More importantly, it meant sexually free. As one gay liberationist proclaimed: "sexual liberation means freeing the homosexual in everyone" (cited in Jay and Young 1992, 331).

Although anticipating somewhat the critique of identity leveled by queer theorists and the queer movement of the 1990s, this formulation of gay liberation posed an interesting challenge for the fledgling gay liberation social movement. Because one of the goals of the movement was to build constituency support, it had an interest in finding strategies to accomplish this. The appeals to gays and lesbians to "come out" functioned to build this constituency—to adopt a public gay identity oriented around same-sex desire. The movement found it much easier to organize around this understanding of gay identity rather than one devoted to "polymorphous perversity." Although also acknowledging that all identities are historical and social constructions, the queer critique of gay identity that emerged in the 1990s focused on how stabilizing gay identity excludes people for whom same-sex desire is not a salient identity but one that intersects with several other marginalized identities.

The relationship of lesbians to the gay liberation movement was more complicated than that of men and can only be understood by placing it in the social movement context of the times. Although the homophile organization of women, The Daughters of Bilitis, always considered how the subordinate position of women created unique problems for lesbians, its insistence on respectability did not lend itself to highly visible tactics and thus it never gained a wide constituency among lesbians. This constituency was constructed through the emergence of second-wave feminism in the mid- to late-1960s.

It is impossible to understand virtually any aspect of the gay liberation movement without situating it within the social movement upsurge of "the sixties" and the counterculture that swirled around these social movements. The language of liberation and oppression and the tactics and strategies of confrontational protest and coalitional politics were direct "spillovers" from the black freedom struggle, the antiwar movement, and the New Left in general. These links, of course, were never direct and unproblematic.

Through its consciousness-raising groups and its insistence that the personal is political, the feminist movement helped bring a whole generation of lesbians to political activity. Unfortunately, some heterosexual feminists were uncomfortable with embracing lesbianism as a feminist issue and this resistance sent scores of these women to gay liberation, where they refashioned the feminist concepts of sexism and patriarchy to underscore the extent to which these dynamics were based on the assumption of heterosexuality. This feminist influence on gay liberation, as noted above, was profound.

Despite this influence, the relationship between lesbians and the male-dominated gay liberation movement was not without conflict. Some men bristled at what they perceived as the constant charges of male bias leveled by gay liberation women; some women bristled at what they perceived as men's excessive concern over issues of police harassment for cruising and public sex.

One fairly well-known incident involving the Gay Liberation Front's support for the Black Panther Party led to a formal break by GLF women and to their movement toward a more separatist lesbian feminist stance on sexual politics. Due to the influence of gay liberation on the other movements of the late 1960s, the chairman of the BPP, Huey Newton, issued a strongly worded statement to the party supporting the cause of gay liberation and its central role as a revolutionary force for social change. As a result of this gesture, the GLF participated in the Panther-sponsored Revolutionary People's Constitutional Convention that took place in Philadelphia in 1970, only to find that the GLF women's caucuses were routinely disrupted and monitored by the Panthers and these women's issues ignored in the platform of the convention. The refusal of the GLF men to support the women was the "straw that broke the camel's back" and some women turned to more lesbian feminist organizations to find support and continue their political work.

The Gay Liberation Front embodied many of the features of the gay liberation movement already mentioned. Primarily, it spoke the language of oppression that was becoming increasingly familiar in the organizations of the New Left in the late 1960s and early 1970s and saw the source of gay oppression in both the structure of social institutions and in the reluctance of homosexuals to "come out of the closet." In this latter regard, the GLF, through its demonstrations, underground newspapers, broadsides, and member socialization, helped transform the meaning of "coming out" from a personal and subcultural process (i.e., "coming out into a gay world") to a political statement (i.e., making known one's gay identity in every aspect of one's life).

In addition, as the name implies, the GLF saw itself as one of a number of revolutionary fronts of the New Left. Its political platform was explicitly multi-issued: it was anti-imperialist, antiwar, antiracist, and antisexist. In fact, it was this multi-issue focus together with its free-wheeling anti-organizational structure that frustrated several members and led them to form another gay liberation organization, the Gay Activists Alliance in 1971 (GAA). Although wedded to several tenets of liberationist politics, the GAA was single-issue focused and coupled its attention-grabbing and confrontational tactics with participation in the lobbying, campaigning, and other activities associated with electoral politics. Not surprisingly, the structure of the GAA also differed from that of the GLF in that it abided by Robert's Rules of Parliamentary Procedure and established a constitution that specified a committee structure, division of labor, terms of office, and so on—in short, a bureaucratic structure.

The GAA signaled the shift to a more reformist politics for lesbians and gays in the mid- to late 1970s. As the New Left with its promise of multidimensional revolutionary change disintegrated, the gay and lesbian movement continued to flourish in altered form. Liberationist politics were replaced by a focus on organization and culture building, the cultivation of a gay identity analogous to an ethnic or racial identity, and a rights-based approach to the political process. This period would persist until the late 1980s, when the unwillingness of the federal government and many mainstream social institutions to respond to the AIDS epidemic unleashed a new form of liberationist politics in the form of the Aids Coalition to Unleash Power (ACTUP) and other confrontational forms of AIDS militancy.

Stephen Valocchi

See also Stonewall Riots

Further Reading:

Abbott, Sidney, and Barbara Love. 1972. *Sappho Was a Right-On Woman.* New York: Stein and Day.

Altman, Dennis. 1971/1993. *Homosexual: Oppression and Liberation.* New York: New York University Press.

Crimp, Douglas, with Adam Rolston. 1990. *AIDS Demo Graphics.* Seattle, WA: Bay Press.

D'Emilio, John. 1983. *Sexual Politics, Sexual Communities: The Making of a Homosexual Minority in the United States, 1940–1970.* Chicago: the University of Chicago Press

———. 2002. *The World Turned: Essays on Gay History, Politics, and Culture.* Durham, NC, and London: Duke University Press.

Jay, Karla, and Allen Young. 1972/1992. *Out of the Closets: Voices of Gay Liberation.* New York: New York University Press.

Kissack, Terrence. 1995. "Freaking Fag Revolutionaries: New York's Gay Liberation Front, 1969–1971." *Radical History Review* 62: 104–34.

Marotta, Toby. 1981. *The Politics of Homosexuality.* Boston: Houghton Mifflin.

Roscoe, Will, ed. 1996. *Radically Gay: Gay Liberation in the Words of Its Founder, Harry Hay.* Boston: Beacon Press.

Stein, Marc. 2000. *City of Brotherly and Sisterly Loves: Lesbian and Gay Philadelphia, 1945–1972.* New York: Basic Books.

Suran, Justin David. 2001. "Coming Out against the War: Antimilitarism and the Politicization of Homosexuality in the Era of Vietnam." *American Quarterly* 53: 452–488.

Teal, Donn. 1971. *The Gay Militants.* New York: St. Martin's Press.

Gay Men

See Homosexuality

Gay-Straight Alliances

Gay-Straight Alliances (GSAs) are a social movement in the form of school clubs occurring mostly in high schools, composed of sexual-minority youth and their allies seeking to end sexual-orientation prejudice. Gay-Straight Alliances attract a diverse range of students aiming to promote safety, tolerance, and acceptance for all students, regardless of sexual orientation or identity. Harassment and institutionalized homophobia experienced by sexual-minority youth lead to higher rates of suicide and suicidal thoughts, depression, absence from school, low grades, dropping out, substance abuse, and running away from home (Ryan and Futterman 1998, 24–26). School authorities generally do not adequately address the factors contributing to these risks. According to supporters, this harsh environment at school for those who vary from sexual or gender norms warrants the formation of GSAs.

Those who are perceived as not conforming to dominant gender and/or sexual norms are likely to be the targets of hatred and harassment. Males, in particular, who do not conform to hegemonic constructions of gender are more often the victims of harsh expressions of homophobia and heterosexism, and men and boys are frequently the perpetrators (Kuehne and Sullivan 2001; National Coalition of Anti-Violence Programs 2002). The homophobic character of hegemonic masculinity has been well documented, theorized (Connell 1995; Kimmel 1994), and applied to the school setting (Friend 1993; Harris 1997; Mac an Ghaill 1994; Martino 2000). In challenging heteronormativity and sexual prejudice, GSAs fundamentally confront hegemonic masculinity as it is currently configured.

There are three major functions that GSAs perform: social support, education, and activism (Lipkin 1999, 273). As a supportive environment for gender or sexually nonconforming youth to talk about their problems, a GSA can act as a safe haven in an otherwise hostile context of the school—a venue for sociability among youth who might otherwise have limited options for connecting with others. Furthermore, a goal of many GSAs is to educate the school community in gender and sexual identity issues, thereby increasing acceptance. Finally, the clubs may advocate for changes in school policies and practices to better address the needs of sexual-minority youth. GSAs vary considerably in which and to what extent each of these functions is emphasized.

Since the formation of the first GSA in 1989, the movement has spread exponentially. High-profile court cases in Salt Lake City, Utah, in 1996 and Orange County, California, in 1999 were initiated when GSAs were banned by school districts (both cases were eventually decided in favor of the GSAs). Visibility from the substantial media coverage of these cases has contributed to the emergence of hundreds of additional GSAs. The 1998 murder of a gay University of Wyoming student, Matthew Shepard, also acted as a major catalyst for the rapid growth of the movement. According to the Gay, Lesbian, and Straight Education Network (GLSEN), more than 1,000 GSAs exist in the United States in 2003 with a heavy concentration in Massachusetts and California.

Earlier support and advocacy programs for sexual-minority youth in schools informed and paved the way for the GSA movement, but none before had such an overt focus on the importance of building coalitions between heterosexual and nonheterosexual youth to combat heterosexism and homophobia.

Jeffrey Sweat

Further Reading:
Connell, Robert W. 1995. *Masculinities.* Cambridge: Polity Press.
Friend, Richard A. 1993. "Choices, Not Closets: Heterosexism and Homophobia in Schools." Pp. 209–236 in *Beyond Silenced Voices: Class, Race*

and Gender in U.S. Schools. Edited by Lois Weiss and Michelle Fine. Albany, NY: SUNY Press.

Gay, Lesbian, and Straight Education Network. "GLSEN Tallies 1,000 Gay-Straight Alliances." At *http://www.glsen.org* (cited 20 November 2001).

Harris, Mary B., ed. 1997. *School Experiences of Gay and Lesbian Youth.* New York: Harrington Park Press.

Kimmel, Michael S. 1994. "Masculinity as Homophobia: Fear, Shame, and Silence in the Construction of Gender Identity." Pp. 119–141 in *Theorizing Masculinities.* Edited by Harry Brod and Michael Kaufman. London: Sage.

Kuehne, Kristen, and Anne Sullivan. 2001. "Patterns of Anti-gay Violence." *Journal of Interpersonal Violence* 16, no. 9: 929–943.

Lipkin, Arthur. 1999. *Understanding Homosexuality, Changing Schools.* Boulder, CO: Westview Press.

Mac an Ghaill, Mairten. 1994. *The Making of Men: Masculinities, Sexualities, and Schooling.* Buckingham, Philadelphia: Open University Press.

Martino, Wayne. 2000. "Policing Masculinities: Investigating the Role of Homophobia and Heteronormativity in the Lives of Adolescent School Boys." *Journal of Men's Studies* 8, no. 2: 213–236.

National Coalition of Anti-Violence Programs. 2002. "Anti-Lesbian, Gay, Bisexual, and Transgender Violence in 2001." At http://www.lambda.org/ (cited 2002).

Perrotti, Jeff, and Kim Westheimer. 2001. *When the Drama Club is Not Enough: Lessons from the Safe Schools Program for Lesbian and Gay Students.* Boston: Beacon Press.

Ryan, Caitlin, and Donna Futterman. 1998. *Lesbian & Gay Youth: Care & Counseling.* New York: Columbia University Press.

Gay-Straight Friendship

See Friendship, Gay-Straight

Gender Differences in Life Expectancy

See Life Expectancy; Men's Health Movement

Gender Equality

Legal privileges and rights are conveyed irrespective of gender, equally recognizing the autonomy of men and women. Originally discussed in terms of *sex equality* the term *gender equality* reflects efforts initiated within the feminist movement to distinguish between sex (that which is strictly biological) and gender (that which is constructed by a host of social, legal, political, and economic arrangements that reflect distinctions based on race, class, ethnicity, sexuality and religion).

A key concept of Western society is the notion that under the "rule of law" all individuals are to be given the same consideration without prejudice. Equality as it is legally articulated and practiced is premised on an Aristotelian framework under which similarly situated individuals are to be treated similarly and dissimilar individuals must be treated differently.

Reflecting the Aristotelian framework, contemporary consideration of gender equality in the United States evolved from a debate begun in the early part of the twentieth century about the extent to which sex equality required women to be treated the same as men without special treatment due to their physical or other differences. Spearheaded by the National Women's Party and its leader, Alice Paul, advocates of the sameness position called for an Equal Rights Amendment (ERA) to the United States Constitution, which stated in part in its original proposed draft before Congress in 1923 that "Men and women shall have equal rights throughout the United States and in every place subject to its jurisdiction." Opponents of the ERA and of the equality (understood as same treatment) it offered included progressive reformers who had been advocating for sex-specific protective labor legislation that afforded women legal protections unavailable to men. These reformers suggested that women's unique physical differences from men, particularly their childbearing abilities, required special protections for wage-earning women who often endured long hours in harsh conditions for very little pay. Among those who articulated this "difference" argument was Ethel Smith of the National Women's Trade Union who believed that equality for women would only be achieved if their distinct experiences as women were recognized and accommodated by gender-specific protective labor legislation. It was within the context of this "sameness/difference" debate that consideration of the legal guarantees for sex equality took form (Silberstein 1995, 139–148).

Without the ratification of the ERA, the U.S. Constitution offers no specific protections against sex discrimination. Early advocates for women's rights had made an effort in the later part of the nineteenth century to use the Fourteenth Amendment, which stated in part that "No state shall abridge the privileges or immunities of citizens of the United States . . . nor deny to any person within its jurisdiction the equal protection of the laws," and was one of three amendments ratified in response to the Civil War. This effort involved the movement to repeal a state statute that prohibited women from becoming lawyers. The U.S. Supreme Court found that the Fourteenth Amendment did not prohibit states from limiting women's ability to practice law because, as one justice explained, "The paramount destiny and mission of woman are to fulfil the noble and benign offices of wife and mother" (*Bradwell v. Illinois,* 83 U.S. [16 Wall.] 130 [Bradley concurring]). Members of the suffrage movement finally achieved their goal of applying the most basic citizenship right in a free democracy, the right to vote, to women with the passage of the Nineteenth Amendment in 1920. Although this amendment did not address the issue of sex equality, some believed that it would serve as a guarantee of women's equality. In 1923 the Supreme Court gave some indication that this would be the case in a decision in which it found that a minimum wage law for women was unconstitutional (*Adkins v. Children's Hospital,* 261 U.S. 525 [1923].) In its decision the Court acknowledged that women might need special legal protections because their physical differences, primarily their maternal functions, made them more susceptible to injuries and work-related illnesses. However, the Court was clear that women were not in need of a broad range of special protections, as the Nineteenth Amendment had essentially eradicated the differences in women's civil, political, and economic status from that of men (*Adkins* at 552). By finding that upon gaining the right to vote women virtually were similarly situated to men, the decision reflected the Aristotelian requirement of treating equals equally and unequals unequally.

Despite the Nineteenth Amendment's potential for generating sex equality, there was very little in the way of constitutional prohibitions against sex-based discrimination until 1971, when the Supreme Court finally recognized that sex-specific rules were suspect and applied the equal protection clause of the Fourteenth Amendment to overturn a statute that gave preference to men in serving as executors of estates (*Reed v. Reed,* 404 U.S. 71 [1971]). Significantly, the Court did not treat sex discrimination as it had race discrimination in large measure because, unlike the case of race where differential treatment is presumably limited to permissible affirmative action, distinctions based on sex were to be tolerated as a means for acknowledging the differences between men and women. As a result, subsequent decisions that considered the constitutionality of sex-based distinctions have not set an absolute bar against discrimination but have tolerated it when, for example, women's role as mothers made different treatment appear necessary. In other instances, the Court has had a difficult time making distinctions between unconstitutional sex discrimination and that which is permissible to compensate for prior discrimination. This has been evident in some initial efforts to challenge those sex stereotypes that have generated inequalities toward men. Nevertheless, there have been significant challenges to gender-based distinctions that have disadvantaged both men and women. For instance, the Supreme Court has found that a state-supported nursing school impermissibly discriminated against men by denying them admission. The Court found that such an exclusion was not only paternalistic toward the women students whom the state argued would be better educated in an all-female classroom environment, but it also denied men equal access to a profession of their own choosing (*Mississippi University for Women v. Hogan*, 458 U.S. 718 [1982]).

The demand for gender equality has challenged the sex-based stereotypical roles assigned to men and women in reproductive families. Thus, the Supreme Court found a law that allowed unwed mothers to block adoptions of their children for any reason but allowed unwed fathers to do so only when the adoption violated the "best interests" of the children to be an unconstitutional violation of the fathers' rights to equal protection (*Caban v. Mohammed*, 441 U.S. 380 [1979]). Fathers are not absolutely equated to mothers in their connection to their children, as indicated by the Supreme Court's decision to uphold a statute that prevented unwed fathers from suing for the wrongful death of their children before they had been legitimized but held no such prohibitions for unwed mothers. Underlying this decision is the assumption that the unwed mother's relationship to the child is "known," whereas that of the unwed father can only be known once it is legally recognized (*Parham v. Hughes*, 441 U.S. 347 [1979]). Although court decisions may continue to reflect a bias against men as primary nurturers of their children, there is legal precedent to require that men be given the same recognition for their relationships with their children as has been assumed to be natural in the case of women.

Beyond the equal protections afforded by the Constitution against sex discrimination, notable pieces of legislation have been instrumental in equalizing the status of men and women. Chief among these has been the Civil Rights Act of 1964, which prohibited discrimination on the basis of sex as well as race in employment under what is commonly called Title VII (42 U.S.C. §§ 2000 et. seq.). Enacted to address the labor-market discrimination most women encounter, the statute has also challenged the gender-based assumptions that have limited men's access to a full range of employment opportunities because of occupational sex segregation. However, the equality enacted by Title VII parallels that afforded by the U.S. Constitution through the equal protection clause in that it includes some allowances for those distinctions necessary to the performance of the job known as "bona fide occupational qualifications" (BFOQs). These qualifications are not applied to race, suggesting that sex differences at times may require differential treatment of men and women. Such exceptions are meant to be rather limited and have been tempered by the prohibition of sex stereotypes as standards for employment and promotion, as the Supreme Court stated that under Title VII "[G]ender must be irrelevant to employment decisions" (*Price Waterhouse v. Hopkins*, 490 U.S. 228, 240 [1989]).

The legal formula for gender equality that relies on similarity as the standard for equal treatment has been criticized as it limits the potential for eradicating gender-based distinctions that prevent men and women from experiencing true equality. Some have suggested that this formula situates maleness as the norm against which women are measured in determining the level of permissible discrimination. Within this context several scholars in men's studies have examined how the normativity of maleness has not only privileged men in relation to women but has disadvantaged them by rigidly defining appropriate masculine behavior (Strecopoulos and Uebel 1997). Instead of the traditional formulation of equality, scholars like Catharine Mackinnon have suggested applying an inequality approach that would find the existence of discrimination whenever there is a systemic deprivation of benefits to one sex because of sex. Others have suggested that the requirements of finding similarities and differences has forced a standardization of gender experiences that ignores the ways in which they are informed by and influence an array of distinctions that include race, sexuality, class, and ethnicity (Wing 1997).

Dara J. Silberstein

See also Backlash; "Glass Ceiling"; "Glass Escalator"; "Masculinity Dividend"; Pay Gap

Further Reading:
Carbado, Devon W., ed. 1999. *Black Men on Race, Gender, and Sexuality.* New York: New York University Press.
Delgado, Richard, and Jean Stefancic, eds. 2000. *Critical Race Theory: The Cutting Edge.* 2d ed. Philadelphia: Temple University Press.
Kimmel, Michael S., and Michael A. Messner. 2001. *Men's Lives.* 5th ed. Boston: Allyn and Bacon.
Mackinnon, Catharine. 1987. *Feminism Unmodified.* Boston: Harvard University Press.
———. 2001. *Sex Equality.* New York: Foundation Press.
Silberstein, Dara J. 1995. "A Legal Historical Analysis of the United States Women's Bureau and Women Workers as Mothers, 1900–1964." (unpublished dissertation).
Strecopoulos, Mary, and Michael Uebel, eds. 1997. *Race and the Subject of Masculinities.* Durham, NC: Duke University Press.
William, Wendy W. 1983. "The Equality Crisis: Some Reflections on Culture, Courts and Feminism." *Women's Rights Law Reporter* 7: 175.
Wing, Adrien Katherine, ed. 1997. *Critical Race Feminism: A Reader.* New York: New York University Press.

Gender Order

The concept of "gender order," which was initially articulated by the Australian social historian Jill Matthews (1984) and further developed and elaborated by Robert Connell (1987) and other social scientists, refers to a historically constructed pattern of power relations between men and women. Two decades after its initial formulation, the concept has by the early 2000s acquired great theoretical complexity and analytical value, and it presents an alternative both to ahistorical notions of "patriarchy" and to deterministic concepts of a "sex/gender system."

In her study of the historical construction of femininity, Matthews (1984) introduces the term *gender order* to name the systematic way in which societies turn barely differentiated babies into social men and women and order the patterns of relationships among and between them (3–29). By analogy, Matthews (1984) notes, "we can talk of an economic order as being the ordering of people's relationships to the means of production and consumption" (14). As this analogy suggests, there are other orderings of relationships within every society, such as economic and racial orderings, which cut across the gender order and deflect and modify it. Thus, for Matthews, *gender order* names an abstraction that simplifies the unruliness of social life, making it possible to talk about one ordering of social relationships in isolation.

In formulating this concept, Matthews's concern was exclusively with women and femininity. Connell (1987) has explicitly linked the concept of gender order to the study of men and masculinities and to a group of other concepts, such as "gender regime" and "gender practice," turning Matthews's relatively isolated notion into an integral part of a unified social theory of gender. Connell's analysis of gender relations in a wide range of organizations, including schools and factories, concludes that these organizations embody an extensive and relatively enduring pattern in their gender arrangements (e.g., most mineworkers are men). Such a pattern in gender arrangements he calls the "gender regime" of an organization. The gender regimes of different organizations within a society are themselves part of wider patterns, which also endure over time, and Connell calls these wider patterns the "gender order" of a society or, on a global level, "world gender order." In this framework, Connell sees masculinities and femininities as "configurations of practice" constructed *within* the context of gender orders.

The concept of gender order is widely used in the international literature on men and masculinities. Particularly, it has been very influential in studies examining the relationship between masculinities and sport, while it is also used in studies that focus on masculinities and violence, gender relations in the workplace, masculinities and globalization, and sexual practices. Also, there has been increased research interest in questions related to the intersection and inseparability of the economic, racial, sexual, and gender orders of societies.

As it is used in contemporary literature, the concept of gender order embodies an anti-essentialist, constructionist, and historicist way of thinking that differentiates it from similar concepts, such as "patriarchy" and "sex/gender system." It is broader and more inclusive than the notion of "patriarchy," which implies an ahistorical state of male oppression over women and ignores varying forms of male domination and female resistance and power. The concept of gender order refers to a society's systemic capacity to order gender relations in a historically specific way, but it does not presuppose the nature of this ordering. Thus, as Matthews (1984) noted, a gender order could be matriarchal or patriarchal or egalitarian, just as an economic order could be feudal or capitalist or communist (14).

The concept of gender order is more similar to Rubin's (1975) celebrated notion of "sex/gender system," defined as a set of arrangements by which societies transform biological sexuality into gender roles and gender stratification. Yet, Rubin's analysis, which draws heavily on Claude Levi-Strauss's structuralist interpretation of kinship systems, underemphasizes the agency of gender subjects and thus portrays the sex/gender system as a deterministic "apparatus which takes up females as raw materials and fashions domesticated women as products" (Rubin 1975, 158). In contrast to such determinism, the concept of gender order entails active construction according to which the orders that constrain and facilitate gender practices are themselves produced and reproduced in gender practice. This has been empirically exemplified in Frank Barrett's (1995) review of a series of studies that address the question of the active transformation of gender orders.

Demetris Z. Demetriou

See also Patriarchy
Further Reading:
Barrett, Frank J. 1995. "Finding Voice within the Gender Order." *Journal of Organizational Change and Management* 8, no. 6: 8–15.
Connell, Robert W. 1987. *Gender and Power: Society, the Person and Sexual Politics.* Stanford, CA: Stanford University Press.
Matthews, Jill J. 1984. *Good and Mad Women: The Historical Construction of Femininity in Twentieth-Century Australia.* Sydney, Australia: Allen and Unwin.
Rubin, Gail. 1975. "The Traffic in Women: Notes on the 'Political Economy' of Sex." Pp. 157–210 in *Towards an Anthropology of Women.* Edited by R. Reiter. New York: Monthly Review Press.

"Gendercide"

The term "gendercide" was first coined by the U.S. scholar Mary Anne Warren in her 1985 book, *Gendercide: The Implications of Sex Selection.* Warren's definition has provided a useful foundation for subsequent research:

The *Oxford American Dictionary* defines genocide as "the deliberate extermination of a race of people." By analogy, gendercide would be the deliberate extermination of persons of a particular sex (or gender). Other terms, such as "gynocide" and "femicide," have been used to refer to the wrongful killing of girls and women. But "gendercide" is a sex-neutral term, in that the victims may be either male or female. There is a need for such a sex-neutral term, since sexually discriminatory killing is just as wrong when the victims happen to be male. The term also calls attention to the fact that gender roles have often had lethal consequences, and that these are in important respects analogous to the lethal consequences of racial, religious, and class prejudice. (Warren 1985, 22)

Warren's terminology never quite took hold in feminist discourse. But in June 2000, the gendercide framework was revived by Adam Jones in an article, "Gendercide and Genocide," for *Journal of Genocide Research* (Jones 2001). In that piece, Jones sought to realize the inclusive promise of Warren's terminology, which largely had been limited in its practical application to "anti-female gendercide" (Warren 1985, 32). Jones contended that it is in fact "non-combatant men [who] have been and continue to be the most frequent targets of mass killing and genocidal slaughter, as well as a host of lesser atrocities and abuses." This "mass killing of males, particularly of 'battle-age' men, has roots deep in the history of conflict between human communities." In many cases, it had resulted in "staggering demographic disproportions of adult males vs. adult females—that is, a wildly skewed underrepresentation of adult men" (Jones 2001, 186–187).

The revival of the gendercide framework has occurred in the broader context of comparative genocide studies. This multidisciplinary field derived from the upsurge of interest in the Jewish holocaust in the 1960s, producing a host of scholars that gradually moved on to explore the global-historical phenomenon of genocide in comparative perspective.

The key preoccupation of this literature, apart from the debate over definitions of genocide, has been to detect reliable early-warning signs of genocide and devise effective strategies of intervention for mass killings already underway. Jones argued in "Gendercide and Genocide" that "gendercides against men and women—but particularly men—may be seen . . . as one of the more common forms of genocide." That is to say, in many circumstances, the genocide *consists* of a campaign in which large-scale killing is limited to or focused upon the "battle-age" male component of the targeted population. In other cases, including the three "classic" genocides of the twentieth century (Armenia, the Jewish Holocaust, and Rwanda), gender-selective killing of younger adult males serves as a harbinger or trip wire for mass killing that eventually targets all group members. It is the "battle-age" male subgroup that is standardly perceived as most dangerous or threatening to the ambitions of the *génocidaires*. (This is evident in the rhetoric of demonization that is deployed in the pregenocidal environment—the "terrorists," "subversives," "demons," "cockroaches," and so on are gendered male.) In such instances, then, this group's elimination is seen as a *necessary but not sufficient* stage in the unfolding of a whole-scale, "root-and-branch" campaign of genocide. Gendercide against "battle-age" men serves to render the remainder of the group effectively defenseless. It may also be a means, as in the Nazi-occupied territories in the summer of 1941, of acclimatizing the killers to their grisly tasks: killing younger noncombatant men evokes few of the qualms attached to the killing of children, women, and the elderly (see Goldhagen 1997, 149–150).

For example, in his controversial work *Hitler's Willing Executioners,* Goldhagen notes that "The *Einsatzgruppen* [Nazi killing-squad] officers . . . could habituate their men into their new vocation as genocidal executioners through a stepwise escalation of the killing. First, by shooting primarily teenage and adult Jewish males, they would be able to acclimate themselves to mass executions without the shock of killing women, young children, and the infirm. . . . They could also believe that they were selectively killing the most dangerous Jews, which was a measure that they could conceive to be reasonable for this apocalyptic war. Once the men became used to slaughtering Jews on this sex-selective and smaller scale, the officers could more easily expand the scope and size of the killing operations" (Goldhagen 1997, 149–150). Note that even with this "acclimating," the extension of the genocide beyond "battle-age" males caused trauma and even breakdowns among the killers. The result was the development of more impersonal, "hands-off" methods of killing, notably gas vans and, subsequently, gas chambers (see also Jones 2001, 203).

If this trend of both "sufficient" and preliminary targeting of "battle-age" men holds true, then one would expect campaigns of violence and repression against this group to be among the most reliable early-warning signs of impending genocide. Some of Jones's subsequent work has sought to explore the implications for humanitarian intervention, offering criticisms of human-rights and media reportage, which, the author alleges, tends to skate over or ignore the selective targeting of males in violent conflicts, up to and including genocide (see, e.g., Jones 2002a).

In February 2000 a web-based educational initiative, Gendercide Watch (*www.gendercide.org*), was launched to provide a clearinghouse for case studies and media coverage of gendercide. The case studies include not just political/military gendercides, but gendercidal *institutions* such as female infanticide, "honor" killings, *corvée* (forced) labor, and incarceration and capital punishment. The attempt here is to expand our understanding of "sexually discriminatory killing" (Warren's phrase) beyond the obvious cases of direct mass killing—in part, to ensure that gendercide against women receives its due, because women appear more likely to be selectively victimized by such "background" institutions than by militarized mass killing. One case study, for example, focuses on maternal mortality (Gendercide Watch 2000–2002a). This phenomenon, which is amenable to relatively easy intervention even by the poorest states, claims the lives of some 600,000 women annually—a death toll almost equal to that of the 1994 Rwanda genocide—and is repeated each year. Likewise, female infanticide "is as old as many cultures, and has likely accounted for millions of gender-selective deaths throughout history" (Gendercide Watch 2000–2002b).

Since 2000, a small but diverse group of scholars has begun to explore, adapt, and criticize the gendercide framework deployed in Jones (2001). These efforts culminated in March 2002 with the publication of a special issue of *Journal of Genocide Research* on "Gendercide and Genocide." True to the multidisciplinary spirit of genocide studies, the issue included contributions from the fileds of sociology, psychology, political science, human rights activism, and queer studies. Evelin Lindner (2002) examined "gendercide and humiliation in honor and human rights societies," linking gendercidal outbreaks against males, male suicidal behavior, and male violence against women to the particular configurations of shame and humiliation in "honor" societies. Øystein Gullvåg Holter offered a sophisticated "theory of gendercide," describing the phenomenon as "an outcome of civil-life processes as well as conflict and war events" (Holter 2002, 12). Jones (2002b) applied the gendercide framework to the genocide in Rwanda, while David Buchanan, a member of Amnesty International, studied the connection between "gendercide and human rights" (Buchanan 2002). Stefanie Rixecker (2002) considered the implications of new biotechnologies for possible gendercidal campaigns against gays and lesbians. Stuart Stein (2002) was more skeptical—questioning, for instance, whether the sex-selective targeting of "battle-age" males was as prominent or significant a feature of the Jewish Holocaust as Jones had argued, and asking whether much was gained by the addition of yet another "-cide" to the genocide literature. Stein's critique has been buttressed by R. Charli Carpenter (forthcoming), who accepts the legitimacy of a focus on sex-selective massacres of men and women, but seeks to move the study of gender and genocide beyond this somewhat limited focus.

It is clear that a great deal more research into gendercide is warranted. Key theoretical issues include the appropriate boundaries of the framework. (How significant is the gender variable in "gendercides" where ethnicity, social class, age, and other factors are also significant? Can gendercidal institutions usefully be studied alongside political/military gendercides?) Another important question, partially addressed by Holter and Lindner, concerns the linkage between patriarchal social structure and gendercides against both women and men. Michael Kimmel has proposed that "gendercidal moments . . . are least likely to happen when patriarchy is in fullest force or when it is completely undermined—that is, when women's equality is very high or very low. It is when patriarchy is destabilized . . . that the most frantic efforts are undertaken to *restore*" patriarchal privilege, including through the selective targeting of other men. This model derives from Kimmel's conviction "that much of mass male violence is psychologically restorative of some status quo ante in which masculine entitlement was more visible and stable" (Kimmel 2002). His line of analysis seems highly promising. The model should perhaps be expanded, however, to allow for enduring gendercidal institutions such as female infanticide and forced labor, and for gendercides that occur in a context of a militarized campaign, crisis, or emergency not necessarily linked to a broader "destabilization" of patriarchy. Examples of this latter phenomenon would include the Japanese mass killings of Chinese men (and mass rapes and smaller-scale killings of Chinese women) in Nanjing in 1937–1938 and the 1971 genocide inflicted on Bengali males by West Pakistani forces in what is today Bangladesh (see Gendercide Watch 2000–2002c, d).

Adam Jones

Further Reading:

Buchanan, David. 2002. "Gendercide and Human Rights." *Journal of Genocide Research* 4, no. 1 (March): 95–108.

Carpenter, Robyn Charli. Forthcoming. "Beyond Gendercide." *International Journal of Human Rights*.

Gendercide Watch. 2000–2002a. "Case Study: Maternal Mortality." At http://www.gendercide.org/case_maternal.html.

———. 2000–2002b. "Case Study: Female Infanticide." At http://www.gendercide.org/case_infanticide.html.

———. 2000–2002c. "Case Study: The Nanjing Massacre, 1937–38." At http://www.gendercide.org/case_nanjing.html.

———. 2000–2002d. "Case Study: Genocide in Bangladesh, 1971." At http://www.gendercide.org/case_bangladesh.html.

Goldhagen, Daniel J. 1997. *Hitler's Willing Executioners: Ordinary Germans and the Holocaust.* New York: Vintage.

Holter, Øystein Gullvåg. 2002. "A Theory of Gendercide." *Journal of Genocide Research* 4, no. 1 (March): 11–38.

Jones, Adam. 2001. "Gendercide and Genocide." *Journal of Genocide Research* 2, no. 2 (June): 185–211.

———. 2002a. "Genocide and Humanitarian Intervention: Incorporating the Gender Variable." *Journal of Humanitarian Assistance* (February). At http://www.jha.ac/articles/a080.htm.

———. 2002b. "Gender and Genocide in Rwanda." *Journal of Genocide Research* 4, no. 1 (March): 65–94.

Kimmel, Michael. 2002. Personal communication, September 24.

Lindner, Evelin. 2002. "Gendercide and Humiliation on Honor and Human Rights Societies." *Journal of Genocide Research* 4, no. 1 (March): 137–155.

Rixecker, Stefanie S. 2002. "Genetic Engineering and Queer Biotechnology: The Eugenics of the Twenty-First Century?" *Journal of Genocide Research* 4, no. 1 (March): 109–126.

Stein, Stuart. 2002. "Geno- and Other Cides: A Cautionary Note on Knowledge Accumulation." *Journal of Genocide Research* 4, no. 1 (March).

Warren, Mary Anne. 1985. *Gendercide: The Implications of Sex Selection.* Totowa, NJ: Rowman & Allanheld.

Gender-Role Conflict

Defined as a "psychological state in which socialized gender roles have negative consequences on the person or others" (O'Neil, Good, and Holmes 1995, 166), gender-role conflict is believed to occur when an individual internalizes sexist or restrictive gender roles, and then devalues, restricts, or violates himself, herself, or others as a result (O'Neil et al. 1995). The term does not represent a single type of conflict, but encompasses a broad range of negative intrapersonal and interpersonal consequences that arise from adopting traditional gender roles. Specifically, a person is said to experience gender-role conflict when the individual devalues himself or herself by feeling ashamed for not living up to traditional gender ideals; restricts himself or herself by avoiding anything that is not gender stereotypical; devalues another who does not act in gender-stereotypical ways; restricts others from acting in gender-atypical ways; violates others through acting in gender-typical ways (e.g., through use of violence); experiences being devalued by others when acting in a gender-atypical way; or is violated by others who are acting in a gender-typical way.

Because the construct encompasses such a broad range of negative consequences, persons, and situations, it inevitably overlaps with several other gender constructs developed to describe difficulties arising from traditional gender-role socialization. The two most notable overlapping constructs are Eisler's (1995) gender-role stress construct (i.e., stress resulting from one's appraisal of failing to live up to traditional gender-role standards) and Pleck's (1981) gender-role strain construct (i.e., strain experienced from gender-role socialization that creates trauma, dysfunction, and feelings of inadequacy when not living up to gender ideals).

Although theoretically applicable to girls and women, theory and research on gender-role conflict has been limited to examining masculine gender-role conflict with boys and men. In the earliest discussions of the construct, O'Neil and his colleagues identified six patterns that result from masculine socialization in which boys and men (a) restrict their own and others' emotions; (b) obsess about achievement and success; (c) restrict their sexual and affectionate behavior; (d) emphasize success, power, and competition; (e) become homophobic; and (e) experience health problems (O'Neil 1981a, 1981b).

To examine these patterns, O'Neil and his colleagues developed the Gender Role Conflict Scale. Factor analysis suggests that the scale measures four gender-role conflict patterns: Success, Power and Competition; Restricted Emotionality; Restricted Affectionate Behavior Between Men; and Conflict Between Work and Family (O'Neil, Helms, David, Gable, and Wrightsman 1986).

Although Betz and Fitzgerald (1993) have criticized the Gender Role Conflict Scale because the items on the first three scales do not assess conflict directly, results from over 150 empirical studies support many of O'Neil's propositions about gender-role conflict's relationship to devaluing self, devaluing others, intrapersonal conflict, interpersonal conflict, and psychological distress (see *www.familystudies.uconn.edu/oneil.htm* for a bibliography of studies using the Gender Role Conflict Scale). For example, empirical studies support the view that gender-role conflict is connected to lower self-esteem; antipathy toward homosexuals and women; immature and externalizing psychological defenses; sexual aggression and violence; and both general psychological distress, as well as specific psychological problems such as depression, anxiety, and substance abuse.

Molly Freitag

See also Gender-Role Conformity; Gender-Role Strain

Further Reading:

Betz, Nancy E., and Louise F. Fitzgerald. 1993. "Individuality and Diversity: Theory and Research in Counseling Psychology." *Annual Review of Psychology* 44: 343–381.

Eisler, Richard M. 1995. "The Relationship between Masculine Gender Role Stress and Men's Health Risk: The Validation of the Construct." Pp. 207–255 in *A New Psychology of Men*. Edited by R. F. Levant and W. S. Pollack. New York: Basic Books.

O'Neil, James M. 1981a. "Male Sex-Role Conflicts, Sexism, and Masculinity: Psychological Implications for Men, Women, and the Counseling Psychologist." *The Counseling Psychologist* 9: 61–81.

———. 1981b. "Patterns of Gender Role Conflict and Strain: Sexism and Fear of

Femininity in Men's Lives." *Personnel and Guidance Journal* 60: 203–210.

O'Neil, James M., Glenn E. Good, and Sarah Holmes. 1995. "Fifteen Years of Theory and Research on Men's Gender Role Conflict: New Paradigms for Empirical Research." Pp. 164–206 in *A New Psychology of Men*. Edited by R. F. Levant and W. S. Pollack. New York: Basic Books.

O'Neil, James M., B. Helms, R. Gable, L. David, and L. Wrightsman. 1986. "Gender Role Conflict Scale: College Men's Fear of Femininity." *Sex Roles* 14: 335–350.

Pleck, Joseph H. 1981. *The Myth of Masculinity.* Cambridge, MA: MIT Press.

Gender-Role Conformity

Gender-role conformity is defined as adhering to gender-role norms (i.e., societal rules and standards) about how to be masculine or feminine in one's public and/or private life. In social psychology, conformity is usually defined as occurring when perceived or real pressure from others causes individuals to act differently from how they would act without such influence (Myers 1996). This fits well with the experiences of males and females when they are beginning the process of gender-role socialization. For example, when a young boy falls down and starts crying, his father or mother might tell him, "big boys don't cry." In this case, when the boy stops crying in response to these pressures, he is conforming to a gender-role norm (i.e., emotional control) by acting differently from how he would otherwise act.

However, because males and females experience constant gender socialization, individuals internalize many of society's rules and standards about gender. Thus, after boys and girls (and men and women) internalize their respective gender-role norms, they are likely to act the same in private as they would in public, despite their original inclinations. To continue the example, when the boy grows up and experiences disappointments that would lead to tears but does not cry about them even when alone, he may be conforming to a gender-role norm that has been internalized.

These rules and standards are believed to be taught to males and females by social agents such as parents, teachers, peers, and the media about how they are supposed to act, think, and feel (Bem 1981). However, because gender-role norms vary as a function of culture, class, race, sexual orientation, economic system, and time in history (Kimmel 1996), the behaviors, thoughts, and feelings that reflect gender-role conformity also vary as a function of these sociocultural variables.

A given person is also likely to experience variability in the gender-role norms of different groups that comprise his or her social network (e.g., playgroups, groups at work, family, religious groups, and classmates). For example, a man may belong to one group in which the normative messages about masculinity include being violent and having sexual conquests. However, he may also belong to a religious group in which the masculine norms involve being a protector of the weak and a faithful husband. In such cases, characteristics of the groups, such as unanimity, size, as well as the similarity and importance of the groups to the individual, are important to consider to understand their influence on conformity (Cialdini and Trost 1999). In this case, the person can be expected to conform to the gender-role norms of the group that is larger, more similar, and important to him or her, and if this groups tends to be more uniform in conforming to gender-role norms.

These consequences of conforming to gender-role norms are often both positive and negative and affect a range of life areas, including one's relationships, self-perceptions, and physical and psychological health. As conformity to social norms leads to group acceptance and group rewards (see Cialdini and Trost 1999), males or females who conform to their respective gender-role norms are likely to be popular or seen as likeable. In real-world terms, the acceptance and rewards from the group might translate into getting asked for a date, picked for the team, perceived as a good parent, or promoted in one's career.

As social norms provide guidance for individuals in ambiguous situations (Cialdini and Trost 1999), another significant benefit for the individual who conforms to gender-role norms includes feeling that he or she has clear guidance in terms of how to act in society. This is no small benefit as the process of identity development is often a difficult one. As such, conformity to gender-role norms helps establish an identity for the individual who is wrestling with this stage of development.

Additionally, research shows that the acceptance by others that comes with conformity to social norms increases persons' feelings of self-worth and self-esteem (Solomon, Greenberg, and Pyszczynski 1991). Other research on managing one's self-concept suggests that conformity to social norms helps persons avoid developing the self-concept of being deviant (Asch 1956). As such, conformity to gender-role norms can help males and females to feel good about themselves and not to see themselves as deviant men or women.

However, as some argue, because living up to gender-role norms is often unattainable and some gender-role norms are dysfunctional (Pleck 1981, 1995), several significant costs are associated with gender-role conformity. In his work describing gender-role strain, Pleck (1981) identified different types of strain that occur from trying to live up gender-role expectations. One type, discrepancy strain, occurs when males or females who hold a given role-norm as salient, fail to live up to it. Pleck (1995) believes that this failure leads to low self-esteem and other negative psychological consequences for men and women who try to conform to these norms. For example, if a boy or a man tries to conform to the masculine norm of being a "winner," he is likely to experience discrepancy strain during those times when he inevitably loses.

Pleck also describes dysfunction strain that produces negative consequences for the individual because fulfilling certain gender-role expectations brings negative consequences to the person or others. For example, conforming to masculine norms such as violence, risk taking, or promiscuity are likely to have many negative psychological and health consequences for individuals, families, and society.

James R. Mahalik

See also Gender-Role Conflict; Gender-Role Strain

Further Reading:

Asch, Solomon. 1956. Studies of Independence and Conformity: A Minority of One against a Unanimous Majority. *Psychological Monographs* 70, no. 9, While No. 416.

Bem, Sandra L. 1981. "Gender Schema Theory: A Cognitive Account of Sex Typing." *Psychological Review* 88: 354–364.

Cialdini, Robert B., and Melanie R. Trost. 1999. "Social Influence: Social Norms, Conformity, and Compliance." Pp. 151–192 in *The Handbook of Social Psychology*. Vol. 2. Edited by D. Gilbert, S. Fiske, and G. Lindzy. Boston: McGraw-Hill.

Kimmel, Michael. 1996. *Manhood in America: A Cultural History*. New York: Free Press.

Myers, David G. 1996. *Social Psychology*. New York: McGraw-Hill.

Pleck, Joseph H. 1981. *The Myth of Masculinity*. Cambridge, MA: MIT Press.

———. 1995. "The Gender Role Strain Paradigm: An Update." Pp. 11–32 in *A New Psychology of Men*. Edited by Ronald F. Levant and William S. Pollack. New York: Basic Books.

Solomon, Sheldon, Jeff Greenberg, and Thomas Pyszczynski. 1991. "A Terror Management Theory of Social Behavior: The Psychological Functions of Self-Esteem and Cultural Worldviews." *Advances in Experimental Social Psychology* 24: 93–159.

Gender-Role Strain

The new psychology of men views gender roles not as biological or even social "givens," but rather as psychologically and socially constructed entities that bring certain advantages and disadvantages, and, most importantly, can change. This perspective acknowledges the biological differences between men and women, but argues that it is not the biological differences of sex that make for "masculinity" and "femininity." These notions are socially constructed from bits and pieces of biological, psychological, and social experience to serve particular purposes. Traditional constructions of gender serve patriarchal purposes; nontraditional constructions, such as those the anthropologist David Gilmore described among the Tahitians and the Semai, serve more equalitarian purposes.

The Gender Role Strain Paradigm, originally formulated by Joseph Pleck in *The Myth of Masculinity* (1981) is the forerunner in the new psychology of men of social constructionism and of modern critical thinking about masculinity, having been formulated before social constructionism emerged as a new perspective on masculinity. His work spawned a number of major research programs that have produced important data that have deepened our understanding of the strain men experience when they attempt to live up the impossibility of the male role.

Pleck demonstrated that the paradigm that had dominated the research on masculinity for fifty years (1930–1980)—the Gender Role Identity Paradigm—not only poorly accounts for the observed data, but also promotes the patriarchal bifurcation of society on the basis of stereotyped gender roles. In its place, Pleck proposed the Gender Role Strain Paradigm.

The older Gender Role Identity Paradigm assumed that people have an inner psychological need to have a gender-role identity, and that optimal personality development hinged on its formation. The extent to which this "inherent" need is met is determined by how completely a person embraces his or her traditional gender role. From such a perspective, the development of appropriate gender-role identity is viewed as a failure-prone process; and, failure for men to achieve a masculine gender-role identity is thought to result in homosexuality, negative attitudes toward women, or defensive hypermasculinity. This paradigm springs from the same philosophical roots as the "essentialist" or "nativist" view of sex roles—the notion

that (in the case of men) there is a clear masculine "essence" that is historically invariant.

In contrast, the Gender Role Strain Paradigm proposes that contemporary gender roles are contradictory and inconsistent; that the proportion of persons who violate gender roles is high; that violation of gender roles leads to condemnation and negative psychological consequences; that actual or imagined violation of gender roles leads people to overconform to them; that violating gender roles has more severe consequences for males than for females; and that certain prescribed gender-role traits (such as male aggression) are often dysfunctional. In this paradigm, appropriate gender roles are determined by the prevailing gender ideology (which is operationally defined by gender-role stereotypes and norms) and are imposed on the developing child by parents, teachers, and peers—the cultural transmitters who subscribe to the prevailing gender ideology. As noted above, this paradigm springs from the same philosophical roots as social constructionism—the perspective that notions of "masculinity" and femininity" are relational, socially constructed, and subject to change.

Thompson and Pleck (1995) proposed the term "masculinity ideology" to characterize the core construct in the corpus of research assessing attitudes toward men and male roles. Masculinity, or gender, ideology is a very different construct from the older notion of gender orientation. Gender orientation arises out of the Identity Paradigm, and presumes that masculinity is rooted in actual differences between men and women. This approach has attempted to assess the personality *traits* more often associated with men than women, using such instruments as the Bem Sex Role Inventory and Spence's Personal Attributes Questionnaire. In contrast, studies of masculinity ideology take a *normative* approach, in which masculinity is viewed as a socially constructed gender ideal for men. Whereas the masculine male in the orientation/trait approach is one who *possesses* particular personality traits, the traditional male in the ideology/normative approach is one who endorses the ideology that men *should* have sex-specific characteristics (and women should not). Empirical evidence supports the notion that gender orientation and gender ideologies are independent and have different correlates.

The Strain Paradigm asserts that there is no single standard for masculinity, nor is there an unvarying masculinity ideology. Rather, because masculinity is a social construction, ideals of manhood may differ for men of different social classes, races, ethnic groups, sexual orientations, life stages, and historical eras. We therefore prefer to speak of masculinity ideologies.

Despite the diversity in masculinity ideology in the contemporary United States, there is a *particular* constellation of standards that have held sway over large sections of the population. It is common to refer to this as "traditional" masculinity ideology, because it was the dominant view of the male role prior to the deconstruction of gender that took place beginning in the 1970s.

Traditional masculinity ideology is thought to be a multidimensional construct. Brannon (1976) identified four components of traditional masculinity ideology: that men should not be feminine ("no sissy stuff"); that men should strive to be respected for successful achievement ("the big wheel"); that men should never show weakness ("the sturdy oak")'; and that men should seek adventure and risk, even accepting violence if necessary ("give 'em hell"). More recently, the Male Role Norms Inventory (MRNI) defined traditional masculinity ideology in terms of seven dimensions: (1) the requirement to avoid all things feminine; (2) the injunction to restrict one's emotional life; (3) the emphasis on toughness and aggression; (4) the injunction to be self-reliant; (5) the emphasis on achieving status above all else; (6) nonrelational, objectifying attitudes toward sexuality; and (7) fear and hatred of homosexuals.

Pleck's formulation of the Gender Role Strain stimulated research on three varieties of male gender-role strain, which he termed "discrepancy strain," "dysfunction strain," and "trauma strain." Discrepancy strain results when one fails to live up to one's internalized manhood ideal, which, among contemporary adult males, is often a close approximation of the traditional code. Dysfunction strain results even when one fulfills the requirements of the male code, because many of the characteristics viewed as desirable in men can have negative side effects on the men themselves and on those close to them. The concept of trauma strain has been applied to certain groups of men whose experiences with gender-role strain are thought to be particularly harsh, such as professional athletes, war veterans, survivors of child abuse, men of color, and gay and bisexual men. But above and beyond the recognition that certain classes of men may experience trauma strain, a perspective on the male role-socialization process has emerged that views socialization under traditional masculinity ideology as *inherently* traumatic. The traumatic aspects are seen most clearly in the emotion-socialization process, through which boys' natural emotional expressivity is suppressed and channeled.

Ronald F. Levant

See also Gender-Role Conflict; Gender-Role Conformity

Further Reading:
Brod, Harry. 1987. *The Making of the Masculinities: The New Men's Studies.* Boston: Unwin Hyman.
David, Deborah, and Robert Brannon, eds. 1976. *The Forty-Nine Percent Majority: The Male Sex Role.* Reading, MA: Addison-Wesley.
Gilmore, David D. 1990. *Manhood in the Making: Cultural Concepts of Masculinity.* New Haven, CT: Yale University Press.
Levant, Ronald F., and Gini Kopecky. 1995. *Masculinity Reconstructed.* New York: Dutton.
Levant, Ronald F., and William S. Pollack, eds. 1995. *A New Psychology of Men.* New York: Basic Books.
Pleck, Joseph H. 1981. *The Myth of Masculinity.* Cambridge, MA: MIT Press.
———. 1995. "The Gender Role Strain Paradigm: An Update." in *A New Psychology of Men.* Edited by Ronald F. Levant and William S. Pollack. New York: Basic Books.

Thompson, Edward H., and Joseph H. Pleck. 1995. "Masculinity Ideology: A Review of Research Instrumentation on Men and Masculinities." Pp. 11–32 in *A New Psychology of Men*. Edited by Ronald F. Levant and William S. Pollack. New York: Basic Books.

George Gordon, Lord Byron

See Byron, George Gordon

GI Joe

Introduced by Hasbro in 1964, the GI Joe doll marked a groundbreaking addition to the toy industry. The twelve-inch military action figure possessed the first fully articulated body, with twenty-one moving parts that allowed the toy to bend at the joints and be manipulated into various lifelike positions (Miller 1998). Although this was an important development for the toy industry, GI Joe was even more noteworthy because it was the first mass-produced doll intended for boys. Mattel's Ken doll was already on the market, but Ken was marketed as a boyfriend for the already successful Barbie doll. In other words, Ken was a male doll for female children. As a male doll for male children, GI Joe was considered a marketing triumph.

During the toy's conception and development, Hasbro was extremely concerned that the toy would be perceived as feminine and actively sought to counter this potential pitfall. The members of the development team were repeatedly reminded that GI Joe was "a moveable fighting man" and were forbidden to use the word *doll*. It was in this context that the phrase *action figure* was coined (Michlig 1998). In addition to utilizing masculine language to describe it, the doll was physically designed to showcase masculine traits. GI Joe was created with broader shoulders and a fuller chest than Mattel's Ken doll, his face was given a more chiseled appearance, and he bore a scar on one cheek. Unlike the Barbie doll, which was marketed without a prescribed occupation (essentially as a toy woman), GI Joe was marketed as a toy soldier. The doll's hypermasculine occupation was central to his branding. The accessories were miniature replicas of regulation military garments, weapons, and gear. In furthering the heroic imagery, Hasbro also falsely claimed that GI Joe's face was a composite design based on the faces of twenty Medal of Honor winners (Miller 1998).

When GI Joe was a freshman on the market, it more than quadrupled the first-year sales of Mattel's Barbie doll, and second-year sales further skyrocketed, bringing Hasbro a remarkable $23 million in 1965 (Michlig 1998; Miller 1998). The success was dampened significantly in the years that followed as a result of the growing antiwar sentiments sparked by the Vietnam War and the efforts of protest groups such as Parents for Responsibility in the Toy Industry, which specifically targeted military toys. The changing social climate led Hasbro to shift the focus of the line from militarism to adventure, with scuba gear and astronaut suits replacing the majority of weapons. The shift in focus was the first in a series of myriad adaptations that kept GI Joe competitive in the market. Some of the many changes included the introduction of GI Joe's "kung fu grip" when martial arts rose in popularity during the early 1970s and the evolution of a much smaller (three-and-three-quarter-inch) action figure inspired by the success of the *Star Wars* toys. Though the line disappeared briefly in the late 1970s, it was flourishing again by the early 1980s and remains in production into the 2000s, nearly forty years after its introduction, as a popular collector's item in its original twelve-inch form (Michlig 1998).

Though GI Joe has been a commercial success and one of the most recognizable pop culture icons in postwar America, the toy has not been without controversy. GI Joe has been perceived by many as a negative role model for boys. Since its inception, the line of toys has been criticized for glorifying war as well as promoting violence and aggression in boys. More recently, GI Joe has been challenged for presenting an unrealistic ideal of male muscularity. Critics point to the dramatic transformations that have taken place in GI Joe's physical appearance. Over the years, in addition to adding gimmicky features such as lifelike hair and an "atomic" eye, the stature of the doll has grown dramatically. While the original GI Joe was scaled to human proportions, newer versions of the doll have become increasingly muscular and more sharply defined. Psychiatrist Harrison Pope made headlines in 1998 when he studied the 1997 Extreme GI Joe, finding that if the toy were a human being, his biceps would measure 26 inches in circumference, while the average male bicep circumference measures approximately 12.5 inches when flexed. Critics contend that unrealistic images of muscularity may prompt young men to develop eating disorders and turn to anabolic steroids in an effort to approximate the ideal (Goldstein 2001).

Sarah Sobieraj

Further Reading:

Goldstein, Joshua S. 2001. *War and Gender: How Gender Shapes the War System and Vice Versa.* Cambridge, UK: Cambridge University Press.

Michlig, John. 1998. *GI Joe: The Complete Story of America's Favorite Man of Action.* San Francisco: Chronicle Books.

Miller, Wayne G. 1998. *Toy Wars.* New York: Times Books.

Pope, Harrison G., Roberto Olivardia, Amanda Gruber, and John Borowiecki. 1999. "Evolving Ideals of Male Body Image as Seen through Action Toys." *International Journal of Eating Disorders* 26: 65–72.

"Glass Ceiling"

A term that describes the barriers to women's upward mobility in organizations, the *glass ceiling* consists of "those artificial barriers, based on attitudinal or organizational bias, that prevent qualified individuals from advancing upward within their organization into management level positions" (Martin 1991, 1).

The glass ceiling keeps women from being promoted equally with men. Women in the United States hold only 7 percent of all corporate board seats. Between 95 percent and 97 percent of all senior managers are men. Of the 4,012 highest paid directors, officers or corporate CEOs in America, only 19— less and one-half of 1 percent—are women. And the glass ceiling's effects are multiplied when race is brought into the equation. In 1970, between 1 percent and 3 percent of all senior management positions in all Fortune 500 companies were held by women and minorities; in 1990, only 5 percent were held by women and minorities. In 1988, 72 percent of all managers in companies with more than 100 employees were white men; 23 percent were white women; 3 percent were black men; and 2 percent were black women.

The glass ceiling occurs under a variety of circumstances. Corporate management may be either unable or unwilling to establish policies and practices that are effective mechanisms to promote workplace diversity. The company may not have adequate job evaluation criteria that allow for determining comparable worth of tasks, or they may rely on traditional gender stereotypes in evaluation. Limited family-friendly workplace policies also inhibit women's ability to rise.

Perhaps the most important element that reinforces the glass ceiling is the informal effort by men to restore or retain the all-male atmosphere of the corporate hierarchy. Equal opportunities for advancement would disrupt the casual friendliness and informality of the homosocial world at the top—the fact that those with whom one interacts share similar basic values and assumptions. "What's important is comfort, chemistry, relationships and collaborations," one manager explained. "That's what makes a shop work. When we find minorities and women who think like we do, we snatch them up" (*Good for Business* 1995). One British study of female MBAs, for example, found that by far the "most significant" and "most resistant" barrier to women's advancement was the "'men's club' network" (Simpson 1996, 199).

Perhaps the most celebrated case involving a corporate glass ceiling was the 1989

Supreme Court decision in *Hopkins v. Price Waterhouse.* Ann Hopkins was denied promotion to partnership in one of the nation's largest and most prestigious accounting firms. Although she had brought more business into the company than any of the men who were promoted, she was perceived as abrasive and demanding. Opponents of her promotion said she was "macho" and that she "overcompensated for being a woman" and that she would benefit from "a course at charm school." One of her supporters told her that she might make partner if she could learn to "walk more femininely, talk more femininely, dress more femininely, wear makeup, have her hair styled, and wear jewelry" (*Hopkins v. Price Waterhouse*). The Court awarded her $400,000 in back pay and fees, and required that she be promoted to partner.

The *Hopkins* case provides a perfect illustration of the ways in which traditional gender stereotypes also impede women's progress. Had Ms. Hopkins *been* more traditionally feminine, she would never have been the aggressive and ambitious success that she became. Thus, either way, women lose. Either they are too aggressive, in which case they are seen as mannish, "ball-busting bitches," or they are too ladylike, and as a result are passed over as being too passive, sweet, and not ambitious enough.

In 1991 Congress passed the Civil Rights Act, which established a Glass Ceiling Commission, the goal of which was to eliminate "artificial barriers based on attitudinal or organizational bias." These barriers included relying on word of mouth to fill upper-level positions (the "old boys' network") and suggested that a system of monetary compensations be instituted for word-of-mouth referrals of qualified women and minorities. Some companies have already instituted their own policies designed to enable women to break through the glass ceiling in all three areas where women experience it—hiring, promotion, and retention. These tend to be among the more forward-looking companies.

The glass ceiling has different impacts on men, depending upon one's political persuasion. Writer Warren Farrell (1993) argues that all the attention to the ways women are held back from promotion by the glass ceiling hides the fact that it is *men* who are the victims of sex discrimination in the workplace. Men, Farrell argues, are the victims of the "glass cellar"—stuck in the most hazardous and dangerous occupations. In fact, Farrell argues, of the 250 occupations ranked by the *Jobs Related Almanac,* the 25 worst jobs (such as truck driver, roofer, boilermaker, construction worker, welder, and football player) were almost all male. Over 90 percent of all occupational deaths happen to men. All the hazardous occupations are virtually all male—including firefighting (99 percent), logging (98 percent), trucking (98 percent), and construction (97 percent)—while the "safest" occupations are those held by women, including secretary (99 percent female) and receptionist (97 percent) (Farrell 1993).

It is true that many of the jobs that men take *are* hazardous—and made more so unnecessarily by an ideology of masculinity that demands that men remain stoic and uncomplaining in the face of danger. Thus, on dangerous construction sites or offshore oil rigs, men frequently shun safety precautions, such as safety helmets, as suitable, perhaps, for sissies or wimps, but not for "real" men. But the jobs that are the most exclusively male are also those that have fought most fiercely the entry of women. And those jobs are also far better paid than the jobs that are almost exclusively female. For example, the nation's fire departments have been especially resistant to women joining their "fraternal order," doing so only under court order and often "welcoming" women with a significant amount of harassment. It is odd to blame women for not entering those occupations from which they have been excluded by men's resistance.

Michael Kimmel

Note: Portions of this entry were adapted from Michael Kimmel, The Gendered Society, *New York: Oxford University Press, 2000.*

See also "Glass Escalator"; Pay Gap
Further Reading:
Farrell, Warren. 1993. *The Myth of Male Power.* New York: Simon & Schuster.

Good for Business: Making Full Use of the Nation's Human Capital. 1995. Washington, DC: U.S. Government Printing Office.

Martin, Lynn. 1991. *A Report on the Glass Ceiling Initiative.* Washington, DC: U.S. Department of Labor.

Meyerson, Debra E., and Joyce K. Fletcher. 2000. "A Modest Manifesto for Shattering the Glass Ceiling." *Harvard Business Review* (January/February).

Simpson, Ruth. 1996. "Does an MBA Help Women? Career Benefits of the MBA." *Gender, Work and Organization* 3, no. 2: 196–204.

"Glass Escalator"

The "glass escalator" is a phrase coined by sociologist Christine Williams to describe what happens to men who enter predominantly female occupations. The term is meant to be contrasted with the "glass ceiling" by which women's mobility is limited. The glass escalator refers to men's enhanced mobility within these female-dominated groups. Men entering mostly female occupations don't bump up against a glass ceiling; they ride the "glass escalator," and have a much easier time being promoted than even women do.

Williams (1992) conducted interviews with seventy-six men and twenty-three women in four occupations—nursing, librarianship, elementary education, and social work. She found that men experienced positive discrimination when entering those fields; several people noted a clear preference for hiring men. And men were promoted to managerial positions more rapidly and frequently, thus making men overrepresented in the managerial ranks. Men who do women's work, it appears, may earn less than men who work in predominantly male occupations, but they earn more and are promoted faster than women in the same occupation.

Men did experience some negative effects, especially in their dealings with the public. For example, male nurses face a common stereotype that they are gay. Male librarians faced images of themselves as "wimpy" and asexual; male social workers were seen as "feminine" or "passive." One male librarian found that he had difficulty establishing enough credibility so that the public would accept him as the children's "storyteller." Ironically, though, Williams found that these negative stereotypes of men doing "women's work" actually added to the glass escalator effect "by pressuring men to move *out* of the most female-identified areas, and *up* to those regarded as more legitimate and prestigious for men" (Williams 1995, 296).

Williams concluded that men "take their gender privilege with them when they enter predominantly female occupations: this translates as an advantage in spite of their numerical rarity" (1995, 296). Men, it seems, win either way. When women are tokens, men retain their numerical superiority and are able to maintain their gender privilege by restricting a woman's entry, promotion, and experiences in the workplace. When men are tokens, they are welcomed into the profession, and use their gender privilege to rise quickly in the hierarchy. "Regardless of the problems that might exist," writes Alfred Kadushin (1976), "it is clear and undeniable that there is a considerable advantage in being a member of the male minority in any female profession" (441).

Michael Kimmel

See also "Glass Ceiling"
Further Reading:
Kadushin, Alfred. 1976. "Men in a Woman's Profession." *Social Work* 21: 441.

Williams, Christine. 1992. "The Glass Escalator: Hidden Advantages for Men in the 'Female' Professions." *Social Problems* 39, no. 3: 253–267.

———. 1995. *Still a Man's World: Men Who Do 'Women's Work.'* Berkeley, CA: University of California Press.

God

The word *God* refers to a symbol foundational to the faiths of Judaism, Christianity, and Islam and central to much of Western culture. This symbol epitomizes core values that provide for social identity and cohesion, psychological stability, and scientific comprehensibility. As such, notions of God are intricately and symbiotically related to ideas about the nature of human beings, as well as to ways their relations ought to be ordered. Consequently, ideas about God often reflect anxieties about social order and one's place in that order.

The impact of critical gender studies, generally, and men's studies, specifically, on ideas about God is best seen in relation to three prevalent patterns by which the relations among God, human nature, and social order have been construed. Those patterns are generally referred to as classical theism, pantheism, and panentheism.

Traditionally, classical theism, most fully developed by medieval and early modern theologians with reference to classical metaphysics, asserts a God that is one (contra polytheism) and is not identified with the world (contra pantheism). As the Supreme Being, this God is understood to be the creator and ruler of the cosmos. Completely transcendent of, or other than, all other finite, contingent, corporeal, temporal, mutable, passible, compound, corruptible, partially knowing, weak created things, God's attributes are understood to be, then, the opposite. "He" is infinite, self-existent, incorporeal, eternal, immutable, impassible, simple, perfect, omniscient, and omnipotent. In the divine-human relation, the emphasis is on the priority of "His" agency over humanity's. The invariable reference to this God with exclusively masculine pronouns is not accidental. In Judaism, Christianity, and Islam, this notion is modeled on the pattern of an absolute monarch, from the medieval period on.

These notions of God and of the divine-human relation have shaped cultural constructions of masculinity and femininity. Dominant masculine norms require men to simulate the pretense of omniscient, dispassionate, unrelated, sovereign, divine agency, while women are cast into the dependent, deficient, accommodating human role. Socially, then, these conceptions rationalize and legitimate patriarchal social arrangements that privilege men's agency over women's. They are also employed to legitimate the privilege of members of economically, culturally, religiously, and sexually dominant groups over members of nondominant groups. In other words, the assertion of God's sovereignty often masks that of members of dominant social groups.

Feminists have critiqued the oppressive uses to which this notion of God has been put, including the polarization of male and female sex roles, the detrimental effects those definitions have on women, and the legitimation of male supremacy, as well as that of other dominant social groups. Antisexist men's studies scholars have followed those analyses and extended them by exploring the deleterious effects on men of various social locations.

On the other end of the spectrum is pantheism ("God is all") or atheism ("God is not at all"). The first stresses the immanence of God, meaning that God and the world are virtually identical, so that the divine essence is the essence of the world. Against the emphasis in classical theism on the agency of God against human agency, pantheism might be seen as an attempt to dignify human agency and history. However, some feminists have criticized this approach, because it has the effect of rendering sacred prevailing, patriarchal arrangements and does not provide a sufficient theoretical basis for human freedom to resist and overturn those arrangements. Certain expressions of atheism function as assertions of human agency and freedom over claims of divine agency that simply mask that of ruling elites. From some feminist and men's studies perspectives, the problem with an atheistic "will to power" is the lack of a notion of underlying unity and, therefore, an affirmation of each as a necessary constitutive part of the whole of reality. That is, it reinforces the notion of an isolated masculine self that dominates whomever it can.

Feminist and men's studies scholars concerned about gender, ecological, and other relations of justice, tend toward the third notion of God: panentheism. *Panentheism* is "[t]he belief that the Being of God includes and penetrates the whole universe, so that every part of it exists in Him, but (as against pantheism) that this Being is more than, and is not exhausted by, the universe" (*Oxford Dictionary of the Christian Church*). The panentheistic notion involves both transcendence and immanence, distinction and unity. In the divine-human relation, God neither subsumes the human (pantheism) nor is subsumed by the human (atheism). Neither does God affect humanity without being affected (classical theism). Rather, the panentheistic model entails mutual influence between the divine and human, although ideas about the extent of that influence vary. For many, working within Jewish, Christian, and Muslim contexts, as well as those exploring various Goddess traditions, panentheistic models of God provide resources that engender respect for diversity and the sovereignty of each human person and for a fundamental vision of unity in which each is necessary for the well-being of the whole. It is a model that affirms a "relational autonomy" within the divine life itself, between God and humanity, among human beings, and between human beings and nonhuman forms of life.

Men's studies scholars have explored such issues as the ways exclusively masculine language and images of God are problematic for men; how more inclusive images might be recovered from dominant religious traditions, as well as nondominant religious traditions, including Goddess traditions; and how more holistic male images might be related to stronger female images.

Future work will most likely include investigations of the relation between notions of God and men as they relate to issues of parenting, global economic justice, ecology, and religious and cultural cooperation.

Stephen Boyd

See also Religion

Further Reading:

Boyd, Stephen, W. Merle Longwood, and Mark Muesse, eds. 1996. *Redeeming Men: Religion and Masculinities*. Louisville, KY: Westminster / John Knox.

Eilberg-Schwartz, Howard. 1994. *God's Phallus*. Boston: Beacon Press.

Johnson, Elizabeth. 1994. *She Who Is: The Mystery of God in Feminist Theological Discourse*. New York: Crossroad.

Gilkey, Langdon. 1992. "God." In *A Handbook of Christian Theology*. Edited by Don Musser. Nashville, TN: Abingdon.

Ramshaw, Gail. 1995. *God beyond Gender*. Minneapolis, MN: Fortress.

Godard, Jean-Luc (1930–)

Jean-Luc Godard ranks among the filmmakers about whom there are the greatest number of books written. Born in Paris in 1930, Jean-Luc Godard began as a film critic for the famous magazine *Les Cahiers du cinéma,* thanks to his friend François Truffaut who introduced him and also gave Godard the film script for his first feature film, *A Bout de Souffle* (*Breathless*) (1960), one of the key movies from the French New Wave (*Nouvelle Vague*).

Godard's early rebellious movies were influenced by American B-movies (Godard dedicated his *A Bout de Souffle* to the directors of an American firm, Monogram Pictures). Godard admired the films of Nicholas Ray, Orson Welles, and Fritz Lang. He tried to imitate them, but something very different emerged in *A Bout de Souffle, Le Petit Soldat* (1960), *Bande à part* (*Band of Outsiders*) (1964), and *Made in USA* (1966).

Many Godard movies deal with the couple, from *A Bout de Souffle* through *Éloge de l'amour* (2001). The man is often despised by the woman he loves: In *A Bout de Souffle*, Patricia (Jean Seberg) betrays Michel, her lover. In *Le Mépris* (*Contempt*) (1963), Camille (Brigitte Bardot) feels contempt for her husband (Michel Piccoli). In *Masculine-Feminine* (1966), Paul (Jean-Pierre Léaud) is weak and can't change the society he doesn't accept; his girlfriend Madeleine is opportunistic, a career woman who wants to become a pop singer. At the end of *Weekend* (1967), the widow played by Mireille Darc eats a human rib that might be her late husband's.

The man's gaze through a woman's body is already present in the unfinished short film shot in *Le Mépris* (*Contempt*) (1963). The camera follows parts of a woman's naked body in *British Sounds* (1969) while we hear simultaneously feminist slogans. Codirected with Anne-Marie Miéville, the provocative *Numéro Deux* (1975) shows almost pornographic images of ordinary people seen naked. Female genuine beauty is also explored in *Passion* (1981) and *Je Vous Salue Marie* (1983). In the collective film *Aria* (1987), Godard still criticizes the standard canons of male and female beauty.

Fatherhood is almost inconceivable in Godard's films. In *Une femme est une femme* (1961), the woman wants a child from her boyfriend, who always refuses. In *A Married Woman* (1964), the young boy is just a prop to show that the couple has a child they must take care of. In the beginning of *Pierrot le Fou* (1965), Anna Karina is a babysitter, but children don't play a major role here. In *Weekend*, the young boy disguised as an Indian is impossible and noisy. An exception is the four-hour series, *France Tour Détour: Deux Enfants* (1978), that includes two ten-year-old characters, but still depicts no parents or families. A family with two children appears in *Numéro Deux* (1975).

Men are immature in many films written by Godard. In *Les Carabiniers* (1963), men want to go to war for material reasons and the will to dominate. In *Pierrot le Fou*, Ferdinand can't find his own identity; he kills himself, as does Paul in *Masculine-Feminine*.

Women are badly treated in many Godard's movies. Some seem to choose prostitution, always portrayed as a normal job, as in *Vivre sa vie* (*My Life to Live*) (1962), *Alphaville* (1965), *Deux ou trois choses que je sais d'elle* (*Two or Three Things I Know about Her*) (1967), and *Sauve qui peut la vie* (1979). In Godard's view, female prostitution is seen as a symbol of capitalist commerce. Women are forced to undress by armed men in *Les Carabiniers* (1963). White women are savagely killed by some members of the Black Power movement in *One + One* (a.k.a. *Sympathy for the Devil*) (1970). Godard overtly criticizes the actress Jane Fonda in his *Letter to Jane* (1972), a one-hour film. Godard was frequently accused of misogyny.

Yves Laberge

Further Reading:
Gauthier, Guy, ed. 2002. *Flash-back Sur la Nouvelle Vague,* Paris: Corlet, *CinémAction,* No 104.

Graham, Sylvester (1795–1851)

Sylvester Graham was a Presbyterian minister who preached on temperance and became one of the nation's leading health reformers and a pioneer in the cereal and food business. Graham developed Graham Flour and the Graham Cracker as an antidote to health problems of American men in the middle of the nineteenth century.

In his book, *A Lecture to Young Men* (1834), and in his magazine, *Graham Journal of Health and Longevity,* Graham laid out an elaborate plan for dietary and behavioral reforms that would allow men to live secure, upright, and productive lives. Sexual desire, Graham believed, "disturbs and disorders all the functions of the system" (39), and so Graham offered a set of bodily prescriptions for physical and sexual temperance. He advocated a diet of farinaceous foods, properly prepared, like "good bread, made of coarsely ground, unbolted wheat, or rye-meal, and hominy, made of cracked wheat, or rye, or Indian corn" (73). Young men were to eat small suppers and no animal meat whatever, because Graham was convinced that one is more susceptible to sin if one eats another's flesh. (Twice, Graham was attacked by a mob of Boston butchers who thought he was ruining their business.)

Graham also advocated strenuous exercise for boys and men, and he believed that socializing boys to bad habits of "luxury, indolence, voluptuousness, and sensuality" would lead them to surrender their "nobleness, dignity, honor and manhood" (34).

Most important, boys and men were to avoid sex. He counseled men to have sex with their wives no more than once a month, and warned boys of the dangers of masturbation in terms that would make anyone wince; masturbation would make one into a

> wretched transgressor [who] sinks into a miserable fatuity, and finally becomes a confirmed and degraded idiot, whose deeply sunken and vacant, glossy eye, and livid shriveled countenance, and ulcerous, toothless gums, and fetid breath, and feeble, broken voice, and emaciated and dwarfish and crooked body, and almost hairless head—covered perhaps with suppurating blisters and running sores—denote a premature old age! A blighted body—and a ruined soul! (25)

Michael Kimmel

See also Kellogg, J. H.; Masturbation
Further Reading:
Graham, Sylvester. 1834. *A Lecture to Young Men.* Providence, RI: Weeden and Cory.

The Great Gatsby

See Fitzgerald, F. Scott; Gatsby, Jay

Grey, Zane (1872–1939)

Zane Grey was among the greatest storytellers and the most successful proselytizers for the American West. Through his dozens of stories, novels, magazines, and films, Grey's westerns became a staple for American boys during the twentieth century.

Film poster for Zane Grey's Wagon Wheels *(Library of Congress)*

Born in Zanesville, Ohio, in 1872, Grey was a semiprofessional baseball player and a half-hearted dentist in his younger days. (He had studied dentistry at the University of Pennsylvania, which he attended on a baseball scholarship.) "All boys love baseball," he famously said. "If they don't, they're not real boys" (Grey 1909, 1). But it was as a writer, memorializing the fast-fading West that Grey excelled.

His first breakthrough success came with *Heritage of the Desert* (1910), and nearly a novel a year followed. Perhaps his most famous book was *Riders of the Purple Sage* (1912), a title that was even appropriated by a spin-off band of the Grateful Dead in the late 1960s. In that story, the hero, Bern Venters, represents the men of the nineteenth century, who "have been enfeebled by the doctrines of a feminized Christianity." As the novel opens, Jane Witherspoon has even taken away his guns. Through his transformation in the novel, "American men are taking their manhood back from the Christian women who have been holding it in thrall" (cited in Tompkins 1992, 167).

In all, Grey wrote sixty western novels, as well as books about fishing, juvenile biographies, and baseball. "Harness the caveman—yes!" Grey wrote in 1924, "but do not kill him. Something of the wild and primitive should remain instinctive in the human race" (cited in Tompkins 1992, 33).

An avid fisherman and hunter, Grey explored some of the world's most renowned fishing spots and wrote constantly until his death in 1939. His works are little read today, less because they celebrate an anachronistic western past than because his portrayals of Native Americans in particular are less than flattering.

Michael Kimmel

See also Wister, Owen

Further Reading:
Grey, Zane. 1909. "Inside Baseball." *Baseball* 3, no. 4.
———. 1912. *Riders of the Purple Sage*. New York: Harper Brothers.
Jackson, Carleton. 1989. *Zane Grey*. New York: Twayne Publishers.
May, Stephen. 1997. *Zane Grey: Romancing the West*. Athens, OH: Ohio University Press.
Tompkins, Jane. 1992. *West of Everything*. New York: Oxford University Press.

Grooms

Groom, short for *bridegroom,* a term that entered the English language in the eleventh century, refers to the male role in marriage customs from betrothal until completion of the wedding rituals. Though commonly referring only to heterosexuals, "groom" can also apply to homosexual (gay *and* lesbian) and transgendered relationships and rites. Because roughly 2.33 million males in the United States alone get legally married each year (NCHS 2002), this term applies to a significant portion of the adult population. The groom role requires much learning about and performing of gender roles, involves gaining gendered privileges and responsibilities, and initiates complex social and economic relationships. As yet, however, little academic attention has focused on this premarital role (whereas research on men *within* marriage is plentiful; see Nock 1998).

Within academia, cross-cultural and anthropological work demonstrates the complexity and diversity of grooms' responsibilities and practices, presently and historically, in diverse regions, from Scotland (Charsley 1991) to Korea (Kendall 1996). Though such research shows how religion, race, ethnicity, region, and class may shape the meanings and practices of grooms, wedding customs involve similar events cross-culturally. Events typically begin with betrothal, whether engagement after courting or through arrangement or matchmaking. Betrothal usually initiates the economic relationship between the couple or their families, involving the giving of rings, gifts, or promises of future exchange. Traditionally, this exchange includes a dowry in which property transfers from the bride's family to the groom's, though in some cultures (China and many Muslim countries) the groom's family gives payment to the bride's. In most cultures, following betrothal, the whole family or the bride's father symbolically or literally "gives" the bride to the groom (though in Mohawk ceremonies mothers give both to the other); thus, the husbands' dominance over wives is symbolically enacted and sometimes legally reinforced. Most marriage and social conventions mark the bride (and sometimes the groom) as married, signaling her property status or unavailability to other men (or women). This may entail wearing wedding rings or necklaces (as in Tamil Hindu ceremonies), displaying forehead marks (like the "Tilak" in Hindu marriages), or linguistically marking women by changing or combining their surnames or addressing them with differing titles or pronouns (e.g., "Mrs." versus "Ms."). Other events involving the groom may include rite of passage ceremonies (like capping rituals in China), the display of financial means (through gifts or providing a feast), and legal or contractual rites (signing wedding licenses or writing letters promising gifts [China]). All of these proceedings function, in varying degrees, to socialize into, symbolize, or enact particular cultural beliefs and practices surrounding gender and labor divisions.

The groom's role also initiates numerous relationships with the larger economy and politics. The role is highly consumer oriented within most industrialized societies, with grooms responsible for providing rings, gifts, and special clothing for the wedding ceremony. Contributing to the wedding industry in this way, some argue, potentially makes the groom complicit (knowingly or not) in exploitative activities, such as the trade in "blood" diamonds from warring nations and the replication of restrictive gender roles (Ingraham 1999). Grooms similarly enter into complex relationships with the state through marriage, including legal associations (like marriage licenses and tacit agreement to handle divorce through courts) and accepting privileges available only to (by U.S. law, heterosexual) married couples (like hospital visitation rights and the ability to refuse testifying against spouses). Given such complex relationships, the impact of the groom's role on men and those around them is prodigious.

The groom role requires further systematic study. For instance, many have examined women's socialization into roles as brides and wives, but little understanding exists of such socialization for males. Chrys Ingraham (1999), for example, claims: "Women are taught from early childhood to plan for 'the happiest day of their lives.' Men are taught, by the *absence* of such socializing mechanisms, that their work is 'other' than that" (81; emphasis added). In actuality, socialization for the groom's work is not "absent," but requires much learning across the lifespan, from childhood through postwedding reflection (Weaver-Hightower 2002). Implicated in this learning are numerous media sources

(like television shows, literacy materials, and movies with weddings as the ultimate culmination), social relationships (such as family modeling of marital interaction or peer pressure to "settle down" or not), and institutions (like schools and curriculum, state-sponsored "encouragement" of marriage, and religious doctrine). Future research might examine these modes and locations of socialization as well as the dividends of getting married for grooms, from perspectives as diverse as language use, health effects, interfamily relationships, or feminist studies of dominance. Future research might also suggest ways to intervene in socialization and institutional structures to eventually produce more equitable, satisfying, and stable marital relationships for both men and women of various sexual orientations.

Marcus Weaver-Hightower

Further Reading:

Charsley, Simon R. 1991. *Rites of Marrying: The Wedding Industry in Scotland.* Manchester, UK: Manchester University Press.

Henslin, James M. 1989. *Marriage and Family in a Changing Society.* 3d ed. New York: Free Press.

Ingraham, Chrys. 1999. *White Weddings: Romancing Heterosexuality in Popular Culture.* New York: Routledge.

Kendall, Laurel. 1996. *Getting Married in Korea: Of Gender, Morality, and Modernity.* Berkeley, CA: University of California Press.

National Center for Health Statistics (NCHS). 2002. "Births, Marriages, Divorces, and Deaths: Provisional Data for 2001." *National Vital Statistics Reports* 50, no. 14: 1–2.

Nock, Steven L. 1998. *Marriage in Men's Lives.* New York: Oxford University Press.

Weaver-Hightower, Marcus B. 2002. "The Truth about Grooms (Or, How to Tell Those Tuxedoed Men Apart)." Pp. 201–217 in *The Foreign Self: Truth Telling as Educational Inquiry.* Edited by Francois V. Tochon. Madison, WI: Atwood Publishing.

Guns

From the first settling of the American colonies, guns became inseparable from masculinity. Plymouth Colony passed laws requiring white men, particularly Scotch and Irish immigrants, to carry firearms and participate in military training. Conversely, lawmakers were quick to deny firearms to Native Americans and African American slaves. Gun ownership and shooting aptitude were standards of frontier life. Using long rifles as part of frontier subsistence, men hunted, trapped, and killed game, thus providing for themselves and their families. Men fulfilled their roles as protectors of wives, children, and property by using firearms defensively against wild game, Native Americans, and the British during the American Revolution. Owning a long rifle bestowed upon men the ability to protect their families when the colony, state, or country could not. Thus entrenched with one another, masculinity and firearms found positions within the traditions of militarism, patriotism, and nationalism.

Presenting opportunities for male bonding since colonial times, firearms cemented father-son, as well as other, paternal relationships. Placing boys at the threshold of manhood, game hunting conferred responsibility, maturity, and autonomy, working as a rite of passage and preparing them for their eventual role as protector and provider. Once skilled in firearms use, a young man often served as head of the household during his father's absence, whether temporary or permanent. Creating a common interest, gunmanship strengthened male relationships with siblings, cousins, uncles, and grandfathers during the precarious age of adolescence—thus reinforcing masculinity. Though limited, this model still thrives in rural areas where hunter's education is part of the public school curriculum.

An early custom, dueling was imported to America from England and Europe where men had defended their honor employing various weapons one on one since the Middle Ages. By the early nineteenth century, dueling was an American feature of the upper class. Elaborate codes evolved that governed procedures and rules for conducting duels.

Using large-caliber, smoothbore flintlock pistols, men preserved their honor and demanded satisfaction from one other for insults to their manhood as well as to any lady under their care or protection. To a great extent, the essence of dueling was male bravado as the likelihood of either man dying was remote; flintlocks often misfired and accuracy was difficult for even the most skilled of shooters. Much as criminals evade gun control laws of today, men of earlier centuries ignored or eluded laws against dueling. Relying upon their proficiency with weapons, men gained public admiration for winning duels, while unlucky opponents were denounced for their cowardice upon their failure to meet the challenge. Disputes between common men—the farmers and merchants—were settled with their fists.

Boys are innately interested in firearms whether they live in a gun-owning family or not. Playing cowboys and Indians or war is commonplace in boys' culture. When toy guns are not available, their imaginations take over, making rifles from sticks or pistols from their hands. Popular Christmas gifts in the past, BB guns are rarities in the tense sociopolitical climate of early twenty-first-century America. Exposed to increasing levels of violence and aggression, boys gain virtual hunting and shooting skills via video and computer games, thus removing the father from his role in masculine socialization.

Although boys easily find inspiration for violence in videogames, action movies and musical genres promote and at times demand gunplay and gun ownership as routes to manhood. However, in many cultures initiation rites for boys were historically violent in nature. As communities and families have dissolved, gangs fulfill traditional roles of masculine socialization, especially in regard to gun ownership. Violence permeates each member's entry and survival within the gang. Gangs enact ritualized group activities that unify men's lives.

Though gangs include men of all ethnic backgrounds, African American men regain both racial and masculine empowerment via gun ownership. And while there is a high correlation between the high murder rate and firearms use in the United States, African American men are more likely to be victims. The easy availability of guns, coupled with poverty and racism, have contributed to an increase in suicide among African American men. Sixty-three percent of African American suicide victims in a recent year used a gun to commit the deed (Lott 1998, 180).

Both class and race predicts membership in the National Rifle Association (NRA), whose members are mostly white, rural, and working class. NRA members view gun control as part of the professional class's war on rural life. Proceeds from turkey shoots and other events sponsored by gun clubs present altruistic outlets for rural men to contribute to their communities as well as offering occasions for socialization. Primarily social events, gun shows provide an arena in which history buffs, gun collectors, historical reenactors, hobbyists, and outdoorsmen connect with others who share their interests. Upper-class men participate in gun culture by shooting both skeet and clays and taking part in fox hunting.

Issues surrounding gun control are school shootings, gang activity, concealed-carry permits, etc. White boys are twice as likely to bring guns to school than black boys.

Though guns are owned for sport, protection, and criminal actives, men are the primary users and owners of firearms. In 1994 the Federal Bureau of Investigation reported that firearms were used in seven out of every ten murders committed in the United States. (Clark and Glick). Men significantly outnumber women in terms of gun ownership and 65 percent of gun owners report having them for protection (Cohen 2000, 33). Paradoxically, handguns frequently kill victims of domestic violence, essentially women and children. Research on domestic violence reveals that gun ownership is a key contributor in the escalation of nonfatal spouse abuse to homicide. Gun control may be primarily an issue of controlling men and masculinity. However, concealed handguns produce an equalizing effect between the sexes.

Rebecca Tolley-Stokes

See also Cowboys; Violence

Further Reading:
Clark, Beth, and Susan Glick. 1996. "Men Who Abuse Women Shouldn't Be Allowed to Own Firearms." Knight-Ridder/Tribune News Service (July 31).
Cohen, Michael D. 2000. "About Four in 10 Americans Report Owning a Gun." *The Gallup Monthly Poll* 421 (October): 32–35.
Garbarino, James. 1999. *Lost Boys: Why Our Sons Turn Violent and How We Can Save Them.* New York: The Free Press.
Lott, John R. 1998. *More Guns Less Crime: Understanding Crime and Gun Control Laws.* Chicago: University of Chicago Press.
"Why Suicide Is Increasing among Young Black Men." 1996. *Jet* 90, no. 13 (August 12): 12 (4).

Hall, G. Stanley (1844–1924)

One of the United States' most celebrated psychologists, G. Stanley Hall coined the term "adolescence" and, as president of Clark University, invited Sigmund Freud to lecture in the United States. Hall's understanding of masculinity and femininity emerged from an unique theoretical perspective known as recapitulation theory, a theoretical framework predicated upon evolutionary principles and generated by Hall to understand the development of mental processes. He, like other functionalist psychologists of his time, used evolution to argue that men and women evolved differently to fit into different roles: men into the world of work with its emphasis upon logic, rationality, and competition, and women into the sphere of the home with nurturance as the dominant quality.

Hall asserted that evolution was the organizing principle that united the phylogenetic emergence of the species with the ontogenetic development of the individual. Thus, each child in the course of her or his individual development recapitulated every stage of development through which the human race from its earliest animal beginnings had passed. But the details of the stages differed for men and women. From this developmental perspective, Hall constructed a pedocentric or child-centered view of education that argued that the best educational environment was one that allowed the free expression of the recapitulated impulses of the male and female child. Of particular interest to Hall was the stage of adolescence where the differences between girls and boys appeared to emerge most strongly and were in most need of free expression. The emergence of woman as the mother of the species, a position to which she was relegated by most functionalist psychologists of the late nineteenth and early twentieth centuries, was for Hall determined by the protection of her reproductive capabilities, as well as her interest in motherhood. Both of these qualities could be damaged in adolescence by education that did not teach to motherhood or by an educational environment that physically and mentally put strain on the health of her reproductive organs. For adolescent boys, the danger was just as great. The presence of girls in the classroom could have a "feminizing" effect on them and female teachers were thought to produce wildness in boys by not allowing free enough expression of their savage impulses. Hall argued that such impulses could find their best expression in activities such as those found in the Boy Scouts and in the masculinizing books of the series. In general, argued Hall, coeducation was bad for both boys and girls. Overexposure of the sexes to one another often resulted in lack of sexual attraction in adulthood.

Hall's stance on recapitulation and its role in the differentiation of the sexes were spelled out fully in a two-volume work published in 1904. The work was entitled *Adolescence: Its Psychology and Its Relations to Physiology, Anthropology, Sociology, Sex, Crime, Religion, and Education*. Although most psychologists of Hall's time were not in disagreement with Hall as to the existence of differences between the sexes and were convinced that such differences were the result of evolutionary dictates and thus the result of innate rather than social forces, Hall's recapitulation spin on evolution did not receive general support among his contemporaries. Hall had little in the way of data to support his theory, a perceived weakness in a field that was moving heavily into research and verifiability. In addition, psychology was rapidly embracing learning theory and research with animal species, while interest in humans took the form of mental testing. Hall was out of step with his profession, but not with society. For practitioners in education such as teachers and social welfare workers and for professional organizations within education such as the National Education Association, the need for separation of the sexes was more acceptable. In addition, parents who learned of his views through articles he wrote for popular magazines such as *Appleton's* and through speeches he made to the public embraced his contention that men and women were different, especially with regard to the superiority of the male in intellectual functioning. Particularly interesting was Hall's rather romantic notion of woman as of strong character and morally superior to man whether educated or not. It was a view not out of step with the social milieu of the time. Whether it had scientific merit was another issue.

Regardless of the social support Hall received, American culture as well as American psychology moved beyond his theory. Coeducation in public schools appeared to be established practice and universities admitted women as well as men at both the undergraduate and graduate levels. Developmental psychology, of which Hall is credited as being the father, was captured for a time by those in schools of home economics and not in traditional departments of psychology. Academic psychology continued its love affair with learning and mental testing well into the twentieth century. Psychoanalytic theory, developed by Sigmund Freud (brought to the United States to speak at Clark University by Hall himself) dominated personality theory and clinical practice prior to and following World War II and continues in evolved forms to capture lay opinion and some clinical practice yet today. Yet when, as a result of the women's movement of the late 1960s and early 1970s, feminist psychologists began to question, analyze, and criticize theory on what is now called gender differences and empirical data assumed to support traditional theory, it appeared that the incorporation of evolutionary theory into psychology to account for the "innate" differences between men and women was alive and well. Aspects of contemporary psychology are rife with the influence of Hall's theory without ever using the word "recapitulation." Consider, for example, the work of Lawrence Kohlberg (1971) on moral development and, more recently, Carol Gilligan's (1982) research on moral reasoning in adolescent women. In the field of education, articles abound in professional journals and newspapers and magazines arguing the merits of single-gender education in high school and college. Although Hall died in 1924, our culture and the social sciences continue to debate the nature of masculinity and femininity. Are they social constructs or, as Hall asserted, biological givens dictated by the evolutionary need to differentiate the sexes into innately given roles of behavior and character, woman as nurturer and man as provider/reasoner?

Lesley A. Diehl

See also Adolescence; Coeducation; Freud, Sigmund

Further Reading:

Diehl, Lesley A. 1987. "G. Stanley Hall: Foe of Coeducation and Educator of Women." *American Psychologist* 41, no. 8: 868–878.

———. 2000. "G. Stanley Hall." Pp. 50–53 in *Encyclopedia of Psychology.* Edited by Alan E. Kazdin. London: Oxford University Press.

Gilligan, Carol. 1982. *In a Different Voice.* Cambridge, MA: Harvard University Press.

Hall, G. Stanley. 1904. *Adolescence: Its Psychology and Its Relations to Physiology, Anthropology, Sociology, Sex, Crime, Religion and Education.* Vols. 1 and 2. New York: Appleton.

Ross, Dorothy. 1972. *G. Stanley Hall: The Psychologist as Prophet.* Chicago: The University of Chicago Press.

Hamlet

Shakespeare's *Hamlet* has always been seen as a play about the complexity of human identity, but more recently, gender-conscious criticism has drawn attention to the questions of masculinity that the play explores. Three main areas may be delineated: the play's relation to Freudian psychology, and in particular to the question of the Oedipus complex in the formation of masculine subjectivity; the play's exploration and elaboration of types of masculine identity in the context of early modern constructions of masculinity; and the deep-rooted gendering of human attributes that the play both articulates and questions.

At the center of *Hamlet* stands a fascination with the self divided against itself: Hamlet is driven both by a desire to avenge the death of his father, the king, and also by a more introspective, sensitive, or circumspect impulse, which causes him continually to delay his revenge and seek safety in a pretend or real madness. Much of the debate about the play, both in published criticism and in interpretive performance, has been about the source of this division. In the mid-twentieth century Ernest Jones's famous psychoanalytical essay, *Hamlet and Oedipus* (1949), provided the first clear analysis of the play in terms of issues of masculinity. According to Jones, Hamlet's madness and his inaction are both symptoms of an unresolved Oedipal complex: At a subconscious level Hamlet's repressed incestuous desires toward his mother implicate him in his uncle's crime, preventing him from carrying out the act of revenge. The notion of an Oedipal Hamlet was attacked by formalist critics for its naively naturalistic approach to dramatic character. Yet an Oedipal reading of *Hamlet* makes good historical sense, as the play itself, along with *Oedipus Rex,* was instrumental in the development of Freud's own thinking about male subjectivity. The narrative patterns of these plays, together with his own clinical investigations, underpin Freud's formulation of the Oedipus complex.

Even without Freud, there are several ways in which *Hamlet* directly addresses issues of masculinity. Throughout the play, Hamlet continually searches for models on which to construct his own masculine identity, while the audience is offered contrasting images whereby to judge the prince. The imagination of young Hamlet is dominated by the idealized memory of old Hamlet, his murdered father, together with its negative image, the demonized Claudius. Other masculine icons also haunt his imagination. In one crucial episode, a group of traveling players recounts a story from the Trojan wars in which the brutal Greek hero Pyrrhus kills King Priam of Troy. Hamlet becomes temporarily obsessed with the image of warrior masculinity that Pyrrhus represents and he berates himself for his effeminacy in not acting likewise. In *Hamlet,* as in many of Shakespeare's plays, masculine and feminine values become polarized, and the language of Hamlet's own introspection reveals his unease that his more humane impulses are somehow effeminate. An influential essay by David Leverenz (1978) argues that Hamlet's revulsion at the feminine passivity within himself eventually becomes displaced into his own brutal behavior toward the women in the play, and in particular toward Ophelia.

Hamlet also seeks meaning in the figure of the Norwegian prince Fortinbras, a warrior-hero who becomes, in Hamlet's eyes, an icon of fully achieved masculinity. In Fortinbras he sees the epitome of masculine "honor." This is a key concept, not only for Hamlet, but for the construction of early modern masculinity in general. The honor codes of the sixteenth and seventeenth centuries comprise a complex set of implicit and explicit rules, assumptions, and conventions. Covering topics from ethical precepts to details of dress and deportment, these codes offer an articulation of masculine gender ideology of the period. Hamlet's dilemma involves a negotiation of the contrasting imperatives of these codes. On the one hand, they imply a warrior ethic, which would dictate the primacy of personal revenge; on the other, they stress self-control and civic duty. Caught between these two dictates, Hamlet reaches eagerly for an exemplar who seems to have solved the problem of masculine gender construction by ignoring its complexities. When, at the end of the play, Fortinbras arrives to take charge of the court to which Hamlet himself was heir, there is a palpable sense of loss.

Michael Mangan

See also Shakespeare, William

Further Reading:

Fletcher, Anthony. 1995. *Gender, Sex, and Subordination in England, 1500–1800.* New Haven, CT: Yale University Press.

Jenkins, Harold, ed. 1999. *William Shakespeare's Hamlet.* London: Arden.

Jones, Ernest. 1949. *Hamlet and Oedipus.* New York: Norton.

Leverenz, David. 1978. "The Woman in Hamlet: An Interpersonal View." *Signs: Journal of Woman in Culture and Society* 4: 302—303.

Mangan, Michael. 1991. *A Preface to Shakespeare's Tragedies.* Harlow, UK: Longman.

Strachey, James, ed. 1953–1966. *The Standard Edition of the Complete Psychological Works of Sigmund Freud.* London: Hogarth Press.

Wells, Robin Headlam. 2000. *Shakespeare on Masculinity.* Cambridge, UK: Cambridge University Press.

Hanks, Tom (1956–)

Although he played an ordinary fellow in more than thirty movies (including *Splash* [1984], *Big* [1988], and *Punchline* [1988]), U.S. actor Tom Hanks is known worldwide for a few characters to whom he gave life in some key films. In *Philadelphia* (1993), directed by Jonathan Demme, he plays a talented lawyer who loses his job when his boss learns that he has AIDS. The double victimization of this positive character brought much sympathy toward Hanks's character, and to gay men generally, as he tried vigorously to respond to the unfair attitude of his employer.

A very popular romance, *Sleepless in Seattle* (1993), written and directed by Nora Ephron, contributed to constructing Hanks's heterosexual character and identity in a subdued role. Hanks plays a fragile widower father of an eight-year-old son, with whom hundreds of women want to get in touch with when he suddenly reveals his loneliness and his cry for love on a radio talk show. Dialogs even feature unexpected reflections about gender roles, for instance when they oppose "male" movies (*The Dirty Dozen*) to "female" films (*An Affair to Remember*).

But Hanks's most durable performance was in *Forrest Gump* (1994), directed by Robert Zimeckis. Told in a flashback over thirty years of American history, the story follows the life of a young man named Forrest Gump, a talented but naive American with a low I.Q., who was always sincere and sometimes abused. He was an amazingly fast runner, in a country where people love to run and admire good runners. He also had the chance to be at the right place at the right moment. With the help of new technology and special effects, the lucky character revisits the 1960s in a realistic mode. He meets many American icons such as President John F. Kennedy, sees the protests against the Vietnam War, and becomes a hero during that same war. The heart of the story is Gump's relationship with Jenny, a girl he meets when they are both children. It is she who helps him find his talent for running and who defends him against the bullies of childhood. Gump falls in love with her, but she—unlike her retarded friend—grows up. The poignancy of Gump's devotion to Jenny over the thirty-year span of the action, during most of which she rejects his romantic suggestions even as she sinks lower into a life of bad choices and drug addiction, is what moves this drama. Ultimately, we see that the measure of a man is not his I.Q., but his capacity to love and to act in fidelity to high principles. Gump, despite his low intelligence, triumphs and in so doing presents a startling and compelling image of manhood. The film *Forrest Gump* was one of the most publicized American movies of the 1990s and achieved huge success and many awards. The reason for that popularity is quite simple: The naive man—the "stupid" man—could have been a loser, but he nonetheless succeeds in many ways, as a fast runner, as a heroic soldier, as a businessman specializing in shrimp, and finally as a husband and father only because he is genuine, honest, and sincere.

Tom Hanks also starred in Ron Howard's *Apollo 13* (1995), in which he played an astronaut, and again as an unpretending hero in Steven Spielberg's *Saving Private Ryan* (1998).

In another Nora Ephron movie, titled *You've Got Mail* (1998), Hanks teams again with actress Meg Ryan, as he did in *Sleepless in Seattle* (1993), in a plot inspired by Ernst Lubitsch's famous film classic *The Shop Around the Corner* (1940), a comedy in which James Stewart starred. In *You've Got Mail* (1998), Tom Hanks appears once more as a desired handsome heterosexual man who can sparkle a beautiful lady. In this light evocation to *Sleepless in Seattle,* both main characters are separated most of the time, even though they somehow feel attracted one by the other; they only know they could love each other, but their contacts are mostly virtual (through email, as the title suggests). After a gay role in *Philadelphia* (1993), both Nora Ephron movies helped Tom Hanks in confirming his heterosexual sex appeal.

As an actor, Tom Hanks fits into the continuum of familiar incarnations of the average American man, in the tradition of the Hollywood cinema. There is a bit of James Stewart, Glenn Ford, Montgomery Clift, or even Robin Williams in some of the characters given to Tom Hanks: He is an "everyman" with whom audiences can easily identify, yet projects a relaxed sexuality, charm, and capacity for heroics that set him apart even in his "ordinary guy" guises. Hanks often appears on television and occasionally works for minor projects as a film director, writer, and producer. In 2002, Tom Hanks received the American Film Institute's Life Achievement Award.

Yves Laberge

Further Reading:

Tom Hanks Appreciation Society Web Site. At http://www.tomhanksweb.com/ (cited 27 July 2003).

Unofficial Tom Hanks website run by fans. At http://www.tomhanksland.com/ (cited 27 July 2003)

Hawthorne, Nathaniel (1804–1864)

Nathaniel Hawthorne was troubled by the style of manliness that achieved dominance during his lifetime, and his writing explores issues of masculinity that remain urgent in the twenty-first century. Hawthorne's gender ambivalence was first noted by feminist scholars like Carolyn Heilbrun (1973) and Nina Baym (1971), who celebrated his portrayal of strong women characters, like Hester Prynne in *The Scarlet Letter* (1850), who rebel against subordination, displaying virtues of independence, self-reliance, and decisive action traditionally associated with men. In other Hawthorne novels—*The Blithedale Romance* (1852) and *The Marble Faun* (1860)—such strong women are coupled with pious and submissive domestic angels.

This polar arrangement is also found in Hawthorne's depiction of men. He portrays strong, worldly men in conjunction with figures that project his fears about his own man-

Nathaniel Hawthorne, best known for his novel The Scarlet Letter, *combined moral seriousness with a conviction that literature could transcend human foibles and suffering. He often turned to the early history of New England for tales he could transform imaginatively into myths concerning the ideals of freedom, equality, and justice. (DoYou Graphics)*

masculinity in Hawthorne, viewing it as a psycho-social structure shaped by historical conditions, not a natural endowment wholly dictated by genes. Leverenz demonstrated that Hawthorne's lifetime (1804–1864) was a period in American life during which the ruling gender arrangements underwent fundamental change. The masculinity of elite, white males in the colonial period was "patrician," keyed to bloodline and landed privilege, a model that yielded precedence during the early years of the nineteenth century to the champions of a new social and economic order. Democracy, urbanization, westward expansion, and unregulated capitalist competition enshrined entrepreneurial self-reliance as the definitive "manly" virtue, and the fine ruffles, wigs, and stockings that were worn by gentry males in the prerevolutionary period were branded "effeminate" and disappeared from public life.

Hawthorne's writing explores the dimensions of this shift, in which the "self-made man" became the central icon of a new style heralded as "natural manhood" in contrast to the "merely conventional" folkways of the traditional patrician elite. *The House of the Seven Gables* (1851) dramatizes this transition. At the outset of the novel, the Pyncheon family—whose social position has depended on traditional privilege—occupies the decaying old house, to be displaced by the self-reliant Holgrave at the end. Yet this seeming celebration of the new masculine ideal is crosscut by the depiction of Jaffrey Pyncheon, the novel's the prime villain.

Though he is a descendant of the patrimonial family, Pyncheon is nonetheless a ruthless worldly competitor and has acquired vast new wealth by exploiting the opportunities of the emerging capitalist order. Hawthorne admired the self-reliant manhood of the new ideal, but he was also appalled by the cruelty, selfishness, emotional poverty, sexual exploitiveness, and illegitimate political power of the "self-made men" that he saw gaining prestige in the public world around him.

hood. These characters—Owen Warland ("The Artist of the Beautiful"), Arthur Dimmesdale (*The Scarlet Letter*), Miles Coverdale (*The Blithedale Romance*), Septimius Felton (from an unfinished manuscript)—are embarrassed by their failure to meet the requirements of conventional masculinity; they are hesitant, introspective, and shy; they are beset by strong passions of desire, guilt, grief and rage; and they are consumed by aesthetic preoccupations. Hawthorne himself created a divided impression on those who knew him well: He was seen to embody staunch and healthy-minded manliness, but also possessed traits considered "feminine."

David Leverenz's *Manhood and the American Renaissance* (1989) inaugurated the study of

The emerging gender system asserted that masterful manliness and submissive womanhood were ordained by nature and that a man or woman possessing contrary traits was abnormal. But in *The House of the Seven Gables* Hawthorne dramatizes the opposite view. Jaffrey Pyncheon's manliness is a masquerade, a mask of masculinity, which he puts on like his fine clothing with an eye to maintaining a public image. Hawthorne notices the bitterness that seeps through this mask, resulting from Pyncheon's effort to suppress emotional responses he cannot afford to display. The horror of Pyncheon's false existence overcomes even Holgrave, the seeming hero of self-reliance, because it is a horror buried within Holgrave's heart as well. In the mid-nineteenth century, thus, Hawthorne recognized that restrictive forms of masculinity may produce severe strain on persons required to live them out in defiance of their native capacities and impulses.

The gay literary scholars Robert Martin (1990) and Edwin Haviland Miller (1993) explore Hawthorne's awareness that the ruling masculine ideal was oppressive, in particular to Hawthorne himself. The exact degree to which Hawthorne was sexually attracted to men, like the question whether his Uncle Robert Manning sexually abused him in childhood, cannot be decisively answered given the available evidence. But as Miller has noted, there are reasons to believe that Herman Melville was attracted to Hawthorne and that Hawthorne's responsive sexual interest can be seen in the phobic recoil to be found in his personal notebooks during the time of their close acquaintance and in *The Blithedale Romance*.

Within his marriage Hawthorne sought to live out the ideal of self-reliant masculinity, and his wife Sophia likewise sought to fulfill the correlative role of domestic angel. In their engagement and marriage, as in the family life they created together, they celebrated their own perfect fulfillment of these ideals. Yet the work of T. Walter Herbert (1993) demonstrates that on both sides there were strong currents of covert resistance and rebellion. Sophia brought an impulse to command into the relationship; Nathaniel yearned to luxuriate in maternal protection; and they both chafed under the sexual self-discipline required of middle-class families.

These issues appear in *The Scarlet Letter,* where Sophia's suppressed strength and boldness become overt in the character of Hester Prynne, while Hawthorne's inwardly divided masculinity gives form to the characters of Roger Chillingworth and Arthur Dimmesdale. These characterizations are not merely autobiographical, however; they convey Hawthorne's insight into the gender dilemmas taking form in the society around him, where the male sexual susceptibility and aesthetic passion displayed by the guilty preacher Dimmesdale were branded unmasculine. The rationally guided and consummately self-reliant Roger Chillingworth portrays the corresponding maladies: the emotional ignorance, stunted capacity for intimacy, homophobic lust, and disposition toward sexual abuse that afflicts compulsively self-governing and self-reliant men. The two characters taken together are a composite, Herbert has argued, representing a manhood split into irreconcilable warring fragments. This chronic dilemma, very much alive in the early twenty-first century, was taking form in Hawthorne's time and resulted from an emerging gender tyranny that Hawthorne resented but could not wholly disavow. It is the tyranny of a manhood based on the traits required for ceaseless individual competition with other men, which subordinates women to its psychic requirements and stigmatizes other masculinities as "unnatural."

T. Walter Herbert

Further Reading:

Baym, Nina. 1971. "Hawthorne's Women: The Tyranny of Social Myths." *Centennial Review* 15: 250–272.

———. 1982. "Nathaniel Hawthorne and his Mother: A Biographical Speculation." *American Literature* 54: 2–27.

———. 1982. "Thwarted Nature: Nathaniel Hawthorne as Feminist." Pp. 58–77 in

American Novelists Revisited: Essays in Feminist Criticism. Edited by Fritz Fleischmann. Boston: G. K. Hall.

Erlich, Gloria C. 1984. *Family Themes and Hawthorne's Fiction: The Tenacious Web.* New Brunswick, NJ: Rutgers University Press.

Heilbrun, Carolyn G. 1973. *Toward a Recognition of Androgyny.* New York: Knopf.

Herbert, T. Walter, Jr. 1993. *Dearest Beloved: The Hawthornes and the Making of the Middle-Class Family.* Berkeley, CA: University of California Press.

———. 2002. *Sexual Violence and American Manhood.* Cambridge, MA: Harvard University Press.

Leverenz, David. 1989. *Manhood and the American Renaissance.* Ithaca, NY: Cornell University Press.

Martin, Robert K. 1990. "Hester Prynne, C'est Moi: Nathaniel Hawthorne and the Anxieties of Gender." Pp. 122–139 in *Engendering Men: The Question of Male Feminist Criticism.* Edited by Joseph A. Boone and Michael Cadden. New York: Routledge.

Miller, Edwin Haviland. 1993. *Salem Is My Dwelling Place: A Life of Nathaniel Hawthorne.* Iowa City: University of Iowa Press.

Traister, Bryce. 2000. "Academic Viagra: The Rise of American Masculinity Studies." *American Quarterly* 52, no. 2: 114–138.

Hazing

Hazing refers to violent or abusive forms of initiation ritual within many military, Greek, and other masculine-typed organizations (including some populated partially or wholly by women). In its pure form, hazing is a highly structured behavior that can be identified and understood by a specific set of criteria that separate it from other social behaviors that are simply painful, humiliating, or mean. Although hazing often has these attributes, its structural nature makes it a fundamentally different category of performance. The general concept of hazing is anathema to most people, yet its central, emotional, deeply personal, and clearly endemic role within many hypermasculine institutions entitles it to a dispassionate review.

The quality that differentiates hazing from other superficially similar behaviors is the specific co-occurrence of *structured ritual, collectively perceived purpose,* and *a unidirectional form of abuse.* Not all social rituals are abusive and some that are abusive are not purposeful. Similarly, some social practices may be reciprocative, rather than unidirectional, or relatively unstructured. Hazing, by contrast, is characterized by all three qualities.

The body of literature on human ritual is enormous, but hazing rituals belong in the subcategory of *rituals of initiation.* Like all such rituals, hazing typically requires a distinct and dichotomous set of individuals: those who *have* power, authority, experience, and group-identity and those who are attempting to *earn* these attributes. Like all true rituals (and unlike most customs or folkways), hazing rituals are limited by time and place, have a definite beginning and end, and usually include a well-rehearsed or at least well-planned script. The overall hazing "process" may include a series of rituals each of which contributes to the perceived organizational project of turning initiates into members, recruits into soldiers, and pledges into "brothers" and "sisters."

Many behaviors commonly identified as hazing lack the essential element of consciously and collectively perceived purpose. Hazing distinguishes itself from other activities in that those participating in the process, both as perpetrator and as recipient, consciously perceive a reason—however expedient or rational—for the practice. This reason is sometimes as simple as the mechanical and highly effective transposition of *meaning* and *experience:* anything suffered for must be worth suffering for; greater suffering equates to greater worth; the more we have suffered together, the more we must value each other and the organization to which we collectively and exclusively belong. Hazing has the power to create perceived meaning out of actual meaninglessness, to force harmony on incoherence, and to form bonds among people on a patently contrived and yet often extremely effective pretext.

Kirby D. Schroeder

See also Hazing, High School and College
Further Reading:

Herdt, Gilbert H. 1998. *Rituals of Manhood: Male Initiation in Papua New Guinea.* New Brunswick, NJ: Transaction.

Morinis, Alan. 1985. "The Ritual Experience: Pain and the Transformation of Consciousness in Ordeals of Initiation." *Ethos* 13, no. 2: 150–174.

Nuwer, Hank. 2001. *Wrongs of Passage: Fraternities, Sororities, Hazing, and Binge Drinking.* Bloomington, IN: Indiana University Press.

Sweet, Stephen. 1999. "Understanding Fraternity Hazing: Insights from Symbolic Interactionist Theory." *Journal of College Student Development* 40, no. 4: 355–365.

Hazing, High School and College

Hazing refers to any activity expected of someone joining a group (or to maintain full status in a group) that humiliates, degrades, or risks emotional and/or physical harm, regardless of the person's willingness to participate. In years past, hazing practices were typically considered harmless pranks or comical antics associated with young men in college fraternities. In the early twenty-first century we know that hazing extends far beyond college fraternities and is experienced by males and females in school groups, university organizations, athletic teams, and military and other social and professional organizations, causing emotional and physical harm and even death. Hazing practices are shaped by power dynamics operating in a group and/or organization within a particular cultural context. As such, hazing also reflects societal norms and expectations around gender and masculinity, in particular.

Behavior that would meet today's definition of hazing has been documented among male educational and military groups for centuries. The term *hazing* however was not commonly used in the United States until the Civil War period when it emerged as a descriptor of initiation jokes played on newcomers to the ranks of the military. After the Civil War, the term *hazing* was used to describe practices of initiating new students to the university and maintaining order within the established hierarchy between classes of students (i.e., upperclassmen vs. freshmen). Such activities typically included expectations of personal servitude and other displays of subordination to students in the upper ranks. Occasionally however, hazing involved what was termed "disorderly conduct" and sometimes escalated into physical brawls causing serious injuries and even fatalities (Nuwer 1999).

Hazing practices in the early 2000s continue to reflect the masculine historical roots of military units and universities. However, documentation of hazing in high schools, organized athletics, as well as professional groups like police academies and firefighting units has grown considerably. Over the last century, and especially the last three decades of the twentieth century, awareness and concern about the dangers of hazing has increased, marked for example by its inclusion in many school and university codes of student conduct. Since the 1970s there has been at least one student fatality each year involving hazing (Nuwer 1999, 237). Such tragedies often led to increased public scrutiny and sometimes resulted in the passage of statutory legislation rendering hazing a criminal act. In the United States in 2003, forty-four states have enacted antihazing laws that vary widely in scope and consequence but are typically restricted to behavior occurring in educational arenas.

Hazing activities are generally considered to be physically abusive, hazardous, and/or sexually violating. The specific behaviors or activities within these categories vary widely among participants, groups, and settings. Alcohol use is common in nearly all types of hazing. Other examples of typical hazing practices include: personal servitude; sleep deprivation; restrictions on personal hygiene; verbal abuse; forced wearing of embarrassing or humiliating attire in public; forced consumption of vile substances or smearing of such on one's skin; brandings; physical beatings; binge drinking and drinking games; and sexual simulation and sexual assault.

Empirical research on hazing is scarce, and as of 2003, no systematic investigation has been done to examine the role of gender in hazing. The most recent and extensive studies have focused on hazing for male and female high school students and intercollegiate athletes. Results of these studies indicated that 48 percent of high school student group members reported being subjected to hazing (Alfred University 2000), and 79 percent of NCAA athlete respondents reported experiencing one or more typical hazing behaviors as part of team initiations (Alfred University 1999). National news accounts of hazing and anecdotal evidence point toward gender differences in hazing activities. In general, a common conclusion drawn is that hazing among men is more likely to be violent in nature and hazing among women is more likely to be psychological/emotional in nature. Such perspectives align with and also reinforce predominant understandings of differences between the genders. The results of the Alfred/NCAA study revealed differences between types of hazing experienced by male and female athletes. Notably, women were less likely than men to be subjected to unacceptable acts, including destroying or stealing property, beatings, being tied up or taped, being confined to small places, paddled, or kidnapped or transported and abandoned (Alfred University 1999). This finding supports the assertion that sex/gender differences in hazing experiences do exist. For some, this distinction is simply attributed to innate biological differences between the sexes. Others, however, draw on a social constructionist perspective to argue that these differences are largely the result of learning to perform gender roles differently (Allan forthcoming).

Several ethnographic and journalistic accounts of fraternity life (Nuwer 1990, 1999) and athletics (Robinson 1998) provide some insights about hazing practices. A number of these examinations rely substantially on theories of gender, sexism, and homophobia to explain aspects of all-male groups that increase the probability of violence against women who come in contact with these groups (Martin 1989; Rhoads 1995). While hazing practices may take many forms (largely influenced by the participants, group, and setting), some common characteristics can be identified and understood in relation to predominant masculinity as practiced in contemporary European and North American society. For instance, when hazing occurs among men, regardless of the type of group, it is often framed as a test of "strength," "courage," and "determination."

How men and women are taught to live in the world affects patterns of violence, abuse, and other behaviors involved in hazing practices. Regardless of race and socioeconomic status, accounts of hazing incidents among boys and men often include tests of physical endurance, forced alcohol consumption, paddling, and other forms of physical assaults. A common rationale in support of hazing is that it is a "tradition" necessary to "weed out" those unworthy of membership.

Research on fraternity cultures and male athletic teams reveals an emphasis on hypermasculinity: physical and mental toughness, endurance of pain and humiliation, obedience to superiors, and the use of physical coercion to obtain compliance (Martin 1989; Messner and Sabo 1989). Gender theory provides a framework for understanding the ways in which hazing is both shaped by and contributes to shaping notions of masculinity and manhood. Some men who have been hazed are firm believers in the abuses endured through the process of hazing and insist that they "enjoyed the challenge." Such arguments are embedded in predominant cultural performances of masculinity and what boys are taught to expect of themselves and others as "real men." Likewise, social anxieties around masculinity also sustain hazing practices. The more males are fearful of being labeled as weak, the more likely they are to participate in hazing activities that are dangerous and even life-threatening. A chronology of hazing fatalities reveals that men are far more likely to die from hazing activities than are women. Of more than sixty documented hazing deaths, only three have been women (Nuwer 1999, 237).

Gendered practices of hazing are supported by the role homophobia plays in reinforcing rigid and confining expectations of masculine and feminine behavior. This dynamic is evidenced when, for instance, high school students are asked to think about what happens if a man is a little bit *too* nurturing or a bit *too* emotional and they are quick to respond, "he's a sissy," "he's a fag." Women who cross the line of normative expectations for femininity face similar social consequences of being called "butch" or "dyke." These terms are unlikely to serve as deterrents unless they are perceived negatively, and homophobia ensures this. Thus, the predominant social construction of masculinity works in tandem with homophobia to create a climate in which violent and demeaning hazing practices are more likely to be tolerated and even considered beneficial for young men (Allan forthcoming).

Understanding masculinity as a dynamic process of "doing" gender helps to illuminate why the eradication of hazing practices can be difficult. Because hazing can serve as an opportunity for men to prove their masculinity (and heterosexuality), the elimination of hazing traditions can be threatening on multiple fronts. Exit costs for leaving a hazing organization increase because young men may lose a major part of their identity by severing ties with the organization. Further, when hazing is so closely tied to the performance of masculinity, those who identify with predominant cultural constructions

of masculinity are likely to fear that their manhood will be called into question if they resist an opportunity to prove it via hazing practices. This also explains, at least in part, why some pledges, rookies, and new members of organizations ask to be hazed even if the group is attempting to eradicate such traditions. Newcomers know they are likely to be subject to scrutiny by members who have proved their manhood through hazing. Such scrutiny is not entirely external—but also self-imposed—as many males have been taught to think of manhood in terms of physical prowess, toughness, and conquest.

Increasingly, reports of hazing among boys and men include acts of sexual victimization. Although reports of hazing have increased over the decade prior to 2003, the humiliation and degradation—along with the threat of group retaliation—continue to make it exceedingly difficult for many to report such abuses. Efforts to curtail harmful hazing have emphasized legal and policy remedies. And although educational and programmatic efforts to discourage hazing are mounting, such efforts are rarely grounded in perspectives linking the performance of gender to the development and maintenance of abusive hazing practices. Making masculinity visible is crucial to further understanding hazing and developing effective prevention strategies.

Elizabeth J. Allan

See also Hazing

Further Reading:

Alfred University. 1999. "Initiation Rites and Athletics for NCAA Sports Teams: A National Survey." At *http://www.alfred.edu/news/html/hazing.*

———. 2000. "Initiation Rites in American High Schools: A National Survey." At *http://www.alfred.edu/news/html/hazing_study.html.*

Allan, Elizabeth J. Forthcoming. "Hazing and Gender: Analyzing the Obvious." In *Examining Hazing.* Edited by Hank Nuwer. Bloomington: Indiana University Press.

Martin, Patricia Y. 1989. "Fraternities and Rape on Campus." *Gender and Society* 3, no. 4: 457–473.

Ernest Hemingway is regarded as the quintessential American novelist and one of the great prose stylists writing in English in the first half of the twentieth century. (National Archive)

Messner, Michael A., and Donald F. Sabo. 1989. *Sex, Violence and Power in Sports.* Freedom, CA: Crossing Press.

Nuwer, Hank. 1990. *Broken Pledges: The Deadly Rite of Hazing.* Atlanta, GA: Longstreet Press.

———. 1999. *Wrongs of Passage: Fraternities, Sororities, Hazing and Binge Drinking.* Bloomington: Indiana University Press.

———. 2000. *High School Hazing: When Rites Become Wrongs.* New York: Grolier.

Rhoads, Robert A. 1995. "Whales Tales, Dog Piles, and Beer Goggles: An Ethnographic Study of Fraternity Life." *Anthropology and Education Quarterly* 26, no. 3: 306–323.

Robinson, Laura. 1998. *Crossing the Line: Violence and Sexual Assault in Canada's National Sport.* Toronto, Canada: McClelland and Stewart.

StopHazing.org. At *http://www.stophazing.org.*

Hemingway, Ernest (1899–1961)

During his lifetime, Ernest Hemingway presented himself as the personification of masculinity. Much of his fiction features protagonists who prefer action to sustained thought and is set in such male worlds as war, bullfighting, boxing, hunting, or fishing. In 1927, in a review of Hemingway's second collection of stories, *Men without Women*, Edmund Wilson noted Hemingway's "appetite for the physical world. . . . his drama always turns on some principle of courage, of pity, of honor—in short, of sportsmanship" (108). Hemingway's protagonists follow a code of "grace under pressure," which Philip Young described as "made of the controls of honor and courage which in a life of tension and pain make a man a man and distinguish him from the people who follow random impulses, let down their hair, and are generally messy, perhaps cowardly, and without inviolable rules for how to live holding tight" (Young 1966, 63–64).

Young considered these "code heroes" as masks for Hemingway himself, thus contributing to the tendency to read Hemingway's fiction as autobiography. And as Hemingway became a celebrity writer, he was not shy about promoting his own heroic exploits. In his column in *Esquire* magazine in the 1930s, he chronicled his experiences as a sports fisherman, hunter of big and small game, bullfighting aficionado and buddy of matadors, and as a gourmet he instructed his readers in his favorite food and drink and where to find it in the world. In *Death in the Afternoon* (1932), his conjoining of the art of writing with the art of bullfighting helped to establish writing as a manly vocation. Physically large and good-looking, Hemingway was frequently photographed, appearing in major publications posed with a huge marlin he had battled; or cradling his Springfield rifle, crouched next to a dead lion; or surveying Spanish trenches as a war correspondent; or with one of the four attractive wives he had wooed and won. Indeed, even his suicide was considered a heroic act.

After his death, however, as his unpublished work became available, a new and more complex Hemingway emerged. The major document that initiated a new reading of Hemingway and his work was the novel *The Garden of Eden,* published in 1986 in a bowdlerized version. Even so, readers were introduced to an unusual couple: writer David Bourne and his wife Catherine, who experiment with bisexuality, indulge in serious tanning, favor look-alike haircuts and bleach jobs, and set up a *ménage a trois* with bisexual Marita. Prior to the publication of *The Garden of Eden,* not much attention had been paid to an entry written by Hemingway in Mary Hemingway's diary in 1953 and published in her autobiography *How It Was* in 1976: "She has always wanted to be a boy and thinks as a boy. . . . She loves me to be her girls, which I love to be. . . . at night we do every sort of thing. . . . Since I have never cared for any man and dislike any tactile contact with men . . . I loved feeling the embrace of Mary" (369–370). Read in this new light, Hemingway's texts reveal a writer exploring issues of gender as well as the price of machismo. For example, critical interest turned to Jake Barnes's dislike of homosexuals in *The Sun Also Rises* as a reflection of his own vexed sexuality, and can be seen as part of the chain of Hemingway's ongoing treatment of homoeroticism, especially evident in *Death in the Afternoon* (1932) and in stories dealing with bullfighters, such as "The Undefeated" (1925) or "The Mother of a Queen" (1933). An early *ménage à trois* consisting of two lesbians and an unmanly poet is found in "Mr. and Mrs. Elliot" (1924), and in "The Sea Change" (1931), the dialogue between and man and a woman in a bar makes clear that the woman, who is leaving to go off for an affair with another woman, is not doing this for the first time. The man asks the bartender for "what the punks drink," to signal his feeling of having been transformed, or unmanned. He terms her actions as "vice," prefiguring the sense of damnation felt by the Bournes after their experiments with sexual changing and partner-swapping in *The Garden of Eden.*

Some critics and biographers saw Hemingway's interest in sexual role-playing, or changing, as evidence of psychic damage caused by Hemingway's mother when she dressed toddler Hemingway and his older sister Marcelline in look-alike "Dutch dolly" outfits. Grace Hemingway proudly recorded her two-year-old son's lisping rejection of this role in her diary: "I not a Dutch dolly, I Pawnee Bill. Bang. I shoot Fweetee." Kenneth Lynn finds that Grace Hemingway, while delighting in her son's desire to be "a real man," confused Ernest by her "wish to conceal his masculinity and her eagerness to encourage it." Hemingway's father, on the other hand, taught his son and three daughters how to hunt and fish, and on vacations in the Michigan woods, all the children dressed in boy's overalls. Both parents strongly supported the code of "muscular Christianity" that prevailed during the early twentieth century, and Hemingway's immersion in that culture helped to shape him as well.

Nancy R. Comley

Further Reading:
Comley, Nancy R., and Robert Scholes. 1994. *Hemingway's Genders.* New Haven: Yale University Press.
Lynn, Kenneth. 1987. *Hemingway.* New York: Simon and Schuster.
Moddelmog, Debra A. 1999. *In Pursuit of Ernest Hemingway.* Ithaca, NY: Cornell University Press.
Raeburn, John. 1984. *Fame Became of Him: Hemingway as Public Writer.* Bloomington: Indiana University Press.
Reynolds, Michael. 1986. *The Young Hemingway.* New York: Blackwell.
———. 1989. *Hemingway: The Paris Years.* New York: Blackwell.
———. 1992. *Hemingway: The American Homecoming.* New York: Blackwell.
———. 1997. *Hemingway: The 1930s.* New York: W. W. Norton.
———. 1999. *Hemingway: The Final Years.* New York: W. W. Norton.
Wilson, Edmund. 1967. "The Sportsman's Tragedy." Pp. 339–344 in *The Shores of Light.* New York: Farrar, Straus and Giroux.

Young, Philip. 1966. *Hemingway: A Reconsideration.* New York: Harcourt, Brace and World.

Hero

The English word and its European equivalents refer both to the principal male character in a story or drama and to a man of superhuman properties. Masculinities, remarks Graham Dawson "are lived out in the flesh, but fashioned in the imagination" (1994, 1). The hero begins as the central carrier of plot, and whether he is in the end victorious or doomed, he provides a template for dominant male roles. The Bronze Age warrior chieftain whose trace is preserved in Greek epics like Homer's *Iliad* was buried with his jewelry, his weapons, and his armor. Subsequently, the idea of the hero dramatized the possibility of fame, of being remembered for his deeds. So heroic action, recalled whether in song, legend, or film, creates its own symbolic descendants.

Onto the figure of the hero as celebrated in social narrative are projected fantasies of a purified and invulnerable identity. He is a model both as a strong, admirable, character, but also because he seeks out and confronts danger. In doing so, this figure molds social perceptions of where danger lies (the realm of the feminine, of the Other, or of the natural environment), and how it may be faced or conquered. As the idea spreads beyond the boundaries of epic text, heroes both reflect and organize collective needs for role models and admirable figures. Minority groups and nations, as well as sports fans, generate heroes who reflect back an idealized self-image.

Numerous reasons demonstrate why masculinity research needs to treat the idealized identity of the hero with suspicion. Unlike women, who through childbearing can defy mortality through a tangible physical link to the future, men have to settle for symbolic influence over the next generation. So being celebrated or textually commemorated may in some sense be a male substitute for being able to produce physical descendants. The memorable, "larger than life" quality of heroes defines and celebrates patriarchy. In addition, the traditional hero dramatizes the male as the performer of "deeds." (The archaic, high register word resonates with the heroic tradition.) The central masculine figure is imagined as a maker, rather than a victim of events: He either triumphs or, if he loses, it is in the struggle against terrible odds. Whichever the outcome, he sets his stamp on the world. In the dualist universe, which is the hero's field of operation (good versus evil, we versus they), domination of the social and the nonhuman world is made to seem natural (Hourihan 1997). In representing strength and hardened boundaries against the chaotic—even treacherous—world on which he sets his mark, the hero glorifies the male body as a phallic weapon. He thus articulates a purified masculine identity achieved through courageous acceptance of risk.

Perhaps celebrations of the hero surface precisely in those historical moments when traditional forms of masculinity are perceived to be at risk. In early Victorian Britain, Emerson's friend Thomas Carlyle urged the revival of hero figures in what he saw as a commercial and compromised age. Conditions of war or national crisis frequently produce hero figures whose cultural function may be to simplify the complications in which society finds itself (for example, in much U.S. cinema following the end of the Vietnam War). At the same time, there have also been lively traditions of cultural inquiry into the failure of male figures to exhibit an undivided self or to live up to expectations of leadership and dominance. Both literature and film have frequently taken as a subject the "antihero": the male who through his clownishness, deviousness, or cowardice fails to live up to the high expectations placed upon the male leader. The film *Catch-22* (1970) or the films of Woody Allen are prime examples. Alongside this tradition, hero icons like Sylvester Stallone and

Superman live on in film and popular culture. The single-minded hero persists in popular and visual cultures especially in representations of warfare, which is itself often contrasted with civilian life as the setting for forms of heroism uncorrupted by evasion and compromise.

Masculine fantasies cannot be seen simply as a form of escape. Since the 1970s, a consistent feminist critique has pointed to the dangers of the heroic tradition as reinforcing male fantasies of omnipotence and violence. Subsequently, the men's movement, too, has expressed doubts about the value of these kinds of role models. Taking a cue from Richard Sennett (1970), we might ask whether human society can any longer afford these longings for uncomplicated identity, or for a masculine subjectivity purified of contradictory elements—so contemptuous of difference, of the feminine, of the coexistence of other identities. John MacInnes (1998) quotes Adam Phillips: "the problems start when we imagine that life could be any other than a mess. We get stuck on the fantasies of what a messless life would comprise rather than appreciating its messiness and making real choices" (21).

Perhaps the current widespread preoccupation in North America and Europe with a supposed crisis in masculinity is in part fueled by nostalgia over the decline of simplified role models—idealized versions of the warrior, the manual worker, the sportsman, or the authoritative father (Faludi 1999). Are the practices and apparatus of domination themselves attempts to solve the problems of masculine frustration? In the twentieth century the heroisms of adventure and warfare were particularly associated with nationalism and with imperial adventures. In more extreme situations, attempts to salvage male pride and heroic values have resulted in forms of totalitarianism. Heroes attempt (by bullying and violence if necessary) to create spaces where the fantasy of purified identity, collective or individual, can be achieved. The hero—whose narra-

tives seem so often to hark back to his violent origins—has a hint of the Bronze Age about him. His persistence as a model for masculinity could turn out to be an environmental and political disaster.

Ben Knights

Further Reading:

Beynon, John. 2002. *Masculinities and Culture.* Buckingham and Philadelphia: Open University Press.

Dawson, Graham. 1994. *Soldier Heroes: British Adventure, Empire and the Imagining of Masculinities.* London: Routledge.

Faludi, Susan. 1999. *Stiffed.* New York: William Morrow.

Hourihan, Margery. 1997. *Deconstructing the Hero: Literary Theory and Children's Literature.* London: Routledge.

MacInnes, John. 1998. *The End of Masculinity: The Confusion of Sexual Genesis and Sexual Difference in Modern Society.* Buckingham and Philadelphia: Open UniversityPress.

Sennett, Richard. 1970. *The Uses of Disorder: Personal Identity and City Life.* Harmondsworth, NY: Knopf.

Heston, Charlton (1924–)

American actor, director, union leader, and political activist, Charlton Heston is known for starring in masculine roles in epic film dramas of the 1950s, 1960s, and 1970s. More recently, Heston has turned his attention to conservative political activity, while appearing in cameo and smaller roles in films that poke fun at his epic status. Heston's string of largely heroic, larger-than-life roles have made him an icon of traditional masculinity (physically tough, handsome, monogamously heterosexual, patriotic, and often religious). Heston's chiseled good-looks, rugged physique, and mellifluous and well-trained voice lead to him being cast as Biblical heroes in films such as *The Ten Commandments* (1956), in which he played Moses, and *The Greatest Story Ever Told* (1965), where he appeared as John the Baptist. He also starred as historical characters such as the Cid in *El Cid* (1961), Andrew Jackson in *The Buccaneer* (1958), Michelangelo in *The Agony and the Ecstasy* (1965), and Cardinal

Richelieu in *The Three Musketeers* (1973) and *The Four Musketeers* (1974). After playing these historical heroes, Heston led a number of 1970s disaster films set in present (*Airport, 1975* [1974]; *Earthquake* [1974]) and science fiction films, (*The Planet of the Apes* [1968], *Beneath the Planet of the Apes* [1970], *The Omega Man* [1971], and *Soylent Green* [1973]. Off screen, Heston has lent his stature to an evolving array of political issues: the Civil Rights movement in the 1950s, gun control in the 1960s, and gun rights in the 1990s. In 1965 Heston became president of the Screen Actors Guild for six years, having been hand-picked by his predecessor, Ronald Reagan. Heston has chaired the American Film Institute and in 1998 became the president of the National Rifle Association. As NRA leader, Heston has championed a number of very conservative causes, often grabbing headlines because of his celebrity status and loaded rhetoric.

Born John Charlton Carter in 1924, Heston became interested in drama during high school and spent a year studying drama at Northwestern University before enlisting in the Army Air Corps in World War II. He did not return to college after the war because he viewed the GI Bill as a government handout. He moved to New York and began getting roles on and off Broadway and in live television, particularly in *Westinghouse Studio One*. He and his wife, Lydia Clarke, spent time in Asheville, North Carolina, managing a theater and acting and directing there. He made his Hollywood debut in *Dark City* (1950). His breakthrough role was as the ringmaster in Cecil B. DeMille's *The Greatest Show on Earth* (1952). Heston won the best actor Oscar for his portrayal of the Jewish prince turned galley slave in *Ben-Hur* (1959). He has also appeared in Shakespearean films, including *Hamlet* (1996), *Julius Caesar* (1970), and *Antony and Cleopatra* (1973), which he also directed. More recent films include *Wayne's World II* (1993), *Any Given Sunday* (1999), and *Planet of the Apes* (2001).

Heston has written several autobiographical works, including *The Actor's Life, Journals 1956–1976* (1978), *Beijing Diary* (1990), and *In the Arena* (1995).

Ashton D. Trice
Samuel A. Holland

Further Reading:
Crowther, Bruce. 1986. *Charlton Heston: The Epic Presence*. London: Columbus Books.
Heston, Charlton. 1978. *The Actor's Life: Journals, 1956–1976*. New York: E. P. Dutton.
———. 1990. *Beijing Diary*. New York: Simon and Schuster.
———. 1995. *In the Arena: An Autobiography*. New York: Simon and Schuster.
Munn, Michael. 1986. *Charlton Heston*. New York: St. Martin's Press.
Solomon, Jon. 1978. *The Ancient World in the Cinema*. New York: A. S. Barnes.

Heteronormativity

When Adrienne Rich coined the phrase "compulsory heterosexuality" (1986), she argued that universal heterosexual desire and practice are certainly assumed, required, and mandated by the combined weight of dozens of social institutions and thousands of individuals, from lawgivers and scholars to teachers and parents to the person who casually asks "are you married?" at the laundromat. Later, in the introduction to *Fear of a Queer Planet: Queer Politics and Social Theory* (1993), Michael Warner coined *heteronormativity* to refer to the practice of organizing patterns of thought, basic awareness, and raw beliefs around the presumption of universal heterosexual desire. Heteronormativity is different from heterosexual desire itself, because men and women who desire each other may still recognize that homoerotic desire exists as a normal and valid variation of human experience. By contrast, heteronormativity acknowledges no variations, no exceptions, no resistance, no dissent; it becomes the way we perceive the world.

The presumption of universal heterosexual desire informs epistemology, determining what can be thought and what can be discussed: The term *man* is meaningless unless it includes "desiring women," and *woman* is meaningless unless it includes "desiring men." In modern societies, men are particularly oppressed by the need to perform heterosexuality every moment of every day: Young boys are incessantly told "you'll meet a nice girl someday and settle down"; teenage boys often mark a first heterosexual experience as an essential step from childhood to manhood (and frequent additional heterosexual experiences as essential to maintaining that manhood); and adult men often recoil from the suggestion that they might harbor homoerotic desire as an affront to their masculine identity—as an indication that they are not really men at all. Even gay men must negotiate this oppressive and ubiquitous universalization of heterosexual desire: every official document they encounter asks them to choose between "single (and heterosexual)" or "married (and heterosexual)"; colleagues nudge them when attractive women pass, because after all every man likes women; they are subject to inquiries about how they "became" gay, or rather changed from their "original" heterosexual state.

But heteronormativity extends far beyond the arena of interpersonal relationships to imbue social institutions, artistic works, discourses of statehood, and individual lives with an underlying, unquestioned, and invisible presumption of universal heterosexual desire. We negotiate a universe of legal and social validation of heterosexual loves, from senior proms to conjugal rights in prison, from couples' discounts at hotels to the immediate immigration rights of foreign marital partners, from a nonchalant goodbye kiss at the airport to incessant male-female couples grinning down from billboards to fairy tales with princes rescuing princesses. It is, indeed, difficult to find any aspect of modern life that does not include men desiring women and women desiring men as a premise, as necessary to being human as breathing and thinking.

Heteronormativity cannot be resisted merely by gay, lesbian, bisexual, or otherwise nonstraight identities, which are usually constructed within the framework of universal heterosexual desire; that is, if all desire is by definition heterosexual desire, if to be a "man" implicitly means "desiring women," then a gay man must *really* be a woman, and his desire arguably heterosexual. Conversely, a gay or bisexual male identity may be constructed as an anomaly: to be a "man" means "desiring women," with the sole exception of this particular man right here in front of me. However, all ideological systems, even the most ingrained and pervasive, are ultimately incoherent and unstable; the presumption of universal heterosexual desire is a myth that can never stand up to serious scrutiny. The project of queer theory seeks to resist heteronormativity by revealing its instability, by finding the nonstraight, antistraight, or contrastraight desire implicit in every heteronormative discourse.

Jeffery P. Dennis

Further Reading:

Jackson, Stevi. 1999. *Heterosexuality in Question.* Thousand Oaks, CA: Sage Publications.

Rich, Adrienne. 1986/1980. "Compulsory Heterosexuality and Lesbian Existence." Pp. 23–75 in *Blood, Bread, and Poetry: Selected Prose 1979–1985.* New York: Norton.

Richardson, Diane. 1996. "Heterosexuality and Social Theory." Pp. 1–20 in *Theorizing Heterosexuality: Telling it Straight.* Edited by Diane Richardson. Buckingham, UK: Open University Press.

Warner, Michael. 1993. "Introduction." Pp. vii-xxxi in *Fear of a Queer Planet: QueerPolitics and Social Theory.* Edited by Michael Warner. Minneapolis, MN: University of Minnesota Press.

Heterosexism

See Heteronormativity; Homophobia

Heterosexuality

See Heteronormativity; Masculinities; Masculinities, Relations among

Hippies at a fair, 1960s (Henry Diltz / Corbis)

Hippies

Is *hippie masculinity* a contradiction in terms? One might presume that hippie men, with their long hair, outlandish costumes, and rejection of competition as "uptightness," were the Americans least concerned with maintaining a sense of masculine identity. After all, exasperated "straight" (conventional) adults frequently remarked at the time (1960s–1970s) that "you can't tell the boys from the girls nowadays!" The image of the soft, "androgynous" hippie male is a fixture in today's popular culture. But in fact, hippie men were cultural radicals whose appearance and behavior signaled a deep, but frequently only partly articulated, commitment to the search for more authentic forms of masculine identity. In post–World War II America, "straight" men struggled to reconcile expec-

tations that men exhibit rugged independence, toughness, and bravado with demands that they be nurturing fathers, emotionally responsive husbands, and team players in the corporate workplace. Hippie men refused to accept the terms of that struggle, questioning the very legitimacy of companionate marriage, careerism, and the nuclear family, identifying them as the *sources* of, not the solution to, a masculine malaise that had given rise after World War II to a much-remarked "crisis of masculinity" (Kimmel 1996). Hippies sought to reclaim an "authentic" and "natural" masculinity by constructing a completely new society, within which they hoped to renew their connection to the natural world and to those parts of human nature that, they believed, modern industrial society had repressed: emotional honesty; spiritual ecstasy; uninhibited sexual expression; and warm, cooperative social relations in close-knit communities. Their efforts generated a diverse range of nonconformist masculinities that still exert significant influence on American culture at the start of the twenty-first century. Hippie masculinities evolved in the context of a completely decentralized phenomenon, which scholars have called "the counterculture." All hippies rejected straight society as "uptight" and unnatural. They further agreed that the most important factor in creating social change was the consciousness of the individual: new structures and institutions would evolve as people freed their minds from old presumptions (Braunstein and Doyle 2002). However, hippies never reached consensus on the precise means and ends by which to liberate human consciousness. Some took an anarchistic approach to creating the new society. They saw freedom as the total absence of imposed authority. Others took a mystical approach. They saw freedom as adherence to natural law; industrial society had erred, they said, because its faith in scientific reason dismissed as superstition the metaphysical realities that defined human existence. Hippie mystics adopted ancient systems of wisdom (such as monastic Buddhism) or borrowed freely from many systems, old and new. The choice between anarchist and mystical approaches to change served as the point of departure for the formation of anarchist and mystical hippie masculinities (Hodgdon 2002).

Anarchist hippies contended that the institutions of straight society promised men a rewarding masculine identity as a breadwinning head of household. Yet, in observing their fathers' lives, they concluded that breadwinning emasculated the men by requiring continual deference to higher authority. Debased by alienating work, a spiritually barren religious life that demanded faith in the absence of ecstatic experience, and the emotional dishonesty of conforming to repressive sexual mores, the career man and the blue-collar "hard hat" alike passively accepted that the big issues were the province of those more successful than themselves.

The anarchist Diggers, a loose collective formed in the Haight-Ashbury district of San Francisco in 1966, encouraged ordinary men to "find their brothers" by slipping free of the breadwinner's yoke. Self-styled "outlaws," they distributed free food, opened "free stores" in which would-be "customers" might experience the exchange of goods without money, and thumbed their noses at the police and the law, using city streets as a theater for pageants that encouraged direct popular participation in the creation of the new society. Like the Beats of the 1950s, the Diggers romanticized marginalized men—gangsters, artists, racial minorities—as those who preserved the spirit of anarchy amid the deference of bourgeois culture. The Diggers admired the swaggering Black Panthers and for a time collaborated with the Hell's Angels motorcycle gang (Coyote 1998).

Spiritual teacher Stephen Gaskin and his followers were good examples of the many experiments in hippie mysticism. They established The Farm, a commune in Summertown, Tennessee, in 1971. It became the largest of the hippie-era communes, reaching a population of perhaps 1,500 in 1980 (Miller 1999, 120). Gaskin taught that straight society overemphasized aggression and assertiveness in men, leaving them incapable of appreciating women's feminine qualities as worthy of genuine respect. The result was the "battle of the sexes," which, by keeping both men and women mired in a low state of metaphysical awareness, led not only to personal unhappiness, but to humankind's greatest problems: pollution, warfare, and inequality. Gaskin rejected Digger "outlaw" manhood and the "sexual revolution" as self-indulgent egoism. The solution, he said, was for men to adopt a disciplined approach to marriage: "household yoga" required of husbands a lifelong, monogamous commitment. The ideal husband was to cultivate "knightly" comportment in his relations with "ladies." The commune's social structure evolved around the promotion, protection, and veneration of childbirth and motherhood, with men's labors dedicated to providing the material support for that sacred fertility (S. Gaskin et al. 1974; I Gaskin et al. 1975).

These and many other colorful variants of hippie masculinity tell us a great deal about the presumptions about gender that prevailed in the United States in the mid-twentieth century. Both Gaskin and the Diggers developed their ideologies of social change in the years just before the inception of the women's liberation movement. The sexism of the counterculture and other youth movements of the time stimulated the development of women's liberation, while at the same time serving as the latter's model for social activism and movement culture building (Evans 1980; Umansky 1996). Feminist criticism of radical men's sexism, in turn, influenced at least some radical men to assume greater participation in household tasks, drop sexist forms of hip usage (such as calling women "chicks" or "old ladies"), and in some cases even to question the once-universal hippie presumption that sexual intercourse was necessarily liberating because pleasurable to men. Hip masculinity, like conventional forms of manhood, has been subject to change over time. Today, it continues to exist as one of many variants in a pluralist system of gender relations (Connell 1995).

Tim Hodgdon

See also Beat Poets

Further Reading:
Braunstein, Peter, and Michael William Doyle, eds. 2002. *Imagine Nation: The American Counterculture of the 1960s and '70s.* New York: Routledge.
Connell, R. W. 1995. *Masculinities.* Cambridge, UK: Polity Press.
Coyote, Peter. 1998. *Sleeping Where I Fall: A Chronicle.* Washington, DC: Counterpoint.
Evans, Sara. 1980. *Personal Politics: The Roots of Women's Liberation in the Civil Rights Movement and the New Left.* New York: Vintage.
Fike, Rupert, ed. 1998. *Voices from The Farm: Adventures in Community Living.* Summertown, TN: Book Publishing Co.
[Gaskin], Ina May, and the Farm Midwives. 1975. *Spiritual Midwifery.* Summertown, TN: Book Publishing Co.
[Gaskin], Stephen, and The Farm. 1974. *Hey Beatnik! This Is the Farm Book.* Summertown, TN: Book Publishing Co.
Hodgdon, Tim. 2002. "Manhood in the Age of Aquarius: Masculinity in Two Countercultural Communities, 1965–1983." (Ph.D. dissertation, Arizona State University, Tempe, Arizona.).
Kimmel, Michael S. 1996. *Manhood in America: A Cultural History.* New York: Free Press.
Miller, Timothy. 1999. *The 60s Communes: Hippies and Beyond.* Syracuse, NY: Syracuse University Press.
Umansky, Lauri. 1996. *Motherhood Reconceived: Feminism and the Legacies of the Sixties.* New York: New York University Press.
Veysey, Laurence. *The Communal Experience: Anarchist and Mystical Counter-Cultures in America.* New York: Harper and Row, 1973.

Hispanic Men

See Latino Masculinities

Hollinghurst, Alan (1954–)

An important chronicler of the gay life in England and contributor to the British literary discourse on masculinities, male sexuality, and AIDS, Alan Hollinghurst is known for his novels, which are by turns raunchy, elegiac, and cerebral, and are equally apt to stir controversy and uphold tradition. In 1988, in the midst of the AIDS epidemic, his incisive, nostalgic look at the lives of gay men in the early 1980s England put Hollinghurst on the literary map.

The intricate narrative of *The Swimming-Pool Library* (1988) encompasses, simultaneously, several months in the life of Will Beckwith, an upper-crust young Londoner whose abundant leisure and good looks allow him to explore the seemingly unlimited sexual possibilities afforded by pre-AIDS London, and several decades of the persecution of gay men in Britain. Defiantly hedonistic and adamantly resistant to any moralizing conclusions, the novel nonetheless engages in a candid exploration of British history and the troubling intersections of sexuality, gender, class, race, power, art, and the law.

Hollinghurst continues to ponder the connections between the public and the private realms, desire and betrayal, history and artistry in his second novel, *The Folding Star,* shortlisted for the Booker Prize in 1994. A brief and doomed love affair between Edward Manners, an English tutor and aspiring writer, and Luc Altidore, his young student, echoes wistfully the Hellenist tradition of erotically charged all-male pedagogy. The subplot involving Edgard Orst, a fictional Belgian-Jewish artist, and his assistant Paul Echevin makes World War II and the Holocaust an unlikely background for a story of sexual awakening, as well as the ultimate test of ethical choices and personal loyalties.

The Spell (1998), Hollinghurst's last novel to date, paints the much-changed landscape of the gay life in the 1990s. Although we occasionally get the glimpse of an Ecstasy-laced London rave, or a half-hearted attempt at an orgy, the novel's most memorable image, two couples watching the sunset on an idyllic Dorset cliff, comes at the end. The novel reconciles gay fathers and sons, forgives unfaithful lovers and buries those lost to AIDS. *The Spell* takes a shot at a traditional happy ending and hopes for the regeneration of a community ravaged by the epidemic.

An ongoing dialogue with the British literary tradition is the trademark of Hollinghurst's writing. His novels invoke a range of voices, from the flamboyant to the sublime. Such writers as E. M. Forster and Oscar Wilde, Ronald Firbank and John Milton, and Thomas Hardy and William Thackeray have inspired Hollinghurst's work in various ways. His keen awareness of his literary and historical legacy makes Hollinghurst a novelist of considerable interest and value to the students of both British literature and masculinities. The evolution of his plots and the predicaments of his characters illustrate the way in which language and history both shape and unsettle our notions of gender and sexuality.

Born in 1954 in Gloucestershire, Alan Hollinghurst read and subsequently taught English at Magdalene College, Oxford. He has also held a teaching position at the University of London and served as an editor at *The Times Literary Supplement.*

Helena Gurfinkel

Further Reading:

Hollinghurst, Alan. 1988. *The Swimming-Pool Library.* New York: Random House.
———. 1994. *The Folding Star.* 1994 New York: Pantheon Books.
———. 1999. *The Spell.* New York: Viking.
The Knitting Circle: Literature, "Alan Hollinghurst." At *http://www.sbu.ac.uk/stafflag/hollinghurst.html* (cited 25 October 2002).

Homicide

Men and boys are far more often the perpetrators and victims of homicide than are women. This pattern is remarkably stable, holding across time and across nations (Newburn and Stanko 1994). Even though gender is the most conspicuous characteristic of homicide, gender is rarely the subject of homicide studies. When gender is considered, women are usually the focus. Because homicide tends to be a masculine matter, it is important to explore the theoretical reasons for this phenomenon. It follows, then, that understanding gender differences is critical to understanding the nature and causes of homicide.

Attempts to understand masculinity and crime at the individual level have emphasized the need to recognize a variety of masculinities (as opposed to one monolithic experience of masculinity), as well as the social construction of masculinity. This involves an acknowledgement of the many forms masculine violence can assume. Scholars who share this perspective suggest that crime is one of the many patterned ways that masculinity is performed. In other words, men "do" masculinity according to their specific situational contexts. In situations in which men commit homicide, murder can be a process of affirming masculinity (Messerschmidt 1993).

Ethnographic evidence further illuminates distinct scenarios of masculine homicide. One common scenario is when men use lethal violence to control the behavior of female sexual partners. It is possible that this stems from the notion that males expect to have a right to possess a woman. In this case, the use of violence is a matter of maintaining control over women, a notion that may be a key aspect of masculine socialization. In the case of male-on-male violence, masculine homicide usually involves a defense of a man's honor. Other times lethal violence is used to resolve a conflict. The conceptual framework that emerges here involves themes of masculine domination, as well as masculine competition for status and honor. What makes these scenarios distinctively masculine is that women rarely commit homicide for the same reasons men do (Polk 1994).

Men are more likely than women to kill strangers or acquaintances. Men are also more likely to commit homicide during the course of arguments that involve status competition or "saving face" (Kruttschnitt 2000). Lifestyle theorists also suggest that because males are less likely than females to be supervised by capable guardians, men are more apt to be in situations that are conducive to offending (Cohen and Felson 1979; Hagan 1990). In other words, as part of the gender socialization process, women are subject to greater surveillance, social control, and supervision than men are.

Sociobiologists contend that there is a biological predisposition among men to commit violent acts, but that this same propensity is not present in women. However, the bulk of evidence indicates that it is not biological factors that determine how men behave, but rather, it is social and cultural factors that influence such gender-specific behavior (Kimbrell 1995). Scholars who have found support for the power of socialization in explaining the link between gender and violence often point out that boys and girls are differentially socialized. Boys are more likely to be encouraged to act aggressively while girls are more likely to be encouraged to act passively. In explaining the link between masculinity and homicide, scholars have also appealed to cultural factors and role expectations. That is, culturally specific behavioral norms are different for boys than they are for girls.

This kind of gender-specific socialization is ultimately constituted through language. Thus, postmodern and poststructuralists emphasize that understanding men's criminality should involve an examination of how a proliferation of discourses are constructed about masculinity and violence (Collier 1998). Once scholars discover how ideas about masculinity and crime are constituted in multiple discourses, a process of deconstruction can begin, which then might reveal those social practices that produce crime.

Because very few men actually commit homicide, gender alone is not a sufficient explanation. Other factors interact with gender to increase the probability of homicide. Class tends to be a significant variable in homicide studies. Polk (1994) found the two most important factors in understanding homicide to be masculinity and lower-class status. The lack of access to power and economic rewards may lead males to use violence as compensation. That is, violence may be an alternate way of securing honor or reputation when it is otherwise unavailable to men in lower-class positions. The need to preserve honor or display bravado may be structured according to where males exist in the social hierarchy. Of course, the emphasis on masculine honor is culturally and historically specific. As notions of hegemonic masculinity change across space and time, the relationship between masculinity and homicide can be expected to assume different forms.

Age is a critical variable in understanding the relationship between masculinity and homicide. Homicide tends to be committed almost exclusively by young people. Individuals between the ages of fifteen and thirty-four commit three-quarters of all homicides. Race and geographic location are also important indicators of homicide. Homicide offenders are disproportionately African American, the majority of which are of low income and live in urban areas. Some researchers contend that race is a stronger predictor of homicide offending and victimization than gender. The high involvement of ethnic minorities (excluding Asians) in homicide is often explained by their marginal status, their lack of access to societal resources, and their concentration in socially disorganized urban areas.

At the macro level, the causes for gender-specific homicide are not as distinct. In cross-national studies, economic inequality, cultural support for violence, and disrupted families are positively associated with homicide rates (Kruttschnitt 2000). This tends to hold for both male and female homicide rates, thus contributing to the growing body of evidence that gender-neutral, macro-structural variables tend to predict both male and female homicide rates, as opposed to gender-specific variables predicting each. Although this advancement has helped to explain changes in male and female homicide rates, it does not explain the gender gap, that is, why males commit more homicide than females do.

Gwen Hunnicutt

See also Violence

Further Reading:

Cohen, Lawrence E., and Marcus Felson. 1979. "Social Change and Crime Rate Trends: A Routine Activity Approach." *American Sociological Review* 44, no. 4: 588–607.

Collier, Richard. 1998. *Masculinities, Crime and Criminology.* Thousand Oaks, CA: Sage.

Hagan, John. 1990. "The Structure of Gender and Deviance: A Power-Control Theory of Vulnerability to Crime and the Search for Deviant Role Exits." *Canadian Review of Sociology and Anthropology* 27, no. 2: 137–157.

Hatty, Suzanne E. 2000. *Masculinities, Violence and Culture.* Thousand Oaks, CA: Sage.

Kimbrell, Andrew. 1995. *The Masculine Mystique.* New York: Ballantine Books.

Kruttschnitt, Candace. 2000. "Gender and Violence." Pp. 77–92 in *Women, Crime and Criminal Justice.* Edited by Claire M. Renzetti and Lynne Goodstein. Los Angeles: Roxbury.

Messerschmidt, James W. 1993. *Masculinities and Crime: Critique and Reconceptualization of Theory.* Lanham, MD: Rowman and Littlefield.

Newburn, Tim, and Elizabeth A. Stanko. 1994. *Just Boys Doing Business? Men, Masculinities and Crime.* New York: Routledge.

Polk, Kenneth. 1994. *When Men Kill: Scenarios of Masculine Violence.* Melbourne, Australia: Cambridge University Press.

Homophobia

Homophobia is classically defined as a fear or hatred of homosexuals (Weinberg 1972), but it has become increasingly clear that this definition fails to capture the full significance of homophobia.

Homophobia is a problematic term that is commonly refers neither to a true phobia nor to a fear of sameness (as the derivation from the Greek *homos* would suggest) (Haaga 1991). Moreover, beyond problems with its literal meaning, the everyday use of the term *homophobia* indicates that its significance extends far beyond being a simple prejudice against homosexuals. It is deeply implicated in the gender order and its influence on contemporary masculinities and male identity is almost universally underestimated (Kimmel 1994). Male homophobia is a resilient, ubiquitous, highly influential taboo, which exerts profound effects on the lives of all men, not just gay men.

In attempting to resolve the difficulties inherent in defining homophobia, some writers have advocated restricting the term to its literal sense and to use it to describe true phobias (Haaga 1991). Others (including this author) prefer to retain the term as a useful "placeholder" for a cluster of social phenomena and to base its definition on the everyday usage of "homophobia" and related words. Eventually new words will be needed to adequately reflect the complicated web of taboos that are currently conflated under the umbrella of *homophobia*.

Uncertainties about the social significance of homophobia and the difficulties in establishing an agreed meaning for the term have prompted some writers to examine antihomosexual prejudice more closely. A number of schools of thought have proposed various theoretical frameworks to explain homophobia. Among these frameworks are ones that assert that homophobia is a manifestation of misogyny, heterosexism, or religious bias (Haaga 1991; Kimmel 1994; Plummer 1999).

Unfortunately each of these frameworks has shortcomings and, although useful, none offers a complete explanation for why homophobia exists or what it is supposed to achieve, and none explains homophobia in its entirety. For example, although homophobia does indeed target homosexuality, it is also triggered by nonsexual behaviors such as the way a man dresses, how he walks, and how flexible his wrists are. Further, while homophobia targets boys who act like girls, misogyny fails to explain why boys are at increased risk of being targeted when they prefer academic pursuits or solo men's sports over team sports. Even more difficult to explain with any of the conventional theories is the observation that boys in junior school regularly report being targeted with homophobia when they mix too much with girls or in later years when they don't mix with girls enough. Certainly antigay, misogynistic, heterosexist, or religious biases don't seem to offer comprehensive explanations for all scenarios in which homophobia is triggered.

An alternative explanation for homophobia has emerged out of observations about the development of boys (Plummer 2001). Using a deceptively simple design, it was possible to trace how the use of homophobic words developed among boys and young men and what meanings were attached to them (Plummer 1999). Importantly, similar patterns were found independently across various states in Australia and New Zealand and these findings were consistent with work from the United States, Britain, and elsewhere (Mac-an-Ghaill 1994; Thorne 1993).

It was observed that boys start using homophobic words like "poofter" and "faggot" during primary school (Plummer 2001). These words become commonplace in boys' talk before puberty, before their sexual identity consolidates, and before they know much (if anything) about homosexuality. Yet, words like "poofter" and "faggot" are not random, meaningless insults—on the contrary, from their earliest appearance they are invested with very specific, powerful meanings. These early meanings and their sequential appearance provide powerful insights into the workings and significance of homophobia. The research found that words like "poofter" and "faggot" are:

- highly gender specific. These words are never used against girls, against whom they lack meaning, whereas they have extreme significance for boys from the outset.
- deeply negative. Boys never consider these words complimentary, and they clearly rank them apart, and fear them more than any other swear words circulating among their peers at the time.
- consistently triggered by an array of nonsexual characteristics and behaviors, including how boys dress, how they style their hair, how polished their shoes are, what school subjects they choose, how well they participate in team sports, whether they are too interested in reading books and doing well in class, whether they are "teacher's pets," and so on.
- ultimately incorporate antihomosexual meaning too, yet earlier connotations from childhood are retained.
- suspended under certain circumstances. This occurs in two classic situations: First, homophobic inhibitions can be relinquished when boys are removed from the risk of peer group scrutiny, and second, special dispensation for some homoerotic activities can be issued

TABLE 1: Meanings Associated with Homophobia

Characteristics	Protective	Risky
Gender *("femophobia")*	Emphasized masculinity	Insufficiently masculine Feminine
Physical development *and physicality*	Physical strength Physical maturity Physically active	Weak Physical immaturity Bookish
Group allegiances	Peer-group member Peer-group loyalty Team sport oriented	Loyalties outside peer group Peer-group betrayal Outsider Loner
Power and authority	Dominant Bold Hypermasculine Rebel	Submissive Cowardly Effeminate Conformist
Sexuality *("true" homphobia)*	Heterosexual	Sexually "deviant"

providing they are conducted according to agreed codes and sanctioned by the group (Plummer 1999, 266).

In addition to targeting boys who are effeminate, homophobia also targets boys who act like babies, particularly when under pressure; who are slow to develop physically; who are not peer-group oriented; whose appearance differs from peer-group standards; who conform too much to the authority of adults at the expense of peer-group loyalty; who distinguish themselves in reading and academic pursuits; who are good at subjects at school that do not solely belong to a boy's domain; who avoid tough team sports; and on the odd occasion homophobic words even target homosexuality! So while perceived femininity and homosexuality in males can trigger homophobia, they are elements among many that can do so. The term *onion skinning* was coined for this highly patterned, successive layering of powerful meaning into homophobic words (Plummer 1999, 44).

Despite antihomosexual prejudice being a central aspect of homophobia, more often than not homophobia is triggered by nonsexual, "surrogate" characteristics in the absence of any evidence of sexual practice. The above research offers an explanation of why this is so: For crucial early periods in a boy's development, homophobic words are deployed against nonsexual targets and these meanings persist into adulthood alongside later antigay connotations. Coherence between the early (nonsexual) and later (antigay) meanings is achieved because all of the meanings (early and late) share the quality of targeting behaviors and characteristics that are deemed inappropriate for boys as they mature. Thus homophobia is rooted in gender dynamics, but rather than specifically marking the *intergender* divide between masculinity and femininity, homophobia marks an *intragender* divide between appropriate, peer-endorsed masculine behavior and a lack of appropriate masculinity (a failure to measure up). In other words, *poofter* and *faggot* are cumulative repositories for everything a growing boy should not be.

The attraction of this model is that it accommodates the antihomosexual, misogynistic, and heterosexist explanations for homophobia and addresses their shortcomings. And rather than being one of many masculinities (Connell 1995), the meanings associated with homophobia indicate that during boys' development, homosexuality is positioned as *contrary* to orthodox masculinity (against the "order of things"—at least in modern Western culture, but unlike many traditional cultures). This positioning explains much of the power that drives homophobia.

Not only do boys attach consistent, powerful meanings to homophobic words, but in turn these words deeply intimidate boys. This dynamic—the fear of homophobia or "homophobiaphobia"—exerts a powerful influence over boys and deeply affects how they behave in front of others, particularly their peers. As a result of this pressure, precise complex codes emerge that even govern how boys gesture, use their eyes, and how they style their appearance and behavior to avoid attracting homophobia (Plummer 1999, 2001). It has been argued that the journey from childhood to adulthood is a "homophobic passage." Homophobic passage refers to the complex social processes extending from early boyhood to adulthood, during which homophobia starts, crescendos, peaks, and moderates, and during which major shifts in homophobic meanings and corresponding reorganizations and restrictions of masculinity take place (Plummer 1999). In modern Western culture, homophobia plays a fundamental role in bullying, the male "pecking order," and ultimately in policing the attainment of manhood (Kimmel 1994; Rofes 1995; Plummer 1999, 2001).

David Plummer

See also Homosexuality

Further Reading:

Connell, R. W. 1995. *Masculinities.* Sydney, Australia: Allen and Unwin.

Haaga, David A. F. 1991. "Homophobia?" *Journal of Social Behavior and Personality* 6, no. 1: 171–174.

Kimmel, Michael S. 1994. "Masculinity as Homophobia." In *Theorising Masculinities.* Edited by H. Brod and M. K. Kaufman. Thousand Oaks, CA: Sage.

Mac-an-Ghaill, Mairtin. 1994. *The Making of Men: Masculinities, Sexualities and Schooling.* Buckingham, UK: Open University Press.

Plummer, David C. 1999. *One of the Boys: Masculinity, Homophobia and Modern Manhood.* New York: Haworth.

———. 2001. "Policing Manhood: New Theories about the Social Significance of Homophobia." In *Sexual Positions: an Australian View.* Edited by C. Wood. Melbourne, Australia: Hill of Content/Collins.

Thorne, Barrie. 1993. *Gender Play: Girls and Boys in School.* Buckingham, UK: Open University Press.

Weinberg, George. 1972. *Society and the Healthy Homosexual.* Boston: Alyson.

Homosexuality

Homosexuality, which has existed in every culture across the span of history, presents an interesting challenge to the study of masculinity. Male homosexuals, in modern times thought to be effeminate, "failed" men, have not always occupied that position in societies around the world. In recent times, gay men have helped to redefine masculinity, to emphasize the idea of multiple masculinities even within the gay community, and have challenged the idea that they do not qualify as masculine.

Homosexuality, the sexual and affectional attraction between members of the same sex, has been and continues to be part of every culture and society in the world. Throughout time and in different places, societies found a role for homosexuals and developed expectations for behavior and demeanor. Among the upper classes in ancient Greek societies, male homosexual relationships played an important role, were accepted as normal, and were part of the education of young males. Elaborate rites in some Greek city-states had young males chosen, "kidnapped," and placed into the tutelage of an adult male for months. Homosexual sex was an integral part of these rites and was considered a masculine coming-of-age endeavor. In ancient Rome, attitudes toward homosexuality varied. Among Romans, however, there was little concern about the object of sexual penetration; it was the act of penetration that defined manhood. Even Christianity had a place for same-sex relationships until approximately the tenth century (Boswell 1980).

In Eastern societies, homoerotic relations were also important. In China, homosexuality was accepted, more so in some eras than others, but on the whole was not condemned. In the Han dynasty, the "passion of the cut sleeve" was the reference for male homosexual behavior that was common in Chinese society until the nineteenth century. In Japan, Samurai warriors and Buddhist monks both incorporated homosexual elements. India, likewise, had an active homosexual culture with legal boy prostitution lasting until Indian independence in 1948.

Native American cultures had a unique and respected place for homosexual men and women—they constituted a special sex. Called *berdache,* males wore female clothing, took the passive role in sex, and were often treated as sacred persons. The Aztecs, Mayans, and Incas all practiced homosexuality, both in ritual and in everyday life.

In all of these societies a subtle tension existed between notions of masculinity and homosexual desire and acts. There were rules of behavior and practice with regard to the active and passive roles in sex between men. Should conventions be broken, the participant's masculinity was called into question. For example, in some ancient Greek societies, adult males who had sex with young males who had not yet grown facial hair were considered within the bounds of acceptability. Should this rule be broken, and there is ample evidence that it was often violated, the participants were open to ridicule.

In general, the active partner, the one playing the dominant sexual role (i.e., the penetrator) was considered masculine, and such behavior was relatively acceptable even in societies that condemned homosexuality.

The male who penetrated was, after all, behaving like a male, and the object of his sexual predation made no difference. The passive partner, on the other hand, was considered less than a man, effeminate, and treated with no respect.

Throughout history sexual behavior was addressed by legal and religious authorities with varying degrees of acceptance or condemnation. Yet, the concept of sexuality did not exist, per se, and was not approached in a systematic manner or studied by scholars until the eighteenth century.

At that time, religious and moral attitudes had begun to condemn all nonprocreative sex (including homosexuality). But the rationalist philosophy of the era attacked these regressive religious attitudes and proscriptions. At the same time, sexuality became an increasing concern of the medical community, which came to the defense of old religious beliefs and standards. It was not until the late nineteenth century that some scholars and scientists began to approach sexuality, including homosexuality, as an area for research and scholarship. In fact, the words "homosexual" and "homosexuality" did not exist prior to 1869.

It is interesting to note that in the middle to late nineteenth century, the earliest calls for homosexual rights were given voice. Karl Heinrich Ulrichs, a researcher and philosopher, wrote many tracts in favor of rights for homosexuals. In 1864 he coined the term "urnings" for homosexuals, whom he considered to be the third sex. Ulrichs theorized that during gestation the male homosexual developed physically as a male but spiritually as a female, thus accounting for same-sex desires. As an essentialist, he was able to argue that because homosexuality was inborn, those with that trait should not be discriminated against or condemned. He also believed that homosexuals were effeminate by nature. This began the first glimmerings of the discussion of masculinity among homosexual men.

A contemporary of Ulrichs with whom he corresponded was Karl Maria Kertbeny, who studied sexuality and theorized about homosexuality. Also an essentialist, he coined the term *homosexual* in 1869 and, like Ulrichs, he worked for homosexual rights. In addition, he believed that homosexual men were superior masculine beings—more virile and hypersexual than ordinary men, particularly because they did not use sex as a weapon against women.

Kertbeny's term *homosexual* was later co-opted by the medical-psychiatric community, which reduced the concept to a condition considered a disease.

At the same time and into the early twentieth century, Magnus Hirschfeld, a sex researcher who is considered the father of the early homosexual rights movement, promulgated his own theories and solutions. He opened the Institute for Sexual Science in 1919 in Berlin, where he also fought passionately for homosexual rights.

Unfortunately, Hirschfeld's work and that of his institute was almost totally destroyed by the Nazis. Indeed, his works were chief among those marked for destruction in the great book-burning spectacles engineered by the Nazi Party.

Decades later a new movement arose in the United States. Groups of homosexual men and women, careful to adhere to traditional sex and gender roles and appearances, walked small picket lines for homosexual rights. The Liberty Bell in Philadelphia was the site of many of these events in the early 1960s. These pioneers sought to normalize the idea of homosexuality in the public consciousness. Their quiet efforts were making headway when events they could not predict took their ideas to the next level. The gay rights movement emerged in 1969 out of occurrences now called the Stonewall Riots. Against type and against all odds, drag queens, lesbians, and gay men fought back against police oppression at the Stonewall Bar in Greenwich Village, and rioting broke out. For three days and nights the rioting disrupted the city, stunning the public and the police, who never expected homosexuals to fight back. The issue was catapulted into the national debate.

The stereotype of the nelly, effeminate male homosexual was shattered, though not totally destroyed, at Stonewall. Afterward even homosexual men had to redefine what it meant to be a man and a homosexual, what masculinity meant in the gay milieu.

Because masculinity is defined, in part, in opposition to femininity, anything that is perceived as feminine can not be masculine. Michael Kimmel and others point out that femininity or effeminacy drives the actions of men and impels them to be the opposite. Increasingly, sexual orientation is used to define masculinity, bringing with it the repression of homosexuality that is used to maintain hegemonic masculinity.

Effeminacy is not something that all gay men exhibit, but among those who do, it is sometimes used to help gay men recognize each other. In the early twentieth century, effeminacy among gay men was thought to be the rule and was more or less tolerated as a harmless aberration. This, however, contributed to the definition of gay men in terms of the absence of masculinity. By extension, anyone that did not seem outwardly masculine was thought to be homosexual.

As a result, gay men were left to reconcile the ideas of homosexuality and masculinity. Heterosexual males see gay men as submissive, compliant, and passive, whereas they see themselves as dominant, forceful, and highly sexual. But Kimmel notes that manhood is based less on specific characteristics and more on the fear of being dominated by others. Masculinity then becomes a type of public display.

Masculinity as a display or as an act becomes more malleable. Thus, whether consciously or not, in the 1970s gay men began to develop their own brands of masculinity. Stonewall had liberated them to experiment with gender.

Gay men are shaped by the same forces as straight men, one of which is traditional masculinity. One gay male expression of this form of masculinity, Martin Levine observes, was the birth of "the clone," which was, in essence, a performance. Homosexual men began to adopt macho, blue-collar clothing—jeans, flannel shirts, and the like. They sported thick moustaches or close-cropped beards, muscled bodies, and sullen expressions. Most of all they aped the heterosexual ideal of constant sex and a "fast-lane" existence. Physical strength, male bonding, and recreational sex are all highly valued masculine traits. The clone embodied these qualities of masculinity to a heightened degree, leading to a variety of hypermasculinity that challenged the notion that they were "failed men."

Around the same time, the artist Tom of Finland began to connect homosexuality and hypermasculinity in his highly sexualized drawings. He depicted gay men as supermasculine, with fantastically bulging muscles and huge genitalia. He portrayed them in a variety of masculine costumes—military men, construction workers, anything macho, powerful, and domineering. His inventions also had sex—all varieties of male-male sex—with a joyous freedom and carefree attitude. His work became iconic in the gay male community.

In the 1980s the AIDS crisis changed sexual practices, if only for a while. Before the crisis gay men had anonymous sex with abandon. After it became clear that AIDS was sexually transmitted, these practices slowed almost to a halt. Bathhouses were closed in many communities. Sex became a thing to fear. Proving their masculinity through sexual prowess became difficult if not impossible for gay men. The clone was gone and something had to take his place.

Other options and differing masculinities needed to be explored. At the same time, the rise of the feminist movement led to new definitions of manhood. Joseph Pleck (1981) points to occupational prowess (rather than performance in the sexual arena), opposite-sex bonding, and a relational sexual style as

hallmarks of a new, modern masculinity. Gays were beginning to "come out" and show that they were members of every group; working in every occupation; able to form lasting, loving relationships; and capable of taking on the duties of parenthood.

There are a variety of masculinities within the gay male community. Though 1970s-style clones are gone, the muscle hunk (one manifestation of which is the Chelsea boy) whose hypermasculine appearance makes him seem the epitome of manliness, still exists. The gym has become the sanctuary of this brand of masculine performance; proving one's masculinity through physical prowess remains an option. Even sexual performance has again become prominent. Safer sex practices make sex possible; however, more recently, there is also a rise in the incidence of bareback sex (sex without condoms or other protection), indicating that sex without limits is still a masculine proving ground for some.

Culturally, the changing shape of gay masculinity is clearly seen in movies and television. The earliest movies portrayed gay men as effeminate and sissified. They minced and pranced and were often seen as evildoers. Almost always they came to a bad end. In the 1970s and 1980s the conception gradually changed. Though there are still stereotypical images and ill-informed portrayals, homosexuals are beginning to be presented as just another part of the human spectrum.

Freed from the fear of being dominated by others because they are a minority and parts of their lives are controlled by heterosexually structured laws and conventions, gay men can reinvent masculinity for their own purposes, to parody gender roles, to mix and match sex-role traits. Studies find that gay men differ from straight men "on conscious, self-reported gender-related identity" (Lippa 2002). This may reflect a divergence from traditional definitions of masculinity and the continuing search for new variations on masculinity within the gay community.

Joseph R. G. DeMarco

See also Heteronormativity

Further Readings: Boswell, John. 1980.
Christianity, Social Tolerance, and Homosexuality.
Chicago: University of Chicago Press.

Chauncey, George. 1992. *Gay New York.* New York:
Basic Books.

Connell. R.W. 1995. *Masculinities.* Berkeley, CA:
University of California Press.

Healey, Murray. 1994. "The Mark of a Man:
Masculine Identities and the Art of Macho
Drag" *Critical Quarterly* 36, no. 1: 86–93.

Lippa, R.A. 2002. *Gender, Nature and Nurture.*
Mahwah, NJ: Earlbaum.

Pleck, Joseph H. 1981. *The Myth of Masculinity.*
Cambridge, MA: MIT Press.

Ramakers, Micha. 2000. *Dirty Pictures: Tom of
Finland, Masculinity, and Homosexuality.* New
York: St. Martin's Press.

Homosociality

Homosociality is the mutual orientation to members of the same sex and "the seeking, enjoyment, and/or preference for the company of the same sex" (Lipman-Blumen 1976, 16), which connects gender-based ties and solidarity. Homosociality has a physical and a symbolic connotation. It refers to the "literal," that is, spatial separation of male spheres from female spheres, and it means that in developing (moral) attitudes, (political) opinions, and systems of values, members of the same sex are the most important significant others. To call a group homosocial, both connotations must be given. The physical copresence of members of the same sex alone does not constitute a homosocial sphere. Even when one woman or few women are physically present in an all-male setting, the homosocial atmosphere can be preserved if the woman becomes "one of the boys" (Fine 1987)—that is, if the woman adapts to the symbolic order of the male majority and their patterns of communication and interaction. On the other hand, a group of men can fail to constitute a homosocial sphere if, despite the physical absence of women, women and their expectations are (omni-)present on a symbolic level. This is (or was) the case in some types of (profemi-

nist) men's consciousness-raising groups, whose discourses are centered on the demands and expectations of women.

Lipman-Blumen (1976), who introduced the notion of homosociality into gender studies, stated that traditionally homosociality is practiced more by men than by women. There were more male homosocial groups than female groups. The higher extent of homosociality among men is an expression of male dominance and, at the same time, contributes to maintaining men's dominant position by excluding women from important realms of society and by strengthening the cohesion among men.

By drawing lines between male and female spheres, physically and symbolically, homosociality founds and maintains habitual security of individual men. "This security manifests itself in a naturally performed, taken for granted positioning in the gender relation—as opposed to a positioning brought about in discourse, by reflecting on the male role. . . . Habitual security . . . is grounded in the everyday order of the taken-for-granted and obvious" (Behnke/Meuser 2001, 159–160). Within homosocial settings, men mutually determine what makes a (normal) man. Usually this is not a matter of explicit discourse—being a man is not the topic of communication—but is embedded in the flow of talk about each and every thing. Often members of homosocial groups are not aware of the fact that belonging to the same gender is a constituting feature of their groups. Rather, ignoring this contributes to the taken-for-grantedness of men's positioning in the gender order.

Homosocial settings are of crucial importance for founding and maintaining a masculine identity. "Masculinity is largely a homosocial enactment" (Kimmel 1996, 7). Peer groups of male juveniles play an important role in the process of developing an adult masculine identity. Among adult males, too, being acknowledged by other men confirms a man's masculinity. Tribute paid by women does not have this impact, because only being acknowledged by someone who is seen as being on a par with oneself counts. There are two interconnected features of homosocial settings on which masculine identity is founded: distinction from the world of females that is often devalued, and conjunction with other men.

Compared with heterosocial interaction, men perceive the atmosphere of the homosocial setting as relaxed. For most men this setting is of high value, a place where a man can have fun and be "oneself." This holds for men from different social classes and milieus. The locations and the internal structures of the homosocial settings are, for example, quite different in a working-class pub and a middle-class Rotary Club, but a central motive for meeting with other males that men from both social worlds express is "simply having fun as men." Further, and most important, the homosocial setting is seen as an authentic male world, as the place where "masculine authenticity" can be lived. According to explanations that members of different homosocial groups gave in group discussions (Meuser 1998), only among men can a man "come to himself" and show his "true face." Here a man would not have to consider feminine feelings and sensitivities. Instead, he could communicate in whatever form or content he likes. Communication among men is perceived as "more frank and more honest" than communication with women. Thus, the homosocial group is experienced as the place where men can be authentic, while in heterosocial interaction more or less pretence is necessary.

The interactional culture of male homosocial groups shows a great variety. It reaches from quite informal structures, as in circles of buddies, to highly formalized structures, as in the military. It can be egalitarian as well as strongly hierarchical. In either case, the homosocial setting meets the described functions. The crucial point is the absence of women. Homosociality as such relieves men of the demands and expectancies they believe confront them when women are present. Considering this, women always are potentially dangerous for homosocial cohesion. "Women can kill," one man states in a group discussion, at least the mood or the "clubby" atmosphere characteristic of all-male groups.

Even if many homosocial groups may have features of an "iron cage," the homosocial association founds habitual security in several ways. It supplies men, according to Gerson and Peiss (1985), "with resources, skills, solidarity and power" (321). Thus, homosociality reinforces the boundaries between the genders and contributes to the "symbolic power" (Bourdieu 1990) of men. The homosocial group is to be seen as a "collective actor" in the construction of difference and of hegemonic masculinity. Especially in an epoch when the dominance of men is more and more questioned, male homosociality helps to reinforce male hegemony. The homosocial group increasingly takes on the function of a refuge where men can mutually affirm the correctness and "normality" of their own perspectives on the gender order. Here the changing gender order can be "normalized," at least symbolically. The homosocial group is, so to say, of high strategic value in the "battle of the sexes."

Because homosociality seems to be more significant to men than to women, we might expect that recent changes in the gender order would lead to increased homosocial relations among women as a source of power, at the same time as it results in increased searching for homosociality among men as a form of resistance to gender equality. But, paradoxically, one consequence of the transformation of the gender order is that more and more formerly all-male institutions, especially those in the workplace, are losing their homosocial character. Thus, men's increased search for homosociality might also become increasingly difficult.

Michael Meuser

See also Male Bonding; "New Lad" Fiction
Further Reading:
Behnke, Cornelia, and Michael Meuser. 2001. "Gender and Habitus: Fundamental Securities

and Crisis Tendencies among Men." Pp. 153–174 in *Gender in Interaction: Perspectives on Femininity and Masculinity in Ethnography and Discourse.* Edited by Bettina Baron and Helga Kotthoff. Amsterdam/Philadelphia: John Benjamins.

Bourdieu, Pierre. 1990. "La Domination Masculine." *Actes de la Recherche en Sciences Sociales* 84: 2–31.

Fine, Gary Alan. 1987. "One of the Boys: Women in Male-Dominated Settings." Pp. 131–147 in *Changing Men: New Directions in Research on Men and Masculinity.* Edited by Michael S. Kimmel. Newbury Park, CA: Sage.

Gerson, Judith M., and Kathy Peiss. 1985. "Boundaries, Negotiation, Consciousness: Reconceptualizing Gender Relations." *Social Problems* 32: 317–331.

Kimmel, Michael. 1996. *Manhood in America.* New York: Free Press.

Lipman-Blumen, Jean. 1976. "Toward a Homosocial Theory of Sex Roles: An Explanation of the Sex Segregation of Social Institutions." *Signs* 1: 15–31.

Meuser, Michael. 1998. *Geschlecht und Sinnlichkeit. Soziologische Theorie und kulturelle Deutungsmuster.* Opladen, Germany: Leske and Budrich.

Honor

Honor has been one of the most basic social codes for prompting and regulating men's competition for status. A mode of social control as well as self-control, it helps to stabilize male hierarchies, especially in small social groups beset by internal instabilities and external threats. Unlike individualism, honor does not idealize solitary self-reliance. Instead, it rests on a man's reputation in his community. The more a man enacts a shared ideal of manliness, the more honor he gains. Especially among the elite, the more he diverges from a quest for glory and prestige, or from a moral or chivalric ideal, the less respect he gets from friends and kin. A man of honor would rather die than know that other men see him as cowardly or humiliated.

In the second volume of *Democracy in America* (1840), Alexis de Tocqueville gives two definitions for honor: "the esteem, glory, or reverence that a man receives from his fellow men;" and also "that peculiar rule" by which "a people or a class allot praise or blame" (1945, 3: 18, 242–243). A man gains honor to the degree that he can exemplify his society's code of manly prowess. Typically this code praises manly valor, independence, and self-control, while blaming and shaming men who seem weak, vulnerable, or dependent. Such codes function most intensely and comprehensively in small villages or kinship units.

At least two kinds of honor occur in most honor-shame societies: (1) ascribed honor, gained through lineage, family connections, and sometimes patronage; and (2) acquired honor, gained through social contests. In most premodern societies, honor presumes a hierarchy of male over female, senior over junior, and dynastic or inherited over acquired wealth, in keeping with reverence for patriarchal ancestors. The code also sharply contrasts free men with slaves, and exalts the warrior over the "gentle" man or the coward. In Renaissance Italy, honor came to a man with *virtú,* loosely translated as forceful boldness, even—or sometimes especially—if he lacked what we would call "virtue." Honor-shame societies tend to devalue compromise and negotiation, while highly valuing confrontation and rituals of public self-display. Paradoxically, honor comes to those who constantly struggle for it. Its hierarchies of social valuing are never stable, especially for younger men. Contestation trains them for the valor that can protect and extend their kinship group or community.

The honor code arose in what anthropologists call "agonistic cultures," particularly around the Mediterranean Sea. From Old Testament cultures through Italian city-states, often in tension with Christ's teachings to turn the other cheek, and currently in the Middle East and Bosnia, peoples that frequently jostle and conflict with other peoples develop a warrior ideal of manhood. At least one historian, Samuel Haber, has argued that modern specialized professions function in similar ways, though with more intellectual- ized forms of honor and valor.

Honor cannot be separated from the so- cial uses of shaming. For J. G. Peristiany (1966), who edited the first major study of these dynamics in Mediterranean societies, "Honour and shame are the constant preoc- cupation of individuals in small scale, exclu- sive societies where face-to-face personal, as opposed to anonymous, relations are of paramount importance" (11). He highlights "the insecurity and instability of the honour- shame ranking"; a man "is constantly 'on show'" to prove himself to his peers (12). By contrast, in the modern world of mobility and urbanization, "*who* are our peers and for how long?" (12 [original emphasis]).

The threat of social shaming also stimu- lates ostentatious benevolence to stabilize and perpetuate small groups, whether fami- lies, clans, villages, city-states, or elites. Marcel Mauss's classic book, *The Gift* (1950), inaugurated the study of premodern honor- shame societies. To show how precapitalist groups use threats of shaming to recirculate surplus wealth, Mauss highlights an extreme instance, the potlatch, in which a man se- cures honor by giving away all his posses- sions. Conversely, an unreciprocated gift brings humiliation. Ritual gift giving can re- store one's honor: "One must act the 'great lord' upon such occasions" (65–66). Surprisingly, the word "honor" probably de- rives from the Latin word *onus*, or "burden." In premodern societies at least, having sur- plus wealth implies the burden of recirculat- ing it, and what seem to be freely offered gifts require the subsequent burden of recip- rocation.

In larger groups, shaming also disciplined elites. From 1200 to 1500 in northern Italy, cities commissioned paintings of aristocratic men who had fled the city as accused crimi- nals or traitors and hung these portraits up- side down on the city walls to deface their names. The specter of family dishonor lured many fugitives back to face trial and even

death. As Samuel Egerton notes, these tactics worked well in feudal, tribelike communes.

Honor-shame codes often intimate the threat or promise of violence and physical combat as a way of resolving conflicts. In the antebellum South, nose-pulling constituted instant shaming, sometimes leading to duels among the elite (Greenberg 1996). Dueling also enacted contests for honor in nine- teenth-century France and Germany. More recently, in the United States and other postindustrial countries, the quest for honor through controlled violence has been out- sourced to spectator sports, particularly football and basketball. For the athletes, "trash talk" claims honor for themselves while shaming potential rivals. In many ur- ban areas, to be "dissed" (disrespected) re- quires assault to avenge the shaming.

In politics, too, the fear of losing honor by displaying vulnerability or incurring shame governs many male self-presentations. In 1972, the Democratic front-runner, Senator Edmund Muskie, had to drop out of the pres- idential primaries because he cried in public after his wife had been slandered. Fear of shame also prolonged the United States' con- tinued involvement in the Vietnam War for al- most a decade, to counter the imputation of national cowardice and defeat. A similar dy- namic may have helped to generate the U.S. government's swerve from Osama bin Laden to Iraq as an object of attack, after having been attacked by unlocatable terrorists on 11 September 2001. More generally, for thou- sands of years, many nations, cultures, com- munities, and individual men have avenged perceived wrongs in the name of honor.

Until very recently, white Americans have often made black men's bodies a particularly intense site of ascribed shame, in part be- cause slavery has been a ubiquitous metaphor for unmanly dependence and submission. After the Civil War, as the prospect of black equality threatened white mastery, white racism functioned as a collective shaming of black people to restore the honor of the defeated Confederacy, as well as to establish cross-regional bonds for what some critics have called a national white imaginary.

In many small, patriarchal societies, a dutiful daughter can serve as a prime gift to secure her father's honor, while an independent or sexually active daughter becomes a prime signifier of her father's and therefore her family's shame. Sometimes fathers and brothers may disown or even kill an unchaste daughter. In 1999, a front-page Sunday *New York Times* story on honor in the Arab world quotes a young Egyptian journalist who recalled a moment in his high school biology class. After sketching the female reproductive system, the teacher pointed out the entrance to the vagina and said, "This is where the family honor lies!" (Jehl 1999, 1). Although the reciprocal expectations animating such sexual prohibitions flagrantly constrain young women's autonomy, they help to secure family alliances that support small groups and clans in conditions of threat and scarcity.

As recently as the Bosnia conflict in the mid-1990s, many armies have used rape to destroy the honor of conquered fathers and brothers, whose inability to protect a kinswoman's virtue brings lifelong shame to the family. In nonsexualized ways, General William T. Sherman's march through Georgia and the Carolinas during the American Civil War undermined the honor and morale of Confederate soldiers, unable to protect their women and their homes. For elite and middle-class men in many modern cultures, including the United States until the 1970s, shame also attaches to a married woman who works outside the home to help support the family, because her pay devalues the man's role as provider.

Many honor-shame societies also develop a subversive element: the shameless trickster. In the antebellum South, some slaves adopted that role (Wyatt 1988). In Shakespeare's *Henry IV, Part 1* (1597), Falstaff muses that honor "pricks me on" but might "prick me off" (V, i, 129–130). As he concludes, honor is only "a word," and words are just "air." Later, in Shakespeare's *All's Well That Ends Well* (1604–1605), Paroles—French for "words"—shrugs off what looks like a life-ending public shaming by saying to himself and the audience, "Simply the thing I am / Shall make me live" (IV, iii, 310–311). The tricksters' pleasure in improvisation and self-refashioning supersedes their concern for honor, shame, or reputation. In that respect, Shakespeare anticipates various modern heroes and antiheroes.

David Leverenz

Further Reading:

Abu-Lughod, Lila. 1986. *Veiled Sentiments: Honor and Poetry in a Bedouin Society.* Berkeley, CA: University of California Press.

Egerton, Samuel. 1985. *Pictures and Punishment: Art and Criminal Prosecution during the Florentine Renaissance.* Ithaca, NY: Cornell University Press.

Freeman, Joanne. 2001. *Affairs of Honor: National Politics in the New Republic.* New Haven, CT: Yale University Press.

Gilmore, David, ed. 1987. *Honor and Shame and the Unity of the Mediterranean.* Washington, DC: American Anthropological Association.

Greenberg, Kenneth. 1996. *Honor and Slavery.* Princeton, NJ: Princeton University Press.

Haber, Samuel. 1991. *The Quest for Authority and Honor in the American Professions, 1750–1900.* Chicago: University of Chicago Press.

Jehl, Douglas. 1999. "Arab Honor's Price: A Woman's Blood," *New York Times,* 20 June, p. 1.

Mauss, Marcel. 1950/1990. *The Gift: The Form and Reason for Exchange in Archaic Societies.* Translated by W. D. Halls. New York: W. W. Norton.

Nye, Robert A. 1993. *Masculinity and Male Codes of Honor in Modern France.* New York: Oxford University Press.

Peristiany, J. G., ed. 1966. *Honour and Shame: The Values of Mediterranean Society.* Chicago: University of Chicago Press.

Tocqueville, Alexis de. 1840/1945. *Democracy in America,* Vol. 2. Book 3. Chapter 18. Edited by Phillips Bradley. Translated by Henry Reeve and Francis Bowen. New York: Modern Library.

Trexler, Richard C. 1980/1991. *Public Life in Renaissance Florence.* Ithaca, NY: Cornell University Press.

Wyatt, Brown. 1988. "The Mask of Obedience: Male Slave Psychology in the Old South," *American Historical Review* 93 (December): 1228–1252.

Horror

The horror genre is always concerned with making human beings fearful and/or uncomfortable and therefore has, from time to time, used tension surrounding images of masculinity to frighten and/or disturb its audience. Sometimes this horror results from seeing the negative sides of the masculine stereotypes magnified to horrible proportions, as in Jason in the *Friday the 13th* series (1980–1989) and Michael Meyers in *Halloween* (1978–1989). Sometimes the horror comes from the confusion between what a man should be and what a man is; this is a horror tapped into by most of Stephen King's best work. It can even be the horror of suddenly being thrust into culturally codified masculine acts as the vacationers of *Deliverance* (1970) are. Regardless of how masculinity is used to create horror, in most cases the creation of horror is paramount to any sort of social message. Therefore, critics looking for an overtly positive or negative agenda in horror will be disappointed, though many interesting insights have been found in exploring the social side effects of manipulating masculinity in horrific ways.

Before the horror genre, there was literature that inspired horrific emotions. Much of this literature was connected to notions of masculinity. For example, the epic poem *Beowulf* (ca. 1000) deals with a horrifying monster, which is defeated by a heroic man. Shakespeare's Hamlet (1603) meets the ghost of his dead father and is sent down a very masculine path toward justice. Neither of these texts has the total devotion to inspiring horror their descendants would have, but one can see beginnings even here, and one can see those beginnings had strong ties to ideas about masculinity.

The horror genre, as it is commonly understood, was not always passionately interested in masculinity. It would not be until the 1800s that horror and masculinity became deeply intertwined. In *Danse Macabre* (1983), Stephen King highlights three novels as being primary to the existence of the horror genre: *Frankenstein* (1818) by Mary Shelley, *Dracula* (1891) by Bram Stoker, and *The Strange Case of Dr. Jekyll and Mr. Hyde* (1887) by Robert Louis Stevenson. *Dracula* is explicitly a novel of sexuality, but *Frankenstein* and *The Strange Case of Dr. Jekyll and Mr. Hyde* seem to focus on horror in relation to masculinity. In Edward Hyde, Stevenson creates an image of monstrous masculinity that King quite arguably states defines masculinity-based horror from its reception on.

As the genre moved westward to America, it became more masculine. Edgar Allen Poe's tales of madness were never explicitly about masculinity, but the horrors of gender conformity were never far from his mind. For example, the narrator of "The Tell-Tale Heart" (1843) is unable to be the cool, calculated, masculine man he wishes to be and confesses to murder.

The genre's next major author, H. P. Lovecraft, moved away from masculine anxieties to focus on his mythos of the Elder Gods: strange, exotic deities who bear more than a passing resemblance to the races Lovecraft was uncomfortable with (the term "racist" does appear in Lovecraftian criticism from time to time). Lovecraft bears mentioning because of his strong impact on the horror genre and because of his lack of interest in explicitly addressing issues of masculinity. Poe's more interior and brooding brand of horror would be the norm as time went by, but Lovecraft and his fellow contributors to *Weird Tales* provided—and continue to provide—an example of what might have been.

In Cold War American culture, anxiety about masculinity became paramount to horror film and fiction. In the literary world, the works of Richard Matheson (specifically *The Shrinking Man* [1956] and *I Am Legend* [1954], which would be filmed twice, most recently as *The Omega Man* [1971]) found much bankable fear in the gap between what the perfect, anti-Communist American man should be and what he really was. Robert Bloch, a friend and peer to the exterior-oriented Lovecraft, would provide the genre with one of its most memorable villains in his novel *Psycho* (1959). Though his Norman Bates differs greatly from the Norman Bates of Hitchcock's (for one, his Norman Bates was chubbier than Anthony Perkins), both of these characters present a powerful image of a man whose anxiety in regards to his gender identity is unbearable.

In the late 1970s, Stephen King's fiction took Richard Matheson's trend and made it into an industry. His novels, specifically those involving the brave men of the Castle Rock police department, are nearly always passionately involved with not only the difficulties of being a "real man" but also the horrors "real men" are famous for inflicting on others (read *The Dark Half* [1989] for a prime example of a "real man" gone horribly wrong).

Finally, in the last twenty or thirty years of the twentieth century, the teen slasher film became the most pointed critique of traditional sex roles within the horror genre to date. As Carol J. Clover brilliantly elucidates in her work *Men, Women, and Chainsaws* (1993), males and females who conform to traditional sex roles suffer in these films, whereas those who are more independently oriented tend to thrive (much has been said about Jamie Lee Curtis—Laurie in the original *Halloween,* but a watchful viewer of the film also notices that the dumb, pretty boyfriends are utterly unmemorable and worthless, whereas the sensitive Dr. Loomis, played by Donald Pleasence, is far more likeable and successful even though he is a far cry from being a pin-up model).

John Axel Kohagen

See also King, Stephen
Further Reading:

Carroll, Noel. 1990. *The Philosophy of Horror: or, Paradoxes of the Heart.* New York: Routledge.

Clover, Carol J. 1993. *Men, Women, and Chainsaws: Gender in the Modern Horror Film.* Princeton, NJ: Princeton University Press.

King, Stephen. 1983. *Danse Macabre.* New York: Berkeley.

Hostile Environment

Hostile environment refers to a type of sexual harassment, originally defined as unwelcome sexual advances, requests for sexual favors, and other verbal or physical conduct of a sexual nature that makes the workplace intimidating, hostile, or offensive (U.S. Equal Employment Opportunity Commission [EEOC] 1980). In 1993, the EEOC specified that harassment need not be sexual in nature, but can be "harassment due to gender-based animus" (51, 267).

Hostile environment harassment is much more common than *quid pro quo* sexual harassment (in which submission to such advances or favors is either explicitly or implicitly used as a term or condition of employment). A hostile environment occurs when an employee is hampered in her or his work by: (1) epithets, slurs, negative stereotyping, or threatening, intimidating, or hostile acts; or (2) written or graphic material that denigrates or shows hostility or aversion toward an individual or group . . . and that is placed on walls, bulletin boards, or elsewhere on the employer's premises or circulated in the workplace (EEOC 1993). Interpretations of the law since 1995 suggest that offensive behavior is not legally harassment unless it is frequent, severe, or physically threatening. However, in *Nadeau v. Rainbow Rugs, Inc.*, 675 A.2d 973 (Me. 1996), the Supreme Judicial Court of Maine held that a single incident of sexual harassment may be sufficient to create a hostile work environment.

Women have always experienced hostile environment harassment, but it was not until the late 1970s that U.S. courts began to recognize it as a legal harm. Catherine MacKinnon's (1979) groundbreaking work defined sexual harassment (both *quid pro quo* and hostile environment) as a form of sex discrimination prohibited by Title VII of the 1964 Civil Rights Act (prohibiting discrimination on the basis of race, color, religion, national origin, and sex). Beyond the workplace, sexual harassment in schools, universities, and colleges is illegal under Title IX of the Federal Education Amendments of the U.S. Civil Rights Act. Although the EEOC defined both *quid pro quo* and hostile environment harassment as prohibited sex discrimination in 1980, it was not considered illegal until the Supreme Court included sexual harassment in the category of gender discrimination in 1986 (*Meritor Savings Bank v. Vinson*, 477 U.S. 57). Since the 1990s attention has focused upon whether the use of a "reasonable person" standard by the courts is appropriate to evaluate whether a set of circumstances create a hostile work environment. Because women and men have varied perceptions of sexual harassment—with women perceiving a broader range of social-sexual behaviors as harassing—and because women are far more often the "harassee," a "reasonable woman" standard might be more appropriate (e.g., *Ellison v. Brady* [1991]).

In the past two decades of the twentieth century, several high-profile cases have focused the nation's attention on sexual harassment. Most prominent is the 1991 Clarence Thomas-Anita Hill dust-up during Thomas's Supreme Court confirmation hearings, but other national cases include the U.S. navy's 1991 Tailhook convention, the 1994 investigation of Senator Bob Packwood, the 1994 Mitsubishi suit, and the case of *Paula Jones v. William Jefferson Clinton* (1998, WL 148370). The number of formal complaints has increased in the same period, in part because of these high-profile cases. For example, Sandler (1997) reports that following the Hill-Thomas hearings, sexual harassment charges filed in the first half of 1992 increased by more than 50 percent over the same period the previous year.

For a variety of reasons, hostile environment harassment is thought to be grossly underreported. Women may be discouraged from identifying it as sexual harassment and may be encouraged to "put up with" objectionable behavior. Women fear embarrassment or stigma and many fear retaliation in the form of more abuse, job loss, or career penalties. Victims worry that they will not be

believed, and some fear that reporting the behavior will make little difference (evidence suggests women are successful in only a small percentage of sexual harassment cases). Conceptual and methodological issues make capturing the extent of hostile environment harassment difficult. Standardized methodology is lacking (Gruber 1998). Some studies look at incidence over a set period of time, others estimate prevalence over a woman's lifetime. Additionally, there is wide variation in the operationalization of hostile environment sexual harassment. Asking directly about sexual harassment results in lower prevalence than asking about particular behaviors experienced in the workplace or educational settings. Estimates from various studies find anywhere between 20 to 70 percent of women have experienced harassing behavior in the workplace; however, the National Council for Research on Women (1991) estimates that half or more of working women can expect to be sexually harassed during their careers. Furthermore, between 30 to 60 percent of female students can expect to experience sexual harassment by teachers, administrators, staff, or peers.

Researchers often focus on specific institutions, such as medicine or academia, in which hostile environments (or "chilly climates" in Sandler's terminology) are entrenched, but much research uses broader population studies to explore who gets harassed. Overall, gender is the best predictor of harassment: Women are far more likely to be victims of hostile environment harassment and men are far more likely to be perpetrators. In particular, women in male-dominated occupations are especially at risk, whether blue-collar or professional. Overall, people with less power are more likely to experience hostile environment harassment, for example, younger women, single women, "racial" or ethnic-minority women, women in subordinate occupational positions, women in sex-imbalanced occupations, women students (both undergraduate and graduate), economically disadvantaged or disabled women, and women who are socially isolated or unassertive (Gruber 1997). Also at risk are men who deviate from ideal masculinity norms, which may be illegal since *Oncale v. Sundowner Oil,* 1998) (Quinn 2000). Some attention has been focused on "contrapower" sexual harassment, which is the harassment of a superior by a subordinate (e.g., a teacher harassed by a student) and almost always perpetrated by men against women.

Although there is variation by social context, harassment is generally a reflection of power stratification between women and men. In her focus on sexual harassment on college campuses, Paludi (1996) defines harassment as "the confluence of authority (power) relations and sexuality (sexism) in a culture stratified by sex" (5). Men create hostile environments in order to establish or maintain social dominance. Masculinity is socially constructed and "the production of a hostile work environment is partially a result of masculine identity performance and male group formation produced through sexist and sexual humor" (Quinn 2000, 1158). In particular, men create hostile environments to reinforce certain forms of masculinity and to enhance group solidarity among men. In short, men gain power by calling attention to women's differences or by calling attention to men who do not fit dominant masculine norms (e.g., gay men and men of color). Furthermore, the hostile environment harassment of heterosexual men is often a tactic to "feminize" men who do not fit dominant cultural ideals of heterosexual masculinity (Lee 2000). Men reinforce their identities as powerful, successful, romantic, and virile by contrasting themselves with men who are wimps and sexual flops. Thus, men who are in feminized occupations or are caring and emotional (i.e., not manly enough) may be especially at risk for hostile environment harassment.

Hostile environment harassment has economic and emotional consequences for individuals and society. A range of studies have documented the lowered productivity of victims, negative health effects (sleeplessness, anxiety, depression, nervousness, headaches, weight gains and losses) and lowered satisfaction with one's job and life. Victims often miss work or quit altogether. At a macro level, governments and corporations can pay a steep price. One study of federal employees (1992–1994) put the price tag of sexual harassment for the government at $327 million in the form of sick leave, job turnover, and lost productivity (Eisaguirre 1993). *Working Women Magazine* estimates that the top 150 Fortune 500 companies lose 6.7 million per year to sexual harassment (Kimmel 2000). And in 1998, Mitsubishi was ordered to pay $34 million to hundreds of women workers.

What deters hostile environments? Vigorous prosecution may prove an effective deterrent (the Mitsubishi settlement stands as the largest on record in a corporate case and sends a strong message to employers), but because hostile environment sexual harassment is about power, achieving gender equity and reducing power imbalances between women and men may be important. In addition, organizational context matters (Gruber 1998). Women in workplaces with proactive harassment strategies are less likely to be physically threatened or to be targets of offensive sexual comments and questions. Clear procedures that punish harassers and support victims can reduce hostile environments, and training in sexual harassment is most effective when accompanied by strong managerial support. Since 2000, a focus by the courts is the extent of employer responsibility. Employers can be held liable for the acts of supervisors if the employer knew or should have known of the conduct and did not take corrective action.

In addition, implementation is key. Beyond being included in the employee handbook or policy manual, workplaces need to regularly communicate the policy to employees through memos, posters, brochures, and newsletters. Organizations must train supervisory personnel, and all employees need to understand the important terms (e.g., *quid pro quo* vs. hostile environment). Workplaces should guarantee in writing that no one who files a complaint will be the target of more harassment or retaliation. Finally, redefining sexual harassment as "sexist" harassment may help employees and students see their experiences as harassment (Lee 2001). Indeed, many court cases have ruled that hostile environment sexual harassment can be nonsexual (e.g., *McKinney v. Dole* 1988; *Hall v. Gus Construction Co., Inc.* 1985; *Campbell v. Kansas State University* 1991).

In the early 2000s, the connection between law, policies, and everyday practice is "contradictory and incomplete" (Quinn 2000, 1182). Consequently, honing policies and educating women and men about the policies will be ineffective until we understand the everyday realities of harassed women and men and until we make visible the gendered realities of changing workplaces and educational arenas.

Susan W. Hinze

See also Sexual Harassment

Further Reading:

Campbell v. Kansas State University, 780 F. Supp. 755 (1991).

Eisaguirre, Lynne. 1993. *Sexual Harassment: A Reference Handbook.* Santa Barbara, CA: ABC-CLIO.

Ellison v. Brady, 924 F.2d 872, 875–876 (9th Cir. 1991).

Gruber, James E. 1990. "Methodological Problems and Policy Implications in Sexual Harassment Research." *Population Research and Policy Review* 9, no. 3: 235–254.

———. 1997. "An Epidemiology of Sexual Harassment: Evidence from North America and Europe." Pp. 84–98 in *Sexual Harassment: Theory, Research and Treatment.* Edited by W. O'Donohue. Needham Heights, MA: Allyn and Bacon.

———. 1998. "The Impact of Male Work Environments and Organizational Policies on Women's Experiences of Sexual Harassment." *Gender & Society* 12, no. 3: 301–320.

Hall v. *Gus Constr. Co.,* 842 F.2d 1010 (8th Cir. 1988).

Kimmel, Michael. 2000. *The Gendered Society.* New York: Oxford University Press.

Lee, Deborah. 2000. "Hegemonic Masculinity and Male Feminization: The Sexual Harassment of Men at Work." *Journal of Gender Studies* 9, no. 2: 141–155.

———. 2001. "'He Didn't Sexually Harass Me, as in Harassed for Sex . . . He was Just Horrible': Women's Definitions of Unwanted Male Sexual Conduct at Work." *Women's Studies International Forum* 24, no. 1: 25–38.

MacKinnon, Catharine A. 1979. *Sexual Harassment of Working Women: A Case of Sex Discrimination.* New Haven, CT: Yale University Press.

McKinney v. Dole, 765 F.2d 1129 (D.C. Cir. 1985).

Meritor Savings Bank v. Vinson, 477 U.S. 57 (1986).

Nadeau v. Rainbow Rugs, Inc., 1996 ME 675 A.2d 973.

National Council for Research on Women. 1991. *Sexual Harassment: Research and Resources.* New York: National Council for Research on Women.

Paludi, Michele, ed. 1996. *Sexual Harassment on College Campuses: Abusing the Ivory Power.* Albany: State University of New York Press.

Paula Jones v. William Jefferson Clinton (1998, WL 148370).

Quinn, Beth A. 2000. "The Paradox of Complaining: Law, Humor, and Harassment in the Everyday Work World." *Law and Social Inquiry: Journal of the American Bar Foundation* 25, no. 4: 1151–1185.

Sandler, Bernice R. 1997. "Student-to-Student Sexual Harassment." In *Sexual Harassment on Campus: A Guide for Administrators, Faculty, and Students.* Edited by Bernice Sandler and Robert Shoop. Boston: Allyn & Bacon.

U.S. Equal Opportunity Commission. 1980. "Guidelines on Discrimination because of Sex." *Federal Register* 45, no. 219: 74676–74677.

U.S. Equal Opportunity Commission. 1993. "Guidelines on Harassment Based on Race, Color, Religion, Gender, National Origin, Age or Disability." *Federal Register* 58: 51266–51269.

Houdini, Harry (1874–1926)

Harry Houdini increasingly is being seen as one of the iconic masculine figures of early twentieth-century popular culture. Starting as a conventional stage conjuror, he developed into a phenomenally popular entertainer whose persona combined masculine roles such as daredevil, hero, magician, strongman, and male nude; and whose per-

Harry Houdini (Library of Congress)

formances encoded complex narratives of masculine display, subjection, and dominance.

Born Ehrich Weiss, Houdini's career as a performer began in the 1890s, when he worked as a traveling conjuror, specializing in the traditional kind of stage magic act that was particularly popular at this time. Typically, this act articulates a gender politics all its own. The (male) conjuror is costumed in the formal evening wear, which signifies both masculine power and class privilege. He pretends to have superhuman abilities and to break natural laws; he conducts transmuta-

tions and disappearances that announce a mastery over the physical realm. Frequently, he has a female assistant, whose presence adds some sexual glamour to the occasion and emphasizes the conjuror's dominant masculinity. In extreme cases, the assistant herself becomes the object upon which the conjuror demonstrates his magical powers: She is made to vanish and reappear, or she is mutilated and then restored. The performance distills an image of masculine power, control, and authority. Houdini's distinctive style is visible in the variation that he soon developed on this theme: In his signature trick, entitled "Metamorphosis," he was bound with ropes and imprisoned in a trunk; then, when the trunk was opened, Houdini had escaped and his assistant (his wife, Bess) was discovered bound inside it. "Metamorphosis" temporarily subverts, and then reaffirms the simpler image of dominant masculinity that the traditional conjuror's act conveys: It positions the magician as victim rather than master, then reestablishes his dominance and control.

This was the blueprint for what became Houdini's typical narrative: the male body is displayed, subjected to imprisonment or danger, and then shown to triumph over its subjection. As he began to specialize in escapology routines, the element of bodily display became increasingly important in Houdini's act, and he would frequently perform his escapes seminaked—ostensibly to demonstrate that he had no hidden keys or picklocks about his person. The effect was to increase the sense both of the performer's vulnerability and also of his power—because Houdini, though short, was physically muscular. An important study by John F. Kasson links Houdini's performances with another form of popular entertainment, that of the professional strongman, and a tradition of masculine physical culture that was exemplified in the late nineteenth century by Eugene Sandow—and in the late twentieth by Arnold Schwarzenegger! The genuine danger that some of Houdini's escapes involved also link him with the emerging tradition of the movie stuntman—though Houdini's own career in films never prospered, despite his attempts to promote himself as a movie hero.

The climax of Houdini performances was frequently a challenge, in which it was stipulated that his opponents should try to restrain him using the apparatuses of their trades. Most commonly, these challenges involved policemen, prison officers, and warders from "insane asylums," but Houdini was also challenged by industrial workers of various kinds. Consequently, his escapes were not only from jail cells, handcuffs, and straitjackets, but also from industrial ropes, locks and chains, bandages, coffins, packing cases, beer barrels, cranes, milk churns, water tanks, and similar industrial products. Various psychological studies of Houdini have commented on escape as a metaphor, seeing in it the articulation of repressed private meanings relating to Houdini's own childhood and family background. However, it may be that for his audience, the key metaphor was that of the "ordinary man" confronting and heroically overcoming, not only authority figures such as policemen and jailers, but the whole repressive apparatus and iconography of early twentieth-century Western industrial society. Houdini himself stressed this sense of his own ordinariness, incorporating it into his own self-mythologizing, and insisting repeatedly that he used strength and trickery, not supernatural powers. Later in his career, this became a serious issue for him in his angry exposes of the fraudulent "female magic" of spiritualist seances.

Michael Mangan

Further Reading:

Brandon, Ruth. 1993. *The Life and Many Deaths of Harry Houdini.* London: Mandarin.

Gibson, Walter B., and Morris N. Young, eds. 1953. *Houdini on Magic.* New York: Dover.

Kasson, John F. 2001. *Houdini, Tarzan and the Perfect Man. The White Male Body and the Challenge of Modernity in America.* New York: Hill and Wang.

Meyer, Bernard C. 1976. *Houdini: A Mind in Chains: A Psychoanalytic Portrait.* New York: E. P. Dutton.

Phillips, Adam. 2001. *Houdini's Box.* London: Faber and Faber.

Silverman, Kenneth. 1996. *Houdini!!! The Career of Ehrich Weiss.* New York: HarperCollins.

Taylor, Rogan P. 1985. *The Death and Resurrection Show: From Shaman to Superstar.* London: Blond.

Housework

Housework, also known as household labor or domestic labor, involves the physical and emotional work required to maintain homes. Housework includes the managerial tasks of designating, scheduling, and monitoring chores and is often performed as unpaid labor in service to family members. Since the beginning of the Industrial Revolution, a distinctively gendered pattern of responsibility for housework has emerged in most Western countries, with women performing most of it. Overall, men spend approximately one-third the amount of time on routine repetitive household labor as their female partners, a fact that is linked to men's better pay and longer hours in the labor force. In general, domestic partners with superior financial and institutional resources can avoid doing the least desirable household tasks. Recent trends suggest that men are performing a larger proportionate share of housework, primarily because employed women are doing less of it. The distribution of domestic work has moved from a culturally mandated division of labor based on gender to an individually negotiated allocation of household chores, but labor-market inequities and cultural stereotypes continue to define housework as women's work.

The Industrial Revolution brought changes in both productive and social reproductive labor. Economic production, previously centered on the family farm and involving both men and women, moved to factories in newly urbanized areas. Men, single women, and immigrant and working-class married women became the country's predominant wage earners. Responsibility for reproducing the paid labor force (known as "social reproduction") fell to wives. The rise of the cultural ideology of separate spheres for the sexes bolstered the conceptual distinction between rational, strong men in control of the public domain and emotional, frail women associated with the private sphere. Correspondingly, the male "family breadwinner" mentality became as ingrained in the masculine mystique as did the female "homemaker" mentality in the feminine. Doing housework came to be seen as part of enacting women's "natural" role.

As modern industry began to produce the majority of goods needed for household survival in the late nineteenth and twentieth centuries, the role of the homemaker shifted from family sustenance to consumption. Electricity and indoor plumbing were gradually introduced into modernized residences, and housework chores centered on the use of "labor-saving" devices. Homemaking, or "home economics," became a science, and middle-class housewives were characterized as domestic professionals, guided by male technology experts. As "ice boxes" forestalled the need to buy food daily and washing machines and electric dryers replaced wringers and washboards, the drudgery of housework decreased. However, actual time spent on housework remained relatively stable as standards for cleanliness and fashion increased, and studies show that women did nearly as much housework in the latter part of the twentieth century as they did in the early part (Strasser 1982). Thus, although women have less time available to do housework because of their increased labor-force participation, the cultural notion that housework is "women's work" persists. As a result, many women find their "working" day continuing after hours into a "second shift" of housework in the home (Hochschild 1989).

Researchers generally categorize housework into "routine" and "occasional" chores, roughly corresponding to traditionally "feminine" and traditionally "masculine" tasks.

Although there is nothing inherently gendered about these tasks, power differences and cultural ideals have tended to allocate different tasks to men and women. Occasional chores typically performed by men include tasks such as yard care, home maintenance, car repair, and paying bills. These chores are less habitual and performed less often than routine tasks, and allow some discretion in scheduling and performance. Routine housework tasks typically performed by women include preparing meals, washing dishes, doing laundry, cleaning house, and shopping for groceries. If there are children in the household, their care and supervision represent additional domestic tasks to be performed, and the presence of children also increases the amount of routine housework that needs to be done. In the United States and other developed nations, married women do two or three times the amount of routine housework and childcare as their husbands. Moreover, women tend to take responsibility for scheduling and monitoring domestic work even when they delegate it or pay others to do it. Although some people find performing such chores enriching, these routine tasks are subject to little discretion and most people see them as time-consuming, repetitive, and boring. When men do not participate in domestic tasks, their female partners tend to be more depressed and to experience increased conflict in the relationship (Coltrane 2000).

Allocation of housework between partners varies depending on issues such as marital status, time availability, relative income, education level, gender egalitarianism, and the number of infants and young children in the home. Unlike women, whose share of housework increases after marriage, men perform more routine housework when they are in cohabiting relationships than when they are married. Men do more housework when they have more education, whereas women with more education do less. Men also do more of the household labor when their female partner works more hours in the paid labor force and, sometimes, when they themselves work less. More sharing occurs when the woman earns a larger proportion of the family income, when she holds gender egalitarian attitudes, and when there are fewer young children in the home. Moreover, having children tends to traditionalize housework allocation, with women doing more and men's housework participation remaining the same or dropping when they become parents. There is some evidence that housework allocation varies by race/ethnicity, as well, with African American men performing a larger share of housework than European American men, although significantly less than African American women. Research is more ambiguous about the household labor participation of Latino/ Hispanic men, with some studies showing that they do more housework and some showing that they do less than European American men. None of these circumstances predict equality in the division of housework, however, and, although men are doing more than they used to, women in the United States continue to do nearly three times the amount of indoor routine housework that men do (Coltrane 2000; Thompson and Walker 1989).

Although most people in the United States say they believe that housework should be divided equally if both partners in the relationship are employed, the actual division of domestic labor remains unequal (Coltrane 1996). Most of the time, however, both husbands and wives perceive this imbalance as fair. Only when wives do about two-thirds of the housework, or twice as much as their husbands do, is there a tendency for them to begin to see the division of labor as unfair (Lennon and Rosenfield 1994). Women continue to feel responsible for care of their homes and families, encouraged by cultural ideals and traditional notions of family caretaking as women's role. This sense of responsibility often translates into adjustments in their workplace participation, leading women into "mommy track" jobs

limited in opportunities for higher pay and advancement.

Men have been the primary beneficiaries of the unequal distribution of housework. Generally having the greater resources and power in relationships, men tend to opt out of performing routine housework. Meanwhile, having a partner available to manage the household and care for children while they devote themselves to careers, allows married men to reap an earnings advantage, or "marriage premium," over nonmarried men (Cohen 2002). At the same time, women pay a "marriage penalty" in the workplace as a result of their real and perceived family responsibilities (England and Farkas 1986).

Women continue to be disadvantaged both in the home and the workplace by cultural perceptions of housework as "women's work" and by a persistently unbalanced division of household labor that places a double burden on employed women. Men continue to reap the benefits of the current distribution of housework in terms of workplace advantage and, because they opt out of most routine housework, increased leisure time in the home (Deutsch 1999). When they can afford it, families today are purchasing more services that used to be provided within the home, using housecleaning and laundry services, and eating out more often. While this alleviates some of the stress on employed middle-class women, it also increases the demand on the global service economy, whose workers tend to be drawn from minority populations who have been historically disadvantaged in terms of pay standards and job benefits. In this way, the unequal allocation of housework is related to issues of race and class stratification, as well as gender inequality. While men's proportion of housework has increased in the past several decades, both nationally and internationally, it still remains far below the amount performed by their female partners, even as women's hours in the paid workforce increase. Over the long term, as women be-

William Dean Howells, best remembered for his novel
The Rise of Silas Lapham, *remained a prolific writer*
for more than six decades. (Library of Congress)

come more equally committed breadwinners
in the workplace, the negative consequences
of unbalanced divisions of housework will
likely only be alleviated if men become more
equal-sharing partners at home.

Michele Adams
Scott Coltrane

Further Reading:

Cohen, Philip. 2002. "Cohabitation and the
Declining Marriage Premium for Men." *Work
and Occupations* 29: 346–363.

Coltrane, Scott. 1996. *Family Man: Fatherhood,
Housework, and Gender Equity.* New York: Oxford
University Press.

———. 2000. "Research on Household Labor:
Modeling and Measuring the Social
Embeddedness of Routine Family Work."
Journal of Marriage and the Family 62:
1208–1233.

Deutsch, Francine. 1999. *Halving It All: How
Equally Shared Parenting Works.* Cambridge, MA:
Harvard University Press.

England, Paula, and George Farkas. 1986.
*Households, Employment, and Gender: A Social,
Economic, and Demographic View.* New York:
Aldine.

Hochschild, Arlie Russell. 1989. *The Second Shift:
Working Parents and the Revolution at Home.* New
York: Viking.

Lennon, Mary Clare, and Sarah Rosenfield. 1994.
"Relative Fairness and the Division of
Housework: The Importance of Options."
American Journal of Sociology 100: 506–531.

Shelton, Beth Anne. 1992. *Women, Men, and Time:
Gender Differences in Paid Work, Housework, and
Leisure.* New York: Greenwood Press.

Strasser, Susan. 1982. *Never Done: A History of
American Housework.* New York: Pantheon
Books.

Thompson, Linda, and Alexis J. Walker. 1989.
"Gender in Families." *Journal of Marriage and the
Family* 51: 845–871.

Howells, William Dean (1837–1920)

In his public image and his writing, William
Dean Howells was a central symbol for particular types of manhood: the self-made
man, the rising Westerner, the breadwinner,
one half of the man-and-wife unit, the artist
as a man of business, and the white male liberal. Howells was the most influential editor
and literary critic of his generation in the
United States and the author of numerous
novels and other books, twenty or so of
which are granted sustained attention by literary critics and cultural historians. In his
role as spokesperson for the nation's literary
establishment, he promoted realism in literature—then a genre considered threateningly
democratic—and he furthered the early careers of female, black, Jewish, and socialist
authors. At the same time he made his particular type of manhood seem a timeless
norm to thousands of readers. The crests and
troughs of his critical reputation are a telling
sign of each generation's attitude toward
Howells's genteel manliness. In the 1890s,
his former proteges Hamlin Garland and
Upton Sinclair objected to his unwillingness
to express his socialist beliefs. And from
1900 to the 1930s, writers like Sherwood
Anderson and Willa Cather targeted Howells

for his prudishness and inability to portray psychological depth—things that they considered cowardly, unmasculine, and therefore unworthy of a great literary artist. Since the 1980s, historicist scholars have taken more seriously Howells's contributions to progressive reform, and feminist and masculinity scholars have demonstrated that Howells's work is a valuable source of representations of and ruminations about genteel men in relation to women, minorities, and twentieth-century men.

Born and raised in Ohio, Howells was the son of a printer active in abolitionist causes and religious dissent. Seeing how his father's radicalism alienated him from his neighbors, the young Howells educated himself instead in literature. In 1865, Howells and his wife, Elinor Mead Howells, moved to Boston, where Howells served on the editorial board of the *Atlantic Monthly,* the most influential American arts and letters magazine of its day. While working as a novelist and critic in the 1880s, Howells formulated his aesthetic of realism. For Howells, realism came to mean representing social problems without rose-colored glasses so that the middle classes and the elite would see themselves as implicated in such problems. He was the lone literary figure to write publicly in defence of the Haymarket anarchists, who were arrested and convicted of murder after a bomb was thrown during a labor strike in Chicago in 1886.

His semi-autobiographical novels depict the social conditions that made it nearly impossible to be a self-made man in the 1880s and 1890s and the challenges these social conditions posed for men's achieved identity (see Hilkey 1997). The husband and wife in *A Modern Instance* (1882) separate partially because of the stress of the husband's journalist life, and in *The Landlord at Lion's Head* (1897) a Harvard student wonders how he will tell his proud country mother that Harvard graduates don't always find jobs. During this time, Howells became a businessman himself, negotiating advantageous contracts with

James R. Osgood and then Harpers and Brothers, contracts that made him one of the first American authors to live off the proceeds of his craft, but which also made him feel like a "kept" man.

Amy Kaplan (1988) lays the groundwork for studying the structural similarities between Howells's best novels, *A Modern Instance, The Rise of Silas Lapham* (1885), and *The Hazard of New Fortunes* (1890), and progressive reformers' class and gender politics. Kaplan demonstrates that Howells's realism was an attempt to engage middle-class readers with a rapidly changing social world. As such, he was on a defensive mission against the popular romances and the mass circulation newspapers that were engaging readers without the intervening hand of a moral guardian.

Focusing on gender in Howells's work, Elsa Nettels (1997) shows how Howells tended to portray men as firm and decisive and women as vague and emotional. In contrast, Michael Davitt Bell (1993) links Howells's prescriptions for realism in literature with the rough, masculine ideal of the early twentieth century. Joseph McElrath Jr.'s (1997) article is one demonstration of the complex power dynamics of Howells's literary mentoring of younger, more oppositional writers.

One line of Howells scholarship focuses on the marginal in Howells, on what he shied away from, and on what this shying away reveals about the respectable male psyche. John Crowley (1989) has excavated Howells's fears and fascinations with sexuality, homosexuality, and the new woman. Henry Wonham (1995) argues that Howells used black characters to explore extreme psychological states that he dared not explore in himself.

Recent scholars see even the official Howells as a matter of contestation. Augusta Rohrbach (2000) shows how Howells's mustachioed image was a conscious performance, and Phillip Barrish (2001) argues that Howells equated irony with masculine intellectual prestige. June Howard (2001) explains how in the early twentieth-century Howells worked comfortably within a publishing industry that was characterized by battles between the sexes but was not gender segregated.

Stephanie C. Palmer

Further Reading:

Barrish, Phillip. 2001. *American Literary Realism, Critical Theory, and Intellectual Prestige, 1880–1995.* Cambridge, UK: Cambridge University Press.

Bell, Michael Davitt. 1993. *The Problem of American Realism: Studies in the Cultural History of a Literary Idea.* Chicago: University of Chicago Press.

Crowley, John W. 1989. *The Mask of Fiction: Essays on W. D. Howells.* Amherst, MA: University of Massachusetts Press.

Hilkey, Judy. 1997. *Character Is Capital: Success Manuals and Manhood in Gilded Age America.* Chapel Hill, NC: University of North Carolina Press.

Howard, June. 2001. *Publishing the Family.* Durham, NC: Duke University Press.

Kaplan, Amy. 1988. *The Social Construction of American Realism.* Chicago: University of Chicago Press.

McElrath, Joseph R., Jr. 1997. "W. D. Howells and Race: Charles W. Chesnutt's Disappointment of the Dean." *Nineteenth-Century Literature* 51: 474–499.

Nettels, Elsa. 1997. *Language and Gender in American Fiction: Howells, James, Wharton, and Cather.* Houndmills, Basingstoke, Hampshire, UK: Macmillan.

Rohrbach, Augusta. 2000. "'You're a Natural-Born Literary Man': Becoming William Dean Howells, Culture Maker and Cultural Marker." *New England Quarterly* 73:625–653.

Wonham, Henry B. 1995. "Writing Realism, Policing Consciousness: Howells and the Black Body." *American Literature* 67: 701–724.

Huck Finn

See Finn, Huckleberry

Hunting

There is something mythically masculine about hunting. Young men, it seems, learn to hunt from their fathers, who learned from their fathers, who learned from their fathers, and so on into the mists of American history.

The actual history of hunting in North America, however—or rather the history of how Anglo-American men have used hunting to define manliness—is more complex than the myth.

Colonial promotional literature invariably portrayed the New World as a hunter's paradise. Virginia, wrote one pamphleteer, being "Earth's only paradise," would yield an "infinite store" of "land and water fowls," as well as "deer, kain, and fallow, stags, coneys, hares, with many fruits and roots good for meat" (Johnson 1963). The great abundance of game, it seemed, would attract gentlemen to America, or, alternatively, it would make plebeian adventurers into gentlemen.

Actual colonists, however, held ambivalent attitudes toward hunting. Hunting, after all, was what Indians did. If, as Protestant clerics and Enlightenment thinkers maintained, Europeans rightfully claimed "heathen" lands by planting crops, then surely men who made hunting a way of life could claim no lands. Hence colonists seldom classified white hunters as heroes; more often, colonists classified them as savages. Moravian farmers of eighteenth-century Virginia, for instance, sought to lift themselves above "the dregs of human society who spend their time in murdering wild beasts" (in Tillson 1991, 10). Protestants, moreover (especially Puritans and Quakers, but others, too), conceived of sport hunting as a wasteful ritual of an arrogant and irreligious European elite. To many, perhaps most, Protestants, hunting was laudable only insofar as it rid the land of pests and predators, making way for agrarian civilization.

Ideas about hunting and its relation to an idealized manliness changed dramatically in the early nineteenth century. Hunter heroes like Daniel Boone, Davy Crockett, and Natty Bumppo appeared in paintings, sculptures, and most of all, in countless books intended to appeal to youths. In part, the celebration of hunters stemmed from Revolutionary-era writers who transformed the image of the Hobbesian backwoodsman—the man who

recognized no authority but his own—into the image of a zealous guardian of natural rights. More important, hunter heroes of the nineteenth-century epitomized a new sort of manliness that hinged on "self-possession," the trait that, according to biographers, marked Daniel Boone for greatness.

Like their hunter heroes, young men of the Jacksonian and antebellum decades became rugged individualists who migrated into the wilderness of the frontier as well as into the wilderness of growing cities. The market revolution broke apart families and communities, demanding that young men live by their own wits and talents. Like the Daniel Boone of literature, young individualists might abstain from tobacco, drink, and sexual allurements—thus showing Boone-like "self-possession"—or, like Davy Crockett, they might give way to all three. Hunter heroes thus represented opposite faces of middle-class manliness (though one might argue with equal logic that the literary Crockett, unlike Boone, epitomized a working-class manliness increasingly popular among boatmen, teamsters, and construction workers).

The new fascination for hunter heroes in turn translated into a new fascination for sport hunting among middle-class and elite men. Sport hunters, however, abjured the hunting techniques of real backwoodsmen, promoting instead a code of sportsmanship that gave the quarry (seemingly) a fair chance to escape. Thus, sport hunters linked themselves with the genteel sportsmen of England as well as with common-man heroes like Boone, all the while setting themselves apart from the common men of the real frontier. Indeed, the great popularizer of antebellum sport hunting and sportsmanship in the United States—Henry William Herbert— was the son of an English aristocrat.

The ambiguous identity of antebellum sport hunters gave way in the Gilded Age to a full-throated celebration of the hunter as American aristocrat. George Armstrong Custer serves as an example. In two 1874

photographs by W. H. Illingworth, Custer, accompanied by his favorite scout, Bloody Knife, stands triumphant over a huge bear, as if to proclaim himself nature's choice to rule the army, the Indian, and American nature. But perhaps a better example of the hunter-aristocrat would be Cornelius Vanderbilt, or George Eastman, or any of the innumerable Gilded Age plutocrats who, as Thorstein Veblen noted, stocked their greenswards with elk and deer instead of utilitarian cows, symbols of a more agrarian, egalitarian America. If Daniel Boone represented the courageous, independent man in a libertarian wilderness—the man who determined his own fate through pluck and determination—the new hunter represented the Darwinian victor of a grand struggle for survival. By stocking vast parks with big game and by joining elite hunting clubs with plush facilities, Gilded Age sport hunters confirmed their hegemony over American society.

Theodore Roosevelt wrote in 1893 that he would "much regret" to see hunting confined to a "system of large private game preserves, kept for the enjoyment of the very rich" (Roosevelt [1893] 1910, 270). Yet there was nothing extraordinary about hunting author Dwight Huntington's assertion in 1900 that, in the future, all hunting would take place on private preserves. The disappearance of big game in the wild had become a fact of life; antelope, elk, bison, and grizzlies—not to mention some species of wild fowl—were well on the way to extinction. Even deer had disappeared from much of the East. Men like Roosevelt, however, remembered that the common man's right to hunt symbolized the common man's political rights, and to take away that right was to concede that America had lost its democratic vitality.

As a consequence of his passion for wildlife, Roosevelt created the Boone and Crockett Club in 1887. Harking back to the virtues epitomized by Daniel Boone, the club promoted "energy, resolution, manliness, self-reliance" and "capacity for self-help" among its elite members (Grinnell 1910). Beyond that, the Boone and Crockett Club lobbied assiduously for conservation. With assistance from the League of American Sportsmen, the American Bison Society, the Camp Fire Club, the American Game Protective Association, and the Permanent Wild Life Protection Fund, Boone and Crockett members helped create federal game protection laws and wildlife preserves.

The campaign to protect game was laced with irony. Indian lands—which had once been appropriated in the name of farming— were now appropriated in the name of game preservation. To protect hunting as a rite of manly self-reliance, meanwhile, hunters had to join conservationist clubs and lobby for the enlargement of government powers. The result of that lobbying was surely better than the alternative, and deer, antelope, bison, bear, and wildfowl were saved for future generations of Americans to enjoy.

In the twentieth century, sport hunting and its relationship to an idealized manliness continued to change. Though the gentleman hunter did not entirely disappear, hunting increasingly became a rural and blue-collar pastime. In part, that change stemmed from conservation laws enacted early in the century. The creation of bag limits and hunting seasons eliminated, at least theoretically, market and subsistence hunting, thus making all hunters—regardless of class—into "sportsmen." Meanwhile, inexpensive firearms, together with paid holidays and vacations and mass-produced automobiles, made hunting trips to distant locales possible for millions of men. In the 1940s, fully one-quarter of the adult male population of the United States qualified as sport hunters. Hunting, however, declined in popularity in the second half of the twentieth century, at least in proportion to the total U.S. population.

In part, hunting was superseded by such team sports as baseball, football, and basketball, which teach corporate manliness rather than manly individualism. In part, hunting was also superseded by backpacking, rock climbing, and kayaking, which provide a less sanguine venue for outdoor recreation to thousands of middle-class males (and females). More important, hunting was superseded by golf, which offers a forum for individualistic competition amid the splendor of nature, yet does not require the death of sentient beings. Millions of American hunters, nonetheless, continue to venture into the woods each fall. Though few share the elite status of their Gilded Age and Progressive era brethren, they—like those brethren— tend to subscribe to conservative or libertarian notions of manliness, notions epitomized in the rite of hunting.

Daniel Justin Herman

Further Reading:

Altherr, Thomas. 1976. "'The Best of All Breathing': Hunting as a Mode of Environmental Perception in American Literature and Thought from James Fenimore Cooper to Norman Mailer." (Ph.D. dissertation, Ohio State University.)

Grinnell, George Bird, ed. 1910. *Brief History of the Boone and Crockett Club, with Officers, Constitution and List of Members for the Year 1910.* New York: Forest and Stream Publishing Company.

Herman, Daniel Justin. 2001. *Hunting and the American Imagination.* Washington, DC: Smithsonian Institution Press.

Johnson, Robert. [1609] 1963. "Nova Britannia. Offering the Most Excellent Fruites by Planting in Virginia. Exciting All Such as Be Well Affected to Further the Same." In *Tracts and Other Papers Relating Principally to the Origin, Settlement, and Progress of the Colonies in North America, from the Discovery to the Year 1776.* Compiled by Peter Force. Vol. 1. Gloucester, MA: P. Smith.

Reiger, John F. 2000. *American Sportsmen and the Origins of Conservation.* 3d ed. Revised and Expanded. Corvallis, OR: Oregon State University Press.

Roosevelt, Theodore. [1893] 1910. *The Wilderness Hunter. Homeward Bound Edition.* New York: Review of Reviews.

Tillson, Albert H. Jr. 1991. *Gentry and Common Folk: Political Culture on the Virginia Frontier, 1740–1789.* Chapel Hill: University of North Carolina Press.

Trefethen, James B. 1975. *An American Crusade for Wildlife.* New York: Winchester Press.

Warren, Louis S. 1997. *The Hunter's Game: Poachers and Conservationists in Twentieth-Century America.* New Haven and London: Yale University Press.

Husbands

Marriage changes men because most other people in our society expect husbands to behave differently than unmarried men. The expectations that influence men and change their lives are what makes marriage a *social institution.* All social institutions consist of broadly shared ideals about what is appropriate and inappropriate. As such, social institutions consist of informal rules that are often called norms. The norms of marriage include expectations about husbands that are ignored or violated by some men, but are never ignored or violated by most men. Compared to the time before they got married, husbands earn and work more, have better physical and mental health, live longer, are more generous, are happier, participate more in community life, attend religious services more frequently, and have better sex lives (Waite and Gallagher 2000) because they are now responding to different incentives and desires as well as different expectations by other people.

In order to understand how and why marriage changes men in these ways, it is necessary to consider the norms that define the institution. Even if every individual marriage differs in subtle ways from every other, all spouses are held to the same expectations of others in the form of norms. A husband may not be very interested in working for a living, for example. But others expect him to do so. And if he does not work, he will be viewed as unusual, as someone who deviates from what is expected. Sociology teaches us that norm-breakers often pay a price for their nonconformity. They are often excluded from groups that embrace the norms (i.e., they are shunned), and those who embrace the norms often distrust them. So

there is pressure to conform to the cultural patterns of institutions. This is obvious with respect to such personal traits as sexual orientation, political ideology, or intimate lifestyle. To varying degrees, and at different times in history, those whose sexual orientation differed from what was expected (basically, heterosexual), those who rejected the prevailing political order and advocated its overthrow, or those who chose to live with another person without being married were treated as deviants and paid a price in terms of their acceptance among others as a result.

The norms that define the institution of marriage are included in our laws, our religious traditions, public opinion, and cultural traditions. They include the following:

1. Marriage is a free choice, based on love. In this country, marriage is presumed to be a personal decision made by two people who are in love. Others do not arrange marriages. As a result, success or failure in marriage is a reflection of personal success or failure. Individuals, that is, are held responsible for whether they marry, and if so, whether their marriage fails.

2. People should not marry until they are mature enough to do so. Historically, American laws have defined a minimum age at which one may marry, and this age is traditionally the same as the age at which parents are no longer legally responsible for the individual—today, at age eighteen in most states. Presumably, when an individual is old enough to be personally legally liable for his actions, this person meets our minimal definition of a mature person. In addition, married couples in America are expected to establish their own dwelling, rather than living with either set of parents. Maturity and independence, in this view, are closely related norms about marriage.

3. Marriage in America is between heterosexuals. Few would deny that two people of the same sex could establish a strong and loving relationship. Still, marriage, per se, has traditionally been viewed as a union of male and female partners. To date, no state in America has legalized homosexual marriages, despite concerted efforts to do so and Vermont's "civil union" law. Where the public has been asked to vote on legalizing homosexual marriages, the idea has failed (Hawaii, Alaska) even when courts or legislatures have been in favor of such legal rights. Whether or not such exclusions are deemed to be fair or equitable to homosexuals, they are a clear reflection of how marriage is understood by the public, as a union of a male and female.

4. The husband is expected to work to support his family, even though his wife is not. The majority of wives today work for pay, but it is still not a social norm that they must. Husbands, however, are expected to work for pay. There will be little scorn for the woman who decides to stay home to raise her children, for example. This is less true for husbands. The married man who cannot work may be pitied. But the married man who will not work is more likely to be seen as deviant. Simply put, working for pay is less optional for husbands than for wives, at least at the dawn of the twenty-first century. Even men who had irregular and unpredictable work histories before marriage typically work more and earn more once they are husbands.

5. Married people are expected to be sexually faithful to their partners. In America, there is only one wife and one husband in each marriage (monogamy). Traditionally, and by law, sex outside of marriage was viewed as unacceptable. Even now that unmarried sexual relations are more acceptable and common, infidelity in marriage is not (Laumann, et al. 1994, Table 515). Essentially, marital fidelity in a monogamous marriage means that husbands and wives have agreed to restrict themselves from searching for other sexual partners so long as they are married. The norm means that no husband or wife may legitimately seek another sexual partner so long as they are married. This may be understood as a form of commitment that pertains only to husbands and wives.

6. Marriage typically involves children. Historically, marriage was the only legitimate outlet for bearing children. And even when large numbers of children are, in fact, born to unmarried women, it is still the case that almost all married partners have children. Only one in ten married women reaches age forty-four without a child. The importance of the norm about children and marriage is that husbands who become fathers are making a public statement that they are assuming the responsibility of parenthood. Men who father children outside of marriage may be required by a court to assume such responsibilities, but this is not automatic as it is with married fathers. In other words, married fathers are publicly accepting responsibility for the care and provision of their offspring (see Nock 1998, Chapter 2 on marital norms).

To each of the norms listed above, husbands are expected to conform. There is certainly no strict legal or financial penalty for most failures to conform. But to the extent that deviation from the norms leads to exclusion (or shunning), most seem unwilling to risk it. Indeed, the threat of isolation appears to be a very effective incentive to induce broad conformity with social norms, whether related to marriage or other issues. Acceptance by others is often necessary for securing a good job, obtaining credit, and being trusted by others generally.

As husbands and wives agree to conform to these norms, there are predictable changes in their lives. For men, in particular, conformity to marital norms leads to the sorts of changes mentioned at the outset. They work more, earn more, give more money and time to others, dedicate themselves more to relatives, and so on. The obvious question is why marriage alters men in such ways.

The answer is that most husbands understand and accept the norms about marriage. Once married, they have different reasons to work, accept responsibility, honor their commitments, and such (i.e., their incentives have been altered). Also, to the extent that husbands accept the legitimacy of marriage norms and internalize them, they want to conform to these standards (i.e., their preferences have been altered). As husbands, they are expected to be more reliable than other men, and they internalize these expectations by thinking and acting like husbands.

Economists call this the "signaling" function of marriage. An economic signal is something one does that alters other people's beliefs, or conveys information to them (Rowthorn 2002, 135). Such economic signals tell others (employers, friends, neighbors) about the type of person one is. To be most effective, such signals must be relatively costly to acquire (e.g., a college degree, a specialized skill). Marriage functions as a symbol because it is costly. Husbands place significant limits on their behaviors both in the present and future by getting married. What, then, is conveyed by the signal of marriage? Among other things, a man signals that he is willing to accept long-term commitments and responsibilities, that he is mature, independent, and faithful, that he is committed to working to support his family, that he is willing to accept responsibility for any children he fathers, and, of course, that he is

heterosexual. Do such signals matter? The answer is found by asking whether husbands are treated differently from other men. Are they trusted more? Given more responsibilities? Offered better jobs? To date, the evidence indicates that the answer to all such questions is yes. This is why married people have historically been given legal rights and privileges not granted to the unmarried (Cott 2000).

Steven L. Nock

See also Bachelors

Further Reading:

Cott, Nancy F. 2000. *Public Vows: A History of Marriage and the Nation*. Cambridge, MA: Harvard University Press.

Laumann, Edward O., John H. Gagnon, Robert T. Michael, and Stuart Michaels. 1994. *The Social Organization of Sexuality: Sexual Practices in the United States*. Chicago: University of Chicago Press.

Nock, Steven L. 1998. *Marriage in Men's Lives*. New York: Oxford University Press.

Rowthorn, Robert. 2002. "Marriage as a Signal." Pp. 132–156 in *The Law and Economics of Marriage and Divorce*. Edited by Anthony W. Dines and Robert Rowthorn. Cambridge, UK: Cambridge University Press.

Waite, Linda J., and Maggie Gallagher. 2000. *The Case for Marriage: Why Married People are Happier, Healthier, and Better Off Financially*. New York: Doubleday.

Hypermasculinity

The term *hypermasculinity* is one of several concepts in the sociological and psychological literature describing compulsive masculine self-identity concerns and behaviors. One of the earliest uses is in a 1974 article by Ira Silverman and Simon Dinitz in *Criminology* in which they use the term *hypermasculine behavior* to describe the antisocial, aggressive, and criminal activities of a sample of delinquent boys. It is preceded by and co-occurs in the literature over the next twenty-five years with the terms *compulsive masculinity* and, much more commonly, *machismo* (though the latter deserves distinction as a specifically Latino form).

One of the earliest attempts to theorize the concept of hypermasculinity specifically is in a 1984 *Psychiatry* article by Leonard Glass. In this article, Glass draws upon psychotherapy sessions with several of his male patients and argues that hypermasculinity has two fundamental (and, by their nature, pathological) forms: The "man's man" is the cowboy/jock—strong, dependable, rough, mystified by women, rigid, unemotional, powerful, dirty; the "ladies' man" is the Casanova—smooth, charming, stylish, sly, seductive, sexually predatory, knowledgeable about what women want, and emotionally counterfeit. "Healthy" men appear in neither category.

Fifteen years later, in her work on masculinity and sport, Varda Burstyn (1999) uses the term *hypermasculinity* to describe "an exaggerated ideal of manhood linked mythically and practically to the role of the warrior" (4), "the ideal man in the masculinist conception" (10), and "the belief that ideal manhood lies in the exercise of force to dominate others" (192). Her work consistently associates hypermasculinity with dominance, violence, physical strength, and compulsive heterosexuality as expressed and reproduced in competitive sport.

The following represents a definition broad enough to encompass all three uses: Hypermasculinity refers to sets of behaviors and beliefs characterized by unusually highly developed masculine forms as defined by existing cultural values. The next several paragraphs break down this definition into its specific parts.

1. "sets of behaviors and beliefs": Hypermasculinity can appear either in the actions of an individual or category of individuals (i.e., "behaviors"), or in their minds ("beliefs"). We would typically expect occurrence in the latter to result in appearance in the former, although this would not necessary follow: A person could hold hypermasculine beliefs without exhibiting them in actual behavior, and could exhibit hypermasculine behaviors without necessarily maintaining hypermasculine beliefs. However, and in either case, the beliefs or behaviors would need to be part of some cultural *set* (see below) in order to warrant the term "hypermasculine."

2. "characterized by usually highly developed masculine forms": Although many beliefs or behaviors may be generally "masculine" in appearance, the prefix "hyper-" implies a sense of extremes, and in so doing it *stigmatizes*: what is "hyper-" masculine has become masculine in the "wrong" way. It is masculinity somehow out of control (criminal, pathological, violent, etc.). Hypermasculinity may take more than one form and a given culture may have a variety of complimentary or overlapping hypermasculine archetypes.

3. "as defined by existing cultural values": The definition of what is "masculine" inevitably varies by culture and over time. Values shift or diverge, and with them the definition of what is masculine or feminine also changes. Hypermasculinity is characterized by one or more *sets* of strong social and cultural agreements on those values and always exists oppositionally in relation to forms of femininity (and, theoretically, hyperfemininity). What is hypermasculine, then, is always hyper-*not*-feminine.

Kirby Schroeder

See also "Adonis Complex"
Further Reading:

Burstyn, Varda. 1999. *Rites of Men: Manhood, Politics, and the Culture of Sport.* Toronto, Canada: University of Toronto Press.

Glass, Leonard L. 1984. "Man's Man/Ladies' Man: Motifs of Hypermasculinity." *Psychiatry* 47, no. 3: 260–278.

Silverman, Ira J., and Simon Dinitz. 1974. "Compulsive Masculinity and Delinquency: An Empirical Investigation." *Criminology* 11, no. 4: 498–515.

I

Ibsen, Henrik (1828–1906)

Henrik Ibsen is considered one of the most important dramatists to shape modern European drama. His long career started in the mid-nineteenth century, when literature was still heavily under the influence of Romanticism. Moving with the trend to a more realistic representation, Ibsen brought the dramatic arts into the Naturalist mode with his prose drama and advocacy of the fourth-wall convention, for which he is mostly known. This innovation in dramatic form was accompanied not only by a transformation in language from verse to prose, but also in a shift of dramatic content from a retrospection of Norwegian folklore and epics in his early plays to a forward-looking approach to social issues in his contemporary Norwegian society. Despite the adaptation of a new language and a progressive shedding of the historical personalities and events for contemporary social issues, Ibsen's body of work bears reading as a whole that embodies a set of values and concerns, presented in different garbs in the individual plays.

Regardless of whether it is the early epic dramas or the more famous "social drama" he wrote in the middle of his long career, whether it is the abstract concept of greatness or the more concrete question of gender relations in the Norwegian society of his day, or whether it is a male character or a female character who is chosen to bear the burden of making the most important decisions in the play, the twenty-six plays Ibsen wrote during his five-decade career deal essentially with a person's relationship with his or her self, often how he or she wills his or her being, and how he or she fights against opposing forces that threaten to change that willed self. Although a few of the memorable heroines Ibsen created grant him the reputation of being a "women's libber," Ibsen himself denied this identity, and his dedication to the theme of selfhood, most often expressed in a masculine sense of creation, can be seen throughout his important plays.

Ibsen's early plays are written in verse, and the content is mostly taken from Norwegian folklore or history. The list includes: *Catilina* (1850), *The Burial Mound* (1850), *Norma* (1851), *St John's Eve* (1853), *Lady Inger of Østraat* (1855), *The Feast at Solhoug* (1856), *Olaf Liljekrans* (1857), *The Vikings at Helgeland* (1858), *Love's Comedy* (1862), and *The Pretenders* (1863); they are lesser known and not much performed. The choice of subject gives ample space for the protagonists to develop and test their theories about their selfhood. Rather close to the structure and format of classical drama, these early plays exhibit male heroes who have larger-than-life egos and kingly thoughts and are not afraid to will their selves into being, even if it means fighting what they perceive as the external opposing forces. Although there are a number of ambitious female characters, the vision of the early plays is that of individuals competing to be themselves through realizing their willed qualities. The heroes' will to compete even with God the Creator makes the matter of self realization a masculine issue.

Brand (1866), *Peer Gynt* (1867), *The League of Youth* (1869), and *Emperor and Galilean* (1873) may be seen as the transitional plays before Ibsen's full emergence into his famous prose drama. Among them, *Brand* and *Peer Gynt* are generally considered the most significant works, both in terms of their establishing Ibsen's position as a great dramatic artist, as well as featuring the typical Ibsen hero for whom it is "all or nothing" regarding his desire to be the full self. This masculine desire for the absolute is to be seen repeatedly in the later prose drama, in some cases even embodied by female characters.

Ibsen's prose drama starts with *Pillars of Society* (1877). Michael Meyer (1971), Ibsen's biographer, regards him as taking up the role of a social critic in the group of plays including *A Doll's House* (1879), *Ghosts* (1881), *An Enemy of the People* (1882), and *The Wild Duck* (1884). Faced with social problems such as greed, hypocrisy, vanity, and corruption, the male protagonists in these plays persist with what they believe to be rightful masculine qualities: moral courage, faith, integrity, and idealism. Yet the complexity of these dramas shows that the high-sounding qualities might be admirable, but they are not always the simple answer to real conditions in human life. The male protagonists face disillusionment and frustration in the external and human resistance to their ideals.

The next phase of Ibsen's drama is described by Michael Meyer as an exploration of the unconscious, for *Rosmersholm* (1886),

The Lady from the Sea (1888), and *Hedda Gabler* (1890) feature powerfully rendered characters whose depth comes from a richly endowed unconscious life, very often incomprehensible even to themselves. Rebecca West, Ellida, and Hedda Gabler are memorable female characters who live a mysterious life of self-exploration, testing their own subjectivity as the male heroes in the previous phase of Ibsen's work. In these plays the negotiation of freedom and the absolute self takes place in the feminine, which can be seen as a refraction of the journey of male exploration in other of Ibsen's plays.

The final phase of Ibsen's work is in many ways a fitting conclusion to his artistic search for an absolute self. *The Master Builder* (1892), *Little Eyolf* (1894), and *When We Dead Awaken* (1899) all show the protagonist artist at the highest point of his career, so successful that he is competing with the Creator for further glory. Although *John Gabriel Borkman* (1896) is not about an artist, the protagonist is shown to be emerging from an undesirable life to new goals. Solness, Allmers, Borkman, and Rubek may be regarded as standing on the cold mountain tops of their lives, seeking to make the ultimate step of their masculine selves. Yet ultimately it is the avalanche that greets these masculine egos, who stretched beyond their limits.

Amy Lee

Further Reading:

Egan, Michael, ed. 1972. *Henrik Ibsen: The Critical Heritage.* London: Routledge.

Eikeland, P. J. 1934. *Ibsen Studies.* New York: Haskell House.

Gerland, Oliver. 1998. *A Freudian Poetics for Ibsen's Theatre: Repetition, Recollection, and Paradox.* Lewiston, NY: Edwin Mellen Press.

Gray, Ronald. 1977. *Ibsen—A Dissenting View: A Study of the Last Twelve Plays.* Cambridge, NY: Cambridge University Press.

Hochman, Stanley. 1984. *McGraw-Hill Encyclopedia of World Drama.* New York: McGraw-Hill, Inc.

Johnston, Brian. 1989. *Text and Supertext in Ibsen's Drama.* University Park, PA: Pennsylvania State University Press.

Lyons, Charles R. 1972. *Henrik Ibsen: The Divided Consciousness.* Carbondale and Edwardsville, IL: Southern Illinois University Press.

McFarlane, James, ed. 1994. *The Cambridge Companion to Ibsen.* Cambridge, NY: Cambridge University Press.

Meyer, Michael. 1971. *Ibsen.* New York: Viking.

Rhodes, Norman. 1995. *Ibsen and the Greeks: The Classical Greek Dimension in Selected Works of Henrik Ibsen as Mediated by German and Scandinavian Culture.* Lewisburg, PA: Bucknell University Press.

Immigration

International migration is a complex trend informed by structural factors operating at a global level and by family and individual decisions at the microlevel. Crossing international borders varies by the gender, class, and racial background of the participants. Some immigrants are professional men from developing countries recruited and/or enticed by opportunities in multinational corporations in developed countries. Others are refugees who move from one country to another to escape persecution or for economic survival. International migration is gendered and has consequences for the gender composition of both host and home countries. Men are more likely to be legal immigrants and receive legal status in the host country and women are more likely to be refugees.

At the beginning of the twenty-first century, the estimated number of immigrants worldwide was over 45 million. Of these, approximately 22 million were refugees (http://www.unhcr.ch). Refugees are either expelled or leave due to fear of persecution. According to the 1951 United Nations Convention, refugees are persons "who, owing to well-founded fear of being persecuted for reasons of race, religion, nationality, membership of particular social group or political opinion" are outside of the country of their nationality and are unable to return to its protection (UNHCR 2002, 11). Like immigrants, most of the refugees are from Asian and African countries and remain there, with very few receiving amnesty in developed countries.

Among theories of immigration, the neoclassical economics model explains immigration as a result of wage differentials and the dynamics of labor-market responses to the supply and demand of workers across international boarders. This follows the push and pull hypothesis; that undesirable socioeconomic conditions at home push those who are capable of moving to destinations that offer desirable pull factors. Network theory stipulates that social networks of family, locality, and ethnic bonds facilitate the flow of populations from their home states to specific host destinations. Network connections provide opportunities for immigration, reduce the cost, and enhance the benefits. World system theory points to globalization that has created various labor niches for professional, skilled, and unskilled workers across international boundaries. In the same vain, dual labor-market theory stipulates that rich industrial economies benefit from immigrant workers who perform mostly undesirable but necessary work. A decline in low-wage immigration does not necessarily increase wages because employers keep these jobs immune from labor-market forces. Historically employers have found ways to keep some labor out of labor market competition, through techniques like slavery, indentured workers, and race, gender, and religious segmentation (discrimination) like that found in agricultural labor in the United States, domestic labor in western Europe, and service labor in the Persian Gulf region.

Feminism has broadened the conceptual framework by pointing out that immigration is gendered, as social relations of economic development, family organization, and government policies are gendered. Feminists acknowledge that a complex network of socioeconomic factors, cultural values, and geographical conditions affect immigration. But they point out that these macrotrends are influenced by gender dynamics regarding productive labor and reproductive values. Feminist theories have formulated how the interaction of capitalism and patriarchy affects immigration policies, which can result in splitting families, underground trafficking of undocumented workers and children, and exploitation of the poor across international boundaries. Although immigration research ignored women, it also assumed a generic man, divorced of ethnicity, class, or other distinctions.

The women's movements and globalization have challenged the classical theories of development and migration. Changing roles of women across the globe have raised questions about the notion of masculinity, men's status at home, and their opportunities in the public domain. Global capitalism, with its demand for cheap labor and open markets, has frustrated many men's traditional ambitions. These trends have affected men and the notion of masculinity in the developed north and the developing or poor south.

Many initial studies of immigration assumed movement of peasant or working-class men from less developed areas to expanding economies in the industrial north. High or low fertility was perceived to account for immigration and emigration. Studies show that, although the growth of manufacturing and industrialization provided opportunities for some men to immigrate, the majority of the movement in the post–Cold War period was of laborers in service and construction industries. Furthermore, the largest immigration volume is between countries marked by high fertility and developing economies. The gender composition of migration in each region of the world is different. The oil-producing countries of the Middle East attract skilled male workers, whereas women converge on Southeast Asian countries to work in textile factories.

Gender affects decisions at the household level as well, regarding who stays or who goes and what happens to those left behind. Each sex's familial and gender roles dictate where, when, how, and why they go. Married men leave their families in search of employment, whereas married women are less likely to leave their husbands and chil-

dren for employment over a long period of time. Distance is another factor influenced by gender. Men are more likely than women to emigrate to distant destinations or difficult, restrictive countries. The single, young adult of both sexes, especially from upper-middle classes in developing countries, immigrates for personal growth. He or she, nevertheless, is expected to help the family back home, either financially or by facilitating opportunities for the immigration of younger siblings. Families' expectations of return benefits depend more on the skills of young emigrants than on their gender. However, families expect that daughters will stay closer to home and marry compatriots.

Married men face more pressure to emigrate in order to provide for their families. They emigrate over longer distances and stay longer. Married women are less likely to be the initial emigrant; rather they follow male members of their families. Married professional men make the move with their families, but skilled immigrant men are more likely to leave their families behind and either return home to them or bring them later at a more opportune time when they have job security or have established legal residency.

For men, international migration is a two-tiered system. Those with specialized education, mostly from upper strata of their society, migrate and are recruited to developed countries. They also have the advantage of a social network in the host country to facilitate their immigration. Peasants and unskilled workers migrate to regional labor magnets to work in sweatshops or on cash-crop plantations. The network theory is more appropriate in explaining the immigration of the former, while the dual labor market fits the immigration of the latter group. The middle-class men in these countries lack the skills and resources of their rich countrymen to emigrate to developed countries, but they find unskilled labor undesirable and economically disadvantageous. It is this group that finds itself shut out of the opportunities abroad and excluded from the small ruling elite at home. Inadequately trained college-educated young men in the developing south face a shrinking job market, blocked mobility, and unresponsive or autocratic governments.

Immigrant men face numerous challenges in the new country. Some of these, such as learning a new language, acquiring new skills, and adjusting to different social and cultural expectations, are predictable. Others are more gradual and subtle. Among these are challenges to their notion of masculinity and their power in the family. In the new country, women may find employment and exert their financial independence for the first time. Children may tune into their new peer culture that disregards traditional values of gender and age. It may also happen that women are the sole breadwinners of the family by finding employment in the service sector, where men find their civil service background or managerial skills unmarketable in the new labor market. This combination is often a recipe for marital dispute and even divorce. On the other hand, single men have the advantage of the double standard, which grants them more sexual freedom than single women.

In immigrant-receiving countries, the native young men from the lower middle class rail against the affluence and status of the newly arrived professional immigrants. They also resent the poor immigrants for loss of jobs and the decline of wages. They blame big business for transferring manufacturing jobs overseas and see the government as the lackey of large corporations for refusing to stand up to them and protect the native workers against immigrants and big business. This group, facing shrinking employment opportunities, is resentful of immigrants for usurping rights and benefits perceived to be rightfully theirs, and they may join nationalistic or supremacist racist groups. These groups are on the rise in western Europe, the United States, Canada, and Australia. At times their tactics are violent toward immigrants or their own governments, as in the case of Timothy McVeigh in the United States, who was angry at the government's handouts to minorities and immigrants.

New innovations in communication and transportation generate new opportunities for transfer of labor across national boundaries, but they also challenge the primacy of geographical boundaries and government sovereignty. The technological divide has generated unique opportunities for professionals in high-tech industries who are mostly men. It has also raised the relative expectations of men who lack skills and/or resources to migrate.

So far immigration has benefited both host and home countries. For the home countries, labor migration has reduced unemployment and its associated social ills, while remittances from workers abroad have boosted the foreign-exchange earnings of a country. For the host countries, it has met their various labor needs. But the unstable global economy and volatile polity in many regions are making international migration both necessary and unpredictable. The developing countries are faced with a young, semieducated population that cannot be absorbed by their struggling economies. Developed countries, while needing the new labor, are more than ever skeptical of immigration. They are restricting their definition of refugees, closing their borders against massively displaced populations, and scrutinizing families. The public opinion among the native population of these countries is turning anti-immigration and nativistic.

Many countries or regions have created free-trade zones to entice foreign capital and international trade, undeterred by labor regulations and government tariffs. These free-trade zones, like the North American Free Trade Agreement (NAFTA), may reduce the labor shortage of the rich and unemployment of the poor countries, but they have not staved off immigration flow. International migration will grow and with it the ideals of masculinities will change to include more flexible gender roles.

Shahin Gerami

Further Reading:

Gabaccia, Donna, ed. 1992. *Seeking Common Ground: Multidisciplinary Studies of Immigrant Women in the United States.* Westport, CT: Greenwood.

Hanassab, Shideh. 1998. "Sexuality, Dating, and Double Standards: Young Iranian Immigrants in Los Angeles." *Iranian Studies* 31, no. 1 (Winter): 65–75.

Kelson, Gregory A., and Debra L. DeLaet. 1999. *Gender and Immigration.* New York: New York University Press.

Mahdi, Ali Akbar. 2001. "Perception of Gender Roles Among Female Iranian Immigrants in the United States." Pp. 185–210 in *Women, Religion, and Culture in Iran.* Edited by Sarah Ansari and Vanessa Martin. London: Curzon Press.

Massey, Douglas S., Arango Joaquin, Hugo Graeme, Ali Kouaouci, Adela Pellegrino, and J. Edward Taylor. 1993. "Theories of International Migration: A Review and Appraisal." *Population and Development Review* 19, no. 3: 431–465.

Sowell, Thomas. 1996. *Migration and Culture: A World View.* New York: Basic Books.

Tietelbaum, Michael S., and Sharon Russell. 1994. "International Migration, Fertility, and Development." Pp. 229–249 in *Population and Development: Old Debates, New Conclusions.* Edited by Robert Cassen. New Branswick, NJ: Transaction Publishers.

United Nations High Commissioner for Refugees (UNHCR). 2002. "Global Appeal 2002." At http://www.unhcr.ch/pubs/fdrs/ga2002toc/htm (cited 20 August 2003).

———. 2002. "Basic Facts." At http://www.unhcr.ch/cgi-bin/texis/vtx/home? (cited 28 August 2003).

Imperialism

See Colonialism

Impotence

See Erectile Dysfunction; Viagra

Infertility

Infertility is medically defined as no pregnancy after a year of trying. In societies where manhood is measured by the number of children fathered, infertility is socially stigmatizing. Male infertility seems to be on the rise and is very difficult to treat.

In men, chemotherapy, ulcer and high blood pressure medications, alcohol, marijuana, and anabolic steroids for bulking up muscles can all lower sperm counts. In the last decade, research from international studies implicates a global environment riddled with toxic pollutants in significantly lowering sperm counts throughout the world.

In both women and men, there is little protection against workplace exposure to fertility-reducing toxins. In 1991, the U.S. Supreme Court decided that employers could not use protection of the fetus as a rationale for barring fertile women from hazardous jobs. The decision to take a job that might cause infertility is now up to workers themselves, including men at risk of sperm deformity. In addition to job-related hazards, sexually transmitted diseases and inadequate health care have contributed to higher rates of infertility among African Americans, and they are less likely to have access to expensive procreative technologies. For all groups, a significant cause of infertility in later life are teen-age chlamydia infections, a very common bacterial sexually transmitted disease that may have no symptoms and therefore go undetected and untreated.

Whether the woman or the man is infertile, the woman is usually the one who initially seeks help. If she is determined to have a biological child with her male partner, she has to ensure his willingness to undergo demands like intercourse at ovulation and masturbation to produce fresh sperm. She will also need sympathy and emotional support throughout the days, months, and often years of repeated attempts to get pregnant. Conversely, if she refuses to undergo fertility treatments, her infertile male partner's opportunity to have a biological child in this relationship is lost. This imbalance in the demands of treatment sets up the dynamics of gender bargaining in male infertility.

There are several assisted reproductive technologies readily available in many coun-

TABLE 1: Assisted Reproductive Technologies, with Success Rates

Technology	Description	Success Rate
Donor Insemination (DI, formerly known as artificial insemination)	Semen from either an unknown donor through a semen bank or from a male friend or relative is inserted either into the vagina (intra cervical insemination) or directly into the cervix (intra uterine insemination). Fresh or frozen semen can be used.	IUI pregnancy rate is 12.4 percent per cycle.
Oocyte Donation (also known as egg donation)	Female donors are given drugs to stimulate the production of eggs. These eggs are harvested at ovulation and inseminated with male partner's or donor sperm. When they develop into embryos, they are implanted into the adopter's womb. Oocyte donation is typically used by women who have premature ovarian failure (under 40 years of age) or who are perimenopausal (over 40 years of age and 5–10 years before menopause).	Pregnancy rates vary depending upon the recipient's age.
In Vitro Fertilization (IVF)	Hormones are administered to increase production of ova. They are removed and fertilized with sperm in a petri dish. Gametes are incubated for a day or two until the resultant cell division produces an embryo that can be implanted into the woman's womb.	24.9 percent live birth rate from the 1998 Centers for Disease Control's survey of 360 ART clinics in the United States.
Intracyto-plasmic Sperm Injection (ICSI)	A single active sperm cell is injected directly into a previously surgically removed oocyte. The resultant embryo is implanted into a woman's body. ICSI allows previously subfertile or infertile men to participate in reproduction with their biological gametes.	Clinical pregnancy rate is between 31.6 percent and 36.8 percent.
Embryo Adoption	A previously created embryo is implanted and gestated in the womb of a woman who did not provide the ovum. The gestational mother is designated as the biological mother. If adopted by a heterosexual couple, the designated father is usually not the sperm donor.	N/A
Surrogacy	A woman carries the fetus for another woman. The fetus may or may not be biologically related to a member of the adoptive family. ART may or may not be used to impregnate the gestational carrier.	N/A

tries. They may or may not be covered under insurance plans or national health services, and some (such as surrogacy) are illegal in some countries. The accompanying table describes these procedures and, where available, their success rates.

Judith Lorber
Lisa Jean Moore

See also Childlessness

Further Reading:

Cayan, S., D. Lee, J. Conaghan, et al. 2001. "A Comparison of ICSI Outcomes with Fresh and Cryopreserved Epididymal Spermatozoa from the Same Couples." *Human Reproduction* 16, no. 3: 495–499.

Hendin, B. N., T. Falcone, J. Hallak, et al. 2000. "The Effect of Patient and Semen Characteristics on Live Birth Rate Following Intrauterine Insemination: A Retrospective Study." *Journal of Assisted Reproductive Genetics* 17, no. 5: 245–252.

Intimacy

The word *intimacy* evolved from the Latin *intimus,* which means "innermost" or "deepest." In modern parlance, it usually refers to "a process in which two caring people share as freely as possible in the exchange of feelings, thoughts, and actions," though other very different definitions are possible. Some people emphatically differentiate intimacy from romance, strong affection, tenderness, eternal love, or sexual passion; they may view this interpersonal connection as contingent upon compassionate acceptance and knowledge of oneself (Masters, Johnson, and Kolodny 1995).

The present review emphasizes how cultural variables affect men's level of intimacy toward men and women. Comprehensive reviews of the intimacy literature are available elsewhere (Masters et al. 1995).

Considerable evidence suggests that American heterosexual men (of European ancestry) are—on average—less likely than women to express intimacy, at least with respect to self-disclosure (Masters et al. 1995; Tognoli 1980). From childhood, these men are socialized to believe that they must prove

their masculine strength to themselves and others at all times, that the expression of intimacy to women is more acceptable than to other men, and that the expression of tender and vulnerable feelings is unmanly. They secretly fear being perceived as homosexual, causing them to minimize overtly intimate expressions toward other men (Tognoli 1980).

Of course, the evidence for group averages and general socialization pressures can be misleading. The expression of intimacy varies greatly among men. Despite childhood socialization, men in general are fully capable of intimacy and, on average, become increasingly concerned with intimacy as they age (Masters et al. 1995).

Taboos against male-to-male intimacy are absent in many cultures. In discussing cultures that value male-to-male intimacy, and undervalue male-to-female intimacy, Williams (1992) described patterns observed in men from Native America (North American Indians), Andalusia (Andorra, Spain), and Java (an Island in Indonesia). Native American men had elaborate ceremonies involving the expression of fondness for each other. Moreover, they had special quarters where they slept together overnight. Within the quarters' confines, they shared emotions and talked candidly about their daily problems. In contrast to male-male relationships, typical marriages apparently served economic and procreation functions more than intimate ones. There was often little expectation that husband and wife would be best friends. Partners sometimes expected economic support despite not being sexually attracted to each other.

Men in Andalusia (Andorra, Spain) typically preferred to express emotions in same-sex friendships (male-male) rather than cross-sex friendships (male-female). They were expected to spend considerable time in the company of other men, where important events were to be discussed. Their leisure time was spent with male friends at the local tavern. Once their sons reached fifteen years of age, these men, rather than their wives, became primarily responsible for child rearing. Similarly, men in Java had emotional needs met by same-sex friends after they married. After working in the village for the entire day, they typically spent the evening in the company of other men, discussing personal issues, playing musical instruments together, and dancing.

Williams (1992) compared men from the three cultures to men living in the United States. He noted that each of these three cultures enforced social roles defined by gender. He emphasized that the results illustrate how cultural background powerfully influences the frequency and type of intimacy that men express. Moreover, Williams concluded that friendships among heterosexual men in the United States have been adversely affected by homophobia and competition within work environments. These variables do not compromise male-male friendships in the three aforementioned cultures. These cultures, however, do not stigmatize homosexual behavior. Indeed, such cultures do not differentiate between homosexual and heterosexual behavior. As such, men are not inhibited in expressing intimacy to other men. It is unclear if men from these cultures engaged in homosexuality. In cultures where there is little or no discrepancy between heterosexual and homosexual acts as expressions of same-sex intimacy, it is often difficult to study only nonsexual intimacy among men.

Little is known about the patterns of intimacy among American men from non-European cultural and ethnic backgrounds. Studies of these nondominant groups are rare. Two studies have investigated intimacy in male-male friendships among African Americans (Franklin 1992) and Iranian American men (Khorrami 2002).

Among African Americans, there are differences between men from working-class and upwardly mobile backgrounds (Franklin 1992). The working-class men exhibit considerable intimacy. Their intimacy reflects a political consciousness based on a shared sense of victimization and oppression. In contrast, the upwardly mobile men tend to adopt less intimate patterns as they succeed within the dominant culture. In general, they increasingly adopt values, traits, and beliefs that parallel those of the mainstream. Although they, too, may experience racism and exclusion, their level of intimacy is moderated by their financial, educational, intellectual, and social ambition.

They frequently avoid intimacy with male friends, preferring to discuss sports, economic ventures, and occupational concerns. In fact, the more such men immerse themselves in mainstream institutions, the less likely they are to express intimacy in male-male friendships. In short, these men are reinforced for being independent, competitive, emotionally inexpressive, and homophobic (Franklin 1992).

Among Iranian Americans, a somewhat similar picture emerges. There are striking differences between men who immigrated to the United States between the late 1970s and early 1980s (the time of the Iranian Revolution) and those who immigrated earlier or later (Khorrami 2002). The majority of men who immigrated during the late 1970s and early 1980s were fleeing their homeland in the midst of violent revolution, turmoil, and trauma. They often left their friends and some of their families behind, in harm's way. When these men arrived in the United States, they experienced hostility, fueled by negative media characterizations and stereotypes of Iranians. Fearing persecution in America, these men formed intimate friendships with each other. Typically, they spent many hours together, discussing their vulnerabilities and fears and reading poetry. Their intimate bonds served as a support system, helping to buffer their collective emotional trauma.

The Iranian men who immigrated before or after the revolution exhibited a different pattern of male-male friendship. Their relative lack of turmoil meant a less traumatic transition to life in America. These individuals showed patterns of intimacy that more closely resembled those of the dominant culture.

Khorrami (2002) also found that the younger the Iranian man was upon entry, the less intimate his male-male friendships were. The younger immigrants tended to have more American friends than Iranian friends. They exhibited more competition, striving for independence, and homophobia than their older counterparts.

Sam Khorrami
David Henry Peterzell

See also Friendship

Further Reading:

Franklin, C. W. 1992. "Hey, Home-Yo, Bro." Pp. 201–214 in *Men's Friendships.* Edited by P. M. Nardi. Newbury Park, CA: Sage.

Khorrami, Sam. 2002. "The Social Construction of Masculinity among Iranian American Men" (unpublished manuscript).

Masters, W. H., V. E. Johnson, and R. C. Kolodny. 1995. *Human Sexuality.* New York: HarperCollins.

Tognoli, J. 1980. "Male Friendship and Intimacy across the Life Span." *Family Relations* 29: 273–279.

Williams, W. L. (1992). "The Relationship between Male-Male Friendship and Male-Female Marriage: American Indian and Asian Comparisons." Pp. 186–200 in *Men's Friendships.* Edited by P. Nardi. Newbury Park, CA: Sage.

Invisible Man

In this acclaimed 1952 novel, Ralph Ellison follows in the tradition of such figures as Frederick Douglass and Richard Wright, African American men for whom the terms "freedom" and "manhood" are nearly synonymous. In the novel's famous first chapter, the nameless first-person narrator recounts his humiliating experience at a battle royal, a spectacle put on for the sadistic entertainment of prominent white businessmen. Believing that he is there to give a dignified speech in the manner of Booker T. Washington on the virtues of lifting oneself up by one's bootstraps, the nameless narrator instead finds himself forced to fight a group of other young black men while blindfolded. The young men are then given contradictory orders; they are both commanded and forbidden to watch as a frightened, naked white woman—the U.S. flag tattooed just above her crotch—dances. The white businessmen reward the narrator's willingness to participate in his own sexualized humiliation by granting him a college scholarship. The scene epitomizes the novel's interest in showing white power's ruthless debasement of black men's relations with each other and white men's responsibility for the conditions of their own paranoia about black men's supposed sexual interest in white women. Although the narrator understands that the naked woman's fear resembles his own, for much of the novel the narrator appears to believe that a woman is "any man's most easily accessible symbol of freedom" (Ellison 1952, 153).

At the all-black college, the narrator inadvertently exposes a wealthy white trustee to the seamier side of poor black life when, while chauffeuring the trustee, he stops at the cabin of a man who has impregnated his own daughter, a fact that strikes a deep and disturbing chord for the trustee. The college's manipulative and sycophantic president, Dr. Bledsoe, considers the narrator's blunder evidence that he is too foolish to remain at the college and expels him. The narrator travels north to New York City under the impression that he will be allowed to return to college after working for a few months. The novel's first major shift occurs when a wealthy white homosexual named Emerson reveals to the narrator that Bledsoe has betrayed him and will never allow him to return to college. Ellison's papers at the Library of Congress reveal that he intended Emerson's homosexuality to enable a sympathetic identification with the narrator's status as a fellow outcast.

In the novel's second section, the narrator obtains employment at the Liberty Paint

Factory, which specializes in white paint for government buildings. Following an explosive accident in the factory's bowels, the narrator awakens in a hospital, apparently having undergone a surgery-free, prefrontal lobotomy. Though he suffers temporarily from amnesia, the narrator escapes from the hospital, regains his memory, and takes up lodging in Harlem with a tradition-minded black woman named Mary Rambo who nurses him back to health. Happening upon the eviction of an elderly black woman, the narrator delivers an impassioned plea for peaceable resistance that inadvertently incites a riot. His "effective" speech is noted by the Brotherhood, an organization modeled on the Communist Party, and the narrator is taken on as a speaker under the tutelage of a leading member, Brother Jack. Brotherhood leaders decide that the narrator thinks too independently and, as a probationary action, assign him to speak on the "Woman Question" downtown, away from Harlem's volatility.

The narrator discovers that a fellow black member of the Brotherhood, Tod Clifton, has disappeared, then finds him selling degrading Sambo dolls on the street. Clifton is shot by police, and the narrator decides on his own initiative to deliver a stirring speech at Clifton's funeral. Brotherhood leaders rebuke him for his independent decision and inflammatory speech. While arguing, the narrator discovers that Brother Jack is literally half blind when his glass eye pops out during a fit of anger. Based on his discovery of a trickster figure named Rinehart, who seems to be many things to many people, the narrator determines at this point to behave superficially like a yes-man and clandestinely to milk the wife or girlfriend of some high-ranking Brotherhood official for confidential information on the organization's intentions. This plan aborts when the narrator actually finds himself in a sexual posture with such a woman, for she insists that he act out her fantasy of being raped by a black man. Here, too, Ellison underscores the disquieting connections between sexual and racial oppression.

The narrator abandons his plan to use the woman for his own ends and, returning uptown, wanders through a race riot incited by a radical nationalist named Ras the Exhorter, a kind of blend of Marcus Garvey and Gordon Parks Sr., whom Ellison knew and collaborated with on a series of photographs for *Life* magazine that represented scenes from the novel (Jackson 2002, 375–376). During the riot, the narrator escapes down a manhole where he realizes the degree to which the Brotherhood has manipulated him. He then hallucinates his own castration at the hands of the novel's most prominent male characters, both black and white. Rather than despair over this loss of manhood, the narrator laughs, asserting that he now understands his castration as the price of their freedom. This opens up the novel's final level of perception, and the narrator recounts his story from an underground apartment, coming to terms with his experience in order to reemerge ready to act more effectively. Gordon Parks's photograph *Man Peeking from Manhole: Harlem, 1949* tentatively stages such a reemergence.

Douglas Steward

Further Reading:

Benston, Kimberly W., ed. 1987. *Speaking for You: The Vision of Ralph Ellison.* Washington, DC: Howard University Press.

Ellison, Ralph. Undated. Container 144, Folder 5, Ralph Ellison Papers. Manuscript Division, Library of Congress, Washington, DC..

———. 1952. *Invisible Man.* New York: Vintage.

———. 1964. *Shadow and Act.* New York: Vintage.

Graham, Maryemma, and Amritjit Singh, eds. 1995. *Conversations with Ralph Ellison.* Jackson, MS: University Press of Mississippi.

Jackson, Lawrence. 2002. *Ralph Ellison: Emergence of Genius.* New York: John Wiley & Sons.

Kim, Daniel Y. 1997. "Invisible Desires: Homoerotic Racism and Its Homophobic Critique in Ralph Ellison's *Invisible Man.*" *Novel* 30: 309–28.

O'Meally, Robert, ed. 1988. *New Essays on Invisible Man.* New York: Cambridge University Press.

Ives, Charles (1874–1954)

One of America's most celebrated composers, Charles Ives was renowned for his efforts to "revirilize" the American musical vernacular.

Born in Danbury, Connecticut, in 1874, Ives studied at Yale and was inspired by transcendentalist philosophy. He used innovative and radical technical components in his compositions, and incorporated bitonal forms, polyrhythms, and quotation techniques he learned from his father.

Ives rejected what he heard as the "sweet" or "feminine" music of the Impressionists, such as Debussy—"easy music for the sissies, the lilypad ears," he wrote. Instead, he derived a masculine musical idiom, incorporating dissonance of strong sounds and virile patriotism. At the end of one composition he wrote, "to strengthen and give more muscle to the ear, brain, heart, limbs and FEAT! Atta boy!" Elsewhere he provided occasional marginal notations like "keep up the fight!" or "don't quit because the ladybirds don't like it" (cited in Cowell and Cowell 1955, 10).

Ives received the Pulitzer Prize for music for his Symphony No. 3 in 1947.

Michael Kimmel

Further Reading:
Cowell, Henry, and Sidney Cowell. 1955. *Charles Ives and His Music.* New York: Oxford University Press.

J

Jackson, Michael (1958–)

American entertainer and one of the most successful solo recording artists of all time, Jackson is as celebrated for his music and music videos as he is derided for radical alterations in his appearance and allegations about improprieties in his private life.

Although best known for a solo career beginning in the late 1970s with *Off the Wall* (1979) and peaking throughout the 1980s with *Thriller* (1982), then the bestselling album of all time, and *Bad* (1987), Jackson began his career performing as a child with his brothers. Coached and managed by their father, "The Jackson Five" emerged from Gary, Indiana, and rose to prominence in the early and mid-1970s with mainstream pop hits including "ABC" and "I'll Be There." Jackson's first solo recording, "Ben" (1972), made him, at age fourteen, among the youngest successful popular American solo artists and certainly one of very few among African American entertainers. In 1978 Jackson costarred with Diana Ross in an African American–themed remake of the classic film *The Wizard of Oz,* called simply *The Wiz.*

Jackson's celebrity continued unabated throughout the early 1980s and first peaked during his performance at the nationally televised twenty-fifth anniversary celebration of Motown Records, where he unveiled what would become his *Thriller*-era image—sequined jacket and high-cuffed pants, white socks, loafers, one sequined glove, and fedora—and where he debuted to universal acclaim the "moonwalk," a dance step of his own creation. With *Thriller,* Jackson became the first international music-video superstar, and at the 1984 Grammy awards, Jackson set a still-undefeated record of eight awards in a single evening.

Throughout the *Thriller* and *Bad* periods, Jackson's seemingly ubiquitous videos—many conceived as "short films" with elaborate sets and feature-length production budgets—introduced innovations in the music-video genre, as well as in electronic technology: his 1991 short film *Black or White* popularized the process of "morphing," an electronic melting of one image into another. A measure of Jackson's contribution to the music-video form came in the late 1980s with the naming of "The Michael Jackson Video Vanguard Award" by MTV, the American-based center of the music-video industry.

Jackson's star continued to rise—and finally fell—around the release of *Dangerous* (1991), when allegations of pedophilia and admissions of prescription drug addiction doomed his promotional tour and cast a

Michael Jackson performs during the Democratic National Committee (DNC) benefit concert, "A Night at the Apollo," at the world-famous Apollo Theater on 24 April 2002 in New York. (AFP/Corbis)

shadow over Jackson's celebrity, which continues to haunt the singer to this day, largely on the basis of Jackson's settlement of the child abuse charges out of court for an undisclosed amount. Much-heralded, so-called "comebacks" with *HIStory: Past, Present, and Future, Book I* (1995) and *Invincible* (2001) have generated less interest than Jackson's personal life and sexuality—he has been married twice and is the father of three children—as well as his radical alterations in appearance, including what is generally believed to be extensive plastic surgery and skin-lightening treatments, the latter of which Jackson has repeatedly insisted is the natural result of the pigmentation disorder vitiligo.

Often noted for his feminine appearance—comparisons to one-time idol Diana Ross abound—and his skin color, Jackson has been routinely lampooned as, in effect, a white woman. Such transformations may be traced back to the mid 1980s, when Jackson's emergence as a superstar spawned gentle ribbing about his high-pitched voice, his playfulness, and his apparent preference for socializing with young children. These quirks seemed slightly more ominous with the alterations in image and appearance that accompanied Jackson's *Bad* period, when noticeable cosmetic surgery encouraged speculation about the singer's racial and sexual identities, and when Jackson's carefully stylized appropriation of SandM fashion introduced a dark erotic edge that complicated the singer's squeaky-clean image. As Jackson's skin continued to lighten, and as his facial features continued to change, the singer found himself increasingly under fire from all sides. International media coverage of his career began to shift away from his artistry and on to his eccentricities, and the British press dubbed him "Wacko Jacko," an appellation that has stuck in popular consciousness for more than a decade.

Surrounding himself with young children, primarily preadolescent boys, by the early 1990s Jackson appeared in public in even more suggestive attire, sporting lamé bikini briefs over dark trousers and thus calling attention to the exaggerated bulge the layers of fabric created in his crotch. Around the same time, Jackson began punctuating many of his dance moves with repeated masturbatory gestures, a move the singer claims to have appropriated from rap musicians in an effort to heighten his ever-eroding "street credibility." Inevitably, Jackson's image and choreography led to concerns about his sexuality and to speculation about the nature of his interest in children. With the breakdown of the tour for *Dangerous* and the allegations of pedophilia that followed, Jackson found himself in the eye of a media storm that continued to engulf him throughout the next decade. In the early 2000s, controversy about Jackson's private proclivities has again shifted, this time away from his sex life and on to his role as a father: whether he is the biological father of all three of his children is not known, and in late 2002, Jackson's dangling of his youngest child over a Paris balcony to the horror of the fans assembled below resulted in legal inquiries in his home state of California about Jackson's suitability as a parent.

Jackson's most dedicated fans continue to support him, yet the larger cultural reign he once claimed slips farther and more obviously out of his control. Part child, part adult, part male, part female, part black, part white, Jackson continues to occupy a highly fraught cultural position. Still, musicians and critics laud him for his contributions to the music and music-video industries, and with the turn of the century, increasing numbers of younger popular American entertainers have begun to cite Jackson's influence, thus registering the pervasive and long-lasting nature of his influence on the entertainment industry.

Samuel Lyndon Gladden

Further Reading:
Andersen, Christopher P. 1995. *Michael Jackson Unauthorized*. New York: Pocket Books.
Jackson, Michael. 1988. *Moonwalk*. New York: Doubleday.
Taraborrelli, J. Randy. 1991. *Michael Jackson: The Magic and the Madness*. Secaucus, NJ: Birch Lane Press.

James, Henry, Jr. (1843–1916)

Henry James is best known as the creator of strong female characters: Daisy Miller, Isabel Archer, Maisie, and the governess in *The Turn of the Screw* (1898), to name just a few. However, he just as assiduously explored masculinity, portraying conventional male characters like Christopher Newman in *The American* (1877) and Basil Ransom of *The Bostonians* (1886) alongside marginal figures like Lambert Strether of *The Ambassadors* (1903) and the narrator of *The Aspern Papers* (1888).

James was born in New York City in 1843. His parents left him and his siblings free to explore the intellectual and spiritual world around them; the exercise of the imagination was to be a central theme in James's work, particularly as it relates to his exploration of masculinity. Such play of the imagination occurred with a back injury the young James suffered while serving as a volunteer fireman in New York. This wound he referred to later as his "obscure hurt," alternately alluding to the manly activity that occasioned the wound and to the physical incapacity that followed. That physical reality could be manipulated by one's imagination became a motif for James.

Heterosexuality being the hallmark of masculinity in the United States of his time, one might wonder if James was himself a lady's man. He was not the marrying kind. Late in life James began to exhibit a certain passion for men, though the evidence points to an unconsummated sexuality: a lavishing of verbal affection, with warm embraces and kisses for the men he held most dear. By his death in 1916 in England, his circle of male friends had included Hendrik Andersen, Hugh Walpole, Morton Fullerton, and Jocelyn Persse.

A central question for men in James's fiction mirrored the question in his own life: how to imaginatively create a space for men who find themselves at the margins of life— men who do not marry, men who do not excel at business endeavors, men who are fond of other men, men who feel and display tender emotions. Many characters in James's work never find a satisfactory place in life to express who they are and so find themselves in maturity looking back over a life devoid of passion. Some do find the embrace of a woman, as in "The Jolly Corner" (1908); others remain with more questions than answers, as in another late James story, "The Beast in the Jungle" (1903), which asks why someone cannot respond to an offer of love.

Rowland Mallet in *Roderick Hudson* (1876) and the narrator of *The Aspern Papers* are examples of marginal male figures who create empowering fictions about themselves. Mallet imagines himself to be a father figure for the younger Roderick, though in reality his is a subservient role. The narrator of *The Aspern Papers* conceives of his underhanded task in heroic terms like "errand," "glory," and "romance." Lambert Strether of *The Ambassadors* is a richer example still of the powers of the imagination. Strether frequently imagines himself not as more masculine than he is, but as less so; he embraces the fiction of submission in the forms, alternately, of little boy, feeble old man, or beast of burden. By imagining himself in more submissive roles than he is in, Strether imaginatively toys with and comes to enjoy his life at the margins of masculinity.

The marginal male in James's work is not without sexual desires, but his desires may be unconventional. So it is with Ralph Touchett in *The Portrait of a Lady* (1881), whose physical disability keeps him from marriage but who finds a voyeuristic satisfaction in observing the twists and turns of Isabel Archer's fate. Committed to a life of passivity, Ralph imaginatively finds pleasure and achieves a degree of power over Isabel, however nonthreatening. Unable to compete aggressively on the masculine stage set before them, such male characters in James's fiction revel in the pleasures of passivity.

James's work asks if, after all, such compensatory pleasures are enough. The answer may lie in James's personal ethic, which was intensely nonaggressive. James himself took pleasure, and saw his marginal characters take pleasure, in a vivid imagination, which James defined as the ability to appreciate difference. The compensation for his marginal characters is their gift of appreciating—and comprehending—lives other than their own.

Coordinately, conventional masculinity is often associated with a lack of imagination in James's work. Scattered throughout his fiction are conventionally masculine characters who lack the ability to appreciate lives other than their own. Such characters are generally taciturn, able to move as they do in the shadows. For example, the uncle in *The Turn of the Screw,* secure in his world of privilege, forbids the governess any communication with him. His presence looms large as a male comfortable in his world, unquestioned in his masculinity, and removed from his charges. Likewise the urbane father in the story "The Pupil" (1891) remains physically and emotionally worlds apart from the pain of his acutely sensitive son and the son's male tutor.

This is not to say that conventional masculinity is always negatively portrayed. However, James never takes gender for granted. Christopher Newman in *The American* is the "new man" confronting old Europe with his masculine energy. James pokes gentle fun at the innocence of this young man and of American men in general. American innocence assumes a boundless enterprise, but European culture will have none of it; for the first time in his life, this American male finds himself before a door permanently closed to him, not despite who he is—rather because of it.

Another character of conventional masculinity, Basil Ransom in *The Bostonians,* appears as the paragon of good taste from the last bastion of manners in America, the Deep South. James juxtaposes Ransom's tastefulness against the apparent tastelessness of American women reformers. Although gender appears to be the theme, it is more a vehicle for James's support of good taste on the part of either sex: Ransom's masculinity is good because it is well mannered; if the re-formers are disparaged, it is more for their methods than their ideas.

Kelly Cannon

Further Reading:

Bradley, John R. 1999. *Henry James and Homo-Erotic Desire.* New York: Macmillan.

Cannon, Kelly. 1996. *Henry James and Masculinity: The Man at the Margins.* New York: St. Martin's Press.

Davis, Lloyd. 1988. *Sexuality and Textuality in Henry James: Reading through the Virginal.* New York: Peter Lang.

Eakin, Paul John. 1988. "Henry James's Obscure Hurt." *New Literary History* 19, no. 3: 675–692.

Edel, Leon. 1953–1972. *Henry James.* 5 vols. Philadelphia: Lippincott.

Hall, Richard. 1985. "Henry James: Interpreting an Obsessive Memory." In *Essays on Gay Literature.* Edited by Stuart Kellogg. New York: Harrington Park Press.

Kaplan, Fred. 1992. *Henry James: The Imagination of Genius, A Biography.* New York: William Morrow.

Sedgwick, Eve Kosofsky. 1986. "The Beast in the Closet: James and the Writing of Homosexual Panic." Pp. 300–338 in *Sex, Politics, and Science in the Nineteenth-Century Novel.* Edited by Ruth Bernard Yeazell. Baltimore, MD: Johns Hopkins University Press.

Seymour, Miranda. 1989. *A Ring of Conspirators: Henry James and His Literary Circle: 1885–1915.* Boston: Houghton Mifflin.

Jay Gatsby

See Gatsby, Jay

Jazz

Jazz provides an exceptional perspective on the multiplicity of male gender-identity possibilities, for although perceptions have shifted somewhat in recent years, the music remains, as it was in its earliest days, a man's world. The 2002 membership figures from the International association of Jazz Educators, the music's predominant professional society, show that of the association's approximately 6,000 members registered worldwide, only about 1,200, or 20 percent, are women. Further, unlike some areas of the arts—the world of symphony orchestras, for instance, where men hold most of the performance chairs but

Ornette Coleman with his saxophone during a rehearsal for his Empty Foxhole *album. (Mosaic Images)*

women constitute the majority of patrons and board members—the gender imbalance in jazz encompasses all areas and levels. Indeed, a 1992 study funded by the National Endowment for the Arts showed that jazz stood as the only benchmark activity in the arts in which men attended performances more often than women did (DeVeaux 1992).

Yet the fact that jazz continues to serve as a professional "boys' club" tells only one small part of the story, as this music has given rise to a number of different—frequently contesting—models of masculinity.

Moreover, in a music genre so deeply connected to African American cultures and musical traditions, issues of gender identity always go hand in hand with issues of racial identity. For example, in the 1930s Hollywood presented mainstream America with two very different images of jazz and jazz musicians. Full-length films portrayed white bandleader Paul Whiteman as a "serious" musician, solemnly conducting his symphonic jazz orchestra. At the same time, a 1933 Betty Boop short depicted a cartoon version of black trumpeter Louis Armstrong as a "jungle savage." Such contrasting representations played into and supported deeply entrenched public understandings that linked white men to intelligence and sophistication and marked black men as primitive and "natural." These stereotypes not only influenced how listeners saw and heard jazz, but also the ways and places in which musicians would be able to present themselves and their music. Recognizing such connections can help us to discern how and why identities are formed, contested, and reformed.

Perhaps the most consequential moment in the configuration of jazz gender identities occurred with the rise of bebop (or bop) in the middle 1940s, as this subgenre marked the emergence of a distinctly African American form of modernism. Where jazz musicians from earlier subgenres had presented themselves predominantly as entertainers, bebop jazzmen considered themselves "artists." Dizzy Gillespie, Howard McGhee, Max Roach, and other early black boppers rejected as "Uncle Toms" those performers, including even Armstrong, who combined a jovial stage presence with dancer-friendly styles. Bop musicians typically maintained an aloof demeanor on stage, even to the point where some, most famously Miles Davis, turned their backs to the audience. This attitude was magnified when scores of men emulated the heroin use of bop saxophonist Charlie Parker, resulting in a "junkie" comportment that was at once impassive and seemingly disdainful of the public.

Musically, bebop reflected modernity's exclusivity by valuing virtuosity and complexity above other musical elements. Correspondingly, the ability to "run changes" (improvise over a preset harmonic progression) served as the established measuring stick for musicianship and functioned as the basis for bop's celebrated "cutting contests," the principal means by which instrumentalists tested one another. In these unofficial battles, musicians attempted to play faster, higher, and louder, while incorporating more intricate lines and complex harmonic substitutions, than their adversaries. Listeners expected those in a cutting contest to play "like men," that is, hard, fast, and loud. Such performances represented more than overt displays of instrumental proficiency; standards of musical excellence become mapped onto general attributes of an individual's power and manhood.

Jazz writers of the bop era picked up on and reinforced these understandings, leading to reviews that drew on such gendered terms as "strength," "virility," and "assertiveness" to describe musical performances. One letter writer to a leading fan magazine got straight to the point: "Good jazz is hard masculine stuff with a whip to it" (Walser 1999, 119). Thus, the prevailing identities of the jazzman during the 1940s and 1950s were marked by an imperturbable front masking a growing sense of African American assertiveness along with a kind of musical "machismo" fueled by fierce competition.

In 1959, Ornette Coleman, a newcomer to the New York scene, challenged bebop identity with a new set of techniques and aesthetics, ultimately forcing many musicians to rethink their established roles, attitudes, and standards of excellence. To be sure, Coleman and the other members of his quartet had absorbed bop's stylistic principals. But they eventually developed their own approach to them: rather than basing improvisations on preset harmonic progressions, as the beboppers before them had done, they focused on melodic considerations, sometimes even dispensing with chords altogether. This new style rendered bop's long-standing markers of musical/masculine identity practically meaningless: there were no chord changes to run, thus, nothing and no one to "conquer." The unusual timbres that these musicians employed distanced themselves even further from their predecessors. Coleman's trumpeter, Don Cherry, developed a particularly idiosyncratic instrumental style. Cherry's tone—thin, pinched, wavering—was, by bop standards, "weak," the antithesis of traditional notions of the virile trumpet king (Gabbard 1995). Still, many listeners found his playing attractive.

By undermining bebop's foundations of musical manhood, Coleman had configured new criteria by which players might understand themselves as jazzmen and laid the groundwork for a new subgenre, eventually known as "free jazz." Those sympathetic to Coleman's style began to equate his brand of musical "freedom" with the struggles in the broader social realm, so that his music became the sound of black civil rights for many listeners, writers, and musicians. At the same time, however, bebop-style jazz performance and heterosexual prowess had been two of the few areas of the popular imagination of the time in which African American males had been perceived to be superior to their white counterparts. Coleman's alternative model of performance had destabilized these former positions of masculinity and prestige. And the dilemma some black musicians faced went beyond simply no longer knowing what to play; many experienced a crisis of identity, engaging the very real question of who to be.

Another illustration of the complex interaction of gender and race can be witnessed in the case of pianist Bill Evans. Evans fully adhered to bebop's "jazz as art music" aesthetic, and he too followed Parker into narcotics. Yet Evans completely eschewed the rougher sounds of his bop-oriented contemporaries, employing a subtly sophisticated harmonic approach influenced by European classical composers. In addition, he maintained a unique comportment at his instrument: shoulders hunched; head bowed almost to the keys; eyes closed. Just as important, Bill Evans was a white man and, as with other musicians before him, he was seen as somehow more cerebral than his black contemporaries. This factor is crucial in understanding Evans as the inspiration for

a "sensitive intellectual" identity prevalent among a number of white pianists, including Denny Zeitlin and Brad Mehldau, to this day (for more on both Coleman and Evans, see Ake 2002).

Parker, Coleman, and Evans represent only a few of the ways in which jazzmen have understood and presented themselves, on stage and off. But if jazz musicians have managed to configure and display a broad range of masculinities, one area remains largely taboo: homosexuality. Despite the fact that writers and musicians have often praised this music as a progressive realm valuing freedom, openness, and interpersonal cooperation, jazz's various communities have shown much less tolerance toward homosexuals than have European classical music and dance, Broadway shows, and other areas of the arts and entertainment. In this regard, jazz has tended to operate much like the world of professional team sports, where a "locker room" mentality can lead all too quickly from a healthy sense of solidarity to cruel denigration of those who are different.

Jazz's homophobia stretches far back into the music's history. Even the earliest New Orleans innovators remained highly conscious of displaying a hearty and unambiguous heterosexuality. Jelly Roll Morton, for instance, described the ambivalence he felt toward taking up the piano as a youth because of the degree to which public perception of that instrument was linked to those of "questionable" tendencies. Interestingly, in order to avoid confusion in this matter, Morton considered taking up the violin, an instrument that was deemed "manly" in his New Orleans Creole neighborhood, but which hardly carries those connotations today (Lomax 1993).

Regardless of the intolerance, homosexual musicians have always written and played jazz. Significant gay contributors include vibraphonist Gary Burton; violinist Stephane Grappelli; pianists Fred Hersch, Don Pullen, and Cecil Taylor; and composer Billy

Strayhorn. Doubtless, there were and are many others; rumors and innuendo continue to swirl around Lester Young, Tony Williams, and even notorious womanizers Miles Davis and Duke Ellington.

Exactly what percentage of the whole homosexual players represent will not be known until attitudes shift such that these musicians no longer feel the need to stay "in the closet" for fear of being ostracized (or worse). Academic and popular writing on jazz has begun to address the topic of homosexuality (Davis 2002), but it is clear that many fans and musicians still hold prejudices (Petranicht 2002).

Finally, any discussion of jazz and gender should consider a population conspicuously absent from the music and the discourse surrounding it: women. We have seen that despite the immense legacy of legendary performers Bessie Smith, Billie Holiday, Mary Lou Williams, and Ella Fitzgerald, or the more recent contributions of Ingrid Jensen, Diana Krall, Maria Schneider, Geri Allen, and others, relatively few women have participated in jazz on any level. A number of factors contribute to this disparity, but social mores have certainly played a major role. For example, some of the earliest and most fertile locations for jazz performance—bars, brothels, gambling halls—were also those locations least accessible to women. Without direct access to these venues, with the invaluable opportunities they provided to listen to, sit in among, and make professional contacts with established players, aspiring female musicians were left at a disadvantage. As early as the 1930s, published debates publicly recognized the practical effects of this double standard (Walser 1999, 111–120).

Meanwhile, the extraordinary case of Dorothy Tipton (1914–1989) reveals the degree to which at least one jazz musician tried to overcome these barriers. Pianist and singer Tipton lived her entire professional (and even much of her private) life as a man, "Billy" Tipton, in large part so that she could have full and equal access to the jazz work environment (Middlebrook 1998).

Even those women who did manage to make names for themselves during the first half of the twentieth century did so largely in one of two roles, either as singer or pianist. Again, societal expectations played a significant part in this process. Parents encouraged their daughters to study voice and keyboard because those skills had emerged during the nineteenth century as positive markers of middle-class respectability. At the same time, music teachers steered young women away from jazz's other predominant instruments—drums, bass, clarinet, saxophone, trumpet, trombone—because striking or blowing into these devices was deemed "unladylike." Such obstacles make the accomplishments of the International Sweethearts of Rhythm, the Darlings of Rhythm, and other "all-girl" bands of the 1940s appear that much more impressive (Tucker 2001). Although women more recently have made notable advances toward employment equality in many fields, their place in jazz remains marginal.

David Ake

See also Jazz Musicians, Representations of

Further Reading:
Ake, David. 2002. *Jazz Cultures.* Berkeley and Los Angeles: University of California Press.
Davis, Francis. 2002. "In the Macho World of Jazz, Don't Ask, Don't Tell." *New York Times,* 1 September, sec. 2, p. 1.
DeVeaux, Scott. 1995. "Jazz in America: Who's Listening?" Research Division Report #31, National Endowment for the Arts. Carson, CA: Seven Locks Press.
Gabbard, Krin. 1991. *Jammin' At the Margins: Jazz and the American Cinema.* Chicago: University of Chicago Press.
———. 1995. "Signifyin(g) the Phallus: Mo' Better Blues and Representations of the Jazz Trumpet." Pp. 104–130 in *Representing Jazz.* Edited by Krin Gabbard. Durham, NC: Duke University Press.
Lomax, Alan. 1993. *Mister Jelly Roll.* New York: Pantheon.
Middlebrook, Diane Wood. 1998. *Suits Me: The Double Life of Billy Tipton.* New York: Houghton Mifflin.

Petranicht, Giovanni. 2002. "Gays in Jazz." *Jazz Times* (May): 28.

Roberts, Matana. "Makes Me Wanna Holler: Gender Issues in Jazz and Improvisational Music." At http://www.Schoolforimprovisationalmusic.org/pages/library/matana1.html (cited 27 July 2003).

Tucker, Sherrie. 2001. *Swing Shift: All-Girl Bands of the 1940s.* Durham, NC: Duke University Press.

Walser, Robert. 1999. *Keeping Time: Readings in Jazz History.* New York: Oxford University Press.

Jazz Musicians, Representations of

The visual culture of jazz—representations of men and by men ranging from painting and sculpture to photography and video—has, until the early twenty-first century, received little critical attention, yet sociocultural issues of race and gender are embedded in the production and reception of these images, in which African American masculinity is constructed, celebrated, and even contradicted.

Some studies have underscored the formal connection between classic jazz and high modernism in the visual arts. To be sure, each genre characterizes the avant-garde and increasingly popular tastes of early-twentieth-century Western culture; moreover, there is recognizable a distinct dialogue between artists and musicians. For example, painters and sculptors, such as Alexander Calder, Stuart Davis, Fernand Léger, Henri Matisse, Joan Miró, Piet Mondrian, and Pablo Picasso, commonly took jazz as their subject, and songwriters frequently provided lyrics and titles marked by a particularly visual vocabulary. Yet the nature of these borrowings was mainly inspirational or celebratory.

Other studies, equally concerned with putting jazz and representation into productive dialogue (though concerned less with issues of style, influence, and iconography and more with sociocultural issues of gender and racial identity), have called attention to the stereotypical and, thus, often problematic performances and representations of masculinity that characterize both of these modernist movements. The machismo exhibited by the action painter Jackson Pollock, for instance, who bodily entered his work, spilling, dripping, and spraying paint onto the canvas in an ejaculatory manner, parallels that of the bebop jazz musicians—contemporaries whose free and loose manner and aloof yet assertive personalities have often been described as aggressive and virile. If such self-presentation contributed to a hyperheterosexual masculinity, it also contradicted that identity insofar as the body, though so central to these constructions of identity, is, within modernist discourse, regarded as problematic—not cerebral and abstract but sexual and emotional, feminine and "Other."

That tension becomes especially palpable in photographic representations of jazz musicians, which, emphasizing corporeality, simultaneously exaggerate and emasculate culturally defined notions of race and gender. Photographic portraiture, in particular, captures the bodily performances and negotiations so crucial to maintaining fictive identities. Photography became the predominant means of representing jazz musicians for reasons of familiarity, economy, and efficiency—but also because, stylistically, the quick, unstudied, and spontaneous technique of photography reflects the unaffected, improvisational arrangement and orchestration of jazz music. Photographers such as William P. Gottlieb, Milt Hinton, Herman Leonard, Herb Snitzer, and Francis Wolff photographed jazz musicians including Louis Armstrong, John Coltrane, Miles Davis, Duke Ellington, Dizzy Gillespie, Thelonious Monk, and Charlie Parker at rehearsal in recording studios and on stage in music clubs in places like Chicago, New Orleans, New York, and Paris, among others. In individual and group portraits, male musicians are shown in a variety of poses, from profile to frontal views, either half-length or full-length. They are set in recognizable spaces, usually crowded smoke-filled interiors, and rarely make direct eye contact with the viewer. Either at play or at rest, jazz musicians are almost always depicted with their instruments; in fact, these attributes—clarinet, drums, piano, saxophone, trombone, and trumpet—often compete with the sitters as subject matter. The overall effect is that of an informal and candid snapshot. Indeed, there is a certain amateur quality to these pictures insofar as the photographers were not always formally trained artists or photojournalists but rather tended to be club owners, fans, or even the jazz musicians themselves.

Yet despite elements of naivete and improvisation, with compositions and arrangements reflecting the character of the music behind these scenes, representations of jazz musicians were often carefully staged. Directed by agents or record executives, such jazz photography was primarily produced and distributed for business purposes. For example, record labels such as Decca and Blue Note commissioned photographs for album covers, posters, and other promotional materials. While economic considerations may in part explain why these representations were produced, sociocultural concerns reveal the implications of such purposefully planned images and suggest a gender and racial politics operating in and against representations of jazz musicians. Provocatively placed instruments, not without phallic overtones, perpetuate stereotypes of African American sexuality, while similarly uncritical and racially charged images of blowing, spitting, gyrating, and sweating black male bodies situate the jazz musician at the margins—corporeal, feminine, Other. These representations simultaneously construct, celebrate, censor, and contradict socially dictated and managed definitions of masculinity.

Allison Levy

See also Jazz
Further Reading:
Appel, Alfred, Jr. 2002. *Jazz Modernism: From Ellington and Armstrong to Matisse and Joyce.* New York: Alfred A. Knopf.
Carner, Gary. 1991. "Jazz Photography: A Conversation with Herb Snitzer." *Black American Literature Forum* 25, no. 3: 561–592.
Cuscuna, Michael, Charlie Lourie, and Oscar Schnider. 2000. *Blue Note Jazz Photography of Francis Wolff.* New York: Universe.
Gabbard, Krin, ed. 1995. *Representing Jazz.* Durham, NC: Duke University Press.
Goldson, Elizabeth, ed. 1997. *Seeing Jazz: Artists and Writers on Jazz.* Foreword by Clark Terry. Introduction by Robert O'Meally. Afterword by Milt Hinton. Compiled by Marquette Folley-Cooper, Deborah Macanic, and Janice McNeil. San Francisco: Chronicle Books in association with the Smithsonian Institution Traveling Exhibition Service.
Friedlander, Lee. 1992. *The Jazz People of New Orleans.* New York: Pantheon Books.
O'Meally, Robert G., ed. 1998. *The Jazz Cadence of American Culture.* New York: Columbia University Press.
Panish, Jon. 1997. *The Color of Jazz: Race and Representation in Postwar American Culture.* Jackson, MS: University Press of Mississippi.

Jewish Men

The story of Jewish men should begin with the foundational Jewish story, the Book of Genesis. As many have noted, much of the plot of Genesis is the story of a single family, one greatly extended through time and space, that would in today's culture be diagnosed as a dysfunctional family, with its intrafamilial history replete with tales of murder, theft, deception, and other crimes too numerous to mention.

Much of the story of Genesis is a story specifically about conflicts among brothers, whether it be the original murder of Abel by Cain, or later struggles among Isaac and Ishmael, Jacob and Esau, or Joseph and his brothers, some of them equally deadly in intent if not in outcome. In these fratricidal struggles, often to seek the blessings of the father, victory usually goes, often surprisingly, not to the older, stronger brother, but to the younger and weaker one, the mother's rather than the father's favorite, the one less traditionally masculine in skill and hirsute in appearance.

This challenge to patriarchal primogeniture, this legacy of reversals of fortune in Jewish culture's foundational narrative in favor of the more feminized over the more masculinized Jewish male leaves a legacy of conflict that runs throughout Jewish history. Within Jewish culture it complicates struggles between patriarchal and egalitarian strains in Judaism, and within the dominant culture it contributes to images and slanders of Jewish men being seen as unmanly.

Various patriarchal practices within Judaism work to privilege Jewish men over Jewish women, including the exclusion of women from central prayers, rituals, and positions of authority, the male ritual of circumcision functioning as the defining mark of being a Jew, and the nonrecognition of the contributions of Jewish women to Jewish history and community. Despite strong proscriptions in Judaism, which raise suspicions of idolatry in the face of any depiction of God, the Divine Presence is nonetheless often pictured as male or masculine, the Divine Source as Heavenly Father.

Simultaneously, Jewish men remain relatively disempowered vis-à-vis non-Jewish men of the hegemonic culture. Sound analyses of Jewish men must integrate their situatedness along both axes of power, wherein they are on the one hand a subordinate but on the other hand a superordinate group. In this vein, one should note that some of the foundational insights of psychoanalysis, particularly regarding the influence of social forces on the formation of the psyche, stem from Freud's analyses of his own dreams and memories regarding his father's power over him as a child but simultaneous shaming in his eyes as a Jew by the dominant culture. Kafka's "Letter to the Father" and other of his writings explore related Jewish father-and-son themes.

Consider, for example, how one must understand the dual dynamics of being subordinate within the dominant culture but superordinate within one's own culture in order to understand the dynamics of overdetermination whereby the hierarchical dichotomy of mind over body, or brains over brawn, comes to loom very large in the lives of Jewish men, resulting in the life of the mind becoming valued and overvalued as a source of Jewish male identity. Given the central importance of the scholarly study of texts within Judaism, this functions as a source of power for Jewish men, who have had access to Jewish learning and thereby claim authority and status against feminist challenge from Jewish women, while simultaneously vis-à-vis the dominant culture this ideal is defended, by Jewish women as well as men, against anti-Semitic attacks on it and the accompanying putative feminization of Jewish men as overly intellectual and insufficiently muscular. This feminization of Jewish men accompanies a historically common occurrence of an intertwining of anti-Semitic and heterosexist/homophobic discourses, practices, and persecutions, made tangible in the smoke rising from the burning of "faggots" at the stake and bodies in the crematoria.

Scholars have turned their attention to a long history of the literal and figurative stigmatizing marking of the male Jew's body, from the mark of Cain and the stigmata of Jesus's wounds to the horns of Michelangelo's *Moses;* from the hooked nose illustrators traditionally use to indicate a Shylock-like character to the stereotypical beard, sallow complexion, and/or glasses of the Jewish intellectual; and from the stooped shoulders, flat feet, and either sunken chest or corpulent girth of the Jewish male unfit for military service to the ungendered, tattooed number and yellow star of the Holocaust.

Some have seen the formative influence of Jewish culture in the development of the radical theories of Freud and Marx, as well as in the general prevalence of Jews in progressive movements for social and political change, citing such factors as Judaism's prophetic and messianic commitments to justice, the biblical tradition of the revelation of theodicean truth through historical narrative, and the insights into the social whole generated by a critical intellectual tradition situated liminally in but not of the culture, illuminating from the margins the workings of unconscious forces not as visible to those centrally ensconced in the system.

Contemporary representations of American Jewish masculinity are central themes in the works of such Jewish male authors as Philip Roth, David Mamet, and Tony Kushner and filmmakers such as Barry Levinson and Woody Allen. The influence on popular culture of Jewish men seeking to work through their ambivalences about their roles in American culture has been enormous. Just in the early twentieth century this ranges from the blackface performances of cantor's son Al Jolson (Asa Yoelson) and self-effacing humor of immigrants' son Jack Benny (Benjamin Kubelsky) to the creation of the character of Superman and with it the entire comic book superhero genre by teenagers Jerry Siegel and Joe Shuster and the role of such moguls as Louis B. Mayer in the creation of the Hollywood film industry.

Creative and critical works by and about Jewish men have been foundational to the construction and deconstruction of masculinities.

Harry Brod

See also Bar Mitzvah; Circumcision

Further Reading:

Biale, David. 1992. *Eros and the Jews: From Biblical Israel to Contemporary America.* New York: Basic Books.

Boyarin, Daniel. 1997. *Unheroic Conduct: The Rise of Heterosexuality and the Invention of the Jewish Man.* Berkeley: University of California Press.

Breines, Paul. 1990. *Tough Jews: Political Fantasies and the Moral Dilemma of American Jewry.* New York: Basic Books.

Brod, Harry, ed. 1988. *A Mensch among Men: Explorations in Jewish Masculinity.* Freedom, CA: Crossing Press.

Eilberg-Schwartz, Howard. 1994. *God's Phallus: And Other Problems for Men and Monotheism.* Boston: Beacon.

Gilman, Sander. 1991. *The Jew's Body.* New York: Routledge.

Ostriker, Alicia Suskin. 1994. *The Nakedness of the Fathers: Biblical Visions and Revisions.* New Brunswick, NJ: Rutgers University Press.

Pitzele, Peter. 1995. *Our Fathers' Wells: A Personal Encounter with the Myths of Genesis.* San Francisco: Harper.

Rosenberg, Warren. 2001. *Legacy of Rage: Jewish Masculinity, Violence, and Culture.* Amherst, MA: University of Massachusetts Press.

Waskow, Arthur. 1978. *Godwrestling.* New York: Schocken.

Jocks

Jock—slang for an athlete and often derogatory in nature—is almost exclusively used to describe male athletes. Although the term originated as a short form of the word "jockey," it is more frequently used to describe athletes in team sports, or contact sports, than athletes of individual sports as the term connotes a hypermacho attitude that is associated with sports like football and basketball. Jocks are given social prestige over nonjocks, and because of their highly athletic and sexualized bodies help men as a whole maintain patriarchal and heterosexual privilege.

The importance of athleticism in the construction of a masculine hierarchy has been shown from early childhood through college. Boys vertically align themselves primarily through athleticism—those who are more athletic are positioned at the top (the jocks) while the unathletic are marginalized as being less masculine and viewed as outsiders (fags and pussies).

Connell (1995) highlights that there exists a belief that "true masculinity" almost always proceeds from men's bodies. As a result, jocks often define what hegemonic masculinity entails. Thus, masculinity and athleticism are interlinked, providing for a cornerstone of contemporary gender ideology, in which patriarchal and heterosexual privilege is maintained through the ability to commit violence against women and gay men. For a by-product of an athletic body is that it is more physically capable of committing violence than a nonathletic body. Much of the social prestige jocks capture comes from awe of their highly sexualized bodies. In fact, the term *jock* is so engendered within the male body that "jock" is also used as slang for "penis" in such terms as "jock strap" or "jock itch," or expressions like, "she was all up on my jock."

Being a jock provides social privileges not only over women and gay men, but over other heterosexual men as well. McGuffey and Rich (1999) show that high-status middle school boys not only gain social prestige among their peers, but they also secure resources for themselves—such as prime playing areas. And in high school and collegiate settings, jocks may be given more institutional leeway when it comes to deviancy than nonathletes because of the entertainment value, and often hero status, that their athleticism brings to the community. Athletes, for example, might find their punishment delivered on the playing field instead of undergoing the institutional punishment a nonathlete would. For example, two high school students who fight in the hallways are likely to receive a five-day suspension, while two athletes fighting on the soccer field get a red card and are ejected from the match.

Although heterosexuality is not a precursor to athletic performance, as gay athletes have been shown to be as good as or better than straight athletes, the image of hyperheterosexuality is compulsory to being a jock. In order to resist suspicion of homosexuality, jocks associate sheer athleticism with heterosexuality. Homosexuality and effeminacy are looked on as being incompatible with sport. Thus, the sheer athleticism and muscular physique of the jock serves to shield him from suspicion of homosexuality.

Presenting an image of being heterosexually hypersexed is an important part of jock culture because it helps deflect attention from the reality that sport is a homoerotic arena. Because of the close contact, communal showering, touching, and male bonding that sport provides, Pronger (1990) theorizes that sport actually serves as a magnet for gay men. He argues that because sports are both highly homophobic and homoerotic,

they provide a good place for a gay male to hide his same-sex desires. A closeted gay jock is socially rewarded for partaking in homoerotic behaviors, yet he helps reproduce the culture of homophobia that marginalized him in the first place.

Because of their ability to use their physically capable bodies as a weapon, jocks often become the unofficial rule enforcers in institutional settings. The "might over right" mentality is particularly useful in setting and enforcing norms that serve the best interest of the jocks. Many of these norms regard gender roles, particularly what it means to be a man. The enforcement of these gender norms comes thorough symbolic violence in the form of homophobic and misogynistic discourse, and in the real threat that a physically strong body embodies.

Because jock culture seems to devalue all things feminine, Burton-Nelson (1995) argues that as women have gradually gained access to arenas once reserved for men, men have reacted by stressing their strength over women. And even though most men do not fit the somatic description of what it takes to be a jock, they rely on the few who do to maintain the male form as being capable of physical violence over the female.

Eric Anderson

Further Reading:

Anderson, Eric. 2000. *Trailblazing: The True Story of America's First Openly Gay Track Coach*. Los Angeles: Alyson Books.

Bissinger, H. G. 1990. *Friday Night Lights: a Town, a Team, and a Dream*. Reading, MA: Addison Wesley.

Bryson, Lois. 1987. "Sport and the Maintenance of Masculine Hegemony." *Women's Studies International Forum* 10: 349–360.

Burton-Nelson, Mariah. 1995. *The Stronger Women Get the More Men Love Football: Sexism and the American Culture of Sports*. New York: Avon Books.

Connell, R. W. 1995. *Masculinities*. Berkeley, CA: University of California Press.

McGuffey, C. Shawn, and Brian Rich. 1999. "Playing in the Gender Transgression Zone: Race, Class, and Hegemonic Masculinity in Middle Childhood." *Gender & Society* 13, no. 5: 608–610.

Messner, Michael. 1992. *Power at Play: Sports and the Problem of Masculinity.* Boston: Beacon Press.

Miracle, Andrew W., and C. Roger Rees. 1994. *Lessons of the Locker Room: The Myth of School Sports.* Amherst, NY: Prometheus Books.

Pronger, Brian. 1990. *The Arena of Masculinity: Sports, Homosexuality, and the Meaning of Sex.* New York: St. Martin's.

Thorne, Barrie. 1993. *Gender Play: Girls and Boys in School.* New Brunswick, NJ: Rutgers University Press.

Juvenile Delinquency

Juvenile delinquency, defined as criminal or status offenses committed by minor youth, is disproportionately carried out by males. Children who commit the more serious of these acts, frequently for extended periods of time, are typically referred to as juvenile delinquents. Of the 2.5 million juvenile arrests in 1999, 73 percent were of males (Snyder 2001, 9). Juvenile males were arrested 4.2 times more often for Violent Crime Index Offenses than females in 2000 (Snyder 2001). Ninety-three percent of juvenile murder offenders from 1980 through 1999 were male (Snyder 2001, 6). The male-female juvenile arrest disparity is referred to as the "gender gap in offending" (Heimer 2000, 427).

Male juveniles also reportedly engage in greater use of alcohol and illicit drugs than do females. Historically, juvenile delinquency and criminal research has concentrated on male offenders primarily because males commit the majority of criminal and delinquent acts, particularly the more serious and violent offenses. Explanations of male offending have focused on biological, psychological, and sociological theories. Biological research on juvenile delinquency conceptualizes criminality as a problem of heredity or genetics specific to some groups. It posits the presence of a physical abnormality to explain juvenile offending and criminality. Early research linked body type with delinquency. Sheldon (1949) published *Varieties of Delinquency* in which he described how male youth with muscular and athletic physiques were prone to have more active, assertive, and aggressive personalities, thus making them more prone to delinquency (Regoli and Hewitt 2000, 83). Early IQ research, much contested by many of today's experts, was used to link intelligence with delinquency, particularly in explanations of the overrepresentation of minority male youth in delinquency statistics. Recent biological explanations of delinquency include attention deficit hyperactivity disorder (ADHD), a diagnosis that is six to nine times more common in boys than in girls and nine times more likely to occur in delinquents than in nondelinquents (91).

Psychological explanations argue that delinquency stems from the individual and his or her relationship with the environment. Albert Bandura's work on social learning theory argues that juvenile delinquency is a learned behavior and that children engage in delinquent acts because they are watching and imitating others. This idea has influenced the attention researchers, parents, educators, and concerned citizens have paid to media influences on children's behavior. For example, a spate of school-yard shootings by male students in the mid- to late 1990s was linked by some to the television show *South Park* as well as to the 1995 film *Basketball Diaries.*

Sociological research on juvenile delinquency has historically focused its attention on juvenile males, particularly those in lower-class communities. Chesney-Lind (1989) addresses this in her article entitled "Girls' Crime and Woman's Place: Toward a Feminist Model of Female Delinquency." She highlights the pivotal research in juvenile delinquency and how it shaped and was shaped by this emphasis on male delinquency. The influential research by Clifford R. Shaw and Henry D. McKay using an ecological perspective to study male delinquency in 1929 narrowed the scope of juvenile delinquency research to focus solely on male delinquents. Evidence of this impact can be found in Frederic M. Thrasher's work on Chicago gangs in the 1930s. Thrasher "spent one page out of 600 on the five or six female gangs he encountered in his field observation of juvenile gangs" (Thrasher, 9). Albert K. Cohen's gang research in the 1950s notes the significance of masculinity in the shaping of adolescent male behavior. He argues that delinquency is an integral mechanism by which male youth may establish their masculinity. Walter B. Miller's work on lower-class youth, as described by Chesney-Lind (1989), also asserts that the "emphasis on importance of trouble, toughness, excitement" within this community "predisposes poor youth (particularly male youth) to criminal misconduct" (10). The work of both Cohen and Miller in the 1950s and 1960s clearly established the importance of conceptualizing masculinity in explanations of male delinquency. Chesney-Lind (1989) also cites Cloward and Ohlin's work in the 1960s. They examined the opportunity structures available to male youth. Their work, using Merton's strain theory, asserts that male delinquency can be traced to both a lack of "legitimate" opportunities available to male working-class youth as well as an outright resistance to femininity (10). Here again, the link between masculinity and delinquency was made. Lastly, the work of Edwin Sutherland using his theory of differential association and that of Travis Hirschi using social control theory further emphasize the location of juvenile delinquency research on male youthful offenders. Their data, like that of all the aforementioned eminent juvenile delinquency researchers, consists of predominantly or fully all-male samples to understand juvenile delinquency.

Sociological research on juvenile delinquency in the 1990s has attempted to explain the characteristics of male gender roles that enhance the propensity for males to offend and to commit more serious crimes than females. Gendered explanations of juvenile delinquency perceive delinquency to be a learned behavior related to the socialization of one's gender role. The fact that males commit more crimes in both number and degree of severity than females is explained as gender-role socialization rather than as a biological distinction. Indeed, the 1990s produced a proliferation of work focusing attention on the relationship between masculinity and the treatment of boys by various social institutions including the family, school, and the criminal justice system. One such work by William Pollack (1998), entitled *Real Boys: Rescuing Our Sons from the Myths of Boyhood*, made the *New York Times* bestseller list. Pollack's work explores the impact of socializing boys to be men and the unintended consequences of this on individual boys and its larger impact on society, including male youths' inability to deal with depression, violence, drugs, alcohol, sexuality, and love. The exploration of masculinity and criminality is also the theme of the film *Tough Guise* (1999). The title refers to the mask men wear to conceal their vulnerability including any behaviors that identify male youth as "real men," particularly in front of their peers.

Feminist sociological work has recently addressed female juvenile offending and its link with patriarchy. Chesney-Lind (1989) argues that the lack of attention to female delinquency has only been within the research and academic community. The juvenile justice system has long paid attention to female delinquency, particularly girls' sexual promiscuity. Feminist theories of delinquency focus our gaze on the victimization of girls (Regoli and Hewitt 2000, 312). Patriarchal families allow prime opportunities for adults, particularly male family members, to abuse girls. These events often precipitate girls' increased risk for running away from home, further heightening their risk for other types of deviance.

Jessica L. Kenty-Drane

See also Gangs
Further Reading:
Chesney-Lind, Meda. 1989. "Girls' Crime and Woman's Place: Toward a Feminist Model of Female Delinquency." *Crime and Delinquency* 35, no. 1: 5–29.

Heimer, Karen. 2000. "Changes in the Gender Gap in Crime and Women's Economic Marginalization." *Criminal Justice* 1: 427–480.

Jhally, Sut, director. 1999. *Tough Guise: Violence, Media, and the Crisis in Masculinity.* Videocassette. Northampton, MA: Media Education Foundation.

Johnston, L. D., P. M. O'Malley, and J. G. Bachman. 1999. *National Survey Results on Drug Use from the Monitoring the Future Study, 1976–1998.* Bethesda, MD: National Institutes of Health, National Institute on Drug Abuse, and Institute for Social Research, University of Michigan.

Pollack, William. 1998. *Real Boys: Rescuing Our Sons from the Myths of Boyhood.* New York: Henry Holt.

Regoli, Robert M., and John D. Hewitt. 2000. *Delinquency in Society.* Boston: McGraw-Hill.

Schoemaker, Donald J. 1996. *Theories of Delinquency: An Examination of Explanations of Delinquent Behavior.* New York: Oxford University Press.

Snyder, Howard N. 2001. "Law Enforcement and Juvenile Crime." *OJJDP Juvenile Justice Bulletin* (December): 1–32.

Thrasher, Frederic M. 2000. *The Gang: A Study of 1,313 Gangs in Chicago.* Imprint Peotone, IL: New Chicago School Press.